BOOK OF QUOTATIONS
ORGANIZED BY THEMES

FIRST EDITION

Revised on January 25, 2019

LARISA KRECHET

Table of Contents

Ability

I do the very best I know how-the very best I can; and I mean to keep doing so until the end. If the end brings me out all right, what is said against me won't amount to anything. If the end brings me out wrong, ten angels swearing I was right would make no difference.
Abraham Lincoln (1809 - 1865), Francis Carpenter, Six Months at the White House, 1867
The less their ability, the more their conceit.
Ahad HaAm
Great ability develops and reveals itself increasingly with every new assignment.
Baltasar Gracian
Natural ability without education has more often attained to glory and virtue than education without natural ability.
Cicero (106 BC - 43 BC)
Be systematically heroic in little unnecessary points, do every day or two something for no other reason than its difficulty, so that, when the hour of need draws nigh, it may find you not unnerved or untrained to stand the test.
Daniel Akst, We Have Met the Enemy: Self-Control in an Age of Excess, 2011
The trick of it, she told herself, is to be courageous and bold and make a difference. Not change the world exactly, just the bit around you. Go out there with your double-first, your passion and your new Smith Corona electric typewriter and work hard at ... something. Change lives through art maybe. Write beautifully. Cherish your friends, stay true to your principles, live passionately and fully well. Experience new things. Love and be loved if at all possible. Eat sensibly. Stuff like that.
David Nicholls, One Day, 2010
It is a great ability to be able to conceal one's ability.
Francois de La Rochefoucauld (1613 - 1680), Maxims, 1665
Martyrdom... is the only way in which a man can become famous without ability.
George Bernard Shaw (1856 - 1950), The Devil's Disciple (1901) act 3
I know of no more encouraging fact than the unquestioned ability of a man to elevate his life by conscious endeavor.
Henry David Thoreau (1817 - 1862)
Ability will never catch up with the demand for it.
Malcolm Forbes (1919 - 1990)
Dressing up is inevitably a substitute for good ideas. It is no coincidence that technically inept business types are known as "suits."
Paul Graham, September 2004
Nerds don't just happen to dress informally. They do it too consistently. Consciously or not, they dress informally as a prophylactic measure against stupidity.
Paul Graham, September 2004
There is something that is much more scarce, something rarer than ability. It is the ability to recognize ability.
Robert Half
Perhaps the most valuable result of all education is the ability to make yourself do the thing you have to do, when it ought to be done, whether you like it or not; it is the first lesson that ought to be learned; and however early a man's training begins, it is probably the last lesson that he learns thoroughly.
Thomas H. Huxley (1825 - 1895)
The Army has carried the American ... ideal to its logical conclusion. Not only do they prohibit discrimination on the grounds of race, creed and color, but also on ability.
Tom Lehrer (1928 -)

Acting;Art;Talent;Television

I do not regret one professional enemy I have made. Any actor who doesn't dare to make an enemy should get out of the business.
Bette Davis (1908 - 1989), The Lonely Life, 1962
Acting is all about honesty. If you can fake that, you've got it made.
George Burns (1896 - 1996)
Talk low, talk slow, and don't talk too much.
John Wayne (1907 - 1979), Advice on acting
Acting is not being emotional, but being able to express emotion.
Kate Reid
Acting is the most minor of gifts and not a very high-class way to earn a living. After all, Shirley Temple could do it at the age of four.
Katharine Hepburn (1907 - 2003)
Being a celebrity has taught me to hide, but being an actor has opened my soul.
Meryl Streep (1949 -), Barnard Commencement Speech, 2010
Empathy is at the heart of the actor's art.
Meryl Streep (1949 -), Barnard Commencement Speech, 2010
One is obliged to do a great deal of kissing in my line of work: air kissing, [butt] kissing, kissing up, and of course actual kissing. Much like hookers, actors have to do it with people we may not like or even know.
Meryl Streep (1949 -), Barnard Commencement Speech, 2010
Pretending is not just play. Pretending is imagined possibility. Pretending, or acting, is a very valuable life skill and we do it all the time.
Meryl Streep (1949 -), Barnard Commencement Speech, 2010
While I am overwhelmingly proud of work that I, believe me, did not do on my own, I can assure you that awards have very little bearing on my own personal happiness, my own sense of well-being and purpose in the world.
Meryl Streep (1949 -), Barnard Commencement Speech, 2010
Women are better at acting then men. Why? Because we have to be. If successfully convincing someone bigger than you are of something he doesn't want to know is a survival skill, this is how women have survived through the millennia.
Meryl Streep (1949 -), Barnard Commencement Speech, 2010

There's a rule in acting called, "Don't play the result." If you have a character who's going to end up in a certain place, don't play that until you get there. Play each scene and each beat as it comes. And that's what you do in life: You don't play the result.
Michael J. Fox (1961 -), Good Housekeeping, June 2011
The most difficult character in comedy is that of a fool, and he must be no simpleton who plays the part.
Miguel de Cervantes (1547 - 1616), Don Quixote, 1605
I love acting. It is so much more real than life.
Oscar Wilde (1854 - 1900), The Picture of Dorian Gray, 1891
Acting like someone you're not is exactly what it takes to realize you're capable of more than you ever knew.
Rob Sheridan, Mad Love, The Young and The Reckless, 2011
I enjoy being a highly overpaid actor.
Roger Moore (1927 -)
Acting is merely the art of keeping a large group of people from coughing.
Sir Ralph Richardson (1902 - 1983), quoted in New York Herald Tribune, May 19, 1946
When a man plays a woman in a dress, you're halfway there. It's inherently funny. When a woman plays a man, for whatever reason, it's not that instant kind of funny.
Tina Fey, ABC-TV World News Now
You can be a little bit darker and rougher on the stage, partly because when you're in the theater, people have come to see you, and so they kind of know what they're in for. In television, you are sort of sneaking into people's homes. So, I think you can be a little bit darker on stage.
Tina Fey, Interview from Second City, 2008
We're actors - we're the opposite of people.
Tom Stoppard (1937 -), Rosencrantz and Guildenstern are Dead (1967)

Actions

We have too many high sounding words, and too few actions that correspond with them.
Abigail Adams (1744 - 1818), letter to John Adams, 1774
I've arrived at this outermost edge of my life by my own actions. Where I am is thoroughly unacceptable. Therefore, I must stop doing what I've been doing.
Alice Koller, An Unknown Woman, 1982
All human actions have one or more of these seven causes: chance, nature, compulsion, habit, reason, passion, and desire.
Aristotle (384 BC - 322 BC)
Men acquire a particular quality by constantly acting a particular way... you become just by performing just actions, temperate by performing temperate actions, brave by performing brave actions.
Aristotle (384 BC - 322 BC)
Actions lie louder than words.
Carolyn Wells
Deliberation is the function of the many; action is the function of one.
Charles de Gaulle (1890 - 1970), War Memoirs, 1960
The superior man is modest in his speech, but exceeds in his actions.
Confucius (551 BC - 479 BC), The Confucian Analects
You cannot have a proud and chivalrous spirit if your conduct is mean and paltry; for whatever a man's actions are, such must be his spirit.
Demosthenes (384 BC - 322 BC), Third Olynthiac
I have long since come to believe that people never mean half of what they say, and that it is best to disregard their talk and judge only their actions.
Dorothy Day (1897 - 1980), The Long Loneliness, 1952
An event had happened, upon which it is difficult to speak, and impossible to be silent.
Edmund Burke (1729 - 1797), Speeches... in the Trial of Warren Hastings, May 5, 1789
Action is character.
F. Scott Fitzgerald (1896 - 1940), The Last Tycoon, 1941
You ask me why I do not write something....I think one's feelings waste themselves in words, they ought all to be distilled into actions and into actions which bring results.
Florence Nightingale (1820 - 1910), in Cecil Woodham-Smith, Florence Nightingale, 1951
Happiness lies not in the mere possession of money. It lies in the joy of achievement, in the thrill of creative effort.
Franklin D. Roosevelt (1882 - 1945), Speeches... in the Trial of Warren Hastings, May 5, 1789
We defend and we build a way of life, not for America alone, but for all mankind.
Franklin D. Roosevelt (1882 - 1945), Fireside chat on national defense, May 26, 1940
When a man asks himself what is meant by action he proves he is not a man of action. Action is a lack of balance. In order to act you must be somewhat insane. A reasonably sensible man is satisfied with thinking.
Georges Clemenceau (1841 - 1929), Conversation with Jean Martet, January 1, 1929
Somewhere deep down we know that in the final analysis we do decide things and that even our decisions to let someone else decide are really our decisions, however pusillanimous.
Harvey Cox, On Not Leaving It to the Snake, 1967
Words without actions are the assassins of idealism.
Herbert Hoover (1874 - 1964)
Only actions give life strength; only moderation gives it a charm.
Jean Paul Richter (1763 - 1825)
I have always thought the actions of men the best interpreters of their thoughts.
John Locke (1632 - 1704)
I was seldom able to see an opportunity until it had ceased to be one.
Mark Twain (1835 - 1910)
Don't be too timid and squeamish about your actions. All life is an experiment. The more experiments you make the better.
Ralph Waldo Emerson (1803 - 1882)
Life is one long process of getting tired.
Samuel Butler (1835 - 1902), Notebooks, 1912

Nothing will ever be attempted if all possible objections must be first overcome.
Samuel Johnson (1709 - 1784), Rasselas, 1759
In this theater of man's life, it is reserved only for God and for angels to be lookers-on.
Sir Francis Bacon (1561 - 1626)
Aggressive fighting for the right is the greatest sport in the world.
Theodore Roosevelt (1858 - 1919)
We are face to face with our destiny and we must meet it with high and resolute courage. For us is the life of action, of strenuous performance of duty; let us live in the harness, striving mightily; let us rather run the risk of wearing out than rusting out.
Theodore Roosevelt (1858 - 1919), Address at the opening of the gubernatorial campaign, New York City, October 5, 1898
Delay is preferable to error.
Thomas Jefferson (1743 - 1826), Letter to George Washington, May 16, 1792
Strong reasons make strong actions.
William Shakespeare (1564 - 1616)

Adversity

Nearly all men can stand adversity, but if you want to test a man's character, give him power.
Abraham Lincoln (1809 - 1865)
If we had no winter, the spring would not be so pleasant: if we did not sometimes taste of adversity, prosperity would not be so welcome.
Anne Bradstreet (1612 - 1672), 'Meditations Divine and Moral,' 1655
By courage I repel adversity.
(Adversa Virtute Repello)
Anonymous
He knows not his own strength that hath not met adversity.
Ben Jonson (1572 - 1637)
Be more prompt to go to a friend in adversity than in prosperity.
Chilo
Friendship make prosperity more shining and lessens adversity by dividing and sharing it.
Cicero (106 BC - 43 BC), On Friendship, 44 B.C.
Adversity is the touchstone of friendship.
French Proverb
Adversity is the trial of principle. Without it a man hardly knows whether he is honest or not.
Henry Fielding (1707 - 1754)
He that can heroically endure adversity will bear prosperity with equal greatness of the soul; for the mind that cannot be dejected by the former is not likely to be transported without the latter.
Henry Fielding (1707 - 1754)
In adversity remember to keep an even mind.
Horace (65 BC - 8 BC), Odes
You will never truly know yourself or the strength of your relationships until both have been tested by adversity.
J. K. Rowling, Harvard Commencement Address, 2008
In prosperity our friends know us; in adversity we know our friends.
John Churton Collins
Adversity does teach who your real friends are.
Lois McMaster Bujold, A Civil Campaign, 1999
By trying we can easily learn to endure adversity – another man's I mean.
Mark Twain (1835 - 1910)
By trying we can easily learn to endure adversity. Another man's, I mean.
Mark Twain (1835 - 1910), Following the Equator (1897)
Always seek out the seed of triumph in every adversity.
Og Mandino (1923 - 1996)
Prosperity makes friends, adversity tries them.
Publilius Syrus (~ 100 BC), Maxims
Adversity is the state in which man most easily becomes acquainted with himself, being especially free of admirers then.
Samuel Johnson (1709 - 1784)
Fire is the test of gold; adversity, of strong men.
Seneca (5 BC - 65 AD), Epistles
Remember that there is nothing stable in human affairs; therefore avoid undue elation in prosperity, or undue depression in adversity.
Socrates (469 BC - 399 BC)
Adversity causes some men to break; others to break records.
William Arthur Ward
A man I am cross'd with adversity.
William Shakespeare (1564 - 1616), The Two Gentlemen of Verona, Act IV, sc.1
A wretched soul, bruised with adversity,
We bid be quiet when we hear it cry;
But were we burdened with like weight of pain,
As much or more we should ourselves complain.
William Shakespeare (1564 - 1616)
Let me embrace thee, sour adversity, for wise men say it is the wisest course.
William Shakespeare (1564 - 1616), Henry VI, Part III, Act III, sc. 1
Sweet are the uses of adversity,
Which like the toad, ugly and venomous,
Wears yet a precious jewel in his head;

And this our life, exempt from public haunt,
Finds tongues in trees, books in the running brooks,
Sermons in stones, and good in everything.
William Shakespeare (1564 - 1616), As You Like It, Act II, sc.1
Sweet are the uses of adversity, which, like a toad, though ugly and venomous, wears yet a precious jewel in its head.
William Shakespeare (1564 - 1616)

Avertising; Journalism; Television
I LIKE ads. It's not that we don't like ads, we just don't like ads when they are out of place.
Bill Barnes, How to Blog for Money by Learning from Comics, SXSW 2006
The very first law in advertising is to avoid the concrete promise and cultivate the delightfully vague.
Bill Cosby (1937 -)
Advertising is the modern substitute for argument; its function is to make the worse appear the better.
George Santayana (1863 - 1952)
If people aren't going to talk about your product, then it's not good enough.
Jeffrey Kalmikoff, Designing for Community with Zero-Advertising Brands, SXSW 2006
Half the money I spend on advertising is wasted; the trouble is I don't know which half.
John Wanamaker (1838 - 1922), (attributed)
Many a small fortune has been made large by the right kind of advertising.
Mark Twain (1835 - 1910), A Connecticut Yankee in King Arthur's Court
You can tell the ideals of a nation by its advertisements.
Norman Douglas, South Wind, 1917
Chess is as elaborate a waste of human intelligence as you can find outside an advertising agency.
Raymond Chandler (1888 - 1959)
Advertising is a valuable economic factor because it is the cheapest way of selling goods, particularly if the goods are worthless.
Sinclair Lewis (1885 - 1951)
Advertising may be described as the science of arresting the human intelligence long enough to get money from it.
Stephen Leacock (1869 - 1944)
Advertisements... contain the only truths to be relied on in a newspaper.
Thomas Jefferson (1743 - 1826), Letter to Nathaniel Macon, January 12, 1819
I read no newspaper now but Ritchie's, and in that chiefly the advertisements, for they contain the only truths to be relied on in a newspaper.
Thomas Jefferson (1743 - 1826), Letter to Nathaniel Macon, January 12, 1819
What is the difference between unethical and ethical advertising? Unethical advertising uses falsehoods to deceive the public; ethical advertising uses truth to deceive the public.
Vilhjalmur Stefansson (1879 - 1962), "Discovery", 1964

Advice
Never trust the advice of a man in difficulties.
Aesop (620 BC - 560 BC)
It is very difficult to live among people you love and hold back from offering them advice.
Anne Tyler (1941 -), Celestial Navigation, 1974
People who ask our advice almost never take it. Yet we should never refuse to give it, upon request, for it often helps us to see our own way more clearly.
Brendan Francis
Ask advice only of your equals.
Danish Proverb
Please give me some good advice in your next letter. I promise not to follow it.
Edna St. Vincent Millay (1892 - 1950), Letters
Don't give advice. It will come back and bite you in the [butt]. Don't take anyone's advice. So, my advice to you is to be true to yourself and everything will be fine.
Ellen DeGeneres, Tulane Commencement Speech, 2009
Write down the advice of him who loves you, though you like it not at present.
English Proverb
Advice is what we ask for when we already know the answer but wish we didn't.
Erica Jong
Good advice is something a man gives when he is too old to set a bad example.
Francois de La Rochefoucauld (1613 - 1680)
I owe my success to having listened respectfully to the very best advice, and then going away and doing the exact opposite.
G. K. Chesterton (1874 - 1936)
Never give advice unless asked.
German Proverb
Some people like my advice so much that they frame it upon the wall instead of using it.
Gordon R. Dickson
There is no human problem which could not be solved if people would simply do as I advise.
Gore Vidal (1925 -)
The true secret of giving advice is, after you have honestly given it, to be perfectly indifferent whether it is taken or not, and never persist in trying to set people right.
Hannah Whitall Smith, 1902
I have found the best way to give advice to your children is to find out what they want and then advise them to do it.
Harry S Truman (1884 - 1972)
No-one wants advice only corroboration.
John Steinbeck (1902 - 1968)
The only thing to do with good advice is pass it on. It is never any use to oneself.

Oscar Wilde (1854 - 1900)
Don't try to solve serious matters in the middle of the night.
Philip K. Dick (1928 - 1982), What The Dead Men Say, 1964
The advice of friends must be received with a judicious reserve; we must not give ourselves up to it and follow it blindly, whether right or wrong.
Pierre Charron
Many receive advice, few profit by it.
Publilius Syrus (~ 100 BC), Maxims
Advice is very easy to give, and even easier not to follow, so I don't fool with it.
Randy Pausch, Carnegie Mellon Commencement Speech, 2008
It seems that bad advice that's fun will always be better known than than good advice that's dull-no matter how useless that fun advice is.
Scott Berkun, Confessions of a Public Speaker, 2009
Never take the advice of someone who has not had your kind of trouble.
Sidney J. Harris
In giving advice, seek to help, not please, your friend.
Solon (638 BC - 559 BC)
Never advise anyone to go to war or to marry.
Spanish Proverb
Be yourself is the worst advice you can give to some people.
Tom Masson
Don't be a dick!
Wil Wheaton, WWdN: In Exile Tagline

Age

Wisdom doesn't automatically come with old age. Nothing does - except wrinkles. It's true, some wines improve with age. But only if the grapes were good in the first place.
Abigail Van Buren (1918 -), 1978
I have enjoyed greatly the second blooming... suddenly you find - at the age of 50, say - that a whole new life has opened before you.
Agatha Christie (1890 - 1976)
The deepest definition of youth is life as yet untouched by tragedy.
Alfred North Whitehead (1861 - 1947)
Growing old is no more than a bad habit which a busy man has no time to form.
Andre Maurois (1885 - 1967), The Art of Living
You can only perceive real beauty in a person as they get older.
Anouk Aimee, O Magazine, October 2003
Young people are in a condition like permanent intoxication, because youth is sweet and they are growing.
Aristotle (384 BC - 322 BC), 'Nicomachean Ethics'
At twenty years of age the will reigns; at thirty the wit; at forty the judgement.
Benjamin Franklin (1706 - 1790)
Beware of the young doctor and the old barber.
Benjamin Franklin (1706 - 1790)
By my rambling digressions I perceive myself to be growing old.
Benjamin Franklin (1706 - 1790)
I will never be an old man. To me, old age is always 15 years older than I am.
Bernard M. Baruch (1870 - 1965)
To me, old age is always 15 years older than I am.
Bernard M. Baruch (1870 - 1965), 1940
Aging is not 'lost youth' but a new stage of opportunity and strength.
Betty Friedan (1921 - 2006)
There is no old age. There is, as there always was, just you.
Carol Matthau, O Magazine, October 2003
Always be nice to those younger than you, because they are the ones who will be writing about you.
Cyril Connolly (1903 - 1974)
The great secret that all old people share is that you really haven't changed in 70 or 80 years. Your body changes, but you don't change at all.
Doris Lessing, O Magazine, October 2003
The surprising thing about young fools is how many survive to become old fools.
Doug Larson
I'm very pleased with each advancing year. It stems back to when I was forty. I was a bit upset about reaching that milestone, but an older friend consoled me. 'Don't complain about growing old - many, many people do not have that privilege.'
Earl Warren (1891 - 1974), Chief Justice
In spite of illness, in spite even of the archenemy sorrow, one can remain alive long past the usual date of disintegration if one is unafraid of change, insatiable in intellectual curiosity, interested in big things, and happy in small ways.
Edith Wharton (1862 - 1937)
Old age, calm, expanded, broad with the haughty breadth of the universe, old age flowing free with the delicious near-by freedom of death.
Edith Wharton (1862 - 1937)
It is a sadness of growing older that we lose our ardent appreciation of what is new and different and difficult.
Elizabeth Aston, The Exploits & Adventures of Miss Alethea Darcy, 2005
With age come the inner, the higher life. Who would be forever young, to dwell always in externals?
Elizabeth Cady Stanton (1815 - 1902), O Magazine, October 2003
Though it sounds absurd, it is true to say I felt younger at sixty than I felt at twenty.
Ellen Glasgow (1873 - 1945), The Woman Within, 1954
That is the greatest fallacy, the wisdom of old men. They do not grow wise. They grow careful.
Ernest Hemingway (1899 - 1961), A Farewell to Arms, 1929

Only when one has lost all curiosity about the future has one reached the age to write an autobiography.
Evelyn Waugh (1903 - 1966)
I grow more intense as I age.
Florida Scott-Maxwell, O Magazine, October 2003
The longer I live the more beautiful life becomes.
Frank Lloyd Wright (1869 - 1959)
You're an old-timer if you can remember when setting the world on fire was a figure of speech.
Franklin P. Jones
Old age is like everything else. To make a success of it, you've got to start young.
Fred Astaire
It is kind of strange watching your personal history become costume.
gadgetgirl, gadgetgirl, 07-25-07
Age to me means nothing. I can't get old; I'm working. I was old when I was twenty-one and out of work. As long as you're working, you stay young. When I'm in front of an audience, all that love and vitality sweeps over me and I forget my age.
George Burns (1896 - 1996)
I was always taught to respect my elders and I've now reached the age when I don't have anybody to respect.
George Burns (1896 - 1996)
It is a mistake to regard age as a downhill grade toward dissolution. The reverse is true. As one grows older, one climbs with surprising strides.
George Sand (1804 - 1876)
Before you contradict an old man, my fair friend, you should endeavor to understand him.
George Santayana (1863 - 1952)
About the only thing that comes to us without effort is old age.
Gloria Pitzer, in Reader's Digest, 1979
Age is not a particularly interesting subject. Anyone can get old. All you have to do is live long enough.
Groucho Marx (1890 - 1977)
The older I grow the more I distrust the familiar doctrine that age brings wisdom.
H. L. Mencken (1880 - 1956)
A young man is embarrassed to question an older one.
Homer (800 BC - 700 BC), The Odyssey
Young men's minds are always changeable, but when an old man is concerned in a matter, he looks both before and after.
Homer (800 BC - 700 BC), The Iliad
The stream is as good as at first; the little rubbish it collects in the turnings is easily moved away.
Jane Austen (1775 - 1817), Persuasion, 1818
I didn't mind getting old when I was young. It's the being old now that's getting to me.
John Scalzi, Old Man's War, 2005
To resist the frigidity of old age one must combine the body, the mind and the heart - and to keep them in parallel vigor one must exercise, study and love.
Karl von Bonstetten
Sure I'm for helping the elderly. I'm going to be old myself some day.
Lillian Carter, in her 80s
The denunciation of the young is a necessary part of the hygiene of older people, and greatly assists in the circulation of their blood.
Logan Pearsall Smith (1865 - 1946), Afterthoughts (1931) "Age and Death"
I never feel age...If you have creative work, you don't have age or time.
Louise Nevelson (1900 - 1988), 1980
The secret of staying young is to live honestly, eat slowly, and lie about your age.
Lucille Ball (1911 - 1989)
No matter how old you are, there's always something good to look forward to.
Lynn Johnston (1947 -), For Better or For Worse, 01-04-04
You're never too old to become younger.
Mae West (1892 - 1980)
I'm having a glorious old age. One of my greatest delights is that I have outlived most of my opposition.
Maggie Kuhn, Speech to Vermont state legislature, 1991
Of all the self-fulfilling prophecies in our culture, the assumption that aging means decline and poor health is probably the deadliest.
Marilyn Ferguson, The Aquarian Conspiracy, 1980
The first half of life consists of the capacity to enjoy without the the chance; the last half consists of the chance without the capacity.
Mark Twain (1835 - 1910)
Young people have an almost biological destiny to be hopeful.
Marshall Ganz, quoted by Sara Rimer in New York Times
Old age is not so bad when you consider the alternatives.
Maurice Chevalier (1888 - 1972)
You don't stop laughing because you grow old. You grow old because you stop laughing.
Michael Pritchard
Age is...wisdom, if one has lived one's life properly.
Miriam Makeba, O Magazine, October 2003
Middle age is when you've met so many people that every new person you meet reminds you of someone else.
Ogden Nash (1902 - 1971)
A person is always startled when he hears himself seriously called an old man for the first time.
Oliver Wendell Holmes (1809 - 1894)
To be 70 years young is sometimes far more cheerful and hopeful than to be 40 years old.

Oliver Wendell Holmes (1809 - 1894)
I am not young enough to know everything.
Oscar Wilde (1854 - 1900)
The old believe everything, the middle-aged suspect everything, and the young know everything.
Oscar Wilde (1854 - 1900)
To get back my youth I would do anything in the world, except take exercise, get up early, or be respectable.
Oscar Wilde (1854 - 1900), The Picture of Dorian Gray, 1891
I am an old man, but in many senses a very young man. And this is what I want you to be, young, young all your life.
Pablo Casals (1876 - 1973), O Magazine, October 2003
At my age the bones are water in the morning until food is given them.
Pearl Buck (1892 - 1973)
Perhaps one has to be very old before one learns how to be amused rather than shocked.
Pearl S. Buck, China, Past and Present, 1972
Yet somehow our society must make it right and possible for old people not to fear the young or be deserted by them, for the test of a civilization is in the way that it cares for its helpless members.
Pearl S. Buck, My Several Worlds, 1954
He who is of calm and happy nature will hardly feel the pressure of age, but to him who is of an opposite disposition youth and age are equally a burden.
Plato (427 BC - 347 BC), The Republic
An old doting fool, with one foot already in the grave.
Plutarch (46 AD - 120 AD), Morals
As we grow old...the beauty steals inward.
Ralph Waldo Emerson (1803 - 1882)
People age even when you're not looking.
Randy K. Milholland, Something Postive, 07-30-08
As for me, except for an occasional heart attack, I feel as young as I ever did.
Robert Benchley (1889 - 1945)
To hold the same views at forty as we did at twenty is to have been stupefied for a score of years, and take rank, not as a prophet, but as an unteachable brat, well birched and none the wiser.
Robert Louis Stevenson (1850 - 1894), Crabbed Age and Youth, 1874
The heads of strong old age are beautiful beyond all grace of youth.
Robinson Jeffers, O Magazine, October 2003
In case you're worried about what's going to become of the younger generation, it's going to grow up and start worrying about the younger generation.
Roger Allen
People who say you're just as old as you feel are all wrong, fortunately.
Russell Baker (1925 -)
The young have aspirations that never come to pass, the old have reminiscences of what never happened.
Saki (1870 - 1916)
The best part about being my age is in knowing how my life worked out. Sure, there's a lot more living to go, but there isn't much doubt that I'll always be the 'Dilbert guy.' Unless I go on a crime spree, in which case I'll be 'that stabbin' Dilbert guy.'
Scott Adams (1957 -), The Benefits of Getting Old, Dilbert Blog, 08-22-06
The older I get, the more I feel almost beautiful...
Sharon Olds, Oprah Magazine, May 2004
There is nothing better than birthday cake. It's like a slice of concentrated love with buttercream frosting.
Takayuki Ikkaku, Arisa Hosaka and Toshihiro Kawabata, Animal Crossing: Wild World, 2005
To keep the heart unwrinkled, to be hopeful, kindly, cheerful, reverent - that is to triumph over old age.
Thomas Bailey Aldrich, O Magazine, October 2003
Where is the path to Grown-Up Land? How do I get there? Or will I just get old, not understanding that I'm no longer young?
Tish Grier, love and hope and sex and dreams, 05-01-07
I think age is a very high price to pay for maturity.
Tom Stoppard (1937 -)
We who are of mature age seldom suspect how unmercifully and yet with what insight the very young judge us.
W. Somerset Maugham (1874 - 1965), The Razor's Edge, 1943
When you have loved as she has loved, you grow old beautifully.
W. Somerset Maugham (1874 - 1965)
When you're eighteen your emotions are violent, but they're not durable.
W. Somerset Maugham (1874 - 1965), The Razor's Edge, 1943

Agreement

My idea of an agreeable person is a person who agrees with me.
Benjamin Disraeli (1804 - 1881)
It is by universal misunderstanding that all agree. For if, by ill luck, people understood each other, they would never agree.
Charles Baudelaire (1821 - 1867)
Those who agree with us may not be right, but we admire their astuteness.
Cullen Hightower
Your very silence shows you agree.
Euripides (484 BC - 406 BC)
We rarely think people have good sense unless they agree with us.
Francois de La Rochefoucauld (1613 - 1680), Maximes (1678)

If men would consider not so much wherein they differ, as wherein they agree, there would be far less of uncharitableness and angry feeling.
Joseph Addison (1672 - 1719)
If two men agree on everything, you may be sure that one of them is doing the thinking.
Lyndon B. Johnson (1908 - 1973)
I don't necessarily agree with everything I say.
Marshall McLuhan (1911 - 1980)
If you can find something everyone agrees on, it's wrong.
Mo Udall
To disagree with three-fourths of the British public is one of the first requisites of sanity.
Oscar Wilde (1854 - 1900)
Whenever people agree with me I always feel I must be wrong.
Oscar Wilde (1854 - 1900)
The greatest mistake is trying to be more agreeable than you can be.
Walter Bagehot (1826 - 1877)
When two men in business always agree, one of them is unnecessary.
William Wrigley Jr. (1861 - 1932)
Ambition;
Ambition is putting a ladder against the sky.
American Proverb
The universe is not required to be in perfect harmony with human ambition.
Carl Sagan (1934 - 1996)
Ambition is a poor excuse for not having sense enough to be lazy.
Edgar Bergen (1903 - 1978), (Charlie McCarthy)
The nature of society is largely determined by the direction in which talent and ambition flow-by the tilt of the social landscape.
Eric Hoffer (1902 - 1983), The Temper of Our Time, 1967
What seems to be generosity is often no more than disguised ambition, which overlooks a small interest in order to secure a great one.
Francois De La Rochefoucauld (1613 - 1680)
Most people would succeed in small things if they were not troubled with great ambitions.
Henry Wadsworth Longfellow (1807 - 1882), Driftwood; Table Talk, 1857
Ambition - it is the last infirmity of noble minds.
James M. Barrie (1860 - 1937)
Ambition often puts men upon doing the meanest offices; so climbing is performed in the same posture with creeping.
Jonathan Swift (1667 - 1745), Miscellanies, 1711
All ambitions are lawful except those that climb upward on the miseries or credulities of mankind.
Joseph Conrad (1857 - 1924)
It's delightful to have ambitions. I'm so glad I have such a lot. And there never seems to be any end to them—that's the best of it. Just as soon as you attain to one ambition you see another one glittering higher up still. It does make life so interesting.
L. M. Montgomery (1874 - 1942), Anne of Green Gables, 1908
Dreams, goals, ambitions - these are the stuff man uses for fuel.
L. Ron Hubbard (1911 - 1986)
Keep away from people who try to belittle your ambitions. Small people always do that, but the really great make you feel that you, too, can become great.
Mark Twain (1835 - 1910)
He who blinded by ambition, raises himself to a position whence he cannot mount higher, must thereafter fall with the greatest loss.
Niccolo Machiavelli (1469 - 1527)
A man without ambition is dead. A man with ambition but no love is dead. A man with ambition and love for his blessings here on earth is ever so alive. Having been alive, it won't be so hard in the end to lie down and rest.
Pearl Bailey (1918 - 1990)
Though ambition itself be a vice, yet it is often times the cause of virtues.
Quintilian
Men are more often bribed by their loyalties and ambitions than by money.
Robert Jackson
Ambition drove many men to become false; to have one thought locked in the breast, another ready on the tongue.
Sallust (86 BC - 34 BC), The War with Catiline
All ambitions are lawful except those which climb upward on the miseries or credulities of mankind.
William Congreve (1670 - 1729)
Ambition, the soldier's virtue, rather makes choice of loss, than gain which darkens him.
William Shakespeare (1564 - 1616), Antony and Cleopatra, Act III, sc.1
I have no spur to prick the sides of my intent, but only vaulting ambition, which o'erleaps itself, and falls on the other.
William Shakespeare (1564 - 1616), Macbeth, Act I, sc. 7
I hold ambition of so light a quality that is is but a shadow's shadow.
William Shakespeare (1564 - 1616), Hamlet, Act II, sc. 2
Lowliness is young ambition's ladder,
Whereto the climber-upward turns his face;
But when he once attains the upmost round,
He then unto the ladder turns his back,
Looks in the clouds, scorning the base degrees
By which he did ascend
William Shakespeare (1564 - 1616), Julius Caesar, Act II, sc.1
Virtue is choked with foul ambition.
William Shakespeare (1564 - 1616), Henry VI, Part II, Act III, sc. 1

America

In America any boy may become President and I suppose it's just one of the risks he takes.
Adlai E. Stevenson Jr. (1900 - 1965), Speech in Indianapolis, 26 Sept. 1952
There is a New America every morning when we wake up. It is upon us whether we will it or not.
Adlai E. Stevenson Jr. (1900 - 1965)
America's greatest strength, and its greatest weakness, is our belief in second chances, our belief that we can always start over, that things can be made better.
Anthony Walton
America is a large, friendly dog in a very small room. Every time it wags its tail, it knocks over a chair.
Arnold Toynbee (1889 - 1975)
America, we are better than these last eight years. We are a better country than this.
Barack Obama (1961 -), Nomination Acceptance Speech, 08-28-08
I know starting careers in troubled times is a challenge, but it is also a privilege. Because it's moments like these that force us to try harder, dig deeper and to discover gifts we never knew we had. To find the greatness that lies within each of us. So don't ever shy away from that endeavor. Don't stop adding to your body of work. I can promise that you will be the better for that continued effort as will be this nation that we all love.
Barack Obama (1961 -), Arizona State Commencement Speech, 2009
In recent years, we've become enamored with our own past success. Lulled into complacency by the glitter of our own achievements. We've become accustomed to the title of Military Superpower, forgetting the qualities that got us there. We've become accustomed to our economic dominance in the world, forgetting that it wasn't reckless deals and get rich quick schemes that got us where we are, but hard work and smart ideas, quality products and wise investments.
Barack Obama (1961 -), Arizona State Commencement Speech, 2009
That is the American story. People, just like you, following their passions, determined to meet the times on their own terms. They weren't doing it for the money. Their titles weren't fancy. But they changed the course of history and so can you.
Barack Obama (1961 -), Arizona State Commencement Speech, 2009
There is nothing wrong with America that cannot be cured by what is right with America.
Bill Clinton (1946 -)
America's one of the finest countries anyone ever stole.
Bobcat Goldthwaite
There's the country of America, which you have to defend, but there's also the idea of America. America is more than just a country, it's an idea. An idea that's supposed to be contagious.
Bono (1960 -), Oprah Winfrey Show, 2002
I see America, not in the setting sun of a black night of despair ahead of us, I see America in the crimson light of a rising sun fresh from the burning, creative hand of God. I see great days ahead, great days possible to men and women of will and vision.
Carl Sandburg (1878 - 1967)
The trouble with America is that there are far too many wide-open spaces surrounded by teeth.
Charles Luckman
America is the greatest, freest and most decent society in existence. It is an oasis of goodness in a desert of cynicism and barbarism. This country, once an experiment unique in the world, is now the last best hope for the world.
Dinesh D'Souza
There is nothing wrong with America that the faith, love of freedom, intelligence and energy of her citizens cannot cure.
Dwight D. Eisenhower (1890 - 1969)
The United States is a nation of laws: badly written and randomly enforced.
Frank Zappa (1940 - 1993)
America is therefore the land of the future, where, in the ages that lie before us, the burden of the World's History shall reveal itself.
Georg W. Hegel (1770 - 1831)
England and America are two countries separated by a common language.
George Bernard Shaw (1856 - 1950)
The business of America is not business. Neither is it war. The business of America is justice and securing the blessings of liberty.
George F. Will (1941 -)
America is a young country with an old mentality.
George Santayana (1863 - 1952)
America has never been an empire. We may be the only great power in history that had the chance, and refused – preferring greatness to power and justice to glory.
George W. Bush (1946 -), speech, November 19, 1999
America has never been united by blood or birth or soil. We are bound by ideals that move us beyond our backgrounds, lift us above our interests and teach us what it means to be citizens.
George W. Bush (1946 -), Inaugural address, 2001
America will never run... And we will always be grateful that liberty has found such brave defenders.
George W. Bush (1946 -)
By heritage and by choice, the United States of America will make that stand.
George W. Bush (1946 -), Speech to the United Nations, September 12, 2002
In the United States there is more space where nobody is than where anybody is. That is what makes America what it is.
Gertrude Stein (1874 - 1946), The Geographical History of America (1936)

What's right about America is that although we have a mess of problems, we have great capacity - intellect and resources - to do some thing about them.
Henry Ford II (1917 - 1987)
America - a great social and economic experiment, noble in motive and far-reaching in purpose.
Herbert Hoover (1874 - 1964)
I'm not going to quit. Why should I quit? This country is worth fighting for.
Hillary Rodham Clinton (1948 -), Ellen DeGeneres interview, 04-07-08
This is the story of America. Everybody's doing what they think they're supposed to do.
Jack Kerouac (1922 - 1969), On the Road
In a country as big as the United States, you can find fifty examples of anything.
Jeffery F. Chamberlain
Americans;America;England
In every American there is an air of incorrigible innocence, which seems to conceal a diabolical cunning.
A. E. Housman (1859 - 1936)
Too many of us look upon Americans as dollar chasers. This is a cruel libel, even if it is reiterated thoughtlessly by the Americans themselves.
Albert Einstein (1879 - 1955)
The people reign over the American political world as God rules over the universe. It is the cause and the end of all things; everything rises out of it and is absorbed back into it.
Alexis De Tocqueville (1805 - 1859), Democracy in America, 1835
Americans will put up with anything provided it doesn't block traffic.
Dan Rather (1931 -)
I was born an American; I will live an American; I shall die an American.
Daniel Webster (1782 - 1852)
How much longer are we going to think it necessary to be "American" before (or in contradistinction to) being cultivated, being enlightened, being humane, and having the same intellectual discipline as other civilized countries?
Edith Wharton (1862 - 1937)
I sometimes think that the saving grace of America lies in the fact that the overwhelming majority of Americans are possessed of two great qualities- a sense of humor and a sense of proportion.
Franklin D. Roosevelt (1882 - 1945)
Americans never quit.
General Douglas Macarthur (1880 - 1964)
Americans adore me and will go on adoring me until I say something nice about them.
George Bernard Shaw (1856 - 1950)
Americans are overreachers; overreaching is the most admirable of the many American excesses.
George F. Will (1941 -), Statecraft as Soulcraft
Half of the American people have never read a newspaper. Half never voted for President. One hopes it is the same half.
Gore Vidal (1925 -)
Nobody ever went broke underestimating the intelligence of the American public.
H. L. Mencken (1880 - 1956)
The character inherent in the American people has done all that has been accomplished; and it would have done somewhat more, if the government had not sometimes got in its way.
Henry David Thoreau (1817 - 1862)
It is, I think, an indisputable fact that Americans are, as Americans, the most self-conscious people in the world, and the most addicted to the belief that the other nations are in a conspiracy to under-value them.
Henry James (1843 - 1916)
Americans are benevolently ignorant about Canada, while Canadians are malevolently well informed about the United States.
J. Bartlett Brebner
George Washington had a vision for this country. Was it three days of uninterrupted shopping?
Jeff Melvoin, Northern Exposure, Bolt from the Blue, 1994
The American, by nature, is optimistic. He is experimental, an inventor and a builder who builds best when called upon to build greatly.
John F. Kennedy (1917 - 1963)
This nation was founded by many men of many nations and backgrounds. It was founded on the principle that all men are created equal, and that the rights of every man are diminished when the rights of one man are threatened.
John F. Kennedy (1917 - 1963), Radio and television report to the American people in civil rights, June 11, 1963
Ninety-eight percent of the adults in this country are decent, hard-working, honest Americans. It's the other lousy two percent that get all the publicity. But then–we elected them.
Lily Tomlin (1939 -)
Sitting at the table doesn't make you a diner, unless you eat some of what's on that plate. Being here in America doesn't make you an American. Being born here in America doesn't make you an American.
Malcolm X (1925 - 1965), Malcolm X Speaks, 1965
An Englishman is a person who does things because they have been done before. An American is a person who does things because they haven't been done before.
Mark Twain (1835 - 1910)
The people of the United States, perhaps more than any other nation in history, love to abase themselves and proclaim their unworthiness, and seem to find refreshment in doing so... That is a dark frivolity, but still frivolity.
Robertson Davies

For the American people are a very generous people and will forgive almost any weakness, with the possible exception of stupidity.
Will Rogers (1879 - 1935), The Illiterate Digest, 1924
Anger;Enemies
Eat a third and drink a third and leave the remaining third of your stomach empty. Then, when you get angry, there will be sufficient room for your rage.
Babylonian Talmud, tractate Gittin
Anger makes you smaller, while forgiveness forces you to grow beyond what you were.
Cherie Carter-Scott, "If Love Is a Game, These Are the Rules"
When anger rises, think of the consequences.
Confucius (551 BC - 479 BC)
Anger makes dull men witty, but it keeps them poor.
Elizabeth I (1533 - 1603), in Francis Bacon, Apophthegms, 1625
Anger as soon as fed is dead-
'Tis starving makes it fat.
Emily Dickinson (1830 - 1886), Poems, Second Series, 1891
If you do not wish to be prone to anger, do not feed the habit; give it nothing which may tend to its increase.
Epictetus (55 AD - 135 AD)
If you would cure anger, do not feed it. Say to yourself: 'I used to be angry every day; then every other day; now only every third or fourth day.' When you reach thirty days offer a sacrifice of thanksgiving to the gods.
Epictetus (55 AD - 135 AD)
I have seen a peaceful expression turn to anger as fast as a whip cracks, and so the look on the face might mean less than what it seems to be.
Erica Eisdorfer, The Wet Nurse's Tale, 2009
Anger at lies lasts forever. Anger at truth can't last.
Greg Evans, Luann (comic), September 27, 2003
Anger is a signal, and one worth listening to.
Harriet Lerner, The Dance of Anger, 1985
Never forget what a man says to you when he is angry.
Henry Ward Beecher (1813 - 1887)
Holding on to anger, resentment and hurt only gives you tense muscles, a headache and a sore jaw from clenching your teeth. Forgiveness gives you back the laughter and the lightness in your life.
Joan Lunden, in Healthy Living Magazine
A child that has a quick temper, just blaze up and cool down, ain't never likely to be sly or deceitful.
L. M. Montgomery (1874 - 1942), Anne of Green Gables, 1908
Speak when you are angry–and you will make the best speech you'll ever regret.
Laurence J. Peter (1919 - 1988)
Usually when people are sad, they don't do anything. They just cry over their condition. But when they get angry, they bring about a change.
Malcolm X (1925 - 1965), Malcolm X Speaks, 1965
How much more grievous are the consequences of anger than the causes of it.
Marcus Aurelius
Never get angry. Never make a threat. Reason with people.
Mario Puzo (1920 - 1999), 'The Godfather'
I have a right to my anger, and I don't want anybody telling me I shouldn't be, that it's not nice to be, and that something's wrong with me because I get angry.
Maxine Waters, in Brian Lanker, I Dream a World, 1989

Apathy

Science may have found a cure for most evils; but it has found no remedy for the worst of them all - the apathy of human beings.
Helen Keller (1880 - 1968), My Religion, 1927
Choosing to live in narrow spaces leads to form of mental agoraphobia and that brings its own terrors. I think the willfully unimaginative see more monsters, they are often more afraid. What is more, those who choose not to empathize enable real monsters. For without ever committing an act of outright evil ourselves, we collude through our own apathy.
J. K. Rowling, Harvard Commencement Address, 2008
The greatest danger to our future is apathy.
Jane Goodall (1934 -)
Is sloppiness in speech caused by ignorance or apathy? I don't know and I don't care.
William Safire (1929 -)
Argument;Balance;Agreement;Communication
How many a dispute could have been deflated into a single paragraph if the disputants had dared to define their terms.
Aristotle (384 BC - 322 BC)
The Argument from Intimidation is a confession of intellectual impotence.
Ayn Rand (1905 - 1982), The Virtue of Selfishness, 1964
My parents only had one argument in forty-five years. It lasted forty-three years.
Cathy Ladman
He who strikes the first blow admits he's lost the argument.
Chinese Proverb
I can win an argument on any topic, against any opponent. People know this, and steer clear of me at parties. Often, as a sign of their great respect, they don't even invite me.
Dave Barry (1947 -)
Use soft words and hard arguments.
English Proverb

The most perfidious way of harming a cause consists of defending it deliberately with faulty arguments.
Friedrich Nietzsche (1844 - 1900), The Gay Science, section 191
The thing I hate about an argument is that it always interrupts a discussion.
G. K. Chesterton (1874 - 1936)
No matter what side of the argument you are on, you always find people on your side that you wish were on the other.
Jascha Heifetz (1901 - 1987)
That's the beauty of argument-if you argue correctly, you're never wrong.
Jason Reitman and Christopher Buckly, Thank You for Smoking, 2006
If you go in for argument, take care of your temper. Your logic, if you have any, will take care of itself.
Joseph Farrell
Silence is one of the hardest arguments to refute.
Josh Billings (1818 - 1885)
Behind every argument is someone's ignorance.
Louis D. Brandeis (1856 - 1941)
Arguments are to be avoided; they are always vulgar and often convincing.
Oscar Wilde (1854 - 1900)
It is not necessary to understand things in order to argue about them.
Pierre Beaumarchais (1732 - 1799)
In a heated argument we are apt to lose sight of the truth.
Publilius Syrus (~ 100 BC)
The argument is at an end.
Saint Augustine (354 AD - 430 AD)
I learned an important lesson in the art of debate. Present your argument clearly, arm yourself with cutting wit and of course, bob and weave!
Takayuki Ikkaku, Arisa Hosaka and Toshihiro Kawabata, Animal Crossing: Wild World, 2005
It is impossible to defeat an ignorant man in argument.
William G. McAdoo (1863 - 1941)
With reasonable men I will reason; with humane men I will plea; but to tyrants I will give no quarter, nor waste arguments where they will certainly be lost.
William Lloyd Garrison (1805 - 1879)
For they are yet ear-kissing arguments.
William Shakespeare (1564 - 1616)
Art;Poetry;Music;Criticism
[Abstract art is] a product of the untalented, sold by the unprincipled to the utterly bewildered.
Al Capp (1909 - 1979)
Art is the imposing of a pattern on experience, and our aesthetic enjoyment is recognition of the pattern.
Alfred North Whitehead (1861 - 1947), Dialogues (1954)
Painting: The art of protecting flat surfaces from the weather and exposing them to the critic.
Ambrose Bierce (1842 - 1914), The Devil's Dictionary
Art is the desire of a man to express himself, to record the reactions of his personality to the world he lives in.
Amy Lowell (1874 - 1925)
Art is a collaboration between God and the artist, and the less the artist does the better.
Andre Gide (1869 - 1951)
I have often thought that if photography were difficult in the true sense of the term – meaning that the creation of a simple photograph would entail as much time and effort as the production of a good watercolor or etching – there would be a vast improvement in total output. The sheer ease with which we can produce a superficial image often leads to creative disaster.
Ansel Adams (1902 - 1984)
Let each man exercise the art he knows.
Aristophanes (450 BC - 388 BC), Wasps, 422 B.C.
The aim of art is to represent not the outward appearance of things, but their inward significance.
Aristotle (384 BC - 322 BC)
Art does not exist only to entertain, but also to challenge one to think, to provoke, even to disturb, in a constant search for truth.
Barbra Streisand (1942 -)
I believe that if it were left to artists to choose their own labels, most would choose none.
Ben Shahn (1898 - 1969)
So you see, imagination needs moodling - long, inefficient, happy idling, dawdling and puttering.
Brenda Ueland
I suppose no matter what I'm drawing, there will always be some sort of question in my mind about it. A work of art (even cartoon art)is never really finished; it is abandoned.
Brooke McEldowney, Pibgorn commentary, 03-31-05
I can't criticize what I don't understand. If you want to call this art, you've got the benefit of all my doubts.
Charles Rosin, Northern Exposure, Aurora Borealis, 1990
Art is born of the observation and investigation of nature.
Cicero (106 BC - 43 BC)
Art forms of the past were really considered elitist. Bach did not compose for the masses, neither did Beethoven. It was always for patrons, aristocrats, and royalty. Now we have a sort of democratic version of that, which is to say that the audience is so splintered in its interests.
David Cronenberg, Rocketboom, 07-19-06
The idea of a mass audience was really an invention of the Industrial Revolution.
David Cronenberg, Rocketboom, 07-19-06

I don't understand why people think everything has to have meaning. While painting the Mona Lisa did Leonardo Da Vinci intend for it to have greater meaning than a work of art that he made?
Devin J. Monroe (1983 -)
If you were in a burning house and there was a cat and a Rembrandt, what would you save? The cat...you would save the cat, because the cat is alive. The art is dead. It's just paint on a canvas, ink on a page. To live for art is to deny life. It's just to destroy life.
Diane Frolov and Andrew Schneider, Northern Exposure, Cicely, 1992
I merely took the energy it takes to pout and wrote some blues.
Duke Ellington (1899 - 1974)
Works of art, in my opinion, are the only objects in the material universe to possess internal order, and that is why, though I don't believe that only art matters, I do believe in Art for Art's sake.
E. M. Forster (1879 - 1970)
Another unsettling element in modern art is that common symptom of immaturity, the dread of doing what has been done before.
Edith Wharton (1862 - 1937)
Art is on the side of the oppressed. Think before you shudder at the simplistic dictum and its heretical definition of the freedom of art. For if art is freedom of the spirit, how can it exist within the oppressors?
Edith Wharton (1862 - 1937)
A painting in a museum hears more ridiculous opinions than anything else in the world.
Edmond de Goncourt (1822 - 1896)
It is all very well, when the pen flows, but then there are the dark days when imagination deserts one, and it is an effort to put anything down on paper. That little you have achieved stares at you at the end of the day, and you know the next morning you will have to scrape it down and start again.
Elizabeth Aston, The True Darcy Spirit, 2006
Illusions are art, for the feeling person, and it is by art that you live, if you do.
Elizabeth Bowen (1899 - 1973)
Artists who seek perfection in everything are those who cannot attain it in anything.
Eugene Delacroix (1798 - 1863)
I don't believe in total freedom for the artist. Left on his own, free to do anything he likes, the artist ends up doing nothing at all. If there's one thing that's dangerous for an artist, it's precisely this question of total freedom, waiting for inspiration and all the rest of it.
Federico Fellini (1920 - 1993)
Art is making something out of nothing and selling it.
Frank Zappa (1940 - 1993)
I paint my own reality. The only thing I know is that I paint because I need to, and I paint whatever passes through my head without any other consideration.
Frida Kahlo (1907 - 1954)
Art, like morality, consists of drawing the line somewhere.
G. K. Chesterton (1874 - 1936)
Without art the crudeness of reality would make the world unbearable.
George Bernard Shaw (1856 - 1950), Back to Methuselah, 1921
Painting is an attempt to come to terms with life. There are as many solutions as there are human beings.
George Tooker
What I dream of is an art of balance.
Henri Matisse (1869 - 1954), O Magazine, April 2003
Every artist dips his brush in his own soul, and paints his own nature into his pictures.
Henry Ward Beecher (1813 - 1887), Proverbs from Plymouth Pulpit, 1887
The more minimal the art, the more maximum the explination.
Hilton Kramer, The New York Times art critic, in the late 1960
Through all the world there goes one long cry from the heart of the artist: Give me leave to do my utmost.
Isak Dineson, 'Babette's Feast'
The painting has a life of its own. I try to let it come through.
Jackson Pollock (1912 - 1956)
It doesn't matter if people are interested. It's about you taking your stuff and shouting out into the void.
Jadelr and Cristina Cordova, Chasing Windmills, 07-11-2006
It's not your painting anymore. It stopped being your painting the moment that you finished it.
Jeff Melvoin, Northern Exposure, Fish Story, 1994
You're confusing product with process. Most people, when they criticize, whether they like it or hate it, they're talking about product. That's not art, that's the result of art. Art, to whatever degree we can get a handle on (I'm not sure that we really can) is a process. It begins in the heart and the mind with the eyes and hands.
Jeff Melvoin, Northern Exposure, Fish Story, 1994
There is no better deliverance from the world than through art; and a man can form no surer bond with it than through art.
Johann Wolfgang von Goethe (1749 - 1832), Elective Affinities
If art is to nourish the roots of our culture, society must set the artist free to follow his vision wherever it takes him.
John F. Kennedy (1917 - 1963), Speech at Amherst College, October 26, 1963
We must never forget that art is not a form of propaganda; it is a form of truth.
John F. Kennedy (1917 - 1963), October 26, 1963
The urge to make art or contemplate philosophy does not go away when you are sick. Those urges just become transfigured by illness.
John Green, The Fault in Our Stars, 2012
Every time I paint a portrait I lose a friend.
John Singer Sargent (1856 - 1925), quoted in Bentley and Esar, Treasury of Humorous Quotations (1951)

To live a creative life, we must lose our fear of being wrong.
Joseph Chilton Pearce
Our creations MUST be shared to be art, and the easiest way to share our art is to sell it.
Laura Moncur (1969 -), Merriton: 35 Minutes from Home, 03-07-12
What we play is life.
Louis Armstrong (1900 - 1971)
The creation of art is not the fulfillment of a need but the creation of a need. The world never needed Beethoven's Fifth Symphony until he created it. Now we could not live without it.
Louis I Kahn
All the arts we practice are apprenticeship. The big art is our life.
M. C. Richards
One reassuring thing about modern art is that things can't be as bad as they are painted.
M. Walthall Jackson
Painting in watercolor is like walking a tight-rope; one must achieve a perfect balance between what the paint wants to do and what the artist wants to do, or all is lost.
Mary C. Taylor, Watercolor Bold and Free
Creativity is...seeing something that doesn't exist already. You need to find out how you can bring it into being and that way be a playmate with God.
Michele Shea
I say that good painters imitated nature; but that bad ones vomited it.
Miguel de Cervantes (1547 - 1616), Exemplary Novels (1613)
Photography, fortunately, to me has not only been a profession but also a contact between people - to understand human nature and record, if possible, the best in each individual.
Nickolas Muray
Art has never been made while thinking of art.
Niko Stumpo, The Wooster Collective, December 2006
I passionately hate the idea of being with it, I think an artist has always to be out of step with his time.
Orson Welles (1915 - 1985)
Every child is an artist. The problem is how to remain an artist once he grows up.
Pablo Picasso (1881 - 1973)
Painting is just another way of keeping a diary.
Pablo Picasso (1881 - 1973)
There are painters who transform the sun to a yellow spot, but there are others who with the help of their art and their intelligence, transform a yellow spot into the sun.
Pablo Picasso (1881 - 1973)
There is no abstract art. You must always start with something. Afterward you can remove all traces of reality.
Pablo Picasso (1881 - 1973)
Art is either plagiarism or revolution.
Paul Gauguin (1848 - 1903)
I shut my eyes in order to see.
Paul Gauguin (1848 - 1903)
Technology adds nothing to art. Two thousand years ago, I could tell you a story, and at any point during the story I could stop, and ask, Now do you want the hero to be kidnapped, or not? But that would, of course, have ruined the story. Part of the experience of being entertained is sitting back and plugging into someone else's vision.
Penn Jillette (1955 -), Interview in WIRED magazine, 1993
Why should I buy expensive art when I can make my own.
Pjero Milani
The position of the artist is humble. He is essentially a channel.
Piet Mondrian (1872 - 1944)
Every artist was first an amateur.
Ralph Waldo Emerson (1803 - 1882), Letters and Social Aims: Progress of Culture, 1876
An authentic work of art must start an argument between the artist and his audience.
Rebecca West (1892 - 1983), The Count and the Castle, 1957
Repetition is the death of art.
Robin Green, Northern Exposure, Burning Down the House, 1992
Creativity is allowing yourself to make mistakes. Art is knowing which ones to keep.
Scott Adams (1957 -), 'The Dilbert Principle'
If I've learned one thing in the 14 years I've been a full-time cartoonist, it's that you can not let anyone else define your professionalism. It has to be a personal ethos to which you adhere despite third party influence or acceptance. The old measuring sticks for professionalism are going away and now more than ever it's time for independent creatives to set the bar. Set it high.
Scott R. Kurtz, PvPonline, 11-28-2011
All art is an imitation of nature.
Seneca (5 BC - 65 AD)
Painting is silent poetry, and poetry is painting with the gift of speech.
Simonides (556 BC - 468 BC)
Creative work is play. It is free speculation using materials of one's chosen form.
Stephen Nachmanovitch
Art is merely the refuge which the ingenious have invented, when they were supplied with food and women, to escape the tediousness of life.
W. Somerset Maugham (1874 - 1965), 'Of Human Bondage', 1915
I never spend more than one hour in a gallery. That is as long as one's power of appreciation persists.
W. Somerset Maugham (1874 - 1965), The Razor's Edge, 1943
Life isn't long enough for love and art.
W. Somerset Maugham (1874 - 1965), The Moon and Sixpence
The art of art, the glory of expression and the sunshine of the light of letters, is simplicity.

Walt Whitman (1819 - 1892)
I know just how frustrating it can be when you're tired and exhausted, but you still want to draw something.
Ward Jenkins, Ward-O-Matic, 03-23-2006
Each painting has its own way of evolving...When the painting is finished, the subject reaveals itself.
William Baziotes
The aim of every artist is to arrest motion, which is life, by artificial means and hold it fixed so that a hundred years later, when a stranger looks at it, it moves again since it is life.
William Faulkner (1897 - 1962), Interview, 1958
Atheism;God;Religion
The worst moment for the atheist is when he is really thankful and has nobody to thank.
Dante Gabriel Rossetti (1828 - 1882)
I always admired atheists. I think it takes a lot of faith.
Diane Frolov and Andrew Schneider, Northern Exposure, Seoul Mates, 1991
The opposite of the religious fanatic is not the fanatical atheist but the gentle cynic who cares not whether there is a god or not.
Eric Hoffer (1902 - 1983)
I believe in God, only I spell it Nature.
Frank Lloyd Wright (1869 - 1959)
If there were no God, there would be no Atheists.
G. K. Chesterton (1874 - 1936)
I have too much respect for the idea of God to make it responsible for such an absurd world.
Georges Duhamel (1884 - 1966)
I'm a born-again atheist.
Gore Vidal (1925 -)
I once wanted to become an atheist, but I gave up - they have no holidays.
Henny Youngman (1906 - 1998)
Nobody talks so constantly about God as those who insist that there is no God.
Heywood Broun (1888 - 1939)
An atheist is a man who has no invisible means of support.
John Buchan (1875 - 1940)
Somebody once asked me if I have anything like faith, and I said I have faith in the narrative. I have a belief in a narrative that is bigger than me, that is alive and I trust will work itself out.
Joss Whedon, Entertainment Weekly, 08-30-13
I don't know if God exists, but it would be better for His reputation if He didn't.
Jules Renard (1864 - 1910)
I'm the world's least happy atheist. I miss having religious faith, but trying to have it seems like trying to be in love with someone that you're not in love with.
Lisa Williams, Learning the Lessons of Nixon, 03-29-08
I am an atheist, myself. A simple faith, but a great comfort to me, in these last days.
Lois McMaster Bujold
I'm still an atheist, thank God.
Luis Bunuel (1900 - 1983)
It is the final proof of God's omnipotence that he need not exist in order to save us.
Peter De Vries, "The Mackerel Plaza," 1958
When I told the people of Northern Ireland that I was an atheist, a woman in the audience stood up and said, "Yes, but is it the God of the Catholics or the God of the Protestants in whom you don't believe?"
Quentin Crisp
Religion is about turning untested belief into unshakeable truth through the power of institutions and the passage of time.
Richard Dawkins (1941 -), "The Root of All Evil", Channel 4 UK, 2006
We are all atheists about most of the gods that societies have ever believed in. Some of us just go one god further.
Richard Dawkins (1941 -), "The Root of All Evil", UK Channel 4, 2006
You've got your phenomenon on one hand. Concrete and knowable. On the other hand you've got the incomprehensible. You call it God, but to me, God or no, it remains just that, the unknowable.
Robin Green and Mitchell Burgess, Northern Exposure, A Wing and a Prayer, 1994
Ask a deeply religious Christian if he'd rather live next to a bearded Muslim that may or may not be plotting a terror attack, or an atheist that may or may not show him how to set up a wireless network in his house. On the scale of prejudice, atheists don't seem so bad lately.
Scott Adams (1957 -), The Dilbert Blog: Atheists: The New Gays, 11-19-06
Shake off all the fears of servile prejudices, under which weak minds are servilely crouched. Fix reason firmly in her seat, and call on her tribunal for every fact, every opinion. Question with boldness even the existence of a God; because, if there be one, he must more approve of the homage of reason than that of blindfolded fear.
Thomas Jefferson (1743 - 1826)
If God did not exist, it would be necessary to invent him.
Voltaire (1694 - 1778)
How can I believe in God when just last week I got my tongue caught in the roller of an electric typewriter?
Woody Allen (1935 -)
If it turns out that there is a God, I don't think that he's evil. But the worst that you can say about him is that basically he's an underachiever.
Woody Allen (1935 -)
To you I'm an atheist; to God, I'm the Loyal Opposition.
Woody Allen (1935 -)
Attitude;Optimism;Pessimism;Forgiveness
Being assertive does not mean attacking or ignoring others feelings. It means that you are willing to hold up for yourself fairly-without attacking others.

Albert Ellis, Michael Abrams, Lidia Dengelegi, The Art & Science of Rational Eating, 1992
Eccentricity is not, as dull people would have us believe, a form of madness. It is often a kind of innocent pride, and the man of genius and the aristocrat are frequently regarded as eccentrics because genius and aristocrat are entirely unafraid of and uninfluenced by the opinions and vagaries of the crowd.
Edith Sitwell (1887 - 1964), Taken Care Of ,1965
A positive attitude may not solve all your problems, but it will annoy enough people to make it worth the effort.
Herm Albright (1876 - 1944)
I happen to feel that the degree of a person's intelligence is directly reflected by the number of conflicting attitudes she can bring to bear on the same topic.
Lisa Alther, Kinflicks, 1975
Complaining is good for you as long as you're not complaining to the person you're complaining about.
Lynn Johnston (1947 -), For Better or For Worse, 11-06-03
I am still determined to be cheerful and happy, in whatever situation I may be; for I have also learned from experience that the greater part of our happiness or misery depends upon our dispositions, and not upon our circumstances.
Martha Washington (1732 - 1802)
A strong positive mental attitude will create more miracles than any wonder drug.
Patricia Neal
Human beings, by changing the inner attitudes of their minds, can change the outer aspects of their lives.
William James (1842 - 1910)
The greatest discovery of my generation is that a human being can alter his life by altering his attitudes of mind.
William James (1842 - 1910)

Authority

No moral system can rest solely on authority.
A. J. Ayer (1910 - 1989), Humanist Outlook
To punish me for my contempt for authority, fate made me an authority myself.
Albert Einstein (1879 - 1955)
The peaceful transfer of authority is rare in history, yet common in our country. With a simple oath, we affirm old traditions and make new beginnings.
George W. Bush (1946 -), Inaugural address, 2001
Truth is the secret of eloquence and of virtue, the basis of moral authority; it is the highest summit of art and life.
Henri-Frédéric Amiel
Show me the man who keeps his house in hand,
He's fit for public authority.
Sophocles (496 BC - 406 BC), Antigone
Every great advance in natural knowledge has involved the absolute rejection of authority.
Thomas H. Huxley (1825 - 1895)
Wherever there is authority, there is a natural inclination to disobedience.
Thomas Haliburton
There is no fettering of authority.
William Shakespeare (1564 - 1616), All's Well that Ends Well, Act II, sc. 3
If you wish to know what a man is, place him in authority.
Yugoslav Proverb

Autumn

Autumn is a second spring when every leaf is a flower.
Albert Camus (1913 - 1960)
When the bold branches
Bid farewell to rainbow leaves -
Welcome wool sweaters.
B. Cybrill
Fall is my favorite season in Los Angeles, watching the birds change color and fall from the trees.
David Letterman (1947 -)
For man, autumn is a time of harvest, of gathering together.
For nature, it is a time of sowing, of scattering abroad.
Edwin Teale
A few days ago I walked along the edge of the lake and was treated to the crunch and rustle of leaves with each step I made. The acoustics of this season are different and all sounds, no matter how hushed, are as crisp as autumn air.
Eric Sloane
The leaves fall, the wind blows, and the farm country slowly changes from the summer cottons into its winter wools.
Henry Beston, Northern Farm
If winter is slumber and spring is birth, and summer is life, then autumn rounds out to be reflection. It's a time of year when the leaves are down and the harvest is in and the perennials are gone. Mother Earth just closed up the drapes on another year and it's time to reflect on what's come before.
Mitchell Burgess, Northern Exposure, Thanksgiving, 1992
I cannot endure to waste anything as precious as autumn sunshine by staying in the house. So I spend almost all the daylight hours in the open air.
Nathaniel Hawthorne (1804 - 1864)
It was one of those perfect English autumnal days which occur more frequently in memory than in life.
P. D. James
There is a harmony
In autumn, and a lustre in its sky,
Which through the summer is not heard or seen,

As if it could not be, as if it had not been!
Percy Bysshe Shelley (1792 - 1822)
In the garden, Autumn is, indeed the crowning glory of the year, bringing us the fruition of months of thought and care and toil. And at no season, safe perhaps in Daffodil time, do we get such superb colour effects as from August to November.
Rose G. Kingsley, The Autumn Garden, 1905
Fiery colors begin their yearly conquest of the hills, propelled by the autumn winds. Fall is the artist.
Takayuki Ikkaku, Arisa Hosaka and Toshihiro Kawabata, Animal Crossing: Wild World, 2005
That time of year thou may'st in me behold,
When yellow leaves, or none, or few, do hang
Upon those boughs which shake against the cold,-
Bare ruin'd choirs, where late the sweet birds sang.
William Shakespeare (1564 - 1616), Sonnet LXXIII

Balance

It may make your blood boil and your mind may not be changed, but the practice of listening to opposing views is essential for effective citizenship. It is essential for our democracy.
Barack Obama (1961 -), University of Michigan Commencement, 2010
The best and safest thing is to keep a balance in your life, acknowledge the great powers around us and in us. If you can do that, and live that way, you are really a wise man.
Euripides (484 BC - 406 BC)
We can be sure that the greatest hope for maintaining equilibrium in the face of any situation rests within ourselves.
Francis J. Braceland, O Magazine, April 2003
What I dream of is an art of balance.
Henri Matisse (1869 - 1954), O Magazine, April 2003
So divinely is the world organized that every one of us, in our place and time, is in balance with everything else.
Johann Wolfgang von Goethe (1749 - 1832)
Order is not pressure which is imposed on society from without, but an equilibrium which is set up from within.
Jose Ortega y Gasset (1883 - 1955)
I've learned that you can't have everything and do everything at the same time.
Oprah Winfrey (1954 -), O Magazine, April 2003

Banks

A bank is a place that will lend you money if you can prove that you don't need it.
Bob Hope (1903 - 2003)
Drive-in banks were established so most of the cars today could see their real owners.
E. Joseph Cossman
A banker is a fellow who lends you his umbrella when the sun is shining, but wants it back the minute it begins to rain.
Mark Twain (1835 - 1910)
I don't have a bank account, because I don't know my mother's maiden name.
Paula Poundstone
I believe that banking institutions are more dangerous to our liberties than standing armies. If the American people ever allow private banks to control the issue of their currency, first by inflation, then by deflation, the banks and corporations that will grow up around [the banks] will deprive the people of all property until their children wake-up homeless on the continent their fathers conquered. The issuing power should be taken from the banks and restored to the people, to whom it properly belongs.
Thomas Jefferson (1743 - 1826), (Attributed)

Beauty

What has a man's face to do with his character? Can a man of good character help having a disagreeable face?
Ann Radcliffe (1764 - 1823), The Mysteries of Udolpho, 1764
Think of all the beauty still left around you and be happy.
Anne Frank (1929 - 1945), Diary of a Young Girl, 1952
Like anyone else, there are days I feel beautiful and days I don't, and when I don't, I do something about it.
Cheryl Tiegs (1947 -), O Magazine, May 2004
Beautiful young people are accidents of nature, but beautiful old people are works of art.
Eleanor Roosevelt (1884 - 1962)
What you look like on the outside is not what makes you cool at all. I mean, I had a mullet and wore parachute pants for a long, long time, and I'm doin' okay.
Ellen DeGeneres, The Ellen Show, 05-17-13
The absence of flaw in beauty is itself a flaw.
Havelock Ellis (1859 - 1939), Impressions and Comments (1914)
The words that enlighten the soul are more precious than jewels.
Hazrat Inayat Khan

Develop interest in life as you see it; in people, things, literature, music - the world is so rich, simply throbbing with rich treasures, beautiful souls and interesting people. Forget yourself.
Henry Miller (1891 - 1980)
An agreeable manner may set off handsome features, but can never alter plain ones.
Jane Austen (1775 - 1817), Persuasion, 1818
I'm tired of all this nonsense about beauty being only skin-deep. That's deep enough. What do you want, an adorable pancreas?
Jean Kerr
I am in control of all decisions that have to do with my image, which means that no one will decide what's right for me except me. I'm not special. We should all feel this way about ourselves.
Jennifer Hudson, I Got This: How I Changed My Ways and Lost What Weighed Me Down, 2012
It can be a real struggle to accept that sometimes appearance can be more important than talent or intelligence.
Jennifer Hudson, I Got This: How I Changed My Ways and Lost What Weighed Me Down, 2012
No matter how big the glam squad, or how dramatic the dress, sometimes things just don't work out.
Jennifer Hudson, I Got This: How I Changed My Ways and Lost What Weighed Me Down, 2012
So many people miss out on true talent because they can't get past a look. At the end of the day, losing weight was easy, but finding talent? Now that's hard.
Jennifer Hudson, I Got This: How I Changed My Ways and Lost What Weighed Me Down, 2012
The first question I ask myself when something doesn't seem to be beautiful is why do I think it's not beautiful. And very shortly you discover that there is no reason.
John Cage (1912 - 1992)
I never saw an ugly thing in my life: for let the form of an object be what it may - light, shade, and perspective will always make it beautiful.
John Constable (1776 - 1837)
I look foreword to an America which will not be afraid of grace and beauty.
John F. Kennedy (1917 - 1963), Remarks upon receiving an honorary degree, Amherst College, October 26, 1963
I love pretty things; and I hate to look in the glass and see something that isn't pretty. It makes me feel so sorrowful—just as I feel when I look at any ugly thing. I pity it because it isn't beautiful.
L. M. Montgomery (1874 - 1942), Anne of Green Gables, 1908
One can dream so much better in a room where there are pretty things.
L. M. Montgomery (1874 - 1942), Anne of Green Gables, 1908
A fine dress on a homely maiden is never enough of a distraction. It can convey a sense of wealth and its accompanying attractions, but it can never truly compensate for a plain face.
Laura Moncur (1969 -), The Secret Heart of Charlotte Lucas, 2014
Beauty and seduction is nature's tool for survival, because we will protect what we love.
Louis Schwartzberg, Marie Curie, 2011
Whatever is in any way beautiful hath its source of beauty in itself, and is complete in itself; praise forms no part of it. So it is none the worse nor the better for being praised.
Marcus Aurelius Antoninus (121 AD - 180 AD), Meditations
Just because you are blind, and unable to see my beauty doesn't mean it does not exist.
Margaret Cho, Margaret Cho's weblog, 03-23-06
Thankfully, beauty is easier to remove than apply, and a swipe of demaquillage in the right direction and you are you once again.
Margaret Cho, weblog, 01-27-04
Ugly. Is irrelevant. It is an immeasurable insult to a woman, and then supposedly the worst crime you can commit as a woman. But ugly, as beautiful, is an illusion.
Margaret Cho, weblog, 01-27-04
Somebody once said that beauty is the passport to success, but it's not a passport. It's a visa and it expires.
Michael J. Mosley and Nicholas Rossiter, The Human Face, 2001
Order is the shape upon which beauty depends.
Pearl Buck (1892 - 1973)
Rarely do great beauty and great virtue dwell together.
Petrarch (1304 - 1374), De Remedies
When I'm working on a problem, I never think about beauty. I think only how to solve the problem. But when I have finished, if the solution is not beautiful, I know it is wrong.
R. Buckminster Fuller (1895 - 1983)
The ability to see beauty is the beginning of our moral sensibility. What we believe is beautiful we will not wantonly destroy.
Reverend Sean Parker Dennison, Ministrare, 2-10-05
Yes, I was fat, but I dealt with it by simply never thinking about it. It is useful, when you are fat, to have a lot of other things to think about.
Roger Ebert (1942 - 2013), People Magazine, 09-19-11
People often say that 'beauty is in the eye of the beholder,' and I say that the most liberating thing about beauty is realizing that you are the beholder. This empowers us to find beauty in places where others have not dared to look, including inside ourselves.
Salma Hayek
What you do, the way you think, makes you beautiful.
Scott Westerfeld, Uglies, 2005
There is no excellent beauty that hath not some strangeness in the proportion.
Sir Francis Bacon (1561 - 1626), "Of Beauty"
There's something almost perfect in the ugly duckling syndrome. Because a sensitivity is tattooed on a part of you no one else can see but can somehow guess is there.
Stephanie Klein, Moose, 2008
Eye contact is the best accessory.

Takayuki Ikkaku, Arisa Hosaka and Toshihiro Kawabata, Animal Crossing: Wild World, 2005
If there is one thing worse than being an ugly duckling in a house of swans, it's having the swans pretend there's no difference.
Teena Booth, Falling From Fire

Belief

What counts now is not just what we are against, but what we are for. Who leads us is less important than what leads us-what convictions, what courage, what faith-win or lose. A man doesn't save a century, or a civilization, but a militant party wedded to a principal can.
Adlai E. Stevenson Jr. (1900 - 1965), Welcoming address before the Democratic national convention, Chicago, Illinois, July 21, 1952
Man is what he believes.
Anton Chekhov (1860 - 1904)
I would never die for my beliefs because I might be wrong.
Bertrand Russell (1872 - 1970)
The public will believe anything, so long as it is not founded on truth.
Edith Sitwell (1887 - 1964)
The thing always happens that you really believe in; and the belief in a thing makes it happen.
Frank Lloyd Wright (1869 - 1959)
With most men, unbelief in one thing springs from blind belief in another.
Georg Christoph Lichtenberg (1742 - 1799)
The fact that a believer is happier than a skeptic is no more to the point than the fact that a drunken man is happier than a sober one.
George Bernard Shaw (1856 - 1950)
I would rather have a mind opened by wonder than one closed by belief.
Gerry Spence, 'How to Argue and Win Every Time'
In the province of the mind, what one believes to be true either is true or becomes true.
John Lilly
Men willingly believe what they wish.
Julius Caesar (100 BC - 44 BC), De Bello Gallico
Oh, what a tangled web we weave when first we practice to believe.
Laurence J. Peter (1919 - 1988), misquoting Sir Walter Scott
I never cease being dumbfounded by the unbelievable things people believe.
Leo Rosten (1908 -)
Sometimes I've believed as many as six impossible things before breakfast.
Lewis Carroll (1832 - 1898), Alice in Wonderland
They were so strong in their beliefs that there came a time when it hardly mattered what exactly those beliefs were; they all fused into a single stubbornness.
Louise Erdrich
Remember that what you believe will depend very much on what you are.
Noah Porter (1811 - 1892)
I can believe anything, provided that it is quite incredible.
Oscar Wilde (1854 - 1900), The Picture of Dorian Gray, 1891
Some things have to be believed to be seen.
Ralph Hodgson, on ESP
Unless you believe, you will not understand.
Saint Augustine (354 AD - 430 AD), De Libero Arbitrio
Every man prefers belief to the exercise of judgement.
Seneca (5 BC - 65 AD), 4 BC-65 AD
Though a good deal is too strange to be believed, nothing is too strange to have happened.
Thomas Hardy
Believe one who has proved it. Believe an expert.
Virgil (70 BC - 19 BC), Aeneid
They can conquer who believe they can.
Virgil (70 BC - 19 BC)
Those who can make you believe absurdities can make you commit atrocities.
Voltaire (1694 - 1778)
Birds;Nature;Pets
It is not only fine feathers that make fine birds.
Aesop (620 BC - 560 BC), The Jay and the Peacock
One swallow does not make a summer.
Aristotle (384 BC - 322 BC), Nichomachean Ethics
How helpless we are, like netted birds, when we are caught by desire!
Belva Plain
I realized that If I had to choose, I would rather have birds than airplanes.
Charles Lindbergh (1902 - 1974), Interview shortly before his death, 1974
A bird does not sing because it has an answer. It sings because it has a song.
Chinese Proverb
Fall is my favorite season in Los Angeles, watching the birds change color and fall from the trees.
David Letterman (1947 -)
I hope you love birds too. It is economical. It saves going to heaven.
Emily Dickinson (1830 - 1886)
The moment a little boy is concerned with which is a jay and which is a sparrow, he can no longer see the birds or hear them sing.
Eric Berne (1910 - 1970)
I once had a sparrow alight upon my shoulder for a moment, while I was hoeing in a village garden, and I felt that I was more distinguished by that circumstance that I should have been by any epaulet I could have worn.
Henry David Thoreau (1817 - 1862)

Use what talents you possess: the woods would be very silent if no birds sang there except those that sang best.
Henry Van Dyke
Those little nimble musicians of the air, that warble forth their curious ditties, with which nature hath furnished them to the shame of art.
Izaak Walton (1593 - 1683)
God loved the birds and invented trees. Man loved the birds and invented cages.
Jacques Deval, Afin de vivre bel et bien
The very idea of a bird is a symbol and a suggestion to the poet. A bird seems to be at the top of the scale, so vehement and intense his life. . . . The beautiful vagabonds, endowed with every grace, masters of all climes, and knowing no bounds – how many human aspirations are realised in their free, holiday-lives – and how many suggestions to the poet in their flight and song!
John Burroughs (1837 - 1921), Birds and Poets, 1887
I value my garden more for being full of blackbirds than of cherries, and very frankly give them fruit for their songs.
Joseph Addison (1672 - 1719), 'The Spectator'
I know why the caged bird sings.
Maya Angelou (1928 -), Quoting a lyric by Paul Laurence Dunbar
Cranes carry this heavy mystical baggage. They're icons of fidelity and happiness. The Vietnamese believe cranes cart our souls up to heaven on our wings.
Mitchell Burgess, Northern Exposure, The Bad Seed, 1992
Our avian brothers are back to roost on the first leg of their annual sojourn south. Why them and not us? Maybe it's because we humans are meant to be rooted in one spot.
Mitchell Burgess, Northern Exposure, The Bad Seed, 1992
There'll be bluebirds over the white cliffs of Dover,
Tomorrow, just you wait and see.
Nat Burton, White Cliffs of Dover (song, 1941)
There is nothing in which the birds differ more from man than the way in which they can build and yet leave a landscape as it was before.
Robert Lynd (1879 - 1949), The Blue Lion and Other Essays
Birds sing after a storm; why shouldn't people feel as free to delight in whatever sunlight remains to them?
Rose Kennedy (1890 - 1995)
Much talking is the cause of danger. Silence is the means of avoiding misfortune. The talkative parrot is shut up in a cage. Other birds, without speech, fly freely about.
Saskya Pandita
I know of only one bird - the parrot - that talks; and it can't fly very high.
Wilbur Wright (1867 - 1912), declining to make a speech in 1908
No bird soars too high if he soars with his own wings.
William Blake (1757 - 1827)
When thou seest an eagle, thou seest a portion of genius; lift up thy head!
William Blake (1757 - 1827)
You cannot fly like an eagle with the wings of a wren.
William Henry Hudson (1841 - 1922), Afoot in England, 1909

Birth

It is true that I was born in Iowa, but I can't speak for my twin sister.
Abigail Van Buren (1918 -), (Dear Abby)
Some people are born on third base and go through life thinking they hit a triple.
Barry Switzer (1937 -)
He not busy being born is busy dying.
Bob Dylan (1941 -)
There is no cure for birth and death save to enjoy the interval.
George Santayana (1863 - 1952), Soliloquies in England, 1922, "War Shrines"
When I was born I was so surprised I didn't talk for a year and a half.
Gracie Allen (1906 - 1964)
We are born charming, fresh and spontaneous and must be civilized before we are fit to participate in society.
Judith Martin, (Miss Manners)
Somewhere on this globe, every ten seconds, there is a woman giving birth to a child. She must be found and stopped.
Sam Levenson (1911 - 1980)
To my embarrassment I was born in bed with a lady.
Wilson Mizner (1876 - 1933)

Body

All we actually have is our body and its muscles that allow us to be under our own power.
Allegra Kent, Once a Dancer...
Oh, darling, let your body in, let it tie you in, in comfort.
Anne Sexton (1928 - 1974)
Be sure that it is not you that is mortal, but only your body. For that man whom your outward form reveals is not yourself; the spirit is the true self, not that physical figure which and be pointed out by your finger.
Cicero (106 BC - 43 BC)
Safeguard the health both of body and soul.
Cleobulus
But the body is deeper than the soul and its secrets inscrutable.
E. M. Forster (1879 - 1970)
I live in company with a body, a silent companion, exacting and eternal.
Eugene Delacroix (1798 - 1863)
Of one thing I am certain, the body is not the measure of healing - peace is the measure.
George Melton

The body is an instrument, the mind its function, the witness and reward of its operation.
George Santayana (1863 - 1952)
The mind's first step to self-awareness must be through the body.
George Sheehan
Each individual woman's body demands to be accepted on its own terms.
Gloria Steinem (1934 -), O Magazine, May 2004
Each body has its art...
Gwendolyn Brooks (1917 -)
Every man is the builder of a temple called his body.
Henry David Thoreau (1817 - 1862)
I stand in awe of my body.
Henry David Thoreau (1817 - 1862)
Our own physical body possesses a wisdom which we who inhabit the body lack.
Henry Miller (1891 - 1980)
A sound mind in a sound body is a short but full description of a happy state in this world.
John Locke (1632 - 1704)
A healthy mind in a healthy body.
Juvenal (55 AD - 127 AD)
You should pray for a sound mind in a sound body.
Juvenal (55 AD - 127 AD), Satires
He who loves the world as his body may be entrusted with the empire.
Lao-tzu (604 BC - 531 BC), The Way of Lao-tzu
Over the years your bodies become walking autobiographies, telling friends and strangers alike of the minor and major stresses of your lives.
Marilyn Ferguson
The body is a sacred garment.
Martha Graham (1894 - 1991)
The body is shaped, disciplined, honored, and in time, trusted.
Martha Graham (1894 - 1991)
The body says what words cannot.
Martha Graham (1894 - 1991)
There is but one temple in the universe and that is the body of man.
Novalis (1772 - 1801)
I finally realized that being grateful to my body was key to giving more love to myself.
Oprah Winfrey (1954 -), O Magazine
It is confidence in our bodies, minds and spirits that allows us to keep looking for new adventures, new directions to grow in, and new lessons to learn - which is what life is all about.
Oprah Winfrey (1954 -), Oprah Magazine, May 2004
It's also helpful to realize that this very body that we have, that's sitting right here right now... with its aches and it pleasures... is exactly what we need to be fully human, fully awake, fully alive.
Pema Chodron
Bodily exercise, when compulsory, does no harm to the body; but knowledge which is acquired under compulsion obtains no hold on the mind.
Plato (427 BC - 347 BC), The Republic
Choose rather to be strong of soul than strong of body.
Pythagoras (582 BC - 507 BC)
I am convinced that life in a physical body is meant to be an ecstatic experience.
Shakti Gawain
Our bodies communicate to us clearly and specifically, if we are willing to listen to them.
Shakti Gawain
[The body is] a marvelous machine...a chemical laboratory, a power-house. Every movement, voluntary or involuntary, full of secrets and marvels!
Theodor Herzl (1860 - 1904)
I'm not only my spirit buy my body, and who can decide how much I, my individual self, am conditioned by the accident of my body? Would Byron have been Byron but for his club foot, or Dostoyevsky Dostoyevsky without his epilepsy?
W. Somerset Maugham (1874 - 1965), The Razor's Edge, 1943
It any thing is sacred the human body is sacred.
Walt Whitman (1819 - 1892)
Our bodies are our gardens to which our wills are gardeners.
William Shakespeare (1564 - 1616)

Books

Reading, after a certain age, diverts the mind too much from its creative pursuits. Any man who reads too much and uses his own brain too little falls into lazy habits of thinking.
Albert Einstein (1879 - 1955)
This paperback is very interesting, but I find it will never replace a hardcover book - it makes a very poor doorstop.
Alfred Hitchcock (1899 - 1980)
The covers of this book are too far apart.
Ambrose Bierce (1842 - 1914), The Devil's Dictionary
In literature as in love, we are astonished at what is chosen by others.
Andre Maurois (1885 - 1967)
You can cover a great deal of country in books.
Andrew Lang (1844 - 1912)
There's a certain kind of conversation you have from time to time at parties in New York about a new book. The word "banal" sometimes rears its by-now banal head; you say "underedited," I say "derivative." The conversation goes around and around various literary criticisms, and by the time it moves on one thing is clear: No one read the book; we just read the reviews.
Anna Quindlen (1953 -)
Books to the ceiling,
Books to the sky,
My pile of books is a mile high.
How I love them! How I need them!
I'll have a long beard by the time I read them.
Arnold Lobel
Wear the old coat and buy the new book.
Austin Phelps
Life-transforming ideas have always come to me through books.
Bell Hooks, O Magazine, December 2003
Many books require no thought from those who read them, and for a very simple reason; they made no such demand upon those who wrote them.
Charles Caleb Colton (1780 - 1832), Lacon, 1820
I've never known any trouble that an hour's reading didn't assuage.
Charles De Secondat (1689 - 1755)
Books are the quietest and most constant of friends; they are the most accessible and wisest of counsellors, and the most patient of teachers.
Charles W. Eliot (1834 - 1926), The Happy Life, 1896
There is no mistaking a real book when one meets it. It is like falling in love.
Christopher Morley (1890 - 1957)
A room without books is like a body without a soul.
Cicero (106 BC - 43 BC), (Attributed)
It was a book to kill time for those who like it better dead.
Dame Rose Macaulay (1881 - 1958)
Nothing can do what a book can do. Lifts you out of your life... to a whole new world, whole new perspective. A book is like a dream you're borrowing from a friend.
Dave Kellett, Sheldon, 08-15-2011
Books...are like lobster shells, we surround ourselves with 'em, then we grow out of 'em and leave 'em behind, as evidence of our earlier stages of development.
Dorothy L. Sayers (1893 - 1957), The Unpleasantness at the Bellona Club, 1928
This is not a novel to be tossed aside lightly. It should be thrown with great force.
Dorothy Parker (1893 - 1967)
Don't join the book burners. Don't think you're going to conceal faults by concealing evidence that they ever existed. Don't be afraid to go in your library and read every book...
Dwight D. Eisenhower (1890 - 1969)
My personal hobbies are reading, listening to music, and silence.
Edith Sitwell (1887 - 1964)
All good books are alike in that they are truer than if they had really happened and after you are finished reading one you will feel that all that happened to you and afterwards it all belongs to you; the good and the bad, the ecstasy, the remorse and sorrow, the people and the places and how the weather was.
Ernest Hemingway (1899 - 1961), Old Newsman Writes, Esquire, December 1934
Most new books are forgotten within a year, especially by those who borrow them.
Evan Esar (1899 - 1995)
Properly, we should read for power. Man reading should be man intensely alive. The book should be a ball of light in one's hand.
Ezra Pound (1885 - 1972)
I think it is good that books still exist, but they do make me sleepy.
Frank Zappa (1940 - 1993)
A good novel tells us the truth about its hero; but a bad novel tells us the truth about its author.
G. K. Chesterton (1874 - 1936)
There is a great deal of difference between an eager man who wants to read a book and the tired man who wants a book to read.
G. K. Chesterton (1874 - 1936)
Woe be to him that reads but one book.
George Herbert (1593 - 1633)
From the moment I picked up your book until I laid it down, I was convulsed with laughter. Some day I intend reading it.
Groucho Marx (1890 - 1977)
I find television very educating. Every time somebody turns on the set, I go into the other room and read a book.
Groucho Marx (1890 - 1977)
Outside of a dog, a book is man's best friend. Inside of a dog it's too dark to read.
Groucho Marx (1890 - 1977)
Reading well is one of the great pleasures that solitude can afford you.
Harold Bloom (1930 -), O Magazine, April 2003
How many a man has dated a new era in his life from the reading of a book.
Henry David Thoreau (1817 - 1862), Walden: Reading, 1854
The only obligation to which in advance we may hold a novel, without incurring the accusation of being arbitrary, is that it be interesting.
Henry James (1843 - 1916)
The love of learning, the sequestered nooks,
And all the sweet serenity of books.
Henry Wadsworth Longfellow (1807 - 1882), 'Morituri Salutamus,' 1875
Where is human nature so weak as in the bookstore?
Henry Ward Beecher (1813 - 1887)
Resolve to edge in a little reading every day, if it is but a single sentence. If you gain fifteen minutes a day, it will make itself felt at the end of the year.
Horace Mann (1796 - 1859)
Never judge a book by its movie.
J. W. Eagan

I declare after all there is no enjoyment like reading! How much sooner one tires of anything than of a book! When I have a house of my own, I shall be miserable if I have not an excellent library.
Jane Austen (1775 - 1817), Pride and Prejudice, 1811
Books are the ultimate Dumpees: put them down and they'll wait for you forever; pay attention to them and they always love you back.
John Green, An Abundance of Katherines, 2008
He liked all books, because he liked the mere act of reading, the magic of turning scratches on a page into words inside his head.
John Green, An Abundance of Katherines, 2008
Sometimes, you read a book and it fills you with this weird evangelical zeal, and you become convinced that the shattered world will never be put back together unless and until all living humans read the book.
John Green, The Fault in Our Stars, 2012
Oh for a book and a shady nook...
John Wilson (1785 - 1854)
Never read a book through merely because you have begun it.
John Witherspoon (1723 - 1794)
Fahrenheit 451 is one of those books that is about how amazing books are and how amazing the people who write books are. Writers love writing books like this, and for some reason, we let them get away with it.
Josh Lieb, I am a Genius of Unspeakable Evil and I Want to be Your Class President, 2009
Just the knowledge that a good book is awaiting one at the end of a long day makes that day happier.
Kathleen Norris, Hands Full of Living, 1931
It's all very well to read about sorrows and imagine yourself living through them heroically, but it's not so nice when you really come to have them, is it?
L. M. Montgomery (1874 - 1942), Anne of Green Gables, 1908
Do give books - religious or otherwise - for Christmas. They're never fattening, seldom sinful, and permanently personal.
Lenore Hershey
People say that life is the thing, but I prefer reading.
Logan Pearsall Smith (1865 - 1946), Afterthoughts (1931) "Myself"
Learn as much by writing as by reading.
Lord Acton
When I step into this library, I cannot understand why I ever step out of it.
Marie de Sevigne, O Magazine, December 2003
Be careful about reading health books. You may die of a misprint.
Mark Twain (1835 - 1910)
Just the omission of Jane Austen's books alone would make a fairly good library out of a library that hadn't a book in it.
Mark Twain (1835 - 1910)
The man who doesn't read good books has no advantage over the man who can't read them.
Mark Twain (1835 - 1910)
When I am attacked by gloomy thoughts, nothing helps me so much as running to my books. They quickly absorb me and banish the clouds from my mind.
Michel de Montaigne (1533 - 1592)
I have read your book and much like it.
Moses Hadas (1900 - 1966)
Thank you for sending me a copy of your book. I'll waste no time reading it.
Moses Hadas (1900 - 1966)
This book fills a much-needed gap.
Moses Hadas (1900 - 1966)
A good book is enjoyable. A great book sets off a bomb inside of you.
Ned Hepburn, Ned Hepburn Tumbler, 11-11-2011
There is no such thing as a moral or an immoral book. Books are well written or badly written.
Oscar Wilde (1854 - 1900), The Picture of Dorian Gray, 1891, preface
Always read stuff that will make you look good if you die in the middle of it.
P. J. O'Rourke (1947 -)
Be as careful of the books you read, as of the company you keep; for your habits and character will be as much influenced by the former as by the latter.
Paxton Hood
Reading this book is like waiting for the first shoe to drop.
Ralph Novak
In the highest civilization, the book is still the highest delight. He who has once known its satisfactions is provided with a resource against calamity.
Ralph Waldo Emerson (1803 - 1882), Letters and Social Aims: Quotation and Originality, 1876
Read at least one book a month. This is self-serving, obviously. It's a proven fact that people who read buy more books than people who don't read. In truth, I wish you'd read ten books a month, or at least buy that many.
Randy Pausch, Carnegie Mellon Commencement Speech, 2008
Books are good enough in their own way, but they are a mighty bloodless substitute for life.
Robert Louis Stevenson (1850 - 1894), An Apology for Idlers, 1874
A truly great book should be read in youth, again in maturity and once more in old age, as a fine building should be seen by morning light, at noon and by moonlight.
Robertson Davies
To be a book-collector is to combine the worst characteristics of a dope fiend with those of a miser.
Robertson Davies, "The Table Talk of Samuel Marchbanks"
A book is a version of the world. If you do not like it, ignore it; or offer your own version in return.
Salman Rushdie (1947 -), O Magazine, April 2003
I read part of it all the way through.
Samuel Goldwyn (1882 - 1974)

Reading is sometimes an ingenious device for avoiding thought.
Sir Arthur Helps
Read not to contradict and confute, nor to find talk and discourse, but to weigh and consider.
Sir Francis Bacon (1561 - 1626)
Some books are to be tasted, others to be swallowed, and some few to be chewed and digested: that is, some books are to be read only in parts, others to be read, but not curiously, and some few to be read wholly, and with diligence and attention.
Sir Francis Bacon (1561 - 1626)
Reading is to the mind what exercise is to the body.
Sir Richard Steele
Live always in the best company when you read.
Sydney Smith (1771 - 1845)
I aimed at the public's heart, and by accident I hit it in the stomach.
Upton Sinclair (1878 - 1968), on his novel, "The Jungle" (1906)
The multitude of books is making us ignorant.
Voltaire (1694 - 1778)
Some books are undeservedly forgotten; none are undeservedly remembered.
W. H. Auden (1907 - 1973)
When I read a book I seem to read it with my eyes only, but now and then I come across a passage, perhaps only a phrase, which has a meaning for me, and it becomes part of me.
W. Somerset Maugham (1874 - 1965), 'Of Human Bondage', 1915
This is my favorite book in all the world, though I have never read it.
William Goldman, The Princess Bride
Knowing I lov'd my books, he furnish'd me
From mine own library with volumes that
I prize above my dukedom.
William Shakespeare (1564 - 1616), "The Tempest", Act 1 scene 2

Boredom

Bore, n.: A person who talks when you wish him to listen.
Ambrose Bierce (1842 - 1914), The Devil's Dictionary
A finished person is a boring person.
Anna Quindlen (1953 -)
A bore is a man who, when you ask him how he is, tells you.
Bert Leston Taylor, The So-Called Human Race (1922)
All God does is watch us and kill us when we get boring. We must never, ever be boring.
Chuck Palahniuk (1962 -), Invisible Monsters, 1999
The cure for boredom is curiosity. There is no cure for curiosity.
Dorothy Parker (1893 - 1967), (attributed)
Someone's boring me. I think it's me.
Dylan Thomas (1914 - 1953), in Rayner Heppenstall, Four Absentees (1960)
Every improvement in communication makes the bore more terrible.
Frank Moore Colby
Good-bye. I am leaving because I am bored.
George Saunders, last words
A bore is a man who deprives you of solitude without providing you with company.
Gian Vincenzo Gravina (1664 - 1718)
The capacity of human beings to bore one another seems to be vastly greater than that of any other animal.
H. L. Mencken (1880 - 1956)
The nice thing about being a celebrity is that when you bore people, they think it's their fault.
Henry Kissinger (1923 -)
A healthy male adult bore consumes each year one and a half times his own weight in other people's patience.
John Updike (1932 -), Assorted Prose (1965)
The penalty for success is to be bored by the people who used to snub you.
Nancy Astor (1879 - 1964)
Every hero becomes a bore at last.
Ralph Waldo Emerson (1803 - 1882)
The secret of being a bore is to tell everything.
Voltaire (1694 - 1778), Discours en vers sur l'homme, 1737
The secret of being boring is to say everything.
Voltaire (1694 - 1778)
Life is as tedious as a twice-told tale
Vexing the dull ear of a drowsy man.
William Shakespeare (1564 - 1616), "King John", Act 3 scene 4
[S]he refused to be bored chiefly because she wasn't boring.
Zelda Fitzgerald, 1922

Brain

What a splendid head, yet no brain.
Aesop (620 BC - 560 BC)
Thinking rationally is often different from "positive thinking," in that it is a realistic assessment of the situation, with a view towards rectifying the problem if possible.
Albert Ellis, Michael Abrams, Lidia Dengelegi, The Art & Science of Rational Eating, 1992
Brain: an apparatus with which we think we think.
Ambrose Bierce (1842 - 1914), The Devil's Dictionary
If there is anything in the world that can really be called a man's property, it is surely that which is the result of his mental activity.
Arthur Schopenhauer (1788 - 1860)
Exercising self-restraint can be depleting, yet it can also be ennobling.
Daniel Akst, We Have Met the Enemy: Self-Control in an Age of Excess, 2011

It's essential to tailor rehab to what impassions someone. The brain gradually learns by riveting its attention-through endless repetitions.
Diane Ackerman, One Hundred Names for Love: A Stroke, A Marriage, and the Language of Healing, 2011
The human brain starts working the moment you are born and never stops until you stand up to speak in public.
George Jessel
Estimated amount of glucose used by an adult human brain each day, expressed in M&Ms: 250
Harper's Index, October 1989
The brain is a wonderful organ. It starts working the moment you get up in the morning and does not stop until you get into the office.
Robert Frost (1874 - 1963)
The human brain is a most unusual instrument of elegant and as yet unknown capacity.
Stuart Seaton
If little else, the brain is an educational toy.
Tom Robbins (1936 -)
Aristotle was famous for knowing everything. He taught that the brain exists merely to cool the blood and is not involved in the process of thinking. This is true only of certain persons.
Will Cuppy

Bureaucracy

The perfect bureaucrat everywhere is the man who manages to make no decisions and escape all responsibility.
Brooks Atkinson (1894 - 1984), Once Around the Sun, 1951
Bureaucrats write memoranda both because they appear to be busy when they are writing and because the memos, once written, immediately become proof that they were busy.
Charles Peters
The only thing that saves us from the bureaucracy is inefficiency. An efficient bureaucracy is the greatest threat to liberty.
Eugene McCarthy (1916 - 2005), Time magazine, Feb. 12, 1979
Bureaucracy defends the status quo long past the time when the quo has lost its status.
Laurence J. Peter (1919 - 1988)
Hell hath no fury like a bureaucrat scorned.
Milton Friedman (1912 - 2006)
The best way to compile inaccurate information that no one wants is to make it up.
Scott Adams (1957 -), Dilbert, 07-12-09
Any sufficiently advanced bureaucracy is indistinguishable from molasses.
Unknown

Business

Talk of nothing but business, and dispatch that business quickly.
Aldus Manutius (1449 - 1515), Placard on the door of the Aldine Press
The gambling known as business looks with austere disfavor upon the business known as gambling.
Ambrose Bierce (1842 - 1914), The Devil's Dictionary
Drive thy business or it will drive thee.
Benjamin Franklin (1706 - 1790)
The chief business of the American people is business.
Calvin Coolidge (1872 - 1933), Speech in Washington, Jan. 17, 1925
There is one person in charge of every office in America and that person is Charles Darwin.
Charlie Grandy, The Office, Get the Girl, March 2012
There's no business like show business, but there are several businesses like accounting.
David Letterman (1947 -)
In the modern world of business, it is useless to be a creative original thinker unless you can also sell what you create. Management cannot be expected to recognize a good idea unless it is presented to them by a good salesman.
David M. Ogilvy
Success in business requires training and discipline and hard work. But if you're not frightened by these things, the opportunities are just as great today as they ever were.
David Rockefeller (1915 -)
Here's my theory about meetings and life; the three things you can't fake are erections, competence and creativity. That's why meetings become toxic they put uncreative people in a situation in which they have to be something they can never be. And the more effort they put into concealing their inabilities, the more toxic the meeting becomes. One of the most common creativity-faking tactics is when someone puts their hands in prayer position and conceals their mouth while they nod at you and say, 'Mmmmmm. Interesting.' If pressed, they'll add, 'I'll have to get back to you on that.' Then they don't say anything else.
Douglas Coupland
Charge less, but charge. Otherwise, you will not be taken seriously, and you do your fellow artists no favours if you undercut the market.

Elizabeth Aston, The True Darcy Spirit, 2006
'Whom are you?' he asked, for he had attended business college.
George Ade (1866 - 1944), "The Steel Box", 1898
Good design can't fix broken business models.
Jeffrey Veen, Designing the Friendly Skies, 06-21-06
I find it rather easy to portray a businessman. Being bland, rather cruel and incompetent comes naturally to me.
John Cleese (1939 -)
You never really hear the truth from your subordinates until after 10 in the evening.
Jurgen Schrempp, Former CEO of DaimlerChrysler
In business, you must remain unattached to the outcome. It matters not who is chosen first and who is chosen second. The only thing that matters is the final verdict.
Laura Moncur (1969 -), The Secret Heart of Charlotte, 2014
The more I know about business, the more I'm convinced that it is conducted in homes and churches far more than in office buildings.
Laura Moncur (1969 -), Merriton: Twelve Hours from San Francisco, 09-17-08
A dinner lubricates business.
Lord William Stowell
To succeed as a team is to hold all of the members accountable for their expertise.
Mitchell Caplan, CEO, E*Trade Group Inc.
My own business always bores me to death; I prefer other people's.
Oscar Wilde (1854 - 1900), Lady Windermere's Fan, 1892
Business has only two basic functions-marketing and innovation.
Peter Drucker (1909 - 2005)
Letting your customers set your standards is a dangerous game, because the race to the bottom is pretty easy to win. Setting your own standards–and living up to them–is a better way to profit. Not to mention a better way to make your day worth all the effort you put into it.
Seth Godin, Seth Godin's Blog, 07-28-06
I ran the wrong kind of business, but I did it with integrity.
Sydney Biddle Barrows, in Marian Christy, "Mayflower Madam' Tells All,' Boston Globe, 1986
Designing your product for monetization first, and people second will probably leave you with neither.
Tara Hunt, HorsePigCow, 07-12-06
No one travelling on a business trip would be missed if he failed to arrive.
Thorstein Veblen (1857 - 1929)
In the business world, the rearview mirror is always clearer than the windshield.
Warren Buffett (1930 -)

Camping;
In all things of nature there is something of the marvelous.
Aristotle (384 BC - 322 BC), Parts of Animals
He maketh me to lie down in green pastures he leadeth me beside the still waters.
Bible, Psalm xxiii. 2.
A lot of people like snow. I find it to be an unnecessary freezing of water.
Carl Reiner
Hunting has opened the earth to me and let me sense the rhythms and hierarchies of nature.
Charles Fergus
Real freedom lies in wildness, not in civilization.
Charles Lindbergh (1902 - 1974)
Camping is nature's way of promoting the motel business.
Dave Barry (1947 -)
There is... nothing greater than touching the shore after crossing some great body of water knowing that I've done it with my own two arms and legs.
Diana Nyad
I would feel more optimistic about a bright future for man if he spent less time proving that he can outwit Nature and more time tasting her sweetness and respecting her seniority.
E. B. White (1899 - 1985)
Mountains inspire awe in any human person who has a soul. They remind us of our frailty, our unimportance, of the briefness of our span upon this earth. They touch the heavens, and sail serenely at an altitude beyond even the imaginings of a mere mortal.
Elizabeth Aston, The Exploits & Adventures of Miss Alethea Darcy, 2005
Kneeling over a trickling mountain stream and pumping every ounce of water you use though a filter can really change your perception of turning on a faucet.
Eric Voorhis, Camping Earth, Backcountry Camping Can Be A Stressful Pursuit, 03-02-12
There is a solitude, or perhaps a solemnity, in the few hours that precede the dawn of day which is unlike that of any others in the twenty-four, and which I cannot explain or account for. Thoughts come to me at this time that I never have at any other.
George Bird Grinnell
Some national parks have long waiting lists for camping reservations. When you have to wait a year to sleep next to a tree, something is wrong.
George Carlin (1937 - 2008)
In wildness is the preservation of the world.
Henry David Thoreau (1817 - 1862)
It is pleasant to have been to a place the way a river went.
Henry David Thoreau (1817 - 1862)
It was the Law of the Sea, they said. Civilization ends at the waterline. Beyond that, we all enter the food chain, and not always right at the top.
Hunter S. Thompson (1939 - 2005)
What nature delivers to us is never stale. Because what nature creates has eternity in it.
Isaac Bashevis Singer (1904 - 1991)
Those little nimble musicians of the air, that warble forth their curious ditties, with which nature hath furnished them to the shame of art.

Izaak Walton (1593 - 1683)
People say to me so often, 'Jane how can you be so peaceful when everywhere around you people want books signed, people are asking these questions and yet you seem peaceful,' and I always answer that it is the peace of the forest that I carry inside.
Jane Goodall (1934 -)
Climb the mountains and get their good tidings. Nature's peace will flow into you as sunshine flows into trees. The winds will blow their own freshness into you, and the storms their energy, while cares will drop away from you like the leaves of Autumn.
John Muir (1838 - 1914), Our National Parks, 1901
Come to the woods, for here is rest. There is no repose like that of the green deep woods. Here grow the wallflower and the violet. The squirrel will come and sit upon your knee, the logcock will wake you in the morning. Sleep in forgetfulness of all ill. Of all the upness accessible to mortals, there is no upness comparable to the mountains.
John Muir (1838 - 1914), Atlantic Monthly, January 1869
Everybody needs beauty as well as bread, places to play in and pray in, where nature may heal and give strength to body and soul alike.
John Muir (1838 - 1914), The Yosemite, 1912
Fresh beauty opens one's eyes wherever it is really seen, but the very abundance and completeness of the common beauty that besets our steps prevents its being absorbed and appreciated. It is a good thing, therefore, to make short excursions now and then to the bottom of the sea among dulse and coral, or up among the clouds on mountain-tops, or in balloons, or even to creep like worms into dark holes and caverns underground, not only to learn something of what is going on in those out-of-the-way places, but to see better what the sun sees on our return to common everyday beauty.
John Muir (1838 - 1914), My First Summer in the Sierra, 1911
In God's wildness lies the hope of the world - the great fresh unblighted, unredeemed wilderness. The galling harness of civilization drops off, and wounds heal ere we are aware.
John Muir (1838 - 1914), John of the Mountains, 1938
Keep close to Nature's heart... and break clear away, once in awhile, and climb a mountain or spend a week in the woods. Wash your spirit clean. None of Nature's landscapes are ugly so long as they are wild.
John Muir (1838 - 1914), Our National Parks, 1901
The clearest way into the Universe is through a forest wilderness.
John Muir (1838 - 1914), John of the Mountains, 1938
When we contemplate the whole globe as one great dewdrop, striped and dotted with continents and islands, flying through space with other stars all singing and shining together as one, the whole universe appears as an infinite storm of beauty.
John Muir (1838 - 1914), Travels in Alaska by John Muir, 1915, chapter 1
When we try to pick out anything by itself, we find it hitched to everything else in the Universe.
John Muir (1838 - 1914), My First Summer in the Sierra, 1911
When one loses the deep intimate relationship with nature, then temples, mosques and churches become important.
Krishnamurti, Beginnings of Learning
Nature has been for me, for as long as I remember, a source of solace, inspiration, adventure, and delight; a home, a teacher, a companion.
Lorraine Anderson
Water, taken in moderation, cannot hurt anybody.
Mark Twain (1835 - 1910)
Eventually, all things merge into one, and a river runs through it. The river was cut by the world's great flood and runs over rocks from the basement of time. On some of the rocks are timeless raindrops. Under the rocks are the words, and some of the words are theirs. I am haunted by waters.
Norman Maclean, A River Runs Through It
You can't stay in your corner of the Forest waiting for others to come to you. You have to go to them sometimes.
Pooh's Little Instruction Book, inspired by A. A. Milne
Live in the sunshine, swim the sea, drink the wild air.
Ralph Waldo Emerson (1803 - 1882)
It is not much for its beauty that makes a claim upon men's hearts, as for that subtle something, that quality of air that emanates from old trees, that so wonderfully changes and renews a weary spirit.
Robert Louis Stevenson (1850 - 1894)
Whosoever is delighted in solitude is either a wild beast or a god.
Sir Francis Bacon (1561 - 1626)
Seeing wildlife is like seeing celebrities, only better.
Tanja Andrews, Freshtopia, 08-19-06
The wild life of today is not ours to do with as we please. The original stock was given to us in trust for the benefit both of the present and the future. We must render an accounting of this trust to those who come after us.
Theodore Roosevelt (1858 - 1919)
After you have exhausted what there is in business, politics, conviviality, and so on - have found that none of these finally satisfy, or permanently wear - what remains? Nature remains.
Walt Whitman (1819 - 1892)
And this our life, exempt from public haunt,
Finds tongues in trees, books in running brooks,
Sermons in stones, and good in everything.
William Shakespeare (1564 - 1616), As You Like It, Act II, Scene i, Lines 15-17
Come unto these yellow sands,
And then take hands:
Courtsied when you have, and kiss'd
The wild waves whist.
William Shakespeare (1564 - 1616), "The Tempest", Act 1 scene 2

Cars

When Solomon said there was a time and a place for everything he had not encountered the problem of parking his automobile.
Bob Edwards
Life is too short for traffic.
Dan Bellack
Americans will put up with anything provided it doesn't block traffic.
Dan Rather (1931 -)
Traffic signals in New York are just rough guidelines.
David Letterman (1947 -)
If all the cars in the United States were placed end to end, it would probably be Labor Day Weekend.
Doug Larson
The best car safety device is a rear-view mirror with a cop in it.
Dudley Moore (1935 - 2002)
Drive-in banks were established so most of the cars today could see their real owners.
E. Joseph Cossman
Normal is getting dressed in clothes that you buy for work and driving through traffic in a car that you are still paying for - in order to get to the job you need to pay for the clothes and the car, and the house you leave vacant all day so you can afford to live in it.
Ellen Goodman (1941 -)
It takes hundreds of nuts to hold a car together, but it takes only one of them to scatter it all over the highway.
Evan Esar (1899 - 1995), Esar's Comic Dictionary
I know a lot about cars. I can look at a car's headlights and tell you exactly which way it's coming.
Mitch Hedberg (1968 - 2005)
If the automobile had followed the same development cycle as the computer, a Rolls-Royce would today cost $100, get a million miles per gallon, and explode once a year, killing everyone inside.
Robert X. Cringely, InfoWorld magazine
Is fuel efficiency really what we need most desperately? I say that what we really need is a car that can be shot when it breaks down.
Russell Baker (1925 -)
I hate the outdoors. To me the outdoors is where the car is.
Will Durst

Cats

If a dog jumps in your lap, it is because he is fond of you; but if a cat does the same thing, it is because your lap is warmer.
Alfred North Whitehead (1861 - 1947)
It's funny how dogs and cats know the inside of folks better than other folks do, isn't it?
Eleanor H. Porter (1868 - 1920), Pollyanna, 1912
I honestly don't know how you live without having a cat inside your house. It's like having a little living piece of art that is also very warm and soft.
Hank Green, Vlogbrothers, Cat GIF Critique, 04-26-13
Cats and monkeys; monkeys and cats; all human life is there.
Henry James (1843 - 1916)
Cats regard people as warmblooded furniture.
Jacquelyn Mitchard, The Deep End of the Ocean
Cats are smarter than dogs. You can't get eight cats to pull a sled through snow.
Jeff Valdez
Nature abhors a vacuum, but not as much as cats do.
Lee Entrekin
Of all God's creatures there is only one that cannot be made the slave of the lash. That one is the cat. If man could be crossed with cat it would improve man, but it would deteriorate the cat.
Mark Twain (1835 - 1910), Mark Twain's Notebook, 1935
I like pigs. Dogs look up to us. Cats look down on us. Pigs treat us as equals.
Sir Winston Churchill (1874 - 1965)
"I meant," said Ipslore bitterly, "what is there in this world that truly makes living worthwhile?"
Death thought about it.
"Cats," he said eventually. "Cats are nice."
Terry Pratchett, Sourcery
Cats are intended to teach us that not everything in nature has a function.
Unknown

Celebrities

A sign of celebrity is that his name is often worth more than his services.
Daniel J. Boorstin (1914 -)
A celebrity is a person who works hard all his life to become well known, then wears dark glasses to avoid being recognized.
Fred Allen (1894 - 1956)
A celebrity is one who is known to many persons he is glad he doesn't know.
H. L. Mencken (1880 - 1956)
The nice thing about being a celebrity is that when you bore people, they think it's their fault.
Henry Kissinger (1923 -)
Living in L.A., everyone likes to mold you and change you. I don't care about fame, I don't care about being a celebrity. I know that's part of the job, but I don't feed into anyone's idea of who I should be.

Jessica Alba
I had an epiphany a few years ago where I was out at a celebrity party and it suddenly dawned on me that I had yet to meet a celebrity who is as smart and interesting as any of my friends.
Moby, quoted on CNN.com, March 2005
When once a man has made celebrity necessary to his happiness, he has put it in the power of the weakest and most timorous malignity, if not to take away his satisfaction, at least to withhold it. His enemies may indulge their pride by airy negligence and gratify their malice by quiet neutrality.
Samuel Johnson (1709 - 1784)

Chance

Men are not prisoners of fate, but only prisoners of their own minds.
Franklin D. Roosevelt (1882 - 1945), Pan American Day address, April 15, 1939
It's choice - not chance - that determines your destiny.
Jean Nidetch
Fortune can, for her pleasure, fools advance,
And toss them on the wheels of Chance.
Juvenal (55 AD - 127 AD)
The moments that we have with friends and family, the chances that we have to make a big difference in the world or even to make a small difference to the ones we love, all those wonderful chances that life gives us, life also takes away. It can happen fast and a whole lot sooner than you think.
Larry Page, University of Michigan Commencement Address, 2009
In the field of observation, chance favors only the prepared mind.
Louis Pasteur (1822 - 1895), lecture 1854
Chance is always powerful. Let your hook be always cast; in the pool where you least expect it, there will be a fish.
Ovid (43 BC - 17 AD)
Work and acquire, and thou hast chained the wheel of Chance.
Ralph Waldo Emerson (1803 - 1882)
The sufferings that fate inflicts on us should be borne with patience, what enemies inflict with manly courage.
Thucydides (471 BC - 400 BC)
Destiny is no matter of chance. It is a matter of choice. It is not a thing to be waited for, it is a thing to be achieved.
William Jennings Bryan (1860 - 1925)

Change

They always say time changes things, but you actually have to change them yourself.
Andy Warhol (1928 - 1987), The Philosophy of Andy Warhol
Only I can change my life. No one can do it for me.
Carol Burnett (1936 -)
Change is the constant, the signal for rebirth, the egg of the phoenix.
Christina Baldwin
The only sense that is common in the long run, is the sense of change-and we all instinctively avoid it.
E. B. White (1899 - 1985)
This isn't good or bad. It's just the way of things. Nothing stays the same.
Gordon Atkinson, RealLivePreacher.com Weblog, January 03, 2004
He who rejects change is the architect of decay. The only human institution which rejects progress is the cemetery.
Harold Wilson (1916 - 1995), Speech to the Consultive Assembly of the Council of Europe, Strasbourg, France, January 23, 1967
We all have big changes in our lives that are more or less a second chance.
Harrison Ford (1942 -), quoted by Garry Jenkins in 'Harrison Ford: Imperfect Hero'
Things do not change; we change.
Henry David Thoreau (1817 - 1862), Walden (1970)
Nothing endures but change.
Heraclitus (540 BC - 480 BC), from Diogenes Laertius, Lives of Eminent Philosophers
It's not that some people have willpower and some don't. It's that some people are ready to change and others are not.
James Gordon, M.D.
Just as I had to go through a transition period, I guess [my friends and family] did, too.
Jennifer Hudson, I Got This: How I Changed My Ways and Lost What Weighed Me Down, 2012
Most people see themselves a certain way their entire lives. When they go through a massive change, such as losing weight, they have to learn to see themselves in a new way. It is one of the biggest struggles her members deal with on their journey.
Jennifer Hudson, I Got This: How I Changed My Ways and Lost What Weighed Me Down, 2012
People get comfortable with the way you are—they have formed their opinion of you based on everything they see and know about you as a person. When you change that up by losing weight, they no longer understand you.
Jennifer Hudson, I Got This: How I Changed My Ways and Lost What Weighed Me Down, 2012
The only way you can sustain a permanent change is to create a new way of thinking, acting, and being.
Jennifer Hudson, I Got This: How I Changed My Ways and Lost What Weighed Me Down, 2012
When other people reject positive changes you make for yourself, there is always some nerve to get to the root of in those other people.
Jennifer Hudson, I Got This: How I Changed My Ways and Lost What Weighed Me Down, 2012

Change has a considerable psychological impact on the human mind. To the fearful it is threatening because it means that things may get worse. To the hopeful it is encouraging because things may get better. To the confident it is inspiring because the challenge exists to make things better.
King Whitney Jr.
We did not change as we grew older; we just became more clearly ourselves.
Lynn Hall, Where Have All the Tigers Gone?, 1989
The universe is change; our life is what our thoughts make it.
Marcus Aurelius Antoninus (121 AD - 180 AD), Meditations
Any transition serious enough to alter your definition of self will require not just small adjustments in your way of living and thinking but a full-on metamorphosis.
Martha Beck, O Magazine, Growing Wings, January 2004
This is your time and it feels normal to you, but really, there is no normal. There's only change and resistance to it and then more change.
Meryl Streep (1949 -), Barnard Commencement Speech, 2010
The more things change, the more they remain... insane.
Michael Fry and T. Lewis, Over the Hedge, 05-09-04
There is nothing like returning to a place that remains unchanged to find the ways in which you yourself have altered.
Nelson Mandela (1918 -), 'A Long Walk to Freedom'
Change your thoughts and you change your world.
Norman Vincent Peale (1898 - 1993)
Turbulence is life force. It is opportunity. Let's love turbulence and use it for change.
Ramsay Clark
Few will have the greatness to bend history itself; but each of us can work to change a small portion of events, and in the total of all those acts will be written the history of this generation.
Robert F. Kennedy (1925 - 1968), Day of Affirmation address delivered at the University of Capetown, South Africa, June 6, 1966
Progress is a nice word. But change is its motivator and change has its enemies.
Robert F. Kennedy (1925 - 1968)
If you want change, you have to make it. If we want progress we have to drive it.
Susan Rice, Stanford University Commencement, 2010
Nothing in the world is permanent, and we're foolish when we ask anything to last, but surely we're still more foolish not to take delight in it while we have it. If change is of the essence of existence one would have thought it only sensible to make it the premise of our philosophy.
W. Somerset Maugham (1874 - 1965), The Razor's Edge, 1943

Character

Character is like a tree and reputation like its shadow. The shadow is what we think of it; the tree is the real thing.
Abraham Lincoln (1809 - 1865), Lincoln's Own Stories
Nearly all men can stand adversity, but if you want to test a man's character, give him power.
Abraham Lincoln (1809 - 1865)
Everyone has the obligation to ponder well his own specific traits of character. He must also regulate them adequately and not wonder whether someone else's traits might suit him better. The more definitely his own a man's character is, the better it fits him.
Cicero (106 BC - 43 BC)
Without an acquaintance with the rules of propriety, it is impossible for the character to be established.
Confucius (551 BC - 479 BC), The Confucian Analects
Many a man's reputation would not know his character if they met on the street.
Elbert Hubbard (1856 - 1915)
People grow through experience if they meet life honestly and courageously. This is how character is built.
Eleanor Roosevelt (1884 - 1962), My Day
Forming characters! Whose? Our own or others? Both. And in that momentous fact lies the peril and responsibility of our existence.
Elihu Burritt
Personality can open doors, but only character can keep them open.
Elmer G. Letterman
I am a man of fixed and unbending principles, the first of which is to flexible at all times.
Everett Mckinley Dirkson
In attempts to improve your character, know what is in your power and what is beyond it.
Francis Thompson (1859 - 1907)
A person reveals his character by nothing so clearly as the joke he resents.
Georg Christoph Lichtenberg (1742 - 1799)
Our character...is an omen of our destiny, and the more integrity we have and keep, the simpler and nobler that destiny is likely to be.
George Santayana (1863 - 1952), "The German Mind: A Philosophical Diagnosis"
Character cannot be developed in ease and quiet. Only through experience of trial and suffering can the soul be strengthened, ambition inspired, and success achieved.
Helen Keller (1880 - 1968)
Of all the properties which belong to honorable men, not one is so highly prized as that of character.
Henry Clay (1777 - 1852)
A man's character is his fate.
Heraclitus (540 BC - 480 BC), On the Universe
People with courage and character always seem sinister to the rest.
Hermann Hesse (1877 - 1962)
The farther behind I leave the past, the closer I am to forging my own character.
Isabelle Eberhardt

You cannot dream yourself into a character; you must hammer and forge yourself one.
James A. Froude (1818 - 1894)
How easy it is for generous sentiments, high courtesy, and chivalrous courage to lose their influence beneath the chilling blight of selfishness, and to exhibit to the world a man who was great in all the minor attributes of character, but who was found wanting when it became necessary to prove how much principle is superior to policy.
James Fenimore Cooper, The Last of the Mohicans, 1826
Character consists of what you do on the third and forth tries.
James Mechener
When the character of a man is not clear to you, look at his friends.
Japanese Proverb
Character - the willingness to accept responsibility for one's own life - is the source from which self respect springs.
Joan Didion (1934 -), "Slouching Towards Bethlehem"
Men show their characters in nothing more clearly than in what they think laughable.
Johann Wolfgang von Goethe (1749 - 1832)
I take it as a man's duty to restrain himself.
Lois McMaster Bujold, Ethan of Athos, 1986
One can acquire everything in solitude - except character.
Marie Henri Beyle (1783 - 1842)
To succeed is nothing, it's an accident. but to feel no doubts about oneself is something very different: it is character.
Marie Leneru, Oprah Magazine, May 2004
The character of a man is known from his conversations.
Menander (342 BC - 292 BC)
I could never think well of a man's intellectual or moral character, if he was habitually unfaithful to his appointments.
Nathaniel Emmons
The character of every act depends upon the circumstances in which it is done.
Oliver Wendell Holmes Jr. (1841 - 1935)
Underneath this flabby exterior is an enormous lack of character.
Oscar Levant (1906 - 1972)
Nature magically suits a man to his fortunes, by making them the fruit of his character.
Ralph Waldo Emerson (1803 - 1882)
People seem not to see that their opinion of the world is also a confession of their character.
Ralph Waldo Emerson (1803 - 1882)
I appreciate people who are civil, whether they mean it or not. I think: Be civil. Do not cherish your opinion over my feelings. There's a vanity to candor that isn't really worth it. Be kind.
Richard Greenberg, NY Times Magazine, 03-26-2006
You can tell a lot about a fellow's character by his way of eating jellybeans.
Ronald Reagan (1911 - 2004), quoted in Observer, March 29 1981
Hard work spotlights the character of people: some turn up their sleeves, some turn up their noses, and some don't turn up at all.
Sam Ewing
You can tell the character of every man when you see how he receives praise.
Seneca (5 BC - 65 AD), Epistles
Put more trust in nobility of character than in an oath.
Solon (638 BC - 559 BC)
Sometimes people carry to such perfection the mask they have assumed that in due course they actually become the person they seem.
W. Somerset Maugham (1874 - 1965), The Moon and Sixpence
Strong feelings do not necessarily make a strong character. The strength of a man is to be measured by the power of the feelings he subdues not by the power of those which subdue him.
William Carleton

Charity

Too many have dispensed with generosity in order to practice charity.
Albert Camus (1913 - 1960)
One of the serious obstacles to the improvement of our race is indiscriminate charity.
Andrew Carnegie (1835 - 1919)
Like threads of silver seen through crystal beads
Let love through good deeds show.
Edwin Arnold
The best thing to give to your enemy is forgiveness; to an opponent, tolerance; to a friend, your heart; to your child, a good example; to a father, deference; to your mother, conduct that will make her proud of you; to yourself, respect; to all men, charity.
Francis Maitland Balfour
The living need charity more than the dead.
George Arnold, The Jolly Old Pedagogue (1866)
Charity sees the need not the cause.
German Proverb
A bone to the dog is not charity. Charity is the bone shared with the dog, when you are just as hungry as the dog.
Jack London (1876 - 1916)
In charity there is no excess.
Sir Francis Bacon (1561 - 1626), Of Goodness, and Goodness of Nature (1625)
Be charitable before wealth makes thee covetous.
Sir Thomas Browne (1605 - 1682)

Charity begins at home.
Terence (185 BC - 159 BC), Andria
The charity that hastens to proclaim its good deeds, ceases to be charity, and is only pride and ostentation.
William Hutton

Charm

Charm is a way of getting the answer yes without asking a clear question.
Albert Camus (1913 - 1960)
You know what charm is: a way of getting the answer yes without having asked any clear question.
Albert Camus (1913 - 1960), La Chute (The Fall),1956
All charming people have something to conceal, usually their total dependence on the appreciation of others.
Cyril Connolly (1903 - 1974), Enemies of Promise (1938)
Charm is the quality in others that makes us more satisfied with ourselves.
Henri-Frédéric Amiel
We are born charming, fresh and spontaneous and must be civilized before we are fit to participate in society.
Judith Martin, (Miss Manners)
It is absurd to divide people into good and bad. People are either charming or tedious.
Oscar Wilde (1854 - 1900), Lady Windermere's Fan, 1892, Act I

Children

There was a time when we expected nothing of our children but obedience, as opposed to the present, when we expect everything of them but obedience.
Anatole Broyard
I would be the most content if my children grew up to be the kind of people who think decorating consists mostly of building enough bookshelves.
Anna Quindlen (1953 -)
Grown-ups never understand anything for themselves, and it is tiresome for children to be always and forever explaining things to them.
Antoine de Saint-Exupery (1900 - 1944), "The Little Prince", 1943
Human beings are the only creatures that allow their children to come back home.
Bill Cosby (1937 -)
People who get nostalgic about childhood were obviously never children.
Bill Watterson (1958 -), Calvin and Hobbes
If you can give your son or daughter only one gift, let it be enthusiasm.
Bruce Barton
To be ignorant of what occurred before you were born is to remain always a child.
Cicero (106 BC - 43 BC), Orator, chapter 34, section 120
The first half of our lives is ruined by our parents, and the second half by our children.
Clarence Darrow (1857 - 1938)
One of the common causes of serious difficulty takes the form of parental self-discovery. The newly adopted child brings out submerged feelings or behavior in his parents that make them dislike themselves. This can be such a severe blow to their self- esteem that they must eradicate the cause of their distress. Sometimes the only way that parents are able to do that is by returning the child.
Claudia Jewett Jarrett, Adopting the Older Child, 1978
The best way to learn to be an honest, responsible adult is to live with adults who act honestly and responsibly.
Claudia Jewett Jarrett, Adopting the Older Child, 1978
Facing a mirror you see merely your own countenance; facing your child you finally understand how everyone else has seen you.
Daniel Raeburn, The New Yorker, 05-01-2006
If your parents never had children, chances are you won't, either.
Dick Cavett (1936 -)
The test of the morality of a society is what it does for its children.
Dietrich Bonhoeffer (1906 - 1945)
The best way to keep children home is to make the home atmosphere pleasant—and let the air out of the tires.
Dorothy Parker (1893 - 1967)
Having a baby's sweet face so close to your own, for so long a time as it takes to nurse 'em, is a great tonic for a sad soul.
Erica Eisdorfer, The Wet Nurse's Tale, 2009
We do our children no favour by keeping them near, coddling them, or showing them off to adult visitors. Not that a nursemaid does not sometimes spoil them. But the greatest favour we can do our children is to give visible example of love and esteem to our spouse. As they grow up, they may then look forward to maturity so they too can find such love.
Eucharista Ward, Match For Mary Bennet, 2009
Ask your child what he wants for dinner only if he's buying.
Fran Lebowitz (1950 -)
I must take issue with the term 'a mere child,' for it has been my invariable experience that the company of a mere child is infinitely preferable to that of a mere adult.
Fran Lebowitz (1950 -)
Never have children, only grandchildren.
Gore Vidal (1925 -)
That's the funny thing about havin' a kid. They come with their own set of problems; make everything else you were worried about seem kinda silly.
Greg Garcia, Raising Hope, Dead Tooth, 09-28-10
Babies are cool, until you've done everything to do with 'em and you get bored. That's why T.V. shows about babies don't last more than a year.

Gregory Thomas Garcia, Alan Kirschenbaum, Raising Hope, Burt Rocks, November 30, 2010
A child of five would understand this. Send someone to fetch a child of five.
Groucho Marx (1890 - 1977)
My mother loved children – she would have given anything if I had been one.
Groucho Marx (1890 - 1977)
I have found the best way to give advice to your children is to find out what they want and then advise them to do it.
Harry S Truman (1884 - 1972)
It is not giving children more that spoils them; it is giving them more to avoid confrontation.
John Gray, "Children Are From Heaven"
That's the great thing about being in the third grade. If you've got one polysyllabic adjective, everyone thinks you're a genius.
John Green, Vlogbrothers, My Name Is John Green. And I am a Nerd., 10-30-07
You know that children are growing up when they start asking questions that have answers.
John J. Plomp
I am amused when goody-goodies proclaim, from the safety of their armchairs, that children are naturally prejudice-free, that they only learn to "hate" from listening to bigoted adults. Nonsense. Tolerance is a learned trait, like riding a bike or playing the piano. Those of us who actually live among children, who see them in their natural environment, know the truth: Left to their own devices, children will gang up on and abuse anyone who is even slightly different from the norm.
Josh Lieb, I am a Genius of Unspeakable Evil and I Want to be Your Class President, 2009
Allowing children to fight their own battles is one of the hardest parenting skills to learn.
Julie A., M.A. Ross and Judy Corcoran, Joint Custody with a Jerk: Raising a Child with an Uncooperative Ex, 2011
Children should feel loved because they exist, not because they've behaved in a certain way.
Julie A., M.A. Ross and Judy Corcoran, Joint Custody with a Jerk: Raising a Child with an Uncooperative Ex, 2011
Children will adapt to nearly any rule or routine as long as it is consistently enforced within that particular household.
Julie A., M.A. Ross and Judy Corcoran, Joint Custody with a Jerk: Raising a Child with an Uncooperative Ex, 2011
Trust that your child is trying to be the best he can be and that he will do this more readily without your criticism. Know that he usually sees his own faults without you continually pointing them out.
Julie A., M.A. Ross and Judy Corcoran, Joint Custody with a Jerk: Raising a Child with an Uncooperative Ex, 2011
When children feel they have to earn our love by what they accomplish, they never feel good about themselves, no matter how much they do, no matter what their age. Indeed, some adults work outrageous hours, make huge salaries, and always strive to accomplish more and yet are never satisfied, no matter what they have achieved. This is because they were never given the free, unconditional love of their parents, the love that is every child's birthright.
Julie A., M.A. Ross and Judy Corcoran, Joint Custody with a Jerk: Raising a Child with an Uncooperative Ex, 2011
Your child can't hurt you if you don't accept the hurt. Let it go.
Julie A., M.A. Ross and Judy Corcoran, Joint Custody with a Jerk: Raising a Child with an Uncooperative Ex, 2011
Be gentle with the young.
Juvenal (55 AD - 127 AD)
The thing that impresses me the most about America is the way parents obey their children.
King Edward VIII (1894 - 1972)
Outings are so much more fun when we can savor them through the children's eyes.
Lawana Blackwell, The Courtship of the Vicar's Daughter, 1998
Youth isn't always all it's touted to be.
Lawana Blackwell, The Dowry of Miss Lydia Clark, 1999
People who say they sleep like a baby usually don't have one.
Leo J. Burke
Children might or might not be a blessing, but to create them and then fail them was surely damnation.
Lois McMaster Bujold, "Barrayar", 1991
Our children change us... whether they live or not.
Lois McMaster Bujold, "Barrayar", 1991
Some men just aren't cut out for paternity. Better they should realize it before and not after they become responsible for a son.
Lois McMaster Bujold, Ethan of Athos, 1986
You don't pay back your parents. You can't. The debt you owe them gets collected by your children, who hand it down in turn. It's a sort of entailment. Or if you don't have children of the body, it's left as a debt to your common humanity. Or to your God, if you possess or are possessed by one.
Lois McMaster Bujold, A Civil Campaign, 1999
Kids are like buckets of disease that live in your house.
Louis C. K., Louis C. K.: Chewed Up, 2008
Level with your child by being honest. Nobody spots a phony quicker than a child.
Mary MacCracken
If you want to see what children can do, you must stop giving them things.
Norman Douglas
Children begin by loving their parents; as they grow older they judge them; sometimes they forgive them.
Oscar Wilde (1854 - 1900), The Picture of Dorian Gray, 1891
Humans are the only animals that have children on purpose with the exception of guppies, who like to eat theirs.

P. J. O'Rourke (1947 -)
Children are the only form of immortality that we can be sure of.
Peter Ustinov (1921 - 2004)
Always be nice to your children because they are the ones who will choose your rest home.
Phyllis Diller
Don't limit a child to your own learning, for he was born in another time.
Rabbinical Saying
Children are all foreigners.
Ralph Waldo Emerson (1803 - 1882)
Learning to dislike children at an early age saves a lot of expense and aggravation later in life.
Robert Byrne
I take my children everywhere, but they always find their way back home.
Robert Orben
Never raise your hand to your children; it leaves your midsection unprotected.
Robert Orben
A happy childhood has spoiled many a promising life.
Robertson Davies, "What's Bred in the Bone"
The reason grandparents and grandchildren get along so well is that they have a common enemy.
Sam Levenson (1911 - 1980)
Anyone who uses the phrase 'easy as taking candy from a baby' has never tried taking candy from a baby.
Unknown
D'you call life a bad job? Never! We've had our ups and downs, we've had our struggles, we've always been poor, but it's been worth it, ay, worth it a hundred times I say when I look round at my children.
W. Somerset Maugham (1874 - 1965), 'Of Human Bondage', 1915
How sharper than a serpent's tooth it is
To have a thankless child!
William Shakespeare (1564 - 1616), "King Lear", Act 1 scene 4
It is a wise father that knows his own child.
William Shakespeare (1564 - 1616), "The Merchant of Venice", Act 2 scene 2

Christmas
I never believed in Santa Claus because I knew no white dude would come into my neighborhood after dark.
Dick Gregory (1932 -)
A turkey never voted for an early Christmas.
Irish Proverb
I don't like green Christmases. They're not green—they're just nasty faded browns and grays.
L. M. Montgomery (1874 - 1942), Anne of Green Gables, 1908
Do give books - religious or otherwise - for Christmas. They're never fattening, seldom sinful, and permanently personal.
Lenore Hershey
Aren't we forgeting the true meaning of Christmas? You know, the birth of Santa.
Matt Groening (1954 -), The Simpsons
Christmas is a time when people of all religions come together to worship Jesus Christ.
Matt Groening (1954 -), The Simpsons
I stopped believing in Santa Claus when my mother took me to see him in a department store, and he asked for my autograph.
Shirley Temple (1928 -)
At Christmas play and make good cheer, For Christmas comes but once a year.
Thomas Tusser

Civilization
Civilization advances by extending the number of important operations which we can perform without thinking of them.
Alfred North Whitehead (1861 - 1947)
Civilization degrades the many to exalt the few.
Amos Bronson Alcott (1799 - 1888), Table Talk (1877)
When several villages are united in a single complete community, large enough to nearly or quite self-sufficing, the state comes into existence, originating in the bare needs of life, and continuing in existence for the sake of a good life.
Aristotle (384 BC - 322 BC), Politics, book 1, chapter 2
Underlying the whole scheme of civilization is the confidence men have in each other, confidence in their integrity, confidence in their honesty, confidence in their future.
Bourke Cockran
The country only has charms for those not obliged to stay there.
Edouard Manet (1832 - 1883)
The history of man is a graveyard of great cultures that came to catastrophic ends because of their incapacity for planned, rational, voluntary reaction to challenge.
Erich Fromm (1900 - 1980)
We must remember that any oppression, any injustice, any hatred, is a wedge designed to attack our civilization.
Franklin D. Roosevelt (1882 - 1945), Letter to Dr. William Allan Nielson, January 9, 1940
Civilization is a race between education and catastrophe.
H. G. Wells (1866 - 1946)
The more rapidly a civilization progresses, the sooner it dies for another to rise in its place.
Havelock Ellis (1859 - 1939), The Dance of Life
It is better for civilization to be going down the drain than to be coming up it.
Henry Allen

But the greatest menace to our civilization today is the conflict between giant organized systems of self-righteousness-each system only too delighted to find that the other is wicked-each only too glad that the sins give it the pretext for still deeper hatred and animosity.
Herbert Butterfield, Christianity, Diplomacy and War
Civilization is a method of living, an attitude of equal respect for all men.
Jane Addams (1860 - 1935), Speech, Honolulu (1933)
Civilization is the art of living in towns of such size the everyone does not know everyone else.
Julian Jaynes, "The Origin of Consciousness"
Civilization is built on a number of ultimate principles...respect for human life, the punishment of crimes against property and persons, the equality of all good citizens before the law...or, in a word justice.
Max Nordau (1849 - 1923)
America is the only country that went from barbarism to decadence without civilization in between.
Oscar Wilde (1854 - 1900)
The end of the human race will be that it will eventually die of civilization.
Ralph Waldo Emerson (1803 - 1882)
The true civilization is where every man gives to every other every right that he claims for himself.
Robert Ingersoll (1833 - 1899)
Speech is civilization itself... It is silence which isolates.
Thomas Mann (1875 - 1955)
Civilization begins with order, grows with liberty, and dies with chaos.
Will Durant (1885 - 1981)
You can't say that civilization don't advance, however, for in every war they kill you in a new way.
Will Rogers (1879 - 1935), New York Times, Dec. 23, 1929
One of the indictments of civilizations is that happiness and intelligence are so rarely found in the same person.
William Feather (1908 - 1976)

Clichés

The computing field is always in need of new cliches.
Alan Perlis
Let's have some new cliches.
Samuel Goldwyn (1882 - 1974)
Any great truth can – and eventually will – be expressed as a cliche – a cliche is a sure and certain way to dilute an idea, For instance, my grandmother used to say, 'The black cat is always the last one off the fence.' I have no idea what she meant, but at one time, it was undoubtedly true.
Solomon Short

Committees

If computers get too powerful, we can organize them into a committee – that will do them in.
Bradley's Bromide
A committee can make a decision that is dumber than any of its members.
David Coblitz
Not even computers will replace committees, because committees buy computers.
Edward Shepherd Mead
Committee–a group of men who individually can do nothing but as a group decide that nothing can be done.
Fred Allen (1894 - 1956)
There is no monument dedicated to the memory of a committee.
Lester J. Pourciau
To get something done, a committee should consist of no more than three men, two of whom are absent.
Robert Copeland
A committee is a cul-de-sac down which ideas are lured and then quietly strangled.
Sir Barnett Cocks (1907 - 1989)

Common sense

Common sense is the collection of prejudices acquired by age eighteen.
Albert Einstein (1879 - 1955), (attributed)
Stupid is forever, ignorance can be fixed.
Don Wood
The last time anybody made a list of the top hundred character attributes of New Yorkers, common sense snuck in at number 79.
Douglas Adams (1952 - 2001), "Mostly Harmless"
Everybody gets so much information all day long that they lose their common sense.
Gertrude Stein (1874 - 1946)
[Common sense] is the best sense I know of.
Lord Chesterfield (1694 - 1773)
The freethinking of one age is the common sense of the next.
Matthew Arnold (1822 - 1888), 'God and the Bible,' 1875

Nowadays most people die of a sort of creeping common sense, and discover when it is too late that the only things one never regrets are one's mistakes.
Oscar Wilde (1854 - 1900), The Picture of Dorian Gray, 1891
Nothing astonishes men so much as common sense and plain dealing.
Ralph Waldo Emerson (1803 - 1882), 'Art,' 1841
If an idea's worth having once, it's worth having twice.
Tom Stoppard (1937 -)

Communication

Good communication is as stimulating as black coffee and just as hard to sleep after.
Anne Morrow Lindbergh, 'Gift From the Sea'
Every improvement in communication makes the bore more terrible.
Frank Moore Colby
The constant free flow of communication amount us-enabling the free interchange of ideas-forms the very bloodstream of our nation. It keeps the mind and body of our democracy eternally vital, eternally young.
Franklin D. Roosevelt (1882 - 1945)
Let us make a special effort to stop communicating with each other, so we can have some conversation.
Judith Martin, (Miss Manners)
Sending important messages via text is the coward's way out. Don't be the person who texts important messages. It's rude, inconsiderate, and, yes, cowardly.
Julie A., M.A. Ross and Judy Corcoran, Joint Custody with a Jerk: Raising a Child with an Uncooperative Ex, 2011
Communication is something so simple and difficult that we can never put it in simple words.
T. S. Matthews
I wish people who have trouble communicating would just shut up.
Tom Lehrer (1928 -)
Think like a wise man but communicate in the language of the people.
William Butler Yeats (1865 - 1939)

Communism

Communism doesn't work because people like to own stuff.
Frank Zappa (1940 - 1993)
Under capitalism, man exploits man. Under communism, it's just the opposite.
John Kenneth Galbraith (1908 - 2006)
Communism is like one big phone company.
Lenny Bruce (1923 - 1966)
Communism is like prohibition, it's a good idea but it won't work.
Will Rogers (1879 - 1935), Weekly Articles (1981), first published 1927

Community

The best political community is formed by citizens of the middle class.
Aristotle (384 BC - 322 BC), Politics
Isn't everyone a part of everyone else?
Budd Schulberg, O Magazine, November 2003
First it is necessary to stand on your own two feet. But the minute a man finds himself in that position, the next thing he should do is reach out his arms.
Kristin Hunter, O Magazine, November 2003
Never doubt that a small group of thoughtful, committed citizens can change the world. Indeed, it is the only thing that ever has.
Margaret Mead (1901 - 1978)
The universal brotherhood of man is our most precious possession.
Mark Twain (1835 - 1910)
But the life that no longer trust another human being and no longer forms ties to the political community is not a human life any longer.
Martha Nussbaum, O Magazine, November 2003
God creates men, but they choose each other.
Niccolo Machiavelli (1469 - 1527), quoted in O Magazine, November 2003

Competence

Incompetents invariably make trouble for people other than themselves.
Larry McMurtry (1936 -), 'Lonesome Dove'
Competence, like truth, beauty and contact lenses, is in the eye of the beholder.
Laurence J. Peter (1919 - 1988), The Peter Principle (1969), chapter 1
Equal opportunity means everyone will have a fair chance at being incompetent.
Laurence J. Peter (1919 - 1988)
Everyone rises to their level of incompetence.
Laurence J. Peter (1919 - 1988), "The Peter Principle"
The incompetent with nothing to do can still make a mess of it.
Laurence J. Peter (1919 - 1988)

Computers

The computing field is always in need of new cliches.
Alan Perlis
Computers make it easier to do a lot of things, but most of the things they make it easier to do don't need to be done.
Andy Rooney (1919 -)
The great thing about a computer notebook is that no matter how much you stuff into it, it doesn't get bigger or heavier.
Bill Gates (1955 -), Business @ The Speed of Thought
If computers get too powerful, we can organize them into a committee – that will do them in.

Bradley's Bromide
Why is it drug addicts and computer afficionados are both called users?
Clifford Stoll
My computer beat me at chess... so I beat it at kickboxing.
Demetri Martin
Home computers are being called upon to perform many new functions, including the consumption of homework formerly eaten by the dog.
Doug Larson
Computer Science is no more about computers than astronomy is about telescopes.
E. W. Dijkstra
The question of whether a computer can think is no more interesting than the question of whether a submarine can swim.
E. W. Dijkstra
Not even computers will replace committees, because committees buy computers.
Edward Shepherd Mead
To err is human, but to really foul things up requires a computer.
Farmers' Almanac, 1978
Compromise used to mean that half a loaf was better than no bread. Among modern statesmen it really seems to mean that half a loaf is better than a whole loaf.
G. K. Chesterton (1874 - 1936), What's Wrong with the World, chapter 3, 1910
Most people believe that if you go in and try to micromanage a forest, it is possible to destroy the very thing that makes it a unique and special place. That's just as true of the Net.
Glen Raphael
I do not fear computers. I fear the lack of them.
Isaac Asimov (1920 - 1992)
Part of the inhumanity of the computer is that, once it is competently programmed and working smoothly, it is completely honest.
Isaac Asimov (1920 - 1992)
Computers can figure out all kinds of problems, except the things in the world that just don't add up.
James Magary
Imagine if every Thursday your shoes exploded if you tied them the usual way. This happens to us all the time with computers, and nobody thinks of complaining.
Jef Raskin, interviewed in Doctor Dobb's Journal
The most overlooked advantage to owning a computer is that if they foul up there's no law against wacking them around a little.
Joe Martin, Porterfield
One would think that if you're anonymous, you'd do anything you want, but groups have their own sense of community and what we can do.
John Allen, A network called 'Internet', CBC, 10-08-93
In all large corporations, there is a pervasive fear that someone, somewhere is having fun with a computer on company time. Networks help alleviate that fear.
John C. Dvorak
There is no reason for any individual to have a computer in his home.
Ken Olsen (1926 -), President, Digital Equipment, 1977
No computer has ever been designed that is ever aware of what it's doing; but most of the time, we aren't either.
Marvin Minsky
The most likely way for the world to be destroyed, most experts agree, is by accident. That's where we come in; we're computer professionals. We cause accidents.
Nathaniel Borenstein (1957 -)
Computers are useless. They can only give you answers.
Pablo Picasso (1881 - 1973)
The computer is a moron.
Peter Drucker (1909 - 2005)
If you put tomfoolery into a computer, nothing comes out of it but tomfoolery. But this tomfoolery, having passed through a very expensive machine, is somehow ennobled and no-one dares criticize it.
Pierre Gallois
Programming today is a race between software engineers striving to build bigger and better idiot-proof programs, and the Universe trying to produce bigger and better idiots. So far, the Universe is winning.
Rick Cook, The Wizardry Compiled
To err is human—and to blame it on a computer is even more so.
Robert Orben
If the automobile had followed the same development cycle as the computer, a Rolls-Royce would today cost $100, get a million miles per gallon, and explode once a year, killing everyone inside.
Robert X. Cringely, InfoWorld magazine
I think computer viruses should count as life. I think it says something about human nature that the only form of life we have created so far is purely destructive. We've created life in our own image.
Stephen Hawking (1942 -)
All programmers are playwrights and all computers are lousy actors.
Unknown
In a few minutes a computer can make a mistake so great that it would have taken many men many months to equal it.
Unknown
Where a calculator on the ENIAC is equipped with 18,000 vacuum tubes and weighs 30 tons, computers in the future may have only 1,000 vaccuum tubes and perhaps weigh 1.5 tons.
unknown, Popular Mechanics, March 1949

Conceit

Self-conceit may lead to self-destruction.
Aesop (620 BC - 560 BC), The Frog and the Ox
The smaller the mind the greater the conceit.
Aesop (620 BC - 560 BC)
When they discover the center of the universe, a lot of people will be disappointed to discover they are not it.
Bernard Bailey
Conceit is God's gift to little men.
Bruce Barton
What is the first business of one who practices philosophy? To get rid of self-conceit. For it is impossible for anyone to begin to learn that which he thinks he already knows.
Epictetus (55 AD - 135 AD), Discourses
The world tolerates conceit from those who are successful, but not from anybody else.
John Blake
An ostentatious man will rather relate a blunder or an absurdity he has committed, than be debarred from talking of his own dear person.
Joseph Addison (1672 - 1719)
We are so vain that we even care for the opinion of those we don't care for.
Marie Ebner von Eschenbach
For God hates utterly
The bray of bragging tongues.
Sophocles (496 BC - 406 BC), Antigone
The greatest of faults, I should say, is to be conscious of none.
Thomas Carlyle (1795 - 1881)

Confidence

There are admirable potentialities in every human being. Believe in your strength and your youth. Learn to repeat endlessly to yourself, 'It all depends on me.'
Andre Gide (1869 - 1951)
I was always looking outside myself for strength and confidence, but it comes from within. It is there all the time.
Anna Freud (1895 - 1982)
Having once decided to achieve a certain task, achieve it at all costs of tedium and distaste. The gain in self-confidence of having accomplished a tiresome labor is immense.
Arnold Bennett
Concentration comes out of a combination of confidence and hunger.
Arnold Palmer (1929 -)
Attempt easy tasks as if they were difficult, and difficult as if they were easy; in the one case that confidence may not fall asleep, in the other that it may not be dismayed.
Baltasar Gracian
If I could give you just one gift ever for the rest of your life it would be this. Confidence. It would be the gift of confidence. Either that or a scented candle.
David Nicholls, One Day, 2010
The man who has confidence in himself gains the confidence of others.
Hasidic Saying
All you need in this life is ignorance and confidence; then success is sure.
Mark Twain (1835 - 1910), Letter to Mrs Foote, Dec. 2, 1887
Believe in yourself! Have faith in your abilities! Without a humble but reasonable confidence in your own powers you cannot be successful or happy
Norman Vincent Peale (1898 - 1993)
Often we don't even realize who we're meant to be because we're so busy trying to live out someone else's ideas. But other people and their opinions hold no power in defining our destiny.
Oprah Winfrey (1954 -), O Magazine, November 2009
Feeling special is the worst kind of cage a person can build for himself.
Paolo Giordano, The Solitude of Prime Numbers: A Novel
It seems to me that people have vast potential. Most people can do extraordinary things if they have the confidence or take the risks. Yet most people don't. They sit in front of the telly and treat life as if it goes on forever.
Philip Adams
If I have lost confidence in myself, I have the universe against me.
Ralph Waldo Emerson (1803 - 1882)
You have to have confidence in your ability, and then be tough enough to follow through.
Rosalynn Carter (1927 -)
You can be confident and secure and know that you do a good job at what you do. But you don't know to be arrogant about it.
Ruben Studdard, Seventeen Magazine, September 2003
Self-confidence is the first requisite to great undertakings.
Samuel Johnson (1709 - 1784)
My intent is simply to know my material so well that I'm very comfortable with it. Confidence, not perfection, is the goal.
Scott Berkun, Confessions of a Public Speaker, 2009
Every time you don't follow your inner guidance, you feel a loss of energy, loss of power, a sense of spiritual deadness.
Shakti Gawain
Getting ahead in a difficult profession requires avid faith in yourself. That is why some people with mediocre talent, but with great inner drive, go much further than people with vastly superior talent.
Sophia Loren (1934 -)

You can't connect the dots looking forward you can only connect them looking backwards. So you have to trust that the dots will somehow connect in your future. You have to trust in something: your gut, destiny, life, karma, whatever. Because believing that the dots will connect down the road will give you the confidence to follow your heart, even when it leads you off the well worn path.
Steve Jobs (1955 - 2011), Stanford Commencement Adress, 2005
Confidence is 10% hard work and 90% delusion.
Tina Fey, Vogue Interview, 2010

Congress

Oh, I don't blame Congress. If I had $600 billion at my disposal, I'd be irresponsible, too.
Lichty and Wagner
It could probably be shown by facts and figures that there is no distinctly American criminal class except Congress.
Mark Twain (1835 - 1910)
Suppose you were an idiot and suppose you were a member of Congress. But I repeat myself.
Mark Twain (1835 - 1910)
I don't mind what Congress does, as long as they don't do it in the streets and frighten the horses.
Victor Hugo (1802 - 1885)
This country has come to feel the same when Congress is in session as when the baby gets hold of a hammer.
Will Rogers (1879 - 1935)

Conscience

A clear conscience is a good pillow.
American Proverb
A conscience is what hurts when all your other parts feel so good.
Anonymous
A guilty conscience needs no accuser.
Anonymous
A good conscience is a continual Christmas.
Benjamin Franklin (1706 - 1790)
If all the world hated you and believed you wicked, while your own conscience approved of you and absolved you from guilt, you would not be without friends.
Charlotte Bronte (1816 - 1855), Jane Eyre pg. 61
A lot of people mistake a short memory for a clear conscience.
Doug Larson
In the courtroom of the conscience, a case is always in progress.
Dutch Proverb
Conscience is God's presence in man.
Emanuel Swedenborg (1688 - 1772)
There is one thing alone
that stands the brunt of life throughout its course:
a quiet conscience.
Euripides (484 BC - 406 BC), Hippolytus, 428 B.C.
Conscience is what makes a boy tell his mother before his sister does.
Evan Esar (1899 - 1995)
Fear is the tax that conscience pays to guilt.
George Sewell
Labor to keep alive in your breast that little spark of celestial fire called conscience.
George Washington (1732 - 1799)
Conscience is a mother-in-law whose visit never ends.
H. L. Mencken (1880 - 1956)
Conscience is the inner voice that warns us somebody may be looking.
H. L. Mencken (1880 - 1956), A Mencken Chrestomathy (1949)
Before I can live with other folks, I've got to live with myself. The one thing that doesn't abide by majority rule is a person's conscience.
Harper Lee (1926 -), To Kill a Mockingbird
The conscience of a people is their power.
John Dryden (1631 - 1700)
All a man can betray is his conscience.
Joseph Conrad (1857 - 1924)
Conscience is the perfect interpreter of life.
Karl Barth (1886 - 1968)
I cannot and will not cut my conscience to fit this year's fashions.
Lillian Hellman (1905 - 1984), letter to Committee on Un-American Activities of the House of Representatives, May 19, 1952
Most people sell their souls, and live with a good conscience on the proceeds.
Logan Pearsall Smith (1865 - 1946), Afterthoughts (1931) "Other People"
Freedom is a clear conscience.
Periander
Conscience is the voice of the soul.
Polish Proverb
There is no witness so dreadful, no accuser so terrible as the conscience that dwells in the heart of every man.
Polybius (205 BC - 118 BC), History
Courage without conscience is a wild beast.
Robert Ingersoll (1833 - 1899)
Conscience and reputation are two things. Conscience is due to yourself, reputation to your neighbour.
Saint Augustine (354 AD - 430 AD)
Conscience is, in most men, an anticipation of the opinion of others.
Sir Henry Taylor

It behoves every man who values liberty of conscience for himself, to resist invasions of it in the case of others; or their case may, by change of circumstances, become his own.
Thomas Jefferson (1743 - 1826), Letters to Benjamin Rush, April 21, 1803
...the safest course is to do nothing against one's conscience. With this secret, we can enjoy life and have no fear from death.
Voltaire (1694 - 1778)
Cowardice asks: Is it safe? Expediency asks: Is it politic? But Conscience asks: Is it right?
William Punshon
Conscience does make cowards of us all, and thus the native hue of resolution is sicklied o'er with the pale cast of thought.
William Shakespeare (1564 - 1616), Hamlet, Act III, sc. 1
I feel within me a peace above all earthly dignities, a still and quiet conscience.
William Shakespeare (1564 - 1616)
I know myself know; and I feel within me a peace above all earthly dignities, a still and quiet conscience.
William Shakespeare (1564 - 1616), Henry VIII, Act III, sc. 2
The play's the thing
Wherein I'll catch the conscience of the king.
William Shakespeare (1564 - 1616), "Hamlet", Act 2 scene 2

Conservatives

A conservative is a man who believes that nothing should be done for the first time.
Alfred E. Wiggam
A conservative government is an organized hypocrisy.
Benjamin Disraeli (1804 - 1881), Speech in the House of Commons, Mar. 3, 1845
I am a Conservative to preserve all that is good in our constitution, a Radical to remove all that is bad. I seek to preserve property and to respect order, and I equally decry the appeal to the passions of the many or the prejudices of the few.
Benjamin Disraeli (1804 - 1881), campaign speech at High Wycombe, England, November 27, 1832
The conservative in financial circles I have often described as a man who thinks nothing new ought ever to be adopted for the first time.
Frank A. Vanderlip, From Farm Boy to Financier, chapter 25, 1935
A conservative is a man with two perfectly good legs who, however, has never learned to walk forward.
Franklin D. Roosevelt (1882 - 1945), radio address, Oct. 26, 1939
The true conservative is the man who has a real concern for injustices and takes thought against the day of reckoning.
Franklin D. Roosevelt (1882 - 1945), Speech in Syracuse, NY Sep. 29, 1936
The most radical revolutionary will become a conservative the day after the revolution.
Hannah Arendt (1906 - 1975)
The radical of one century is the conservative of the next. The radical invents the views. When he has worn them out the conservative adopts them.
Mark Twain (1835 - 1910), Notebook, 1935
When you are right you cannot be too radical; when you are wrong, you cannot be too conservative.
Martin Luther King Jr. (1929 - 1968)
Men are conservatives when they are least vigorous, or when they are most luxurious. They are conservatives after dinner.
Ralph Waldo Emerson (1803 - 1882), New England Reformers, 1844
It only takes 20 years for a liberal to become a conservative without changing a single idea.
Robert Anton Wilson
I never dared to be radical when young
For fear it would make me conservative when old.
Robert Frost (1874 - 1963), 'Ten Mills,' A Further Range, 1936
A conservative is a man who sits and thinks, mostly sits.
Woodrow Wilson (1856 - 1924)

Conversation

Bore: one who has the power of speech but not the capacity for conversation.
Benjamin Disraeli (1804 - 1881)
Talking with you is sort of the conversational equivalent of an out of body experience.
Bill Watterson (1958 -), Calvin & Hobbes
Saying what we think gives us a wider conversational range than saying what we know.
Cullen Hightower
Each person's life is lived as a series of conversations.
Deborah Tannen
The real art of conversation is not only to say the right thing at the right place but to leave unsaid the wrong thing at the tempting moment.
Dorothy Nevill
Education begins a gentleman, conversation completes him.
Dr. Thomas Fuller (1654 - 1734), Gnomologia, 1732
Few are agreeable in conversation, because each thinks more of what he intends to say than of what others are saying, and listens no more when he himself has a chance to speak.
Francois de La Rochefoucauld (1613 - 1680)
To listen closely and reply well is the highest perfection we are able to attain in the art of conversation.
Francois de La Rochefoucauld (1613 - 1680)
I often quote myself. It adds spice to my conversation.
George Bernard Shaw (1856 - 1950)

There isn't much better in this life than finding a way to spend a few hours in conversation with people you respect and love. You have to carve this time out of your life because you aren't really living without it.
Gordon Atkinson, RealLivePreacher.com Weblog, August 27, 2003

Anecdotes and maxims are rich treasures to the man of the world, for he knows how to introduce the former at fit place in conversation.
Johann Wolfgang von Goethe (1749 - 1832)

One of the best rules in conversation is, never to say a thing which any of the company can reasonably wish had been left unsaid.
Jonathan Swift (1667 - 1745)

Let us make a special effort to stop communicating with each other, so we can have some conversation.
Judith Martin, (Miss Manners)

Don't knock the weather. If it didn't change once in a while, nine out of ten people couldn't start a conversation.
Kin Hubbard (1868 - 1930)

Spoken words evaporated into the air just as easily as burned letters, but the sound of them seemed immortal. It was as if a word spoken could not be destroyed.
Laura Moncur (1969 -), The Secret Heart of Charlotte Lucas, 2014

Most conversations are simply monologues delivered in the presence of witnesses.
Margaret Millar

The character of a man is known from his conversations.
Menander (342 BC - 292 BC)

Conversation is food for the soul.
Mexican Proverb

You can discover more about a person in an hour of play than in a year of conversation.
Plato (427 BC - 347 BC)

Conversation is an art in which a man has all mankind for his competitors, for it is that which all are practising every day while they live.
Ralph Waldo Emerson (1803 - 1882)

I don't know how to have casual conversation. You think you're talking about one thing, and either you are and it's incredibly boring, or you're not because it's subtext and you need a decoder ring.
Sara B. Cooper, House M.D., Love Hurts, 2004

Your ignorance, cramps my conversation.
Sir Anthony Hawkins (1863 - 1933)

He had occasional flashes of silence, that made his conversation perfectly delightful.
Sydney Smith (1771 - 1845), referring to Macaulay

Silence is one of the great arts of conversation, as allowed by Cicero himself, who says, 'there is not only an art, but an eloquence in it.' A well bred woman may easily and effectually promote the most useful and elegant conversation without speaking a word. The modes of speech are scarcely more variable than the modes of silence.
Tom Blair

It's always difficult to make conversation with a drunk, and there's no denying it, the sober are at a disadvantage with him.
W. Somerset Maugham (1874 - 1965), The Razor's Edge, 1943

Conversation should be pleasant without scurrility, witty without affectation, free without indecency, learned without conceitedness, novel without falsehood.
William Shakespeare (1564 - 1616)

Courage

Courage is the price that Life exacts for granting peace.
Amelia Earhart (1897 - 1937), Courage, 1927

Life shrinks or expands in proportion to one's courage.
Anais Nin (1903 - 1977), The Diary of Anais Nin, volume 3, 1939-1944

Courage is not simply one of the virtues , but the form of every virtue at the testing point.
C. S. Lewis (1898 - 1963)

Live as brave men; and if fortune is adverse, front its blows with brave hearts.
Cicero (106 BC - 43 BC)

Courage is the ladder on which all the other virtues mount.
Clare Booth Luce (1903 - 1987), in Reader's Digest, 1979

The bravest thing you can do when you are not brave is to profess courage and act accordingly.
Corra Harris

Courage is fear that has said its prayers.
Dorothy Bernard

I would rather be a coward than brave because people hurt you when you are brave.
E. M. Forster (1879 - 1970), as a small child

Courage is doing what you're afraid to do. There can be no courage unless you're scared.
Eddie Rickenbacker (1890 - 1973)

Few men are willing to brave the disapproval of their fellows, the censure of their colleagues, the wrath of their society. Moral courage is a rarer commodity than bravery in battle or great intelligence. Yet it is the one essential, vital quality of those who seek to change a world which yields most painfully to change
Ernest Hemingway (1899 - 1961), A Farewell to Arms, 1929

A coward turns away, but a brave man's choice is danger.
Euripides (484 BC - 406 BC), Iphigenia in Tauris, circa 412 B.C.

Perfect courage means doing unwitnessed what he would be capable of with the world looking on.
Francois de La Rochefoucauld (1613 - 1680)

Courage is the art of being the only one who knows you're scared to death.

Harold Wilson (1916 - 1995)

I wanted you to see what real courage is, instead of getting the idea that courage is a man with a gun in his hand. It's when you know you're licked before you begin but you begin anyway and you see it through no matter what.
Harper Lee (1926 -), To Kill a Mockingbird, 1960

A timid person is frightened before a danger, a coward during the time, and a courageous person afterward.
Jean Paul Richter (1763 - 1825)

The stories of past courage can define that ingredient-they can teach, they can offer hope, they can provide inspiration. But they cannot supply courage itself. For this each man must look into his own soul.
John F. Kennedy (1917 - 1963)

Courage and perseverance have a magical talisman, before which difficulties disappear and obstacles vanish into air.
John Quincy Adams (1767 - 1848)

Courage is being scared to death - but saddling up anyway.
John Wayne (1907 - 1979)

The worst thing of all is standing by when folks are doing something wrong.
Kirby Larson, Hattie Big Sky, 2006

If courage wasn't a standard result of aging, it meant that the young could somehow acquire it as well.
Lawana Blackwell, The Courtship of the Vicar's Daughter, 1998

Courage is resistance to fear, mastery of fear - not absence of fear.
Mark Twain (1835 - 1910)

It is curious that physical courage should be so common in the world and moral courage so rare.
Mark Twain (1835 - 1910)

Let bravery be thy choice, but not bravado.
Menander (342 BC - 292 BC)

The strongest, most generous, and proudest of all virtues is true courage.
Michel de Montaigne (1533 - 1592)

The only courage that matters is the kind that gets you from one moment to the next.
Mignon McLaughlin, The Second Neurotic's Notebook, 1966

A hero is no braver than an ordinary man, but he is braver five minutes longer.
Ralph Waldo Emerson (1803 - 1882)

When you meet your antagonist, do everything in a mild and agreeable manner. Let your courage be as keen, but at the same time as polished, as your sword.
Richard Brinsley Sheridan (1751 - 1816)

Keep your fears to yourself, but share your courage with others.
Robert Louis Stevenson (1850 - 1894)

Fortune helps the brave.
Terence (185 BC - 159 BC), Phormio

Far better is it to dare mighty things, to win glorious triumphs, even though checkered by failure , than to take rank with those poor spires who neither enjoy much nor suffer much because they live in the gray twilight that knows not victory or defeat.
Theodore Roosevelt (1858 - 1919)

He that will not sail until all dangers are over, will never put to sea.
Thomas Fuller (1608 - 1661)

Many would be cowards if they had courage enough.
Thomas Fuller (1608 - 1661)

Some have been thought brave because they were afraid to run away.
Thomas Fuller (1608 - 1661)

Fortune favors the brave.
Virgil (70 BC - 19 BC), Aeneid

'Tis much he dares; and, to that dauntless temper of his mind, he hath a wisdom that doth guide his valour to act in safety.
William Shakespeare (1564 - 1616), Macbeth, Act III, sc. 1

When valour preys on reason, it eats the sword it fights with.
William Shakespeare (1564 - 1616), Antony and Cleopatra

Cowardice

He who despairs over an event is a coward, but he who holds hope for the human condition is a fool.
Albert Camus (1913 - 1960), The Rebel (1951)

I would rather be a coward than brave because people hurt you when you are brave.
E. M. Forster (1879 - 1970), as a small child

A coward turns away, but a brave man's choice is danger.
Euripides (484 BC - 406 BC), Iphigenia in Tauris, circa 412 B.C.

None but a coward dares to boast that he has never known fear.
Ferdinand Foch (1851 - 1929)

Patience has its limits. Take it too far, and it's cowardice.
George Jackson (1941 - 1971)

A timid person is frightened before a danger, a coward during the time, and a courageous person afterward.
Jean Paul Richter (1763 - 1825)

There are several good protections against temptations, but the surest is cowardice.
Mark Twain (1835 - 1910), Following the Equator (1897)

A brave man dies but once, a coward many times.
Native American Proverb

Many would be cowards if they had courage enough.
Thomas Fuller (1608 - 1661)

The real hero is always a hero by mistake; he dreams of being an honest coward like everybody else.
Umberto Eco (1932 -), Travels in Hyperreality (Harcourt)

Cowardice asks: Is it safe? Expediency asks: Is it politic? But Conscience asks: Is it right?
William Punshon

A thought which, quarter'd, hath but one part wisdom and ever three parts coward.
William Shakespeare (1564 - 1616), Hamlet, Act IV, sc. 4
Conscience does make cowards of us all, and thus the native hue of resolution is sicklied o'er with the pale cast of thought.
William Shakespeare (1564 - 1616), Hamlet, Act III, sc. 1
Cowards die many times before their deaths;
The valiant never taste of death but once.
William Shakespeare (1564 - 1616), "Julius Caesar", Act II Scene 2
Cowards die many times before their deaths;
The valiant never taste of death but once.
Of all the wonders that I yet have heard,
It seems to me most strange that men should fear;
Seeing that death, a necessary end,
Will come when it will come.
William Shakespeare (1564 - 1616), "Julius Caesar", Act 2 scene 2
Cowards die many times before their deaths; the valiant never taste of death but once.

William Shakespeare (1564 - 1616), Julius Caesar, Act II, sc. 2

Creativity

The secret to creativity is knowing how
  to hide your sources.
Albert Einstein (1879 - 1955)
Frugality without creativity is deprivation.
Amy Dacyczyn
So you see, imagination needs moodling - long, inefficient, happy idling, dawdling and puttering.
Brenda Ueland
The creation of something new is not accomplished by the intellect but by the play instinct acting from inner necessity. The creative mind plays with the objects it loves.
Carl Jung (1875 - 1961)
Creativity is a drug I cannot live without.
Cecil B. DeMille (1881 - 1959)
The problem is never how to get new, innovative thoughts into your mind, but how to get old ones out. Every mind is a building filled with archaic furniture. Clean out a corner of your mind and creativity will instantly fill it.
Dee Hock
There were always people like the pope. They serve a certain function, of course. They subsidize us. But, they don't create anything and they must never be allowed to stop the artist from creating.
Diane Frolov and Andrew Schneider, Northern Exposure, Mite Makes Right, 1994
Humanity can be quite cold to those whose eyes see the world differently.
Eric A. Burns, Gossamer Commons, 08-24-05
Observe Everything.
Communicate Well.
Draw, Draw, Draw.
Frank Thomas, Disney Animator, When asked to give advice to young animators
Creativity can solve almost any problem. The creative act, the defeat of habit by originality, overcomes everything.
George Lois
When Alexander the Great visited Diogenes and asked whether he could do anything for the famed teacher, Diogenes replied: 'Only stand out of my light.' Perhaps some day we shall know how to heighten creativity. Until then, one of the best things we can do for creative men and women is to stand out of their light.
John W. Gardner (1912 - 2002)
To live a creative life, we must lose our fear of being wrong.
Joseph Chilton Pearce
Creativity is...seeing something that doesn't exist already. You need to find out how you can bring it into being and that way be a playmate with God.
Michele Shea
Creativity represents a miraculous coming together of the uninhibited energy of the child with its apparent opposite and enemy, the sense of order imposed on the disciplined adult intelligence.
Norman Podhoretz
Every child is an artist. The problem is how to remain an artist once he grows up.
Pablo Picasso (1881 - 1973)
I started concentrating so hard on my vision that I lost sight.
Robin Green, Northern Exposure, Burning Down the House, 1992
Creativity is allowing yourself to make mistakes. Art is knowing which ones to keep.
Scott Adams (1957 -), 'The Dilbert Principle'
Every time we say, "Let there be!" in any form, something happens.
Stella Terrill Mann
Creative work is play. It is free speculation using materials of one's chosen form.
Stephen Nachmanovitch
The most potent muse of all is our own inner child.
Stephen Nachmanovitch
The noun of self becomes a verb. This flashpoint of creation in the present moment is where work and play merge.
Stephen Nachmanovitch
Don't let the fear of not pleasing someone stop you from being creative.
Wil Wheaton, WIL WHATON dot NET, 12-07-13
The goal isn't to make something everyone will love; the goal is to get excited, and make a thing where something wasn't before.
Wil Wheaton, WIL WHATON dot NET, 12-07-13

Crime

The reason there is so little crime in Germany is that it's against the law.
Alex Levin
Crime does not pay ... as well as politics.
Alfred E. Newman
Life is nothing but a competition to be the criminal rather than the victim.
Bertrand Russell (1872 - 1970)
When you think of the long and gloomy history of man, you will find more hideous crimes have been committed in the name of obedience than have ever been committed in the name of rebellion.
C. P. Snow (1905 - 1980)
Crooks are early adopters.
Craig Newmark (1952 -), Keynote Speech, SXSW 2006
History is indeed little more than the register of the crimes, follies and misfortunes of mankind.
Edward Gibbon (1737 - 1794)
Crime is naught but misdirected energy.
Emma Goldman (1869 - 1940), Anarchism (1910)
Obviously crime pays, or there'd be no crime.
G. Gordon Liddy
Criminals do not die by the hands of the law. They die by the hands of other men.
George Bernard Shaw (1856 - 1950)
Behind every great fortune there is a crime.
Honore de Balzac (1799 - 1850)
Criminal: A person with predatory instincts who has not sufficient capital to form a corporation.
Howard Scott (1926 -)
Going to trial with a lawyer who considers your whole life-style a Crime in Progress is not a happy prospect.
Hunter S. Thompson (1939 - 2005)
A crime which is the crime of many none avenge.
Lucan (39 AD - 65 AD)
We have a criminal jury system which is superior to any in the world; and its efficiency is only marred by the difficulty of finding twelve men every day who don't know anything and can't read.
Mark Twain (1835 - 1910)
The most dangerous criminal may be the man gifted with reason, but with no morals.
Martin Luther King, jr., The Purpose of Education, Maroon Tiger, January-February 1947
Crime butchers innocence to secure a throne, and innocence struggles with all its might against the attempts of crime.
Maximilien Robespierre (1758 - 1794)
The judge is condemned when the criminal is absolved.
Publilius Syrus (~100 BC), Maxims
There is no den in the wide world to hide a rogue. Commit a crime and the earth is made of glass. Commit a crime, and it seems as if a coat of snow fell on the ground, such as reveals in the woods the track of every partridge, and fox, and squirrel.
Ralph Waldo Emerson (1803 - 1882)
The key is to commit crimes so confusing that police feel too stupid to even write a crime report about them.
Randy K. Milholland, Something Positive Comic, 10-30-03
Indeed, history is nothing more than a tableau of crimes and misfortunes.
Voltaire (1694 - 1778)
Murder is unique in that it abolishes the party it injures, so that society has to take the place of the victim and on his behalf demand atonement or grant forgiveness; it is the one crime in which society has a direct interest.
W. H. Auden (1907 - 1973)
Organized crime in America takes in over forty billion dollars a year and spends very little on office supplies.
Woody Allen (1935 -)

Criticism

How much easier it is to be critical than to be correct.
Benjamin Disraeli (1804 - 1881), speech, January 24, 1860
Asking a working writer what he thinks about critics is like asking a lamppost how it feels about dogs.
Christopher Hampton
Any fool can criticize, condemn, and complain - and most fools do.
Dale Carnegie
If you are not criticized, you may not be doing much.
Donald H. Rumsfeld (1932 -), Secretary of Defense
After all, one knows one's weak points so well, that it's rather bewildering to have the critics overlook them and invent others.
Edith Wharton (1862 - 1937)
To avoid criticism do nothing, say nothing, be nothing.
Elbert Hubbard (1856 - 1915)
Do what you feel in your heart to be right - for you'll be criticized anyway. You'll be damned if you do, and damned if you don't.
Eleanor Roosevelt (1884 - 1962)
Honest criticism is hard to take, particularly from a relative, a friend, an acquaintance, or a stranger.
Franklin P. Jones
Criticism is prejudice made plausible.
H. L. Mencken (1880 - 1956)

No degree of dullness can safeguard a work against the determination of critics to find it fascinating.
Harold Rosenberg
Now, in reality, the world have paid too great a compliment to critics, and have imagined them to be men of much greater profundity than they really are.
Henry Fielding (1707 - 1754)
Pay no attention to what the critics say... Remember, a statue has never been set up in honor of a critic!
Jean Sibelius (1865 - 1957), quoted in Bengt de Torne "Sibelius: A Close-Up" 1937
Against criticism a man can neither protest nor defend himself; he must act in spite of it, and then it will gradually yield to him.
Johann Wolfgang von Goethe (1749 - 1832)
Any reviewer who expresses rage and loathing for a novel is preposterous. He or she is like a person who has put on full armor and attacked a hot fudge sundae.
Kurt Vonnegut (1922 - 2007)
Never criticize a man until you've walked a mile in his moccasins.
Native American Proverb
I never met anybody who said when they were a kid, "I wanna grow up and be a critic."
Richard Pryor (1940 - 2005), Guardian Unlimited (UK) August 9, 2004
One cannot review a bad book without showing off.
W. H. Auden (1907 - 1973)
People ask for criticism, but they only want praise.
W. Somerset Maugham (1874 - 1965), "Of Human Bondage", 1915
Criticism comes easier than craftsmanship.
Zeuxis (~400 BC), from Pliny the Elder, Natural History

Curiosity

The cure for boredom is curiosity. There is no cure for curiosity.
Dorothy Parker (1893 - 1967), (attributed)
Only the curious will learn and only the resolute overcome the obstacles to learning. The quest quotient has always excited me more than the intelligence quotient.
Eugene S. Wilson
Curiosity killed the cat, but for a while I was a suspect.
Steven Wright (1955 -)
What we have to do is to be forever curiously testing new opinions and courting new impressions.
Walter Pater (1839 - 1894), 1873
Seize the moment of excited curiosity on any subject to solve your doubts; for if you let it pass, the desire may never return, and you may remain in ignorance.
William Wirt (1772 - 1834)

Cynicism

Idealism is what precedes experience; cynicism is what follows.
David T. Wolf (1943 -)
The power of accurate observation is commonly called cynicism by those who have not got it.
George Bernard Shaw (1856 - 1950)
A cynic is a man who, when he smells flowers, looks around for a coffin.
H. L. Mencken (1880 - 1956)
My pessimism extends to the point of even suspecting the sincerity of the pessimists.
Jean Rostand (1894 - 1977), Journal of a Character, 1931
Cynicism is an unpleasant way of saying the truth.
Lillian Hellman (1905 - 1984), The Little Foxes, 1939
No matter how cynical you get, it is impossible to keep up.
Lily Tomlin (1939 -)
What is a cynic? A man who knows the price of everything and the value of nothing.
Oscar Wilde (1854 - 1900), Lady Windermere's Fan, 1892, Act III
Cynicism is not realistic and tough. It's unrealistic and kind of cowardly because it means you don't have to try.
Peggy Noonan (1950 -), in Good Housekeeping
Cynics regarded everybody as equally corrupt... Idealists regarded everybody as equally corrupt, except themselves.
Robert Anton Wilson
A cynic is not merely one who reads bitter lessons from the past, he is one who is prematurely disappointed in the future.
Sidney J. Harris
Never be a cynic, even a gentle one. Never help out a sneer, even at the devil.
Vachel Lindsay (1879 - 1931)

Dance

I would not know what the spirit of a philosopher might wish more to be than a good dancer.
Friedrich Nietzsche (1844 - 1900), The Gay Science, section 381
If you cannot get rid of the family skeleton, you may as well make it dance.
George Bernard Shaw (1856 - 1950)
Almost nobody dances sober, unless they happen to be insane.

H. P. Lovecraft (1890 - 1937)
Dance is the hidden language of the soul.
Martha Graham (1894 - 1991)
The dance is a poem of which each movement is a word.
Mata Hari (1876 - 1917)
Every day brings a chance for you to draw in a breath, kick off your shoes, and dance.
Oprah Winfrey (1954 -), O Magazine, February 2003
A sympathetic Scot summed it all up very neatly in the remark, "You should make a point of trying every experience once, excepting incest and folk dancing."
Sir Arnold Bax (1883 - 1953), Farewell my Youth (1943)

Death

Death is more universal than life; everyone dies but not everyone lives.
A. Sachs
When I pass, speak freely of my shortcomings and my flaws. Learn from them, for I'll have no ego to injure.
Aaron McGruder, Boondocks, 07-04-04
Death is better, a milder fate than tyranny.
Aeschylus (525 BC - 456 BC), Agamemnon
There is some comfort in dying surrounded by one's children.
Ann Radcliffe (1764 - 1823), The Mysteries of Udolpho, 1764
We do not die because we have to die; we die because one day, and not so long ago, our consciousness was forced to deem it necessary.
Antonin Artaud (1896 - 1948)
Do not fear death so much, but rather the inadequate life.
Bertolt Brecht (1898 - 1956), The Mother, 1932
For certain is death for the born
And certain is birth for the dead;
Therefore over the inevitable
Thou shouldst not grieve.
Bhagavad Gita (250 BC - 250 AD), Chapter 2
He not busy being born is busy dying.
Bob Dylan (1941 -)
I'd rather get my brains blown out in the wild than wait in terror at the slaughterhouse.
Craig Volk, Northern Exposure, A-Hunting We Will Go, 1991
The killing was the best part. It was the dying I couldn't take.
Craig Volk, Northern Exposure, A-Hunting We Will Go, 1991
Be open to your dreams, people. Embrace that distant shore. Because our mortal journey is over all too soon.
David Assael, Northern Exposure, It Happened in Juneau, 1992
A man should not leave this earth with unfinished business. He should live each day as if it was a pre-flight check. He should ask each morning, am I prepared to lift-off?
Diane Frolov and Andrew Schneider, Northern Exposure, All is Vanity, 1991
Death is the enemy. I spent 10 years of my life singlemindedly studying, practicing, fighting hand to hand in close quarters to defeat the enemy, to send him back bloodied and humble and I am not going to roll over and surrender.
Diane Frolov and Andrew Schneider, Northern Exposure, First Snow, 1993
I am going to concentrate on what's important in life. I'm going to strive everyday to be a kind and generous and loving person. I'm going to keep death right here, so that anytime I even think about getting angry at you or anybody else, I'll see death and I'll remember.
Diane Frolov and Andrew Schneider, Northern Exposure, Do The Right Thing, 1992
It's no accident that the church and the graveyard stand side by side. The city of the dead sleeps encircled by the city of the living.
Diane Frolov and Andrew Schneider, Northern Exposure, Lost and Found, 1992
If wild my breast and sore my pride,
I bask in dreams of suicide,
If cool my heart and high my head
I think "How lucky are the dead.
Dorothy Parker (1893 - 1967)
I'm afraid I'm being an awful nuisance.
Edith Sitwell (1887 - 1964), Her last words, as quoted in The Last Years of a Rebel : A Memoir of Edith Sitwell by Elizabeth Salter, 1967
Death is nothing to us, since when we are, death has not come, and when death has come, we are not.
Epicurus (341 BC - 270 BC), from Diogenes Laertius, Lives of Eminent Philosophers
I hope the leaving is joyful; and I hope never to return.
Frida Kahlo (1907 - 1954)
There's a strange sort of quiet when you're dying. It's as if you're in a glass room, and the walls keep getting thicker and thicker.
Gabrielle Zevin, Love Is Hell: Fan Fictions, 2008
Life does not cease to be funny when people die any more than it ceases to be serious when people laugh.
George Bernard Shaw (1856 - 1950)
If you live to be one hundred, you've got it made. Very few people die past that age.
George Burns (1896 - 1996)
There is no cure for birth and death save to enjoy the interval.
George Santayana (1863 - 1952), Soliloquies in England, 1922, "War Shrines"
Pale Death with impartial tread beats at the poor man's cottage door and at the palaces of kings.
Horace (65 BC - 8 BC), Odes
Death can sneak up on you like a silent kitten, surprising you with it's touch and you have a right to act surprised. Other times death stomps in the front door, unwanted and unannounced, and makes it's noisy way to your seat on the sofa.
Hugh Elliott, Bible Versus, 11-27-08

I am not dying, not anymore than any of us are at any moment. We run, hopefully as fast as we can, and then everyone must stop. We can only choose how we handle the race.
Hugh Elliott, Standing Room Only weblog comments, 06-11-04
Life is pleasant. Death is peaceful. It's the transition that's troublesome.
Isaac Asimov (1920 - 1992)
I can't talk about our love story, so I will talk about math. I am not a mathematician, but I know this: There are infinite numbers between 0 and 1. There's .1 and .12 and .112 and an infinite collection of others. Of course, there is a bigger infinite set of numbers between 0 and 2, or between 0 and a million. Some infinities are bigger than other infinities. A writer we used to like taught us that. There are days, many of them, when I resent the size of my unbounded set. I want more numbers than I'm likely to get. But, my love, I cannot tell you how thankful I am for our little infinity. I wouldn't trade it for the world. You gave me a forever within the numbered days, and I'm grateful.
John Green, The Fault in Our Stars, 2012
If the inevitability of human oblivion worries you, I encourage you to ignore it.
John Green, The Fault in Our Stars, 2012
If you were to go [to the Rijksmuseum], and hopefully someday you will, you would see a lot of paintings of dead people. You'd see Jesus on the cross, and you'd see a dude getting stabbed in the neck, and you'd see people dying at sea and in battle and a parade of martyrs. But Not. One. Single. Cancer. Kid. Nobody biting it from the plague or smallpox or yellow fever or whatever, because there is no glory in illness. There is no meaning to it. There is no honor in dying of.
John Green, The Fault in Our Stars, 2012
It's almost as if the way you imagine my dead self says more about you than it says about either the person I was or the whatever I am now.
John Green, The Fault in Our Stars, 2012
Nostalgia is a side effect of dying.
John Green, The Fault in Our Stars, 2012
That was the worst part about having cancer, sometimes: The physical evidence of disease separates you from other people.
John Green, The Fault in Our Stars, 2012
The pleasure of remembering had been taken from me, because there was no longer anyone to remember with. It felt like losing your co-rememberer meant losing the memory itself, as if the things we'd done were less real and important than they had been hours before.
John Green, The Fault in Our Stars, 2012
There will come a time, when all of us are dead. All of us. There will come a time when there are no human beings remaining to remember that anyone ever existed or that our species ever did anything.
John Green, The Fault in Our Stars, 2012
Thinking you won't die is yet another side effect of dying.
John Green, The Fault in Our Stars, 2012
You clench your teeth. You look up. You tell yourself that if they see you cry, it will hurt them, and you will be nothing but A Sadness in their lives, and you must not become a mere sadness, so you will not cry, and you say all of this to yourself while looking up at the ceiling, and then you swallow even though your throat does not want to close and you look at the person who loves you and smile.
John Green, The Fault in Our Stars, 2012
[Not smoking the cigarette is] a metaphor, see: You put the killing thing right between your teeth, but you don't give it the power to do its killing.
John Green, The Fault in Our Stars, 2012
When you lose someone you love, you die too, and you wait around for your body to catch up.
John Scalzi, Old Man's War, 2005
For three days after death hair and fingernails continue to grow but phone calls taper off.
Johnny Carson (1925 - 2005)
It is impossible that anything so natural, so necessary, and so universal as death, should ever have been designed by Providence as an evil to mankind.
Jonathan Swift (1667 - 1745)
A single death is a tragedy; a million deaths is a statistic.
Joseph Stalin (1879 - 1953)
Everything we do really is just a little marker on the long road to death. And sometimes that's overwhelmingly depressing to me, and sometimes it makes me feel kinship and forgiveness. We've all got the same ending to the story. The way we make that story more elaborate, I got to respect.
Joss Whedon, Entertainment Weekly, 08-30-13
We resent the thought that anything can please us when someone we love is no longer here to share the pleasure with us, and we almost feel as if we were unfaithful to our sorrow when we find our interest in life returning to us.
L. M. Montgomery (1874 - 1942), Anne of Green Gables, 1908
As a well-spent day brings happy sleep, so life well used brings happy death.
Leonardo da Vinci (1452 - 1519)
The dead cannot cry out for justice; it is a duty of the living to do so for them.
Lois McMaster Bujold, Diplomatic Immunity, 2002
Out of the people that ever were, almost all of them are dead. There are way more dead people, and you're all gonna die and then you're gonna be dead for way longer than you're alive. Like that's mostly what you're ever gonna be. You're just dead people that didn't die yet.
Louis C. K., Louis C. K.: Hilarious, 2011
It is not death that a man should fear, but he should fear never beginning to live.
Marcus Aurelius Antoninus (121 AD - 180 AD)
Think not disdainfully of death, but look on it with favor; for even death is one of the things that Nature wills.
Marcus Aurelius Antoninus (121 AD - 180 AD), Meditations

The report of my death was an exaggeration.
Mark Twain (1835 - 1910), New York Journal, June 2, 1897
Never knock on Death's door: ring the bell and run away! Death really hates that!
Matt Frewer, as Dr. Mike Stratford in "Doctor, Doctor"
If you don't think your life is worth more than someone else's, sign your donor card and kill yourself now.
Matthew V, Lewis, House M.D., Last Resort, 2008
How his death hung over that house. It's part of what I know to be true—your absence is greater than your presence.
Michael Hainey, After Visiting Friends: A Son's Story, 2013
I suppose that I shall have to die beyond my means.
Oscar Wilde (1854 - 1900), upon being told the cost of an operation
It's sad when our daddies die. Makes us one less person inside.
Pamela Ribon, Why Girls Are Weird, 2003
Must not all things at the last be swallowed up in death?
Plato (427 BC - 347 BC), Dialogues, Phaedo
As men, we are all equal in the presence of death.
Publilius Syrus (~ 100 BC), Moral Sayings, First Century B.C.
The fear of death is more to be dreaded than death itself.
Publilius Syrus (~ 100 BC), Maxims
Being prepared for loss is never the same as being ready for it.
Randy K. Milholland, Something Positive, 10-20-09
Death likes it when you play hard to get.
Randy K. Milholland, Something Positive, 09-20-12
I guess that's how death works. It doesn't matter if we're ready or not. It just happens.
Randy K. Milholland, Something Positive, 11-29-2006
I've accepted that I'm not going to die of natural causes, [but] getting killed 'cuz you're naturally a dick seems like natural causes to me.
Randy K. Milholland, Something Positive, Natural Causes, 06-07-13
The fact that when we die we are nothing more than worm meat—I just don't think about it.
Robin Green and Mitchell Burgess, Northern Exposure, Grosse Pointe 48230, 1993
As we look deeply within, we understand our perfect balance. There is no fear of the cycle of birth, life and death. For when you stand in the present moment, you are timeless.
Rodney Yee
I know death is coming, and I do not fear it. I was perfectly content before I was born, and I think of death as the same state. I am grateful for the gifts of intelligence, love, wonder and laughter. You can't say it wasn't interesting.
Roger Ebert (1942 - 2013), People Magazine, 09-19-11
If I could drop dead right now, I'd be the happiest man alive.
Samuel Goldwyn (1882 - 1974)
There was something awesome in the thought of the solitary mortal standing by the open window and summoning in from the gloom outside the spirits of the nether world.
Sir Arthur Conan Doyle (1859 - 1930)
Death is not the worst; rather, in vain
To wish for death, and not to compass it.
Sophocles (496 BC - 406 BC), Electra
When we die, no one remembers us for what we weighed. Our weight isn't etched into our headstones.
Stephanie Klein, Moose, 2008
Remembering that I'll be dead soon is the most important tool I've ever encountered to help me make the big choices in life.
Steve Jobs (1955 - 2011), Stanford Commencement Adress, 2005
I couldn't kill myself, couldn't let go like so many others had. I wonder if in their last moments they'd changed their minds, but there was no boulder to grab on to.
Suzanne Young, The Program. 2013
The bad end unhappily, the good unluckily. That is what tragedy means.
Tom Stoppard (1937 -), Rosencrantz and Guildenstern are Dead, 1967
Dying is a very dull, dreary affair. And my advice to you is to have nothing whatever to do with it.
W. Somerset Maugham (1874 - 1965)
The dead look so terribly dead when they're dead.
W. Somerset Maugham (1874 - 1965), The Razor's Edge, 1943
Life isn't fair. It's just fairer than death, that's all.
William Goldman, "The Princess Bride"
Against self-slaughter there is a prohibition so divine that cravens my weak hand.
William Shakespeare (1564 - 1616), Cymbeline, Act III, sc. 4
Is it sin to rush into the secret house of death, ere death dare come to us?
William Shakespeare (1564 - 1616), Antony and Cleopatra, Act IV, sc. 15
So every bondman in his own hand bears the power to cancel his captivity.
William Shakespeare (1564 - 1616), Julius Caesar, Act I, sc. 3
There is left us ourselves to end ourselves.
William Shakespeare (1564 - 1616), Antony and Cleopatra, Act IV, sc. 14
Those who welcome death have only tried it from the ears up.
Wilson Mizner (1876 - 1933)
I don't want to achieve immortality through my work... I want to achieve it through not dying.
Woody Allen (1935 -)
It is impossible to experience one's death objectively and still carry a tune.
Woody Allen (1935 -)
On the plus side, death is one of the few things that can be done just as easily lying down.
Woody Allen (1935 -)

There are worse things in life than death. Have you ever spent an evening with an insurance salesman?
Woody Allen (1935 -)

Decisions

The more alternatives, the more difficult the choice.
Abbe' D'Allanival
The first step to getting the things you want out of life is this: Decide what you want.
Ben Stein
Our choices add up; each one influences others, and cumulatively a series of delightful short-term choices can leave us much worse off in the long run.
Daniel Akst, We Have Met the Enemy: Self-Control in an Age of Excess, 2011
A person has three choices in life. You can swim against the tide and get exhausted, or you can tread water and let the tide sweep you away, or you can swim with the tide, and let it take you where it wants you to go.
Diane Frolov and Andrew Schneider, Northern Exposure, Northern Lights, 1993
I think that somehow, we learn who we really are and then live with that decision.
Eleanor Roosevelt (1884 - 1962)
The strongest principle of growth lies in human choice.
George Eliot (1819 - 1880)
Destiny is a name often given in retrospect to choices that had dramatic consequences.
J. K. Rowling, J. K. Rowling Official Website
It is our choices...that show what we truly are, far more than our abilities.
J. K. Rowling, Harry Potter and The Chamber of Secrets, 1999
A pessimist, confronted with two bad choices, chooses both.
Jewish Proverb
The self is not something ready-made, but something in continuous formation through choice of action.
John Dewey (1859 - 1952)
An executive is a person who always decides; sometimes he decides correctly, but he always decides.
John H, Patterson
A weak man has doubts before a decision, a strong man has them afterwards.
Karl Kraus (1874 - 1936)
When I make up my mind to do a thing it stays made up.
L. M. Montgomery (1874 - 1942), Anne of Green Gables, 1908
When it is not necessary to make a decision, it is necessary not to make a decision.
Lord Falkland (1610 - 1643)
Check your ego at the door and check your gut instead. Every right decision I have ever made has come from my gut. Every wrong decision I've made was the result of me not listening to the greater voice of myself
Oprah Winfrey (1954 -), Stanford Commencement Adress, 2008
If it doesn't feel right, don't do it. That's the lesson. That lesson alone, will save you a lot of grief. Even doubt means don't.
Oprah Winfrey (1954 -), Stanford Commencement Adress, 2008
When you don't know what to do, get still. Get very still until you do know what to do.
Oprah Winfrey (1954 -), Stanford Commencement Adress, 2008
When yu' can't have why you choose, yu' just choose what you have.
Owen Wister, The Virginian, Chapter 13, 1929
Choices are made in brief seconds and paid for in the time that remains.
Paolo Giordano, The Solitude of Prime Numbers: A Novel
Give no decision till both sides thou'st heard.
Phocylides
We must give lengthy deliberation to what has to be decided once and for all.
Publilius Syrus (~ 100 BC)
If you limit your choices only to what seems possible or reasonable, you disconnect yourself from what you truly want, and all that is left is a compromise.
Robert Fritz
Remembering that I'll be dead soon is the most important tool I've ever encountered to help me make the big choices in life.
Steve Jobs (1955 - 2011), Stanford Commencement Adress, 2005

Defeat

Do not be afraid of defeat. you are never so near victory as when defeated in a good cause
Henry Ward Beecher (1813 - 1887)
Exile, for no other motive than ease, would be the last defeat, with no seed of future victory in it.
Lois McMaster Bujold, "Shards of Honor", 1986
Victory attained by violence is tantamount to a defeat, for it is momentary.
Mahatma Gandhi (1869 - 1948), 'Satyagraha Leaflet No. 13,' May 3, 1919
There are some defeats more triumphant than victories.
Michel de Montaigne (1533 - 1592)
You can take from every experience what it has to offer you. And you cannot be defeated if you just keep taking one breath followed by another.
Oprah Winfrey (1954 -), O Magazine, What I Know For Sure, January 2004
When defeat is inevitable, it is wisest to yield.
Quintilian
Be careful that victories do not carry the seed of future defeats.
Ralph W. Sockman
A good man would prefer to be defeated than to defeat injustice by evil means.

Sallust (86 BC - 34 BC), 'Jugurthine War,' 41 B.C.
Victorious warriors win first and then go to war, while defeated warriors go to war first and then seek to win.
Sun-tzu (~ 400 BC), The Art of War. Strategic Assessments
Far better it is to dare mighty things, to win glorious triumphs even though checkered by failure, than to rank with those poor spirits who neither enjoy nor suffer much because they live in the gray twilight that knows neither victory nor defeat.
Theodore Roosevelt (1858 - 1919)
What is defeat? Nothing but education; nothing but the first step to something better.
Wendell Phillips (1811 - 1884)

Democracy

Self-criticism is the secret weapon of democracy, and candor and confession are good for the public soul
Adlai E. Stevenson Jr. (1900 - 1965)
Democracy consists of choosing your dictators, after they've told you what you think it is you want to hear.
Alan Corenk
If liberty and equality, as is thought by some are chiefly to be found in democracy, they will be best attained when all persons alike share in the government to the utmost.
Aristotle (384 BC - 322 BC), Politics
The great thing about democracy is that it gives every voter a chance to do something stupid.
Art Spander
Democracy means government by discussion, but it is only effective if you can stop people talking.
Clement Atlee
Democracy is the recurrent suspicion that more than half of the people are right more than half the time.
E. B. White (1899 - 1985), New Yorker, July 3, 1944
Democracy means government by the uneducated, while aristocracy means government by the badly educated.
G. K. Chesterton (1874 - 1936)
Democracy is a device that ensures we shall be governed no better than we deserve.
George Bernard Shaw (1856 - 1950)
Democracy substitutes election by the incompetent many for appointment by the corrupt few.
George Bernard Shaw (1856 - 1950), Man and Superman (1903) "Maxims for Revolutionists"
The whole dream of democracy is to raise the proletarian to the level of stupidity attained by the bourgeois.
Gustave Flaubert (1821 - 1880)
Democracy is the theory that the common people know what they want and deserve to get it good and hard.
H. L. Mencken (1880 - 1956)
The cure for the evils of democracy is more democracy!
H. L. Mencken (1880 - 1956), Notes on Democracy, 1926
Under democracy one party always devotes its chief energies to trying to prove that the other party is unfit to rule - and both commonly succeed, and are right.
H. L. Mencken (1880 - 1956)
Democracy is based upon the conviction that there are extraordinary possibilities in ordinary people.
Harry Emerson Fosdick (1878 - 1969)
The idea of an election is much more interesting to me than the election itself...The act of voting is in itself the defining moment.
Jeff Melvoin, Northern Exposure, Democracy in America, 1992
Democracy is a process by which the people are free to choose the man who will get the blame.
Laurence J. Peter (1919 - 1988)
Men write many fine and plausible arguments in support of monarchy, but the fact remains that where every man has a voice, brutal laws are impossible.
Mark Twain (1835 - 1910)
Democracy is the name we give the people whenever we need them.
Marquis de Flers Robert and Armon de Caillavet
In democracy it's your vote that counts; In feudalism it's your count that votes.
Mogens Jallberg
Many forms of Government have been tried, and will be tried in this world of sin and woe. No one pretends that democracy is perfect or all-wise. Indeed, it has been said that democracy is the worst form of government except all those other forms that have been tried from time to time.
Sir Winston Churchill (1874 - 1965), Hansard, November 11, 1947
A republican government is slow to move, yet once in motion it's momentum becomes irresistible.
Thomas Jefferson (1743 - 1826)
It's not the voting that's democracy, it's the counting.
Tom Stoppard (1937 -), Jumpers (1972) act 1
On account of being a democracy and run by the people, we are the only nation in the world that has to keep a government four years, no matter what it does.
Will Rogers (1879 - 1935)

Design
Luck is the residue of design.
Branch Rickey (1881 - 1965), Lecture title, 1950
To dismiss front-end design as mere 'icing' is to jeopardize the success of any site.
Curt Cloninger, 2001

Design is directed toward human beings. To design is to solve human problems by identifying them and executing the best solution.
Ivan Chermayeff
To design is to communicate clearly by whatever means you can control or master.
Milton Glaser
Design can be art. Design can be aesthetics. Design is so simple, that's why it is so complicated.
Paul Rand, 1997
Design is not just what it looks like and feels like. Design is how it works.
Steve Jobs (1955 - 2011)
In most people's vocabularies, design means veneer. It's interior decorating. It's the fabric of the curtains of the sofa. But to me, nothing could be further from the meaning of design. Design is the fundamental soul of a human-made creation that ends up expressing itself in successive outer layers of the product or service.
Steve Jobs (1955 - 2011)
It's really hard to design products by focus groups. A lot of times, people don't know what they want until you show it to them.
Steve Jobs (1955 - 2011), BusinessWeek, May 25 1998

Desire

The wise man will love; all others will desire.
Afranius
One must not lose desires. They are mighty stimulants to creativeness, to love, and to long life.
Alexander A. Bogomoletz
Man is an animal which, alone among the animals, refuses to be satisfied by the fulfilment of animal desires.
Alexander Graham Bell (1847 - 1922)
Dwell not upon thy weariness, thy strength shall be according to the measure of thy desire.
Arab Proverb
Again, men in general desire the good, and not merely what their fathers had.
Aristotle (384 BC - 322 BC), Politics
I count him braver who overcomes his desires than him who overcomes his enemies.
Aristotle (384 BC - 322 BC), In Stobaeus, Florilegium
It is the nature of desire not to be satisfied, and most men live only for the gratification of it.
Aristotle (384 BC - 322 BC), Politics
How helpless we are, like netted birds, when we are caught by desire!
Belva Plain
If you greatly desire something, have the guts to stake everything on obtaining it.
Brendan Francis
In men of the highest character and noblest genius there is to be found an insatiable desire for honour, command, power, and glory.
Cicero (106 BC - 43 BC)
Let your desires be ruled by reason.
(Appetitus Rationi Pareat)
Cicero (106 BC - 43 BC)
He who desires is always poor.
Claudianus
While we don't have much say over the desires that we have, we certainly can decide which we prefer-and then search for ways to act on that basis.
Daniel Akst, We Have Met the Enemy: Self-Control in an Age of Excess, 2011
There are two tragedies in life. One is not to get your heart's desire. The other is to get it.
George Bernard Shaw (1856 - 1950), "Man and Superman" (1903), act 4
If we desire to avoid insult, we must be able to repel it; if we desire to secure peace, one of the most powerful instruments of our rising prosperity, it must be known, that we are at all times ready for War.
George Washington (1732 - 1799), Fifth annual address to Congress, December 13, 1793
Man is the only animal whose desires increase as they are fed; the only animal that is never satisfied.
Henry George (1839 - 1897)
Manifest plainness,
Embrace simplicity,
Reduce selfishness,
Have few desires.
Lao-tzu (604 BC - 531 BC), The Way of Lao-tzu
There is no calamity greater than lavish desires.
There is no greater guilt than discontentment.
And there is no greater disaster than greed.
Lao-tzu (604 BC - 531 BC), The Way of Lao-tzu
Some prices are just too high, no matter how much you may want the prize. The one thing you can't trade for your heart's desire is your heart.
Lois McMaster Bujold, "Memory", 1996
One must desire something to be alive.
Margaret Deland, O Magazine, September 2002
A human being has a natural desire to have more of a good thing than he needs.
Mark Twain (1835 - 1910), Following the Equator
When you relinquish the desire to control your future, you can have more happiness.
Nicole Kidman, in The Scotsman
Desires are only the lack of something: and those who have the greatest desires are in a worse condition than those who have none, or very slight ones.
Plato (427 BC - 347 BC)

We desire nothing so much as what we ought not to have.
Publilius Syrus (~ 100 BC), Maxims
Desire creates the power.
Raymond Holliwell
Life ought to be a struggle of desire toward adventures whose nobility will fertilize the soul.
Rebecca West (1892 - 1983)
What makes the engine go? Desire, desire, desire.
Stanley Kunitz, O Magazine, September 2003
Those who restrain desire, do so because theirs is weak enough to be restrained.
William Blake (1757 - 1827), The Marriage of Heaven and Hell (c. 1790-1793)
Every man has business and desire,
Such as it is.
William Shakespeare (1564 - 1616), "Hamlet", Act 1 scene 5

Destiny

Destiny waits alike for the free man as well as for him enslaved by another's might.
Aeschylus (525 BC - 456 BC), The Libation Bearers
No trumpets sound when the important decisions of our life are made. Destiny is made known silently.
Agnes de Mille (1909 - 1993)
Destiny is but a phrase of the weak human heart - the dark apology for every error. The strong and virtuous admit no destiny. On earth conscience guides; in heaven God watches. And destiny is but the phantom we invoke to silence the one and dethrone the other.
Edward Bulwer-Lytton (1803 - 1873)
There is a mysterious cycle in human events. To some generations much is given. Of other generations much is expected. This generation of Americans has a rendezvous with destiny.
Franklin D. Roosevelt (1882 - 1945)
Destiny is a name often given in retrospect to choices that had dramatic consequences.
J. K. Rowling, J. K. Rowling Official Website
It's choice - not chance - that determines your destiny.
Jean Nidetch
Our problems are man-made, therefore they may be solved by man. No problem of human destiny is beyond human beings.
John F. Kennedy (1917 - 1963)
I think it's absolutely a blessing when you just know what your purpose is and your destiny. I don't think it's a curse at all.
Lady Gaga (1986 -), The Today Show, 12-08-08
A man that don't believe in destiny don't need to know what his destiny is.
Laura Moncur (1969 -), Merriton: Twelve Hours from San Francisco, 08-20-08
Young people have an almost biological destiny to be hopeful.
Marshall Ganz, quoted by Sara Rimer in New York Times
Often we don't even realize who we're meant to be because we're so busy trying to live out someone else's ideas. But other people and their opinions hold no power in defining our destiny.
Oprah Winfrey (1954 -), O Magazine, November 2009
Man is asked to make of himself what he is supposed to become to fulfill his destiny.
Paul Tillich (1886 - 1965)
Great people and great athletes realize early in their lives their destiny, and accept it. Even if they do not consciously realize the how, the where, the what.
Percy Cerutty
Destiny is for people who are too lazy to create alternate timelines.
R. Stevens, Diesel Sweeties, 10-05-11
Anatomy is destiny.
Sigmund Freud (1856 - 1939), Collected Writings, 1924
It is a mistake to try to look too far ahead. The chain of destiny can only be grasped one link at a time.
Sir Winston Churchill (1874 - 1965)
We are face to face with our destiny and we must meet it with high and resolute courage. For us is the life of action, of strenuous performance of duty; let us live in the harness, striving mightily; let us rather run the risk of wearing out than rusting out.
Theodore Roosevelt (1858 - 1919), Address at the opening of the gubernatorial campaign, New York City, October 5, 1898
Watch your thoughts, they become words.
Watch your words, they become actions.
Watch your actions, they become habits.
Watch your habits, they become your character.
Watch your character, it becomes your destiny.
Unknown
Destiny is no matter of chance. It is a matter of choice. It is not a thing to be waited for, it is a thing to be achieved.
William Jennings Bryan (1860 - 1925)
The ancient saying is no heresy, hanging and wiving goes by destiny.
William Shakespeare (1564 - 1616), The Merchant of Venice, Act II, sc. 9

Differences

A great marriage is not when the 'perfect couple' comes together. It is when an imperfect couple learns to enjoy their differences.
Dave Meurer, "Daze of Our Wives"
Differences of habit and language are nothing at all if our aims are identical and our hearts are open.
J. K. Rowling, Harry Potter and the Goblet of Fire

Toward no crime have men shown themselves so cold-bloodedly cruel as in punishing differences of belief.
James Russell Lowell (1819 - 1891)
If we cannot end now our differences, at least we can help make the world safe for diversity.
John F. Kennedy (1917 - 1963)
So, let us not be blind to our differences - but let us also direct attention to our common interests and to the means by which those differences can be resolved.
John F. Kennedy (1917 - 1963)
Honest differences are often a healthy sign of progress.
Mahatma Gandhi (1869 - 1948)

Dignity

Dignity consists not in possessing honors, but in the consciousness that we deserve them.
Aristotle (384 BC - 322 BC)
No race can prosper till it learns that there is as much dignity in tilling a field as in writing a poem.
Booker T. Washington (1856 - 1915)
Where is there dignity unless there is honesty?
Cicero (106 BC - 43 BC)
The only kind of dignity which is genuine is that which is not diminished by the indifference of others.
Dag Hammarskjold (1905 - 1961)
Dignity comes not from control, but from understanding who you are and taking your rightful place in the world.
Gordon Atkinson, Real Live Preacher weblog, 05-01-05
Human Dignity has gleamed only now and then and here and there, in lonely splendor, throughout the ages, a hope of the better men, never an achievement of the majority.
James Thurber (1894 - 1961)
Be mild with the mild, shrewd with the crafty, confiding to the honest, rough to the ruffian, and a thunderbolt to the liar. But in all this, never be unmindful of your own dignity.
John Brown
Remember this-that there is a proper dignity and proportion to be observed in the performance of every act of life.
Marcus Aurelius Antoninus (121 AD - 180 AD)
One's dignity may be assaulted, vandalized and cruelly mocked, but cannot be taken away unless it is surrendered.
Michael J. Fox (1961 -), in "Saving Milly" by Morton Kondrake
Dignity and love do not blend well, nor do they continue long together.
Ovid (43 BC - 17 AD)
Self-respect is the fruit of discipline; the sense of dignity grows with the ability to say no to oneself.
Rabbi Abraham Heschel
Let not a man guard his dignity, but let his dignity guard him.
Ralph Waldo Emerson (1803 - 1882)
It is not wealth one asks for, but just enough to preserve one's dignity, to work unhampered, to be generous, frank and independent.
W. Somerset Maugham (1874 - 1965), 'Of Human Bondage', 1915
There is a healthful hardiness about real dignity that never dreads contact and communion with others, however humble.
Washington Irving (1783 - 1859)

Discovery

One of the advantages of being disorderly is that one is constantly making exciting discoveries.
A. A. Milne (1882 - 1956)
A discovery is said to be an accident meeting a prepared mind.
Albert Szent-Gyorgyi (1893 - 1986)
Discovery consists of seeing what everybody has seen and thinking what nobody has thought.
Albert Szent-Gyorgyi (1893 - 1986), in Irving Good, The Scientist Speculates (1962)
One doesn't discover new lands without consenting to lose sight of the shore for a very long time.
Andre Gide (1869 - 1951)
The more original a discovery, the more obvious it seems afterwards.
Arthur Koestler (1905 - 1983)
The greatest obstacle to discovery is not ignorance - it is the illusion of knowledge.
Daniel J. Boorstin (1914 -)
There is a theory which states that if ever anybody discovers exactly what the Universe is for and why it is here, it will instantly disappear and be replaced by something even more bizarre and inexplicable. There is another theory which states that this has already happened.
Douglas Adams (1952 - 2001)
The beginning of knowledge is the discovery of something we do not understand.
Frank Herbert (1920 - 1986)
All truths are easy to understand once they are discovered; the point is to discover them.

Galileo Galilei (1564 - 1642)
The most exciting phrase to hear in science, the one that heralds new discoveries, is not 'Eureka!' (I found it!) but 'That's funny ...'
Isaac Asimov (1920 - 1992)
I do not know what I may appear to the world; but to myself I seem to have been only like a boy playing on the seashore, and diverting myself in now and then finding a smoother pebble or a prettier shell than ordinary, whilst the great ocean of truth lay all undiscovered before me.
Isaac Newton (1642 - 1727), From Brewster, Memoirs of Newton (1855)
If I have ever made any valuable discoveries, it has been owing more to patient attention, than to any other talent.
Isaac Newton (1642 - 1727)
Mistakes are the portals of discovery.
James Joyce (1882 - 1941)
The real voyage of discovery consists not in seeking new landscapes but in having new eyes.
Marcel Proust (1871 - 1922)
There is no harm in doubt and skepticism, for it is through these that new discoveries are made.
Richard Feynman (1918 - 1988), Letter to Armando Garcia J, December 11, 1985
He who never made a mistake never made a discovery.
Samuel Smiles

Dogs

If a dog jumps in your lap, it is because he is fond of you; but if a cat does the same thing, it is because your lap is warmer.
Alfred North Whitehead (1861 - 1947)
Don't accept your dog's admiration as conclusive evidence that you are wonderful.
Ann Landers (1918 - 2002)
I loathe people who keep dogs. They are cowards who haven't got the guts to bite people themselves.
August Strindberg (1849 - 1912), A Madman's Diary, 1895
Yet the dogs eat of the crumbs which fall from their masters' table.
Bible, Matthew xv. 27.
Yesterday I was a dog. Today I'm a dog. Tomorrow I'll probably still be a dog. Sigh! There's so little hope for advancement.
Charles M. Schulz (1922 - 2000), (Snoopy)
You can't surprise a man with a dog.
Cindy Chupack, Sex and the City, Don't Ask, Don't Tell, 2000
It's funny how dogs and cats know the inside of folks better than other folks do, isn't it?
Eleanor H. Porter (1868 - 1920), Pollyanna, 1912
If you are a dog and your owner suggests that you wear a sweater, suggest that he wear a tail.
Fran Lebowitz (1950 -)
When a dog runs at you, whistle for him.
Henry David Thoreau (1817 - 1862)
The dog was created especially for children. He is the god of frolic.
Henry Ward Beecher (1813 - 1887)
A dog owns nothing, yet is seldom dissatisfied.
Irish Proverb
Cats are smarter than dogs. You can't get eight cats to pull a sled through snow.
Jeff Valdez
Who knew that dog saliva can mend a broken heart?
Jennifer Neal, nakedjen, 07-22-08
Old age means realizing you will never own all the dogs you wanted to.
Joe Gores
My dog is worried about the economy because Alpo is up to 99 cents a can. That's almost $7.00 in dog money.
Joe Weinstein
When a dog bites a man, that is not news, because it happens so often. But if a man bites a dog, that is news.
John B. Bogart (1848 - 1921)
A dog is the greatest gift a parent can give a child. OK, a good education, then a dog.
John Grogan, An Interview with John Grogan, 2008
A person can learn a lot from a dog, even a loopy one like ours. Marley taught me about living each day with unbridled exuberance and joy, about seizing the moment and following your heart. He taught me to appreciate the simple things - a walk in the woods, a fresh snowfall, a nap in a shaft of winter sunlight. And as he grew old and achy, he taught me about optimism in the face of adversity. Mostly, he taught me about friendship and selflessness and, above all else, unwavering loyalty.
John Grogan, Marley and Me, 2005
We could have bought a small yacht with what we spent on our dog an dall the things he destroyed. Then again, how many yachts wait by the door all day for your return?
John Grogan, Marley and Me, 2005
A dog is the only thing on earth that loves you more than he loves himself.
Josh Billings (1818 - 1885)
If you pick up a starving dog and make him prosperous, he will not bite you. This is the principal difference between a dog and a man.
Mark Twain (1835 - 1910)
We are alone, absolutely alone on this chance planet: and, amid all the forms of life that surround us, not one, excepting the dog, has made an alliance with us.
Maurice Maeterlinck (1862 - 1949)
A door is what a dog is perpetually on the wrong side of.
Ogden Nash (1902 - 1971)
On the Internet, nobody knows you're a dog.
Peter Steiner, cartoon in The New Yorker, July 5, 1993

I wonder if other dogs think poodles are members of a weird religious cult.
Rita Rudner
A boy can learn a lot from a dog: obedience, loyalty, and the importance of turning around three times before lying down.
Robert Benchley (1889 - 1945)
Dogs are not our whole life, but they make our lives whole.
Roger Caras
I like pigs. Dogs look up to us. Cats look down on us. Pigs treat us as equals.
Sir Winston Churchill (1874 - 1965)
Did you ever walk into a room and forget why you walked in? I think that's how dogs spend their lives.
Sue Murphy

Doubt

Doubt 'til thou canst doubt no more...doubt is thought and thought is life. Systems which end doubt are devices for drugging thought.
Albert Guerard
There are two ways to slide easily through life; to believe everything or to doubt everything. Both ways save us from thinking.
Alfred Korzybski (1879 - 1950)
A mind troubled by doubt cannot focus on the course to victory.
Arthur Golden, Memoirs of a Geisha
I think we ought always to entertain our opinions with some measure of doubt. I shouldn't wish people dogmatically to believe any philosophy, not even mine.
Bertrand Russell (1872 - 1970)
The whole problem with the world is that fools and fanatics are always so certain of themselves, but wiser people so full of doubts.
Bertrand Russell (1872 - 1970)
Doubt whom you will, but never yourself.
Christine Bovee
Just think of the tragedy of teaching children not to doubt.
Clarence Darrow (1857 - 1938)
To have doubted one's own first principles is the mark of a civilized man.
Oliver Wendell Holmes Jr. (1841 - 1935)
Beliefs are what divide people. Doubt unites them.
Peter Ustinov (1921 - 2004)
If you would be a real seeker after truth, it is necessary that at least once in your life you doubt, as far as possible, all things.
Rene Descartes (1596 - 1650)
I show you doubt, to prove that faith exists.
Robert Browning (1812 - 1889)
To believe with certainty we must begin with doubting.
Stanislaw Leszczynski (1677 - 1766)
Doubt is not a pleasant condition, but certainty is absurd.
Voltaire (1694 - 1778)
Our doubts are traitors,
And make us lose the good we oft might win
By fearing to attempt.
William Shakespeare (1564 - 1616), "Measure for Measure", Act 1 scene 4
I respect faith, but doubt is what gets you an education.
Wilson Mizner (1876 - 1933)

Dreams

I know how men in exile feed on dreams of hope.
Aeschylus (525 BC - 456 BC), Agamemnon
To accomplish great things, we must not only act, but also dream; not only plan, but also believe.
Anatole France (1844 - 1924)
Hope is a waking dream.
Aristotle (384 BC - 322 BC), from Diogenes Laertius, Lives of Eminent Philosophers
Dreams that do come true can be as unsettling as those that don't.
Brett Butler, 'Knee Deep in Paradise'
To want to be what one can be is purpose in life.
Cynthia Ozick, O Magazine, September 2002
He felt that his whole life was some kind of dream and he sometimes wondered whose it was and whether they were enjoying it.
Douglas Adams (1952 - 2001), "The Hitchhiker's Guide to the Galaxy"
Those who dream by day are cognizant of many things which escape those who dream only by night.
Edgar Allan Poe (1809 - 1849), "Eleonora"
The wisest men follow their own direction.
Euripides (484 BC - 406 BC)
Keep true to the dreams of thy youth.
Friedrich von Schiller (1759 - 1805)
You see things; and you say, 'Why?' But I dream things that never were; and I say, "Why not?"
George Bernard Shaw (1856 - 1950), "Back to Methuselah" (1921), part 1, act 1
Human beings have an inalienable right to invent themselves.
Germaine Greer, O Magazine, September 2002

They say dreams are the windows of the soul–take a peek and you can see the inner workings, the nuts and bolts.
Henry Bromel, Northern Exposure, The Big Kiss, 1991
Dreams surely are difficult, confusing, and not everything in them is brought to pass for mankind. For fleeting dreams have two gates: one is fashioned of horn and one of ivory. Those which pass through the one of sawn ivory are deceptive, bringing tidings which come to nought, but those which issue from the one of polished horn bring true results when a mortal sees them.
Homer (800 BC - 700 BC), The Odyssey
We need men who can dream of things that never were.
John F. Kennedy (1917 - 1963), speech in Dublin, Ireland, June 28, 1963
Dreams come true. Without that possibility, nature would not incite us to have them.
John Updike (1932 -)
I do not want to die... until I have faithfully made the most of my talent and cultivated the seed that was placed in me until the last small twig has grown.
Kathe Kollwitz, O Magazine, September 2002
My bounce-around life had taught me that dreams were dangerous things - they look solid in your mind, but you just try to reach for them. It's like gathering clouds.
Kirby Larson, Hattie Big Sky, 2006
There should be fireworks, at least, when a dream dies.
Kirby Larson, Hattie Big Sky, 2006
I think it is often easier to make progress on mega-ambitious dreams. Since no one else is crazy enough to do it, you have little competition. In fact, there are so few people this crazy that I feel like I know them all by first name.
Larry Page, University of Michigan Commencement Address, 2009
You know what it's like to wake up in the middle of the night with a vivid dream? And you know that if you don't have a pencil and pad by the bed, it will be completely gone by the next morning. Sometimes it's important to wake up and stop dreaming. When a really great dream shows up, grab it.
Larry Page, University of Michigan Commencement Address, 2009
You never lose a dream. It just incubates as a hobby.
Larry Page, University of Michigan Commencement Address, 2009
It has never been my object to record my dreams, just to realize them.
Man Ray, O Magazine, September 2002
One must desire something to be alive.
Margaret Deland, O Magazine, September 2002
Now, I say to you today my friends, even though we face the difficulties of today and tomorrow, I still have a dream. It is a dream deeply rooted in the American dream. I have a dream that one day this nation will rise up and live out the true meaning of its creed: - 'We hold these truths to be self-evident, that all men are created equal.'
Martin Luther King Jr. (1929 - 1968), Speech at Civil Rights March on Washington, August 28, 1963
My dreams were all my own; I accounted for them to nobody; they were my refuge when annoyed - my dearest pleasure when free.
Mary Shelly
I've come to believe that each of us has a personal calling that's as unique as a fingerprint - and that the best way to succeed is to discover what you love and then find a way to offer it to others in the form of service, working hard, and also allowing the energy of the universe to lead you.
Oprah Winfrey (1954 -), O Magazine, September 2002
The key to realizing a dream is to focus not on success but significance - and then even the small steps and little victories along your path will take on greater meaning.
Oprah Winfrey (1954 -), O Magazine, September 2002
The aim of life is self-development. To realize one's nature perfectly - that is what each of us is here for.
Oscar Wilde (1854 - 1900)
If you stop dreaming, you're just sleeping.
Ralph Green and Gregory Garcia, Raising Hope, Dream Hoarders, October 5, 2010

Dreams

It hurts to find out that what you wanted doesn't match what you dreamed it would be.
Randy K. Milholland, Something Positive Comic, 09-07-04
You gotta dream? You gotta protect it. People can't do somethin' themselves, they wanna tell you you can't do it. If you want somethin', go get it, period.
Steven Conrad, Pursuit of Happyness, 2006
Last night I dreamed I ate a ten-pound marshmallow, and when I woke up the pillow was gone.
Tommy Cooper
There is nothing like dream to create the future. Utopia to-day, flesh and blood tomorrow.
Victor Hugo (1802 - 1885), Les Miserables, 1862
Dreaming permits each and every one of us to be quietly and safely insane every night of our lives.
William Dement, in Newsweek, 1959
There are more things in heaven and earth, Horatio,
Than are dreamt of in your philosophy.
William Shakespeare (1564 - 1616), "Hamlet", Act 1 scene 5
The things that one most wants to do are the things that are probably most worth doing.
Winifred Holtby, O Magazine, September 2002
What if nothing exists and we're all in somebody's dream? Or what's worse, what if only that fat guy in the third row exists?
Woody Allen (1935 -), "Without Feathers"

Drinking

And malt does more than Milton can
To justify God's ways to man.
A. E. Housman (1859 - 1936)
Drink no longer water, but use a little wine for thy stomach's sake.
Bible, 1 Timothy v. 23.
Electricity is actually made up of extremely tiny particles called electrons, that you cannot see with the naked eye unless you have been drinking.
Dave Barry (1947 -), "The Taming of the Screw"
If you drink, don't drive. Don't even putt.
Dean Martin
Bacchus hath drowned more men than Neptune.
Dr. Thomas Fuller (1654 - 1734), Gnomologia, 1732
Always do sober what you said you'd do drunk. That will teach you to keep your mouth shut.
Ernest Hemingway (1899 - 1961)
Great people talk about ideas, average people talk about things, and small people talk about wine.
Fran Lebowitz (1950 -)
My Grandmother is over eighty and still doesn't need glasses. Drinks right out of the bottle.
Henny Youngman (1906 - 1998)
When I read about the evils of drinking, I gave up reading.
Henny Youngman (1906 - 1998)
[Water is] the only drink for a wise man.
Henry David Thoreau (1817 - 1862)
It is better to hide ignorance, but it is hard to do this when we relax over wine.
Heraclitus (540 BC - 480 BC), On the Universe
The wine urges me on, the bewitching wine, which sets even a wise man to singing and to laughing gently and rouses him up to dance and brings forth words which were better unspoken.
Homer (800 BC - 700 BC), The Odyssey
Nothing anyone says in a bar is true.
Mark Ruffalo, In Style Magazine, 11-08
The trouble with jogging is that the ice falls out of your glass.
Martin Mull (1943 -)
One reason I don't drink is that I want to know when I am having a good time.
Nancy Astor (1879 - 1964)
I envy people who drink. At least they have something to blame everything on.
Oscar Levant (1906 - 1972)
Work is the curse of the drinking classes.
Oscar Wilde (1854 - 1900), In Life of Oscar Wilde, H. Pearson
Slap a mask on a drunk and you're going to have trouble. It's like having a live reenactment of anonymous forum comments.
Randy K. Milholland, Something Positive, Masquerade, 09-09-13
Drinking makes such fools of people, and people are such fools to begin with, that it's compounding a felony.
Robert Benchley (1889 - 1945)
I always keep a supply of stimulant handy in case I see a snake—which I also keep handy.
W. C. Fields (1880 - 1946)
Reminds me of my safari in Africa. Somebody forgot the corkscrew and for several days we had to live on nothing but food and water.
W. C. Fields (1880 - 1946)
It's always difficult to make conversation with a drunk, and there's no denying it, the sober are at a disadvantage with him.
W. Somerset Maugham (1874 - 1965), The Razor's Edge, 1943

Drugs

I believe that God left certain drugs growing naturally upon our planet to help speed up and facilitate our evolution.
Bill Hicks
Half of the modern drugs could well be thrown out of the window, except that the birds might eat them.
Dr. Martin Henry Fischer
I never took hallucinogenic drugs because I never wanted my consciousness expanded one unnecessary iota.
Fran Lebowitz (1950 -)
I hate to advocate drugs, alcohol, violence, or insanity to anyone, but they've always worked for me.
Hunter S. Thompson (1939 - 2005)
Everything is a drug. Family, art, causes, new shoes... We're all just tweaking our chem to avoid the void.
Joss Whedon, Twitter, 06-27-13
Reality is a crutch for people who can't cope with drugs.
Lily Tomlin (1939 -)
I love drugs, but I hate hangovers, and the hatred of the hangover wins by a landslide every time.
Margaret Cho, weblog, 10-30-03
Drugs have taught an entire generation of Americans the metric system.
P. J. O'Rourke (1947 -)

[Addiction's] not about placating the bad dog - it's about feeding the good dog. You still have to feed the bad dog, but only enough so that the ASPCA doesn't bring you up on charges.
Robert Downey Jr., Entertainment Weekly, 11-21-08
The last time somebody said, 'I find I can write much better with a word processor.', I replied, 'They used to say the same thing about drugs.'
Roy Blount Jr.
Junkies might be easy to knock down, but they're never fragile. They have souls like old leather shoes studded with steel, and they're about as much good as friends.
Scott Westerfeld, The Last Days, 2006
The truth is, marijuana probably isn't going to make you kill people. Most likely isn't going to fund terrorists, but pot makes you feel fine with being bored and it's when you're bored that you should be learning a new skill or some new science or being creative. If you smoke pot you may grow up to find out that you're not good at anything.
Trey Parker and Matt Stone, South Park, My Future Self n' Me, 2002

Duty

We only know of one duty, and that is to love.
Albert Camus (1913 - 1960)
It is the duty of every citizen according to his best capacities to give validity to his convictions in political affairs.
Albert Einstein (1879 - 1955), 'Treasury for the Free World,' 1946
The first duty of a leader is to make himself be loved without courting love. To be loved without 'playing up' to anyone - even to himself.
Andre Malraux (1901 - 1976)
I came to realize that life lived to help others is the only one that matters and that it is my duty...This is my highest and best use as a human.
Ben Stein, E! Online, 12-20-03
A sense of duty is useful in work, but offensive in personal relations. People wish to be liked, not be endured with patient resignation.
Bertrand Russell (1872 - 1970), Conquest of Happiness (1930) ch. 10
The first duty of a man is the seeking after and the investigation of truth.
Cicero (106 BC - 43 BC)
There are some duties we owe even to those who have wronged us. There is, after all, a limit to retribution and punishment.
Cicero (106 BC - 43 BC)
There is no duty more obligatory than the repayment of kindness.
Cicero (106 BC - 43 BC)
There is no such thing as luck. It's a fancy name for being always at our duty, and so sure to be ready when good time comes.
Edward Bulwer-Lytton (1803 - 1873)
Majesty: when a stupid man is doing something he is ashamed of, he always declares it as his duty.
George Bernard Shaw (1856 - 1950), Caesar and Cleopatra, act III
When a stupid man is doing something he is ashamed of, he always declares that it is his duty.
George Bernard Shaw (1856 - 1950), Caesar and Cleopatra (1901) Act III
The reward of one duty is the power to fulfill another.
George Eliot (1819 - 1880)
We have no eternal allies, and we have no perpetual enemies. Our interests are eternal and perpetual, and those interests it is our duty to follow.
Henry John Temple Palmerston, Remarks in the House of Commons, March 1, 1848
The paths of glory at least lead to the grave, but the paths of duty may not get you any where.
James Thurber (1894 - 1961)
The strongest is never strong enough to be always the master, unless he transforms strength into right, and obedience into duty.
Jean Jacques Rousseau (1712 - 1778), The Social Contract, 1762
How can you come to know yourself? Never by thinking, always by doing. Try to do your duty, and you'll know right away what you amount to.
Johann Wolfgang von Goethe (1749 - 1832)
Duty is ours, results are God's.
John Quincy Adams (1767 - 1848)
Life is not so important as the duties of life.
John Randolph (1773 - 1833)
A duty dodged is like a debt unpaid; it is only deferred, and we must come back and settle the account at last.
Joseph F. Newton
When you have a number of disagreeable duties to perform, always do the most disagreeable first.
Josiah Quincy
Attention to our duties provides far greater rewards than beauty and wit. Self-control is what differentiates us from the beasts. Without it, we are merely animals.
Laura Moncur (1969 -), The Secret Heart of Charlotte Lucas, 2014
I take it as a man's duty to restrain himself.
Lois McMaster Bujold, Ethan of Athos, 1986
The dead cannot cry out for justice; it is a duty of the living to do so for them.
Lois McMaster Bujold, Diplomatic Immunity, 2002
Do something every day that you don't want to do; this is the golden rule for acquiring the habit of doing your duty without pain.
Mark Twain (1835 - 1910)
The first duty of love is to listen.
Paul Tillich (1886 - 1965)
Duty then is the sublimest word in the English language. You should do your duty in all things. You can never do more, you should never wish to do less.
Robert E. Lee (1807 - 1870)

There is no duty we so much underrate as the as the duty of being happy.
Robert Louis Stevenson (1850 - 1894), An Apology for Idlers, 1874
There is no duty we so much underrate as the duty of being happy.
Robert Louis Stevenson (1850 - 1894)
Be eager to fulfill the smallest duty and flee from transgression for one duty includes another and one transgression induces another transgression.
The Talmud, We Have Met the Enemy: Self-Control in an Age of Excess, 2011
Property has its duties as well as its rights.
Thomas Brummond
He that would make his own liberty secure, must guard even his enemy from oppression; for if he violates this duty, he establishes a precedent that will reach to himself.
Thomas Paine (1737 - 1809)
Where duty is plain, delay is both foolish and hazardous; where it is not, delay may provide both wisdom and safety.
Tryon Edwards (1809 - 1894)
Remember that it is nothing to do your duty, that is demanded of you and is no more meritorious than to wash your hands when they are dirty; the only thing that counts is the love of duty; when love and duty are one, then grace is in you and you will enjoy a happiness which passes all understanding.
W. Somerset Maugham (1874 - 1965), The Painted Veil, 1925
...it is as hard to do your duty when men are sneering at you as when they are shooting at you.
Woodrow Wilson (1856 - 1924)
We live in an age disturbed, confused, bewildered, afraid of its own forces, in search not merely of its road but even of its direction. There are many voices of counsel, but few voices of vision; there is much excitement and feverish activity, but little concert of thoughtful purpose. We are distressed by our own ungoverned, undirected energies and do many things, but nothing long. It is our duty to find ourselves.
Woodrow Wilson (1856 - 1924), Baccalaureate address, Princeton University, Princeton, New Jersey, June 9, 1907

Economics

An economist is a man who states the obvious in terms of the incomprehensible.
Alfred A. Knopf
Acts of sacrifice and decency without regard to what's in it for you create ripple effects. Ones that lift up families and communities, that spread opportunity and boost our economy.
Barack Obama (1961 -), Arizona State Commencement Speech, 2009
There can be no real individual freedom in the presence of economic insecurity.
Chester Bowles (1901 - 1986)
If all economists were laid end to end, they would not reach a conclusion.
George Bernard Shaw (1856 - 1950)
Economics is extremely useful as a form of employment for economists.
John Kenneth Galbraith (1908 - 2006)
Isn't it interesting that the same people who laugh at science fiction listen to weather forecasts and economists?
Kelvin Throop III
An economist is an expert who will know tomorrow why the things he predicted yesterday didn't happen today.
Laurence J. Peter (1919 - 1988)
Socialism failed because it couldn't tell the economic truth; capitalism may fail because it couldn't tell the ecological truth.
Lester Brown, Fortune Brainstorm Conference, 2006
An economist is a surgeon with an excellent scalpel and a rough-edged lancet, who operates beautifully on the dead and tortures the living.
Nicholas Chamfort (1741 - 1794)
In all recorded history there has not been one economist who has had to worry about where the next meal would come from.
Peter Drucker (1909 - 2005)
There are 10^11 stars in the galaxy. That used to be a huge number. But it's only a hundred billion. It's less than the national deficit! We used to call them astronomical numbers. Now we should call them economical numbers.
Richard Feynman (1918 - 1988)

Education

You don't need fancy highbrow traditions or money to really learn. You just need people with the desire to better themselves.
Adam Cooper and Bill Collage, Accepted, 2006
It is possible to store the mind with a million facts and still be entirely uneducated.
Alec Bourne
An education isn't how much you have committed to memory, or even how much you know. It's being able to differentiate between what you do know and what you don't.
Anatole France (1844 - 1924)
A well-informed mind is the best security against the contagion of folly and of vice. The vacant mind is ever on the watch for relief, and ready to plunge into error, to escape from the languor of idleness.
Ann Radcliffe (1764 - 1823), The Mysteries of Udolpho, 1764
Education is the best provision for old age.
Aristotle (384 BC - 322 BC), from Diogenes Laertius, Lives of Eminent Philosophers

It is the mark of an educated mind to be able to entertain a thought without accepting it.
Aristotle (384 BC - 322 BC)
Education is what survives when what has been learned has been forgotten.
B. F. Skinner (1904 - 1990), New Scientist, May 21, 1964
The strength of the United States is not the gold at Fort Knox or the weapons of mass destruction that we have, but the sum total of the education and the character of our people.
Claiborne Pell (1918 -)
Everyone has a right to a university degree in America, even if it's in Hamburger Technology.
Clive James
School is learning things you don't want to know, surrounded by people you wish you didn't know, while working toward a future you don't know will ever come.
Dave Kellett, Sheldon, 10-09-11
The number of books will grow continually, and one can predict that a time will come when it will be almost as difficult to learn anything from books as from the direct study of the whole universe. It will be almost as convenient to search for some bit of truth concealed in nature as it will be to find it hidden away in an immense multitude of bound volumes.
Denis Diderot (1713 - 1784)
The foundation of every state is the education of its youth.
Diogenes Laertius
Education begins a gentleman, conversation completes him.
Dr. Thomas Fuller (1654 - 1734), Gnomologia, 1732
I didn't go to college at all, any college, and I'm not saying you wasted your time or money, but look at me, I'm a huge celebrity.
Ellen DeGeneres, Tulane Commencement Speech, 2009
Only the educated are free.
Epictetus (55 AD - 135 AD), Discourses
America believes in education: the average professor earns more money in a year than a professional athlete earns in a whole week.
Evan Esar (1899 - 1995)
Education is simply the soul of a society as it passes from one generation to another.
G. K. Chesterton (1874 - 1936)
Education... has produced a vast population able to read but unable to distinguish what is worth reading.
G. M. Trevelyan (1876 - 1962), English Social History (1942)
Good teaching is one-fourth preparation and three-fourths theater.
Gail Godwin
A fool's brain digests philosophy into folly, science into superstition, and art into pedantry. Hence University education.
George Bernard Shaw (1856 - 1950)
Human history becomes more and more a race between education and catastrophe.
H. G. Wells (1866 - 1946), Outline of History (1920)
College isn't the place to go for ideas.
Helen Keller (1880 - 1968)
Education has for its object the formation of character.
Herbert Spencer (1820 - 1903)
The great aim of education is not knowledge but action.
Herbert Spencer (1820 - 1903)
Next in importance to freedom and justice is popular education, without which neither freedom nor justice can be permanently maintained.
James A. Garfield (1831 - 1881), July 12, 1880
Bachelor's degrees make pretty good placemats if you get 'em laminated.
Jeph Jacques, Questionable Content, 01-04-07
That's what college is for - getting as many bad decisions as possible out of the way before you're forced into the real world. I keep a checklist of 'em on the wall in my room.
Jeph Jacques, Questionable Content, 01-04-07
A university is what a college becomes when the faculty loses interest in students.
John Ciardi (1916 - 1986)
It has been my experience that maximizing income is a helluva lot less important than maximizing passion and fulfillment in your both professionally and personally.
John Green, Vlogbrothers, Is College Worth It?, 08-21-12
When I was in college, I remember fearing that the dreary grind of adulthood would feature infinitely more existential dread than frat parties had, but the opposite has been true for me. I'm much less likely to feel that gnawing fear of aimlessness and nihilism than I used to be and that's partly because education gave me job opportunities, but it's mostly because education gave me perspective and context.
John Green, Vlogbrothers, Is College Worth It?, 08-21-12
She knows what is the best purpose of education: not to be frightened by the best but to treat it as part of daily life.
John Mason Brown (1900 - 1969)
Fathers send their sons to college either because they went to college or because they didn't.
L. L. Henderson
Education is a method whereby one acquires a higher grade of prejudices.
Laurence J. Peter (1919 - 1988)
Education's purpose is to replace an empty mind with an open one.
Malcolm Forbes (1919 - 1990), in Forbes Magazine
I have never let my schooling interfere with my education.
Mark Twain (1835 - 1910)
Training is everything. The peach was once a bitter almond; cauliflower is nothing but cabbage with a college education.
Mark Twain (1835 - 1910), Pudd'nhead Wilson (1894)
To repeat what others have said, requires education; to challenge it, requires brains.

Mary Pettibone Poole, A Glass Eye at a Keyhole, 1938
I prefer the company of peasants because they have not been educated sufficiently to reason incorrectly.
Michel de Montaigne (1533 - 1592)
Education is the guardian genius of democracy. It is the only dictator that free men recognize, and the only ruler that free men require.
Mirabeau Buonaparte Lamar
Education is a state-controlled manufactory of echoes.
Norman Douglas
Education is when you read the fine print. Experience is what you get if you don't.
Pete Seeger
When a subject becomes totally obsolete we make it a required course.
Peter Drucker (1909 - 2005)
The direction in which education starts a man will determine his future life.
Plato (427 BC - 347 BC), The Republic
The very spring and root of honesty and virtue lie in good education.
Plutarch (46 AD - 120 AD), Morals
It is only the ignorant who despise education.
Publilius Syrus (~ 100 BC), Maxims
The secret of all success is to know how to deny yourself. Prove that you can control yourself, and you are an educated man; and without this all other education is good for nothing.
R. D. Hitchcock
A college degree is not a sign that one is a finished product but an indication a person is prepared for life.
Reverend Edward A. Malloy, Monk's Reflections
Education is the ability to listen to almost anything without losing your temper or your self-confidence.
Robert Frost (1874 - 1963)
If you feel that you have boy feet planted on the ground, then the university has failed you.
Robert Goheen
Education is a kind of continuing dialogue, and a dialogue assumes, in the nature of the case, different points of view.
Robert Hutchins (1899 - 1977)
The advantage of a classical education is that it enables you to despise the wealth that it prevents you from achieving.
Russell Green
To educate a man in mind and not in morals is to educate a menace to society.
Theodore Roosevelt (1858 - 1919)
Perhaps the most valuable result of all education is the ability to make yourself do the thing you have to do, when it ought to be done, whether you like it or not; it is the first lesson that ought to be learned; and however early a man's training begins, it is probably the last lesson that he learns thoroughly.
Thomas H. Huxley (1825 - 1895)
I know no safe depository of the ultimate powers of the society but the people themselves; and if we think them not enlightened enough to exercise their control with a wholesome discretion, the remedy is not to take it from them, but to inform their discretion by education.
Thomas Jefferson (1743 - 1826)
Education is a progressive discovery of our own ignorance.
Will Durant (1885 - 1981)
There is nothing as stupid as an educated man if you get him off the thing he was educated in.
Will Rogers (1879 - 1935)
The great thing, then, in all education, is to make our nervous system our ally instead of our enemy.
William James (1842 - 1910), The Principles of Psychology
I respect faith, but doubt is what gets you an education.
Wilson Mizner (1876 - 1933)
Education is like a double-edged sword. It may be turned to dangerous uses if it is not properly handled.
Wu Ting-Fang

Emotions

Sadness is poetic. You're lucky to live sad moments. When you let yourself be sad, your body has antibodies. It has happiness that comes rushing in to meet the sadness.
C. K. Louis, The Conan O'Brien Show, 09-20-13
Where we have strong emotions, we're liable to fool ourselves.
Carl Sagan (1934 - 1996), Cosmos (Blues for a Red Planet)
When dealing with people, let us remember we are not dealing with creatures of logic. We are dealing with creatures of emotion, creatures bustling with prejudices and motivated by pride and vanity.
Dale Carnegie
When a man is not amused, he feels an involuntary contempt for those who are.
Edward Bulwer-Lytton (1803 - 1873)
If you want to make people weep, you must weep yourself. If you want to make people laugh, your face must remain serious.
Giovanni Jacopo Casanova
When you own or take responsibility for your feelings, you place yourself in a position of power and control.
Julie A., M.A. Ross and Judy Corcoran, Joint Custody with a Jerk: Raising a Child with an Uncooperative Ex, 2011

When you understand that your feelings are triggered by what you think about an event and not by the event itself, you gain a measure of control. Although you cannot control the things (events) that happen to you, or change your feelings (after all, you feel the way you feel), you can change your thoughts. A change in thoughts often radically alters your feelings.
Julie A., M.A. Ross and Judy Corcoran, Joint Custody with a Jerk: Raising a Child with an Uncooperative Ex, 2011
The sign of an intelligent people is their ability to control emotions by the application of reason.
Marya Mannes
Feelings are really your GPS system for life. When your supposed to do something, or not supposed to do something, your emotional guidance system lets you know.
Oprah Winfrey (1954 -), Stanford Commencement Adress, 2008
The advantage of the emotions is that they lead us astray, and the advantage of science is that it is not emotional.
Oscar Wilde (1854 - 1900), The Picture of Dorian Gray, 1891
Cherish your own emotions and never undervalue them.
Robert Henri (1865 - 1929)
When you're eighteen your emotions are violent, but they're not durable.
W. Somerset Maugham (1874 - 1965), The Razor's Edge, 1943

Enemies

The shaft of the arrow had been feathered with one of the eagle's own plumes. We often give our enemies the means of our own destruction.
Aesop (620 BC - 560 BC), The Eagle and the Arrow
He who has a thousand friends has not a friend to spare,
And he who has one enemy will meet him everywhere.
Ali ibn-Abi-Talib (602 AD - 661 AD), A Hundred Sayings
Above all things, never be afraid. The enemy who forces you to retreat is himself afraid of you at that very moment.
Andre Maurois (1885 - 1967)
Observe your enemies, for they first find out your faults.
Antisthenes (445 BC - 365 BC)
A wise man gets more use from his enemies than a fool from his friends.
Baltasar Gracian
Love your enemies; for they shall tell you all your faults.
Benjamin Franklin (1706 - 1790)
I do not regret one professional enemy I have made. Any actor who doesn't dare to make an enemy should get out of the business.
Bette Davis (1908 - 1989), The Lonely Life, 1962
The meeting of two personalities is like the contact of two chemical substances: if there is any reaction, both are transformed.
Carl Jung (1875 - 1961)
He hasn't an enemy in the world - but all his friends hate him.
Eddie Cantor (1892 - 1964)
Never explain—your friends do not need it and your enemies will not believe you anyway.
Elbert Hubbard (1856 - 1915)
You can discover what your enemy fears most by observing the means he uses to frighten you.
Eric Hoffer (1902 - 1983)
At times one remains faithful to a cause only because its opponents do not cease to be insipid.
Friedrich Nietzsche (1844 - 1900)
Rejoice not at thine enemy's fall - but don't rush to pick him up either.
Jewish Proverb
Forgive your enemies, but never forget their names.
John F. Kennedy (1917 - 1963)
Now the trumpet summons us again—not as a call to bear arms, though arms we need; not as a call to battle, though embattled we are—but a call to bear the burden of a long twilight struggle, year in and year out, "rejoicing in hope, patient in tribulation"—a struggle against the common enemies of man: tyranny, poverty, disease, and war itself.
John F. Kennedy (1917 - 1963), Inaugural Adress, January 20, 1961
The enemy is anybody who's going to get you killed, no matter which side he's on.
Joseph Heller (1923 - 1999), Catch 22
The rule is perfect: in all matters of opinion our adversaries are insane.
Mark Twain (1835 - 1910), in Christian Science
If you want to make peace, you don't talk to your friends. You talk to your enemies.
Moshe Dayan (1915 - 1981)
Never interrupt your enemy when he is making a mistake.
Napoleon Bonaparte (1769 - 1821)
A man cannot be too careful in the choice of his enemies.
Oscar Wilde (1854 - 1900), The Picture of Dorian Gray, 1891
Always forgive your enemies; nothing annoys them so much.
Oscar Wilde (1854 - 1900)
We can learn even from our enemies.
Ovid (43 BC - 17 AD), Metamorphoses
Use your enemy's hand to catch a snake.
Persian Proverb
Treat your friend as if he might become an enemy.
Publilius Syrus (~ 100 BC), Maxims
Reveal not every secret you have to a friend, for how can you tell but that friend may hereafter become an enemy. And bring not all mischief you are able to upon an enemy, for he may one day become your friend.
Saadi (1184 - 1291)
It is hard to fight an enemy who has outposts in your head.

Sally Kempton
Money can't buy friends, but it can get you a better class of enemy.
Spike Milligan
Friends may come and go, but enemies accumulate.
Thomas Jones (1892 - 1969)
I have never made but one prayer to God, a very short one: 'O Lord, make my enemies ridiculous.' And God granted it.
Voltaire (1694 - 1778)
It is easier to forgive an enemy than to forgive a friend.
William Blake (1757 - 1827)
The man who is swimming against the stream knows the strength of it.
Woodrow Wilson (1856 - 1924)

Energy
Energy and persistence conquer all things.
Benjamin Franklin (1706 - 1790)
Love the moment, and the energy of that moment will spread beyond all boundaries.
Corita Kent
Crime is naught but misdirected energy.
Emma Goldman (1869 - 1940), Anarchism (1910)
...happiness gives us the energy which is the basis of health.
Henri-Frédéric Amiel
Energy is the essence of life. Every day you decide how you're going to use it by knowing what you want and what it takes to reach that goal, and by maintaining focus.
Oprah Winfrey (1954 -), O Magazine, July 2003
Life engenders life. Energy creates energy. It is by spending oneself that one becomes rich.
Sarah Bernhardt (1844 - 1923)
Energy is eternal delight.
William Blake (1757 - 1827)
Don't get me wrong: I love nuclear energy! It's just that I prefer fusion to fission. And it just so happens that there's an enormous fusion reactor safely banked a few million miles from us. It delivers more than we could ever use in just about 8 minutes. And it's wireless!
William McDonough, Fortune Brainstorm Conference, 2006

Engineering

Engineering is not merely knowing and being knowledgeable, like a walking encyclopedia; engineering is not merely analysis; engineering is not merely the possession of the capacity to get elegant solutions to non-existent engineering problems; engineering is practicing the art of the organized forcing of technological change... Engineers operate at the interface between science and society...
Dean Gordon Brown
Engineering is the art of organizing and directing men and controlling the forces and materials of nature for the benefit of the human race.
Henry G. Stott, 1907
Engineering is a great profession. There is the satisfaction of watching a figment of the imagination emerge through the aid of science to a plan on paper. Then it moves to realisation in stone or metal or energy. Then it brings homes to men or women. Then it elevates the standard of living and adds to the comforts of life. This is the engineer's high privilege.
Herbert Hoover (1874 - 1964)
I don't care what it is, when it has an LCD screen, it makes it better.
Kevin Rose, Diggnation, Our Lip Dub Is Better Than Yours, 2008
Engineers participate in the activities which make the resources of nature available in a form beneficial to man and provide systems which will perform optimally and economically.
L. M. K. Boelter, 1957
The ideal engineer is a composite ... He is not a scientist, he is not a mathematician, he is not a sociologist or a writer; but he may use the knowledge and techniques of any or all of these disciplines in solving engineering problems.
N. W. Dougherty, 1955
Engineering is an activity other than purely manual and physical work which brings about the utilization of the materials and laws of nature for the good of humanity.
R. E. Hellmund, 1929
Engineering is the professional art of applying science to the optimum conversion of natural resources to the benefit of man.
Ralph J. Smith
Engineering is the practice of safe and economic application of the scientific laws governing the forces and materials of nature by means of organization, design and construction, for the general benefit of mankind.
S. E. Lindsay, 1920
The engineer is the key figure in the material progress of the world. It is his engineering that makes a reality of the potential value of science by translating scientific knowledge into tools, resources, energy and labor to bring them into the service of man ... To make contributions of this kind the engineer requires the imagination to visualize the needs of society and to appreciate what is possible as well as the technological and broad social age understanding to bring his vision to reality.
Sir Eric Ashby
Engineering is the professional and systematic application of science to the efficient utilization of natural resources to produce wealth.

T. J. Hoover and J. C. L. Fish, 1941
Engineering is the science of economy, of conserving the energy, kinetic and potential, provided and stored up by nature for the use of man. It is the business of engineering to utilize this energy to the best advantage, so that there may be the least possible waste.
William A. Smith, 1908

England

He was born an Englishman and remained one for years.
Brendan Behan (1923 - 1964), Hostage (1958)
England and America are two countries separated by a common language.
George Bernard Shaw (1856 - 1950)
The English have no respect for their language, and will not teach their children to speak it.
George Bernard Shaw (1856 - 1950), Pygmalion (1916) preface
We don't bother much about dress and manners in England, because as a nation we don't dress well and we've no manners.
George Bernard Shaw (1856 - 1950), "You Never Can Tell" (1898), act I
We have really everything in common with America nowadays except, of course, language.
Oscar Wilde (1854 - 1900), The Canterville Ghost, 1882
This England never did, nor never shall,
Lie at the proud foot of a conqueror.
William Shakespeare (1564 - 1616), "King John", Act 5 scene 7
This royal throne of kings, this sceptred isle,
This earth of majesty, this seat of Mars,
This other Eden, demi-paradise,
This fortress built by Nature for herself
Against infection and the hand of war,
This happy breed of men, this little world,
This precious stone set in the silver sea,
Which serves it in the office of a wall
Or as a moat defensive to a house,
Against the envy of less happier lands,–
This blessed plot, this earth, this realm, this England.
William Shakespeare (1564 - 1616), "King Richard II", Act 2 scene 1

English
Even if you do learn to speak correct English, whom are you going to speak it to?
Clarence Darrow (1857 - 1938)
The English language was carefully, carefully cobbled together by three blind dudes and a German dictionary.
Dave Kellett, Sheldon, 02-01-09
If the English language made any sense, a catastrophe would be an apostrophe with fur.
Doug Larson
England and America are two countries separated by a common language.
George Bernard Shaw (1856 - 1950)
The English have no respect for their language, and will not teach their children to speak it.
George Bernard Shaw (1856 - 1950), Pygmalion (1916) preface
Every English poet should master the rules of grammar before he attempts to bend or break them.
Robert Graves (1895 - 1985)
Here will be an old abusing of God's patience and the king's English.
William Shakespeare (1564 - 1616), "The Merry Wives of Windsor", Act 1 scene 4

Environment
The animals of the planet are in desperate peril... Without free animal life I believe we will lose the spiritual equivalent of oxygen.
Alice Walker (1944 -), Living by the Word, 1988
I am the Lorax, and I'll yell and I'll shout for the fine things on earth that are on their way out!
Dr. Seuss (1904 - 1991), The Lorax
I speak for the trees, for the trees have no tongues.
Dr. Seuss (1904 - 1991), The Lorax
Unless someone like you cares a whole awful lot, nothing is going to get better. It's not.
Dr. Seuss (1904 - 1991), The Lorax
What is the use of a house if you haven't got a tolerable planet to put it on?
Henry David Thoreau (1817 - 1862)
For in the final analysis, our most basic common link, is that we all inhabit this small planet, we all breathe the same air, we all cherish our children's futures, and we are all mortal.
John F. Kennedy (1917 - 1963), Speech at The American University, Washington, D.C., June 10, 1963
We shall never understand the natural environment until we see it as a living organism. Land can be healthy or sick, fertile or barren, rich or poor, lovingly nurtured or bled white. Our present attitudes and laws governing the ownership and use of land represent an abuse of the concept of private property.... Today you can murder land for private profit. You can leave the corpse for all to see and nobody calls the cops.
Paul Brooks, The Pursuit of Wilderness (1971)

Equality

Unless man is committed to the belief that all mankind are his brothers, then he labors in vain and hypocritically in the vineyards of equality.
Adam Clayton Powell Jr. (1908 - 1972), 'Black Power: A Form of Godly Power,' 1967
Before God we are all equally wise - and equally foolish.
Albert Einstein (1879 - 1955)
That all men are equal is a proposition which, at ordinary times, no sane individual has ever given his assent.
Aldous Huxley (1894 - 1963)
If liberty and equality, as is thought by some are chiefly to be found in democracy, they will be best attained when all persons alike share in the government to the utmost.
Aristotle (384 BC - 322 BC), Politics
The only stable state is the one in which all men are equal before the law.
Aristotle (384 BC - 322 BC)
In the state of nature...all men are born equal, but they cannot continue in this equality. Society makes them lose it, and they recover it only by the protection of the law.
Charles de Montesquieu (1689 - 1755)
The love of democracy is that of equality.
Charles de Montesquieu (1689 - 1755)
All animals are equal but some animals are more equal than others.
George Orwell (1903 - 1950), "Animal Farm"
Equality...is the result of human organization. We are not born equal.
Hannah Arendt (1906 - 1975)
It is not true that equality is a law of nature. Nature has no equality. Its sovereign law is subordination and dependence.
Marquis de Vauvenargues
As men, we are all equal in the presence of death.
Publilius Syrus (~100 BC), Moral Sayings, First Century B.C.
We hold these truths to be self-evident that all men are created equal; that they are endowed by their Creator with certain inalienable rights; that among these are life, liberty, and the pursuit of happiness.
US Declaration of Independence
Men are equal; it is not birth but virtue that makes the difference.
Voltaire (1694 - 1778)

Etiquette

Politeness, n. The most acceptable hypocrisy.
Ambrose Bierce (1842 - 1914), The Devil's Dictionary
That's the secret of entertaining. You make your guests feel welcome and at home. If you do that honestly, the rest takes care of itself.
Barbara Hall, Northern Exposure, Northern Hospitality, 1994
Cleanliness and order are not matters of instinct; they are matters of education, and like most great things, you must cultivate a taste for them.
Benjamin Disraeli (1804 - 1881)
Good manners will open doors that the best education cannot.
Clarence Thomas (1948 -)
It is wise to apply the oil of refined politeness to the mechanisms of friendship.
Colette (1873 - 1954), The Pure and the Impure, 1932
Rudeness is the weak man's imitation of strength.
Eric Hoffer (1902 - 1983)
We don't bother much about dress and manners in England, because as a nation we don't dress well and we've no manners.
George Bernard Shaw (1856 - 1950), "You Never Can Tell" (1898), act I
There is hardly any personal defect which an agreeable manner might not gradually reconcile one to.
Jane Austen (1775 - 1817), Persuasion, 1818
One of the greatest victories you can gain over someone is to beat him at politeness.
Josh Billings (1818 - 1885)
Doesn't matter what a person's name is as long as he behaves himself.
L. M. Montgomery (1874 - 1942), Anne of Green Gables, 1908
To have respect for ourselves guides our morals; and to have a deference for others governs our manners.
Lawrence Sterne (1713 - 1768)
Don't reserve your best behavior for special occasions. You can't have two sets of manners, two social codes - one for those you admire and want to impress, another for those whom you consider unimportant. You must be the same to all people.
Lillian Eichler Watson
If you aren't going to say something directly to someone's face, than don't use online as an opportunity to say it. It is this sense of bravery that people get when they are anonymous that gives the blogosphere a bad reputation.
Mena Trott, Times Online, 12-06-06
Associate with well-mannered persons and your manners will improve. Run around with decent folk and your own decent instincts will be strengthened.
Stanley Walker
Politeness and consideration for others is like investing pennies and getting dollars back.
Thomas Sowell (1930 -), Creators Syndicate
Manners maketh man.
William of Wykeham (1324 - 1404), Motto of Winchester College and New College, Oxford

Evil

Evil brings men together.
Aristotle (384 BC - 322 BC), (attributed)
Evil draws men together.
Aristotle (384 BC - 322 BC), Rhetoric
We must as second best...take the least of the evils.
Aristotle (384 BC - 322 BC), Nichomachean Ethics
The evil of the world is made possible by nothing but the sanction you give it.
Ayn Rand (1905 - 1982), Atlas Shrugged, 1957
The spread of evil is the symptom of a vacuum, whenever evil wins, it is only by default: by the moral failure of those who evade the fact that there can be no compromise on basic principles.
Ayn Rand (1905 - 1982), Capitalism: The Unknown Ideal, 1966
I have discovered that all human evil comes from this, man's being unable to sit still in a room.
Blaise Pascal (1623 - 1662)
Men never do evil so completely and cheerfully as when they do it from a religious conviction.
Blaise Pascal (1623 - 1662)
We are all capable of evil thoughts, but only very rarely of evil deeds: we can all do good deeds, but very few of us can think good thoughts.
Cesare Pavese (1908 - 1950)
All that is necessary for the triumph of evil is that good men do nothing.
Edmund Burke (1729 - 1797)
I know indeed what evil I intend to do,
but stronger than all my afterthoughts is my fury,
fury that brings upon mortals the greatest evils.
Euripides (484 BC - 406 BC), Medea, 431 B.C.
Every minute you are thinking of evil, you might have been thinking of good instead. Refuse to pander to a morbid interest in your own misdeeds. Pick yourself up, be sorry, shake yourself, and go on again.
Evelyn Underhill
Nothing is easier than to denounce the evildoer; nothing is more difficult than to understand him.
Fyodor Dostoevsky (1821 - 1881)
Evil is obvious only in retrospect.
Gloria Steinem (1934 -), Outrageous Acts and Everyday Rebellions, 1983
Do not seek evil gains; evil gains are the equivalent of disaster.
Hesiod (~800 BC), Works and Days
He harms himself who does harm to another, and the evil plan is most harmful to the planner.
Hesiod (~800 BC), Works and Days
Often an entire city has suffered because of an evil man.
Hesiod (~800 BC), Works and Days
Evil deeds do not prosper; the slow man catches up with the swift.
Homer (800 BC - 700 BC), The Odyssey
A person may cause evil to others not only by his action but by his inaction, and in either case he is justly accountable to them for the injury.
John Stuart Mill (1806 - 1873)
The belief in a supernatural source of evil is not necessary; men alone are quite capable of every wickedness.
Joseph Conrad (1857 - 1924), Under Western Eyes, 1911
Evil to him who evil thinks.
(Honi Soit Qui Mal Pense)
King Edward the Third (1312 - 1377), Motto of the order of the Garter
A scoundrel will forever be a scoundrel, no matter which coat he wears.
Laura Moncur (1969 -), The Secret Heart of Charlotte Lucas, 2014
Whenever evil befalls us, we ought to ask ourselves, after the first suffering, how we can turn it into good. So shall we take occasion, from one bitter root, to raise perhaps many flowers.
Leigh Hunt (1784 - 1859)
Between two evils, I always pick the one I never tried before.
Mae West (1892 - 1980), Klondike Annie (1936 film)
It is bitter to lose a friend to evil, before one loses him to death.
Mary Renault, The Praise Singer, 1978
Don't let us make imaginary evils, when you know we have so many real ones to encounter.
Oliver Goldsmith (1730 - 1774)
All things may corrupt when minds are prone to evil.
Ovid (43 BC - 17 AD)
No evil can happen to a good man, either in life or after death.
Plato (427 BC - 347 BC), Dialogues, Apology
Every sweet has its sour; every evil its good.
Ralph Waldo Emerson (1803 - 1882)
Evil when we are in its power is not felt as evil but as a necessity, or even a duty.
Simone Weil (1909 - 1943), Gravity and Grace, 1947
The end excuses any evil.
Sophocles (496 BC - 406 BC), Electra (c.409 BC)
No man is justified in doing evil on the ground of expediency.
Theodore Roosevelt (1858 - 1919), 'The Strenuous Life,' 1900
Of two evils we must always choose the least.
Thomas a Kempis (1380 - 1471)
The evil that we know is best.
Titus Maccius Plautus (254 BC - 184 BC)

Evolution

There is nothing sadder in this world than the waste of human potential. The purpose of evolution is to raise us out of the mud, not have us grovelling in it.
Diane Frolov and Andrew Schneider, Northern Exposure, Cicely, 1992
Today, the theory of evolution is an accepted fact for everyone but a fundamentalist minority, whose objections are based not on reasoning but on doctrinaire adherence to religious principles.
James D. Watson (1928 -)
There are an awful lot of scientists today who believe that before very long we shall have unraveled all the secrets of the universe. There will be no puzzles anymore. To me it'd be really, really tragic because I think one of the most exciting things is this feeling of mystery, feeling of awe, the feeling of looking at a little live thing and being amazed by it and how its emerged through these hundreds of years of evolution and there it is and it is perfect and why.
Jane Goodall (1934 -)
If we are going to teach creation science as an alternative to evolution, then we should also teach the stork theory as an alternative to biological reproduction.
Judith Hayes
The theory of evolution by cumulative natural selection is the only theory we know of that is in principle capable of explaining the existence of organized complexity.
Richard Dawkins (1941 -)
Creationist critics often charge that evolution cannot be tested, and therefore cannot be viewed as a properly scientific subject at all. This claim is rhetorical nonsense.
Stephen Jay Gould (1941 - 2002)
My theory of evolution is that Darwin was adopted.
Steven Wright (1955 -)
It is an error to imagine that evolution signifies a constant tendency to increased perfection. That process undoubtedly involves a constant remodelling of the organism in adaptation to new conditions; but it depends on the nature of those conditions whether the directions of the modifications effected shall be upward or downward.
Thomas H. Huxley (1825 - 1895)

Excellence

It is only in your mind that you have to excel, at anything or everything. Of course, it would be very nice to excel at most things. Indeed, we recommend that you try and do your best. But realistically, you are entitled to do the bare minimum to get by. All your accomplishments are just a bonus, something to enjoy, not requirements. You don't have to do anything to prove that you are worthy of existing.
Albert Ellis, Michael Abrams, Lidia Dengelegi, The Art & Science of Rational Eating, 1992
To enjoy the things we ought and to hate the things we ought has the greatest bearing on excellence of character.
Aristotle (384 BC - 322 BC), Nichomachean Ethics
With regard to excellence, it is not enough to know, but we must try to have and use it.
Aristotle (384 BC - 322 BC), Nichomachean Ethics
Sports serve society by providing vivid examples of excellence.
George F. Will (1941 -)
Strive for excellence, not perfection.
H. Jackson Brown Jr., O Magazine, December 2003
In every power, of which taste is the foundation, excellence is pretty fairly divided between the sexes.
Jane Austen (1775 - 1817), Northanger Abbey, 1818
The ancient Greek definition of happiness was the full use of your powers along lines of excellence.
John F. Kennedy (1917 - 1963)
I am careful not to confuse excellence with perfection. Excellence, I can reach for; perfection is God's business.
Michael J. Fox (1961 -), quoted by Lorne A. Adrain in 'The Most Important Thing I Know'
The secret of joy in work is contained in one word - excellence. To know how to do something well is to enjoy it.
Pearl Buck (1892 - 1973), The Joy of Children, 1964
It takes a long time to bring excellence to maturity.
Publilius Syrus (~ 100 BC), Maxims
The renown which riches or beauty confer is fleeting and frail; mental excellence is a splendid and lasting possession.
Sallust (86 BC - 34 BC), The War with Catiline
The sad truth is that excellence makes people nervous.
Shana Alexander
It's not enough that we do our best; sometimes we have to do what's required.
Sir Winston Churchill (1874 - 1965)

Exercise

Nothing's better than the wind to your back, the sun in front of you, and your friends beside you.
Aaron Douglas Trimble
I think that anyone who comes upon a Nautilus machine suddenly will agree with me that its prototype was clearly invented at some time in history when torture was considered a reasonable alternative to diplomacy.
Anna Quindlen (1953 -)

I believe that every human has a finite number of heart-beats. I don't intend to waste any of mine running around doing exercises.
Buzz Aldrin (1930 -)
Control's a funny thing. It comes and goes. Some days I had it, some days I didn't. It felt like every time I did something healthy, I had this in satiable need to counterbalance it by doing something unhealthy.
Edward Ugel, I'm With Fatty: Losing Fifty Pounds in Fifty Miserable Weeks, 2010
Worrying about gray hair when your weight's soaring out of control is like mowing your lawn while your house is on fire.
Edward Ugel, I'm With Fatty: Losing Fifty Pounds in Fifty Miserable Weeks, 2010
Walking isn't a lost art: one must, by some means, get to the garage.
Evan Esar (1899 - 1995)
Exercise alone provides psychological and physical benefits. However, if you also adopt a strategy that engages your mind while you exercise, you can get a whole host of psychological benefits fairly quickly.
James Rippe, M.D.
Mach-S, the speed at which stress can't keep up, is simply forward motion. But it has to be self- propelled. Note that people in cars are still stressed.
Jef Mallett, Frazz, 08-26-05
Extreme exercise doesn't save you from poor food choices. It can be difficult to exercise and erase away that chocolate cake or pizza pie. It doesn't work that way.
Jennifer Hudson, I Got This: How I Changed My Ways and Lost What Weighed Me Down, 2012
The important message I heard about working out and what I want to share is that you create your own opportunities and your own limitations.
Jennifer Hudson, I Got This: How I Changed My Ways and Lost What Weighed Me Down, 2012
Whenever I'd try to talk myself out of going for a walk, and there were a few days like that, I'd take myself through a series of simple tasks so I would get up and go.
1. Get up.
2. Find your house keys.
3. Put on some shoes.
4. Grab your iPod.
5. Walk out the front door.
Jennifer Hudson, I Got This: How I Changed My Ways and Lost What Weighed Me Down, 2012
There is nothing so good for the inside of a man as the outside of a horse.
John Lubbock, The Use of Life, 1894
Dig where the gold is...unless you just need some exercise.
John M. Capozzi, Why Climb the Corporate Ladder When You Can Take the Elevator?
Exercise ferments the humors, casts them into their proper channels, throws off redundancies, and helps nature in those secret distributions, without which the body cannot subsist in its vigor, nor the soul act with cheerfulness.
Joseph Addison (1672 - 1719), The Spectator, July 12, 1711
Running cross country is the closest man will ever get to flying.
Joseph Vanderstel
You learn a lot about people when you play games with them.
Laura Moncur (1969 -), Pick Me! 02-11-09
Why do strong arms fatigue themselves with frivolous dumbbells? To dig a vineyard is worthier exercise for men.
Marcus Valerius Martialis (40 AD - 103 AD)
There's no easy way out. If there were, I would have bought it. And believe me, it would be one of my favorite things!
Oprah Winfrey (1954 -), O Magazine, February 2005
Nothing like a lot of exercise to make you realize you'd rather be lazy and dead sooner.
Randy K. Milholland, Something Positive, Casting Call, 10-21-13
Exercise is medicine. Literally. Just like a pill, it reliably changes brain function by altering the activity of key brain chemicals and hormones.
Stephen S. Ilardi PhD, The Depression Cure: The 6-Step Program to Beat Depression without Drugs, 2009
Medication isn't the only way to correct brain abnormalities in depression. Physical exercise also brings about profound changes in the brain—changes that rival those seen with the most potent antidepressant medications.
Stephen S. Ilardi PhD, The Depression Cure: The 6-Step Program to Beat Depression without Drugs, 2009
I like weights. You know where you stand with them. Well, sometimes you're lying under them, trying not to let them crush you, but you see, you KNOW they'd crush you if they could. There's honesty.
T. Campbell and Gisele Lagace, Penny and Aggie, 09-12-05
Walking is the best possible exercise. Habituate yourself to walk very far.
Thomas Jefferson (1743 - 1826)

Experience

We know nothing of what will happen in the future, but in the analogy of experience.
Abraham Lincoln (1809 - 1865), Speech on the sub-Treasury, December 26, 1839
You cannot acquire experience by making experiments. You cannot create experience. You must undergo it.
Albert Camus (1913 - 1960)
Experience is not what happens to a man. It is what a man does with what happens to him.
Aldous Huxley (1894 - 1963), Reader's Digest, March 1956
Experience is not what happens to a man; it is what a man does with what happens to him.
Aldous Huxley (1894 - 1963), "Texts and Pretexts", 1932
Experience teaches only the teachable.
Aldous Huxley (1894 - 1963)
Good judgment comes from experience, and experience comes from bad judgment.
Barry LePatner

Human beings, who are almost unique in having the ability to learn from the experience of others, are also remarkable for their apparent disinclination to do so.
Douglas Adams (1952 - 2001), "Last Chance to See"
You gain strength, courage and confidence by every experience in which you really stop to look fear in the face. You are able to say to yourself, 'I have lived through this horror. I can take the next thing that comes along.' You must do the thing you think you cannot do.
Eleanor Roosevelt (1884 - 1962)
Experience is that marvelous thing that enables you to recognize a mistake when you make it again.
Franklin P. Jones
Experience teaches slowly and at the cost of mistakes.
James A. Froude (1818 - 1894)
Men are wise in proportion, not to their experience, but to their capacity for experience.
James Boswell (1740 - 1795), Life of Samuel Johnson, 1791
Experience is the name everyone gives to their mistakes.
Oscar Wilde (1854 - 1900), Lady Windermere's Fan, 1892, Act III
I have but one lamp by which my feet are guided; and that is the lamp of experience. I know way of judging the future but by the past.
Patrick Henry (1736 - 1799), Speech to the Virginia Convention, March 23, 1775
By far the best proof is experience.
Sir Francis Bacon (1561 - 1626)
Experience is a hard teacher because she gives the test first, the lesson afterwards.
Vernon Sanders Law

Experts

An expert is a person who avoids small error as he sweeps on to the grand fallacy.
Benjamin Stolberg
Where facts are few, experts are many.
Donald R. Gannon
An expert is a person who has made all the mistakes that can be made in a very narrow field.
Niels Bohr (1885 - 1962)
My definition of an expert in any field is a person who knows enough about what's really going on to be scared.
P. J. Plauger, Computer Language, March 1983
If the world should blow itself up, the last audible voice would be that of an expert saying it can't be done.
Peter Ustinov (1921 - 2004)
Always listen to experts. They'll tell you what can't be done and why. Then do it.
Robert Heinlein (1907 - 1988)
In the beginner's mind there are many possibilities. In the expert's mind there are few.
Shunryu Suzuki
Believe one who has proved it. Believe an expert.
Virgil (70 BC - 19 BC), Aeneid

Exploration

One doesn't discover new lands without consenting to lose sight of the shore for a very long time.
Andre Gide (1869 - 1951)
Equipped with his five senses, man explores the universe around him and calls this adventure Science.
Edward Powell Hubble, The Nature of Science, 1954
No pessimist ever discovered the secret of the stars or sailed an uncharted land, or opened a new doorway for the human spirit.
Helen Keller (1880 - 1968)
In human life, art may arise from almost any activity, and once it does so, it is launched on a long road of exploration, invention, freedom to the limits of extravagance, interference to the point of frustration, finally discipline, controlling constant change and growth.
Susanne Langer (1895 - 1985)
We shall not cease from exploration. And the end of all our exploring will be to arrive where we started and know the place for the first time.
T. S. Eliot (1888 - 1965), Little Gidding
I'm of the mind that even people who have limitations, if they have a curiosity, they will find a way to explore it.
Tish Grier, love and hope and sex and dreams, 04-12-2006
Emergencies have always been necessary to progress. It was darkness which produced the lamp. It was fog that produced the compass. It was hunger that drove us to exploration. And it took a depression to teach us the real value of a job.
Victor Hugo (1802 - 1885)

Facts

If the facts don't fit the theory, change the facts.
Albert Einstein (1879 - 1955), (attributed)

Facts do not cease to exist because they are ignored.
Aldous Huxley (1894 - 1963), "Proper Studies", 1927
Where facts are few, experts are many.
Donald R. Gannon
Get the facts, or the facts will get you. And when you get them, get them right, or they will get you wrong.
Dr. Thomas Fuller (1654 - 1734), Gnomologia, 1732
Generally the theories we believe we call facts, and the facts we disbelieve we call theories.
Felix Cohen
Delete the adjectives and [you'll] have the facts.
Harper Lee (1926 -)
Facts are facts and will not disappear on account of your likes.
Jawaharlal Nehru (1889 - 1964)
Facts are stubborn things; and whatever may be our wishes, our inclinations, or the dictates of our passion, they cannot alter the state of facts and evidence.
John Adams (1735 - 1826), 'Argument in Defense of the Soldiers in the Boston Massacre Trials,' December 1770
We can have facts without thinking but we cannot have thinking without facts.
John Dewey (1859 - 1952)
Count Hermann Keyserling once said truly that the greatest American superstition was belief in facts.
John Gunther (1901 - 1970)
Let us take things as we find them: let us not attempt to distort them into what they are not. We cannot make facts. All our wishing cannot change them. We must use them.
John Henry Cardinal Newman (1801 - 1890)
Get your facts first, and then you can distort them as much as you please.
Mark Twain (1835 - 1910)
He is indebted to his memory for his jests and to his imagination for his facts.
Richard Brinsley Sheridan (1751 - 1816)
Facts are stupid things.
Ronald Reagan (1911 - 2004)
The trouble with facts is that there are so many of them.
Samuel McChord Crothers, The Gentle Reader
Facts have a cruel way of substituting themselves for fancies. There is nothing more remorseless, just as there is nothing more helpful, than truth.
William C. Redfield, Address at Case School, Cleveland, Ohio, May 27, 1915

Failure

Nobody cleared a path for themselves by giving up.
Alacia Bessette, Simply from Scratch, 2010
If we don't succeed, we run the risk of failure.
Anonymous, often attributed to Dan Quayle
It is possible to fail in many ways...while to succeed is possible only in one way.
Aristotle (384 BC - 322 BC), Nichomachean Ethics
You may be disappointed if you fail, but you are doomed if you don't try.
Beverly Sills (1929 -)
I don't know the key to success, but the key to failure is trying to please everybody.
Bill Cosby (1937 -)
If at first you don't succeed, find out if the loser gets anything.
Bill Lyon
Nothing has a stronger influence psychologically on their environment and especially on their children than the unlived life of the parent.
Carl Jung (1875 - 1961)
I think you actually get a kick out of being disappointed and under-achieving, because it's easier, isn't it? Failure and unhappiness is easier because you can make a joke out of it.
David Nicholls, One Day, 2010
Act as if it were impossible to fail.
Dorothea Brande
If you're willing to fail interestingly, you tend to succeed interestingly.
Edward Albee
Behind many acts that are thought ridiculous there lie wise and weighty motives.
Francois de La Rochefoucauld (1613 - 1680)
It is not enough to succeed. Others must fail.
Gore Vidal (1925 -)
Men are born to succeed, not fail.
Henry David Thoreau (1817 - 1862)
I can't give you a sure-fire formula for success, but I can give you a formula for failure: try to please everybody all the time.
Herbert Bayard Swope (1882 - 1958)
Failure meant a stripping away of the inessential. I stopped pretending to myself that I was anything other than I was and began diverting all my energy into finishing the only work that mattered to me.
J. K. Rowling, Harvard Commencement Address, 2008
It is impossible to live without failing at something, unless you live so cautiously that you might as well not lived at all. In which case, you've failed by default.
J. K. Rowling, Harvard Commencement Address, 2008
Ultimately, we all have to decide for ourselves what constitutes failure, but the world is quite eager to give you a set of criteria if you let it.
J. K. Rowling, Harvard Commencement Address, 2008
Don't be discouraged by a failure. It can be a positive experience. Failure is, in a sense, the highway to success, inasmuch as every discovery of what is false leads us to seek earnestly after what is true, and every fresh experience points out some form of error which we shall afterwards carefully avoid.
John Keats (1795 - 1821)

Next to trying and winning, the best thing is trying and failing.
L. M. Montgomery (1874 - 1942), Anne of Green Gables, 1908
If you have made mistakes, even serious ones, there is always another chance for you. What we call failure is not the falling down but the staying down.
Mary Pickford (1893 - 1979)
You always pass failure on the way to success.
Mickey Rooney (1920 -)
Success isn't permanent, and failure isn't fatal.
Mike Ditka (1939 -)
If at first you don't succeed, failure may be your style.
Quentin Crisp
We all have a few failures under our belt. It's what makes us ready for the successes.
Randy K. Milholland, Midnight Macabre, 10-18-05
A minute's success pays the failure of years.
Robert Browning (1812 - 1889)
Try as hard as we may for perfection, the net result of our labors is an amazing variety of imperfectness. We are surprised at our own versatility in being able to fail in so many different ways.
Samuel McChord Crothers
Success is the ability to go from one failure to another with no loss of enthusiasm.
Sir Winston Churchill (1874 - 1965)
Many of life's failures are people who did not realize how close they were to success when they gave up.
Thomas A. Edison (1847 - 1931)
Have you heard that it was good to gain the day? I also say it is good to fall, battles are lost in the same spirit in which they are won.
Walt Whitman (1819 - 1892)
Good people are good because they've come to wisdom through failure.
William Saroyan (1908 - 1981)

Faith

Hold faithfulness and sincerity as first principles.
Confucius (551 BC - 479 BC), The Confucian Analects
Faith is a cop-out. If the only way you can accept an assertion is by faith, then you are conceding that it can't be taken on its own merits.
Dan Barker, "Losing Faith in Faith", 1992
I always admired atheists. I think it takes a lot of faith.
Diane Frolov and Andrew Schneider, Northern Exposure, Seoul Mates, 1991
If you can't have faith in what is held up to you for faith, you must find things to believe in yourself, for a life without faith in something is too narrow a space to live.
George E. Woodberry
And so faith is closing your eyes and following the breath of your soul down to the bottom of life, where existence and nonexistence have merged into irrelevance. All that matters is the little part you play in the vast drama.
Gordon Atkinson, reallivepreacher.com weblog, September 4, 2003
God, I don't have great faith, but I can be faithful. My belief in you may be seasonal, but my faithfulness will not. I will follow in the way of Christ. I will act as though my life and the lives of others matter. I will love. I have no greater gift to offer than my life. Take it.
Gordon Atkinson, RealLivePreacher.com Weblog, December 26, 2002
The universe seems wondrous to me, with or without God. It has powerful lines and uncompromising ways. Patience and time sit like sages on the planets, strong and impersonal. There is a stark beauty to all of this.
Gordon Atkinson, reallivepreacher.com weblog, September 4, 2003
We think having faith means being convinced God exists in the same way we are convinced a chair exists. People who cannot be completely convinced of God's existence think faith is impossible for them. Not so. People who doubt can have great faith because faith is something you do, not something you think. In fact, the greater your doubt the more heroic your faith.
Gordon Atkinson, RealLivePreacher.com Weblog, December 26, 2002
Treat the other man's faith gently; it is all he has to believe with. His mind was created for his own thoughts, not yours or mine.
Henry S. Haskins
Faithless is he that says farewell when the road darkens.
J. R. R. Tolkien (1892 - 1973)
You have to accept the plan and realize that if you slip, and you might, you can't use that as a reason to give up or stop.
Jennifer Hudson, I Got This: How I Changed My Ways and Lost What Weighed Me Down, 2012
What I am actually saying is that we need to be willing to let our intuition guide us, and then be willing to follow that guidance directly and fearlessly.
Shakti Gawain
To believe in God or in a guiding force because someone tells you to is the height of stupidity. We are given senses to receive our information within. With our own eyes we see, and with our own skin we feel. With our intelligence, it is intended that we understand. But each person must puzzle it out for himself or herself.
Sophy Burnham
Faith is, at one and the same time, absolutely necessary and altogether impossible.
Stanislaw Lem (1921 - 2006)
Desire, ask, believe, receive.
Stella Terrill Mann
Whatever God's dream about man may be, it seems certain it cannot come true unless man cooperates.
Stella Terrill Mann
If you think you can win, you can win. Faith is necessary to victory.

William Hazlitt (1778 - 1830)
He wears his faith but as the fashion of his hat.
William Shakespeare (1564 - 1616), "Much Ado about Nothing", Act 1 scene 1
I respect faith, but doubt is what gets you an education.
Wilson Mizner (1876 - 1933)

Fame

Never suffer youth to be an excuse for inadequacy, nor age and fame to be an excuse for indolence.
Benjamin Haydon
He who pursues fame at the risk of losing his self is not a scholar.
Chuang-tzu (369 BC - 286 BC), The Great Supreme
You can't choose what you're famous for in life.
Dave Kellett, Sheldon, 10-11-09
To have had fame, even very minor fame, and to have lost it, got older and maybe put on a little weight is a kind of living death.
David Nicholls, One Day, 2010
The glory of great men should always be measured by the means they have used to acquire it.
Francois de La Rochefoucauld (1613 - 1680)
Rather than love, than money, than fame, give me truth.
Henry David Thoreau (1817 - 1862)
If you're holding out for universal popularity, I'm afraid you will be in this cabin for a very long time.
J. K. Rowling, Harry Potter and the Goblet of Fire
Living in L.A., everyone likes to mold you and change you. I don't care about fame, I don't care about being a celebrity. I know that's part of the job, but I don't feed into anyone's idea of who I should be.
Jessica Alba
How you matter is defined by the things that matter to you. You matter as much as the things that matter to you do.
John Green, An Abundance of Katherines, 2008
The future will erase everything—there's no level of fame or genius that allows you to transcend oblivion. The infinite future makes that kind of mattering impossible.
John Green, An Abundance of Katherines, 2008
The voracious ambition of humans is never sated by dreams coming true, because there is always the thought that everything might be done better and again.
John Green, The Fault in Our Stars, 2012
We are like a bunch of dogs squirting on fire hydrants. We poison the groundwater with our toxic piss, marking everything MINE in a ridiculous attempt to survive our deaths.
John Green, The Fault in Our Stars, 2012
I could not conceive that [fans] actually wanted me to sign something. It took a long time for me to figure out (a) just say 'Thank you' and sign the thing, and (b) smile in the picture, because if you try to just half-smile you're going to look constipated.
Joss Whedon, Entertainment Weekly, 08-30-13
If you're a misfit within a group of misfits, does that mean you're actually popular and normal?
Laura Preble, The Queen Geek Social Club, 2006
Glory is fleeting, but obscurity is forever.
Napoleon Bonaparte (1769 - 1821)
I think the promise of fame and what it holds to you as a child and dreaming of it is not what it is. What it is, I'm not complaining about, but it's just different than the reality you dreamed.
Rosie O'Donnell, Today Show interview, 04-08-08
It's going to come true like you knew it, but it's not going to feel like you think.
Rosie O'Donnell, Today Show interview, 04-08-08
I'm a bit of an abstract figure that people can project their fantasies on; it's pretty much what we all are, otherwise we wouldn't be stars, and people wouldn't be interested. But people project things on you that have nothing to do with what you really are, or they see a little something and then exaggerate it. And you can't really control that.
Salma Hayek
Famous I don't know about. It's hard to be famous and alive. I just want to play music every day and hear someone say, 'Thanks, that was great, here's some money, same time tomorrow, okay?'
Terry Pratchett, Soul Music, page 151
Popularity? It is glory's small change.
Victor Hugo (1802 - 1885)
Glory is like a circle in the water,
Which never ceaseth to enlarge itself,
Till by broad spreading it disperses to naught.
William Shakespeare (1564 - 1616)

Family

It is dismal coming home, when there is nobody to welcome one!
Ann Radcliffe (1764 - 1823), The Mysteries of Udolpho, 1764
I can't think of anything to write about except families. They are a metaphor for every other part of society.
Anna Quindlen (1953 -)
They say that blood is thicker than water. Maybe that's why we battle our own with more energy and gusto than we would ever expend on strangers.
David Assael, Northern Exposure, Family Feud, 1993

Caregiver: that word should weigh more than others on a page, sag it down a bit and wrinkle it, because the simple-sounding job frazzles as it consumes and depletes. Not that it's only gloomy. Caregiving offers many fringe benefits, including the sheer sensory delight of nourishing and grooming, sharing, and playing. There's something uniquely fulfilling about being a lodestar, feeling so deeply needed, and it's fun finding creative ways to gladden a loved one's life. But caregiving does buttonhole you; you're stitched in one place.
Diane Ackerman, One Hundred Names for Love: A Stroke, A Marriage, and the Language of Healing, 2011

We al have family disfunction. It's why we're successful, to fill that hole.
Eli Attie, House M.D., Parents, 11-14-2011

Having a baby's sweet face so close to your own, for so long a time as it takes to nurse 'em, is a great tonic for a sad soul.
Erica Eisdorfer, The Wet Nurse's Tale, 2009

Losing a baby is not a thing that you could ever get used to.
Erica Eisdorfer, The Wet Nurse's Tale, 2009

If you cannot get rid of the family skeleton, you may as well make it dance.
George Bernard Shaw (1856 - 1950)

Happiness is having a large, loving, caring, close-knit family in another city.
George Burns (1896 - 1996)

Family connexions were always worth preserving, good company always worth seeking.
Jane Austen (1775 - 1817), Persuasion, 1818

Call it a clan, call it a network, call it a tribe, call it a family. Whatever you call it, whoever you are, you need one.
Jane Howard, "Families"

If you ever start feeling like you have the goofiest, craziest, most dysfunctional family in the world, all you have to do is go to a state fair. Because five minutes at the fair, you'll be going, 'you know, we're alright. We are dang near royalty.'
Jeff Foxworthy

Happy families are all alike; every unhappy family is unhappy in its own way.
Leo Tolstoy (1828 - 1910), Anna Karenina, Chapter 1, first line

A family is a unit composed not only of children but of men, women, an occasional animal, and the common cold.
Ogden Nash (1902 - 1971)

No matter where you live, brothers are brothers and sisters are sisters. The bonds that keep family close are the same no matter where you are.
Takayuki Ikkaku, Arisa Hosaka and Toshihiro Kawabata, Animal Crossing: Wild World, 2005

Family isn't about whose blood you have. It's about who you care about.
Trey Parker and Matt Stone, South Park, Ike's Wee Wee, 1998

I think people that have a brother or sister don't realize how lucky they are. Sure, they fight a lot, but to know that there's always somebody there, somebody that's family.
Trey Parker and Matt Stone, South Park, Cat Orgy, 1999

Fashion

There's never a new fashion but it's old.
Geoffrey Chaucer (1342 - 1400)

A fashion is nothing but an induced epidemic.
George Bernard Shaw (1856 - 1950)

I base my fashion taste on what doesn't itch.
Gilda Radner (1946 - 1989)

Every generation laughs at the old fashions, but follows religiously the new.
Henry David Thoreau (1817 - 1862), "Walden", 1854

I once had a sparrow alight upon my shoulder for a moment, while I was hoeing in a village garden, and I felt that I was more distinguished by that circumstance that I should have been by any epaulet I could have worn.
Henry David Thoreau (1817 - 1862)

I'd rather look ridiculous when everybody else does than plain and sensible all by myself.
L. M. Montgomery (1874 - 1942), Anne of Green Gables, 1908

It is ever so much easier to be good if your clothes are fashionable.
L. M. Montgomery (1874 - 1942), Anne of Green Gables, 1908

A fine dress on a homely maiden is never enough of a distraction. It can convey a sense of wealth and its accompanying attractions, but it can never truly compensate for a plain face.
Laura Moncur (1969 -), The Secret Heart of Charlotte Lucas, 2014

Appearances are not the full cloth of a woman, but they are the most readily seen.
Laura Moncur (1969 -), The Secret Heart of Charlotte Lucas, 2014

I cannot and will not cut my conscience to fit this year's fashions.
Lillian Hellman (1905 - 1984), letter to Committee on Un-American Activities of the House of Representatives, May 19, 1952

Fashion is a form of ugliness so intolerable that we have to alter it every six months.
Oscar Wilde (1854 - 1900)

Fashion is something that goes in one year and out the other.
Unknown

The average American can get into the kingdom of heaven much more easily than he can get into the Boulevard St. Germain.
W. Somerset Maugham (1874 - 1965), The Razor's Edge, 1943

What a deformed thief this fashion is.
William Shakespeare (1564 - 1616), "Much Ado About Nothing", Act III scene iii

Fate

There is no fate that cannot be surmounted by scorn.
Albert Camus (1913 - 1960)

To punish me for my contempt for authority, fate made me an authority myself.
Albert Einstein (1879 - 1955)

If you can't change your fate, change your attitude.
Amy Tan (1952 -)

Men are not prisoners of fate, but only prisoners of their own minds.
Franklin D. Roosevelt (1882 - 1945), Pan American Day address, April 15, 1939

I do not believe in a fate that falls on all men however they act; but I do believe in a fate that falls on them unless they act.
G. K. Chesterton (1874 - 1936), On Holland, Generally Speaking, 1928

I do not believe in a fate that falls on men however they act; but I do believe in a fate that falls on them unless they act.
G. K. Chesterton (1874 - 1936), Generally Speaking, Chapter 20, 1929

A man's character is his fate.
Heraclitus (540 BC - 480 BC), On the Universe

The fates have given mankind a patient soul.
Homer (800 BC - 700 BC), The Iliad

Talent and intelligence never yet inoculated anyone against the caprice of the fates.
J. K. Rowling, Harvard Commencement Address, 2008

Fate chooses your relations, you choose your friends.
Jacques Delille

'If it's meant for me, it will be.' Those words are my mantra in life, and it has never let me down.
Jennifer Hudson, I Got This: How I Changed My Ways and Lost What Weighed Me Down, 2012

Man is his own star and the soul that can render an honest and perfect man commands all light, all influence, all fate.
John Fletcher (1579 - 1625), 1647

That consciousness is everything and that all things begin with a thought. That we are responsible for our own fate, we reap what we sow, we get what we give, we pull in what we put out. I know these things for sure.
Madonna (1958 -), O Magazine, January 2004

Maybe our mistakes are what make our fate. Without them, what would shape our lives? Perhaps, if we never veered off course, we wouldn't fall in love or have babies or be who we are.
Michael Patrick King, Sex and the City, I Heart NY, 2002

Naming one thing after another cannot, logically, increase the chances of the new thing turning out like the old thing.
Ned Beauman, The Teleportation Accident, 2013

Whatever limits us, we call Fate.
Ralph Waldo Emerson (1803 - 1882), Fate, The Conduct of Life, 1860

Fate rules the affairs of mankind with no recognizable order.
Seneca (5 BC - 65 AD)

While the fates permit, live happily; life speeds on with hurried step, and with winged days the wheel of the headlong year is turned.
Seneca (5 BC - 65 AD)

I am not an adventurer by choice but by fate.
Vincent van Gogh (1853 - 1890)

If fate means you to lose, give him a good fight anyhow.
William McFee

Men at some time are the masters of their fates: The fault, dear Brutus, is not in our stars, but in ourselves, that we are underlings.
William Shakespeare (1564 - 1616), Julius Caesar, Act I, sc. 2

Fear

When you have the courage to tell the truth about what you're really afraid of, fear doesn't have control over your life.
Ali Vincent, Believe It, Be It: How Being the Biggest Loser Won Me Back My Life, 2009

When one can hear people moving, one does not so much mind, about one's fears.
Ann Radcliffe (1764 - 1823), The Mysteries of Udolpho, 1764

When the mind has once begun to yield to the weakness of superstition, trifles impress it with the force of conviction.
Ann Radcliffe (1764 - 1823), The Mysteries of Udolpho, 1764

Fear is the main source of superstition, and one of the main sources of cruelty. To conquer fear is the beginning of wisdom.
Bertrand Russell (1872 - 1970), Unpopular Essays (1950), "Outline of Intellectual Rubbish"

Courage is fear that has said its prayers.
Dorothy Bernard

Remember that fear always lurks behind perfectionism. Confronting your fears and allowing yourself the right to be human can, paradoxically, make you a far happier and more productive person.
Dr. David M. Burns

No passion so effectually robs the mind of all its powers of acting and reasoning as fear.
Edmund Burke (1729 - 1797), "A Philosophical Inquiry into the Origin of Our Ideas of the Sublime and Beautiful", 1756

One need not be a chamber to be haunted;
One need not be a house;
The brain has corridors surpassing
Material place.
Emily Dickinson (1830 - 1886)

It is when power is wedded to chronic fear that it becomes formidable.
Eric Hoffer (1902 - 1983), The Passionate State of Mind, 1954

You can discover what your enemy fears most by observing the means he uses to frighten you.
Eric Hoffer (1902 - 1983)
If you forgo your plan, you also have to forgo fear.
Eric Schmidt, University of Pennsylvania Commencement Address, 2009
In life we don't get what we want, we get in life what we are. If we want more we have to be able to be more, in order to be more you have to face rejection.
Farrah Gray
None but a coward dares to boast that he has never known fear.
Ferdinand Foch (1851 - 1929)
Even the fear of death is nothing compared to the fear of not having lived authentically and fully.
Frances Moore Lappe, O Magazine, May 2004
I've grown certain that the root of all fear is that we've been forced to deny who we are.
Frances Moore Lappe, O Magazine, May 2004
Let the fear of danger be a spur to prevent it; he that fears not, gives advantage to the danger.
Francis Quarles (1592 - 1644)
There are nights when the wolves are silent and only the moon howls.
George Carlin (1937 - 2008)
Fear is the tax that conscience pays to guilt.
George Sewell
Fear plays an interesting role in our lives. How dare we let it motivate us? How dare we let it into our decision making; into our livelihoods; into our relationships? It's funny isn't it? We take a day a year to dress up, in costume and celebrate fear.
Greg Daniels, Carrie Kemper, Ricky Gervais, Stephen Merchant, The Office, Spooked, October 2011
Fear sometimes stops you from doing stupid things. But it can also stop you from doing creative or exciting or experimental things. It can cloud your judgment of others, and lead to all kinds of evil. The control and understanding of our personal fears is one of the most important undertakings in our life.
Helen Mirren
A timid person is frightened before a danger, a coward during the time, and a courageous person afterward.
Jean Paul Richter (1763 - 1825)
Let us never negotiate out of fear. But let us never fear to negotiate.
John F. Kennedy (1917 - 1963), Inaugural Adress, January 20, 1961
Fear not those who argue but those who dodge.
Marie Ebner von Eschenbach, Aphorisms, 1905
Fear is a question: What are you afraid of, and why? Just as the seed of health is in illness, because illness contains information, your fears are a treasure house of self-knowledge if you explore them.
Marilyn Ferguson
Fear is that little darkroom where negatives are developed.
Michael Pritchard
To use fear as the friend it is, we must retrain and reprogram ourselves...We must persistently and convincingly tell ourselves that the fear is here–with its gift of energy and heightened awareness–so we can do our best and learn the most in the new situation.
Peter McWilliams, Life 101
The fear of death is more to be dreaded than death itself.
Publilius Syrus (~ 100 BC), Maxims
Almost everything: all external expectations, all pride all fear of embarrassment or failure. These tings just fall away in the face of death, leaving only what is truly important. Remembering that you are going to die is the best way I know to avoid the trap of thinking you have something to lose.
Steve Jobs (1955 - 2011), Stanford Commencement Adress, 2005
Feel the fear and do it anyway.
Susan Jeffers, Feel the Fear and Do It Anyway, 1988
Everyone has certain fears, certain things that one cannot abide.
Takayuki Ikkaku, Arisa Hosaka and Toshihiro Kawabata, Animal Crossing: Wild World, 2005
"Fearless" is living in spite of those things that scare you to death.
Taylor Swift
At first cock-crow the ghosts must go
Back to their quiet graves below.
Theodosia Garrison
Suspicion always haunts the guilty mind; the thief doth fear each bush an officer.
William Shakespeare (1564 - 1616), Henry VI, Part III, Act V, sc. 6

Fishing

Fishing is a delusion entirely surrounded by liars in old clothes.
Don Marquis (1878 - 1937)
If people concentrated on the really important things in life, there'd be a shortage of fishing poles.
Doug Larson
Many go fishing without knowing it is fish they are after.
Henry David Thoreau (1817 - 1862)
A fishing rod is a stick with a hook at one end and a fool at the other.
Samuel Johnson (1709 - 1784)
Last year I went fishing with Salvador Dali. He was using a dotted line. He caught every other fish.
Steven Wright (1955 -)
There's a fine line between fishing and just standing on the shore like an idiot.
Steven Wright (1955 -)

Flowers

Autumn is a second spring when every leaf is a flower.
Albert Camus (1913 - 1960)
Arranging a bowl of flowers in the morning can give a sense of quiet in a crowded day - like writing a poem, or saying a prayer.
Anne Morrow Lindbergh
If you enjoy the fruit, pluck not the flower.
Anonymous
A bit of fragrance clings to the hand that gives flowers.
Chinese Proverb
Gardens and flowers have a way of bringing people together, drawing them from their homes.
Clare Ansberry, The Women of Troy Hill
Nobody sees a flower - really - it is so small it takes time - we haven't time - and to see takes time, like to have a friend takes time.
Georgia O'Keeffe (1887 - 1986)
A cynic is a man who, when he smells flowers, looks around for a coffin.
H. L. Mencken (1880 - 1956)
I hope that while so many people are out smelling the flowers, someone is taking the time to plant some.
Herbert Rappaport
Flowers never emit so sweet and strong a fragrance as before a storm. When a storm approaches thee, be as fragrant as a sweet-smelling flower.
Jean Paul Richter (1763 - 1825)
Stretching his hand out to catch the stars, he forgets the flowers at his feet.
Jeremy Bentham (1748 - 1832)
I have seen flowers come in stony places
And kind things done by men with ugly faces
And the gold cup won by the worst horse at the races,
So I trust too.
John Masefield (1878 - 1967)
Flowers are words even a baby can understand.
Quentin Crisp
Money is a powerful aphrodisiac. But flowers work almost as well.
Robert Heinlein (1907 - 1988)
A morning-glory at my window satisfies me more than the metaphysics of books.
Walt Whitman (1819 - 1892)
This bud of love, by summer's ripening breath,
May prove a beauteous flower when next we meet.
William Shakespeare (1564 - 1616), "Romeo and Juliet", Act 2 scene 2

Food

It's amazing how pervasive food is. Every second commercial is for food. Every second TV episode takes place around a meal. In the city, you can't go ten feet without seeing or smelling a restaurant. There are 20 foot high hamburgers up on billboards. I am acutely aware of food, and its omnipresence is astounding.
Adam Scott, The Monkey Chow Diaries, June 2006
Eat breakfast like a king, lunch like a prince, and dinner like a pauper.
Adelle Davis (1904 - 1974)
We are indeed much more than what we eat, but what we eat can nevertheless help us to be much more than what we are.
Adelle Davis (1904 - 1974)
Although I have been prevented by outward circumstances from observing a strictly vegetarian diet, I have long been an adherent to the cause in principle. Besides agreeing with the aims of vegetarianism for aesthetic and moral reasons, it is my view that a vegetarian manner of living by its purely physical effect on the human temperament would most beneficially influence the lot of mankind.
Albert Einstein (1879 - 1955), Translation of letter to Hermann Huth, December 27, 1930
Eating is always a decision, nobody forces your hand to pick up food and put it into your mouth.
Albert Ellis, Michael Abrams, Lidia Dengelegi, The Art & Science of Rational Eating, 1992
Fat is a barrier, a bellicose statement to others that, to some, justifies hostility in kind. The world says to the fat person, "Your fatness is an affront to me, so we have the right to treat you as offensively as you appear." Fat is not merely viewed as another type of tissue, but as a diagnostic sign, a personal statement, and a measure of personality. Too little fat and we see you as being antisocial, fearful and sexless. Too much fat and we see you as slothful, stupid, and sexually hung up.
Albert Ellis, Michael Abrams, Lidia Dengelegi, The Art & Science of Rational Eating, 1992
Fat people, it is commonly held, should be punished because they offend our aesthetic sensibilities. They take up too much space on subways, buses, airplanes, and elevators. They consume more than they contribute to society. They become ill and need to be taken care of, or they die early and their families are left unsupported. The only way fat people can gain some acceptance and forgiveness for their crime of overeating is to at least try, or look like they are trying, to lose weight. They must never eat an ice cream cone in public, never be seen eating a normal sized portion of non-diet food!
Albert Ellis, Michael Abrams, Lidia Dengelegi, The Art & Science of Rational Eating, 1992
Tomatoes and oregano make it Italian; wine and tarragon make it French. Sour cream makes it Russian; lemon and cinnamon make it Greek. Soy sauce makes it Chinese; garlic makes it good.
Alice May Brock

Tell me what you eat, and I will tell you what you are.
Anthelme Brillat-Savarin (1755 - 1826), The Physiology of Taste, 1825
The moral virtues, then, are produced in us neither by nature nor against nature.
Nature, indeed, prepares in us the ground for their reception, but their complete
formation is the product of habit.
Aristotle (384 BC - 322 BC)
Health food makes me sick.
Calvin Trillin (1935 -)
The most remarkable thing about my mother is that for thirty years she served the
family nothing but leftovers. The original meal has never been found.
Calvin Trillin (1935 -)
Subdue your appetites, my dears, and you've conquered human nature.
Charles Dickens (1812 - 1870)
I no longer prepare food or drink with more than one ingredient.
Cyra McFadden
Eating is really one of your indoor sports. You play three times a day, and it's well
worth while to make the game as pleasant as possible.
Dorothy Draper
My ability to tolerate shame, to compartmentalize it, to swallow it, increased right
along with my belt size. it came with the territory of being heavy. Obese people have
a lifetime of experience with shame.
Edward Ugel, I'm With Fatty: Losing Fifty Pounds in Fifty Miserable Weeks, 2010
The people who can most successfully lose weight and maintain a healthy life style
are foodies. When it comes to healthy eating, people who know how to cook and
make ingredients taste good have a distinct advantage over those who can't.
Edward Ugel, I'm With Fatty: Losing Fifty Pounds in Fifty Miserable Weeks, 2010
He who comes first, eats first. [Familiar as: First come first served.]
Eike von Repkow (~ 1220), Sachsenspiegel
Bear in mind that you should conduct yourself in life as at a feast.
Epictetus (55 AD - 135 AD)
Preach not to others what they should eat, but eat as becomes you, and be silent.
Epictetus (55 AD - 135 AD)
I have never cared much for fish - it floats in the belly as much as in the pond.
Erica Eisdorfer, The Wet Nurse's Tale, 2009
If the divine creator has taken pains to give us delicious and exquisite things to eat,
the least we can do is prepare them well and serve them with ceremony.
Fernand Point
Food is an important part of a balanced diet.
Fran Lebowitz (1950 -)
My favorite animal is steak.
Fran Lebowitz (1950 -)
Music with dinner is an insult both to the cook and the violinist.
G. K. Chesterton (1874 - 1936)
Just as animal research tells us that gluttony and sloth are side effects of a drive to
accumulate body fat, it also says that eating in moderation and being physically
active (literally, having the energy to exercise) are not evidence of moral rectitude.
Rather, they're the metabolic benefits of a body that's programmed to remain lean.
Gary Taubes, Why We Get Fat: And What to Do About It, 2010
We don't get fat because we overeat; we overeat because we're getting fat.
Gary Taubes, Why We Get Fat: And What to Do About It, 2010
Good food ends with good talk.
Geoffrey Neighor, Northern Exposure, Duets, 1993
There is no love sincerer than the love of food.
George Bernard Shaw (1856 - 1950), Man and Superman (1903) act 1
What some call health, if purchased by perpetual anxiety about diet, isn't much better
than tedious disease.
George Dennison Prentice
It's important to begin a search on a full stomach.
Henry Bromel, Northern Exposure, The Big Kiss, 1991
If more of us valued food and cheer and song above hoarded gold, it would be a
merrier world.
J. R. R. Tolkien (1892 - 1973)
Food is our common ground, a universal experience.
James Beard
I went into a McDonald's yesterday and said, 'I'd like some fries.' The girl at the
counter said, 'Would you like some fries with that?'
Jay Leno (1950 -)
Avoidance is a great tool to get away from food in my face all day long.
Jennifer Hudson, I Got This: How I Changed My Ways and Lost What Weighed Me Down, 2012
He liked the idea of coffee quite a lot—a warm drink that gave you energy and had
been for centuries associated with sophisticates and intellectuals. But coffee itself
tasted to him like caffeinated stomach bile.
John Green, An Abundance of Katherines, 2008
Talking of Pleasure, this moment I was writing with one hand, and with the other
holding to my Mouth a Nectarine – how good how fine. It went down all pulpy, slushy,
oozy, all its delicious embonpoint melted down my throat like a large, beautified
Strawberry.
John Keats (1795 - 1821)
The only man who is really free is the one who can turn down an invitation to dinner
without giving an excuse.
Jules Renard (1864 - 1910)
You don't have to cook fancy or complicated masterpieces - just good food from fresh
ingredients.
Julia Child (1912 - 2004)
Water is the most neglected nutrient in your diet but one of the most vital.
Kelly Barton
It's the company, not the cooking, that makes a meal.

Kirby Larson, Hattie Big Sky, 2006
Cakes have such a terrible habit of turning out bad just when you especially want
them to be good.
L. M. Montgomery (1874 - 1942), Anne of Green Gables, 1908
A dinner lubricates business.
Lord William Stowell
What is food to one, is to others bitter poison.
Lucretius (96 BC - 55 BC), De Rerum Natura
Man is what he eats.
Ludwig Feuerbach
Sharing food with another human being is an intimate act that should not be indulged
in lightly.
M. F. K. Fisher
New Orleans food is as delicious as the less criminal forms of sin.
Mark Twain (1835 - 1910)
Part of the secret of success in life is to eat what you like and let the food fight it out
inside.
Mark Twain (1835 - 1910)
There are people who strictly deprive themselves of each and every eatable,
drinkable, and smokable which has in any way acquired a shady reputation. They pay
this price for health. And health is all they get for it. How strange it is. It is like paying
out your whole fortune for a cow that has gone dry.
Mark Twain (1835 - 1910)
The art of dining well is no slight art, the pleasure not a slight pleasure.
Michel de Montaigne (1533 - 1592)
Never eat more than you can lift.
Miss Piggy
I like rice. Rice is great if you're hungry and want 2000 of something.
Mitch Hedberg (1968 - 2005)
When I walk into my kitchen today, I am not alone. Whether we know it or not, none
of us is. We bring fathers and mothers and kitchen tables, and every meal we have
ever eaten. Food is never just food. It's also a way of getting at something else: who
we are, who we have been, and who we want to be.
Molly Wizenberg, A Homemade Life: Stories and Recipes from My Kitchen Table, 2009
Ask not what you can do for your country. Ask what's for lunch.
Orson Welles (1915 - 1985)
My doctor told me to stop having intimate dinners for four. Unless there are three
other people.
Orson Welles (1915 - 1985)
Fish is the only food that is considered spoiled once it smells like what it is.
P. J. O'Rourke (1947 -)
At my age the bones are water in the morning until food is given them.
Pearl Buck (1892 - 1973)
A way to a man's heart is through his stomach, that shit true as gold. You put some
love in your food and a fool can taste it.
Raelle Tucker, True Blood, Cold Ground, 2008
What's sad about not eating is the experience, whether at a family reunion or at
midnight by yourself in a greasy spoon under the L tracks. The loss of dining, not the
loss of food.
Roger Ebert (1942 - 2013), People Magazine, 09-19-11
You can tell a lot about a fellow's character by his way of eating jellybeans.
Ronald Reagan (1911 - 2004), quoted in Observer, March 29 1981
There ain't no such thing as wrong food.
Sean Stewart, Perfect Circle, 2004
If hunger makes you irritable, better eat and be pleasant.
Sefer Hasidim
Food is the most primitive form of comfort.
Sheila Graham
Bad men live that they may eat and drink, whereas good men eat and drink that they
may live.
Socrates (469 BC - 399 BC), from Plutarch, How a Young Man Ought to Hear Poems
Thou shouldst eat to live; not live to eat.
Socrates (469 BC - 399 BC)
Make hunger thy sauce, as a medicine for health.
Thomas Tusser, 1524
I've been on a diet for two weeks and all I've lost is two weeks.
Totie Fields
At a dinner party one should eat wisely but not too well, and talk well but not too
wisely.
W. Somerset Maugham (1874 - 1965)
There are few things so pleasant as a picnic eaten in perfect comfort.
W. Somerset Maugham (1874 - 1965), The Razor's Edge, 1943
I once read cooking is something you do for your family. But when you're alone you
sometimes have to treat yourself like family. And now that my apartment's redolent
with the smell of food it feels more like a home than a box where I hang my hat.
Waiter Rant, Waiter Rant, 01-10-10
He hath eaten me out of house and home.
William Shakespeare (1564 - 1616), "King Henry IV Part II", Act 2 scene 1
The sweetest honey Is loathsome in his own deliciousness And in the taste confounds
the appetite.
William Shakespeare (1564 - 1616), Romeo and Juliet

Forgiveness

Forgive many things in others; nothing in yourself.
Ausonius
Anger makes you smaller, while forgiveness forces you to grow beyond what you
were.

Cherie Carter-Scott, "If Love Is a Game, These Are the Rules"
If you haven't forgiven yourself something, how can you forgive others?
Dolores Huerta
To err is human; to forgive, infrequent.
Franklin P. Adams (1881 - 1960)
Forgiveness does not always lead to a healed relationship. Some people are not
capable of love, and it might be wise to let them go along with your anger. Wish them
well, and let them go their way.
Gordon Atkinson, RealLivePreacher.com Weblog, July 7, 2003
Forgiveness is the healing of wounds caused by another. You choose to let go of a
past wrong and no longer be hurt by it. Forgiveness is a strong move to make, like
turning your shoulders sideways to walk quickly on a crowded sidewalk. It's your
move.
Gordon Atkinson, RealLivePreacher.com Weblog, July 7, 2003
It really doesn't matter if the person who hurt you deserves to be forgiven.
Forgiveness is a gift you give yourself. You have things to do and you want to move
on.
Gordon Atkinson, RealLivePreacher.com Weblog, July 7, 2003
No one forgives with more grace and love than a child.
Gordon Atkinson, Real Live Preacher weblog, 02-15-06
'Tis the most tender part of love, each other to forgive.
John Sheffield
There is no revenge so complete as forgiveness.
Josh Billings (1818 - 1885)
It makes you feel very virtuous when you forgive people, doesn't it?
L. M. Montgomery (1874 - 1942), Anne of Green Gables, 1908
Forgiveness is almost a selfish act because of its immense benefits to the one who
forgives.
Lawana Blackwell, The Dowry of Miss Lydia Clark, 1999
The hatred you're carrying is a live coal in your heart - far more damaging to yourself
than to them.
Lawana Blackwell, The Dowry of Miss Lydia Clark, 1999
The weak can never forgive. Forgiveness is the attribute of the strong.
Mahatma Gandhi (1869 - 1948)
Life is an adventure in forgiveness.
Norman Cousins (1915 - 1990)
Always forgive your enemies; nothing annoys them so much.
Oscar Wilde (1854 - 1900)
It is easier to get forgiveness than permission.
Stuart's Law of Retroaction
The stupid neither forgive nor forget; the naive forgive and forget; the wise forgive
but do not forget.
Thomas Szasz, The Second Sin (1973) "Personal Conduct"
A woman can forgive a man for the harm he does her...but she can never forgive him
for the sacrifices he makes on her account.
W. Somerset Maugham (1874 - 1965), The Moon and Sixpence
It is easier to forgive an enemy than to forgive a friend.
William Blake (1757 - 1827)
Pray you now, forget and forgive.
William Shakespeare (1564 - 1616), "King Lear", Act 4 scene 7

Fortune

Calamities are of two kinds: misfortunes to ourselves, and good fortune to others.
Ambrose Bierce (1842 - 1914), The Devil's Dictionary
We should manage our fortunes as we do our health - enjoy it when good, be patient
when it is bad, and never apply violent remedies except in an extreme necessity.
Francois de La Rochefoucauld (1613 - 1680)
Behind every great fortune there is a crime.
Honore de Balzac (1799 - 1850)
Many men can make a fortune but very few can build a family.
J. S. Bryan
Fortune can, for her pleasure, fools advance,
And toss them on the wheels of Chance.
Juvenal (55 AD - 127 AD)
Depend not on fortune, but on conduct.
Publilius Syrus (~100 BC)
Nature magically suits a man to his fortunes, by making them the fruit of his
character.
Ralph Waldo Emerson (1803 - 1882)
Every man is the architect of his own fortune.
Sallust (86 BC - 34 BC)
Of all human ills, greatest is fortune's wayward tyranny.
Sophocles (496 BC - 406 BC), Ajax
Fortune does not change men, it unmasks them.
Suzanne Necker (1739 - 1794)
Fortune helps the brave.
Terence (185 BC - 159 BC), Phormio
Fortune favors the brave.
Virgil (70 BC - 19 BC), Aeneid
Henceforth I ask not good fortune. I myself am good fortune.
Walt Whitman (1819 - 1892)

Freedom

My definition of a free society is a society where it is safe to be unpopular.
Adlai E. Stevenson Jr. (1900 - 1965), Speech in Detroit, 7 Oct. 1952
Freedom is just Chaos, with better lighting.
Alan Dean Foster, "To the Vanishing Point"
Everything that is really great and inspiring is created by the individual who can labor
in freedom.
Albert Einstein (1879 - 1955), 'Out of My Later Years,' 1950
The basis of a democratic state is liberty.
Aristotle (384 BC - 322 BC), Politics
Because you are in control of your life. Don't ever forget that. You are what you are
because of the conscious and subconscious choices you have made.
Barbara Hall, A Summons to New Orleans, 2000
Those who would give up essential liberty to purchase a little temporary safety
deserve neither liberty nor safety.
Benjamin Franklin (1706 - 1790), Historical Review of Pennsylvania, 1759
If you want to be free, there is but one way; it is to guarantee an equally full measure
of liberty to all your neighbors. There is no other.
Carl Schurz (1829 - 1906)
When we lose the right to be different, we lose the privilege to be free.
Charles Evans Hughes, Address at Faneuil Hall, Boston, Massachusetts, June 17, 1925
You can only protect your liberties in this world by protecting the other man's
freedom. You can only be free if I am free.
Clarence Darrow (1857 - 1938), Address to the jury, trial of Communists, Chicago, Illinois, 1920
We hold in our hands, the most precious gift of all: Freedom. The freedom to express
our art. Our love. The freedom to be who we want to be. We are not going to give that
freedom away and no one shall take it from us!
Diane Frolov and Andrew Schneider, Northern Exposure, Cicely, 1992
Only the educated are free.
Epictetus (55 AD - 135 AD), Discourses
In the truest sense, freedom cannot be bestowed; it must be achieved.
Franklin D. Roosevelt (1882 - 1945), Speech, September 22, 1936
Liberty means responsibility. That is why most men dread it.
George Bernard Shaw (1856 - 1950)
Some tourists think Amsterdam is a city of sin, but in truth it is a city of freedom. And
in freedom, most people find sin.
John Green, The Fault in Our Stars, 2012
The only freedom which deserves the name, is that of pursuing our own good in our
own way, so long as we do not attempt to deprive others of theirs, or impede their
efforts to obtain it.
John Stuart Mill (1806 - 1873), On Liberty, 1859
The First Amendment is often inconvenient. But that is besides the point.
Inconvenience does not absolve the government of its obligation to tolerate speech.
Justice Anthony Kennedy (1936 -)
Patterning your life around other's opinions is nothing more than slavery.
Lawana Blackwell, The Dowry of Miss Lydia Clark, 1999
While the State exists, there can be no freedom. When there is freedom there will be
no State.
Lenin (1870 - 1924), "State and Revolution", 1919
Liberty is not a means to a higher political end. It is itself the highest political end.
Lord Acton, Lecture, February 26, 1877
The most certain test by which we judge whether a country is really free is the amount
of security for the minorities.
Lord Acton
Nobody can give you freedom. Nobody can give you equality or justice or anything. If
you're a man, you take it.
Malcolm X (1925 - 1965), Malcolm X Speaks, 1965
You can't separate peace from freedom because no one can be at peace unless he has
his freedom.
Malcolm X (1925 - 1965), Malcolm X Speaks, 1965
It is by the goodness of God that in our country we have those three unspeakably
precious things: freedom of speech, freedom of conscience, and the prudence never to
practice either of them.
Mark Twain (1835 - 1910), Following the Equator (1897)
This liberty will look easy by and by when nobody dies to get it.
Maxwell Anderson (1888 - 1959), Valley Forge, Act III, 1937
Self-reliance is the only road to true freedom, and being one's own person is its
ultimate reward.
Patricia Sampson
To know what you prefer instead of humbly saying Amen to what the world tells you
you ought to prefer, is to have kept your soul alive.
Robert Louis Stevenson (1850 - 1894)
People demand freedom of speech as a compensation for the freedom of thought
which they seldom use.
Soren Kierkegaard (1813 - 1855)
A man's worst difficulties begin when he is able to do as he likes.
Thomas H. Huxley (1825 - 1895), Address on university education, Baltimore, Maryland,
September 12, 1876
I would rather be exposed to the inconveniences attending too much liberty than to
those attending too small a degree of it.
Thomas Jefferson (1743 - 1826), to Archibald Stuart, 1791
We fight not to enslave, but to set a country free, and to make room upon the earth
for honest men to live in.
Thomas Paine (1737 - 1809), The Crisis, no. 4, September 11, 1777
My definition of a free society is a society where it is safe to be unpopular.

Adlai E. Stevenson Jr. (1900 - 1965), Speech in Detroit, 7 Oct. 1952
Freedom is just Chaos, with better lighting.
Alan Dean Foster, "To the Vanishing Point"
Everything that is really great and inspiring is created by the individual who can labor in freedom.
Albert Einstein (1879 - 1955), 'Out of My Later Years,' 1950
The basis of a democratic state is liberty.
Aristotle (384 BC - 322 BC), Politics
Because you are in control of your life. Don't ever forget that. You are what you are because of the conscious and subconscious choices you have made.
Barbara Hall, A Summons to New Orleans, 2000
Those who would give up essential liberty to purchase a little temporary safety deserve neither liberty nor safety.
Benjamin Franklin (1706 - 1790), Historical Review of Pennsylvania, 1759
If you want to be free, there is but one way; it is to guarantee an equally full measure of liberty to all your neighbors. There is no other.
Carl Schurz (1829 - 1906)
When we lose the right to be different, we lose the privilege to be free.
Charles Evans Hughes, Address at Faneuil Hall, Boston, Massachusetts, June 17, 1925
You can only protect your liberties in this world by protecting the other man's freedom. You can only be free if I am free.
Clarence Darrow (1857 - 1938), Address to the jury, trial of Communists, Chicago, Illinois, 1920
We hold in our hands, the most precious gift of all: Freedom. The freedom to express our art. Our love. The freedom to be who we want to be. We are not going to give that freedom away and no one shall take it from us!
Diane Frolov and Andrew Schneider, Northern Exposure, Cicely, 1992
Only the educated are free.
Epictetus (55 AD - 135 AD), Discourses
In the truest sense, freedom cannot be bestowed; it must be achieved.
Franklin D. Roosevelt (1882 - 1945), Speech, September 22, 1936
Liberty means responsibility. That is why most men dread it.
George Bernard Shaw (1856 - 1950)
Some tourists think Amsterdam is a city of sin, but in truth it is a city of freedom. And in freedom, most people find sin.
John Green, The Fault in Our Stars, 2012
The only freedom which deserves the name, is that of pursuing our own good in our own way, so long as we do not attempt to deprive others of theirs, or impede their efforts to obtain it.
John Stuart Mill (1806 - 1873), On Liberty, 1859
The First Amendment is often inconvenient. But that is besides the point. Inconvenience does not absolve the government of its obligation to tolerate speech.
Justice Anthony Kennedy (1936 -)
Patterning your life around other's opinions is nothing more than slavery.
Lawana Blackwell, The Dowry of Miss Lydia Clark, 1999
While the State exists, there can be no freedom. When there is freedom there will be no State.
Lenin (1870 - 1924), "State and Revolution", 1919
Liberty is not a means to a higher political end. It is itself the highest political end.
Lord Acton, Lecture, February 26, 1877
The most certain test by which we judge whether a country is really free is the amount of security for the minorities.
Lord Acton
Nobody can give you freedom. Nobody can give you equality or justice or anything. If you're a man, you take it.
Malcolm X (1925 - 1965), Malcolm X Speaks, 1965
You can't separate peace from freedom because no one can be at peace unless he has his freedom.
Malcolm X (1925 - 1965), Malcolm X Speaks, 1965
It is by the goodness of God that in our country we have those three unspeakably precious things: freedom of speech, freedom of conscience, and the prudence never to practice either of them.
Mark Twain (1835 - 1910), Following the Equator (1897)
This liberty will look easy by and by when nobody dies to get it.
Maxwell Anderson (1888 - 1959), Valley Forge, Act III, 1937
Self-reliance is the only road to true freedom, and being one's own person is its ultimate reward.
Patricia Sampson
To know what you prefer instead of humbly saying Amen to what the world tells you you ought to prefer, is to have kept your soul alive.
Robert Louis Stevenson (1850 - 1894)
People demand freedom of speech as a compensation for the freedom of thought which they seldom use.
Soren Kierkegaard (1813 - 1855)
A man's worst difficulties begin when he is able to do as he likes.
Thomas H. Huxley (1825 - 1895), Address on university education, Baltimore, Maryland, September 12, 1876
I would rather be exposed to the inconveniences attending too much liberty than to those attending too small a degree of it.
Thomas Jefferson (1743 - 1826), to Archibald Stuart, 1791
We fight not to enslave, but to set a country free, and to make room upon the earth for honest men to live in.
Thomas Paine (1737 - 1809), The Crisis, no. 4, September 11, 1777

Friendship

He who has a thousand friends has not a friend to spare,
And he who has one enemy will meet him everywhere.
Ali ibn-Abi-Talib (602 AD - 661 AD), A Hundred Sayings
Misfortune shows those who are not really friends.
Aristotle (384 BC - 322 BC), Eudemian Ethics
Without friends no one would choose to live, though he had all other goods.
Aristotle (384 BC - 322 BC), Nichomachean Ethics
A good friend can tell you what is the matter with you in a minute. He may not seem such a good friend after telling.
Arthur Brisbane, "The Book of Today"
The meeting of two personalities is like the contact of two chemical substances: if there is any reaction, both are transformed.
Carl Jung (1875 - 1961)
Friendship make prosperity more shining and lessens adversity by dividing and sharing it.
Cicero (106 BC - 43 BC), On Friendship, 44 B.C.
The shifts of Fortune test the reliability of friends.
Cicero (106 BC - 43 BC), De Amicitia
It is wise to apply the oil of refined politeness to the mechanisms of friendship.
Colette (1873 - 1954), The Pure and the Impure, 1932
Being friendless taught me how to be a friend. Funny how that works.
Colleen Wainwright, Communicatrix, 11-09-07
Have no friends not equal to yourself.
Confucius (551 BC - 479 BC), The Confucian Analects
Do not protect yourself by a fence, but rather by your friends.
Czech Proverb
You can make more friends in two months by becoming interested in other people than you can in two years by trying to get other people interested in you.
Dale Carnegie
My mother used to say that there are no strangers, only friends you haven't met yet. She's now in a maximum security twilight home in Australia.
Dame Edna Everage (1934 -)
Friends were like clothes: fine while they lasted but eventually they wore thin or you grew out of them.
David Nicholls, One Day, 2010
You're supposed to trust friends. You have no reason to be his friend? That is part of the pleasure of friendship: trusting without absolute evidence and then being rewarded for that trust.
David Shore, House M.D., Not Cancer, 2008
Never explain—your friends do not need it and your enemies will not believe you anyway.
Elbert Hubbard (1856 - 1915)
Nothing changes your opinion of a friend so surely as success - yours or his.
Franklin P. Jones, Saturday Evening Post, November 29, 1953
Be courteous to all, but intimate with few, and let those few be well tried before you give them your confidence. True friendship is a plant of slow growth, and must undergo and withstand the shocks of adversity before it is entitled to the appellation.
George Washington (1732 - 1799)
Nobody sees a flower - really - it is so small it takes time - we haven't time - and to see takes time, like to have a friend takes time.
Georgia O'Keeffe (1887 - 1986)
There isn't much better in this life than finding a way to spend a few hours in conversation with people you respect and love. You have to carve this time out of your life because you aren't really living without it.
Gordon Atkinson, RealLivePreacher.com Weblog, August 27, 2003
When someone allows you to bear his burdens, you have found deep friendship.
Gordon Atkinson, RealLivePreacher.com Weblog, January 4, 2003
You can forget a lot of things, but you cannot forget a woman's name and claim to love her.
Gordon Atkinson, RealLivePreacher.com Weblog, October 20, 2003
All people want is someone to listen.
Hugh Elliott, Standing Room Only weblog, May 8, 2003
Friendship is certainly the finest balm for the pangs of disappointed love.
Jane Austen (1775 - 1817), Northanger Abbey
Good company requires only birth, education, and manners, and with regard to education is not very nice. Birth and good manners are essential; but a little learning is by no means a dangerous thing in good company; on the contrary, it will do very well.
Jane Austen (1775 - 1817), Persuasion, 1818
Here and there, human nature may be great in times of trial; but generally speaking, it is its weakness and not its strength that appears in a sick chamber: it is selfishness and impatience rather than generosity and fortitude, that one hears of. There is so little real friendship in the world! and unfortunately, there are so many who forget to think seriously till it is almost too late.
Jane Austen (1775 - 1817), Persuasion, 1818
My idea of good company is the company of clever, well-informed people, who have a great deal of conversation; that is what I call good company.
Jane Austen (1775 - 1817), Persuasion, 1818
She felt that she could so much more depend upon the sincerity of those who sometimes looked or said a careless or a hasty thing, than of those whose presence of mind never varied, whose tongue never slipped.
Jane Austen (1775 - 1817), Persuasion, 1818
To flatter and follow others, without being flattered and followed in turn, is but a state of half enjoyment.
Jane Austen (1775 - 1817), Persuasion, 1818
When the character of a man is not clear to you, look at his friends.
Japanese Proverb

Go through your phone book, call people and ask them to drive you to the airport. The ones who will drive you are your true friends. The rest aren't bad people; they're just acquaintances.
Jay Leno (1950 -)
In prosperity our friends know us; in adversity we know our friends.
John Churton Collins
The thing about chameleoning your way through life is that it gets to where nothing is real.
John Green, An Abundance of Katherines, 2008
True happiness is of a retired nature, and an enemy to pomp and noise; it arises, in the first place, from the enjoyment of one's self, and in the next from the friendship and conversation of a few select companions.
Joseph Addison (1672 - 1719), The Spectator, March 17, 1911
Kindred spirits are not so scarce as I used to think. It's splendid to find out there are so many of them in the world.
L. M. Montgomery (1874 - 1942), Anne of Green Gables, 1908
An old friend is like a tender memory or a comfortable shoe. It takes years of caring to get to that point.
Laura Moncur (1969 -), The Secret Heart of Charlotte Lucas, 2014
However difficult it is to be the homely friend of a reputed beauty, there are certain benefits. Most days, the humiliation of being the second choice is outweighed by the overflow of disappointed gentlemen.
Laura Moncur (1969 -), The Secret Heart of Charlotte Lucas, 2014
There is nothing like the razor sharp tongue of a good friend to cut through the lies we tell ourselves.
Laura Moncur (1969 -), Merriton: Twelve Hours from San Francisco, 02-25-09
You don't get to pick your own nickname. They've gotta give you one. It's like we're all tryin' to make pets out of each other and we're not comfortable unless we get to name 'em.
Laura Moncur (1969 -), Merriton: Twelve Hours from San Francisco, 03-26-08
It isn't kind to cultivate a friendship just so one will have an audience.
Lawana Blackwell, The Courtship of the Vicar's Daughter, 1998
A good friend of my son's is a son to me.
Lois McMaster Bujold, Ethan of Athos, 1986
Adversity does teach who your real friends are.
Lois McMaster Bujold, A Civil Campaign, 1999
If you make it plain you like people, it's hard for them to resist liking you back.
Lois McMaster Bujold, Diplomatic Immunity, 2002
Never refuse any advance of friendship, for if nine out of ten bring you nothing, one alone may repay you.
Madame de Tencin
An enemy can partly ruin a man, but it takes a good-natured injudicious friend to complete the thing and make it perfect.
Mark Twain (1835 - 1910), Pudd'nhead Wilson
It's the friends you can call up at four a.m. that matter.
Marlene Dietrich (1901 - 1992)
Don't flatter yourself that friendship authorizes you to say disagreeable things to your intimates. The nearer you come into relation with a person, the more necessary do tact and courtesy become. Except in cases of necessity, which are rare, leave your friend to learn unpleasant things from his enemies; they are ready enough to tell them.
Oliver Wendell Holmes (1809 - 1894), The Autocrat of the Breakfast-Table, 1858
I always like to know everything about my new friends, and nothing about my old ones.
Oscar Wilde (1854 - 1900)
The advice of friends must be received with a judicious reserve; we must not give ourselves up to it and follow it blindly, whether right or wrong.
Pierre Charron
Friends have all things in common.
Plato (427 BC - 347 BC), Dialogues, Phaedrus
Prosperity makes friends, adversity tries them.
Publilius Syrus (~100 BC), Maxims
Treat your friend as if he might become an enemy.
Publilius Syrus (~100 BC), Maxims
The ornament of a house is the friends who frequent it.
Ralph Waldo Emerson (1803 - 1882)
Friendship is being there when someone's feeling low and not being afraid to kick them.
Randy K. Milholland, Something Positive, 11-04-10
It's a lot like nature. You only have as many animals as the ecosystem can support and you only have as many friends as you can tolerate the bitching of.
Randy K. Milholland, Something Positive Comic, 08-16-05
Sometimes the measure of friendship isn't your ability to not harm but your capacity to forgive the things done to you and ask forgiveness for your own mistakes.
Randy K. Milholland, Something Positive Comic, 11-07-05
The only thing that lasts longer than a friend's love is the stupidity that keeps us from knowing any better.
Randy K. Milholland, Something Positive Comic, 09-07-06
We did not start as friends, but as people who respected and admired each other. Crucial, absolutely crucial for a partnership. As soon as we could afford it, we ceased sharing lodgings. Equally crucial.
Raymond Joseph Teller, Fury Letter written to Brian Brushwood, 10-18-93
There was a definite process by which one made people into friends, and it involved talking to them and listening to them for hours at a time.
Rebecca West (1892 - 1983)

Reveal not every secret you have to a friend, for how can you tell but that friend may hereafter become an enemy. And bring not all mischief you are able to upon an enemy, for he may one day become your friend.
Saadi (1184 - 1291)
The friendship that can cease has never been real.
Saint Jerome (374 AD - 419 AD), Letter
To like and dislike the same things, that is indeed true friendship.
Sallust (86 BC - 34 BC), The War with Catiline
If a man does not make new acquaintances as he advances through life, he will soon find himself alone. A man should keep his friendships in constant repair.
Samuel Johnson (1709 - 1784)
Get not your friends by bare compliments, but by giving them sensible tokens of your love.
Socrates (469 BC - 399 BC)
Friends, in my experience, are like ladies' fashions. They come and go with the seasons, and are rarely of such stout stuff as bears repeated wearing.
Stephanie Barron, Jane and the Unpleasantness at Scargrave Manor, 1996
We are like oil and water, but all my other relationships are like oil and vinegar! Delicious!
Takayuki Ikkaku, Arisa Hosaka and Toshihiro Kawabata, Animal Crossing: Wild World, 2005
Purchase not friends by gifts; when thou ceasest to give, such will cease to love.
Thomas Fuller (1608 - 1661)
Friends may come and go, but enemies accumulate.
Thomas Jones (1892 - 1969)
We secure our friends not by accepting favors but by doing them.
Thucydides (471 BC - 400 BC), Peloponnesian War
I've learned that all a person has in life is family and friends. If you lose those, you have nothing, so friends are to be treasured more than anything else in the world.
Trey Parker and Matt Stone, South Park, Prehistoric Ice Man, 1999
Don't walk behind me, I may not lead. Don't walk in front of me, I may not follow. Just walk beside me and be my friend.
Unknown, (often attributed to Albert Camus)
I no doubt deserved my enemies, but I don't believe I deserved my friends.
Walt Whitman (1819 - 1892)
We are advertis'd by our loving friends.
William Shakespeare (1564 - 1616)

Genius

But the fact that some geniuses were laughed at does not imply that all who are laughed at are geniuses. They laughed at Columbus, they laughed at Fulton, they laughed at the Wright brothers. But they also laughed at Bozo the Clown.
Carl Sagan (1934 - 1996)
Genius is of no country.
Charles Churchill
Everyone is born with genius, but most people only keep it a few minutes.
Edgard Varese (1883 - 1965)
Genius may have its limitations, but stupidity is not thus handicapped.
Elbert Hubbard (1856 - 1915)
All these words we use, anybody can be a genius now. It used to be you had to have a thought no one ever had before or you had to invent a number. Now, it's like, "Hey, I've got a cup in case we need another cup." "Dude, you're a genius!"
Louis C. K., Louis C. K.: Hilarious, 2011
Genius hath electric power which earth can never tame.
Lydia M. Child
There's a fine line between genius and insanity. I have erased this line.
Oscar Levant (1906 - 1972)
The public is wonderfully tolerant. It forgives everything except genius.
Oscar Wilde (1854 - 1900), The Critic as Artist, 1891
He was a genius - that is to say, a man who does superlatively and without obvious effort something that most people cannot do by the uttermost exertion of their abilities.
Robertson Davies, "Fifth Business"
Genius might be described as a supreme capacity for getting its possessors into trouble of all kinds.
Samuel Butler (1835 - 1902)
There is no great genius without some touch of madness.
Seneca (5 BC - 65 AD), Epistles
Mediocrity knows nothing higher than itself, but talent instantly recognizes genius.
Sir Arthur Conan Doyle (1859 - 1930), (Sherlock Holmes) Valley of Fear, 1915
Genius is one per cent inspiration, ninety-nine per cent perspiration.
Thomas A. Edison (1847 - 1931), Harper's Monthly, 1932
Genius is one percent inspiration, ninety-nine percent perspiration.
Thomas A. Edison (1847 - 1931), Harper's Monthly, 1932
Men of genius do not excel in any profession because they labor in it, but they labor in it because they excel.
William Hazlitt (1778 - 1830)

Giving

You must give some time to your fellow men. Even if it's a little thing, do something for others - something for which you get no pay but the privilege of doing it.
Albert Schweitzer (1875 - 1965)
The great art of giving consists in this: the gift should cost very little and yet be greatly coveted, so that it may be the more highly appreciated.
Baltasar Gracian
The excellence of a gift lies in its appropriateness rather than in its value.
Charles Dudley Warner (1829 - 1900), 'Eleventh Study,' Backlog Studies, 1873

A compliment is a gift, not to be thrown away carelessly, unless you want to hurt the giver.
Eleanor Hamilton
There is no benefit in the gifts of a bad man.
Euripides (484 BC - 406 BC), Medea, 431 B.C.
One must be poor to know the luxury of giving.
George Eliot (1819 - 1880)
Give what you have. To someone, it may be better than you dare to think.
Henry Wadsworth Longfellow (1807 - 1882)
Make all you can, save all you can, give all you can.
John Wesley (1703 - 1791)
Generosity is giving more than you can, and pride is taking less than you need.
Kahlil Gibran (1883 - 1931)
Do give books - religious or otherwise - for Christmas. They're never fattening, seldom sinful, and permanently personal.
Lenore Hershey
You try to give away what you want yourself.
Lois McMaster Bujold, "Memory", 1996
If we have the opportunity to be generous with our hearts, ourselves, we have no idea of the depth and breadth of love's reach.
Margaret Cho, weblog, 03-09-04
If you want to see what children can do, you must stop giving them things.
Norman Douglas
What a child doesn't receive he can seldom later give.
P. D. James, Time to Be in Earnest
Gifts allow us to demonstrate exactly how little we know about a person. And nothing pisses a person off more than being shoved into the wrong pigeonhole.
Pam Davis, House M.D., It's A Wonderful Lie, 2008
A gift in season is a double favor to the needy.
Publilius Syrus (~100 BC), Moral Sayings, 100 B.C.
He doubly benefits the needy who gives quickly.
Publilius Syrus (~100 BC), Maxims
The spirit in which a thing is given determines that in which the debt is acknowledged; it's the intention, not the face-value of the gift, that's weighed.
Seneca (5 BC - 65 AD), Letters to Lucilius, 100 A.D.
We make a living by what we get, we make a life by what we give.
Sir Winston Churchill (1874 - 1965)
Purchase not friends by gifts; when thou ceasest to give, such will cease to love.
Thomas Fuller (1608 - 1661)
Rich gifts wax poor when givers prove unkind.
William Shakespeare (1564 - 1616), Hamlet, 1600

Goals

A goal without a plan is just a wish.
Antoine de Saint-Exupery (1900 - 1944)
It is a paradoxical but profoundly true and important principle of life that the most likely way to reach a goal is to be aiming not at that goal itself but at some more ambitious goal beyond it.
Arnold Toynbee (1889 - 1975)
The person who makes a success of living is the one who see his goal steadily and aims for it unswervingly. That is dedication.
Cecil B. DeMille (1881 - 1959)
The reason most people never reach their goals is that they don't define them, or ever seriously consider them as believable or achievable. Winners can tell you where they are going, what they plan to do along the way, and who will be sharing the adventure with them.
Denis Watley
Achievable goals are the first step to self improvement.
J. K. Rowling, Harvard Commencement Address, 2008
Before you begin a thing, remind yourself that difficulties and delays quite impossible to foresee are ahead. If you could see them clearly, naturally you could do a great deal to get rid of them but you can't. You can only see one thing clearly and that is your goal. Form a mental vision of that and cling to it through thick and thin.
Kathleen Norris
A successful individual typically sets his next goal somewhat but not too much above his last achievement. In this way he steadily raises his level of aspiration.
Kurt Lewin (1890 - 1947)
Let me tell you the secret that has led me to my goal. My strength lies solely in my tenacity.
Louis Pasteur (1822 - 1895)
We find no real satisfaction or happiness in life without obstacles to conquer and goals to achieve.
Maxwell Maltz, Communication Bulletin for Managers & Supervisors, June 2004
To will is to select a goal, determine a course of action that will bring one to that goal, and then hold to that action till the goal is reached. The key is action.
Michael Hanson
Energy is the essence of life. Every day you decide how you're going to use it by knowing what you want and what it takes to reach that goal, and by maintaining focus.
Oprah Winfrey (1954 -), O Magazine, July 2003
The big secret in life is that there is no big secret. Whatever your goal, you can get there if you're willing to work.
Oprah Winfrey (1954 -), O Magazine
Do not turn back when you are just at the goal.

Publilius Syrus (~100 BC), Maxims
In the absence of clearly-defined goals, we become strangely loyal to performing daily trivia until ultimately we become enslaved by it.
Robert Heinlein (1907 - 1988)
The goal of life is living in agreement with nature.
Zeno (335 BC - 264 BC), from Diogenes Laertius, Lives of Eminent Philosophers

God

This only is denied to God: the power to undo the past.
Agathon (448 BC - 400 BC), from Aristotle, Nicomachean Ethics
At any rate, I am convinced that He [God] does not play dice.
Albert Einstein (1879 - 1955), In a letter to Max Born, 1926
Before God we are all equally wise - and equally foolish.
Albert Einstein (1879 - 1955)
O ye of little faith, who believe that somehow the birth of Christ is dependent upon acknowledgment in a circular from OfficeMax!
Anna Quindlen (1953 -), Newsweek, 01-02-06
Or what about the statue in California currently said to be crying bloody tears? Why worry about the alleged weeping of a plaster effigy when so many actual human beings have reason to cry?
Anna Quindlen (1953 -), Newsweek, 01-02-06
God is not dead but alive and well and working on a much less ambitious project.
Anonymous, Graffito
The gods too are fond of a joke.
Aristotle (384 BC - 322 BC)
Think of yourself as an incandescent power, illuminated and perhaps forever talked to by God and his messengers.
Brenda Ueland
When you want something really bad and you close your eyes and wish for it— God's the guy who ignores you.
Caspian Tredwell-Owen, and Alex Kurtzman, The Island, 2005
All God does is watch us and kill us when we get boring. We must never, ever be boring.
Chuck Palahniuk (1962 -), Invisible Monsters, 1999
You talk to God, you're religious. God talks to you, you're psychotic.
Doris Egan, House M.D., House vs. God, 2006
They say that God is everywhere, and yet we always think of Him as somewhat of a recluse.
Emily Dickinson (1830 - 1886)
Slow but sure moves the might of the gods.
Euripides (484 BC - 406 BC), The Bacchae, circa 407 B.C.
Everyone ought to worship God according to his own inclinations, and not to be constrained by force.
Flavius Josephus (37 AD - 100 AD), Life
Pray as if everything depended upon God and work as if everything depended upon man.
Francis Cardinal Spellman (1889 - 1967)
I could prove God statistically.
George Gallup (1901 - 1984)
Doubting God's existence is okay and perfectly acceptable within Christianity as long as the person doubting remains obedient and committed to the Christian path.
Gordon Atkinson, Real Live Preacher weblog, 06-10-04
EVERY path may lead you to God, even the weird ones. Most of us are on a journey. We're looking for something, though we're not always sure what that is. The way is foggy much of the time. I suggest you slow down and follow some of the side roads that appear suddenly in the mist.
Gordon Atkinson, RealLivePreacher.com Weblog, February 13, 2003
I'm searching through all that has ever been hoped, in praise of what can never be known.
Gordon Atkinson, RealLivePreacher.com Weblog, February 13, 2004
When someone is giving you their theology, their God words, you should listen hard and be very gentle. The time to deliver your God words is when you are asked.
Gordon Atkinson, Real Live Preacher weblog, 03-25-05
The glorious gifts of the gods are not to be cast aside.
Homer (800 BC - 700 BC), The Iliad
The gods, likening themselves to all kinds of strangers, go in various disguises from city to city, observing the wrongdoing and the righteousness of men.
Homer (800 BC - 700 BC), The Odyssey
Whoever obeys the gods, to him they particularly listen.
Homer (800 BC - 700 BC), The Iliad
If there's one thing I know it's God does love a good joke.
Hugh Elliott, Standing Room Only weblog, 05-01-04
Call on God, but row away from the rocks.
Indian Proverb
What can you say about a society that says that God is dead and Elvis is alive?
Irv Kupcinet
God gives every bird its food, but He does not throw it into its nest.
J. G. Holland
I want to believe in intelligent design, and hence I am suspicious of anything that seems to confirm my desire to believe.
James Lileks, The Bleat web log, September 15, 2003
If God lived on earth, people would break his windows.
Jewish Proverb
God must become an activity in our consciousness.

Joel S. Goldsmith
How very odd, to believe God gave you life, and yet not think that life asks more of you than watching TV.
John Green, An Abundance of Katherines, 2008
I don't think God gives a shit if we have a dog or if a woman wears shorts. I think He gives a shit about whether you're a good person.
John Green, An Abundance of Katherines, 2008
In God's wildness lies the hope of the world - the great fresh unblighted, unredeemed wilderness. The galling harness of civilization drops off, and wounds heal ere we are aware.
John Muir (1838 - 1914), John of the Mountains, 1938
No synonym for God is so perfect as Beauty. Whether as seen carving the lines of the mountains with glaciers, or gathering matter into stars, or planning the movements of water, or gardening - still all is Beauty!
John Muir (1838 - 1914), Atlantic Monthly, January 1869
We all flow from one fountain Soul. All are expressions of one Love. God does not appear, and flow out, only from narrow chinks and round bored wells here and there in favored races and places, but He flows in grand undivided currents, shoreless and boundless over creeds and forms and all kinds of civilizations and peoples and beasts, saturating all and fountainizing all.
John Muir (1838 - 1914), Badè's Life and Letters of John Muir: June 9, 1872 letter to Miss Catharine Merrill, from New Sentinel Hotel, Yosemite Valley
We must accept that this creative pulse within us is God's creative pulse itself.
Joseph Chilton Pearce
If I really wanted to pray I'll tell you what I'd do. I'd go out into a great big field all alone or into the deep, deep, woods, and I'd look up into the sky—up—up—up—into that lovely blue sky that looks as if there was no end to its blueness. And then I'd just FEEL a prayer.
L. M. Montgomery (1874 - 1942), Anne of Green Gables, 1908
Or perhaps she's just softening me up: she's a Baptist, she'd like me to find Jesus, or vice versa, before it's too late. That kind of thing doesn't run in her family: her mother Reenie never went in much for God. There was mutual respect, and if you were in trouble, naturally you'd call on him, as with lawyers, but as with lawyers, it would have to be bad trouble. Otherwise it didn't pay to get too mixed up with him.
Margaret Atwood (1939 -), The Blind Assassin
It is the creative potential itself in human beings that is the image of God.
Mary Daly
Sometimes it seems like God is difficult to find and impossibly far away. We get so caught up in our small daily duties and irritations that they become the only things that we can focus on. What we forget is that God's love and beauty are all around us, every day, if only we would take the time to look up and see them.
Matthias, Correction Weblog, 11-01-03
I think there's a god and I know it's not me.
Michael J. Fox (1961 -), Good Housekeeping, June 2011
No matter how slow the film, Spirit always stands still long enough for the photographer It has chosen.
Minor White
I know God will not give me anything I can't handle. I just wish that He didn't trust me so much.
Mother Teresa (1910 - 1997)
I think that God in creating Man somewhat overestimated his ability.
Oscar Wilde (1854 - 1900)
God made everything out of nothing, but the nothingness shows through.
Paul Valery (1871 - 1945)
How do you define God? Like this. A God I could understand, at least potentially, was infinitely more interesting and relevant than one that defied comprehension.
Robert J. Sawyer (1960 -), "Calculating God", 2000
You can't be angry with God and not believe in him at the same time.
Sara B. Cooper, House, Damned If You Do, 2004
Live among men as if God beheld you; speak to God as if men were listening.
Seneca (5 BC - 65 AD), Epistles
The universe will reward you for taking risks on its behalf.
Shakti Gawain
Operationally, God is beginning to resemble not a ruler but the last fading smile of a cosmic Cheshire cat.
Sir Julian Huxley (1887 - 1975)
To believe in God or in a guiding force because someone tells you to is the height of stupidity. We are given senses to receive our information within. With our own eyes we see, and with our own skin we feel. With our intelligence, it is intended that we understand. But each person must puzzle it out for himself or herself.
Sophy Burnham
Whatever God's dream about man may be, it seems certain it cannot come true unless man cooperates.
Stella Terrill Mann
When a man takes one step toward God, God takes more steps toward that man than there are sands in the worlds of time.
The Work of the Chariot
God is a comedian playing to an audience too afraid to laugh.
Voltaire (1694 - 1778)
A God that can be understood is no God. Who can explain the Infinite in words?
W. Somerset Maugham (1874 - 1965), The Razor's Edge, 1943
We didn't think much in the air corps of a fellow who wangled a cushy job out of his C.O. by buttering him up. It was hard for me to believe that God thought much of a man who tried to wangle salvation by fulsome flattery. I should have thought the worship most pleasing to him was to do your best according to your lights.
W. Somerset Maugham (1874 - 1965), The Razor's Edge, 1943

We want God to come and save us. But he won't. God doesn't stop levees from failing, he doesn't stay the force of tsunamis, and he doesn't stop planes from smashing into buildings. Deus Ex Machina is overrated.
Waiter Rant, Waiter Rant weblog, 09-09-05
I say to mankind, Be not curious about God. For I, who am curious about each, am not curious about God - I hear and behold God in every object, yet understand God not in the least.
Walt Whitman (1819 - 1892)
I myself do nothing. The Holy Spirit accomplishes all through me.
William Blake (1757 - 1827)
If only God would give me some clear sign! Like making a large deposit in my name in a Swiss bank.
Woody Allen (1935 -)

Golf

The place of the father in the modern suburban family is a very small one, particularly if he plays golf.
Bertrand Russell (1872 - 1970)
If you watch a game, it's fun. If you play at it, it's recreation. If you work at it, it's golf.
Bob Hope (1903 - 2003)
Golf isn't a game, it's a choice that one makes with one's life.
Charles Rosin, Northern Exposure, Aurora Borealis, 1990
There's something intrinsically therapeutic about choosing to spend your time in a wide, open park- like setting that non-golfers can never truly understand.
Charles Rosin, Northern Exposure, Aurora Borealis, 1990
Although golf was originally restricted to wealthy, overweight Protestants, today it's open to anybody who owns hideous clothing.
Dave Barry (1947 -)
It is impossible to imagine Goethe or Beethoven being good at billiards or golf.
H. L. Mencken (1880 - 1956)
Golf and sex are about the only things you can enjoy without being good at.
Jimmy Demaret
The income tax has made more liars out of the American people than golf has.
Will Rogers (1879 - 1935), Illiterate Digest (1924), "Helping the Girls with their Income Taxes"

Gossip
May no portent of evil be attached to the words I say.
Anonymous
To harken to evil conversation is the road to wickedness.. (Pravis Assuescere Sermonibus Est Via Ad Rem Ipsam)
Anonymous
No one gossips about other people's secret virtues.
Bertrand Russell (1872 - 1970)
We cannot control the evil tongues of others; but a good life enables us to disregard them.
Cato the Elder (234 BC - 149 BC)
There is so much good in the worst of us,
And so much bad in the best of us,
That it hardly behooves any of us
To talk about the rest of us.
Edward Wallis Hoch (1849 - 1925), Marion (Kansas) Record
Facts or opinions which are to pass through the hands of so many, to be misconceived by folly in one, and ignorance in another, can hardly have much truth left.
Jane Austen (1775 - 1817), Persuasion, 1818
Never tell evil of a man, if you do not know it for certainty, and if you know it for a certainty, then ask yourself, 'Why should I tell it?'
Johann K. Lavater
A rumor without a leg to stand on will get around some other way.
John Tudor
Many species reciprocate, but only humans gossip, and much of what we gossip about is the vale of other people as partners for reciprocal relationships.
Jonathan Haidt, The Happiness Hypothesis: Finding Modern Truth in Ancient Wisdom, 2005
Once you have listened to the gossip for some time, you will soon feel as if you know everyone, even if you have never met them.
Monica Fairview, Darcy Cousins, 2010
Scandal is gossip made tedious by morality.
Oscar Wilde (1854 - 1900), Lady Windermere's Fan, 1892, Act III
Have I inadvertently said some evil thing?
Phocion (402 BC - 318 BC), from Plutarch, Apothegms
No sword bites so fiercely as an evil tongue.
Sir Philip Sidney (1554 - 1586)
Whoever gossips to you will gossip about you.
Spanish Proverb
Live in such a way that you would not be ashamed to sell your parrot to the town gossip.
Will Rogers (1879 - 1935)
Rumor travels faster, but it don't stay put as long as truth.
Will Rogers (1879 - 1935), 'Politics Getting Ready to Jell,' The Illiterate Digest, 1924
The only time people dislike gossip is when you gossip about them.
Will Rogers (1879 - 1935)
Ill deeds are doubled with an evil word.
William Shakespeare (1564 - 1616)

Government

There is an important sense in which government is distinctive from administration. One is perpetual, the other is temporary and changeable. A man may be loyal to his government and yet oppose the particular principles and methods of administration.
Abraham Lincoln (1809 - 1865), Congressional Record, April 15, 1942
While the people retain their virtue, and vigilance, no administration, by any extreme of wickedness or folly, can very seriously injure the government, in the short space of four years.
Abraham Lincoln (1809 - 1865), First Inaugural Adress, march 4, 1861
What we should be asking is not whether we need a big government or small government, but how we can create a smarter and better government.
Barack Obama (1961 -), University of Michigan Commencement, 2010
When our government is spoken of as some menacing, threatening, foreign entity, it ignores the fact that in our democracy, government is us.
Barack Obama (1961 -), University of Michigan Commencement, 2010
There is no nonsense so arrant that it cannot be made the creed of the vast majority by adequate governmental action.
Bertrand Russell (1872 - 1970)
For every action there is an equal and opposite government program.
Bob Wells
Government is too big and too important to be left to the politicians.
Chester Bowles (1901 - 1986)
Many people consider the things which government does for them as social progress, but they consider the things government does for others as socialism.
Earl Warren (1891 - 1974)
After two years in Washington, I often long for the realism and sincerity of Hollywood.
Fred Thompson, Speech before the Commonwealth Club of California
You know what's interesting about Washington? It's the kind of place where second-guessing has become second nature.
George W. Bush (1946 -), Speech on May 17, 2002
I believe that truth is the glue that holds government together , not only our government but civilization itself. That bond, though strained, is unbroken at home and abroad.
Gerald R. Ford (1913 - 2006), Remarks on taking the oath of office, August 9, 1974 `
If the government is big enough to give you everything you want, it is big enough to take away everything you have.
Gerald R. Ford (1913 - 2006)
In a political sense, there is one problem that currently underlies all of the others. That problem is making Government sufficiently responsive to the people. If we dont make government responsive to the people, we dont make it believable. And we must make government believable if we are to have a functioning democracy.
Gerald R. Ford (1913 - 2006), Address at Jacksonville University, December 16, 1971
The American wage earner and the American housewife are a lot better economists than most economists care to admit. They know that a government big enough to give you everything you want is a government big enough to take from you everything you have.
Gerald R. Ford (1913 - 2006), Remarks to a Joint Session of Congress, August 12, 1974
Every decent man is ashamed of the government he lives under.
H. L. Mencken (1880 - 1956)
I believe that all government is evil, and that trying to improve it is largely a waste of time.
H. L. Mencken (1880 - 1956)
The government consists of a gang of men exactly like you and me. They have, taking one with another, no special talent for the business of government; they have only a talent for getting and holding office.
H. L. Mencken (1880 - 1956)
Whenever you have an efficient government you have a dictatorship.
Harry S Truman (1884 - 1972), Lecture at Columbia University, 28 Apr. 1959
If men were angels, no government would be necessary. If angels were to govern men, neither external nor internal controls on government would be necessary. In framing a government which is to be administered by men over men, the great difficulty lies in this: you must first enable the government to control the governed; and in the next place oblige it to control itself.
James Madison (1751 - 1836), The Federalist Papers, 1788
Before my term has ended, we shall have to test anew whether a nation organized and governed such as ours can endure. The outcome is by no means certain.
John F. Kennedy (1917 - 1963), Annual message to Congress on the State of the Union, January 30, 196]
You will find that the State is the kind of organization which, though it does big things badly, does small things badly, too.
John Kenneth Galbraith (1908 - 2006)
The mystery of government is not how Washington works but how to make it stop.
P. J. O'Rourke (1947 -)
Sure there are dishonest men in local government. But there are dishonest men in national government too.
Richard M. Nixon (1913 - 1994)
The best minds are not in government. If any were, business would hire them right away.
Ronald Reagan (1911 - 2004)
So they [the Government] go on in strange paradox, decided only to be undecided, resolved to be irresolute, adamant for drift, solid for fluidity, all-powerful to be impotent.
Sir Winston Churchill (1874 - 1965), Hansard, November 12, 1936
We must judge of a form of government by its general tendency, not by happy accidents.
Thomas Babington Macaulay (1800 - 1859), Speech on Parliamentary reform, March 2, 1831

In the long-run every Government is the exact symbol of its People, with their wisdom and unwisdom; we have to say, Like People like Government.
Thomas Carlyle (1795 - 1881), Past and Present, 1843
Any government is potentially the worst client in the world you could ever possibly want to have.
Thomas Heatherwick, TED, Building the Seed Cathedral, March 2011
Disbelief in magic can force a poor soul into believing in government and business.
Tom Robbins (1936 -)
It is dangerous to be right when the government is wrong.
Voltaire (1694 - 1778)
I don't make jokes. I just watch the government and report the facts.
Will Rogers (1879 - 1935), quoted in Saturday Review, Aug. 25, 1962
There's no trick to being a humorist when you have the whole government working for you.
Will Rogers (1879 - 1935)
The marvel of all history is the patience with which men and women submit to burdens unnecessarily laid upon them by their governments.
William H. Borah

Gratitude

Gratitude is born in hearts that take time to count up past mercies.
Charles E. Jefferson (1860 - 1937)
Gratitude is not only the greatest of virtues, but the parent of all others.
Cicero (106 BC - 43 BC), 'Pro Plancio,' 54 B.C.
Gratitude is merely the secret hope of further favors.
Francois de La Rochefoucauld (1613 - 1680)
Gratitude is the most exquisite form of courtesy.
Jacques Maritain (1882 - 1973), Reflections on America, 1958
There but for the grace of God go [I].
John Bradford, Encyclopedia of Word and Phrase Origins
I was thinking about the universe wanting to be noticed, and how I had to notice it as best I could. I felt that I owed a debt to the universe that only my attention could repay, and also that I owed a debt to everybody who didn't get to be a person anymore and everyone who hadn't gotten to be a person yet.
John Green, The Fault in Our Stars, 2012
Gratitude can sometimes be as annoying as whininess.
Josh Lieb, I am a Genius of Unspeakable Evil and I Want to be Your Class President, 2009
It's a sign of mediocrity when you demonstrate gratitude with moderation.
Roberto Benigni (1952 -), in Newsweek

Greatness

Some are born great, some achieve greatness, and some hire public relations officers.
Daniel J. Boorstin (1914 -)
It is the nature of all greatness not to be exact.
Edmund Burke (1729 - 1797)
Greatness is more than potential. It is the execution of that potential. Beyond the raw talent. You need the appropriate training. You need the discipline. You need the inspiration. You need the drive.
Eric A. Burns, Gossamer Commons, 08-12-05
By constant self-discipline and self-control you can develop greatness of character.
Grenville Kleiser
I don't confuse greatness with perfection. To be great anyhow is...the higher achievement.
Lois McMaster Bujold, "Mirror Dance", 1994
There are some men who lift the age they inhabit, till all men walk on higher ground in that lifetime.
Maxwell Anderson (1888 - 1959), Valley Forge, Act II, scene ii, 1937
There be three things which make a nation great and prosperous: a fertile soil, busy workshops, easy conveyance for men and goods from place to place.
Sir Francis Bacon (1561 - 1626)
The price of greatness is responsibility.
Sir Winston Churchill (1874 - 1965)
Do not trust people. They are capable of greatness.
Stanislaw Lem (1921 - 2006), "Holiday", September 1963
We have, I fear, confused power with greatness.
Stewart L. Udall (1920 -), commencement address, Dartmouth College, June 13, 1965
The measure of a country's greatness is its ability to retain compassion in times of crisis.
Thurgood Marshall (1908 - 1993)
The secret of greatness is simple: do better work than any other man in your field - and keep on doing it.
Wilfred A. Peterson
Be not afraid of greatness: some men are born great, some achieve greatness and some have greatness thrust upon them.
William Shakespeare (1564 - 1616), 'Twelfth Night'

Greed

Not greedy of filthy lucre.
Bible, 1 Timothy iii. 3.
Greedy eaters dig their graves with their teeth.
French Proverb
The chief weapon of sea pirates, however, was their capacity to astonish. Nobody else could believe, until it was too late, how heartless and greedy they were.
Kurt Vonnegut (1922 - 2007), Breakfast of Champions
Seek not happiness too greedily, and be not fearful of happiness.

Lao-tzu (604 BC - 531 BC)
There is no calamity greater than lavish desires.
There is no greater guilt than discontentment.
And there is no greater disaster than greed.
Lao-tzu (604 BC - 531 BC), The Way of Lao-tzu

Grief

Employment is the surest antidote to sorrow.
Ann Radcliffe (1764 - 1823), The Mysteries of Udolpho, 1764
It is light grief that can take counsel.
Anonymous
Grief is the agony of an instant, the indulgence of grief the blunder of a life.
Benjamin Disraeli (1804 - 1881)
These days grief seems like walking on a frozen river; most of the time he feels safe enough, but there is always that danger he will plunge through.
David Nicholls, One Day, 2010
Grief is Newark. It's there. Can't avoid it. The idea is to hold your nose, hope the traffic's not too bad and get on to Manhattan as quickly as possible.
Eli Attie, House M.D., Dying Changes Everything, 2008
Waste not fresh tears over old griefs.
Euripides (484 BC - 406 BC)
The only cure for grief is action.
George Henry Lewes
Even his griefs are a joy long after to one that remembers all that he wrought and endured.
Homer (800 BC - 700 BC), The Odyssey
Grief does not change you, it reveals you.
John Green, The Fault in Our Stars, 2012
It seems the misfortune of one can plow a deeper furrow in the heart than the misfortune of millions.
Kirby Larson, Hattie Big Sky, 2006
Grief can take care of itself; but to get the full value of a joy you must have someone to divide it with.
Mark Twain (1835 - 1910)
While grief is fresh, every attempt to divert only irritates. You must wait till it be digested, and then amusement will dissipate the remains of it.
Samuel Johnson (1709 - 1784)
Grief teaches the steadiest minds to waver.
Sophocles (496 BC - 406 BC), Antigone
The greatest griefs are those we cause ourselves.
Sophocles (496 BC - 406 BC), Oedipus Rex
I just realized that there's going to be a lot of painful times in life, so I better learn to deal with it the right way.
Trey Parker and Matt Stone, South Park, Raisins, 2003
What's gone and what's past help
Should be past grief.
William Shakespeare (1564 - 1616), "The Winter's Tale", Act 3 scene 2

Guilt

I don't believe in guilt, I believe in living on impulse as long as you never intentionally hurt another person, and don't judge people in your life. I think you should live completely free.
Angelina Jolie (1975 -)
A guilty conscience needs no accuser.
Anonymous
Guilt is a rope that wears thin.
Ayn Rand (1905 - 1982)
If all the world hated you and believed you wicked, while your own conscience approved of you and absolved you from guilt, you would not be without friends.
Charlotte Bronte (1816 - 1855), Jane Eyre pg. 61
Guilt is helpful only when it keeps us acting in line with our beliefs and morals. Otherwise, it creates needless suffering.
Julie A., M.A. Ross and Judy Corcoran, Joint Custody with a Jerk: Raising a Child with an Uncooperative Ex, 2011
Peace visits not the guilty mind.
(Nemo Malus Felix)
Juvenal (55 AD - 127 AD)
Guilt is anger directed at ourselves--at what we did or did not do.
Peter McWilliams, Life 101
Many people weigh the guilt they will feel against the pleasure of the forbidden action they want to take.
Peter McWilliams, Life 101
When they call the roll in the Senate, the Senators do not know whether to answer 'Present' or 'Not guilty.'
Theodore Roosevelt (1858 - 1919)
Nothing is more wretched than the mind of a man conscious of guilt.
Titus Maccius Plautus (254 BC - 184 BC)
Glory built on selfish principles is shame and guilt.
William Cowper (1731 - 1800)
So full of artless jealousy is guilt,
It spills itself in fearing to be spilt.
William Shakespeare (1564 - 1616), "Hamlet", Act 4 scene 5
Suspicion always haunts the guilty mind.
William Shakespeare (1564 - 1616)
Suspicion always haunts the guilty mind; the thief doth fear each bush an officer.
William Shakespeare (1564 - 1616), Henry VI, Part III, Act V, sc. 6

Habits

Curious things, habits. People themselves never knew they had them.
Agatha Christie (1890 - 1976)
Good habits result from resisting temptation.
Ancient Proverb
My problem lies in reconciling my gross habits with my net income.
Errol Flynn (1909 - 1959)
Habit is habit and not to be flung out of the window by any man, but coaxed downstairs a step at a time.
Mark Twain (1835 - 1910)
Habit is habit, and not to be flung out the window by man, but coaxed downstairs, a step at a time.
Mark Twain (1835 - 1910)
Nothing is stronger than habit.
Ovid (43 BC - 17 AD), Ars Amatoria
The chains of habit are too weak to be felt until they are too strong to be broken.
Samuel Johnson (1709 - 1784)
How use doth breed a habit in a man!
William Shakespeare (1564 - 1616), "The Two Gentlemen of Verona", Act 5 scene 4

Happiness

Most folks are about as happy as they make up their minds to be.
Abraham Lincoln (1809 - 1865)
The secret of happiness is to make others believe they are the cause of it.
Al Batt, in National Enquirer
Happiness is nothing more than good health and a bad memory.
Albert Schweitzer (1875 - 1965)
The happiness of a man in this life does not consist in the absence but in the mastery of his passions.
Alfred Lord Tennyson (1809 - 1892)
A person is never happy except at the price of some ignorance.
Anatole France (1844 - 1924)
Happiness arises in a state of peace, not of tumult.
Ann Radcliffe (1764 - 1823), The Mysteries of Udolpho, 1764
The discovery of a new dish does more for human happiness than the discovery of a new star.
Anthelme Brillat-Savarin (1755 - 1826), Physiologie du Gout, 1825
Happiness depends upon ourselves.
Aristotle (384 BC - 322 BC)
Happiness is that state of consciousness which proceeds from the achievement of one's values.
Ayn Rand (1905 - 1982)
Do not weep; do not wax indignant. Understand.
Baruch Spinoza (1632 - 1677)
Content makes poor men rich; discontentment makes rich men poor.
Benjamin Franklin (1706 - 1790)
If there were in the world today any large number of people who desired their own happiness more than they desired the unhappiness of others, we could have paradise in a few years.
Bertrand Russell (1872 - 1970)
All I can say about life is, Oh God, enjoy it!
Bob Newhart (1929 -)
The pursuit of happiness is a most ridiculous phrase; if you pursue happiness you'll never find it.
C. P. Snow (1905 - 1980)
Happiness is not the absence of problems, but the ability to deal with them.
Charles de Montesquieu (1689 - 1755)
Cherish all your happy moments: they make a fine cushion for old age.
Christopher Morley (1890 - 1957)
This is the best kind of voyeurism, hearing joy from your neighbors.
Chuck Sigars, The World According to Chuck weblog, October 14, 2003
With coarse rice to eat, with water to drink, and my bended arm for a pillow - I have still joy in the midst of these things. Riches and honors acquired by unrighteousness are to me as a floating cloud.
Confucius (551 BC - 479 BC), The Confucian Analects
Sometimes it's hard to avoid the happiness of others.
David Assael, Northern Exposure, Our Tribe, 1992
He wanted to live life in such a way that if a photograph were taken at random it would be a cool photograph. Things should look right. Fun; there should be a lot of fun and no more sadness than absolutely necessary.
David Nicholls, One Day, 2010
All sanity depends on this: that it should be a delight to feel heat strike the skin, a delight to stand upright, knowing the bones are moving easily under the flesh.
Doris Lessing
Slow down and enjoy life. It's not only the scenery you miss by going too fast - you also miss the sense of where you are going and why.
Eddie Cantor (1892 - 1964)
Happiness is a mystery like religion, and should never be rationalized.
G. K. Chesterton (1874 - 1936)
A lifetime of happiness! No man alive could bear it: it would be hell on earth.
George Bernard Shaw (1856 - 1950), "Man and Superman" (1903), act I
Happiness is having a large, loving, caring, close-knit family in another city.
George Burns (1896 - 1996)
Happiness is the only sanction of life; where happiness fails, existence remains a mad and lamentable experiment.
George Santayana (1863 - 1952)

To be stupid, selfish, and have good health are three requirements for happiness, though if stupidity is lacking, all is lost.
<u>Gustave Flaubert</u> (1821 - 1880)
Many persons have a wrong idea of what constitutes true happiness. It is not attained through self-gratification but through fidelity to a worthy purpose.
<u>Helen Keller</u> (1880 - 1968)
Man is the artificer of his own happiness.
<u>Henry David Thoreau</u> (1817 - 1862), Journal, January 21, 1838
If we cannot live so as to be happy, let us least live so as to deserve it.
<u>Immanuel Hermann Fichte</u>
I am a kind of paranoiac in reverse. I suspect people of plotting to make me happy.
<u>J. D. Salinger</u> (1919 -)
Personal happiness lies in knowing that life is not a checklist of acquisition or achievement. Your qualifications are not your life.
<u>J. K. Rowling</u>, Harvard Commencement Address, 2008
The foolish man seeks happiness in the distance, the wise grows it under his feet.
<u>James Oppenheim</u>
At the height of laughter, the universe is flung into a kaleidoscope of new possibilities.
<u>Jean Houston</u>
Happiness: a good bank account, a good cook and a good digestion.
<u>Jean Jacques Rousseau</u> (1712 - 1778)
The bird of paradise alights only upon the hand that does not grasp.
<u>John Berry</u>, Flight of White Crows
Why not be happy after a while? You get to a certain age where you prepare yourself for happiness. Sometimes you never remember to get happy.
<u>John Mayer</u>, The Ellen DeGeneres Show, 05-14-12
Nothing is miserable unless you think it so; and on the other hand, nothing brings happiness unless you are content with it.
<u>Jonathan Haidt</u>, The Happiness Hypothesis: Finding Modern Truth in Ancient Wisdom, 2005
The final moment of success is often no more thrilling than taking off a heavy backpack at the end of a long hike. If you went on the hike only to feel that pleasure, you are a fool. Yet people sometimes do just this. They work hard at a task and expect some special euphoria at the end. But when they achieve success and find only moderate and short-lived pleasure, they ask is that all there is? They devalue their accomplishments as a striving after wind. We can call this the progress principle: Pleasure comes more from making progress toward goals than from achieving them.
<u>Jonathan Haidt</u>, The Happiness Hypothesis: Finding Modern Truth in Ancient Wisdom, 2005
True happiness is of a retired nature, and an enemy to pomp and noise; it arises, in the first place, from the enjoyment of one's self, and in the next from the friendship and conversation of a few select companions.
<u>Joseph Addison</u> (1672 - 1719), The Spectator, March 17, 1911
It is an aspect of happiness to suppose we all deserve it.
<u>Joseph Joubert</u>
Laughing is the sensation of feeling good all over and showing it principally in one spot.
<u>Josh Billings</u> (1818 - 1885)
Your primary goal should be to have a great life. You can still have a good day, enjoy your child, and ultimately find happiness, whether your ex is acting like a jerk or a responsible person. Your happiness is not dependent upon someone else.
<u>Julie A., M.A. Ross and Judy Corcoran, Joint Custody with a Jerk: Raising a Child with an Uncooperative Ex</u>, 2011
It is pretty hard to tell what does bring happiness; poverty and wealth have both failed.
<u>Kin Hubbard</u> (1868 - 1930)
Seek not happiness too greedily, and be not fearful of happiness.
<u>Lao-tzu</u> (604 BC - 531 BC)
I've decided that the key to happiness is low expectations.
<u>Laura Moncur</u> (1969 -), Merriton: Twelve Hours from San Francisco, 06-04-08
Joy is not a commodity to be hoarded and protected. It is like a muscle. It must be used daily to keep strong and vigorous. For all my hardships, I have been able to remain quite joyful, for my muscles are strong.
<u>Laura Moncur</u> (1969 -), The Secret Heart of Charlotte Lucas, 2014
I've grown to realize the joy that comes from little victories is preferable to the fun that comes from ease and the pursuit of pleasure.
<u>Lawana Blackwell</u>, The Courtship of the Vicar's Daughter, 1998
I cannot believe that the inscrutable universe turns on an axis of suffering; surely the strange beauty of the world must somewhere rest on pure joy!
<u>Louise Bogan</u>
Happiness is when what you think, what you say, and what you do are in harmony.
<u>Mahatma Gandhi</u> (1869 - 1948)
Very little is needed to make a happy life.
<u>Marcus Aurelius Antoninus</u> (121 AD - 180 AD), Meditations
Happiness is not a state to arrive at, but a manner of traveling.
<u>Margaret Lee Runbeck</u>
In order for people to be happy, sometimes they have to take risks. It's true these risks can put them in danger of being hurt.
<u>Meg Cabot</u>, The Boy Next Door, 2002
If we only wanted to be happy it would be easy; but we want to be happier than other people, which is almost always difficult, since we think them happier than they are.
<u>Montesquieu</u>
When you relinquish the desire to control your future, you can have more happiness.
<u>Nicole Kidman</u>, in The Scotsman
I define joy as a sustained sense of well-being and internal peace - a connection to what matters.
<u>Oprah Winfrey</u> (1954 -), O Magazine

In order to be truly happy, you must live along with, and you must stand for something larger than yourself.
<u>Oprah Wintrey</u> (1954 -), Stanford Commencement Adress, 2008
Happiness isn't something you experience; it's something you remember.
<u>Oscar Levant</u> (1906 - 1972)
And isn't that, at it's core, what the princess fantasy is about for all of us? "Princess" is how we tell little girls that they are special, precious. "Princess" is the wish that we could protect them from pain, that they would never know sorrow, that they will live happily ever after ensconces in lace and innocence.
<u>Peggy Orenstein</u>, Cinderella Ate My Daughter: Dispatches from the Front Lines of the New Girlie-Girl Culture, 2011
No man is happy who does not think himself so.
<u>Publilius Syrus</u> (100 BC), Maxims
One of the keys to happiness is a bad memory.
<u>Rita Mae Brown</u>
Happiness makes up in height for what it lacks in length.
<u>Robert Frost</u> (1874 - 1963)
Most of us believe in trying to make other people happy only if they can be happy in ways which we approve.
<u>Robert S. Lynd</u>
Happiness is always a by-product. It is probably a matter of temperament, and for anything I know it may be glandular. But it is not something that can be demanded from life, and if you are not happy you had better stop worrying about it and see what treasures you can pluck from your own brand of unhappiness.
<u>Robertson Davies</u>
Remember that happiness is a way of travel - not a destination.
<u>Roy M. Goodman</u>
Happiness comes of the capacity to feel deeply, to enjoy simply, to think freely, to risk life, to be needed.
<u>Storm Jameson</u>
Depend not on another, but lean instead on thyself...True happiness is born of self-reliance.
<u>The laws of Manu</u>
Happiness is an imaginary condition, formerly attributed by the living to the dead, now usually attributed by adults to children, and by children to adults.
<u>Thomas Szasz</u>, The Second Sin (1973) "Emotions"
Life's greatest happiness is to be convinced we are loved.
<u>Victor Hugo</u> (1802 - 1885), Les Miserables, 1862
Remember that it is nothing to do your duty, that is demanded of you and is no more meritorious than to wash your hands when they are dirty; the only thing that counts is the love of duty; when love and duty are one, then grace is in you and you will enjoy a happiness which passes all understanding.
<u>W. Somerset Maugham</u> (1874 - 1965), The Painted Veil, 1925
The only true happiness comes from squandering ourselves for a purpose.
<u>William Cowper</u> (1731 - 1800)
The greatest happiness you can have is knowing that you do not necessarily require happiness.
<u>William Saroyan</u> (1908 - 1981)
It is better to be hated for what you are than to be loved for what you are not.
<u>Andre Gide</u> (1869 - 1951)
We hate some persons because we do not know them; and we will not know them because we hate them.
<u>Charles Caleb Colton</u> (1780 - 1832)
If you hate a person, you hate something in him that is part of yourself. What isn't part of ourselves doesn't disturb us.
<u>Hermann Hesse</u> (1877 - 1962)
Hate no one; hate their vices, not themselves.
<u>J. G. C. Brainard</u>
Always remember others may hate you but those who hate you don't win unless you hate them. And then you destroy yourself.
<u>Richard M. Nixon</u> (1913 - 1994), in his White House farewell

Hatred

Truth is the mother of hatred.
<u>Ausonius</u>
Why is propaganda so much more successful when it stirs up hatred than when it tries to stir up friendly feeling?
<u>Bertrand Russell</u> (1872 - 1970)
Hatred does not cease in this world by hating, but by not hating; this is an eternal truth.
<u>Buddha</u> (563 BC - 483 BC), The Dhammapada
No hatred is so bitter as that of near relations.
<u>Cornelius Tacitus</u> (55 AD - 117 AD)
We must remember that any oppression, any injustice, any hatred, is a wedge designed to attack our civilization.
<u>Franklin D. Roosevelt</u> (1882 - 1945)
Hatred is a very underestimated emotion.
<u>Jim Morrison</u> (1943 - 1971)
Any time and energy you spend hating and being angry at your ex will ultimately take a toll on you without effecting any positive changes in your ex or your relationship.
<u>Julie A., M.A. Ross and Judy Corcoran, Joint Custody with a Jerk: Raising a Child with an Uncooperative Ex</u>, 2011
The hatred you're carrying is a live coal in your heart - far more damaging to yourself than to them.
<u>Lawana Blackwell</u>, The Dowry of Miss Lydia Clark, 1999

Hatred paralyzes life; love releases it. Hatred confuses life; love harmonizes it. Hatred darkens life; love illuminates it.
Martin Luther King Jr. (1929 - 1968)
Where there is hatred, let me sow love. Where there is injury, pardon. Where there is doubt, faith.
Saint Francis of Assisi (1181 - 1226)
The human heart is a strange vessel. Love and hatred can exist side by side.
Scott Westerfeld, Peeps, 2005
Dangerous is wrath concealed. Hatred proclaimed doth lose its chance of wreaking vengeance.
Seneca (5 BC - 65 AD)

Health

As I see it, every day you do one of two things: build health or produce disease in yourself.
Adelle Davis (1904 - 1974)
Every patient carries her or his own doctor inside.
Albert Schweitzer (1875 - 1965)
Happiness is nothing more than good health and a bad memory.
Albert Schweitzer (1875 - 1965)
Behind weight gain are the larger hurts and questions that have to be explored, probed, and understood before weight loss and maintenance is a possibility. It's a bigger issue than just calories in, calories out.
Ali Vincent, Believe It, Be It: How Being the Biggest Loser Won Me Back My Life, 2009
Big, sweeping life changes really boil down to small, everyday decisions.
Ali Vincent, Believe It, Be It: How Being the Biggest Loser Won Me Back My Life, 2009
Chicken exits are self-sabotage. They give you a false explanation for why you don't have something you want.
Ali Vincent, Believe It, Be It: How Being the Biggest Loser Won Me Back My Life, 2009
Getting enough sleep can be just as important as working out.
Ali Vincent, Believe It, Be It: How Being the Biggest Loser Won Me Back My Life, 2009
In order to truly give to others, you have to give to yourself first.
Ali Vincent, Believe It, Be It: How Being the Biggest Loser Won Me Back My Life, 2009
It gets a lot easier to deal with life's curveballs when you're not hiding under layers of fat.
Ali Vincent, Believe It, Be It: How Being the Biggest Loser Won Me Back My Life, 2009
Making excuses is not going to get me any closer to my goals.
Ali Vincent, Believe It, Be It: How Being the Biggest Loser Won Me Back My Life, 2009
Resistance is never the agent of change. You have to embrace the actions that are going to get you closer to your goal.
Ali Vincent, Believe It, Be It: How Being the Biggest Loser Won Me Back My Life, 2009
The only battle to win is the battle within, that place where we realize that we deserve to have and create all that we want in our lives.
Ali Vincent, Believe It, Be It: How Being the Biggest Loser Won Me Back My Life, 2009
There's something fundamental you have to understand about yourself before you can change your life for good.
Ali Vincent, Believe It, Be It: How Being the Biggest Loser Won Me Back My Life, 2009
When I was overweight and unhappy, I thought about being smaller, I thought about fitting into different clothes and feeling comfortable in any environment or social situation. But I didn't do anything about it. I was letting myself fall victim to not planning, not clarifying steps to reach my goals. Don't go on just wanting something. Start consciously planning where you want to be.
Ali Vincent, Believe It, Be It: How Being the Biggest Loser Won Me Back My Life, 2009
When weight loss becomes a goal in your life, eating right and exercising are just two pieces of the puzzle. Figuring out why you've put on the extra weight is the hardest part.
Ali Vincent, Believe It, Be It: How Being the Biggest Loser Won Me Back My Life, 2009
You have to track every single thing you eat if you want to keep posting big numbers on the scale each week.
Ali Vincent, Believe It, Be It: How Being the Biggest Loser Won Me Back My Life, 2009
You just have to start putting one foot in front of the other, making an effort to get healthy every day.
Ali Vincent, Believe It, Be It: How Being the Biggest Loser Won Me Back My Life, 2009
The refreshing pleasure from the first view of nature, after the pain of illness, and the confinement of a sick-chamber, is above the conceptions, as well as the descriptions, of those in health.
Ann Radcliffe (1764 - 1823), The Mysteries of Udolpho, 1764
Fitness - If it came in a bottle, everybody would have a great body.
Cher (1946 -)
Health is not valued till sickness comes.
Dr. Thomas Fuller (1654 - 1734), Gnomologia, 1732
Be not slow to visit the sick.
Ecclesiastes
I have never cared much for fish - it floats in the belly as much as in the pond.
Erica Eisdorfer, The Wet Nurse's Tale, 2009
Preserving health by too severe a rule is a worrisome malady.
Francois de La Rochefoucauld (1613 - 1680)
It is amazing how much crisper the general experience of life becomes when your body is given a chance to develop a little strength.
Frank Duff, A Coder in Courierland, 03-20-05
What some call health, if purchased by perpetual anxiety about diet, isn't much better than tedious disease.
George Dennison Prentice
Health is not simply the absence of sickness.
Hannah Green
[Water is] the only drink for a wise man.
Henry David Thoreau (1817 - 1862)

A wise man should consider that health is the greatest of human blessings, and learn how by his own thought to derive benefit from his illnesses.
Hippocrates (460 BC - 377 BC), Regimen in Health
Look to your health; and if you have it, praise God and value it next to conscience; for health is the second blessing that we mortals are capable of, a blessing money can't buy.
Izaak Walton (1593 - 1683)
It's no longer a question of staying healthy. It's a question of finding a sickness you like.
Jackie Mason (1934 -)
If you trust Google more than your doctor then maybe it's time to switch doctors.
Jadelr and Cristina Cordova, Chasing Windmills, 08-21-06
Now there are more overweight people in America than average-weight people. So overweight people are now average. Which means you've met your New Year's resolution.
Jay Leno (1950 -)
'Where and how can I make this meal better for me?' I asked myself that question before every meal—especially in the beginning.
Jennifer Hudson, I Got This: How I Changed My Ways and Lost What Weighed Me Down, 2012
Anyone can lose a few pounds, but not everyone has the tools to stick with it.
Jennifer Hudson, I Got This: How I Changed My Ways and Lost What Weighed Me Down, 2012
Gaining control over your health and well-being is one of those times in your life that you get to be completely selfish and not feel bad about it. If you want to meet your goals, you have to make it about you. You have to make it work for you and you alone. Anything less is a setup for failure.
Jennifer Hudson, I Got This: How I Changed My Ways and Lost What Weighed Me Down, 2012
If you can't take responsibility for your own well-being, you will never take control over it.
Jennifer Hudson, I Got This: How I Changed My Ways and Lost What Weighed Me Down, 2012
If you're not eating the right foods in the right amounts, all the exercise in the world won't combat the caloric intake.
Jennifer Hudson, I Got This: How I Changed My Ways and Lost What Weighed Me Down, 2012
People get comfortable with the way you are—they have formed their opinion of you based on everything they see and know about you as a person. When you change that up by losing weight, they no longer understand you.
Jennifer Hudson, I Got This: How I Changed My Ways and Lost What Weighed Me Down, 2012
Permanent weight loss doesn't come with an on and off switch. It is not something you do for a little while and think it is going to change your body.
Jennifer Hudson, I Got This: How I Changed My Ways and Lost What Weighed Me Down, 2012
What I learned from Weight Watchers is that food was meant to be used as fuel for our bodies. If we are using it for any other reasons, it is time to take a step back and ask ourselves what's up.
Jennifer Hudson, I Got This: How I Changed My Ways and Lost What Weighed Me Down, 2012
When someone wants to lose weight, they will do whatever it takes. They can't do it for anyone else but themselves. It has to be for them alone. Without that understanding, they will fail.
Jennifer Hudson, I Got This: How I Changed My Ways and Lost What Weighed Me Down, 2012
You cannot just work out and then eat poorly and expect to lose weight. It doesn't work that way.
Jennifer Hudson, I Got This: How I Changed My Ways and Lost What Weighed Me Down, 2012
You can't make a life-altering decision for someone else and expect it to stick.
Jennifer Hudson, I Got This: How I Changed My Ways and Lost What Weighed Me Down, 2012
You have to want weight-loss success so badly that no mountain, river, or ocean could keep you from reaching your goals. If you have that drive, passion, and commitment, there is no way you won't get there.
Jennifer Hudson, I Got This: How I Changed My Ways and Lost What Weighed Me Down, 2012
You can either hold yourself up to the unrealistic standards of others, or ignore them and concentrate on being happy with yourself as you are.
Jeph Jacques, Questionable Content webcomic, #352, 05-04-05
Water is the most neglected nutrient in your diet but one of the most vital.
Kelly Barton
Better to look weak and be strong than to look strong and be weak.
Laura Moncur (1969 -), Merriton: 35 Minutes from Home, 05-19-12
Whether you are healthy or ill, your thoughts can drive you. If you are feeling ill, it may be your mind that has made you so.
Laura Moncur (1969 -), The Secret Heart of Charlotte Lucas, 2014
Be careful about reading health books. You may die of a misprint.
Mark Twain (1835 - 1910)
Water, taken in moderation, cannot hurt anybody.
Mark Twain (1835 - 1910)
When I walk into my kitchen today, I am not alone. Whether we know it or not, none of us is. We bring fathers and mothers and kitchen tables, and every meal we have ever eaten. Food is never just food. It's also a way of getting at something else: who we are, who we have been, and who we want to be.
Molly Wizenberg, A Homemade Life: Stories and Recipes from My Kitchen Table, 2009
Getting my lifelong weight struggle under control has come from a process of treating myself as well as I treat others in every way.
Oprah Winfrey (1954 -), O Magazine, August 2004
A vigorous five-mile walk will do more good for an unhappy but otherwise healthy adult than all the medicine and psychology in the world.
Paul Dudley White
Pain (any pain—emotional, physical, mental) has a message. The information it has about our life can be remarkably specific, but it usually falls into one of two categories: "We would be more alive if we did more of this," and, "Life would be more lovely if we did less of that." Once we get the pain's message, and follow its advice, the pain goes away.
Peter McWilliams, Life 101

The more severe the pain or illness, the more severe will be the necessary changes. These may involve breaking bad habits, or acquiring some new and better ones.
Peter McWilliams, Life 101
Health consists of having the same diseases as one's neighbors.
Quentin Crisp
One of the most sublime experiences we can ever have is to wake up feeling healthy after we have been sick.
Rabbi Harold Kushner
Health nuts are going to feel stupid someday, lying in hospitals dying of nothing.
Redd Foxx (1922 - 1991)
Quit worrying about your health. It'll go away.
Robert Orben
Make your own recovery the first priority in your life.
Robin Norwood
A Hospital is no place to be sick.
Samuel Goldwyn (1882 - 1974)
Most men's awareness doesn't extend past their dinner plates.
Scott Westerfeld, Leviathan, 2009
I'm actually way more funny now, because I'm hungry... If comedy comes from pain, I should be funnier now than I ever was.
Seth Rogen, on his weight loss
I already knew to eat clean and listen to my body, to only eat when I was in a calm mental state. Everyone knew. But when you're fat in the head, it's never about knowing the answers. It's about living them.
Stephanie Klein, Moose, 2008
I'd heard it all the time, 'Live in the moment.' But if I did that, I'd weigh more than a dump truck. Losing weight wasn't about the moment at all; it was about having faith in the future. It was about knowing there would be another meal in a few hours.
Stephanie Klein, Moose, 2008
That's the thing about being a former fat camp champ: when asked if I'd change my past if I could, I always answer no. The pain of being an overweight kid, the humiliation, make you think twice before ever cutting anyone else down.
Stephanie Klein, Moose, 2008
Beauty isn't something on the outside. It's your insides that count! You gotta eat green stuff to make sure you're pretty on the inside.
Takayuki Ikkaku, Arisa Hosaka and Toshihiro Kawabata, Animal Crossing: Wild World, 2005
Exercise relieves stress. Nothing relieves exercise.
Takayuki Ikkaku, Arisa Hosaka and Toshihiro Kawabata, Animal Crossing: Wild World, 2005
I don't want to live in a world where I have to eat sugar-free sugar cookies.
Takayuki Ikkaku, Arisa Hosaka and Toshihiro Kawabata, Animal Crossing: Wild World, 2005
Keeping your body healthy is an expression of gratitude to the whole cosmos - the trees, the clouds, everything.
Thich Nhat Hanh
Health is worth more than learning.
Thomas Jefferson (1743 - 1826), letter to his cousin John Garland Jefferson, June 11, 1790
Eating everything you want is not that much fun. When you live a life with no boundaries, there's less joy. If you can eat anything you want to, what's the fun in eating anything you want to?
Tom Hanks (1956 -), Esquire, June 2006

Heroes

The whole point in bein' a hero is to do somethin' greater than yerself. It'd be easy to do it for the glory or the girls. We're bigger men than that.
Alexander Woo, True Blood, Beyond Here Lies Nothing, 2009
Nurture your mind with great thoughts; to believe in the heroic makes heroes.
Benjamin Disraeli (1804 - 1881)
There are new words now that excuse everybody. Give me the good old days of heroes and villains, the people you can bravo or hiss. There was a truth to them that all the slick credulity of today cannot touch.
Bette Davis (1908 - 1989), The Lonely Life, 1962
I think of a hero as someone who understands the degree of responsibility that comes with his freedom.
Bob Dylan (1941 -)
Everyone is necessarily the hero of his own life story.
John Barth (1930 -)
A hero is no braver than an ordinary man, but he is braver five minutes longer.
Ralph Waldo Emerson (1803 - 1882)
Every hero becomes a bore at last.
Ralph Waldo Emerson (1803 - 1882)
Our heroes are people and people are flawed. Don't let that taint the thing you love.
Randy K. Milholland, Midnight Macabre, 09-27-07
The real hero is always a hero by mistake; he dreams of being an honest coward like everybody else.
Umberto Eco (1932 -), Travels in Hyperreality
America's present need is not heroics, but healing; not nostrums but normalcy; not revolution, but restoration.
Warren G. Harding (1865 - 1923), Speech in Boston, 1920
Heroing is one of the shortest-lived professions there is.
Will Rogers (1879 - 1935), Newspaper article, Feb. 15, 1925
We can't all be heroes because somebody has to sit on the curb and clap as they go by.
Will Rogers (1879 - 1935)

History

History is the witness that testifies to the passing of time; it illumines reality, vitalizes memory, provides guidance in daily life and brings us tidings of antiquity.
Cicero (106 BC - 43 BC), Pro Publio Sestio
History is indeed little more than the register of the crimes, follies and misfortunes of mankind.
Edward Gibbon (1737 - 1794)
Hegel was right when he said that we learn from history that man can never learn anything from history.
George Bernard Shaw (1856 - 1950)
Those who cannot remember the past are condemned to repeat it.
George Santayana (1863 - 1952), The Life of Reason, Volume 1, 1905
Human history becomes more and more a race between education and catastrophe.
H. G. Wells (1866 - 1946), The Outline of History, vol.2, chapter 41, 1921
History is more or less bunk. It's tradition. We don't want tradition. We want to live in the present and the only history that is worth a tinker's dam is the history we made today.
Henry Ford (1863 - 1947), Interview in Chicago Tribune, May 25th, 1916
For four-fifths of our history, our planet was populated by pond scum.
J. W. Schopf
That is the supreme value of history. The study of it is the best guarantee against repeating it.
John Buchan, Baron Tweedsmuir
I thought about how wonderfully strange it would be to live in a place where almost everything had been built by the dead.
John Green, The Fault in Our Stars, 2012
History never looks like history when you are living through it.
John W. Gardner (1912 - 2002), quoted by Bill Moyers
If you write a post and put it on a blog, that's a historical document. If you change your template, then that entry looks completely different. It's the same words, but not the same meaning. This all depends on what historical questions that people will be asking and we can't know what they will want.
Josh Greenberg, Digital Preservation and Blogs, SXSW 2006
History is the short trudge from Adam to atom.
Leonard Louis Levinson
History is the version of past events that people have decided to agree upon.
Napoleon Bonaparte (1769 - 1821)
Some people make headlines while others make history.
Philip Elmer-DeWitt, in Time Magazine
History will be kind to me for I intend to write it.
Sir Winston Churchill (1874 - 1965)
Want of foresight, unwillingness to act when action would be simple and effective, lack of clear thinking, confusion of counsel until the emergency comes, until self-preservation strikes its jarring gong-these are the features which constitute the endless repetition of history.
Sir Winston Churchill (1874 - 1965), Speech, House of Commons, May 2, 1935
Indeed, history is nothing more than a tableau of crimes and misfortunes.
Voltaire (1694 - 1778)

Hollywood

You can't find any true closeness in Hollywood, because everybody does the fake closeness so well.
Carrie Fisher (1956 -)
Hollywood is a place where people from Iowa mistake each other for stars.
Fred Allen (1894 - 1956)
You can take all the sincerity in Hollywood, place it in the navel of a firefly and still have room enough for three caraway seeds and a producer's heart.
Fred Allen (1894 - 1956)
After two years in Washington, I often long for the realism and sincerity of Hollywood.
Fred Thompson, Speech before the Commonwealth Club of California
Hollywood is a place where they'll pay you a thousand dollars for a kiss and fifty cents for your soul.
Marilyn Monroe (1926 - 1962)
Behind the phony tinsel of Hollywood lies the real tinsel.
Oscar Levant (1906 - 1972)
In Hollywood a marriage is a success if it outlasts milk.
Rita Rudner
Hollywood is a place where they place you under contract instead of under observation.
Walter Winchell (1897 - 1972)

Home

A man's homeland is wherever he prospers.
Aristophanes (450 BC - 388 BC), Plutus, 388 B.C.
Not going home is already like death.
E. Catherine Tobler, Vanishing Act
Luxuries are never so comfortable as are the familiar, ordinary things of home.
Eucharista Ward, Match For Mary Bennet, 2009
A man travels the world over in search of what he needs and returns home to find it.
George Moore
The most important work you and I will ever do will be within the walls of our own homes.
Harold B. Lee (1899 - 1973)
Life's a voyage that's homeward bound.
Herman Melville (1819 - 1891)
The weird thing about houses is that they almost always look like nothing is happening inside of them, even though they contain most of our lives.
John Green, The Fault in Our Stars, 2012
Ya gotta live somewhere, but also you GET to live somewhere.

John Green, VlogBrothers, A Poem for Spring, 03-26-13
Mid pleasures and palaces though we may roam,
Be it ever so humble, there's no place like home.
John Howard Payne (1791 - 1852)
A good home must be made, not bought.
Joyce Maynard, "Domestic Affairs"
An old house with its windows gone always makes me think of something dead with its eyes picked out.
L. M. Montgomery (1874 - 1942), Anne of Green Gables, 1908
As difficult as it is to have company within one's house, the absence of company is more so. The quiet echoing of solitary footsteps within the halls is suddenly amplified without the voices of excited guests. The clinking of plates and silver has narrowed to individual forks and spoons instead of the enchanting din of dining. The natural creaks and squeaks of the home are louder and more surprising.
Laura Moncur (1969 -), The Secret Heart of Charlotte Lucas, 2014
My home is not a place, it is people.
Lois McMaster Bujold, "Barrayar", 1991
A house that does not have one worn, comfy chair in it is soulless.
May Sarton
In everyone's heart stirs a great homesickness.
Rabbi Seymour Siegel

Honesty

The best measure of a man's honesty isn't his income tax return. It's the zero adjust on his bathroom scale.
Arthur C. Clarke (1917 -)
Where is there dignity unless there is honesty?
Cicero (106 BC - 43 BC)
Maybe coming clean is the ultimate selfish act. A way to absolve yourself by hurting someone who doesn't deserve to be hurt.
Cindy Chupack, Sex and the City, Don't Ask, Don't Tell, 2000
Honesty is a good thing, but it is not profitable to its possessor unless it is kept under control.
Don Marquis (1878 - 1937)
The day is for honest men, the night for thieves.
Euripides (484 BC - 406 BC), Iphigenia in Tauris, circa 412 B.C.
I would rather be accused of breaking precedents than breaking promises.
John F. Kennedy (1917 - 1963)
Honesty pays, but it doesn't seem to pay enough to suit some people.
Kin Hubbard (1868 - 1930)
If the truth doesn't save us, what does that say about us?
Lois McMaster Bujold, Diplomatic Immunity, 2002
Friends should always tell you the truth. But please don't.
Louis C. K., Vanity Fair interview, 2013
Honesty is the best policy - when there is money in it.
Mark Twain (1835 - 1910)
If you tell the truth you don't have to remember anything.
Mark Twain (1835 - 1910)
When in doubt, tell the truth.
Mark Twain (1835 - 1910)
Level with your child by being honest. Nobody spots a phony quicker than a child.
Mary MacCracken
When something that honest is said it usually needs a few minutes of silence to dissipate.
Pamela Ribon, Why Girls Are Weird, 2003
Son, always tell the truth. Then you'll never have to remember what you said the last time.
Sam Rayburn (1882 - 1961), quoted Washingtonian, November 1978
Any fool can tell the truth, but it requires a man of some sense to know how to lie well.
Samuel Butler (1835 - 1902)
Being entirely honest with oneself is a good exercise.
Sigmund Freud (1856 - 1939)
An honest man can feel no pleasure in the exercise of power over his fellow citizens.
Thomas Jefferson (1743 - 1826), letter to John Melish, January 13, 1813
There are only two ways of telling the complete truth–anonymously and posthumously.
Thomas Sowell (1930 -)
Honesty is the best image.
Tom Wilson, Ziggy (comic)
Our lives improve only when we take chances - and the first and most difficult risk we can take is to be honest with ourselves.
Walter Anderson
I have always noticed that people will never laugh at anything that is not based on truth.
Will Rogers (1879 - 1935)
Every man has his fault, and honesty is his.
William Shakespeare (1564 - 1616), "Timon of Athens", Act 3 scene 1
I thank God I am as honest as any man living that is an old man and no honester than I.
William Shakespeare (1564 - 1616), "Much Ado about Nothing", Act 3 scene 1
No legacy is so rich as honesty.
William Shakespeare (1564 - 1616), "All's Well that Ends Well", Act 3 scene 5
Though I am not naturally honest,
I am so sometimes by chance.
William Shakespeare (1564 - 1616)

Honor

Be not ashamed of thy virtues; honor's a good brooch to wear in a man's hat at all times.
Ben Jonson (1572 - 1637)
The difference between a moral man and a man of honor is that the latter regrets a discreditable act, even when it has worked and he has not been caught.
H. L. Mencken (1880 - 1956), 'Prejudices: Fourth Series,' 1924
Don't look for more honor than your learning merits.
Jewish Proverb
An honor is not diminished for being shared.
Lois McMaster Bujold, "Shards of Honor", 1986
Guard your honor. Let your reputation fall where it will. And outlive the bastards.
Lois McMaster Bujold, "A Civil Campaign", 1999
If the truth doesn't save us, what does that say about us?
Lois McMaster Bujold, Diplomatic Immunity, 2002
Reputation is what other people know about you. Honor is what you know about yourself.
Lois McMaster Bujold, "A Civil Campaign", 1999
Real integrity is doing the right thing, knowing that nobody's going to know whether you did it or not.
Oprah Winfrey (1954 -), in Good Housekeeping
What is left when honor is lost?
Publilius Syrus (~ 100 BC), Maxims
The louder he talked of his honor, the faster we counted our spoons.
Ralph Waldo Emerson (1803 - 1882)
Honor does not have to be defended.
Robert J. Sawyer (1960 -), "Calculating God", 2000
Be honorable yourself if you wish to associate with honorable people.
Welsh Proverb

Hope

I know how men in exile feed on dreams of hope.
Aeschylus (525 BC - 456 BC), Agamemnon
He who despairs over an event is a coward, but he who holds hope for the human condition is a fool.
Albert Camus (1913 - 1960), The Rebel (1951)
Until the day when God shall deign to reveal the future to man, all human wisdom is summed up in these two words,–'Wait and hope'.
Alexandre Dumas (1802 - 1870), The Count of Monte Cristo
Hope doesn't come from calculating whether the good news is winning out over the bad. It's simply a choice to take action.
Anna Lappe, O Magazine, June 2003
Hope begins in the dark, the stubborn hope that if you just show up and try to do the right thing, the dawn will come. You wait and watch and work: You don't give up.
Anne Lamott
Hope is a waking dream.
Aristotle (384 BC - 322 BC), from Diogenes Laertius, Lives of Eminent Philosophers
We have been told we cannot do this by a chorus of cynics. They will only grow louder and more dissonant in the weeks to come. We've been asked to pause for a reality check; we've been warned against offering the people of this nation false hope. But in the unlikely story that is America, there has never been anything false about hope.
Barack Obama (1961 -), New Hampshire Democratic Primary Speech, 01-08-08
He that lives upon hope will die fasting.
Benjamin Franklin (1706 - 1790)
While there's life, there's hope.
Cicero (106 BC - 43 BC), Ad Atticum
There are no hopeless situations; there are only men who have grown hopeless about them.
Clare Booth Luce (1903 - 1987)
Hope is the thing with feathers
That perches in the soul.
And sings the tune
Without the words,
and never stops at all.
Emily Dickinson (1830 - 1886)
Do not spoil what you have by desiring what you have not; but remember that what you now have was once among the things you only hoped for.
Epicurus (341 BC - 270 BC)
He who has never hoped can never despair.
George Bernard Shaw (1856 - 1950), Caesar and Cleopatra (1901) act 4
History is moving, and it will tend toward hope, or tend toward tragedy.
George W. Bush (1946 -)
Never deprive someone of hope; it might be all they have.
H. Jackson Brown Jr.
Hope is only the love of life.
Henri-Frédéric Amiel
Even in the darkness, every color can be found. And every day of rain brings water flowing to things growing in the ground.
Joss Whedon, Zack Whedon, Maurissa Tancharoen, and Jed Whedon, Dr. Horrible's Sing Along Blog, 2008
Young people have an almost biological destiny to be hopeful.
Marshall Ganz, quoted by Sara Rimer in New York Times
Hope, like the gleaming taper's light,
Adorns and cheers our way;
And still, as darker grows the night,
Emits a brighter ray.

Oliver Goldsmith (1730 - 1774)
Take hope from the heart of man, and you make him a beast of prey.
Quida
It is difficult to say what is impossible, for the dream of yesterday is the hope of today and the reality of tomorrow.
Robert H. Goddard (1882 - 1945)
To travel hopefully is a better thing than to arrive.
Robert Louis Stevenson (1850 - 1894)
Hope is necessary in every condition.
Samuel Johnson (1709 - 1784)
The past is a source of knowledge, and the future is a source of hope. Love of the past implies faith in the future.
Stephen Ambrose (1936 - 2002), in Fast Company
Cease, every joy, to glimmer on my mind,
But leave—oh! leave the light of Hope behind.
Thomas Campbell (1777 - 1844)
Appetite, with an opinion of attaining, is called hope; the same, without such opinion, despair.
Thomas Hobbes (1588 - 1679)
Never lose hope.
Unknown, Polish Slogan
True hope is swift, and flies with swallow's wings;
Kings it makes gods, and meaner creatures kings.
William Shakespeare (1564 - 1616), "King Richard III", Act 5 scene 2
I can endure my own despair,
but not another's hope.
William Walsh

Humility

He who speaks without modesty will find it difficult to make his words good.
Confucius (551 BC - 479 BC), The Confucian Analects
The firm, the enduring, the simple, and the modest are near to virtue.
Confucius (551 BC - 479 BC), The Confucian Analects
The superior man is modest in his speech, but exceeds in his actions.
Confucius (551 BC - 479 BC), The Confucian Analects
Modesty is the citadel of beauty.
Demades
I have often wished I had time to cultivate modesty... But I am too busy thinking about myself.
Edith Sitwell (1887 - 1964), As quoted in The Observer (30 April 1950)
Humility is no substitute for a good personality.
Fran Lebowitz (1950 -), Metropolitan Life, 1978
Life is a long lesson in humility.
James M. Barrie (1860 - 1937)
The loss of one's dignified bearing is often sudden.
Jerry Van Amerongen, Ballard Street, 09-02-06
Be modest! It is the kind of pride least likely to offend.
Jules Renard (1864 - 1910)
In America, they want you to accomplish these great feats, to pull off these David Copperfield-type stunts. You want me to be great, but you don't ever want me to say I'm great?
Kanye West, Rolling Stone, 2006
You couldn't be that good and not know it, somewhere in your secret heart, however much you'd been abused into affecting public humility.
Lois McMaster Bujold, A Civil Campaign, 1999
Modesty is a shining light; it prepares the mind to receive knowledge, and the heart for truth.
Madam Guizot
Always acknowledge a fault. This will throw those in authority off their guard and give you an opportunity to commit more.
Mark Twain (1835 - 1910)
I am no more humble than my talents require.
Oscar Levant (1906 - 1972)
If I only had a little humility, I'd be perfect.
Ted Turner
If you ever start to feel too good about yourself, they have this thing called the Internet, and you can find a lot of people there who don't like you.
Tina Fey, Golden Globes Acceptance Speech, 2009
It well becomes a young man to be modest.
Titus Maccius Plautus (254 BC - 184 BC)
In peace there's nothing so becomes a man as modest stillness and humility.
William Shakespeare (1564 - 1616)

Humor

That is the saving grace of humor, if you fail no one is laughing at you.
A. Whitney Brown
Humor is the only test of gravity, and gravity of humor; for a subject which will not bear raillery is suspicious, and a jest which will not bear serious examination is false wit.
Aristotle (384 BC - 322 BC)
Humor is everywhere, in that there's irony in just about anything a human does.
Bill Nye, Interview with Wired.com, April 2005
All I need to make a comedy is a park, a policeman and a pretty girl.
Charlie Chaplin (1889 - 1977), in My Autobiography (1964)
Total absence of humor renders life impossible.
Colette (1873 - 1954), Chance Acquaintances, 1952

A joke was not a single-use item but something you brought out again and again until it fell apart in your hand like a cheap umbrella.
David Nicholls, One Day, 2010
If you're at school and you're not that bright or good-looking or popular or whatever, and one day you say something and someone laughs, well, you sort of grab onto it, don't you? you think, well I run funny and I've got this stupid big face and big thighs and no-one fancies me, but at least I can make people laugh, And It's such a nice feeling, making someone laugh, that maybe you get a bit reliant on it. Like, if you're not funny then you're not... anything.
David Nicholls, One Day, 2010
Humor is always based on a modicum of truth. Have you ever heard a joke about a father-in-law?
Dick Clark
A sense of humor is part of the art of leadership, of getting along with people, of getting things done.
Dwight D. Eisenhower (1890 - 1969)
Humor can be dissected as a frog can, but the thing dies in the process and the innards are discouraging to any but the pure scientific mind.
E. B. White (1899 - 1985), Some Remarks on Humor, introduction
Humor is by far the most significant activity of the human brain.
Edward De Bono
There's nothing like a gleam of humor to reassure you that a fellow human being is ticking inside a strange face.
Eva Hoffman
The world is a tragedy to those who feel, but a comedy to those who think.
Horace Walpole (1717 - 1797)
If there's one thing I know it's God does love a good joke.
Hugh Elliott, Standing Room Only weblog, 05-01-04
The only rules comedy can tolerate are those of taste, and the only limitations those of libel.
James Thurber (1894 - 1961)
The wit makes fun of other persons; the satirist makes fun of the world; the humorist makes fun of himself.
James Thurber (1894 - 1961), in Edward R. Murrow television interview
What's the point of havin' a rapier wit if I can't use it to stab people?
Jeph Jacques, Questionable Content, #1615, March 2010
Where humor is concerned there are no standards - no one can say what is good or bad, although you can be sure that everyone will.
John Kenneth Galbraith (1908 - 2006)
The best defence against misguided arrogance is a keen sense of humour.
Kathryn L. Nelson, Pemberley Manor, 2006
One doesn't have a sense of humor. It has you.
Larry Gelbart
Humor is our way of defending ourselves from life's absurdities by thinking absurdly about them.
Lewis Mumford (1895 - 1990)
Humor is the great thing, the saving thing. The minute it crops up, all our irritations and resentments slip away and a sunny spirit takes their place.
Mark Twain (1835 - 1910)
Humor is a rubber sword - it allows you to make a point without drawing blood.
Mary Hirsch
Humor is just another defense against the universe.
Mel Brooks (1926 -)
Tragedy is when I cut my finger. Comedy is when you walk into an open sewer and die.
Mel Brooks (1926 -)
Comedy is simply a funny way of being serious.
Peter Ustinov (1921 - 2004)
Comedy is nothing more than tragedy deferred.
Pico Iyer, Time
Wit makes its own welcome, and levels all distinctions. No dignity, no learning, no force of character, can make any stand against good wit.
Ralph Waldo Emerson (1803 - 1882), Letters and Social Aims: The Comic, 1876
Defining and analyzing humor is a pastime of humorless people.
Robert Benchley (1889 - 1945)
Life is tough, and if you have the ability to laugh at it you have the ability to enjoy it.
Salma Hayek

Humor

Humor is also a way of saying something serious.
T. S. Eliot (1888 - 1965)
There's no trick to being a humorist when you have the whole government working for you.
Will Rogers (1879 - 1935)

Hunting

A peculiar virtue in wildlife ethics is that the hunter ordinarily has no gallery to applaud or disapprove of his conduct. Whatever his acts, they are dictated by his own conscience, rather than by a mob of onlookers. It is difficult to exaggerate the importance of this fact.
Aldo Leopold, A Sand County Almanac
If some animals are good at hunting and others are suitable for hunting, then the Gods must clearly smile on hunting.
Aristotle (384 BC - 322 BC)
No culture has yet solved the dilemma each has faced with the growth of a conscious mind: how to live a moral and compassionate existence when one is fully aware of

the blood, the horror inherent in all life, when one finds darkness not only in one's own culture but within oneself... There are simply no answers to some of the great pressing questions. You continue to live them out, making your life a worthy expression of a leaning into the light.
Barry Lopez, Arctic Dreams

Civilized life has altogether grown too tame, and, if it is to be stable, it must provide a harmless outlets for the impulses which our remote ancestors satisfied in hunting.
Bertrand Russell (1872 - 1970)

All the sounds of this valley run together into one great echo, a song that is sung by all the spirits of this valley. Only a hunter hears it.
Chaim Potok

There is a passion for hunting something deeply implanted in the human breast.
Charles Dickens (1812 - 1870)

Hunting has opened the earth to me and let me sense the rhythms and hierarchies of nature.
Charles Fergus

The land comes alive through its wild creatures.
Charles Fergus

I'd rather get my brains blown out in the wild than wait in terror at the slaughterhouse.
Craig Volk, Northern Exposure, A-Hunting We Will Go, 1991

I kill when I hunt and do not apologize for that, although I reserve the right to think about its implications. I also hunt without killing- whether by accident or design-and I do not apologize for that either. There is room in longbow country for a spectrum of tastes and attitudes, and that is as it should be.
E. Donnall Thomas, Jr.

I don't regard nature as a spectator sport.
Ed Zern

Whenever I see a photograph of some sportsman grinning over his kill, I am always impressed by the striking moral and esthetic superiority of the dead animal to the live one.
Edward Abbey (1927 - 1989), A Voice Crying in the Wilderness

The true trophy hunter is a self-disciplined perfectionist seeking a single animal, the ancient patriarch well past his prime that is often an outcast from his own kind... If successful, he will enshrine the trophy in a place of honor. This is a more noble and fitting end than dying on some lost and lonely ledge where the scavengers will pick his bones, and his magnificent horns will weather away and be lost forever.
Elgin Gates, Trophy Hunter in Asia

Certainly there is no hunting like the hunting of man and those who have hunted armed men long enough and liked it, never really care for anything else thereafter.
Ernest Hemingway (1899 - 1961), "On the Blue Water," Esquire, April 1936

When you have shot one bird flying you have shot all birds flying. They are all different and they fly in different ways but the sensation is the same and the last one is as good as the first.
Ernest Hemingway (1899 - 1961), Winner Take Nothing

When a man wants to murder a tiger he calls it sport; when a tiger wants to murder him he calls it ferocity.
George Bernard Shaw (1856 - 1950), Man and Superman

There is a solitude, or perhaps a solemnity, in the few hours that precede the dawn of day which is unlike that of any others in the twenty-four, and which I cannot explain or account for. Thoughts come to me at this time that I never have at any other.
George Bird Grinnell

We cannot but pity the boy who has never fired a gun; he is no more humane, while his education has been sadly neglected.
Henry David Thoreau (1817 - 1862)

When some of my friends have asked me anxiously about their boys, whether they should let them hunt, I have answered yes– remembering that it was one of the best parts of my education– make them hunters.
Henry David Thoreau (1817 - 1862)

Wild animals never kill for sport. Man is the only one to whom the torture and death of his fellow creatures is amusing in itself.
James A. Froude (1818 - 1894)

The emotions that good hunters need to cultivate are love and service more than courage. The sentiments of the hunt then become translated into art.
James Swan, In Defense of Hunting

If there is a sacred moment in the ethical pursuit of game, it is the moment you release the arrow or touch off the fatal shot.
Jim Posewitz

The pleasure of the sportsman in the chase is measured by the intelligence of the game and its capacity to elude pursuit and in the labor involved in the capture.
John Dean Caton

Keep close to Nature's heart... and break clear away, once in awhile, and climb a mountain or spend a week in the woods. Wash your spirit clean. None of Nature's landscapes are ugly so long as they are wild.
John Muir (1838 - 1914), Our National Parks, 1901

One does not hunt in order to kill; on the contrary, one kills in order to have hunted...If one were to present the sportsman with the death of the animal as a gift he would refuse it. What he is after is having to win it, to conquer the surly brute through his own effort and skill with all the extras that this carries with it: the immersion in the countryside, the healthfulness of the exercise, the distraction from his job.
Jose Ortega y Gasset (1883 - 1955), Meditations on Hunting

I never know which is worse: the sorrow when you hit the bird or the shame when you miss it.
Julian Fellowes, Downton Abbey, Season 2, Episode 9, 2010

When I was twelve, I went hunting with my father and we shot a bird. He was laying there and something struck me. Why do we call this fun to kill this creature who was as happy as I was when I woke up this morning.
Marv Levy

It is very strange, and very melancholy, that the paucity of human pleasures should persuade us ever to call hunting one of them.
Samuel Johnson (1709 - 1784), Anecdotes of Samuel Johnson

In a civilized and cultivated country, wild animals only continue to exist at all when preserved by sportsmen.
Theodore Roosevelt (1858 - 1919)

Idealism

I'm an idealist. I don't know where I'm going, but I'm on my way.
Carl Sandburg (1878 - 1967), Incidentals (1907)

Idealism is what precedes experience; cynicism is what follows.
David T. Wolf (1943 -)

An idealist is one who, on noticing that a rose smells better than a cabbage, concludes that it will also make better soup.
H. L. Mencken (1880 - 1956)

An idealist is a person who helps other people to be prosperous.
Henry Ford (1863 - 1947)

When they come downstairs from their Ivory Towers, Idealists are very apt to walk straight into the gutter.
Logan Pearsall Smith (1865 - 1946), Afterthoughts (1931) "Other People"

Cynics regarded everybody as equally corrupt... Idealists regarded everybody as equally corrupt, except themselves.
Robert Anton Wilson

Ideas

He can compress the most words into the smallest ideas of any man I ever met.
Abraham Lincoln (1809 - 1865)

The vitality of thought is in adventure. Ideas won't keep. Something must be done about them.
Alfred North Whitehead (1861 - 1947)

It is by acts and not by ideas that people live.
Anatole France (1844 - 1924)

Ideals are like stars: you will not succeed in touching them with your hands, but like the seafaring man on the ocean desert of waters, you choose them as your guides, and following them, you reach your destiny.
Carl Schurz (1829 - 1906)

There are only two kinds of scholars; those who love ideas and those who hate them.
Emile Chartier

An idea is salvation by imagination.
Frank Lloyd Wright (1869 - 1959)

Everyone is a genius at least once a year. The real geniuses simply have their bright ideas closer together.
Georg Christoph Lichtenberg (1742 - 1799)

I said to myself, I have things in my head that are not like what anyone has taught me - shapes and ideas so near to me - so natural to my way of being and thinking that it hasn't occurred to me to put them down. I decided to start anew, to strip away what I had been taught.
Georgia O'Keeffe (1887 - 1986)

Any man who afflicts the human race with ideas must be prepare to see them misunderstood.
H. L. Mencken (1880 - 1956)

To die for an idea; it is unquestionably noble. But how much nobler it would be if men died for ideas that were true!
H. L. Mencken (1880 - 1956)

Every composer knows the anguish and despair occasioned by forgetting ideas which one had no time to write down.
Hector Berlioz (1803 - 1869)

College isn't the place to go for ideas.
Helen Keller (1880 - 1968)

This is my answer to the gap between ideas and action - I will write it out.
Hortense Calisher

Don't worry about people stealing an idea. If it's original, you will have to ram it down their throats.
Howard Aiken (1900 - 1973)

Good ideas are not adopted automatically. They must be driven into practice with courageous patience.
Hyman Rickover (1900 - 1986)

So many new ideas are at first strange and horrible, though ultimately valuable that a very heavy responsibility rests upon those who would prevent their dissemination.
J. B. S. Haldane (1892 - 1964)

Do something. If it doesn't work, do something else. No idea is too crazy.
Jim Hightower, The New York Times, March 9, 1986

When ideas fail, words come in very handy.
Johann Wolfgang von Goethe (1749 - 1832)

I can't understand why people are frightened of new ideas. I'm frightened of the old ones.
John Cage (1912 - 1992)

Ideas are like rabbits. You get a couple and learn how to handle them, and pretty soon you have a dozen.
John Steinbeck (1902 - 1968)

A handsome parson is fit for nothing but ti put ideas into the young woman's heads.
Judith Brocklehurst, Darcy And Anne

Lack of money is no obstacle. Lack of an idea is an obstacle.
Ken Hakuta
People laugh at me because I use big words. But if you have big ideas you have to use big words to express them, haven't you?
L. M. Montgomery (1874 - 1942), Anne of Green Gables, 1908
Man's mind, once stretched by a new idea, never regains its original dimensions.
Oliver Wendell Holmes (1809 - 1894)
The human mind treats a new idea the same way the body treats a strange protein; it rejects it.
P. B. Medawar (1915 -)
All opening moves were the same, like in chess. You don't have to come up with anything new, there's no point, because you're both after the same thing anyway. The game soon finds its own way and it's only at that point that you need a strategy.
Paolo Giordano, The Solitude of Prime Numbers: A Novel
The key to every man is his thought.... He can only be reformed by showing him a new idea which commands his own.
Ralph Waldo Emerson (1803 - 1882), Circles, Essays: First Series, 1903
I had a monumental idea this morning, but I didn't like it.
Samuel Goldwyn (1882 - 1974)
The best ideas are common property.
Seneca (5 BC - 65 AD), Epistles
A committee is a cul-de-sac down which ideas are lured and then quietly strangled.
Sir Barnett Cocks (1907 - 1989)
No one has ever had an idea in a dress suit.
Sir Frederick G. Banting (1891 - 1941)
If an idea's worth having once, it's worth having twice.
Tom Stoppard (1937 -)
An invasion of armies can be resisted, but not an idea whose time has come.
Victor Hugo (1802 - 1885), 'Histoire d'un crime,' 1852
One of the greatest pains to human nature is the pain of a new idea.
Walter Bagehot (1826 - 1877)
Books won't stay banned. They won't burn. Ideas won't go to jail. in the long run of history, the censor and the inquisitor have always lost. The only sure weapon against bad ideas is better ideas. The source of better ideas is wisdom. The surest path to wisdom is a liberal education.
Whitney Griswold, Address to students at Phillips Academy, 1952
The way to combat noxious ideas is with other ideas. The way to combat falsehoods is with truth.
William O. Douglas (1898 - 1980)

Ignorance

I believe in the forgiveness of sin and the redemption of ignorance.
Adlai E. Stevenson Jr. (1900 - 1965), retort to a heckler asking him to state his beliefs, Time, November 1, 1963
Not ignorance, but ignorance of ignorance, is the death of knowledge.
Alfred North Whitehead (1861 - 1947)
A person is never happy except at the price of some ignorance.
Anatole France (1844 - 1924)
Ignorance never settles a question.
Benjamin Disraeli (1804 - 1881)
To be conscious that you are ignorant is a great step to knowledge.
Benjamin Disraeli (1804 - 1881), Sybil, 1845
Consistency requires you to be as ignorant today as you were a year ago.
Bernard Berenson (1865 - 1959)
A little learning is a dangerous thing but a lot of ignorance is just as bad.
Bob Edwards
Ignorance is the night of the mind, but a night without moon and star.
Confucius (551 BC - 479 BC)
Stupid is forever, ignorance can be fixed.
Don Wood
It is no good to try to stop knowledge from going forward. Ignorance is never better than knowledge.
Enrico Fermi (1901 - 1954)
Nothing is so firmly believed as that which is least known.
Francis Jeffrey (1773 - 1850)
I have never met a man so ignorant that I couldn't learn something from him.
Galileo Galilei (1564 - 1642)
Ignorance gives one a large range of probabilities.
George Eliot (1819 - 1880)
It is better to confess ignorance than provide it.
Homer Hickam, The Coalwood Way
Ignorance of certain subjects is a great part of wisdom.
Hugo De Groot (1583 - 1645)
If knowledge can create problems, it is not through ignorance that we can solve them.
Isaac Asimov (1920 - 1992)
My whole career can be summed up with 'Ignorance is bliss.' When you do not know better, you do not really worry about failing.
Jeff Foxworthy
It is impossible to make people understand their ignorance; for it requires knowledge to perceive it and therefore he that can perceive it hath it not.
Jeremy Taylor (1613 - 1667)
Nothing is worse than active ignorance.
Johann Wolfgang von Goethe (1749 - 1832)
Ignorance and inconsideration are the two great causes of the ruin of mankind.

John Tillotson (1630 - 1694)
Beware of the man who works hard to learn something, learns it, and finds himself no wiser than before.
Kurt Vonnegut (1922 - 2007)
Against logic there is no armor like ignorance.
Laurence J. Peter (1919 - 1988)
All you need in this life is ignorance and confidence; then success is sure.
Mark Twain (1835 - 1910), Letter to Mrs Foote, Dec. 2, 1887
Whenever you find that you are on the side of the majority, it is time to pause and reflect.
Mark Twain (1835 - 1910)
Nothing in all the world is more dangerous than sincere ignorance and conscientious stupidity.
Martin Luther King Jr. (1929 - 1968), Strength to Love, 1963
We allow our ignorance to prevail upon us and make us think we can survive alone, alone in patches, alone in groups, alone in races, even alone in genders.
Maya Angelou (1928 -)
It's innocence when it charms us, ignorance when it doesn't.
Mignon McLaughlin, The Neurotic's Notebook
Ignorance, the root and the stem of every evil.
Plato (427 BC - 347 BC)
Better be ignorant of a matter than half know it.
Publilius Syrus (~100 BC), Maxims
There are many things of which a wise man might wish to be ignorant.
Ralph Waldo Emerson (1803 - 1882)
Ignorance is not innocence but sin.
Robert Browning (1812 - 1889)
Nothing is so good for an ignorant man as silence; and if he was sensible of this he would not be ignorant.
Saadi (1184 - 1291)
It is worse still to be ignorant of your ignorance.
Saint Jerome (374 AD - 419 AD)
A great deal of intelligence can be invested in ignorance when the need for illusion is deep.
Saul Bellow (1915 - 2005)
The greater the ignorance the greater the dogmatism.
Sir William Osler (1849 - 1919)
The only good is knowledge and the only evil is ignorance.
Socrates (469 BC - 399 BC)
Ignorant men don't know what good they hold in their hands until they've flung it away.
Sophocles (496 BC - 406 BC)
Theories that diseases are caused by mental states and can be cured by will power, are always an index of how much is not understood about the physical terrain of a disease.
Susan Sontag (1933 - 2004), Illness as Metaphor, 1978
Have the courage to be ignorant of a great number of things, in order to avoid the calamity of being ignorant of everything.
Sydney Smith (1771 - 1845)
That there should one Man die ignorant who had capacity for Knowledge, this I call a tragedy.
Thomas Carlyle (1795 - 1881)
The multitude of books is making us ignorant.
Voltaire (1694 - 1778)
Education is a progressive discovery of our own ignorance.
Will Durant (1885 - 1981)
An ignorant person is one who doesn't know what you have just found out.
Will Rogers (1879 - 1935)
You know everybody is ignorant, only on different subjects.
Will Rogers (1879 - 1935), New York Times Aug. 31 1924
Innocence dwells with Wisdom, but never with Ignorance.
William Blake (1757 - 1827)
It is impossible to defeat an ignorant man in argument.
William G. McAdoo (1863 - 1941)

Imagination
Imagination is more important than knowledge...
Albert Einstein (1879 - 1955)
Memory feeds imagination.
Amy Tan (1952 -)
So you see, imagination needs moodling - long, inefficient, happy idling, dawdling and puttering.
Brenda Ueland
Our imagination is the only limit to what we can hope to have in the future.
Charles F. Kettering (1876 - 1958)
An idea is salvation by imagination.
Frank Lloyd Wright (1869 - 1959)
Imagination is the beginning of creation. You imagine what you desire, you will what you imagine and at last you create what you will.
George Bernard Shaw (1856 - 1950)
Choosing to live in narrow spaces leads to form of mental agoraphobia and that brings its own terrors. I think the willfully unimaginative see more monsters, they are often more afraid. What is more, those who choose not to empathize enable real monsters. For without ever committing an act of outright evil ourselves, we collude through our own apathy.
J. K. Rowling, Harvard Commencement Address, 2008

Imagination is not only the uniquely human capacity to envision that which is not, and, therefore, the foundation of all invention and innovation. In its arguably most transformative and relevetory capacity, it is the power that enables us to empathize with humans whose experiences we have never shared.
J. K. Rowling, Harvard Commencement Address, 2008
We do not need magic to transform our world. We carry all the power we need inside ourselves already. We have the power to imagine better.
J. K. Rowling, Harvard Commencement Address, 2008
There is nothing more dreadful than imagination without taste.
Johann Wolfgang von Goethe (1749 - 1832)
Imagination is the one weapon in the war against reality.
Jules de Gaultier
But the worst of imagining things is that the time comes when you have to stop and that hurts.
L. M. Montgomery (1874 - 1942), Anne of Green Gables, 1908
You cannot depend on your eyes when your imagination is out of focus.
Mark Twain (1835 - 1910), A Connecticut Yankee in King Arthur's Court
Everything you can imagine is real.
Pablo Picasso (1881 - 1973)
There is only one admirable form of the imagination: the imagination that is so intense that it creates a new reality, that it makes things happen.
Sean O'Faolain (1900 - 1991)
Skill without imagination is craftsmanship and gives us many useful objects such as wickerwork picnic baskets. Imagination without skill gives us modern art.
Tom Stoppard (1937 -), "Artist Descending a Staircase"

Immortality

The average man, who does not know what to do with his life, wants another one which will last forever.
Anatole France (1844 - 1924)
The only thing wrong with immortality is that it tends to go on forever.
Herb Caen
If all else fails, immortality can always be assured by spectacular error.
John Kenneth Galbraith (1908 - 2006)
Ten thousand fools proclaim themselves into obscurity, while one wise man forgets himself into immortality.
Martin Luther King Jr. (1929 - 1968)
Seek not, my soul, the life of the immortals; but enjoy to the full the resources that are within thy reach.
Pindar (522 BC - 443 BC), 518-438 B.C.
The soul of man is immortal and imperishable.
Plato (427 BC - 347 BC), The Republic
Immortality. I notice that as soon as writers broach this question they begin to quote. I hate quotation. Tell me what you know.
Ralph Waldo Emerson (1803 - 1882), Journal (May 1849)
The first condition of immortality is death.
Stanislaw J. Lec (1909 - 1966), "Unkempt Thoughts"
Millions long for immortality who don't know what to do with themselves on a rainy Sunday afternoon.
Susan Ertz, Anger in the Sky
Our existence is but a brief crack of light between two eternities of darkness.
Vladimir Nabokov (1899 - 1977)
I have
Immortal longings in me.
William Shakespeare (1564 - 1616), "Antony and Cleopatra", Act 5 scene 2
I don't want to achieve immortality through my work... I want to achieve it through not dying.
Woody Allen (1935 -)

Inspiration

Inspiration may be a form of superconsciousness, or perhaps of subconsciousness - I wouldn't know. But I am sure it is the antithesis of self- consciousness.
Aaron Copland (1900 - 1990)
We should be taught not to wait for inspiration to start a thing. Action always generates inspiration. Inspiration seldom generates action.
Frank Tibolt
You can't wait for inspiration. You have to go after it with a club.
Jack London (1876 - 1916)
Inspiration is wonderful when it happens, but the writer must develop an approach for the rest of the time... The wait is simply too long.
Leonard Bernstein (1918 - 1990)
I decided that it was not wisdom that enabled [poets] to write their poetry, but a kind of instinct or inspiration, such as you find in seers and prophets who deliver all their sublime messages without knowing in the least what they mean.
Socrates (469 BC - 399 BC), In "Apology," sct. 21, by Plato.
Genius is one per cent inspiration, ninety-nine per cent perspiration.
Thomas A. Edison (1847 - 1931), Harper's Monthly, 1932
Genius is one percent inspiration, ninety-nine percent perspiration.
Thomas A. Edison (1847 - 1931), Harper's Monthly, 1932

Instinct

If a man is offered a fact which goes against his instincts, he will scrutinize it closely, and unless the evidence is overwhelming, he will refuse to believe it. If, on the other hand, he is offered something which affords a reason for acting in accordance to his instincts, he will accept it even on the slightest evidence. The origin of myths is explained in this way.

Bertrand Russell (1872 - 1970)
The wise are instructed by reason; ordinary minds by experience; the stupid, by necessity; and brutes by instinct.
Cicero (106 BC - 43 BC)
It is only by following your deepest instinct that you can lead a rich life, and if you let your fear of consequence prevent you from following your deepest instinct, then your life will be safe, expedient and thin.
Katharine Butler Hathaway
There can be as much value in the blink of an eye as in months of rational analysis.
Malcolm Gladwell, Blink: The Power of Thinking Without Thinking, 2005
Truly successful decision making relies on a balance between deliberate and instinctive thinking.
Malcolm Gladwell, Blink: The Power of Thinking Without Thinking, 2005
Creativity comes from trust. Trust your instincts.
Rita Mae Brown
I decided that it was not wisdom that enabled [poets] to write their poetry, but a kind of instinct or inspiration, such as you find in seers and prophets who deliver all their sublime messages without knowing in the least what they mean.
Socrates (469 BC - 399 BC), In "Apology," sct. 21, by Plato.

Integrity

Though the vicious can sometimes pour affliction upon the good, their power is transient and their punishment certain; and that innocence, though oppressed by injustice, shall, supported by patience, finally triumph over misfortune!
Ann Radcliffe (1764 - 1823), The Mysteries of Udolpho, 1764
What are riches - grandeur - health itself, to the luxury of a pure conscience, the health of the soul; - and what the sufferings of poverty, disappointment, despair - to the anguish of an afflicted one!
Ann Radcliffe (1764 - 1823), The Mysteries of Udolpho, 1764
Our character...is an omen of our destiny, and the more integrity we have and keep, the simpler and nobler that destiny is likely to be.
George Santayana (1863 - 1952), "The German Mind: A Philosophical Diagnosis"
Integrity combined with faithfulness is a powerful force and worthy of great respect.
Gordon Atkinson, RealLivePreacher.com Weblog, January 27, 2003
In silence man can most readily preserve his integrity.
Meister Eckhart
Real integrity is doing the right thing, knowing that nobody's going to know whether you did it or not.
Oprah Winfrey (1954 -), in Good Housekeeping
Integrity without knowledge is weak and useless, and knowledge without integrity is dangerous and dreadful.
Samuel Johnson (1709 - 1784)
I ran the wrong kind of business, but I did it with integrity.
Sydney Biddle Barrows, in Marian Christy, "'Mayflower Madam' Tells All,' Boston Globe, 1986

Intelligence

Intelligence appears to be the thing that enables a man to get along without education. Education enables a man to get along without the use of his intelligence.
Albert Edward Wiggam
Great spirits have always found violent opposition from mediocrities. The latter cannot understand it when a man does not thoughtlessly submit to hereditary prejudices, but honestly and courageously uses his intelligence and fulfills the duty to express the results of his thought in clear form.
Albert Einstein (1879 - 1955), quoted in New York Times, March 19, 1940
It has yet to be proven that intelligence has any survival value.
Arthur C. Clarke (1917 -)
Men fear thought as they fear nothing else on earth – more than ruin – more even than death.... Thought is subversive and revolutionary, destructive and terrible, thought is merciless to privilege, established institutions, and comfortable habit. Thought looks into the pit of hell and is not afraid. Thought is great and swift and free, the light of the world, and the chief glory of man.
Bertrand Russell (1872 - 1970)
So far as I can remember, there is not one word in the Gospels in praise of intelligence.
Bertrand Russell (1872 - 1970)
Sometimes I think the surest sign that intelligent life exists elsewhere in the universe is that none of it has tried to contact us.
Bill Watterson (1958 -), cartoonist, "Calvin and Hobbes"
There is nobody so irritating as somebody with less intelligence and more sense than we have.
Don Herold
An intellectual is a man who takes more words than necessary to tell more than he knows.
Dwight D. Eisenhower (1890 - 1969)
The test of a first-rate intelligence is the ability to hold two opposed ideas in the mind at the same time, and still retain the ability to function.
F. Scott Fitzgerald (1896 - 1940), "The Crack-Up" (1936)
It is not worth an intelligent man's time to be in the majority. By definition, there are already enough people to do that.
G. H. Hardy (1877 - 1947)
One man that has a mind and knows it can always beat ten men who haven't and don't.
George Bernard Shaw (1856 - 1950), "The Apple Cart" (1930), act I
Readers are plentiful; thinkers are rare.
Harriet Martineau (1802 - 1876)
Truly great madness cannot be achieved without significant intelligence.

Henrik Tikkanen
There is no such thing as an underestimate of average intelligence.
Henry Adams (1838 - 1918)
The intelligence is proved not by ease of learning, but by understanding what we learn.
Joseph Whitney
You don't have to be a genius when you're surrounded by morons.
Josh Lieb, I am a Genius of Unspeakable Evil and I Want to be Your Class President, 2009
An intelligence test sometimes shows a man how smart he would have been not to have taken it.
Laurence J. Peter (1919 - 1988)
I happen to feel that the degree of a person's intelligence is directly reflected by the number of conflicting attitudes she can bring to bear on the same topic.
Lisa Alther, Kinflicks, 1975
To repeat what others have said, requires education; to challenge it, requires brains.
Mary Pettibone Poole, A Glass Eye at a Keyhole, 1938
The more intelligent a man is, the more originality he discovers in men. Ordinary people see no difference between men.
Pascal
Beware when the great God lets loose a thinker on this planet.
Ralph Waldo Emerson (1803 - 1882)
The ability to focus attention on important things is a defining characteristic of intelligence.
Robert J. Shiller, Irrational Exuberance
A mind too active is no mind at all.
Theodore Roethke (1908 - 1963)
I not only use all the brains that I have, but all that I can borrow.
Woodrow Wilson (1856 - 1924)

Internet

When I took office, only high energy physicists had ever heard of what is called the Worldwide Web.... Now even my cat has its own page.
Bill Clinton (1946 -), announcement of Next Generation Internet initiative, 1996
I sense an insatiable demand for connectivity. Maybe all these people have discovered important uses for the Internet. Perhaps some of them feel hungry for a community that our real neighborhoods don't deliver. At least a few must wonder what the big deal is.
Clifford Stoll, Silicon Snake Oil, 1995
It shouldn't be too much of a surprise that the Internet has evolved into a force strong enough to reflect the greatest hopes and fears of those who use it. After all, it was designed to withstand nuclear war, not just the puny huffs and puffs of politicians and religious fanatics.
Denise Caruso, (digital commerce columnist, New York Times)
The Internet is like alcohol in some sense. It accentuates what you would do anyway. If you want to be a loner, you can be more alone. If you want to connect, it makes it easier to connect.
Esther Dyson, Interview in Time Magazine, October 2005
My favorite thing about the Internet is that you get to go into the private world of real creeps without having to smell them.
Penn Jillette (1955 -), in a Compuserve chat
I think the Internet is uniquely suited to this free market idea; that everyone on the Internet that exchanges the traffic back and forth, big or small, we all need each other.
Pete Ashdown, Utah Geek Dinner Speech, 08-22-06
On the Internet, nobody knows you're a dog.
Peter Steiner, cartoon in The New Yorker, July 5, 1993
We've heard that a million monkeys at a million keyboards could produce the complete works of Shakespeare; now, thanks to the Internet, we know that is not true.
Robert Wilensky, speech at a 1996 conference
If you ever start to feel too good about yourself, they have this thing called the Internet, and you can find a lot of people there who don't like you.
Tina Fey, Golden Globes Acceptance Speech, 2009
The 'Net is a waste of time, and that's exactly what's right about it.
William Gibson (1948 -)

Invention

I don't think necessity is the mother of invention - invention, in my opinion, arises directly from idleness, possibly also from laziness. To save oneself trouble.
Agatha Christie (1890 - 1976), An Autobiography, 1977
The best way to predict the future is to invent it.
Alan Kay
An inventor is simply a fellow who doesn't take his education too seriously.
Charles F. Kettering (1876 - 1958)
We are more ready to try the untried when what we do is inconsequential. Hence the fact that many inventions had their birth as toys.
Eric Hoffer (1902 - 1983)
Getting caught is the mother of invention.
Robert Byrne
To invent, you need a good imagination and a pile of junk.
Thomas A. Edison (1847 - 1931)
Invention is the mother of necessity.
Thorstein Veblen (1857 - 1929)

Jealousy

It is in the character of very few men to honor without envy a friend who has prospered.
Aeschylus (525 BC - 456 BC), Agamemnon
Our envy of others devours us most of all.
Alexander Solzhenitsyn (1918 -)
Such is the inconsistency of real love, that it is always awake to suspicion, however unreasonable; always requiring new assurances from the object of its interest.
Ann Radcliffe (1764 - 1823), The Mysteries of Udolpho, 1764
Do not envy a sinner; you don't know what disaster awaits him.
Bible, Old Testament
Jealousy is all the fun you think they had.
Erica Jong, Fear of Flying, 1973
Moral indignation is jealousy with a halo.
H. G. Wells (1866 - 1946), The Wife of Sir Isaac Harman (1914)
It is better to be envied than pitied.
Herodotus (484 BC - 430 BC), The Histories of Herodotus
I am completely in charge of the choices I make about what I am doing to lose weight and get healthy. And you know what? We all have this power. Don't be angry with me for something good I've done for myself. Be angry with yourself for not having the courage to do the same in your own life.
Jennifer Hudson, I Got This: How I Changed My Ways and Lost What Weighed Me Down, 2012
Papa said that I should never be jealous of another's marriage. Whatever joys I imagine them having are just my imaginings. The reality is far more complicated and vast.
Laura Moncur (1969 -), The Secret Heart of Charlotte Lucas, 2014
Envy can be a positive motivator. Let it inspire you to work harder for what you want.
Robert Bringle, quoted in Redbook
They envy the distinction I have won; let them therefore, envy my toils, my honesty, and the methods by which I gained it.
Sallust (86 BC - 34 BC)
Envy is the ulcer of the soul.
Socrates (469 BC - 399 BC)
O, beware, my lord, of jealousy!
It is the green-eyed monster which doth mock
The meat it feeds on.
William Shakespeare (1564 - 1616), "Othello", Act 3 scene 3

Journalism

People everywhere confuse what they read in newspapers with news.
A. J. Liebling (1904 - 1963)
To read a newspaper is to refrain from reading something worthwhile. The first discipline of education must therefore be to refuse resolutely to feed the mind with canned chatter.
Aleister Crowley (1875 - 1947)
Trying to be a first-rate reporter on the average American newspaper is like trying to play Bach's 'St. Matthew's Passion' on a ukulele.
Bagdikian's Observation
Trying to determine what is going on in the world by reading newspapers is like trying to tell the time by watching the second hand of a clock.
Ben Hecht (1893 - 1964)
Literature is the art of writing something that will be read twice; journalism what will be read once.
Cyril Connolly (1903 - 1974), Enemies of Promise (1938)
USA Today has come out with a new survey - apparently, three out of every four people make up 75% of the population.
David Letterman (1947 -)
Editor: a person employed by a newspaper, whose business it is to separate the wheat from the chaff, and to see that the chaff is printed.
Elbert Hubbard (1856 - 1915)
Rock journalism is people who can't write interviewing people who can't talk for people who can't read.
Frank Zappa (1940 - 1993), quoted in Linda Botts, "Loose Talk" (1980)
Journalism largely consists of saying 'Lord Jones is Dead' to people who never knew that Lord Jones was alive.
G. K. Chesterton (1874 - 1936)
Half of the American people have never read a newspaper. Half never voted for President. One hopes it is the same half.
Gore Vidal (1925 -)
All successful newspapers are ceaselessly querulous and bellicose. They never defend anyone or anything if they can help it; if the job is forced on them, they tackle it by denouncing someone or something else.
H. L. Mencken (1880 - 1956)
A newspaper consists of just the same number of words, whether there be any news in it or not.
Henry Fielding (1707 - 1754)
It's amazing that the amount of news that happens in the world every day always just exactly fits the newspaper.
Jerry Seinfeld (1954 -)
Rage is the only quality which has kept me, or anybody I have ever studied, writing columns for newspapers.
Jimmy Breslin
You must have a room, or a certain hour or so a day, where you don't know what was in the newspapers that morning... a place where you can simply experience and bring forth what you are and what you might be.
Joseph Campbell (1904 - 1987)
Once a newspaper touches a story, the facts are lost forever, even to the protagonists.
Norman Mailer (1923 - 2007), "Esquire", June 1960
But what is the difference between literature and journalism?
...Journalism is unreadable and literature is not read. That is all.

Oscar Wilde (1854 - 1900), The Critic as Artist, 1891
Every journalist has a novel in him, which is an excellent place for it.
Russel Lynes
Newspapermen learn to call a murderer 'an alleged murderer' and the King of England 'the alleged King of England' to avoid libel suits.
Stephen Leacock (1869 - 1944)
Advertisements... contain the only truths to be relied on in a newspaper.
Thomas Jefferson (1743 - 1826), Letter to Nathaniel Macon, January 12, 1819
I do not take a single newspaper, nor read one a month, and I feel myself infinitely the happier for it.
Thomas Jefferson (1743 - 1826)
I read no newspaper now but Ritchie's, and in that chiefly the advertisements, for they contain the only truths to be relied on in a newspaper.
Thomas Jefferson (1743 - 1826), Letter to Nathaniel Macon, January 12, 1819
The man who reads nothing at all is better educated than the man who reads nothing but newspapers.
Thomas Jefferson (1743 - 1826)

Joy

The only joy in the world is to begin.
Cesare Pavese (1908 - 1950)
This is the best kind of voyeurism, hearing joy from your neighbors.
Chuck Sigars, The World According to Chuck weblog, October 14, 2003
Give not over thy soul to sorrow; and afflict not thyself in thy own counsel. Gladness of heart is the life of man and the joyfulness of man is length of days.
Ecclesiastes
Do not judge men by mere appearances; for the light laughter that bubbles on the lip often mantles over the depths of sadness, and the serious look may be the sober veil that covers a divine peace and joy.
Edward Chapin
Short is the joy that guilty pleasure brings.
Euripides (484 BC - 406 BC)
During [these] periods of relaxation after concentrated intellectual activity, the intuitive mind seems to take over and can produce the sudden clarifying insights which give so much joy and delight.
Fritjof Capra, physicist
This is the true joy in life, the being used for a purpose recognized by yourself as a mighty one; the being thoroughly worn out before you are thrown on the scrap heap; the being a force of Nature instead of a feverish selfish little clod of ailments and grievances complaining that the world will not devote itself to making you happy.
George Bernard Shaw (1856 - 1950), Man and Superman, Epistle Dedicatory
We could never learn to be brave and patient, if there were only joy in the world.
Helen Keller (1880 - 1968)
I feel like a tiny bird with a big song!
Jerry Van Amerongen, Ballard Street, 08-18-05
I'm always sorry when pleasant things end. Something still pleasanter may come after, but you can never be sure.
L. M. Montgomery (1874 - 1942), Anne of Green Gables, 1908
Isn't it good just to be alive on a day like this? I pity the people who aren't born yet for missing it.
L. M. Montgomery (1874 - 1942), Anne of Green Gables, 1908
It's been my experience that you can nearly always enjoy things if you make up your mind firmly that you will.
L. M. Montgomery (1874 - 1942), Anne of Green Gables, 1908
Looking forward to things is half the pleasure of them. You mayn't get the things themselves; but nothing can prevent you from having the fun of looking forward to them.
L. M. Montgomery (1874 - 1942), Anne of Green Gables, 1908
Joy is not a commodity to be hoarded and protected. It is like a muscle. It must be used daily to keep strong and vigorous. For all my hardships, I have been able to remain quite joyful, for my muscles are strong.
Laura Moncur (1969 -), The Secret Heart of Charlotte Lucas, 2014
I've grown to realize the joy that comes from little victories is preferable to the fun that comes from ease and the pursuit of pleasure.
Lawana Blackwell, The Courtship of the Vicar's Daughter, 1998
I cannot believe that the inscrutable universe turns on an axis of suffering; surely the strange beauty of the world must somewhere rest on pure joy!
Louise Bogan
Grief can take care of itself, but to get the full value of a joy you must have somebody to divide it with.
Mark Twain (1835 - 1910)
May your walls know joy; May every room hold laughter and every window open to great possibility.
Maryanne Radmacher-Hershey, 1995
The most profound joy has more of gravity than of gaiety in it.
Michel de Montaigne (1533 - 1592)
Joy is prayer - Joy is strength - Joy is love - Joy is a net of love by which you can catch souls.
Mother Teresa (1910 - 1997)
The joy of a spirit is the measure of its power.
Ninon de Lenclos (1620 - 1705)
I define joy as a sustained sense of well-being and internal peace - a connection to what matters.
Oprah Winfrey (1954 -), O Magazine
There is an alchemy in sorrow. It can be transmuted into wisdom, which, if it does not bring joy, can yet bring happiness.
Pearl Buck (1892 - 1973)

Winning is important to me, but what brings me real joy is the experience of being fully engaged in whatever I'm doing.
Phil Jackson
Joy is not in things; it is in us.
Richard Wagner
Learning to live in the present moment is part of the path of joy.
Sarah Ban Breathnach
My mind to me a kingdom is,
Such present joys therein I find,
That it excels all other bliss.
Sir Edward Dyer
Real joy comes not from ease or riches or from the praise of men, but from doing something worthwhile.
Sir Wilfred Grenfell (1865 - 1940)
There is no greater joy nor greater reward than to make a fundamental difference in someone's life.
Sister Mary Rose McGeady
When you jump for joy, beware that no one moves the ground from beneath your feet.
Stanislaw J. Lec (1909 - 1966), "Unkempt Thoughts"
Cease, every joy, to glimmer on my mind,
But leave—oh! leave the light of Hope behind.
Thomas Campbell (1777 - 1844)
Things won are done; joy's soul lies in the doing.
William Shakespeare (1564 - 1616), Troilus and Cressida, Act 1, Scene 2

Justice;

I have always found that mercy bears richer fruits than strict justice.
Abraham Lincoln (1809 - 1865), speech in Washington D.C., 1865
Courage is of no value unless accompanied by justice; yet if all men became just, there would be no need for courage.
Agesilaus the Second
The sword of justice has no scabbard.
Antione De Riveral
It is in justice that the ordering of society is centered.
Aristotle (384 BC - 322 BC)
Justice does not come from the outside. It comes from inner peace.
Barbara Hall, A Summons to New Orleans, 2000
In the state of nature, indeed, all men are born equal, but they cannot continue in this equality. Society makes them lose it, and they recover it only by the protection of the laws.
Charles de Montesquieu (1689 - 1755), The Spirit of Laws, 1748
Justice is the constant and perpetual will to allot to every man his due.
Domitus Ulpian (100 AD - 228 AD)
It is the spirit and not the form of law that keeps justice alive.
Earl Warren (1891 - 1974)
Justice is a contract of expediency, entered upon to prevent men harming or being harmed.
Epicurus (341 BC - 270 BC)
Military justice is to justice what military music is to music.
Groucho Marx (1890 - 1977)
Liberty, equality - bad principles! The only true principle for humanity is justice; and justice to the feeble is protection and kindness.
Henri-Frédéric Amiel
Under a government which imprisons unjustly, the true place for a just man is also a prison.
Henry David Thoreau (1817 - 1862), Civil Disobedience, 1849
If it were not for injustice, men would not know justice.
Heraclitus (540 BC - 480 BC)
Many that live deserve death. And some die that deserve life. Can you give it to them? Then be not too eager to deal out death in the name of justice, fearing for your own safety. Even the wise cannot see all ends.
J. R. R. Tolkien (1892 - 1973), The Lord Of the Rings, Book Four, Chapter One
Gossip and reputation make sure that what comes around-a person who is cruel will find that the others are cruel back to him, and a person who is kind will find others are kind in return. Gossip paired with reciprocity allow karma to work here on earth, not in the next life.
Jonathan Haidt, The Happiness Hypothesis: Finding Modern Truth in Ancient Wisdom, 2005
The greatest justice in life is that your vision and looks tend to go simultaneously.
Kevin Bacon, People, 06-13-2011
The dead cannot cry out for justice; it is a duty of the living to do so for them.
Lois McMaster Bujold, Diplomatic Immunity, 2002
Nobody can give you freedom. Nobody can give you equality or justice or anything. If you're a man, you take it.
Malcolm X (1925 - 1965), Malcolm X Speaks, 1965
Injustice anywhere is a threat to justice everywhere.
Martin Luther King Jr. (1929 - 1968), Letter from Birmingham Jail, April 16, 1963
Justice requires that to lawfully constituted Authority there be given that respect and obedience which is its due; that the laws which are made shall be in wise conformity with the common good; and that, as a matter of conscience all men shall render obedience to these laws.
Pope Pius XI (1857 - 1939)
Justice consists not in being neutral between right and wrong, but in finding out the right and upholding it, wherever found, against the wrong.
Theodore Roosevelt (1858 - 1919), 1916 (quoted in the Theodore Roosevelt Centennial CD-ROM)
Justice delayed, is justice denied.
William Gladstone (1809 - 1898)

Kindness

No act of kindness, no matter how small, is ever wasted.
Aesop (620 BC - 560 BC), The Lion and the Mouse

The ideals which have lighted my way, and time after time have given me new courage to face life cheerfully, have been Kindness, Beauty, and Truth. The trite subjects of human efforts, possessions, outward success, luxury have always seemed to me contemptible.
Albert Einstein (1879 - 1955)

Moments of kindness and reconciliation are worth having, even if the parting has to come sooner or later.
Alice Munro

The end result of kindness is that it draws people to you.
Anita Roddick, A Revolution in Kindness, 2003

Ask yourself: Have you been kind today? Make kindness your daily modus operandi and change your world.
Annie Lennox

There are no thanks for a kindness, which has been delayed.
Anonymous

Compassion is the basis of all morality.
Arthur Schopenhauer (1788 - 1860)

There is no duty more obligatory than the repayment of kindness.
Cicero (106 BC - 43 BC)

Forget injuries, never forget kindnesses.
Confucius (551 BC - 479 BC)

Recompense injury with justice, and recompense kindness with kindness.
Confucius (551 BC - 479 BC), The Confucian Analects

To be able to practice five things everywhere under heaven constitutes perfect virtue...[They are] gravity, generosity of soul, sincerity, earnestness, and kindness.
Confucius (551 BC - 479 BC), The Confucian Analects

He who confers a favor should at once forget it, if he is not to show a sordid ungenerous spirit. To remind a man of a kindness conferred and to talk of it, is little different from reproach.
Demosthenes (384 BC - 322 BC)

Carry out a random act of kindness, with no expectation of reward, safe in the knowledge that one day someone might do the same for you.
Diana Spencer

I expect to pass through this world but once; any good thing therefore that I can do, or any kindness that I can show to any fellow creature, let me do it now; let me not defer or neglect it, for I shall not pass this way again.
Ettiene De Grellet

Guard well within yourself that treasure, kindness. Know how to give without hesitation, how to lose without regret, how to acquire without meanness.
George Sand (1804 - 1876)

I have learnt silence from the talkative, toleration from the intolerant, and kindness from the unkind; yet strange, I am ungrateful to these teachers.
Kahlil Gibran (1883 - 1931)

Sometimes when we are generous in small, barely detectable ways it can change someone else's life forever.
Margaret Cho, weblog, 03-11-04

Beginning today, treat everyone you meet as if they were going to be dead by midnight. Extend them all the care, kindness and understanding you can muster. Your life will never be the same again.
Og Mandino (1923 - 1996), The Greatest Miracle in the World

To become acquainted with kindness one must be prepared to learn new things and feel new feelings. Kindness is more than a philosophy of the mind. It is a philosophy of the spirit.
Robert J. Furey

Getting money is not all a man's business: to cultivate kindness is a valuable part of the business of life.
Samuel Johnson (1709 - 1784)

I have always depended on the kindness of strangers.
Tennessee Williams (1911 - 1983), A Streetcar Named Desire (1947)

If you want others to be happy, practice compassion. If you want to be happy, practice compassion.
The Dalai Lama (1935 -)

When you are kind to someone in trouble, you hope they'll remember and be kind to someone else. And it'll become like a wildfire.
Whoopi Goldberg

Yet do I fear thy nature;
It is too full o' the milk of human kindness.
William Shakespeare (1564 - 1616), "Macbeth", Act 1 scene 5

Yet I do fear thy nature; it is too full o' the milk of human kindness.
William Shakespeare (1564 - 1616), Macbeth, Act I, sc. 5

That best portion of a good man's life,
His little, nameless, unremembered acts of kindness and of love.
William Wordsworth (1770 - 1850)

That best portion of a good man's life, His little, nameless, unremembered acts of kindness and of love.
William Wordsworth (1770 - 1850)

The best portion of a good man's life is his little, nameless, unremembered acts of kindness and of love.
William Wordsworth (1770 - 1850)

Knowledge

If we value the pursuit of knowledge, we must be free to follow wherever that search may lead us. The free mind is no barking dog to be tethered on a ten-foot chain.
Adlai E. Stevenson Jr. (1900 - 1965)

If we value the pursuit of knowledge, we must be free to follow wherever that search may lead us. The free mind is not a barking dog, to be tethered on a ten-foot chain.
Adlai E. Stevenson Jr. (1900 - 1965), speech at the University of Wisconsin, Madison, October 8, 1952

Knowledge is like a garden; if it is not cultivated, it cannot be harvested.
African Proverb

Whoever undertakes to set himself up as a judge of Truth and Knowledge is shipwrecked by the laughter of the Gods.
Albert Einstein (1879 - 1955), (attributed)

Knowledge comes, but wisdom lingers.
Alfred Lord Tennyson (1809 - 1892)

Knowledge is essential to conquest; only according to our ignorance are we helpless. Thought creates character. Character can dominate conditions. Will creates circumstances and environment.
Anne Besant (1847 - 1933)

All men by nature desire knowledge.
Aristotle (384 BC - 322 BC), Metaphysics

Our feelings are our most genuine paths to knowledge.
Audre Lorde

It is knowledge that influences and equalizes the social condition of man; that gives to all, however different their political position, passions which are in common, and enjoyments which are universal.
Benjamin Disraeli (1804 - 1881)

The more extensive a man's knowledge of what has been done, the greater will be his power of knowing what to do.
Benjamin Disraeli (1804 - 1881)

To be conscious that you are ignorant is a great step to knowledge.
Benjamin Disraeli (1804 - 1881), Sybil, 1845

An investment in knowledge always pays the best interest.
Benjamin Franklin (1706 - 1790)

If a man empties his purse into his head no one can take it away from him. An investment in knowledge always pays the best interest.
Benjamin Franklin (1706 - 1790)

There is much pleasure to be gained from useless knowledge.
Bertrand Russell (1872 - 1970)

Wisdom is the right use of knowledge. To know is not to be wise. Many men know a great deal, and are all the greater fools for it. There is no fool so great a fool as a knowing fool. But to know how to use knowledge is to have wisdom.
Charles Haddon Spurgeon (1834 - 1892)

Mediocre men often have the most acquired knowledge.
Claude Bernard (1813 - 1878)

I am not one who was born in the possession of knowledge; I am one who is fond of antiquity, and earnest in seeking it there.
Confucius (551 BC - 479 BC), The Confucian Analects

When you know a thing, to hold that you know it; and when you do not know a thing, to allow that you do not know it - this is knowledge.
Confucius (551 BC - 479 BC), The Confucian Analects

Consider your origin; you were not born to live like brutes, but to follow virtue and knowledge.
Dante Alighieri (1265 - 1321), The Divine Comedy

Convinced myself, I seek not to convince.
Edgar Allan Poe (1809 - 1849), Berenice

It is no good to try to stop knowledge from going forward. Ignorance is never better than knowledge.
Enrico Fermi (1901 - 1954)

None of us is as smart as all of us.
Eric Schmidt, University of Pennsylvania Commencement Address, 2009

We have an opportunity for everyone in the world to have access to all the world's information. This has never before been possible. Why is ubiquitous information so profound? It's a tremendous equalizer. Information is power.
Eric Schmidt, University of Pennsylvania Commencement Address, 2009

We have come out of the time when obedience, the acceptance of discipline, intelligent courage, and resolution were most important, into that more difficult time when it is a man's duty to understand his world rather than to simply fight for it.
Ernest Hemingway (1899 - 1961), 1946

Knowledge is power, if you know it about the right person.
Ethel Mumford

The beginning of knowledge is the discovery of something we do not understand.
Frank Herbert (1920 - 1986)

A learned man is an idler who kills time with study. Beware of his false knowledge: it is more dangerous than ignorance.
George Bernard Shaw (1856 - 1950), Man and Superman, 1903

We are here and it is now. Further than that all human knowledge is moonshine.
H. L. Mencken (1880 - 1956)

If money is your hope for independence you will never have it. the only real security that a man can have in this world is a reserve of knowledge, experience, and ability.
Henry Ford (1863 - 1947)

Abundance of knowledge does not teach men to be wise.
Heraclitus (540 BC - 480 BC)

Science is organized knowledge.
Herbert Spencer (1820 - 1903)

Knowledge can be communicated, but wisdom cannot. A man can find it, he can live it, he can be filled and sustained by it, but he cannot utter or teach it.
Hermann Hesse (1877 - 1962)

This is the bitterest pain among men, to have much knowledge but no power.
Herodotus (484 BC - 430 BC), The Histories of Herodotus

If knowledge can create problems, it is not through ignorance that we can solve them.
Isaac Asimov (1920 - 1992)
His priority did not seem to be to teach them what he knew, but rather to impress upon them that nothing, not even... knowledge, was foolproof.
J. K. Rowling, Harry Potter and the Order of the Phoenix
Knowledge speaks, but wisdom listens.
Jimi Hendrix (1942 - 1970)
Knowledge is the only instrument of production that is not subject to diminishing returns.
John Clarke, Economist
We set sail on this new sea because there is knowledge to be gained.
John F. Kennedy (1917 - 1963)
There's a place in the brain for knowing what cannot be remembered.
John Green, An Abundance of Katherines, 2008
When a true genius appears in this world you may know him by this sign, that the dunces are all in confederacy against him.
Jonathan Swift (1667 - 1745)
In completing one discovery we never fail to get an imperfect knowledge of others of which we could have no idea before, so that we cannot solve one doubt without creating several new ones.
Joseph Priestley
Perplexity is the beginning of knowledge.
Kahlil Gibran (1883 - 1931), The Voice of the Master
The ending of sorrow is the beginning of wisdom. Knowledge is always within the shadow of ignorance. Meditation is freedom from thought and a movement in the ecstasy of truth. Meditation is explosion of intelligence.
Krishnamurti
New knowledge is the most valuable commodity on earth. The more truth we have to work with, the richer we become.
Kurt Vonnegut (1922 - 2007), Breakfast of Champions
People are difficult to govern because they have too much knowledge.
Lao-tzu (604 BC - 531 BC), The Way of Lao-tzu
Knowledge is a comfortable and necessary retreat and shelter for us in advanced age, and if we do not plant it while young, it will give us no shade when we grow old.
Lord Chesterfield (1694 - 1773)
The knowledge of the world is only to be acquired in the world, and not in the closet.
Lord Chesterfield (1694 - 1773)
Truth is eternal, knowledge is changeable. It is disastrous to confuse them.
Madeleine L'Engle (1918 -), An Acceptable Time
If you have knowledge, let others light their candles at it.
Margaret Fuller (1810 - 1850)
Education: that which reveals to the wise, and conceals from the stupid, the vast limits of their knowledge.
Mark Twain (1835 - 1910)
I would rather have my ignorance than another man's knowledge, because I have got so much more of it.
Mark Twain (1835 - 1910)
We have not the reverent feeling for the rainbow that a savage has, because we know how it is made. We have lost as much as we gained by prying into that matter.
Mark Twain (1835 - 1910), A Tramp Abroad, vol. 2, 1879
To be absolutely certain about something, one must know everything or nothing about it.
Olin Miller
Knowledge and timber shouldn't be much used till they are seasoned.
Oliver Wendell Holmes (1809 - 1894), The Autocrat of the Breakfast-Table, 1858
Knowledge, if it does not determine action, is dead to us.
Plotinus (205 AD - 270 AD)
All our progress is an unfolding, like a vegetable bud. You have first an instinct, then an opinion, then a knowledge as the plant has root, bud, and fruit. Trust the instinct to the end, though you can render no reason.
Ralph Waldo Emerson (1803 - 1882)
Our knowledge is the amassed thought and experience of innumerable minds.
Ralph Waldo Emerson (1803 - 1882)
I was born not knowing and have had only a little time to change that here and there.
Richard Feynman (1918 - 1988), Letter to Armando Garcia J, December 11, 1985
You can know the name of a bird in all the languages of the world, but when you're finished, you'll know absolutely nothing whatever about the bird... So let's look at the bird and see what it's doing – that's what counts. I learned very early the difference between knowing the name of something and knowing something.
Richard Feynman (1918 - 1988)
He who is not aware of his ignorance will only be misled by his knowledge.
Richard Whatley
Knowledge is of two kinds. We know a subject ourselves, or we know where we can find information on it.
Samuel Johnson (1709 - 1784), quoted in Boswell's Life of Johnson
Mankind have a great aversion to intellectual labor; but even supposing knowledge to be easily attainable, more people would be content to be ignorant than would take even a little trouble to acquire it.
Samuel Johnson (1709 - 1784), quoted in Boswell's Life of Johnson
Rules are just helpful guidelines for stupid people who can't make up their own minds.
Seth Hoffman, House M.D., 2010
I have taken all knowledge to be my province.
Sir Francis Bacon (1561 - 1626)
Knowledge is power.
Sir Francis Bacon (1561 - 1626), Religious Meditations, Of Heresies, 1597
Knowledge is power.

(Ipsa Scientia Potestas Est)
Sir Francis Bacon (1561 - 1626), Meditationes Sacræ. De Hæresibus. (1597)
The only good is knowledge and the only evil is ignorance.
Socrates (469 BC - 399 BC)
There is only one good, knowledge, and one evil, ignorance.
Socrates (469 BC - 399 BC), from Diogenes Laertius, Lives of Eminent Philosophers
Knowledge must come through action; you can have no test which is not fanciful, save by trial.
Sophocles (496 BC - 406 BC), Trachiniae
The greatest enemy of knowledge is not ignorance, it is the illusion of knowledge.
Stephen Hawking (1942 -)
The great end of life is not knowledge, but action.
Thomas Fuller (1608 - 1661)
If a little knowledge is dangerous, where is the man who has so much as to be out of danger.
Thomas H. Huxley (1825 - 1895)
A little learning is not a dangerous thing to one who does not mistake it for a great deal.
William Allen White

Language

We have too many high sounding words, and too few actions that correspond with them.
Abigail Adams (1744 - 1818), letter to John Adams, 1774
He can compress the most words into the smallest ideas of any man I ever met.
Abraham Lincoln (1809 - 1865)
Words calculated to catch everyone may catch no one.
Adlai E. Stevenson Jr. (1900 - 1965), speech to Democratic National Convention, Chicago, Illinois, July 21, 1952
Words are the physicians of the mind diseased.
Aeschylus (525 BC - 456 BC), Prometheus Bound
Language is the source of misunderstandings.
Antoine de Saint-Exupery (1900 - 1944)
Let thy speech be short, comprehending much in a few words.
Aprocrypha
High thoughts must have high language.
Aristophanes (450 BC - 388 BC), Frogs, 405 B.C.
Grasp the subject, the words will follow.
Cato the Elder (234 BC - 149 BC)
Use soft words and hard arguments.
English Proverb
Great literature is simply charged with meaning to the utmost possible degree.
Ezra Pound (1885 - 1972)
The great enemy of clear language is insincerity. When there is a gap between one's real and one's declared aims, one turns as it were instinctively to long words and exhausted idioms, like a cuttlefish spurting out ink.
George Orwell (1903 - 1950), "Politics and the English Language", 1946
A man thinks that by mouthing hard words he understands hard things.
Herman Melville (1819 - 1891)
For me, words are a form of action, capable of influencing change.
Ingrid Bengis
When ideas fail, words come in very handy.
Johann Wolfgang von Goethe (1749 - 1832)
Deeds, not words shall speak me.
John Fletcher (1579 - 1625)
Words ought to be a little wild for they are the assaults of thought on the unthinking.
John Maynard Keynes (1883 - 1946)
The great thing about human language is that it prevents us from sticking to the matter at hand.
Lewis Thomas (1913 - 1993)
Man invented language to satisfy his deep need to complain.
Lily Tomlin (1939 -)
We have really everything in common with America nowadays except, of course, language.
Oscar Wilde (1854 - 1900), The Canterville Ghost, 1882
Words have a longer life than deeds.
Pindar (522 BC - 443 BC), Nemean Odes
Language exerts hidden power, like a moon on the tides.
Rita Mae Brown, Starting From Scratch, 1988
Drawing on my fine command of the English language, I said nothing.
Robert Benchley (1889 - 1945)
No one has a finer command of language than the person who keeps his mouth shut.
Sam Rayburn (1882 - 1961)
Do not accustom yourself to use big words for little matters.
Samuel Johnson (1709 - 1784)
Works of imagination should be written in very plain language; the more purely imaginative they are the more necessary it is to be plain.
Samuel Taylor Coleridge (1772 - 1834)
Broadly speaking, the short words are the best, and the old words best of all.
Sir Winston Churchill (1874 - 1965)
Think like a wise man but communicate in the language of the people.
William Butler Yeats (1865 - 1939)
Speak properly, and in as few words as you can, but always plainly; for the end of speech is not ostentation, but to be understood.
William Penn (1644 - 1718)
I understand a fury in your words,
But not the words.

William Shakespeare (1564 - 1616), "Othello", Act 4 scene 2
My words fly up, my thoughts remain below:
Words without thoughts never to heaven go.
William Shakespeare (1564 - 1616), "Hamlet", Act 3 scene 3
They have been at a great feast of languages, and stolen the scraps.
William Shakespeare (1564 - 1616), "Love's Labour's Lost", Act 5 scene 1

Laughter

We cannot really love anybody with whom we never laugh.
Agnes Repplier (1855 - 1950), Americans and Others, 1912
He deserves Paradise who makes his companions laugh.
Anonymous, (wrongly attributed to the Koran)
We laugh a lot. That's for sure. Sure beats the alternative, doesn't it?
Betty White, Mark Twain Prize, 2010
The more you find out about the world, the more opportunities there are to laugh at it.
Bill Nye, Interview with Wired.com, April 2005
Laughter gives us distance. It allows us to step back from an event, deal with it and then move on.
Bob Newhart (1929 -)
Total absence of humor renders life impossible.
Colette (1873 - 1954), Chance Acquaintances, 1952
Laughter is by definition healthy.
Doris Lessing
The most wasted of all days is one without laughter.
e e cummings (1894 - 1962)
If you don't learn to laugh at trouble, you won't have anything to laugh at when you're old.
Edgar Watson Howe (1853 - 1937)
Laugh at yourself first, before anyone else can.
Elsa Maxwell, September 28, 1958
You cannot be mad at somebody who makes you laugh - it's as simple as that.
Jay Leno (1950 -), O Magazine, February 2003
If we couldn't laugh, we would all go insane.
Jimmy Buffett
In this life he laughs longest who laughs last.
John Masefield (1878 - 1967), "Window in Bye Street", 1912
Man is distinguished from all other creatures by the faculty of laughter.
Joseph Addison (1672 - 1719), The Spectator, September 26, 1712
One doesn't have a sense of humor. It has you.
Larry Gelbart
Always laugh when you can. It is cheap medicine.
Lord Byron (1788 - 1824)
The human race has one really effective weapon, and that is laughter.
Mark Twain (1835 - 1910)
He who laughs, lasts!
Mary Pettibone Poole
You don't stop laughing because you grow old. You grow old because you stop laughing.
Michael Pritchard
Laughter is inner jogging.
Norman Cousins (1915 - 1990)
I was irrevocably betrothed to laughter, the sound of which has always seemed to me to be the most civilized music in the world.
Peter Ustinov (1921 - 2004)
The most wasted day of all is that in which we have not laughed.
Sebastian R. N. Chamfort
You can't deny laughter; when it comes, it plops down in your favorite chair and stays as long as it wants.
Stephen King (1947 -), "Hearts in Atlantis"
Beware of too much laughter, for it deadens the mind and produces oblivion.
The Talmud
Laughter is the closest distance between two people.
Victor Borge (1909 - 2000)
Among those whom I like or admire, I can find no common denominator, but among those whom I love, I can: all of them make me laugh.
W. H. Auden (1907 - 1973)

Laws

Let me not be understood as saying that there are no bad laws, nor that grievances may not arise for the redress of which no legal provisions have been made. I mean to say no such thing. But I do mean to say that although bad laws, if they exist, should be repealed as soon as possible, still, while they continue in force, for the sake of example they should be religiously observed.
Abraham Lincoln (1809 - 1865)
Laws alone can not secure freedom of expression; in order that every man present his views without penalty there must be spirit of tolerance in the entire population.
Albert Einstein (1879 - 1955)
Good laws have their origins in bad morals.
Ambrosius Macrobius
The law, in its majestic equality, forbids the rich as well as the poor to sleep under bridges, to beg in the streets, and to steal bread.
Anatole France (1844 - 1924), The Red Lily, 1894, chapter 7
Where you find the laws most numerous, there you will find also the greatest injustice.
Arcesilaus

Law is order in liberty, and without order liberty is social chaos.
Archbishop Ireland
Even when laws have been written down, they ought not always to remain unaltered.
Aristotle (384 BC - 322 BC), Politics
I have gained this by philosophy: that I do without being commanded what others do only from fear of the law.
Aristotle (384 BC - 322 BC), from Diogenes Laertius, Lives of Eminent Philosophers
Law is mind without reason.
Aristotle (384 BC - 322 BC)
Law is order, and good law is good order.
Aristotle (384 BC - 322 BC), Politics
When men are pure, laws are useless; when men are corrupt, laws are broken.
Benjamin Disraeli (1804 - 1881)
A law is something which must have a moral basis, so that there is an inner compelling force for every citizen to obey.
Chaim Weizmann (1874 - 1952)
In the state of nature...all men are born equal, but they cannot continue in this equality. Society makes them lose it, and they recover it only by the protection of the law.
Charles de Montesquieu (1689 - 1755)
Law stands mute in the midst of arms.
Cicero (106 BC - 43 BC), Pro Milone
The people's good is the highest law.
Cicero (106 BC - 43 BC), De Legibus
The strictest law often causes the most serious wrong.
Cicero (106 BC - 43 BC)
The welfare of the people is the ultimate law.
(Salus Populi Suprema Est Lex)
Cicero (106 BC - 43 BC)
It is found by experience that admirable laws and right precedents among the good have their origin in the misdeeds of others.
Cornelius Tacitus (55 AD - 117 AD)
It is the spirit and not the form of law that keeps justice alive.
Earl Warren (1891 - 1974)
Fragile as reason is and limited as law is as the institutionalised medium of reason, that's all we have between us and the tyranny of mere will and the cruelty of unbridled, undisciplined feelings.
Felix Frankfurter (1882 - 1965)
The United States is a nation of laws: badly written and randomly enforced.
Frank Zappa (1940 - 1993)
What power has law where only money rules.
Gaius Petronius (~ 66 AD)
The problem with any unwritten law is that you don't know where to go to erase it.
Glaser and Way
A judge is a law student who marks his own examination papers.
H. L. Mencken (1880 - 1956)
The trouble with fighting for human freedom is that one spends most of one's time defending scoundrels. For it is against scoundrels that oppressive laws are first aimed, and oppression must be stopped at the beginning if it is to be stopped at all.
H. L. Mencken (1880 - 1956)
It was the boast of Augustus that he found Rome of brick and left it of marble. But how much nobler will be the sovereign's boast when he shall have it to say that he found law... a sealed book and left it a living letter; found it the patrimony of the rich and left it the inheritance of the poor; found it the two-edged sword of craft and oppression and left it the staff of honesty and the shield of innocence.
Henry Brougham (1778 - 1868)
There are not enough jails, not enough policemen, not even enough courts too enforce a law not supported by the people.
Hubert H. Humphrey (1911 - 1978)
Good laws lead to the making of better ones; bad ones bring about worse.
Jean Jacques Rousseau (1712 - 1778)
The law is not so much carved in stone as it is written in water, flowing in and out with the tide.
Jeff Melvoin, Northern Exposure, Crime and Punishment, 1992
Facts are stubborn things; and whatever may be our wishes, our inclinations, or the dictates of our passions, they cannot alter the state of facts and evidence.
John Adams (1735 - 1826)
Ignorance of the law excuses no man: Not that all men know the law, but because 'tis an excuse every man will plead, and no man can tell how to refute him.
John Selden (1584 - 1654)
The more laws and order are made prominent,
The more thieves and robbers there will be.
Lao-tzu (604 BC - 531 BC), The Way of Lao-tzu
I submit that an individual who breaks a law that conscience tells him is unjust, and who willingly accepts the penalty of imprisonment in order to arouse the conscience of the community over its injustice, is in reality expressing the highest respect for the law.
Martin Luther King Jr. (1929 - 1968)
Laws are like sausages. It's better not to see them being made.
Otto von Bismarck (1815 - 1898)
Laws are partly formed for the sake of good men, in order to instruct them how they may live on friendly terms with one another, and partly for the sake of those who refuse to be instructed, whose spirit cannot be subdued, or softened, or hindered from plunging into evil.
Plato (427 BC - 347 BC)
Justice requires that to lawfully constituted Authority there be given that respect and obedience which is its due; that the laws which are made shall be in wise conformity

with the common good; and that, as a matter of conscience all men shall render obedience to these laws.
Pope Pius XI (1857 - 1939)
A jury consists of twelve persons chosen to decide who has the better lawyer.
Robert Frost (1874 - 1963), (attributed)
Law is experience developed by reason and applied continually to further experience.
Roscoe Pound (1870 - 1964)
The law must be stable, but it must not stand still.
Roscoe Pound (1870 - 1964)
Laws do not persuade just because they threaten.
Seneca (5 BC - 65 AD)
Let us consider the reason of the case. For nothing is law that is not reason.
Sir John Powell
The decisions of the courts on economic and social questions depend on their economic and social philosophy.
Theodore Roosevelt (1858 - 1919)
Laws and institutions must go hand in hand with the general progress of the human mind.
Thomas Jefferson (1743 - 1826)
Law is the embodiment of the moral sentiment of the people.
William Blackstone (1723 - 1780)
Necessity has no law.
William Langland (1332 - 1400)
Pity is the virtue of the law, and none but tyrants use it cruelly.
William Shakespeare (1564 - 1616)
The law hath not been dead, though it hath slept.
William Shakespeare (1564 - 1616), "Measure for Measure", Act 2 scene 2
The law that will work is merely the summing up in legislative form of the moral judgement that the community has already reached.
Woodrow Wilson (1856 - 1924)

Laziness

I don't think necessity is the mother of invention - invention, in my opinion, arises directly from idleness, possibly also from laziness. To save oneself trouble.
Agatha Christie (1890 - 1976), An Autobiography, 1977
Ambition is a poor excuse for not having sense enough to be lazy.
Edgar Bergen (1903 - 1978), (Charlie McCarthy)
Idleness is not doing nothing. Idleness is being free to do anything.
Floyd Dell
Idleness and lack of occupation tend - nay are dragged - towards evil.
Hippocrates (460 BC - 377 BC), Decorum
Failure is not the only punishment for laziness; there is also the success of others.
Jules Renard (1864 - 1910)
Laziness is nothing more than the habit of resting before you get tired.
Jules Renard (1864 - 1910)
Indolence is a delightful but distressing state; we must be doing something to be happy.
Mahatma Gandhi (1869 - 1948)
There is no pleasure in having nothing to do; the fun is in having lots to do and not doing it.
Mary Wilson Little
That indolent but agreeable condition of doing nothing.
Pliny the Younger (62 AD - 114 AD), Letters
I'm not sure about whether I shall go. I am the most incurably lazy devil that ever stood in shoe leather – that is, when the fit is on me, for I can be spry enough at times.
Sir Arthur Conan Doyle (1859 - 1930), Sherlock Holmes in "A Study in Scarlet"
Far from idleness being the root of all evil, it is rather the only true good.
Soren Kierkegaard (1813 - 1855)
Never be entirely idle; but either be reading, or writing, or praying or meditating or endeavoring something for the public good.
Thomas a Kempis (1380 - 1471)
He that is busy is tempted by but one devil; he that is idle, by a legion.
Thomas Fuller (1608 - 1661), Gnomologia, 1732
Determine never to be idle...It is wonderful how much may be done if we are always doing.
Thomas Jefferson (1743 - 1826)

Leadership

What luck for rulers that men do not think.
Adolf Hitler (1889 - 1945)
The first duty of a leader is to make himself be loved without courting love. To be loved without 'playing up' to anyone - even to himself.
Andre Malraux (1901 - 1976)
The key to being a good manager is keeping the people who hate me away from those who are still undecided.
Casey Stengel (1890 - 1975)
Self-regulation will always be a challenge, but if somebody's going to be in charge, it might as well be me.
Daniel Akst, We Have Met the Enemy: Self-Control in an Age of Excess, 2011
A sense of humor is part of the art of leadership, of getting along with people, of getting things done.
Dwight D. Eisenhower (1890 - 1969)
The crowd gives the leader new strength.
Evenius

Faith in the ability of a leader is of slight service unless it be united with faith in his justice.
George Goethals (1858 - 1928)
The question, "Who ought to be boss?" is like asking "Who ought to be the tenor in the quartet?" Obviously, the man who can sing tenor.
Henry Ford (1863 - 1947)
It is hard to look up to a leader who keeps his ear to the ground.
James H. Boren
Leadership and learning are indispensable to each other.
John F. Kennedy (1917 - 1963), speech prepared for delivery in Dallas the day of his assassination, November 22, 1963
Leaders make things possible. Exceptional leaders make them inevitable.
Lance Morrow
We will make them think it's their idea. That's how all great leaders fool people.
Laura Preble, The Queen Geek Social Club, 2006
Management is nothing more than motivating other people.
Lee Iacocca (1924 -)
An Army of lions commanded by a deer will never be an army of lions.
Napoleon Bonaparte (1769 - 1821)
So much of what we call management consists in making it difficult for people to work.
Peter Drucker (1909 - 2005)
A leader takes people where they want to go. A great leader takes people where they don't necessarily want to go but where they ought to be.
Rosalynn Carter (1927 -)
The history of the world is but the biography of great men.
Thomas Carlyle (1795 - 1881)

Learning

Learning is not attained by chance, it must be sought for with ardor and attended to with diligence.
Abigail Adams (1744 - 1818), 1780
It is always safe to learn, even from our enemies; seldom safe to venture to instruct, even our friends.
Charles Caleb Colton (1780 - 1832)
Learning without thought is labor lost; thought without learning is perilous.
Confucius (551 BC - 479 BC), The Confucian Analects
That is what learning is. You suddenly understand something you've understood all your life, but in a new way.
Doris Lessing
Only the curious will learn and only the resolute overcome the obstacles to learning. The quest quotient has always excited me more than the intelligence quotient.
Eugene S. Wilson
Whoso neglects learning in his youth,
Loses the past and is dead for the future.
Euripides (484 BC - 406 BC), Phrixus
Whoever ceases to be a student has never been a student.
George Iles
The wisest mind has something yet to learn.
George Santayana (1863 - 1952)
Much learning does not teach understanding.
Heraclitus (540 BC - 480 BC), On the Universe
Never seem more learned than the people you are with. Wear your learning like a pocket watch and keep it hidden. Do not pull it out to count the hours, but give the time when you are asked.
Lord Chesterfield (1694 - 1773)
We learn by example and by direct experience because there are real limits to the adequacy of verbal instruction.
Malcolm Gladwell, Blink: The Power of Thinking Without Thinking, 2005
Anyone who stops learning is old, whether twenty or eighty. Anyone who keeps learning stays young. The greatest thing you can do is keep your mind young.
Mark Twain (1835 - 1910)
Never learn to do anything: if you don't learn, you'll always find someone else to do it for you.
Mark Twain (1835 - 1910)
What is important is to keep learning, to enjoy challenge, and to tolerate ambiguity. In the end there are no certain answers.
Martina Horner, President of Radcliffe College
Whenever you are asked if you can do a job, tell 'em, 'Certainly I can!' Then get busy and find out how to do it.
Theodore Roosevelt (1858 - 1919)
Learning is not compulsory... neither is survival.
W. Edwards Deming (1900 - 1993)
You learn more quickly under the guidance of experienced teachers. You waste a lot of time going down blind alleys if you have no one to lead you.
W. Somerset Maugham (1874 - 1965), The Razor's Edge, 1943

Legacy

Abraham Lincoln and Millard Fillmore had the same title. They were both presidents of the United States, but their tenure in office and their legacy could not be more different.
Barack Obama (1961 -), Arizona State Commencement Speech, 2009
Let us develop the resources of our land, call forth our powers, build up its institutions, promote all its great interests, and see whether we also, in our day and generation, may not perform something worthy to be remembered.

Daniel Webster (1782 - 1852), Address at the laying of the cornerstone of the bunker hill monument
When you have told anyone you have left him a legacy the only decent thing to do is to die at once.
Samuel Butler (1835 - 1902), In Festing Jones, Samuel Butler : A Memoir
No legacy is so rich as honesty.
William Shakespeare (1564 - 1616), "All's Well that Ends Well", Act 3 scene 5

Liberals

Liberals are very broadminded: they are always willing to give careful consideration to both sides of the same side.
Anonymous
I am a Conservative to preserve all that is good in our constitution, a Radical to remove all that is bad. I seek to preserve property and to respect order, and I equally decry the appeal to the passions of the many or the prejudices of the few.
Benjamin Disraeli (1804 - 1881), campaign speech at High Wycombe, England, November 27, 1832
The most radical revolutionary will become a conservative the day after the revolution.
Hannah Arendt (1906 - 1975)
The radical of one century is the conservative of the next. The radical invents the views. When he has worn them out the conservative adopts them.
Mark Twain (1835 - 1910), Notebook, 1935
When you are right you cannot be too radical; when you are wrong, you cannot be too conservative.
Martin Luther King Jr. (1929 - 1968)
It only takes 20 years for a liberal to become a conservative without changing a single idea.
Robert Anton Wilson
A liberal is a man too broadminded to take his own side in a quarrel.
Robert Frost (1874 - 1963)
I never dared to be radical when young
For fear it would make me conservative when old.
Robert Frost (1874 - 1963), 'Ten Mills,' A Further Range, 1936
A liberal is a person whose interests aren't at stake at the moment.
Willis Player

Liars

Liars when they speak the truth are not believed.
Aristotle (384 BC - 322 BC), from Diogenes Laertius, Lives of Eminent Philosophers
Sometimes the lies you tell are less frightening than the loneliness you might feel if you stopped telling them.
Brock Clarke, An Arsonist's Guide to Writers' Homes in New England, 2007
Lying increases the creative faculties, expands the ego, and lessens the frictions of social contacts.
Clare Booth Luce (1903 - 1987)
Repetition does not transform a lie into a truth.
Franklin D. Roosevelt (1882 - 1945), radio address, October 26, 1939
The visionary lies to himself, the liar only to others.
Friedrich Nietzsche (1844 - 1900)
All men are frauds. The only difference between them is that some admit it. I myself deny it.
H. L. Mencken (1880 - 1956)
Hoaxes are nothing new. News media isn't hard to fool. It's fun to fool and people like to mess with people. It all goes to show you that we're not all that hard to fool. I think we should just accept that and trust people anyway.
Hank Green, Vlogbrothers, The Top 10 Greatest Hoaxes of All Time, 10-22-09
It is always the best policy to speak the truth–unless, of course, you are an exceptionally good liar.
Jerome K. Jerome (1859 - 1927)
Being manipulative is dishonest and immature. We often end up having to make up more lies to cover for inconsistencies in our original manipulation. In addition, it sets a terrible example for our children. While it may solve your initial problem, the tangled web that grows from such dishonesty is more trouble than it's worth.
Julie A., M.A. Ross and Judy Corcoran, Joint Custody with a Jerk: Raising a Child with an Uncooperative Ex, 2011
A lie told often enough becomes the truth.
Lenin (1870 - 1924)
A lie can travel halfway around the world while the truth is putting on its shoes.
Mark Twain (1835 - 1910), (attributed)
The history of our race, and each individual's experience, are sown thick with evidence that a truth is not hard to kill and that a lie told well is immortal.
Mark Twain (1835 - 1910), Advice to Youth
Lies are like children: they're hard work, but it's worth it because the future depends on them.
Pam Davis, House M.D., It's A Wonderful Lie, 2008
False words are not only evil in themselves, but they infect the soul with evil.
Plato (427 BC - 347 BC), Dialogues, Phaedo
A liar should have a good memory.
Quintilian, De Institutione Oratoria
Truth is beautiful, without doubt; but so are lies.
Ralph Waldo Emerson (1803 - 1882)
Lies are like children. If you don't nurture them, they'll never be useful later.
Randy K. Milholland, Something Positive, 07-26-2012
Ambition drove many men to become false; to have one thought locked in the breast, another ready on the tongue.

Sallust (86 BC - 34 BC), The War with Catiline
Any fool can tell the truth, but it requires a man of some sense to know how to lie well.
Samuel Butler (1835 - 1902)
The best liar is he who makes the smallest amount of lying go the longest way.
Samuel Butler (1835 - 1902)
Oh what a tangled web we weave,
When first we practise to deceive!
Sir Walter Scott (1771 - 1832), Marmion, Canto vi. Stanza 17.
Truly, to tell lies is not honorable;
but when the truth entails tremendous ruin,
To speak dishonorably is pardonable.
Sophocles (496 BC - 406 BC), Creusa

Life

Life isn't simple. But the beauty of it is, you can always start over. It'll get easier.
Alacia Bessette, Simply from Scratch, 2010
Life is indeed difficult, partly because of the real difficulties we must overcome in order to survive, and partly because of our own innate desire to always do better, to overcome new challenges, to self-actualize. Happiness is experienced largely in striving towards a goal, not in having attained things, because our nature is always to want to go on to the next endeavor.
Albert Ellis, Michael Abrams, Lidia Dengelegi, The Art & Science of Rational Eating, 1992
There are two ways to slide easily through life: to believe everything or to doubt everything; both ways save us from thinking.
Alfred Korzybski (1879 - 1950)
You're alive. Do something. The directive in life, the moral imperative was so uncomplicated. It could be expressed in single words, not complete sentences. It sounded like this: Look. Listen. Choose. Act.
Barbara Hall, A Summons to New Orleans, 2000
The first step to getting the things you want out of life is this: Decide what you want.
Ben Stein
Man is born to live, not to prepare for life.
Boris Pasternak (1890 - 1960), Doctor Zhivago, 1958
Not a shred of evidence exists in favor of the idea that life is serious.
Brendan Gill
You don't have to live your life so that your life is suitable for small talk. Life can be lived in ways that circumnavigate a myriad of colors and landscapes.
Cherie Ve Ard, Technomadia, 04-04-2013
Life is a foreign language; all men mispronounce it.
Christopher Morley (1890 - 1957)
Life is full of surprises and and serendipity. Being open to unexpected turns in the road is an important part of success. If you try to plan every step, you may miss those wonderful twists and turns. Just find your next adventure-do it well, enjoy it-and then, not now, think about what comes next.
Condoleeza Rice
In matters of self-control as we shall see again and again, speed kills. But a little friction really can save lives.
Daniel Akst, We Have Met the Enemy: Self-Control in an Age of Excess, 2011
When we exercise self-control on a given occasion, we win for ourselves a little credibility we can rely on the next time around. Pretty soon we develop a reputation to ourselves that we want badly to uphold. With each test that we meet, our resolve gains momentum, fueled by the fear that we may succumb and establish a damaging precedent for our own weakness.
Daniel Akst, We Have Met the Enemy: Self-Control in an Age of Excess, 2011
Life is a thing that mutates without warning, not always in enviable ways. All part of the improbable adventure of being alive, of being a brainy biped with giant dreams on a crazy blue planet.
Diane Ackerman, One Hundred Names for Love: A Stroke, A Marriage, and the Language of Healing, 2011
The purpose of life is to fight maturity.
Dick Werthimer
Oh, life is a glorious cycle of song,
A medley of extemporanea;
And love is a thing that can never go wrong;
And I am Marie of Romania.
Dorothy Parker (1893 - 1967), Not So Deep as a Well (1937), "Comment"
It's not true that life is one damn thing after another; it is one damn thing over and over.
Edna St. Vincent Millay (1892 - 1950)
Life improves slowly and goes wrong fast, and only catastrophe is clearly visible.
Edward Teller (1908 - 2003)
Life is just one damned thing after another.
Elbert Hubbard (1856 - 1915)
Life is like one big Mardi Gras. But instead of showing your boobs, show people your brain, and if they like what they'll, you'll have more beads than you know what to do with.
Ellen DeGeneres, Tulane Commencement Speech, 2009
Life is something that happens when you can't get to sleep.
Fran Lebowitz (1950 -)
Life is not a spectacle or feast; it is a predicament.
George Santayana (1863 - 1952)
Life is something that everyone should try at least once.
Henry J. Tillman
Life is pleasant. Death is peaceful. It's the transition that's troublesome.
Isaac Asimov (1920 - 1992)

Life is difficult and complicated and beyond anyone's total control, and the humility to
know that will enable you to survive its vicissitudes.
J. K. Rowling, Harvard Commencement Address, 2008
Life is a long lesson in humility.
James M. Barrie (1860 - 1937)
He only earns his freedom and existence who daily conquers them anew.
Johann Wolfgang von Goethe (1749 - 1832)
Life is what happens to you while you're busy making other plans.
John Lennon (1940 - 1980), "Beautiful Boy"
In real life, however, you don't react to what someone did; you react only to what you
think she did, and the gap between action and perception is bridged by the art of
impression management. If life itself is but what you deem it, then why not focus
your efforts on persuading others to believe that you are a virtuous and trustworthy
cooperator?
Jonathan Haidt, The Happiness Hypothesis: Finding Modern Truth in Ancient Wisdom, 2005
The lessons this life has planted in my heart pertain more to caring than crops, more
to Golden Rule than gold, more to the proper choice than to the popular choice.
Kirby Larson, Hattie Big Sky, 2006

Life

Life ain't like books. Books got somebody writin' 'em and tryin' to entertain ya. Life is
more like a set of Legos. Unless you take care of 'em, you lose a few pieces and you
end up steppin' on 'em with bare feet. You gotta take care of your life.
Laura Moncur (1969 -), Merriton: 35 Minutes Away From Home, 02-29-12
Nature has invented reproduction as a mechanism for life to move forward. As a life
force that passes right through us and makes us a link in the evolution of life.
Louis Schwartzberg, TED, the hidden beauty of pollination, March 2011
Life is fickle; the fair man doesn't invariably win.
Mark Hodder, The Strange Affair of Spring Heeled Jack (Burton & Swinburne in), 2010
The more I study the world, the more I am convinced of the inability of brute force to
create anything durable.
Napoleon Bonaparte (1769 - 1821)
The secret of a good life is to have the right loyalties and hold them in the right scale
of values.
Norman Thomas (1884 - 1968)
Life is a fatal complaint, and an eminently contagious one.
Oliver Wendell Holmes (1809 - 1894), "The Poet at the Breakfast-Table", 1872
Difficulties come when you don't pay attention to life's whisper. Life always whispers
to you first, but if you ignore the whisper, sooner or later you'll get a scream.
Oprah Winfrey (1954 -), Stanford Commencement Adress, 2008
Feelings are really your GPS system for life. When your supposed to do something, or
not supposed to do something, your emotional guidance system lets you know.
Oprah Winfrey (1954 -), Stanford Commencement Adress, 2008
Life is a reciprocal exchange. To move forward, you have to give back.
Oprah Winfrey (1954 -), Stanford Commencement Adress, 2008
Nobody's journey is seamless or smooth. We all stumble. We all have setbacks. It's
just life's way of saying, "Time to change course."
Oprah Winfrey (1954 -), Stanford Commencement Adress, 2008
The world has so many lessons to teach you. I consider the world, our earth, to be like
a school, and our life, the classrooms. Sometimes on our planet life school, the
lessons often come dressed up as detours and road blocks and sometimes as full
blown crises. And the secret I've learned to getting ahead is being open to the lessons.
Oprah Winfrey (1954 -), Stanford Commencement Adress, 2008
Walk through life eager and open to self-improvement and that which is going to best
help you evolve, because that's really why were here: to evolve as human beings.
Oprah Winfrey (1954 -), Stanford Commencement Adress, 2008
You really haven't changed, you've just become more of yourself. That is really what
were all trying to do: become more of ourselves.
Oprah Winfrey (1954 -), Stanford Commencement Adress, 2008
Life is far too important a thing ever to talk seriously about.
Oscar Wilde (1854 - 1900), Lady Windermere's Fan, 1892, Act I
Life is a zoo in a jungle.
Peter De Vries
Life is a sexually transmitted disease.
R. D. Laing
We don't beat the Grim Reaper by living longer, we beat the Reaper by living well and
living fully, for the Reaper will come for all of us. The question is what do we do
between the time we are born and the time he shows up. It's too late to do all the
things that you're gonna kinda get around to.
Randy Pausch, Carnegie Mellon Commencement Speech, 2008
The supreme irony of life is that hardly anyone gets out of it alive.
Robert Heinlein (1907 - 1988), "Job", 1984
Every one lives by selling something, whatever be his right to it.
Robert Louis Stevenson (1850 - 1894), Beggars, 1903
Life is just a bowl of pits.
Rodney Dangerfield (1921 - 2004)
Life is like playing a violin in public and learning the instrument as one goes on.
Samuel Butler (1835 - 1902)
Life is the art of drawing sufficient conclusions from insufficient premises.
Samuel Butler (1835 - 1902)
Life was mostly made up of things you couldn't control, full of surprises, and they
weren't always good. Life wasn't what you made it. You were what life made you.
Sara Zarr, Sweethearts, 2008
We make a living by what we get, we make a life by what we give.
Sir Winston Churchill (1874 - 1965)
The unexamined life is not worth living.
Socrates (469 BC - 399 BC), in Plato, Dialogues, Apology

If you had to define stress, it would not be far off if you said it was the process of
living. The process of living is the process of having stress imposed on you and
reacting to it.
Stanley J. Sarnoff, Man Under Stress, 1963
No one wants to die. Even people who want to go to heaven don't want to die to get
there. And yet, death is the destination we all share. No one has ever escaped it, and
that is how it should be, because death is very likely the single best invention of life.
It's life's change agent. It clears out the old to make way for the new.
Steve Jobs (1955 - 2011), Stanford Commencement Adress, 2005
Sometimes life is going to hit you in the head with a brick. Don't lose faith.
Steve Jobs (1955 - 2011), Stanford Commencement Adress, 2005
Your time is limited, so don't waste it living someone else's life. Don't be trapped by
dogma, which is living with the results of other people's thinking. Don't let the noise
of other's opinions drown out your inner voice. And most important, have the courage
to follow your heart and intuition. They somehow already know what you truly want
to become. Everything else is secondary.
Steve Jobs (1955 - 2011), Stanford Commencement Adress, 2005
When I hear somebody sigh, "Life is hard," I am always tempted to ask, "compared
to what?"
Sydney J. Harris
Life is an unbroken succession of false situations.
Thornton Wilder (1897 - 1975)
Life is a moderately good play with a badly written third act.
Truman Capote (1924 - 1984)
It is a funny thing about life; if you refuse to accept anything but the best, you very
often get it.
W. Somerset Maugham (1874 - 1965)
Life is just a mirror, and what you see out there, you must first see inside of you.
Wally 'Famous' Amos (1936 -)
Life isn't fair. It's just fairer than death, that's all.
William Goldman, "The Princess Bride"
The great use of a life is to spend for something that outlasts it.
William James (1842 - 1910)
And so from hour to hour, we ripe and ripe, and then, from hour to hour, we rot and
rot; and thereby hangs a tale.
William Shakespeare (1564 - 1616), As You Like It, Act II, sc. 7
I am sure care's an enemy to life.
William Shakespeare (1564 - 1616), Twelfth Night, Act I, sc. 3
Life is as tedious as a twice-told tale
Vexing the dull ear of a drowsy man.
William Shakespeare (1564 - 1616), "King John", Act 3 scene 4
Life is as tedious as a twice-told tale vexing the dull ear of a drowsy man.
William Shakespeare (1564 - 1616), King John, Act III, sc. 4
The cloud-capp'd towers, the gorgeous palaces,
The solemn temples, the great globe itself,
Yea, all which it inherit, shall dissolve,
And, like this insubstantial pageant faded,
Leave not a rack behind. We are such stuff
As dreams are made on; and our little life
Is rounded with a sleep.
William Shakespeare (1564 - 1616), The Tempest, Act IV, sc. 1
The web of our life is of a mingled yarn, good and ill together.
William Shakespeare (1564 - 1616), All's Well that Ends Well, Act IV, sc. 3
The world's mine oyster, which I with sword will open.
William Shakespeare (1564 - 1616), The Merry Wives of Windsor, Act II, sc. 2
Life is divided into the horrible and the miserable.
Woody Allen (1935 -)
Life is full of misery, loneliness, and suffering - and it's all over much too soon.
Woody Allen (1935 -)
The goal of life is living in agreement with nature.
Zeno (335 BC - 264 BC), from Diogenes Laertius, Lives of Eminent Philosophers

Light

In the right light, at the right time, everything is extraordinary.
Aaron Rose
You can't have a light without a dark to stick it in.
Arlo Guthrie (1947 -)
In the beginning there was nothing. God said, 'Let there be light!' And there was light.
There was still nothing, but you could see it a whole lot better.
Ellen DeGeneres, (attributed)
There are two kinds of light—the glow that illuminates, and the glare that obscures.
James Thurber (1894 - 1961)
What I give form to in daylight is only one per cent of what I have seen in darkness.
M. C. Escher (1898 - 1972), Quoted in Comic Sections, D. MacHale (Dublin 1993)
Let your light shine. Shine within you so that it can shine on someone else. Let your
light shine.
Oprah Winfrey (1954 -), O Magazine, January 2004
Any one who has common sense will remember that the bewilderments of the eyes
are of two kinds, and arise from two causes, either from coming out of the light or
from going into the light, which is true of the mind's eye, quite as much as of the
bodily eye; and he who remembers this when he sees any one whose vision is
perplexed and weak, will not be too ready to laugh; he will first ask whether that soul
of man has come out of the brighter light, and is unable to see because unaccustomed
to the dark, or having turned from darkness to the day is dazzled by excess of light.
Plato (427 BC - 347 BC), The Republic
We burn daylight.
William Shakespeare (1564 - 1616), "The Merry Wives of Windsor", Act 1 scene 4

Listening

There are people who, instead of listening to what is being said to them, are already listening to what they are going to say themselves.
Albert Guinon (1863 - 1923)
No man ever listened himself out of a job.
Calvin Coolidge (1872 - 1933)
Make sure you have finished speaking before your audience has finished listening.
Dorothy Sarnoff
When people talk, listen completely. Most people never listen.
Ernest Hemingway (1899 - 1961)
To listen closely and reply well is the highest perfection we are able to attain in the art of conversation.
Francois de La Rochefoucauld (1613 - 1680)
Be a good listener. Your ears will never get you in trouble.
Frank Tyger
Listen. Do not have an opinion while you listen because frankly, your opinion doesn't hold much water outside of Your Universe. Just listen. Listen until their brain has been twisted like a dripping towel and what they have to say is all over the floor.
Hugh Elliott, Standing Room Only weblog, 02-14-2003
A good listener is a good talker with a sore throat.
Katharine Whitehorn
A good listener is usually thinking about something else.
Kin Hubbard (1868 - 1930)
Maybe I wanted to hear it so badly that my ears betrayed my mind in order to secure my heart.
Margaret Cho, weblog, 03-03-04
No one really listens to anyone else, and if you try it for a while you'll see why.
Mignon McLaughlin
Everybody lies, but it doesn't matter because nobody listens.
Nick Diamos
It is the province of knowledge to speak and it is the privilege of wisdom to listen.
Oliver Wendell Holmes (1809 - 1894)
Know how to listen, and you will profit even from those who talk badly.
Plutarch (46 AD - 120 AD)
As I get older, I've learned to listen to people rather than accuse them of things.
Po Bronson, quoted in Publishers Weekly
My parents taught me how to listen to everybody before I made up my own mind. When you listen, you learn. You absorb like a sponge-and your life becomes so much better than when you are just trying to be listened to all the time.
Steven Spielberg
A good listener is not only popular everywhere, but after a while he gets to know something.
Wilson Mizner (1876 - 1933)

Loneliness

Pray that your loneliness may spur you into finding something to live for, great enough to die for.
Dag Hammarskjold (1905 - 1961)
When you close your doors, and make darkness within, remember never to say that you are alone, for you are not alone; nay, God is within, and your genius is within. And what need have they of light to see what you are doing?
Epictetus (55 AD - 135 AD), Discourses
To be an adult is to be alone.
Jean Rostand (1894 - 1977), Thoughts of a biologist (1939)
Disappearing can be quite the coping mechanism for those of us who fear abandonment the very most of all. If we disappear, you have to find us. You're the one who worries. We know where we are, but you can't leave me. I'm in charge and doing the leaving. Not the other way around.
Jennifer Neal, nakedjen, Disappearing Act, 03-06-12
People drain me, even the closest of friends, and I find loneliness to be the best state in the union to live in.
Margaret Cho, weblog, 10-30-03
The worst loneliness is not to be comfortable with yourself.
Mark Twain (1835 - 1910)
Inside myself is a place where I live all alone and that's where you renew your springs that never dry up.
Pearl Buck (1892 - 1973)
They are never alone that are accompanied with noble thoughts.
Sir Philip Sidney (1554 - 1586)
To be alone is to be different, to be different is to be alone.
Suzanne Gordon, Lonely in America, 1976
No matter how lonely you get or how many birth announcements you receive, the trick is not to get frightened. There's nothing wrong with being alone.
Wendy Wasserstein (1950 - 2005), Isn't It Romantic, 1983

Love

Never pretend to a love which you do not actually feel, for love is not ours to command.
Alan Watts
Such is the inconsistency of real love, that it is always awake to suspicion, however unreasonable; always requiring new assurances from the object of its interest.
Ann Radcliffe (1764 - 1823), The Mysteries of Udolpho, 1764
To love deeply in one direction makes us more loving in all others.
Anne-Sophie Swetchine

Perhaps the feelings that we experience when we are in love represent a normal state. Being in love shows a person who he should be.
Anton Chekhov (1860 - 1904)
To fear love is to fear life, and those who fear life are already three parts dead.
Bertrand Russell (1872 - 1970), Marriage and Morals (1929) ch. 19
Love is not enough. It must be the foundation, the cornerstone - but not the complete structure. It is much too pliable, too yielding.
Bette Davis (1908 - 1989)
Clarity of mind means clarity of passion, too; this is why a great and clear mind loves ardently and sees distinctly what it loves.
Blaise Pascal (1623 - 1662)
The meeting of two personalities is like the contact of two chemical substances: if there is any reaction, both are transformed.
Carl Jung (1875 - 1961)
Nothing takes the taste out of peanut butter quite like unrequited love.
Charles M. Schulz (1922 - 2000), Charlie Brown in "Peanuts"
It is the caring and sharing that count—love is not prevented by the things and the time that you haven't shared.
Claudia Jewett Jarrett, Adopting the Older Child, 1978
There's an evolutionary imperative why we give a crap about our family and friends. And there's an evolutionary imperative why we don't give a crap about anybody else. If we loved all people indiscriminately, we couldn't function.
David Foster, House M.D., TB or Not TB, 2005
To love and be loved is to feel the sun from both sides.
David Viscott, How to Live with Another Person, 1974
Couples are jigsaw puzzles that hang together by touching in just enough points. They're never total fits or misfits.
Diane Ackerman, One Hundred Names for Love: A Stroke, A Marriage, and the Language of Healing, 2011
There's a lot to be said for self-delusionment when it comes to matters of the heart.
Diane Frolov and Andrew Schneider, Northern Exposure, First Snow, 1993
Oh, life is a glorious cycle of song,
A medley of extemporanea;
And love is a thing that can never go wrong;
And I am Marie of Romania.
Dorothy Parker (1893 - 1967), Not So Deep as a Well (1937), "Comment"
One's first love is always perfect until one meets one's second love.
Elizabeth Aston, The Exploits & Adventures of Miss Alethea Darcy, 2005
All love that has not friendship for its base, is like a mansion built upon sand.
Ella Wheeler Wilcox, O Magazine, February 2004
Love is everything it's cracked up to be...It really is worth fighting for, being brave for, risking everything for.
Erica Jong, O Magazine, February 2004
People are such great mysteries. Just when we think we have understood them, a wonderful new aspect shows in them.
Eucharista Ward, Match For Mary Bennet, 2009
When love is in excess it brings a man no honor nor worthiness.
Euripides (484 BC - 406 BC), Medea, 431 B.C.
There is always some madness in love. But there is also always some reason in madness.
Friedrich Nietzsche (1844 - 1900), "On Reading and Writing"
What else is love but understanding and rejoicing in the fact that another person lives, acts, and experiences otherwise than we do...?
Friedrich Nietzsche (1844 - 1900)
I believe love is primarily a choice and only sometimes a feeling. If you want to feel love, choose to love and be patient.
Gordon Atkinson, RealLivePreacher.com Weblog, December 16, 2002
I don't think anyone can DO anything that would make him worthy of love. Love is a gift and cannot be earned. It can only be given.
Gordon Atkinson, RealLivePreacher.com Weblog, January 20, 2003
You can't love anyone until you understand that you can't love everyone.
Gordon Atkinson, RealLivePreacher.com Weblog, October 20, 2003
They wouldn't call it falling in love if you didn't get hurt sometimes, but you just pick yourself up and move on.
Gregory Thomas Garcia, Elijah Aron, Jordan Young, Raising Hope, Cheaters, April 2011
Love is the triumph of imagination over intelligence.
H. L. Mencken (1880 - 1956)
Sometimes when you look back on a situation, you realize it wasn't all you thought it was. A beautiful girl walked into your life. You fell in love. Or did you? Maybe it was only a childish infatuation, or maybe just a brief moment of vanity.
Henry Bromel, Northern Exposure, The Big Kiss, 1991
There is no remedy for love but to love more.
Henry David Thoreau (1817 - 1862), Journal, July 25, 1839
Just because you love someone doesn't mean you have to be involved with them. Love is not a bandage to cover wounds.
Hugh Elliott, Standing Room Only weblog, February 16, 2004
Passion makes the world go round. Love just makes it a safer place.
Ice T, The Ice Opinion
A kiss is a lovely trick, designed by nature, to stop words when speech becomes unnecessary.
Ingrid Bergman (1915 - 1982)
Love is the difficult realization that something other than oneself is real.
Iris Murdoch (1919 - 1999)
We can only learn to love by loving.
Iris Murdoch (1919 - 1999), O Magazine, February 2004
When you have seen as much of life as I have, you will not underestimate the power of obsessive love.

J. K. Rowling, Harry Potter and the Half-Blood Prince, 2005
But when a young lady is to be a heroine, the perverseness of forty surrounding families cannot prevent her. Something must and will happen to throw a hero in her way.
Jane Austen (1775 - 1817), Northanger Abbey
Friendship is certainly the finest balm for the pangs of disappointed love.
Jane Austen (1775 - 1817), Northanger Abbey
I cannot think well of a man who sports with any woman's feelings; and there may often be a great deal more suffered than a stander-by can judge of.
Jane Austen (1775 - 1817), Mansfield Park
I pay very little regard...to what any young person says on the subject of marriage. If they profess a disinclination for it, I only set it down that they have not yet seen the right person.
Jane Austen (1775 - 1817), Mansfield Park
The enthusiasm of a woman's love is even beyond the biographer's.
Jane Austen (1775 - 1817), Mansfield Park
The more I know of the world, the more am I convinced that I shall never see a man whom I can really love. I require so much!
Jane Austen (1775 - 1817), Sense and Sensibility, 1811
We certainly do not forget you as soon as you forget us. It is, perhaps, our fate rather than our merit. We cannot help ourselves. We live at home, quiet, confined, and our feelings prey upon us. You are forced on exertion. You have always a profession, pursuits, business of some sort or other, to take you back into the world immediately, and continual occupation and change soon weaken impressions. All the privilege I claim for my own sex (it is not a very enviable one; you need not covet it), is that of loving longest, when existence or when hope is gone.
Jane Austen (1775 - 1817), Persuasion, 1818
Love is, above all else, the gift of oneself.
Jean Anouilh (1910 - 1987)
Age does not protect you from love. But love, to some extent, protects you from age.
Jeanne Moreau
Is love supposed to last throughout all time, or is it like trains changing at random stops. If I loved her, how could I leave her? If I felt that way then, how come I don't feel anything now?
Jeff Melvoin, Northern Exposure, Altered Egos, 1993
What is it about possessing things? Why do we feel the need to own what we love, and why do we become jerks when we do? We've all been there– you want something, to possess it. By possessing something you lose it. You finally win the girl of your dreams, the first thing you do is change her. The little things she does with her hair, the way she wears her clothes or the way she chews her gum. Pretty soon what you like, what you changed, what you don't like, blends together like a watercolor in the rain.
Jeff Melvoin, Northern Exposure, Dateline: Cicely, 1992
True love brings up everything - you're allowing a mirror to be held up to you daily.
Jennifer Aniston, O Magazine, February 2004
'Light fuse and get away' may work for a Roman candle, but not so much for the wrath of a woman scorned.
Jeph Jacques, Questionable Content webcomic, #678, 08-02-06
A good relationship is like fireworks: loud, explosive, and liable to maim you if you hold on too long.
Jeph Jacques, Questionable Content, 11-14-08
Love is the delightful interval between meeting a beautiful girl and discovering that she looks like a haddock.
John Barrymore (1882 - 1942)
Breaking up isn't something that gets done to you; it's something that happens with you.
John Green, An Abundance of Katherines, 2008
I'm in love with you, and I know that love is just a shout into the void, and that oblivion is inevitable, and that we're all doomed and that there will come a day when all our labor has been returned to dust, and I know the sun will swallow the only earth we'll ever have, and I am in love with you.
John Green, The Fault in Our Stars, 2012
That's who you really like. The people you can think out loud in front of.
John Green, An Abundance of Katherines, 2008
The best way to get people to like you is not to like them too much.
John Green, An Abundance of Katherines, 2008
There's some people in this world who you can just love and love and love no matter what.
John Green, An Abundance of Katherines, 2008
When you're a teenager and you're in love, it's obvious to everyone but you and the person you're in love with.
John Scalzi, Old Man's War, 2005
'Tis the most tender part of love, each other to forgive.
John Sheffield
Gravity. It keeps you rooted to the ground. In space, there's not any gravity. You just kind of leave your feet and go floating around. Is that what being in love is like?
Josh Brand and John Falsey, Northern Exposure, The Pilot, 1990
How we treasure (and admire) the people who acknowledge us!
Julie Morgenstern, O Magazine, Belatedly Yours, January 2004
To love is to receive a glimpse of heaven.
Karen Sunde
Passion is seldom the end of any story, for it cannot long endure if it is not soon supplemented with true affection and mutual respect.
Kathryn L. Nelson, Pemberley Manor, 2006
She makes me love her and I like people who make me love them. It saves me so much trouble in making myself love them.
L. M. Montgomery (1874 - 1942), Anne of Green Gables, 1908

There is no use in loving things if you have to be torn from them, is there? And it's so hard to keep from loving things, isn't it?
L. M. Montgomery (1874 - 1942), Anne of Green Gables, 1908
When people mean to be good to you, you don't mind very much when they're not quite—always.
L. M. Montgomery (1874 - 1942), Anne of Green Gables, 1908
Our hearts can deceive us. Our hearts cannot reason. They cannot judge a man's character. All they can do is see a man and think, 'There is a fine specimen. He is handsome and attentive. He will father healthy children.' It is only our mind that we can trust. Our mind can catch him in lies. Our mind can fathom his honesty and honor.
Laura Moncur (1969 -), The Secret Heart of Charlotte Lucas, 2014
Honesty is the only way with anyone, when you'll be so close as to be living inside each other's skins.
Lois McMaster Bujold, A Civil Campaign, 1999
When you give each other everything, it becomes an even trade. Each wins all.
Lois McMaster Bujold, A Civil Campaign, 1999
Love is an exploding cigar we willingly smoke.
Lynda Barry
Real love is a permanently self-enlarging experience.
M. Scott Peck, O Magazine, February 2004
To be brave is to love someone unconditionally, without expecting anything in return. To just give. That takes courage, because we don't want to fall on our faces or leave ourselves open to hurt.
Madonna (1958 -), O Magazine, January 2004
Love is the big booming beat which covers up the noise of hate.
Margaret Cho, weblog, 01-15-04
Hatred paralyzes life; love releases it. Hatred confuses life; love harmonizes it. Hatred darkens life; love illuminates it.
Martin Luther King Jr. (1929 - 1968)
Think about a woman. Doesn't know you're thinking about her. Doesn't care you're thinking about her. Makes you think about her even more.
Martin Sage and Sybil Adelman, Northern Exposure, The Bumpy Road to Love, 1991
Love is a snowmobile racing across the tundra and then suddenly it flips over, pinning you underneath. At night, the ice weasels come.
Matt Groening (1954 -), "Life in Hell"
Learning to love yourself is the greatest love of all.
Michael Masser and Linda Creed
I always like a good math solution to any love problem.
Michael Patrick King, Sex and the City, Take Me Out To The Ballgame, 1999
The perversity of the human spirit is such that when a young lady longs for one specific partner, every other partner counts for nothing.
Monica Fairview, Darcy Cousins, 2010
When a person is uncertain in love, there is nothing easier than for him to put one and one together and to make three out of them.
Monica Fairview, Darcy Cousins, 2010
Fall not in love, therefore; it will stick to your face.
National Lampoon, "Deteriorata"
She hadn't chosen him over all the others. The truth was that she hadn't even thought about anyone else.
Paolo Giordano, The Solitude of Prime Numbers
The love of those we don't love in return settles on the surface and from there quickly evaporates.
Paolo Giordano, The Solitude of Prime Numbers: A Novel
The first duty of love is to listen.
Paul Tillich (1886 - 1965)
Love is an act of endless forgiveness, a tender look which becomes a habit.
Peter Ustinov (1921 - 2004)
Love is not blind - it sees more, not less. But because it sees more, it is willing to see less.
Rabbi Julius Gordon
For one human being to love another; that is perhaps the most difficult of all our tasks, the ultimate, the last test and proof, the work for which all other work is but preparation.
Rainer Maria Rilke (1875 - 1926)
He who is in love is wise and is becoming wiser, sees newly every time he looks at the object beloved, drawing from it with his eyes and his mind those virtues which it possesses.
Ralph Waldo Emerson (1803 - 1882), Address on The Method of Nature, 1841
Could you imagine how horrible things would be if we always told others how we felt? Life would be intolerably bearable.
Randy K. Milholland, Something Positive Comic, 12-09-05
You can't show love to someone at the expense of someone else who loves you.
Randy K. Milholland, Something Positive, 01-19-10
You make me understand how wonderful it is for little lizards when they find that one special rock that's perfect for sunning themselves on. You make me lizard-happy.
Randy K. Milholland, Something Positive, 02-23-10
Before I met my husband, I'd never fallen in love, though I'd stepped in it a few times.
Rita Rudner
Love is an irresistible desire to be irresistibly desired.
Robert Frost (1874 - 1963)
Where there is hatred, let me sow love. Where there is injury, pardon. Where there is doubt, faith.
Saint Francis of Assisi (1181 - 1226)

In the end, I decide that the mark we've left on each other is the color and shape of love. That the unfinished business between us. Because love, love is never finished. It circles and circles, the memories out of order and not always complete.
Sara Zarr, Sweethearts, 2008
Maybe kissing is sort of like nature's coffee.
Scott Westerfeld, Midnighters: Blue Noon, 2005
The human heart is a strange vessel. Love and hatred can exist side by side.
Scott Westerfeld, Peeps, 2005
We don't always get to choose what we love.
Scott Westerfeld, The Last Days, 2006
One word frees us of all the weight and pain of life: That word is love.
Sophocles (496 BC - 406 BC)
Some relationships start with fights... But, usually only in romantic comedies. Life's not the movies.
Takayuki Ikkaku, Arisa Hosaka and Toshihiro Kawabata, Animal Crossing: Wild World, 2005
Love is or it ain't. Thin love ain't love at all.
Toni Morrison (1931 -), Beloved
Love isn't a decision. It's a feeling. If we could decide who we loved, it would be much simpler, but much less magical.
Trey Parker and Matt Stone, South Park, Chef Aid, 1998
Life's greatest happiness is to be convinced we are loved.
Victor Hugo (1802 - 1885), Les Miserables, 1862
Love is a canvas furnished by Nature and embroidered by imagination.
Voltaire (1694 - 1778)
A woman can forgive a man for the harm he does her...but she can never forgive him for the sacrifices he makes on her account.
W. Somerset Maugham (1874 - 1965), The Moon and Sixpence
The important thing was to love rather than to be loved.
W. Somerset Maugham (1874 - 1965), 'Of Human Bondage', 1915
There's always one who loves and one who lets himself be loved.
W. Somerset Maugham (1874 - 1965), 'Of Human Bondage', 1915
Women are often under the impression that men are much more madly in love with them than they really are.
W. Somerset Maugham (1874 - 1965), The Painted Veil, 1925
Never marry but for love; but see that thou lovest what is lovely.
William Penn (1644 - 1718)
Against love's fire fear's frost hath dissolution.
William Shakespeare (1564 - 1616), The Rape of Lucrece
Alas, their love may be call'd appetite. No motion of the liver, but the palate.
William Shakespeare (1564 - 1616), Twelfth Night, Act II, sc. 4
All fancy-sick she is and pale of cheer, with sighs of love, that costs the fresh blood dear.
William Shakespeare (1564 - 1616), A Midsummer Night's Dream, Act III, sc. 2
And ruin'd love when it is built anew,
Grows fairer than at first, more strong, far greater.
William Shakespeare (1564 - 1616), Sonnet CXIX
Belike you thought our love would last too long, if it were chain'd together.
William Shakespeare (1564 - 1616), The Comedy of Errors, Act IV, sc. 1
But love is blind and lovers cannot see
The pretty follies that themselves commit;
For if they could, Cupid himself would blush
To see me thus transformed to a boy.
William Shakespeare (1564 - 1616), The Merchant of Venice, Act II Scene 6
But miserable most, to love unloved? This you should pity rather than despise.
William Shakespeare (1564 - 1616), A Midsummer Night's Dream
But the strong base and building of my love is as the very centre of the earth, drawing all things to it.
William Shakespeare (1564 - 1616), Troilus and Cressida, Act IV, sc. 2
By heaven, I do love: and it hath taught me to rhyme, and to be melancholy.
William Shakespeare (1564 - 1616), Love's Labour's Lost, Act IV, sc. 3
Doubt that the stars are fire;
Doubt that the sun doth move;
Doubt truth to be a liar;
But never doubt I love.
William Shakespeare (1564 - 1616), Hamlet, Act II, sc. 2
Even as one heat another heat expels, or as one nail by strength drives out another, so the remembrance of my former love is by a newer object quite forgotten.
William Shakespeare (1564 - 1616), The Two Gentlemen of Verona, Act II, sc. 4
For aught that I could ever read, could ever hear by tale or history, the course of true love never did run smooth.
William Shakespeare (1564 - 1616), A Midsummer Night's Dream, Act I, sc. 1
Friendship is constant in all other things
Save in the office and affairs of love:
Therefore all hearts in love use their own tongues;
Let every eye negotiate for itself,
And trust no agent.
William Shakespeare (1564 - 1616), Much Ado About Nothing, Act II, sc. 1
I will wear my heart upon my sleeve for daws to peck at.
William Shakespeare (1564 - 1616), Othello, Act I, sc. 1
If love be blind, it best agrees with night.
William Shakespeare (1564 - 1616), Romeo and Juliet, Act III, sc. 2
If love be blind, love cannot hit the mark.
William Shakespeare (1564 - 1616), Romeo and Juliet, Act II, sc. 1
If that the world and love were young,
And truth in every shepherd's tongue,
These pretty pleasures might me move
To live with thee and be thy love.

William Shakespeare (1564 - 1616), The Passionate Pilgrim
If they love they know not why, they hate upon no better ground, they hate upon no better a ground.
William Shakespeare (1564 - 1616), Coriolanus, Act II, sc. 2
Is love a tender thing? It is too rough, too rude, too boist'rous, and it pricks like a thorn.
William Shakespeare (1564 - 1616), Romeo and Juliet, Act I, sc. 4
Let me not to the marriage of true minds
Admit impediments: love is not love
Which alters when it alteration finds.
William Shakespeare (1564 - 1616), Sonnet cxvi
Let me not to the marriage of true minds
Admit impediments: love is not love
Which alters when it alteration finds,
Or bends with the remover to remove :
O, no! it is an ever fixed mark.
William Shakespeare (1564 - 1616), Sonnet CXVI
Love all, trust a few. Do wrong to none.
William Shakespeare (1564 - 1616), "All's Well That Ends Well", Act 1 Scene 1
Love is begun by time; and that I see in passages of proof, time qualifies the spark and fire of it. There lives within the very flame of love a kind of wick or snuff that will abate it.
William Shakespeare (1564 - 1616), Hamlet, Act IV, sc. 7
Love is blind, and lovers cannot see the pretty follies that themselves commit.
William Shakespeare (1564 - 1616), The Merchant of Venice, Act II, sc. 6
Love lacked a dwelling, and made him her place;
And when in his fair parts she did abide,
She was lodged and newly deified.
William Shakespeare (1564 - 1616), A Lover's Complaint
Love looks not with the eyes, but with the mind; and therefore is winged Cupid painted blind.
William Shakespeare (1564 - 1616), A Midsummer Night's Dream, Act I, sc. 1
Love sought is good, but given unsought is better.
William Shakespeare (1564 - 1616), Twelfth Night, Act III, sc. 1
Love surfeits not, Lust like a glutton dies;
Love is all truth, Lust full of forged lies.
William Shakespeare (1564 - 1616), Venus and Adonis
Love thrives not in the heart that shadows dreadeth.
William Shakespeare (1564 - 1616), The Rape of Lucrece
Love's best habit is a soothing tongue.
William Shakespeare (1564 - 1616), The Passionate Pilgrim
Love's not Time's fool, though rosy lips and cheeks
Within his bending sickle's compass come;
Love alters not with his brief hours and weeks,
But bears it out even to the edge of doom.
William Shakespeare (1564 - 1616), Sonnet CXVI
Love's reason's without reason.
William Shakespeare (1564 - 1616), Cymbeline, Act IV, sc. 2
My bounty is as boundless as the sea, my love love as deep; the more I give to thee, the more I have, for both are infinite.
William Shakespeare (1564 - 1616), Romeo and Juliet, Act II, sc. 2
My love admits no qualifying dross.
William Shakespeare (1564 - 1616), Troilus and Cressida, Act IV, sc. 4
My love is strengthen'd, though more weak in seeming;
I love not less, though less the show appear:
That love is merchandised whose rich esteeming
The owner's tongue doth publish every where.
William Shakespeare (1564 - 1616), Sonnet CII
My mistress' eyes are nothing like the sun;
Coral is far more red than her lips' red...
I love to hear her speak, yet well I know
That music hath a far more pleasing sound.
William Shakespeare (1564 - 1616), Sonnet CXXX
Now my love is thaw'd; which, like a waxen image 'gainst a fire, bears no impression of the thing it was.
William Shakespeare (1564 - 1616), The Two Gentlemen of Verona, Act II, sc. 4
O, how this spring of love resembleth the uncertain glory of an April day!
William Shakespeare (1564 - 1616), The Two Gentlemen of Verona, Act I, sc. 3
O, then, what graces in my love do dwell, that he hath turn'd a heaven unto hell!
William Shakespeare (1564 - 1616), A Midsummer Night's Dream, Act I, sc. 1
Perdition catch my soul, but I do love thee! and when I love thee not, Chaos is come again.
William Shakespeare (1564 - 1616), Othello, Act III, sc. 3
Self-love, my liege, is not so vile a sin as self-neglecting.
William Shakespeare (1564 - 1616), Henry V, Act 2, sc. 4
She cannot love, nor take no shape nor project or affection, she is so self-endeared.
William Shakespeare (1564 - 1616), Much Ado About Nothing, Act III, sc. 1
Some cupid kills with arrows, some with traps.
William Shakespeare (1564 - 1616), Much Ado About Nothing, Act III, sc. 1
The chameleon Love can feed on the air.
William Shakespeare (1564 - 1616), The Two Gentlemen of Verona, Act II, sc.1
The hind that would be mated by the lion must die for love.
William Shakespeare (1564 - 1616), All's Well that Ends Well, Act I, sc. 1
The ostentation of our love, which, left unshown, is often left unloved.
William Shakespeare (1564 - 1616), Antony and Cleopatra, Act III, sc. 6
There's beggary in the love that can be reckon'd.
William Shakespeare (1564 - 1616), Antony and Cleopatra, Act I, sc. 1

Things base and vile, holding no quantity, love can transpose to form and dignity.
William Shakespeare (1564 - 1616), A Midsummer Night's Dream, Act I, sc. 1
This thou perceivest, which makes thy love more strong, to love that well which thou must leave ere long.
William Shakespeare (1564 - 1616), Sonnet LXXIII
This world is not for aye, nor 'tis not strange
That even our loves should with our fortunes change.
For 'tis a question left us yet to prove,
Whether love lead fortune, or else fortune love.
William Shakespeare (1564 - 1616), Hamlet, Act III, sc. 2
What power is it which mounts my love so high, that makes me see, and cannot feed mine eye?
William Shakespeare (1564 - 1616), All's Well that Ends Well, Act I, sc. 1
When love begins to sicken and decay, it useth an enforced ceremony.
William Shakespeare (1564 - 1616), Julius Caesar, Act IV, sc. 2
When, in disgrace with fortune and men's eyes...
Haply I think on thee, and then my state,
Like to the lark at break of day arising
From sullen earth, sings hymns at heaven's gate;
For thy sweet love remember'd such wealth brings
That then I scorn to change my state with kings.
William Shakespeare (1564 - 1616), Sonnet XXIX
Where love is great, the littlest doubts are fear; where little fear grows great, great love grows there.
William Shakespeare (1564 - 1616), Hamlet, Act III, sc. 2
Who ever loved that loved not at first sight?
William Shakespeare (1564 - 1616), As You Like It, Act III, sc. 5

Luck

People always call it luck when you've acted more sensibly than they have.
Anne Tyler (1941 -), Celestial Navigation
The only thing that overcomes hard luck is hard work.
Harry Golden (1902 - 1981)
A pound of pluck is worth a ton of luck.
James A. Garfield (1831 - 1881)
We must believe in luck. For how else can we explain the success of those we don't like?
Jean Cocteau (1889 - 1963)
True luck consists not in holding the best of the cards at the table; luckiest is he who knows just when to rise and go home.
John Hay (1838 - 1905), Distichs, latter 19th century
Luck is what you have left over after you give 100 percent.
Langston Coleman
Shallow men believe in luck. Strong men believe in cause and effect.
Ralph Waldo Emerson (1803 - 1882)
I'm a great believer in luck, and I find the harder I work the more I have of it.
Thomas Jefferson (1743 - 1826), (attributed)

Magic

Books may well be the only true magic.
Alice Hoffman
Any sufficiently advanced technology is indistinguishable from magic.
Arthur C. Clarke (1917 -), "Profiles of the Future", 1961 (Clarke's third law)
As a scientist, I am not sure anymore that life can be reduced to a class struggle, to dialectical materialism, or any set of formulas. Life is spontaneous and it is unpredictable, it is magical. I think that we have struggled so hard with the tangible that we have forgotten the intangible.
Diane Frolov and Andrew Schneider, Northern Exposure, Zarya, 1994
It's not enough to create magic. You have to create a price for magic, too. You have to create rules.
Eric A. Burns, Gossamer Commons, 06-15-05
Ah, music. A magic beyond all we do here!
J. K. Rowling, Harry Potter and the Sorcerer's Stone, 1997
We do not need magic to transform our world. We carry all the power we need inside ourselves already. We have the power to imagine better.
J. K. Rowling, Harvard Commencement Address, 2008
Formerly, when religion was strong and science weak, men mistook magic for medicine; now, when science is strong and religion weak, men mistake medicine for magic.
Thomas Szasz, The Second Sin (1973) "Science and Scientism"
Disbelief in magic can force a poor soul into believing in government and business.
Tom Robbins (1936 -)

Mankind

Every man has three characters-that which he exhibits, that which he has, and that which he thinks he has.
Alphonse Karr (1808-1890)
So long as we live among men, let us cherish humanity.
Andre Gide (1869 - 1951)
One man with courage makes a majority.
Andrew Jackson (1767 - 1845)
To deny our own impulses is to deny the very thing that makes us human.
Andy and Larry Wachowski, The Matrix, 1999
It has been said that man is a rational animal. All my life I have been searching for evidence which could support this.
Bertrand Russell (1872 - 1970)

I have discovered that all human evil comes from this, man's being unable to sit still in a room.
Blaise Pascal (1623 - 1662)
Our notion of symmetry is derived from the human face. Hence, we demand symmetry horizontally and in breath only, not vertically nor in depth.
Blaise Pascal (1623 - 1662)
It is vain to say human beings might be satisfied with tranquillity; they must have action, and they will make it if they can not find it.
Charlotte Bronte (1816 - 1855)
What mattered was not what happens to you, but how you handle it. Self-command is required to overcome the dangerous misinformation of our emotions, and because for the most part the self is the only thing that we can command. We have no control, ultimately, over what people do or think. What we can influence is our understanding of these circumstances and how we respond to them.
Daniel Akst, We Have Met the Enemy: Self-Control in an Age of Excess, 2011
What others think of us would be of little moment did it not, when known, so deeply tinge what we think of ourselves.
George Santayana (1863 - 1952)
The fates have given mankind a patient soul.
Homer (800 BC - 700 BC), The Iliad
From such crooked wood as that which man is made of, nothing straight can be fashioned.
Immanuel Kant (1724 - 1804)
I hate mankind, for I think myself one of the best of them, and I know how bad I am.
Joseph Baretti, quoted in Boswell's Life of Samuel Johnson
You must not lose faith in humanity. Humanity is an ocean; if a few drops of the ocean are dirty, the ocean does not become dirty.
Mahatma Gandhi (1869 - 1948)
It was enough to make a body ashamed of the human race.
Mark Twain (1835 - 1910), The Adventures of Huckleberry Finn
Man is the Only Animal that Blushes. Or needs to.
Mark Twain (1835 - 1910), Following the Equator (1897)
A curious part of the human psyche is that the moment that a person presumed to be in danger is discovered to be safe, everyone's anxiety turns into anger.
Monica Fairview, Darcy Cousins, 2010
His passions make man live, his wisdom merely makes him last.
Nicholas Chamfort (1741 - 1794)
People are governed by the head; a kind heart is of little value in chess.
Nicholas Chamfort (1741 - 1794)
I think that God in creating Man somewhat overestimated his ability.
Oscar Wilde (1854 - 1900)
Man is the only animal that laughs and has a state legislature.
Samuel Butler (1835 - 1902)
As I know more of mankind I expect less of them, and am ready now to call a man a good man upon easier terms than I was formerly.
Samuel Johnson (1709 - 1784)
A man's worst difficulties begin when he is able to do as he likes.
Thomas Henry Huxley
The world is my country, all mankind are my brethren, and to do good is my religion.
Thomas Paine (1737 - 1809)
People are not an interruption of our business. People are our business.
Walter E. Washington, Mayor of Washington, D.C., c. 1971
There is no more miserable human being than one in whom nothing is habitual but indecision.
William James (1842 - 1910)
In the last analysis, my fellow country men, as we in America would be the first to claim, a people are responsible for the acts of their government.
Woodrow Wilson (1856 - 1924), Address, Columbus, Ohio, September 4, 1919

Marriage

The conception of two people living together for twenty-five years without having a cross word suggests a lack of spirit only to be admired in sheep.
Alan Patrick Herbert
A successful marriage is an edifice that must be rebuilt every day.
Andre Maurois (1885 - 1967)
All married couples should learn the art of battle as they should learn the art of making love. Good battle is objective and honest - never vicious or cruel. Good battle is healthy and constructive, and brings to a marriage the principle of equal partnership.
Ann Landers (1918 - 2002)
A simple enough pleasure, surely, to have breakfast alone with one's husband, but how seldom married people in the midst of life achieve it.
Anne Morrow Lindbergh
I used to believe that marriage would diminish me, reduce my options. That you had to be someone less to live with someone else when, of course, you have to be someone more.
Candice Bergen (1946 -)
All marriages are mixed marriages.
Chantal Saperstein
There's only one way to have a happy marriage and as soon as I learn what it is I'll get married again.
Clint Eastwood (1930 -)
A great marriage is not when the 'perfect couple' comes together. It is when an imperfect couple learns to enjoy their differences.
Dave Meurer, "Daze of Our Wives"
Though we marry as adults, we don't marry adults. We marry children who have grown up and still rejoice in being children, especially if we're creative.

Diane Ackerman, One Hundred Names for Love: A Stroke, A Marriage, and the Language of Healing, 2011

Marriage. It's like a cultural hand-rail. It links folks to the past and guides them to the future.
Diane Frolov and Andrew Schneider, Northern Exposure, Our Wedding, 1992

I wonder, among all the tangles of this mortal coil, which one contains tighter knots to undo, and consequently suggests more tugging, and pain, and diversified elements of misery, than the marriage tie.
Edith Wharton (1862 - 1937)

What is right for one couple is wrong for another. I would say that there are many more important factors to a happy marriage.
Elizabeth Aston, The Second Mrs. Darcy, 2007

When a man is ready to marry, he is often not too particular about the lady.
Eucharista Ward, Match For Mary Bennet, 2009

Man's best possession is a sympathetic wife.
Euripides (484 BC - 406 BC), Antigone

Never say that marriage has more of joy than pain.
Euripides (484 BC - 406 BC), Alcestis, 438 B.C.

One man's folly is another man's wife.
Helen Rowland (1876 - 1950)

Nearly all marriages, even happy ones, are mistakes: in the sense that almost certainly (in a more perfect world, or even with a little more care in this very imperfect one) both partners might be found more suitable mates. But the real soul-mate is the one you are actually married to.
J. R. R. Tolkien (1892 - 1973), Letter to Michael Tolkien, March 1941

I pay very little regard...to what any young person says on the subject of marriage. If they profess a disinclination for it, I only set it down that they have not yet seen the right person.
Jane Austen (1775 - 1817), Mansfield Park

I would rather have young people settle on a small income at once, and have to struggle with a few difficulties together, than be involved in a long engagement.
Jane Austen (1775 - 1817), Persuasion, 1818

Knowing their feelings as she did, it was a most attractive picture of happiness to her. She always watched them as long as she could, delighted to fancy she understood what they might be talking of, as they walked along in happy independence, or equally delighted to see the Admiral's hearty shake of the hand when he encountered an old friend, and observe their eagerness of conversation when occasionally forming into a little knot of the navy, Mrs Croft looking as intelligent and keen as any of the officers around her.
Jane Austen (1775 - 1817), Persuasion, 1818

The only time I ever really suffered in body or mind, the only time that I ever fancied myself unwell, or had any ideas of danger, was the winter that I passed by myself. As long as we could be together, nothing ever ailed me, and I never met with the smallest inconvenience.
Jane Austen (1775 - 1817), Persuasion, 1818

When any two young people take it into their heads to marry, they are pretty sure by perseverance to carry their point, be they ever so poor, or ever so imprudent, or ever so little likely to be necessary to each other's ultimate comfort.
Jane Austen (1775 - 1817), Persuasion, 1818

My marriage had its ups and downs like anyone's, but when it came down to it, I knew it was solid. I miss that sort of security, and that sort of connection with someone.
John Scalzi, Old Man's War, 2005

Intimacy is what makes a marriage, not a ceremony, not a piece of paper from the state.
Kathleen Norris

Ain't never seen a ski trip fix a marriage.
Laura Moncur (1969 -), Merriton: Twelve Hours from San Francisco, 07-11-2007

Papa said that I should never be jealous of another's marriage. Whatever joys I imagine them having are just my imaginings. The reality is far more complicated and vast.
Laura Moncur (1969 -), The Secret Heart of Charlotte Lucas, 2014

If there was strife and contention in the home, very little else in life could compensate for it.
Lawana Blackwell, The Courtship of the Vicar's Daughter, 1998

Marriage is a great institution, but I'm not ready for an institution yet.
Mae West (1892 - 1980)

Don't waste too much time trying' to be a better man, ' cause you ain't never gonna be one without a good woman.
Mark Roberts, Mike & Molly, Peggy's New Beau, May 16, 2011

Always get married early in the morning. That way, if it doesn't work out, you haven't wasted a whole day.
Mickey Rooney (1920 -)

A successful marriage requires falling in love many times, always with the same person.
Mignon McLaughlin

My toughest fight was with my first wife.
Muhammad Ali (1942 -)

We were happily married for eight months. Unfortunately, we were married for four and a half years.
Nick Faldo

If you would marry suitably, marry your equal.
Ovid (43 BC - 17 AD)

That is what marriage really means: helping one another to reach the full status of being persons, responsible and autonomous beings who do not run away from life.
Paul Tournier

A good marriage is one which allows for change and growth in the individuals and in the way they express their love.
Pearl Buck (1892 - 1973)

You get married at twenty, you're going to be shocked who you're living with at thirty.
Peter Blake, House M.D., Fools For Love, 2006

That's the thing about marriage. It's a shell game we play with ourselves. We're the suckers and we have to lose, but we play anyway because we lie to ourselves that we can win.
Randy K. Milholland, Something Positive, Family's A Gamble Part 5, 07-25-13

I love being married. It's so great to find that one special person you want to annoy for the rest of your life.
Rita Rudner

In Hollywood a marriage is a success if it outlasts milk.
Rita Rudner

When I meet a man I ask myself, 'Is this the man I want my children to spend their weekends with?'
Rita Rudner

Happiness just wasn't part of the job description back then. You tried to find a helpmate to keep the cold wind and dogs at bay. Happiness just wasn't part of the equation. Survival was.
Robin Green, Northern Exposure, Burning Down the House, 1992

Such is the common process of marriage. A youth and maiden exchange meeting by chance, or brought together by artifice, exchange glances, reciprocate civilities, go home, and dream of one another. Having little to divert attention, or diversify thought, they find themselves uneasy when they are apart, and therefore conclude that they shall be happy together. They marry, and discover what nothing but voluntary blindness had before concealed; they wear out life in altercations, and charge nature with cruelty.
Samuel Johnson (1709 - 1784), Rasselas

There is no observation more frequently made by such as employ themselves in surveying the conduct of mankind, than that marriage, though the dictate of nature, and the institution of Providence, is yet very often the cause of misery, and that those who enter into that state can seldom forbear to express their repentance, and their envy of those whom either chance or caution hath withheld from it.
Samuel Johnson (1709 - 1784), Rambler #18

Remember, that if thou marry for beauty, thou bindest thyself all thy life for that which perchance will neither last nor please thee one year; and when thou hast it, it will be to thee of no price at all; for the desire dieth when it is attained, and the affection perisheth when it is satisfied.
Sir Walter Raleigh (1552 - 1618)

By all means marry: if you get a good wife, you'll be happy. If you get a bad one, you'll become a philosopher.
Socrates (469 BC - 399 BC)

Dude, marriage is the 'get out of loneliness free' card in the Monopoly game of life.
Veronica Pare and Ferrett Steinmetz, Home on the Strange, 11-09-07

Marriage is the only adventure open to the cowardly.
Voltaire (1694 - 1778)

American women expect to find in their husbands a perfection that English women only hope to find in their butlers.
W. Somerset Maugham (1874 - 1965), The Razor's Edge, 1943

I'm not a real movie star. I've still got the same wife I started out with twenty-eight years ago.
Will Rogers (1879 - 1935)

Never marry but for love; but see that thou lovest what is lovely.
William Penn (1644 - 1718)

By this marriage, all little jealousies, which now seem great , and all great fears, which now import their dangers would then be nothing.
William Shakespeare (1564 - 1616), Antony and Cleopatra, Act II, sc. 2

I have wedded her, not bedded her; and sworn to make the 'not' eternal.
William Shakespeare (1564 - 1616), All's Well that Ends Well, Act III, sc. 2

I will fasten on this sleeve of thine: thou art an elm, my husband, I a vine.
William Shakespeare (1564 - 1616), The Comedy of Errors, Act II, sc. 2

If there be no great love in the beginning, yet heaven may decrease it upon better acquaintance, when we are married and have more occasion to know one another...upon familiarity will grow more contempt.
William Shakespeare (1564 - 1616), The Merry Wives of Windsor, Act I, sc. 1

Men are April when they woo, December when they wed: maids are may when they are maids, but the sky changes when they are wives.
William Shakespeare (1564 - 1616), As You Like It, Act IV, sc. 1

O curse of marriage, that we can call these delicate creatures ours, and not their appetites.
William Shakespeare (1564 - 1616), Othello, Act III, sc. 3

The ancient saying is no heresy, hanging and wiving goes by destiny.
William Shakespeare (1564 - 1616), The Merchant of Venice, Act II, sc. 9

Though I want a kingdom, yet in marriage I may not prove inferior to yourself.
William Shakespeare (1564 - 1616), Henry VI, Part III, Act IV, sc. 1

[Marriage is] a world-without-end bargain.
William Shakespeare (1564 - 1616), Love's Labour's Lost

I tended to place my wife under a pedestal.
Woody Allen (1935 -)

I know nothing about sex because I was always married.
Zsa Zsa Gabor (1919 -)

Mathematics

As far as the laws of mathematics refer to reality, they are not certain; and as far as they are certain, they do not refer to reality.

Albert Einstein (1879 - 1955), "Geometry and Experience", January 27, 1921
Do not worry about your difficulties in Mathematics. I can assure you mine are still greater.
Albert Einstein (1879 - 1955)
Mathematics may be defined as the subject in which we never know what we are talking about, nor whether what we are saying is true.
Bertrand Russell (1872 - 1970), Mysticism and Logic (1917) ch. 4
Mathematics, rightly viewed, possesses not only truth, but supreme beauty - a beauty cold and austere, like that of sculpture.
Bertrand Russell (1872 - 1970)
Mathematics is the queen of the sciences.
Carl Friedrich Gauss (1777 - 1855), from Sartorius von Waltershausen, "Gauss zum Gedachtniss" [1856]
I went off to college planning to major in math or philosophy– of course, both those ideas are really the same idea.
Frank Wilczek (1951 -)
In mathematics you don't understand things. You just get used to them.
Johann von Neumann (1903 - 1957)
I have hardly ever known a mathematician who was capable of reasoning.
Plato (427 BC - 347 BC), The Republic
Proof is the idol before whom the pure mathematician tortures himself.
Sir Arthur Eddington (1882 - 1944), The Nature of the Physical World
The mathematics is not there till we put it there.
Sir Arthur Eddington (1882 - 1944), The Philosophy of Physical Science
We used to think that if we knew one, we knew two, because one and one are two. We are finding that we must learn a great deal more about 'and'.
Sir Arthur Eddington (1882 - 1944), The Harvest of a Quiet Eye (A. L. Mackay), 1977
If scientific reasoning were limited to the logical processes of arithmetic, we should not get very far in our understanding of the physical world. One might as well attempt to grasp the game of poker entirely by the use of the mathematics of probability.
Vannevar Bush (1890 - 1974)

Maturity

What I look forward to is continued immaturity followed by death.
Dave Barry (1947 -)
The purpose of life is to fight maturity.
Dick Werthimer
There's no point in being grown up if you can't be childish sometimes.
Doctor Who
By the time I'd grown up, I naturally supposed that I'd be grown up.
Eve Babitz
To be mature means to face, and not evade, every fresh crisis that comes.
Fritz Kunkel
Every human being on this earth is born with a tragedy, and it isn't original sin. He's born with the tragedy that he has to grow up. That he has to leave the nest, the security, and go out to do battle. He has to lose everything that is lovely and fight for a new loveliness of his own making, and it's a tragedy. A lot of people don't have the courage to do it.
Helen Hayes (1900 - 1993), in Roy Newquist, Showcase, 1966
I thought being an adult meant knowing what you believe, but that has not been my experience.
John Green, The Fault in Our Stars, 2012
Maturity is only a short break in adolescence.
Jules Feiffer (1929 -)
My Father taught me how to be a man – and not by instilling in me a sense of machismo or an agenda of dominance. He taught me that a real man doesn't take, he gives; he doesn't use force, he uses logic; doesn't play the role of trouble-maker, but rather, trouble-shooter; and most importantly, a real man is defined by what's in his heart, not his pants.
Kevin Smith, My Boring Ass Life, 06-01-05
That's the worst of growing up, and I'm beginning to realize it. The things you wanted so much when you were a child don't seem half so wonderful to you when you get them.
L. M. Montgomery (1874 - 1942), Anne of Green Gables, 1908
Age is no guarantee of maturity.
Lawana Blackwell, The Courtship of the Vicar's Daughter, 1998
Adulthood isn't an award they'll give you for being a good child. You can waste... years, trying to get someone to give that respect to you, as though it were a sort of promotion or raise in pay. If only you do enough, if only you are good enough. No. You have to just... take it. Give it to yourself, I suppose. Say, I'm sorry you feel like that and walk away. But that's hard.
Lois McMaster Bujold, A Civil Campaign, 1999
When we were children, we used to think that when we were grown-up we would no longer be vulnerable. But to grow up is to accept vulnerability... To be alive is to be vulnerable.
Madeleine L'Engle (1918 -), "Walking on Water: Reflections on Faith and Art", 1980
The grass is always greener once you don't have to mow a lawn anymore.
Randy K. Milholland, Something Positive, Young Hope, 04-26-13

Medicine

One has a greater sense of intellectual degradation after an interview with a doctor than from any human experience.
Alice James
Let's not kid ourselves. Whatever we diagnose, most patients, if they don't die, get well by themselves. Our job is mainly to try to make them feel better; do no harm.
Diane Frolov and Andrew Schneider, Northern Exposure, Wake Up Call, 1992

Half of the modern drugs could well be thrown out of the window, except that the birds might eat them.
Dr. Martin Henry Fischer
The cure for anything is salt water... tears, sweat or the sea.
Isak Dinesen, Seven Gothic Tales, 1934
Don't live in a town where there are no doctors.
Jewish Proverb
That's the thing about pain, it demands to be felt.
John Green, The Fault in Our Stars, 2012
[Medicine is] a collection of uncertain prescriptions the results of which, taken collectively, are more fatal than useful to mankind.
Napoleon Bonaparte (1769 - 1821)
Orthodox medicine has not found an answer to your complaint. However, luckily for you, I happen to be a quack.
Richter cartoon caption
One of the first duties of the physician is to educate the masses not to take medicine.
Sir William Osler (1849 - 1919), Aphorisms from his Bedside Teachings (1961) p. 105
The desire to take medicine is perhaps the greatest feature which distinguishes man from animals.
Sir William Osler (1849 - 1919), In H. Cushing, Life of Sir William Osler (1925)
Formerly, when religion was strong and science weak, men mistook magic for medicine; now, when science is strong and religion weak, men mistake medicine for magic.
Thomas Szasz, The Second Sin (1973) "Science and Scientism"
The art of medicine consists in amusing the patient while nature cures the disease.
Voltaire (1694 - 1778)

Memory

[Memory is] a man's real possession...In nothing else is he rich, in nothing else is he poor.
Alexander Smith (1830 - 1867)
Own only what you can carry with you; know language, know countries, know people. Let your memory be your travel bag.
Alexander Solzhenitsyn (1918 -)
Memory feeds imagination.
Amy Tan (1952 -)
The memory should be specially taxed in youth, since it is then that it is strongest and most tenacious. But in choosing the things that should be committed to memory the utmost care and forethought must be exercised; as lessons well learnt in youth are never forgotten.
Arthur Schopenhauer (1788 - 1860)
Creditors have better memories than debtors.
Benjamin Franklin (1706 - 1790), Poor Richard's Almanac (1758)
The palest ink is better than the best memory.
Chinese Proverb
We can remember minutely and precisely only the things which never really happened to us.
Eric Hoffer (1902 - 1983), The New York Times Magazine, April 25, 1971
Why is it that our memory is good enough to retain the least triviality that happens to us, and yet not good enough to recollect how often we have told it to the same person?
Francois de La Rochefoucauld (1613 - 1680)
One must have a good memory to be able to keep the promises one makes.
Friedrich Nietzsche (1844 - 1900)
The advantage of a bad memory is that one enjoys several times the same good things for the first time.
Friedrich Nietzsche (1844 - 1900)
There is not any memory with less satisfaction than the memory of some temptation we resisted.
James Branch Cabell (1879 - 1958)
If any one faculty of our nature may be called more wonderful than the rest, I do think it is memory. There seems something more speakingly incomprehensible in the powers, the failures, the inequalities of memory, than in any other of our intelligences. The memory is sometimes so retentive, so serviceable, so obedient; at others, so bewildered and so weak; and at others again, so tyrannic, so beyond control! We are, to be sure, a miracle every way; but our powers of recollecting and of forgetting do seem peculiarly past finding out.
Jane Austen (1775 - 1817), Mansfield Park
You don't remember what happened. What you remember becomes what happened.
John Green, An Abundance of Katherines, 2008
Nothing is so admirable in politics as a short memory.
John Kenneth Galbraith (1908 - 2006)
It's a poor sort of memory that only works backward.
Lewis Carroll (1832 - 1898)
When I was younger, I could remember anything, whether it had happened or not.
Mark Twain (1835 - 1910)
He who is not very strong in memory should not meddle with lying.
Michel de Montaigne (1533 - 1592)
Nothing fixes a thing so intensely in the memory as the wish to forget it.
Michel de Montaigne (1533 - 1592)
It was one of those perfect English autumnal days which occur more frequently in memory than in life.
P. D. James
You can fall ill with just a memory.
Paolo Giordano, The Solitude of Prime Numbers: A Novel
For the sense of smell, almost more than any other, has the power to recall memories and it is a pity that you use it so little.

Rachel Carson (1907 - 1964)
Memories can be sad, but sometimes they can also save you.
Takayuki Ikkaku, Arisa Hosaka and Toshihiro Kawabata, Animal Crossing: Wild World, 2005
The secret of a good memory is attention, and attention to a subject depends upon our interest in it. We rarely forget that which has made a deep impression on our minds.
Tryon Edwards (1809 - 1894)
I would forget it fain; But, O, it presses to my memory, like damned guilty deeds to a sinners mind.
William Shakespeare (1564 - 1616), Romeo and Juliet, Act III, sc. 2
Though yet of Hamlet our dear brother's death the memory be green.
William Shakespeare (1564 - 1616), Hamlet, Act I, sc. 2
When to the sessions of sweet silent thought
I summon up remembrance of things past,
I sigh the lack of many things I sought,
And with old woes new wail my dear time's waste.
William Shakespeare (1564 - 1616), Sonnet XXX
When wasteful war shall statues overturn,
And broils root out the work of masonry,
Nor Mars his sword nor wars quick fire shall burn
The living record of your memory.
William Shakespeare (1564 - 1616), Sonnet LV

Men and Women

There can be no spirituality, no sanctity, no truth without the female sex.
Diane Frolov and Andrew Schneider, Northern Exposure, Revelations, 1993
I'm just a person trapped inside a woman's body.
Elayne Boosler
How close the sexes sometimes come to one another. It is as much a matter of behaviour and the spere in which they move that separates the masculine part of humanity from the feminine.
Elizabeth Aston, The Exploits & Adventures of Miss Alethea Darcy, 2005
Women upset everything. When you let them into your life, you find that the woman is driving at one thing and you're driving at another.
George Bernard Shaw (1856 - 1950), "Pygmalion" (1913)
Misogynist: A man who hates women as much as women hate one another.
H. L. Mencken (1880 - 1956)
I hate women because they always know where things are.
James Thurber (1894 - 1961)
I hate to hear you talking so like a fine gentleman, and as if women were all fine ladies, instead of rational creatures.
Jane Austen (1775 - 1817), Persuasion, 1818
We certainly do not forget you as soon as you forget us. It is, perhaps, our fate rather than our merit. We cannot help ourselves. We live at home, quiet, confined, and our feelings prey upon us. You are forced on exertion. You have always a profession, pursuits, business of some sort or other, to take you back into the world immediately, and continual occupation and change soon weaken impressions. All the privilege I claim for my own sex (it is not a very enviable one; you need not covet it), is that of loving longest, when existence or when hope is gone.
Jane Austen (1775 - 1817), Persuasion, 1818
The male is a domestic animal which, if treated with firmness, can be trained to do most things.
Jilly Cooper
Funny business, a woman's career: the things you drop on the way up the ladder so you can move faster. You forget you'll need them again when you get back to being a woman. It's one career all females have in common, whether we like it or not: being a woman. Sooner or later, we've got to work at it, no matter how many other careers we've had or wanted.
Joseph L. Mankiewicz (1909 - 1993), in All About Eve
For all their strength, men were sometimes like little children.
Lawana Blackwell, The Dowry of Miss Lydia Clark, 1999
Male and female represent the two sides of the great radical dualism. But in fact they are perpetually passing into one another. Fluid hardens to solid, solid rushes to fluid. There is no wholly masculine man, no purely feminine woman.
Margaret Fuller (1810 - 1850), Woman in the Nineteenth Century, 1845
When I think of talking, it is of course with a woman. For talking at its best being an inspiration, it wants a corresponding divine quality of receptiveness, and where will you find this but in a woman?
Oliver Wendell Holmes (1809 - 1894)
If women are expected to do the same work as men, we must teach them the same things.
Plato (427 BC - 347 BC)
When the candles are out all women are fair.
Plutarch (46 AD - 120 AD), Morals
Don't accept rides from strange men, and remember that all men are strange.
Robin Morgan
Men live in a fantasy world. I know this because I am one, and I actually receive my mail there.
Scott Adams (1957 -)
What is most beautiful in virile men is something feminine; what is most beautiful in feminine women is something masculine.
Susan Sontag (1933 - 2004), Against Interpretation, 1966
Women who seek to be equal with men lack ambition.
Timothy Leary (1920 - 1996)
For most of history, Anonymous was a woman.
Virginia Woolf (1882 - 1941)
Heaven has no rage like love to hatred turned,
Nor hell a fury like a woman scorned.

William Congreve (1670 - 1729), The Mourning Bride, 1697, act III scene 8
A woman impudent and mannish grown is not more loathed than an effeminate man in time of action.
William Shakespeare (1564 - 1616), Troilus and Cressida, Act III, sc. 3
A woman mov'd is like a fountain troubled, muddy,
ill-seeming, thick, bereft of beauty.
William Shakespeare (1564 - 1616), Taming of the Shrew, Act V, sc. 2
Age cannot wither her, nor custom stale her infinite variety.
William Shakespeare (1564 - 1616), Antony and Cleopatra, Act II, sc. 2
Art thou a man? thy form cries out thou art:
Thy tears are womanish; thy wild acts denote
The unreasonable fury of a beast:
Unseemly woman in a seeming man!
Or ill-beseeming beast in seeming both!
William Shakespeare (1564 - 1616), Romeo and Juliet, Act III, sc. 3
Frailty, thy name is woman!
William Shakespeare (1564 - 1616), "Hamlet", Act 1 scene 2
Give me that man that is not passion's slave, and I will wear him in my hearts core.
William Shakespeare (1564 - 1616), Hamlet, Act III, sc. 2
Have you not heard it said full oft, a woman's nay doth stand for naught.
William Shakespeare (1564 - 1616), The Passionate Pilgrim
He is the half part of a blessed man,
Left to be finished by such as she;
And she a fair divided excellence,
Whose fulness of perfection lies in him.
William Shakespeare (1564 - 1616), King John, Act II, sc. 4
His life was gentle, and the elements so mix'd in him that Nature might stand up and say to all the world 'This was a man!'
William Shakespeare (1564 - 1616), Julius Caesar, Act I, sc. 2
How ever do we praise ourselves, our fancies are more giddy and uniform, more longing, wavering, sooner lost and worn, than women's are.
William Shakespeare (1564 - 1616), Twelfth Night, Act II, sc. 4
How hard it is for women to keep counsel!
William Shakespeare (1564 - 1616), The Passionate Pilgrim
I have a man's mind, but a woman's might.
William Shakespeare (1564 - 1616), Julius Caesar, Act II, sc. 4
I thank God I am not a woman, to be touched in so many giddy offences as He hath generally taxed their whole their whole sex withal.
William Shakespeare (1564 - 1616), As You Like It, Act III, sc. 2
Let me have men about me that are fat,
Sleek-headed men, and such as sleep o' nights:
Yond Cassius has a lean and hungry look;
He thinks too much: such men are dangerous.
William Shakespeare (1564 - 1616), Julius Caesar, Act I, sc. 2
Men have marble, women waxen, minds.
William Shakespeare (1564 - 1616), The Rape of Lucrece
Men's vows are women's traitors!
William Shakespeare (1564 - 1616), Cymbeline, Act III, sc. 4
Sigh no more, ladies, sigh no more,
Men were decievers ever,-
One foot in the sea and one on shore,
To one thing constant never.
William Shakespeare (1564 - 1616), Much Ado About Nothing, Act II, sc. 3
There's daggers in men's smiles.
William Shakespeare (1564 - 1616), Macbeth, Act II, sc. 3
Though men can cover crimes with bold stern looks, poor women's faces are their own faults' books.
William Shakespeare (1564 - 1616), The Rape of Lucrece
To be slow in words is a woman's only virtue.
William Shakespeare (1564 - 1616), The Passionate Pilgrim
What is a man, if his chief good and market of his time be but to sleep and feed? a beast, no more.
William Shakespeare (1564 - 1616), Hamlet, Act IV, sc. 4
Women being the weaker vessels, are ever thrust to the walls.
William Shakespeare (1564 - 1616), Romeo and Juliet, Act I, sc. 1
Women may fall when there's no strength in men.
William Shakespeare (1564 - 1616), Romeo and Juliet, Act II, sc. 3

Mercy

I have always found that mercy bears richer fruits than strict justice.
Abraham Lincoln (1809 - 1865), speech in Washington D.C., 1865
Cowards are cruel, but the brave
Love mercy, and delight to save.
John Gay (1685 - 1732)
We shall show mercy, but we shall not ask for it.
Sir Winston Churchill (1874 - 1965), speech in the House of Commons, July 14, 1940
Nothing emboldens sin so much as mercy.
William Shakespeare (1564 - 1616)
Sweet mercy is nobility's true badge.
William Shakespeare (1564 - 1616), "Titus Andronicus", Act 1 scene 2
The quality of mercy is not strain'd,
It droppeth as the gentle rain from heaven
Upon the place beneath. It is twice blest:
It blesseth him that gives and him that takes.
'T is mightiest in the mightiest: it becomes
The throned monarch better than his crown;
His sceptre shows the force of temporal power,

The attribute to awe and majesty,
Wherein doth sit the dread and fear of kings;
But mercy is above this sceptred sway,
It is enthroned in the hearts of kings,
It is an attribute to God himself;
And earthly power doth then show likest God's,
When mercy seasons justice. Therefore, Jew,
Though justice be thy plea, consider this,
That in the course of justice none of us
Should see salvation: we do pray for mercy;
And that same prayer doth teach us all to render
The deeds of mercy.
William Shakespeare (1564 - 1616), "The Merchant of Venice", Act 4 scene 1

Mistakes

Mistakes are a part of being human. Appreciate your mistakes for what they are:
precious life lessons that can only be learned the hard way. Unless it's a fatal
mistake, which, at least, others can learn from.
Al Franken, "Oh, the Things I Know", 2002
Anyone nit-picking enough to write a letter of correction to an editor doubtless
deserves the error that provoked it.
Alvin Toffler
Great services are not canceled by one act or by one single error.
Benjamin Disraeli (1804 - 1881)
An expert is a person who avoids small error as he sweeps on to the grand fallacy.
Benjamin Stolberg
Wise men profit more from fools than fools from wise men; for the wise men shun the
mistakes of fools, but fools do not imitate the successes of the wise.
Cato the Elder (234 BC - 149 BC), from Plutarch, Lives
We must not say every mistake is a foolish one.
Cicero (106 BC - 43 BC)
Be not ashamed of mistakes and thus make them crimes.
Confucius (551 BC - 479 BC)
Laughing at our mistakes can lengthen our own life. Laughing at someone else's can
shorten it.
Cullen Hightower
We're all capable of mistakes, but I do not care to enlighten you on the mistakes we
may or may not have made.
Dan Quayle (1947 -)
No one who cannot rejoice in the discovery of his own mistakes deserves to be called a
scholar.
Donald Foster
Assert your right to make a few mistakes. If people can't accept your imperfections,
that's their fault.
Dr. David M. Burns
The greatest mistake you can make in life is to be continually afraid you will make
one.
Elbert Hubbard (1856 - 1915)
The greatest mistake you can make in life is to be continually fearing you will make
one.
Elbert Hubbard (1856 - 1915)
Experience is that marvelous thing that enables you to recognize a mistake when you
make it again.
Franklin P. Jones
It's always helpful to learn from your mistakes because then your mistakes seem
worthwhile.
Garry Marshall, 'Wake Me When It's Funny'
A life spent making mistakes is not only more honorable, but more useful than a life
spent doing nothing.
George Bernard Shaw (1856 - 1950)
While one person hesitates because he feels inferior, the other is busy making
mistakes and becoming superior.
Henry C. Link
She had an unequalled gift... of squeezing big mistakes into small opportunities.
Henry James (1843 - 1916)
When you make a mistake, don't look back at it long. Take the reason of the thing
into your mind and then look forward. Mistakes are lessons of wisdom. The past
cannot be changed. The future is yet in your power.
Hugh White (1773 - 1840)
I have learned throughout my life as a composer chiefly through my mistakes and
pursuits of false assumptions, not by my exposure to founts of wisdom and
knowledge.
Igor Stravinsky (1882 - 1971)
Any man whose errors take ten years to correct is quite a man.
J. Robert Oppenheimer (1904 - 1967), speaking of Albert Einstein
Experience teaches slowly and at the cost of mistakes.
James A. Froude (1818 - 1894)
Mistakes are the portals of discovery.
James Joyce (1882 - 1941)
If all else fails, immortality can always be assured by spectacular error.
John Kenneth Galbraith (1908 - 2006)
There must be a limit to the mistakes one person can make, and when I get to the end
of them, then I'll be through with them. That's a very comforting thought.
L. M. Montgomery (1874 - 1942), Anne of Green Gables, 1908
Freedom is not worth having if it does not include the freedom to make mistakes.
Mahatma Gandhi (1869 - 1948)

There are sadistic scientists who hurry to hunt down errors instead of establishing the
truth.
Marie Curie (1867 - 1934)
If you have made mistakes, even serious ones, there is always another chance for
you. What we call failure is not the falling down but the staying down.
Mary Pickford (1893 - 1979)
If I had my life to live over... I'd dare to make more mistakes next time.
Nadine Stair
Never interrupt your enemy when he is making a mistake.
Napoleon Bonaparte (1769 - 1821)
An expert is a person who has made all the mistakes that can be made in a very
narrow field.
Niels Bohr (1885 - 1962)
Experience is the name everyone gives to their mistakes.
Oscar Wilde (1854 - 1900), Lady Windermere's Fan, 1892, Act III
Nowadays most people die of a sort of creeping common sense, and discover when it
is too late that the only things one never regrets are one's mistakes.
Oscar Wilde (1854 - 1900), The Picture of Dorian Gray, 1891
Every great mistake has a halfway moment, a split second when it can be recalled
and perhaps remedied.
Pearl Buck (1892 - 1973)
Mistakes, obviously, show us what needs improving. Without mistakes, how would we
know what we had to work on?
Peter McWilliams, Life 101
To avoid situations in which you might make mistakes may be the biggest mistake of
all.
Peter McWilliams, Life 101
Creativity is allowing yourself to make mistakes. Art is knowing which ones to keep.
Scott Adams (1957 -), 'The Dilbert Principle'
Mistakes are part of the dues one pays for a full life.
Sophia Loren (1934 -)
There are grammatical errors even in his silence.
Stanislaw J. Lec (1909 - 1966), "Unkempt Thoughts"
If I had to live my life again, I'd make the same mistakes, only sooner.
Tallulah Bankhead (1903 - 1968)
Love truth, and pardon error.
Voltaire (1694 - 1778)
I daresay one profits more by the mistakes one makes off one's own bat than by
doing the right thing on somebody's else advice.
W. Somerset Maugham (1874 - 1965), 'Of Human Bondage', 1915
The greatest mistake is trying to be more agreeable than you can be.
Walter Bagehot (1826 - 1877)
When you make a mistake, admit it. If you don't, you only make matters worse.
Ward Cleaver

Money

Too many of us look upon Americans as dollar chasers. This is a cruel libel, even if it
is reiterated thoughtlessly by the Americans themselves.
Albert Einstein (1879 - 1955)
Poverty cannot deprive us of many consolations. It cannot rob us of the affection we
have for each other, or degrade us in our own opinion, of in that of any person,
whose opinion we ought to value.
Ann Radcliffe (1764 - 1823), The Mysteries of Udolpho, 1764
There is some magic in wealth, which can thus make persons pay their court to it,
when it does not even benefit themselves. How strange it is, that a fool or knave, with
riches, should be treated with more respect by the world, than a good man, or a wise
man in poverty!
Ann Radcliffe (1764 - 1823), The Mysteries of Udolpho, 1764
I feel good about taking things to Goodwill and actually, I do like shopping at
Goodwill. It's so cheap that it feels like a library where I am just checking things out
for awhile until I decide to take them back.
April Foiles
He that is of the opinion money will do everything may well be suspected of doing
everything for money.
Benjamin Franklin (1706 - 1790)
If you would be wealthy, think of saving as well as getting.
Benjamin Franklin (1706 - 1790)
Who is rich? He that is content. Who is that? Nobody.
Benjamin Franklin (1706 - 1790)
Riches may enable us to confer favours, but to confer them with propriety and grace
requires a something that riches cannot give.
Charles Caleb Colton (1780 - 1832), Lacon, 1825
Annual income twenty pounds, annual expenditure nineteen six, result happiness.
Annual income twenty pounds, annual expenditure twenty pound ought and six,
result misery.
Charles Dickens (1812 - 1870), David Copperfield, 1849
Subdue your appetites, my dears, and you've conquered human nature.
Charles Dickens (1812 - 1870)
If all the rich people in the world divided up their money among themselves there
wouldn't be enough to go around.
Christina Stead (1903 - 1983), House of All Nations (1938) "Credo"
Endless money forms the sinews of war.
Cicero (106 BC - 43 BC), Philippics
Money was never a big motivation for me, except as a way to keep score. The real
excitement is playing the game.
Donald Trump (1946 -), "Trump: Art of the Deal"
If you want to know what God thinks of money, just look at the people he gave it to.

Dorothy Parker (1893 - 1967)
Money is the sinew of love as well as war.
Dr. Thomas Fuller (1654 - 1734), Gnomologia, 1732
I'm living so far beyond my income that we may almost be said to be living apart.
e e cummings (1894 - 1962)
The only way not to think about money is to have a great deal of it.
Edith Wharton (1862 - 1937)
Save a little money each month and at the end of the year you'll be surprised at how little you have.
Ernest Haskins
My problem lies in reconciling my gross habits with my net income.
Errol Flynn (1909 - 1959)
The mint makes it first, it is up to you to make it last.
Evan Esar (1899 - 1995)
The rich are the scum of the earth in every country.
G. K. Chesterton (1874 - 1936), Flying Inn (1914)
Lack of money is the root of all evil.
George Bernard Shaw (1856 - 1950)
One must be poor to know the luxury of giving.
George Eliot (1819 - 1880)
Money frees you from doing things you dislike. Since I dislike doing nearly everything, money is handy.
Groucho Marx (1890 - 1977)
The chief value of money lies in the fact that one lives in a world in which it is overestimated.
H. L. Mencken (1880 - 1956)
Make money your god and it will plague you like the devil.
Henry Fielding (1707 - 1754)
Make money, money by fair means if you can, if not, but any means money.
Horace (65 BC - 8 BC), Epistles
If you can count your money, you don't have a billion dollars.
J. Paul Getty (1892 - 1976)
I have enough money to last me the rest of my life, unless I buy something.
Jackie Mason (1934 -)
A large income is the best recipe for happiness I ever heard of.
Jane Austen (1775 - 1817), Mansfield Park
A large income is the best recipe for happiness I ever heard of.
Jane Austen (1775 - 1817), Mansfield Park
Nothing amuses me more than the easy manner with which everybody settles the abundance of those who have a great deal less than themselves.
Jane Austen (1775 - 1817), Mansfield Park
That isn't about money, fame, or power. It's about will, dedication, commitment, and knowing your self-worth. You can be poor as dirt and have those traits. Money can't buy you values. You just need to know what is important to you and then feel secure in your pursuit to achieve that.
Jennifer Hudson, I Got This: How I Changed My Ways and Lost What Weighed Me Down, 2012
One of the greatest disservices you can do to a man is to lend him money that he can't pay back.
Jesse H. Jones, The New York Times Magazine, July 2, 1939
All the perplexities, confusions, and distress in America arise, not from defects in their constitution or confederation, not from want of honor or virtue, so much as from the downright ignorance of the nature of coin, credit, and circulation.
John Adams (1735 - 1826), Letter to Thomas Jefferson, August 25, 1787
A wise man should have money in his head, but not in his heart.
Jonathan Swift (1667 - 1745)
All my businesses are scrupulously legal. Not because I have any moral problems with crime. It just makes my life easier to obey the law. Crime is for poor people; you don't need to rob the bank if you own it.
Josh Lieb, I am a Genius of Unspeakable Evil and I Want to be Your Class President, 2009
This is something that I do consider to be good advice: I took my first paycheck and I put it in the goddamn bank. Then I took my second paycheck and put it in the goddamn bank. I had seen the roller coaster of my father's career - top of the world, then unemployed - and I never wanted to take a job because I needed money.
Joss Whedon, Entertainment Weekly, 08-30-13
Do not be fooled into believing that because a man is rich he is necessarily smart. There is ample proof to the contrary.
Julius Rosenwald (1862 - 1932)
Be rich to yourself and poor to your friends.
Juvenal (55 AD - 127 AD)
It is not easy for men to rise whose qualities are thwarted by poverty.
Juvenal (55 AD - 127 AD), Satires
The easiest way for your children to learn about money is for you not to have any.
Katharine Whitehorn
Lack of money is no obstacle. Lack of an idea is an obstacle.
Ken Hakuta
It is pretty hard to tell what does bring happiness; poverty and wealth have both failed.
Kin Hubbard (1868 - 1930)
The safest way to double your money is to fold it over and put it in your pocket.
Kin Hubbard (1868 - 1930)
He had learned over the years that poor people did not feel so poor when allowed to give occasionally.
Lawana Blackwell, The Courtship of the Vicar's Daughter, 1998
Money can't buy happiness, but neither can poverty.
Leo Rosten (1908 -)
It is the wretchedness of being rich that you have to live with rich people.
Logan Pearsall Smith (1865 - 1946), Afterthoughts (1931) "In the World"

You don't have to die in order to make a living.
Lynn Johnston (1947 -), For Better or For Worse, 10-14-05
Riches cover a multitude of woes.
Menander (342 BC - 292 BC), Lady of Andros
No matter how rich you become, how famous or powerful, when you die the size of your funeral will still pretty much depend on the weather.
Michael Pritchard
The more you chase money, the harder it is to catch it.
Mike Tatum, Cashing In or Selling Out, SXSW 2006
It is better to have a permanent income than to be fascinating.
Oscar Wilde (1854 - 1900), The Model Millionaire, 1912
Wealth is the parent of luxury and indolence, and poverty of meanness and viciousness, and both of discontent.
Plato (427 BC - 347 BC), The Republic
Money alone sets all the world in motion.
Publilius Syrus (~ 100 BC), Maxims
Money is the opposite of the weather. Nobody talks about it, but everybody does something about it.
Rebecca Johnson, in 'Vogue'
Someday I want to be rich. Some people get so rich they lose all respect for humanity. That's how rich I want to be.
Rita Rudner
Finance is the art of passing money from hand to hand until it finally disappears.
Robert W. Sarnoff
It has been said that the love of money is the root of all evil. The want of money is so quite as truly.
Samuel Butler (1835 - 1902), Erewhon (1872)
Money's the same, whoever gives it to you. That was the point of money, after all: crisp and clean or wrinkled or disintegrated into quarters - a dollar was always worth a hundred cents.
Scott Westerfeld, The Last Days, 2006
A billion here, a billion there, pretty soon it adds up to real money.
Senator Everett Dirksen (1896 - 1969)
The art of living easily as to money is to pitch your scale of living one degree below your means.
Sir Henry Taylor
A little wanton money, which burned out the bottom of his purse.
Sir Thomas More (1478 - 1535), Works
Money: There's nothing in the world so demoralizing as money.
Sophocles (496 BC - 406 BC), Antigone
Money can't buy friends, but it can get you a better class of enemy.
Spike Milligan
I choose the likely man in preference to the rich man; I want a man without money rather than money without a man.
Themistocles (527 BC - 460 BC), from Plutarch, Lives
Never spend your money before you have it.
Thomas Jefferson (1743 - 1826)
He had heard people speak contemptuously of money: he wondered if they had ever tried to do without it.
W. Somerset Maugham (1874 - 1965), 'Of Human Bondage', 1915
Money is like a sixth sense without which you cannot make a complete use of the other five.
W. Somerset Maugham (1874 - 1965), 'Of Human Bondage', 1915
Perhaps the most important use of money - It saves time. Life is so short, and there's so much to do, one can't afford to waste a minute; and just think how much you waste, for instance, in walking from place to place instead of going by bus and in going by bus instead of by taxi.
W. Somerset Maugham (1874 - 1965), The Razor's Edge, 1943
That's the thing about Mother Nature, she really doesn't care what economic bracket you're in.
Whoopi Goldberg
Be you in what line of life you may, it will be amongst your misfortunes if you have not time properly to attend to pecuniary [monetary] matters. Want of attention to these matters has impeded the progress of science and of genius itself.
William Cobbett (1763 - 1835)
No one can earn a million dollars honestly.
William Jennings Bryan (1860 - 1925)
Money is better than poverty, if only for financial reasons.
Woody Allen (1935 -)

Morality

No moral system can rest solely on authority.
A. J. Ayer (1910 - 1989), Humanist Outlook
Ethics, too, are nothing but reverence for life. That is what gives me the fundamental principle of morality, namely, that good consists in maintaining, promoting, and enhancing life, and that destroying, injuring, and limiting life are evil.
Albert Schweitzer (1875 - 1965), Civilization and Ethics, Preface
Good laws have their origins in bad morals.
Ambrosius Macrobius
Compassion is the basis of all morality.
Arthur Schopenhauer (1788 - 1860)
The people who are regarded as moral luminaries are those who forego ordinary pleasures themselves and find compensation in interfering with the pleasures of others.
Bertrand Russell (1872 - 1970)
We have, in fact, two kinds of morality side by side: one which we preach but do not practice, and another which we practice but seldom preach.

Bertrand Russell (1872 - 1970), Sceptical Essays (1928), "Eastern and Western Ideals of Happiness"
There is no moral precept that does not have something inconvenient about it.
Denis Diderot (1713 - 1784)
Morality is herd instinct in the individual.
Friedrich Nietzsche (1844 - 1900), The Gay Science, section 116
I say that a man must be certain of his morality for the simple reason that he has to suffer for it.
G. K. Chesterton (1874 - 1936)
An Englishman thinks he is moral when he is only uncomfortable.
George Bernard Shaw (1856 - 1950), Man and Superman (1903) act 3
The difference between a moral man and a man of honor is that the latter regrets a discreditable act, even when it has worked and he has not been caught.
H. L. Mencken (1880 - 1956), 'Prejudices: Fourth Series,' 1924
Truth is the secret of eloquence and of virtue, the basis of moral authority; it is the highest summit of art and life.
Henri-Frédéric Amiel
Aim above morality. Be not simply good; be good for something.
Henry David Thoreau (1817 - 1862), Walden, 1854
Do not be too moral. You may cheat yourself out of much life. Aim above morality. Be not simply good; be good for something.
Henry David Thoreau (1817 - 1862)
Never let your sense of morals get in the way of doing what's right.
Isaac Asimov (1920 - 1992)
History is a voice forever sounding across the centuries the laws of right and wrong. Opinions alter, manners change, creeds rise and fall, but the moral law is written on the tablets of eternity.
James A. Forude
Taste is not only a part and index of morality, it is the only morality. The first, and last, and closest trial question to any living creature is "What do you like?" Tell me what you like, I'll tell you what you are.
John Ruskin (1819 - 1900)
Scandal is great entertainment because it allows people to feel contempt, a moral emotion that gives feeling of moral superiority while asking nothing in return.
Jonathan Haidt, The Happiness Hypothesis: Finding Modern Truth in Ancient Wisdom, 2005
The higher the buildings, the lower the morals.
Noel Coward (1899 - 1973)
Morality, like art, means drawing a line someplace.
Oscar Wilde (1854 - 1900)
Scandal is gossip made tedious by morality.
Oscar Wilde (1854 - 1900), Lady Windermere's Fan, 1892, Act III
The ability to see beauty is the beginning of our moral sensibility. What we believe is beautiful we will not wantonly destroy.
Reverend Sean Parker Dennison, Ministrare, 2-10-05
I believe that in this generation those with the courage to enter the conflict will find themselves with companions in every corner of the world.
Robert F. Kennedy (1925 - 1968), Day of affirmation, address delivered at the University of Capetown, South Africa, June 6, 1966
If your morals make you dreary, depend on it , they are wrong.
Robert Louis Stevenson (1850 - 1894)
Perfection of moral virtue does not wholly take away the passions, but regulates them.
Saint Thomas Aquinas (1225 - 1274)
The soul is the captain and ruler of the life of morals.
Sallust (86 BC - 34 BC)
'Wrong' is one of those concepts that depends on witnesses.
Scott Adams (1957 -), Dilbert, 11-05-09
I have never believed there was one code of morality for a public and another for a private man.
Thomas Jefferson (1743 - 1826)
All sects are different, because they come from men; morality is everywhere the same, because it comes from God.
Voltaire (1694 - 1778)

Morning

Arranging a bowl of flowers in the morning can give a sense of quiet in a crowded day - like writing a poem, or saying a prayer.
Anne Morrow Lindbergh
I get up every morning determined to both change the world and have one hell of a good time. Sometimes this makes planning my day difficult.
E. B. White (1899 - 1985)
I have a problem about being nearly sixty: I keep waking up in the morning and thinking I'm thirty-one.
Elizabeth Janeway, Between Myth and Morning, 1974
Some mornings it just doesn't seem worth it to gnaw through the leather straps.
Emo Phillips
In a real dark night of the soul it is always three o'clock in the morning, day after day.
F. Scott Fitzgerald (1896 - 1940), "The Crack-Up" (1936)
I feel sorry for people who do not drink. When they wake up in the morning it is as good as they are going to feel all day.
Frank Sinatra (1915 - 1998), Quoted in The Sydney Morning Herald
Take a two-mile walk every morning before breakfast.
Harry S Truman (1884 - 1972)
Never rely on the glory of the morning nor the smiles of your mother-in-law.
Japanese Proverb

The average, healthy, well-adjusted adult gets up at seven-thirty in the morning feeling just plain terrible.
Jean Kerr
On a lazy Saturday morning when you're lying in bed, drifting in and out of sleep, there is a space where fantasy and reality become one. Are you awake, or are you dreaming? You see people and things; some are familiar; some are strange. You talk, you feel, but you move without walking; you fly without wings. Your mind and your body exist, but on separate planes. Time stands still. For me, this is the feeling I have when ideas come.
Lynn Johnston (1947 -), Lynn on Ideas
In the morning, when you are sluggish about getting up, let this thought be present: 'I am rising to a man's work.'
Marcus Aurelius Antoninus (121 AD - 180 AD), Meditations
Never face facts; if you do, you'll never get up in the morning.
Marlo Thomas
My future starts when I wake up every morning... Every day I find something creative to do with my life.
Miles Davis (1926 - 1991)
I have always felt that the moment when first you wake up in the morning is the most wonderful of the twenty-four hours.
Monica Baldwin
At my age the bones are water in the morning until food is given them.
Pearl Buck (1892 - 1973)
The brain is a wonderful organ. It starts working the moment you get up in the morning and does not stop until you get into the office.
Robert Frost (1874 - 1963)
I had a monumental idea this morning, but I didn't like it.
Samuel Goldwyn (1882 - 1974)
What a beautiful, sunny morning. It makes you happy to be alive, doesn't it? We can't let the sun outshine us! We have to beam, too!
Takayuki Ikkaku, Arisa Hosaka and Toshihiro Kawabata, Animal Crossing: Wild World, 2005
Early morning cheerfulness can be extremely obnoxious.
William Feather (1908 - 1976)

Music

The whole problem can be stated quite simply by asking, 'Is there a meaning to music?' My answer would be, 'Yes.' And 'Can you state in so many words what the meaning is?' My answer to that would be, 'No.'
Agron Copland (1900 - 1990)
After silence, that which comes nearest to expressing the inexpressible is music.
Aldous Huxley (1894 - 1963), "Music at Night", 1931
[T]here's no bad day that can't be overcome by listening to a barbershop quartet; this is just truth, plain and simple.
Chuck Sigars, The World According to Chuck weblog, September 30, 2003
An intellectual snob is someone who can listen to the William Tell Overture and not think of The Lone Ranger.
Dan Rather (1931 -)
But then there's a moment like tonight, a profound and transcendent experience, the feeling as if a door has opened, and it's all because of that instrument, that incredible, magical instrument.
Diane Frolov and Andrew Schneider, Northern Exposure, Mite Makes Right, 1994
Opera is when a guy gets stabbed in the back and, instead of bleeding, he sings.
Ed Gardner
Wagner's music is better than it sounds.
Edgar Wilson Nye (1850 - 1896), quoted in Mark Twain's Autobiography, 1924
My personal hobbies are reading, listening to music, and silence.
Edith Sitwell (1887 - 1964)
I don't know anything about music. In my line you don't have to.
Elvis Presley (1935 - 1977)
Only sick music makes money today.
Friedrich Nietzsche (1844 - 1900), Der Fall Wagner, Section 5
Music with dinner is an insult both to the cook and the violinist.
G. K. Chesterton (1874 - 1936)
Hell is full of musical amateurs.
George Bernard Shaw (1856 - 1950)
Hell is full of musical amateurs: music is the brandy of the damned.
George Bernard Shaw (1856 - 1950), Man and Superman (1903) act 3
I think I should have no other mortal wants, if I could always have plenty of music. It seems to infuse strength into my limbs and ideas into my brain. Life seems to go on without effort, when I am filled with music.
George Eliot (1819 - 1880)
There is no feeling, except the extremes of fear and grief, that does not find relief in music.
George Eliot (1819 - 1880), The Mill on the Floss, 1860
Music is essentially useless, as life is.
George Santayana (1863 - 1952), Life of Reason (1905) vol. 4, ch. 4
Music is essentially useless, as life is: but both have an ideal extension which lends utility to its conditions.
George Santayana (1863 - 1952), Life of Reason (1905) vol. 4, ch. 4
Military justice is to justice what military music is to music.
Groucho Marx (1890 - 1977)
Among all men on the earth bards have a share of honor and reverence, because the muse has taught them songs and loves the race of bards.
Homer (800 BC - 700 BC), The Odyssey
My music is best understood by children and animals.
Igor Stravinsky (1882 - 1971), In Observer 8 Oct. 1961
Ah, music. A magic beyond all we do here!

J. K. Rowling, Harry Potter and the Sorcerer's Stone, 1997
I think everyone should have a Beatles phase in their life. I think it's part of growing up in the Western world.
Jadelr and Cristina Cordova, Chasing Windmills, 07-24-06
Music like religion, unconditionally brings in its train all the moral virtues to the heart it enters, even though that heart is not in the least worthy.
Jean Baptiste Montegut
I hate music, especially when it's played.
Jimmy Durante (1893 - 1980)
If you develop an ear for sounds that are musical it is like developing an ego. You begin to refuse sounds that are not musical and that way cut yourself off from a good deal of experience.
John Cage (1912 - 1992)
Music is the only language in which you cannot say a mean or sarcastic thing.
John Erskine (1879 - 1951)
Classical music is the kind we keep thinking will turn into a tune.
Kin Hubbard (1868 - 1930)
Music is a discipline, and a mistress of order and good manners, she makes the people milder and gentler, more moral and more reasonable.
Martin Luther (1483 - 1546)
My heart, which is so full to overflowing, has often been solaced and refreshed by music when sick and weary.
Martin Luther (1483 - 1546)
Take a music bath once or twice a week for a few seasons, and you will find that it is to the soul what the water bath is to the body.
Oliver Wendell Holmes (1809 - 1894)
Music makes one feel so romantic - at least it always gets on one's nerves - which is the same thing nowadays.
Oscar Wilde (1854 - 1900)
If a thing isn't worth saying, you sing it.
Pierre Beaumarchais (1732 - 1799)
Music is the wine that fills the cup of silence.
Robert Fripp
Of all noises, I think music is the least disagreeable.
Samuel Johnson (1709 - 1784)
I don't mind what language an opera is sung in so long as it is a language I don't understand.
Sir Edward Appleton (1892 - 1965)
A musicologist is a man who can read music but can't hear it.
Sir Thomas Beecham (1879 - 1961)
Brass bands are all very well in their place - outdoors and several miles away.
Sir Thomas Beecham (1879 - 1961)
The way to write American music is simple. All you have to do is be an American and then write any kind of music you wish.
Virgil Thomson (1896 - 1989)
My loathings are simple: stupidity, oppression, crime, cruelty, soft music.
Vladimir Nabokov (1899 - 1977)
No opera plot can be sensible, for people do not sing when they are feeling sensible.
W. H. Auden (1907 - 1973)
Music has charms to soothe the savage breast
To soften rocks, or bend a knotted oak.
William Congreve (1670 - 1729), The Mourning Bride, Act 1 Scene 1
I can sing, and speak to him in many sorts of music.
William Shakespeare (1564 - 1616), Twelfth Night, Act I, sc. 2
If music be the food of love, play on;
Give me excess of it, that, surfeiting,
The appetite may sicken, and so die.
That strain again! it had a dying fall:
O, it came o'er my ear like the sweet sound
That breathes upon a bank of violets,
Stealing and giving odour!
William Shakespeare (1564 - 1616), "Twelfth Night", Act 1 scene 1
If music be the food of love, play on; give me excess of it, that, surfeiting, the appetite may sicken, and so die.
William Shakespeare (1564 - 1616), Twelfth Night, Act I, sc. 1
In sweet music is such art: killing care and grief of heart fall asleep, or hearing, die.
William Shakespeare (1564 - 1616), Henry VIII, Act III, sc. 1
Music, moody food of us that trade in love.
William Shakespeare (1564 - 1616), Antony and Cleopatra, Act II, sc. 5
Their savage eyes turn'd to a modest gaze
By the sweet power of music: therefore the poet
Did feign that Orpheus drew trees, stones and floods;
Since nought so stockish, hard and full of rage,
But music for the time doth change his nature.
The man that hath no music in himself,
Nor is not moved with concord of sweet sounds,
Is fit for treasons, stratagems and spoils.
William Shakespeare (1564 - 1616), The Merchant of Venice, Act V, sc. 1
To know the cause why music was ordain'd! Was it not to refresh the mind of a man after his studies or his usual pain?
William Shakespeare (1564 - 1616), The Taming of the Shrew, Act III, sc. 1
When griping grief the heart doth wound,
and doleful dumps the mind opresses,
then music, with her silver sound,
with speedy help doth lend redress.
William Shakespeare (1564 - 1616)
I can't listen to that much Wagner. I start getting the urge to conquer Poland.

Woody Allen (1935 -)
The refreshing pleasure from the first view of nature, after the pain of illness, and the confinement of a sick-chamber, is above the conceptions, as well as the descriptions, of those in health.
Ann Radcliffe (1764 - 1823), The Mysteries of Udolpho, 1764
And then, the unspeakable purity and freshness of the air! There was just enough heat to enhance the value of the breeze, and just enough wind to keep the whole sea in motion, to make the waves come bounding to the shore, foaming and sparkling, as if wild with glee.
Anne Bronte (1820 - 1849), Agnes Grey
Our land is more valuable than your money. As long as the sun shines and the waters flow, this land will be here to give life to men and animals; therefore, we cannot sell this land. It was put here for us by the Great Spirit and we cannot sell it because it does not belong to us.
Anonymous, Blackfoot chief (c. 1880)
Nature is just enough; but men and women must comprehend and accept her suggestions.
Antoinette Brown Blackwell (1825 - 1921)
In all things of nature there is something of the marvelous.
Aristotle (384 BC - 322 BC), Parts of Animals
Nature does nothing uselessly.
Aristotle (384 BC - 322 BC), Politics
He maketh me to lie down in green pastures he leadeth me beside the still waters.
Bible, Psalm xxiii, 2.
A lot of people like snow. I find it to be an unnecessary freezing of water.
Carl Reiner
Real freedom lies in wildness, not in civilization.
Charles Lindbergh (1902 - 1974)
Art is born of the observation and investigation of nature.
Cicero (106 BC - 43 BC)
Nature herself makes the wise man rich.
Cicero (106 BC - 43 BC)
The materials of wealth are in the earth, in the seas, and in their natural and unaided productions.
Daniel Webster (1782 - 1852), Remarks in the Senate, march 12, 1838
I speak for the trees, for the trees have no tongues.
Dr. Seuss (1904 - 1991), The Lorax
I would feel more optimistic about a bright future for man if he spent less time proving that he can outwit Nature and more time tasting her sweetness and respecting her seniority.
E. B. White (1899 - 1985)
Mountains inspire awe in any human person who has a soul. They remind us of our frailty, our unimportance, of the briefness of our span upon this earth. They touch the heavens, and sail serenely at an altitude beyond even the imaginings of a mere mortal.
Elizabeth Aston, The Exploits & Adventures of Miss Alethea Darcy, 2005
I believe in God, only I spell it Nature.
Frank Lloyd Wright (1869 - 1959)
Adapt or perish, now as ever, is nature's inexorable imperative.
H. G. Wells (1866 - 1946)
In wildness is the preservation of the world.
Henry David Thoreau (1817 - 1862)
It is pleasant to have been to a place the way a river went.
Henry David Thoreau (1817 - 1862)
Nature is wont to hide herself.
Heraclitus (540 BC - 480 BC), On the Universe
It was the Law of the Sea, they said. Civilization ends at the waterline. Beyond that, we all enter the food chain, and not always right at the top.
Hunter S. Thompson (1939 - 2005)
What nature delivers to us is never stale. Because what nature creates has eternity in it.
Isaac Bashevis Singer (1904 - 1991)
One cannot fix one's eyes on the commonest natural production without finding food for a rambling fancy.
Jane Austen (1775 - 1817), Mansfield Park
My mission is to create a world where we can live in harmony with nature.
Jane Goodall (1934 -)
People say to me so often, 'Jane how can you be so peaceful when everywhere around you people want books signed, people are asking these questions and yet you seem peaceful,' and I always answer that it is the peace of the forest that I carry inside.
Jane Goodall (1934 -)
You think Nature is some Disney movie? Nature is a killer. Nature is a bitch. It's feeding time out there 24 hours a day, every step that you take is a gamble with death. If it isn't getting hit with lightning today, it's an earthquake tomorrow or some deer tick carrying Lime disease. Either way, you're ending up on the wrong end of the food chain.
Jeff Melvoin, Northern Exposure, Bolt from the Blue, 1994
Climb the mountains and get their good tidings. Nature's peace will flow into you as sunshine flows into trees. The winds will blow their own freshness into you, and the storms their energy, while cares will drop away from you like the leaves of Autumn.
John Muir (1838 - 1914), Our National Parks, 1901
Come to the woods, for here is rest. There is no repose like that of the green deep woods. Here grow the wallflower and the violet. The squirrel will come and sit upon your knee, the logcock will wake you in the morning. Sleep in forgetfulness of all ill. Of all the upness accessible to mortals, there is no upness comparable to the mountains.

John Muir (1838 - 1914), Atlantic Monthly, January 1869
Everybody needs beauty as well as bread, places to play in and pray in, where nature
may heal and give strength to body and soul alike.
John Muir (1838 - 1914), The Yosemite, 1912
Fresh beauty opens one's eyes wherever it is really seen, but the very abundance and
completeness of the common beauty that besets our steps prevents its being absorbed
and appreciated. It is a good thing, therefore, to make short excursions now and then
to the bottom of the sea among dulse and coral, or up among the clouds on
mountain-tops, or in balloons, or even to creep like worms into dark holes and
caverns underground, not only to learn something of what is going on in those out-of-
the-way places, but to see better what the sun sees on our return to common everyday
beauty.
John Muir (1838 - 1914), My First Summer in the Sierra, 1911
I know that our bodies were made to thrive only in pure air, and the scenes in which
pure air is found. There is not a "fragment" in all nature, for every relative fragment
of one thing is a full harmonious unit in itself.
John Muir (1838 - 1914), A Thousand Mile Walk to the Gulf, 1916
In God's wildness lies the hope of the world - the great fresh unblighted, unredeemed
wilderness. The galling harness of civilization drops off, and wounds heal ere we are
aware.
John Muir (1838 - 1914), John of the Mountains, 1938
Keep close to Nature's heart... and break clear away, once in awhile, and climb a
mountain or spend a week in the woods. Wash your spirit clean. None of Nature's
landscapes are ugly so long as they are wild.
John Muir (1838 - 1914), Our National Parks, 1901
No synonym for God is so perfect as Beauty. Whether as seen carving the lines of the
mountains with glaciers, or gathering matter into stars, or planning the movements of
water, or gardening - still all is Beauty!
John Muir (1838 - 1914), Atlantic Monthly, January 1869
The clearest way into the Universe is through a forest wilderness.
John Muir (1838 - 1914), John of the Mountains, 1938
The wrongs done to trees, wrongs of every sort, are done in the darkness of ignorance
and unbelief, for when the light comes, the heart of the people is always right.
John Muir (1838 - 1914), My First Summer in the Sierra, 1911
When we contemplate the whole globe as one great dewdrop, striped and dotted with
continents and islands, flying through space with other stars all singing and shining
together as one, the whole universe appears as an infinite storm of beauty.
John Muir (1838 - 1914), Travels in Alaska by John Muir, 1915, chapter 1
When we try to pick out anything by itself, we find it hitched to everything else in the
Universe.
John Muir (1838 - 1914), My First Summer in the Sierra, 1911
When one loses the deep intimate relationship with nature, then temples, mosques
and churches become important.
Krishnamurti, Beginnings of Learning
Nature has been for me, for as long as I remember, a source of solace, inspiration,
adventure, and delight; a home, a teacher, a companion.
Lorraine Anderson
Water, taken in moderation, cannot hurt anybody.
Mark Twain (1835 - 1910)
Eventually, all things merge into one, and a river runs through it. The river was cut by
the world's great flood and runs over rocks from the basement of time. On some of
the rocks are timeless raindrops. Under the rocks are the words, and some of the
words are theirs. I am haunted by waters.
Norman Maclean, A River Runs Through It
Live in the sunshine, swim the sea, drink the wild air.
Ralph Waldo Emerson (1803 - 1882)
In nature there are neither rewards or punishments - there are consequences.
Robert Green Ingersoll
It is not much for its beauty that makes a claim upon men's hearts, as for that subtle
something, that quality of air that emanates from old trees, that so wonderfully
changes and renews a weary spirit.
Robert Louis Stevenson (1850 - 1894)
It's amazing how quickly nature consumes human places after we turn our backs on
them. Life is a hungry thing.
Scott Westerfeld, Peeps, 2005
Whosoever is delighted in solitude is either a wild beast or a god.
Sir Francis Bacon (1561 - 1626)
I'm terribly sorry, but nature is not always family friendly.
Takayuki Ikkaku, Arisa Hosaka and Toshihiro Kawabata, Animal Crossing: Wild World, 2005
Seeing wildlife is like seeing celebrities, only better.
Tanja Andrews, Freshtopia, 08-19-06
A vacuum is a hell of a lot better than some of the stuff that nature replaces it with.
Tennessee Williams (1911 - 1983), Cat on a Hot Tin Roof (1955)
After you have exhausted what there is in business, politics, conviviality, and so on -
have found that none of these finally satisfy, or permanently wear - what remains?
Nature remains.
Walt Whitman (1819 - 1892)
You must not know too much or be too precise or scientific about birds and trees and
flowers and watercraft; a certain free-margin, and even vagueness - ignorance,
credulity - helps your enjoyment of these things.
Walt Whitman (1819 - 1892)
And this our life, exempt from public haunt,
Finds tongues in trees, books in running brooks,
Sermons in stones, and good in everything.
William Shakespeare (1564 - 1616), As You Like It, Act II, Scene i, Lines 15-17
Come unto these yellow sands,
And then take hands:

Courtsied when you have, and kiss'd
The wild waves whist.
William Shakespeare (1564 - 1616), "The Tempest", Act 1 scene 2
Nature does require her times of preservation.
William Shakespeare (1564 - 1616), Henry VIII, Act III, sc. 2
Where the bee sucks, there suck I:
In a cowslip's bell I lie;
There I couch when owls do cry.
On the bat's back I do fly
After summer merrily.
Merrily, merrily shall I live now
Under the blossom that hangs on the bough.
William Shakespeare (1564 - 1616), The Tempest, Act V, sc. 1
The goal of life is living in agreement with nature.
Zeno (335 BC - 264 BC), from Diogenes Laertius, Lives of Eminent Philosophers

Nenessity

Not even the gods fight against necessity.
Simonides (556 BC - 468 BC), from Plato, Dialogues, Protagoras
Necessity has no law.
William Langland (1332 - 1400)
Necessity is the plea for every infringement of human freedom. It is the argument of
tyrants; it is the creed of slaves.
William Pitt

Neighbors

This is the best kind of voyeurism, hearing joy from your neighbors.
Chuck Sigars, The World According to Chuck weblog, October 14, 2003
Virtue is not left to stand alone. He who practices it will have neighbors.
Confucius (551 BC - 479 BC), The Confucian Analects
There are many who dare not kill themselves for fear of what the neighbors will say.
Cyril Connolly (1903 - 1974)
The Bible tells us to love our neighbors, and also to love our enemies; probably
because they are generally the same people.
G. K. Chesterton (1874 - 1936)
Some people did what their neighbors did so that if any lunatics were at large, one
might know and avoid them.
George Eliot (1819 - 1880), Middlemarch
A bad neighbor is a misfortune, as much as a good one is a great blessing.
Hesiod (~800 BC), Works and Days
The impersonal hand of government can never replace the helping hand of a
neighbor.
Hubert H. Humphrey (1911 - 1978)
Ask about your neighbors, then buy the house.
Jewish Proverb
How much time he saves who does not look to see what his neighbor says or does or
thinks.
Marcus Aurelius Antoninus (121 AD - 180 AD)
The good neighbor looks beyond the external accidents and discerns those inner
qualities that make all men human and, therefore, brothers.
Martin Luther King Jr. (1929 - 1968), 'Strength to Love,' 1963
It is folly to punish your neighbor by fire when you live next door.
Publilius Syrus (~100 BC)
Don't buy the house; buy the neighborhood.
Russian Proverb
No matter how much you disagree with your kin, if you are a thoroughbred you will
not discuss their shortcomings with the neighbors.
Tom Thompson
A nation is a society united by delusions about its ancestry and by common hatred of
its neighbors.
William Ralph Inge (1860 - 1954)

Night

Oh, treacherous night! thou lendest thy ready veil to every treason, and teeming
mischief's beneath thy shade.
Aaron Hill
Sometimes I lie awake at night, and I ask, "Where have I gone wrong?"
Then a voice says to me, "This is going to take more than one night."
Charles M. Schulz (1922 - 2000), Charlie Brown in "Peanuts"
Ignorance is the night of the mind, but a night without moon and star.
Confucius (551 BC - 479 BC)
Those who dream by day are cognizant of many things which escape those who
dream only by night.
Edgar Allan Poe (1809 - 1849), "Eleonora"
For the night was not impartial. No, the night loved some more than others, served
some more than others.
Eudora Welty (1909 -)
Wait until it is night before saying that it has been a fine day.
French Proverb
You never really hear the truth from your subordinates until after 10 in the evening.
Jurgen Schrempp, Former CEO of DaimlerChrysler
Not being able to sleep is terrible. You have the misery of having partied all night...
without the satisfaction.
Lynn Johnston (1947 -), For Better or For Worse, 07-22-06
I think wholeness comes from living your life consciously during the day and then
exploring your inner life or unconscious at night.

Margery Cuyler
Don't try to solve serious matters in the middle of the night.
Philip K. Dick (1928 - 1982), What the Dead Men Say, 1954
I like the night. Without the dark, we'd never see the stars.
Stephenie Meyer, Twilight, 2005

Nobility

Noble life demands a noble architecture for noble uses of noble men. Lack of culture means what it has always meant: ignoble civilization and therefore imminent downfall.
Frank Lloyd Wright (1869 - 1959)
It is nobler to declare oneself wrong than to insist on being right - especially when one is right.
Friedrich Nietzsche (1844 - 1900), Thus Spoke Zarathustra
I too shall lie in the dust when I am dead, but now let me win noble renown.
Homer (800 BC - 700 BC), The Iliad
Whenever a man does a thoroughly stupid thing, it is always from the noblest motives.
Oscar Wilde (1854 - 1900), The Picture of Dorian Gray, 1891
Life ought to be a struggle of desire toward adventures whose nobility will fertilize the soul.
Rebecca West (1892 - 1983)
They are never alone that are accompanied with noble thoughts.
Sir Philip Sidney (1554 - 1586)
Put more trust in nobility of character than in an oath.
Solon (638 BC - 559 BC)
The truth is that there is nothing noble in being superior to somebody else. The only real nobility is in being superior to your former self.
Whitney Young (1921 - 1971)
No one can build his security upon the nobleness of another person.
Willa Cather (1873 - 1947)
Sweet mercy is nobility's true badge.
William Shakespeare (1564 - 1616), "Titus Andronicus", Act 1 scene 2

Opinions

When men exercise their reason coolly and freely on a variety of distinct questions, they inevitably fall into different opinions on some of them. When they are governed by a common passion, their opinions, if they are to be called, will be the same.
Alexander Hamilton (1755 - 1804)
It is not advisable, James, to venture unsolicited opinions. You should spare yourself the embarrassing discovery of their exact value to your listener.
Ayn Rand (1905 - 1982), Atlas Shrugged, 1957
Every man has a right to his opinion, but no man has a right to be wrong in his facts.
Bernard M. Baruch (1870 - 1965)
I think we ought always to entertain our opinions with some measure of doubt. I shouldn't wish people dogmatically to believe any philosophy, not even mine.
Bertrand Russell (1872 - 1970)
The opinions that are held with passion are always those for which no good ground exists; indeed the passion is the measure of the holders lack of rational conviction. Opinions in politics and religion are almost always held passionately.
Bertrand Russell (1872 - 1970), Sceptical Essays, 1961
I'm not sure I want popular opinion on my side — I've noticed those with the most opinions often have the fewest facts.
Bethania McKenstry
Fight for your opinions, but do not believe that they contain the whole truth, or the only truth.
Charles A. Dana (1819 - 1897)
The recipe for perpetual ignorance is: be satisfied with your opinions and content with your knowledge.
Elbert Hubbard (1856 - 1915)
The moment we begin to fear the opinions of others and hesitate to tell the truth that is in us, and from motives of policy are silent when we should speak, the divine floods of light and life no longer flow into our souls.
Elizabeth Cady Stanton (1815 - 1902), 1890
There is probably an element of malice in our readiness to overestimate people - we are, as it were, laying up for ourselves the pleasure of later cutting them down to size.
Eric Hoffer (1902 - 1983), The New York Times Magazine, April 25, 1971
Opinions founded on prejudice are always sustained with the greatest of violence.
Francis Jeffrey (1773 - 1850)
It is hard enough to remember my opinions, without also remembering my reasons for them!
Friedrich Nietzsche (1844 - 1900)
Don't judge a man by his opinions, but what his opinions have made of him.
Georg Christoph Lichtenberg (1742 - 1799)
Nothing is more conducive to peace of mind than not having any opinions at all.
Georg Christoph Lichtenberg (1742 - 1799)
I have opinions of my own – strong opinions – but I don't always agree with them.
George Bush (1924 -)
This imputation of inconsistency is one to which every sound politician and every honest thinker must sooner or later subject himself. The foolish and the dead alone never change their opinion.
James Russell Lowell (1819 - 1891), My Study Windows,1899
Where there is much desire to learn, there of necessity will be much arguing, much writing, many opinions; for opinions in good men is but knowledge in the making.
John Milton (1608 - 1674)

Risk! Risk anything! Care no more for the opinions of others, for those voices. Do the hardest thing on earth for you. Act for yourself. Face the truth.
Katherine Mansfield (1888 - 1923)
Patterning your life around other's opinions is nothing more than slavery.
Lawana Blackwell, The Dowry of Miss Lydia Clark, 1999
I am not one of those who in expressing opinions confine themselves to facts.
Mark Twain (1835 - 1910), Wearing White Clothes speech, 1907
Our opinions do not really blossom into fruition until we have expressed them to someone else.
Mark Twain (1835 - 1910), quoted in Mark Twain and I, Opie Read, 1940
Sane and intelligent human beings are like all other human beings, and carefully and cautiously and diligently conceal their private real opinions from the world and give out fictitious ones in their stead for general consumption.
Mark Twain (1835 - 1910), Mark Twain In Eruption
It is much easier to break the rules when one s surrounded by strangers. One does not know any of them, so one cannot really care for their opinion.
Monica Fairview, Darcy Cousins, 2010
You are, you are young, my son, and, as the years go by, time will change and even reverse many of your present opinions. Refrain therefore awhile from setting yourself up as a judge of the highest matters.
Plato (427 BC - 347 BC), Dialogues, Theaetetus
You get fifteen democrats in a room, and you get twenty opinions.
Senator Patrick Leahy (1940 -), May 1990
There is no greater mistake than the hasty conclusion that opinions are worthless because they are badly argued.
Thomas H. Huxley (1825 - 1895)
Every difference of opinion is not a difference of principle.
Thomas Jefferson (1743 - 1826), First Inaugural Adress, 1801
Literature is strewn with the wreckage of men who have minded beyond reason the opinions of others.
Virginia Woolf (1882 - 1941), A Room of One's Own (1929)
What we have to do is to be forever curiously testing new opinions and courting new impressions.
Walter Pater (1839 - 1894), 1873

Opportunity

Next to knowing when to seize an opportunity, the most important thing in life is to know when to forego an advantage.
Benjamin Disraeli (1804 - 1881)
Seize opportunity by the beard, for it is bald behind.
Bulgarian Proverb
Small opportunities are often the beginning of great enterprises.
Demosthenes (384 BC - 322 BC)
You have to recognize when the right place and the right time fuse and take advantage of that opportunity. There are plenty of opportunities out there. You can't sit back and wait.
Ellen Metcalf
There is no security on this earth, there is only opportunity.
General Douglas MacArthur (1880 - 1964)
Trouble is only opportunity in work clothes.
Henry J. Kaiser (1882 - 1967)
She had an unequalled gift... of squeezing big mistakes into small opportunities.
Henry James (1843 - 1916)
Too many people are thinking of security instead of opportunity. They seem more afraid of life than death.
James F. Byrnes (1879 - 1972)
The Chinese use two brush strokes to write the word 'crisis.' One brush stroke stands for danger; the other for opportunity. In a crisis, be aware of the danger - but recognize the opportunity.
John F. Kennedy (1917 - 1963), Speech in Indianapolis, April 12, 1959
We are continually faced with a series of great opportunities brilliantly disguised as insoluble problems.
John W. Gardner (1912 - 2002)
Equal opportunity means everyone will have a fair chance at being incompetent.
Laurence J. Peter (1919 - 1988)
You create your opportunities by asking for them.
Patty Hansen, Prevention Magazine, 11-05
While we stop to think, we often miss our opportunity.
Publilius Syrus (~ 100 BC), Maxims
No great man ever complains of want of opportunity.
Ralph Waldo Emerson (1803 - 1882)
A wise man will make more opportunities than he finds.
Sir Francis Bacon (1561 - 1626)
Opportunity is missed by most people because it is dressed in overalls and looks like work.
Thomas A. Edison (1847 - 1931)
THERE ARE NO MISTAKES, only opportunities.
Tina Fey, Bossypants, 2011
We are confronted with insurmountable opportunities.
Walt Kelly (1913 - 1973), "Pogo" (comic strip)

Optimism

Perpetual optimism is a force multiplier.
Colin Powell (1937 -)
The place where optimism most flourishes is the lunatic asylum.
Havelock Ellis (1859 - 1939)

The optimist proclaims that we live in the best of all possible worlds; and the pessimist fears this is true.
James Branch Cabell (1879 - 1958), The Silver Stallion, 1926
The reason we all like to think so well of others is that we are all afraid for ourselves. The basis of optimism is sheer terror.
Oscar Wilde (1854 - 1900), The Picture of Dorian Gray, 1891
I find nothing more depressing than optimism.
Paul Fussell
The point of living and of being an optimist, is to be foolish enough to believe the best is yet to come.
Peter Ustinov (1921 - 2004)
Many an optimist has become rich by buying out a pessimist.
Robert G. Allen
For myself I am an optimist - it does not seem to be much use being anything else.
Sir Winston Churchill (1874 - 1965), speech at the Lord Mayor's banquet, London, November 9, 1954
An optimist is the human personification of spring.
Susan J. Bissonette

Painting

Painting: The art of protecting flat surfaces from the weather and exposing them to the critic.
Ambrose Bierce (1842 - 1914), The Devil's Dictionary
A painting in a museum hears more ridiculous opinions than anything else in the world.
Edmond de Goncourt (1822 - 1896)
Painting is an attempt to come to terms with life. There are as many solutions as there are human beings.
George Tooker
Every artist dips his brush in his own soul, and paints his own nature into his pictures.
Henry Ward Beecher (1813 - 1887), Proverbs from Plymouth Pulpit, 1887
The painting has a life of its own. I try to let it come through.
Jackson Pollock (1912 - 1956)
It's not your painting anymore. It stopped being your painting the moment that you finished it.
Jeff Melvoin, Northern Exposure, Fish Story, 1994
Every time I paint a portrait I lose a friend.
John Singer Sargent (1856 - 1925), quoted in Bentley and Esar, Treasury of Humorous Quotations (1951)
A man paints with his brains and not with his hands.
Michelangelo Buonarroti (1475 - 1564)
I say that good painters imitated nature; but that bad ones vomited it.
Miguel de Cervantes (1547 - 1616), Exemplary Novels (1613)
Painting is just another way of keeping a diary.
Pablo Picasso (1881 - 1973)
There are painters who transform the sun to a yellow spot, but there are others who with the help of their art and their intelligence, transform a yellow spot into the sun.
Pablo Picasso (1881 - 1973)
Painting is silent poetry, and poetry is painting with the gift of speech.
Simonides (556 BC - 468 BC)
Each painting has its own way of evolving...When the painting is finished, the subject reaveals itself.
William Baziotes

Parents

How simple a thing it seems to me that to know ourselves as we are, we must know our mothers' names.
Alice Walker (1944 -), O Magazine, May 2003
The world is full of women blindsided by the unceasing demands of motherhood, still flabbergasted by how a job can be terrific and torturous.
Anna Quindlen (1953 -), O Magazine, May 2003
Sometimes the laughter in mothering is the recognition of the ironies and absurdities. Sometime, though, it's just pure, unthinking delight.
Barbara Schapiro, O Magazine, May 2003
Sooner or later we all quote our mothers.
Bern Williams
The place of the father in the modern suburban family is a very small one, particularly if he plays golf.
Bertrand Russell (1872 - 1970)
The most remarkable thing about my mother is that for thirty years she served the family nothing but leftovers. The original meal has never been found.
Calvin Trillin (1935 -)
My parents only had one argument in forty-five years. It lasted forty-three years.
Cathy Ladman
By the time a man realizes that maybe his father was right, he usually has a son who thinks he's wrong.
Charles Wadsworth
Your parents, they give you your life, but then they try to give you their life.
Chuck Palahniuk (1962 -), Invisible Monsters, 1999
The first half of our lives is ruined by our parents, and the second half by our children.
Clarence Darrow (1857 - 1938)
There's something unnatural about a woman finding babies or, more specifically, conversation about babies, boring. They'll think she's bitter, jealous, lonely. But she's also bored of everybody telling her how lucky she is, what with all that sleep and all that freedom and spare time, the ability to go on dates or head off to Paris at a

moments notice. It sounds like they're consoling her, and she resents this and feels patronized by it.
David Nicholls, One Day, 2010
If your parents never had children, chances are you won't, either.
Dick Cavett (1936 -)
A mother is not a person to lean on but a person to make leaning unnecessary.
Dorothy C. Fisher (1879 - 1958), quoted in O Magazine, May 2003
The art of mothering is to teach the art of living to children.
Elain Heffner, O Magazine, May 2003
The central struggle of parenthood is to let our hopes for our children outweigh our fears.
Ellen Goodman (1941 -)
Having a baby's sweet face so close to your own, for so long a time as it takes to nurse 'em, is a great tonic for a sad soul.
Erica Eisdorfer, The Wet Nurse's Tale, 2009
Losing a baby is not a thing that you could ever get used to.
Erica Eisdorfer, The Wet Nurse's Tale, 2009
The gods visit the sins of the fathers upon the children.
Euripides (484 BC - 406 BC), Phrixus
There is...nothing to suggest that mothering cannot be shared by several people.
H. R. Schaffer, O Magazine, May 2003
That's sort of a cliché about parents. We all believe that our children are the most beautiful children in the world. But the thing is, what no one really talks about is the fact that we all really believe it.
Heather Armstrong, Dooce, 05-04-06
This is part of the essence of motherhood, watching your kid grow into her own person and not being able to do anything about it. Otherwise children would be nothing more than pets.
Heather Armstrong, Dooce, 11-15-05
For rarely are sons similar to their fathers: most are worse, and a few are better than their fathers.
Homer (800 BC - 700 BC), The Odyssey
The most important thing she'd learned over the years was that there was no way to be a perfect mother and a million ways to be a good one.
Jill Churchill, O Magazine, May 2003
Just a word of advice. Whenever you're furious with your parents or you think they're terrible, just remember, you vomited on them and they kept you.
John Green, Vlogbrothers, The Five Worst Places to Vomit, 09-04-12
It's interesting, on your second day of existence, to realize that your father is going to blame all the future failures of his life on you.
Josh Lieb, I am a Genius of Unspeakable Evil and I Want to be Your Class President, 2009
Fostering a spirit of cooperation with your ex means laying down your weapons in the war of divorce in order to protect your children.
Julie A., M.A. Ross and Judy Corcoran, Joint Custody with a Jerk: Raising a Child with an Uncooperative Ex, 2011
It's helpful to imagine your relationship with him or her as a business relationship rather than a personal one. Just as you wouldn't share that you're feeling fat, ugly, and depressed with a client or tell her that you've just met the love of your life and you've never been happier, these thoughts and feelings should be kept to yourself and not shared with your ex. Finally, as in any good business relationship, be honest and prepared to deliver what you promise.
Julie A., M.A. Ross and Judy Corcoran, Joint Custody with a Jerk: Raising a Child with an Uncooperative Ex, 2011
The point is that no matter what your feelings are, your children will be better off if you make them your central focus and work diligently at keeping the parenting relationship civil and cooperative.
Julie A., M.A. Ross and Judy Corcoran, Joint Custody with a Jerk: Raising a Child with an Uncooperative Ex, 2011
It does not always follow that good men are good fathers.
Kathryn L. Nelson, Pemberley Manor, 2006
The thing that impresses me the most about America is the way parents obey their children.
King Edward VIII (1894 - 1972)
Folks that has brought up children know that there's no hard and fast method in the world that'll suit every child. But them as never have think it's all as plain and easy as Rule of Three—just set your three terms down so fashion, and the sum'll work out correct.
L. M. Montgomery (1874 - 1942), Anne of Green Gables, 1908
Some men just aren't cut out for paternity. Better they should realize it before and not after they become responsible for a son.
Lois McMaster Bujold, Ethan of Athos, 1986
My mother had a great deal of trouble with me, but I think she enjoyed it.
Mark Twain (1835 - 1910)
Parents are never as bad as kids think they are.
Matt Witten, House M.D., Cursed, 2004
Parents were invented to make children happy by giving them something to ignore.
Ogden Nash (1902 - 1971)
Some are kissing mothers and some are scolding mothers, but it is love just the same.
Pearl Buck (1892 - 1973), quoted in O Magazine, May 2003
My father hated radio and could not wait for television to be invented so he could hate that too.
Peter De Vries
Call home at least once a week. It's a proven fact that we call home less the older we get. And that's wrong. It should be the other way around. As we get older, our parents get older.
Randy Pausch, Carnegie Mellon Commencement Speech, 2008
Most turkeys taste better the day after; my mother's tasted better the day before.

Rita Rudner
Neurotics build castles in the air, psychotics live in them. My mother cleans them.
Rita Rudner
The reason grandparents and grandchildren get along so well is that they have a common enemy.
Sam Levenson (1911 - 1980)
What children take from us, they give...We become people who feel more deeply, question more deeply, hurt more deeply, and love more deeply.
Sonia Taitz, O Magazine, May 2003as
If everyone had a dad like mine, no one would have sex tapes.
Tina Fey, David Letterman Interview, 2011
A mother only does her children harm if she makes them the only concern of her life.
W. Somerset Maugham (1874 - 1965), The Razor's Edge, 1943
It is a wise father that knows his own child.
William Shakespeare (1564 - 1616), "The Merchant of Venice", Act 2 scene 2

Passion

The happiness of a man in this life does not consist in the absence but in the mastery of his passions.
Alfred Lord Tennyson (1809 - 1892)
My passions were all gathered together like fingers that made a fist. Drive is considered aggression today; I knew it then as purpose.
Bette Davis (1908 - 1989), The Lonely Life, 1962
He only employs his passion who can make no use of his reason.
Cicero (106 BC - 43 BC)
Be still when you have nothing to say; when genuine passion moves you, say what you've got to say, and say it hot.
D. H. Lawrence (1885 - 1930)
Only passions, great passions, can elevate the soul to great things.
Denis Diderot (1713 - 1784)
The worst sin - perhaps the only sin - passion can commit, is to be joyless.
Dorothy L. Sayers (1893 - 1957), Gaudy Night
Judgement, not passion should prevail.
Epicharmus
Nothing great in the world has been accomplished without passion.
Georg Wilhelm, O Magazine, September 2003
Passion makes the world go round. Love just makes it a safer place.
Ice T, The Ice Opinion
Blaze with the fire that is never extinguished.
Luisa Sigea, O Magazine, September 2003
Waste no more time talking about great souls and how they should be. Become one yourself!
Marcus Aurelius Antoninus (121 AD - 180 AD)
When the habitually even-tempered suddenly fly into a passion, that explosion is apt to be more impressive than the outburst of the most violent amongst us.
Margery Allingham, Death of a Ghost, 1934
I had learnt to seek intensity...more of life, a concentrated sense of life.
Nina Berberova, O Magazine, September 2003
Do the one thing you think you cannot do. Fail at it. Try again. Do better the second time. The only people who never tumble are those who never mount the high wire. This is your moment. Own it.
Oprah Winfrey (1954 -), O Magazine, September 2003
I believe that one of life's greatest risks is never daring to risk.
Oprah Winfrey (1954 -), O Magazine, September 2003
You will need to find your passion. Don't give up on finding it because then all you're doing is waiting for the Reaper.
Randy Pausch, Carnegie Mellon Commencement Speech, 2008
You will not find your passion in things and you will not find your passion in money. The more things and the more money you have, the more you will look around and use that as the metric and there will be someone with more.
Randy Pausch, Carnegie Mellon Commencement Speech, 2008
Your pasion must come from the things that fuel you from the inside. Honors and awards are nice things, but only to the extent that they regard the real respect from your peers.
Randy Pausch, Carnegie Mellon Commencement Speech, 2008
It's the soul's duty to be loyal to its own desires. It must abandon itself to its master passion.
Rebecca West (1892 - 1983)
Passion is the quickest to develop, and the quickest to fade. Intimacy develops more slowly, and commitment more gradually still.
Robert Sternberg
The biggest thing [Frida] brought into my life was this peacefulness. I still get passionate about things, but my passion is not so scattered and it's not needy. It's a lot more powerful because it comes with this groundedness and peacefulness. That it's about the process, not about the results.
Salma Hayek, Conversation with Salma Hayek, 2002
There was a disturbance in my heart, a voice that spoke there and said, I want, I want, I want! It happened every afternoon, and when I tried to suppress it it got even stronger.
Saul Bellow (1915 - 2005), O Magazine, September 2003
It is easier to exclude harmful passions than to rule them, and to deny them admittance than to control them after they have been admitted.
Seneca (5 BC - 65 AD)
What makes the engine go? Desire, desire, desire.
Stanley Kunitz, O Magazine, September 2003
Passion kept one fully in the present, so that time became a series of mutually exclusive 'nows.'

Sue Halpern, O Magazine, September 2003
patience; sanity; balance
Learn the art of patience. Apply discipline to your thoughts when they become anxious over the outcome of a goal. Impatience breeds anxiety, fear, discouragement and failure. Patience creates confidence, decisiveness, and a rational outlook, which eventually leads to success.
Brian Adams
Patience is the greatest of all virtues.
Cato the Elder (234 BC - 149 BC)
A handful of patience is worth more than a bushel of brains.
Dutch Proverb
Our patience will achieve more than our force.
Edmund Burke (1729 - 1797)
It is very strange that the years teach us patience - that the shorter our time, the greater our capacity for waiting.
Elizabeth Taylor (1932 -), "A Wreath of Roses"
There art two cardinal sins from which all others spring: Impatience and Laziness.
Franz Kafka (1883 - 1924)
Patience has its limits. Take it too far, and it's cowardice.
George Jackson (1941 - 1971)
We could never learn to be brave and patient, if there were only joy in the world.
Helen Keller (1880 - 1968)
The fates have given mankind a patient soul.
Homer (800 BC - 700 BC), The Iliad
If I have ever made any valuable discoveries, it has been owing more to patient attention, than to any other talent.
Isaac Newton (1642 - 1727)
Patience serves as a protection against wrongs as clothes do against cold. For if you put on more clothes as the cold increases, it will have no power to hurt you. So in like manner you must grow in patience when you meet with great wrongs, and they will then be powerless to vex your mind.
Leonardo da Vinci (1452 - 1519)
I am extraordinarily patient, provided I get my own way in the end.
Margaret Thatcher (1925 -), in Observer April 4, 1989
There will be a time when loud-mouthed, incompetent people seem to be getting the best of you. When that happens, you only have to be patient and wait for them to self destruct. It never fails.
Richard Rybolt
Patience is the companion of wisdom.
Saint Augustine (354 AD - 430 AD)
Have patience with all things, but chiefly have patience with yourself. Do not lose courage in considering your own imperfections but instantly set about remedying them - every day begin the task anew.
Saint Francis de Sales (1567 - 1622)
You must first have a lot of patience to learn to have patience.
Stanislaw J. Lec (1909 - 1966), "Unkempt Thoughts"
Patience is the best remedy for every trouble.
Titus Maccius Plautus (254 BC - 184 BC), Rudens
Have courage for the great sorrows of life and patience for the small ones; and when you have laboriously accomplished your daily task, go to sleep in peace. God is awake.
Victor Hugo (1802 - 1885)
A high hope for a low heaven: God grant us patience!
William Shakespeare (1564 - 1616), Love's Labour's Lost, Act I, sc. 1
A very little thief of occasion will rob you of a great deal of patience.
William Shakespeare (1564 - 1616), Coriolanus, Act II, sc. 1
Had it pleas'd heaven to try me with affliction... I should have found in some place of my soul a drop of patience.
William Shakespeare (1564 - 1616), Othello, Act IV, sc. 2
How poor are they that have not patience! What wound did ever heal but by degrees?
William Shakespeare (1564 - 1616), Othello, Act II, sc. 3
How poor are they who have not patience! What wound did ever heal but by degrees.
William Shakespeare (1564 - 1616)
I do oppose my patience to his fury, and am arm'd to suffer with a quietness of spirit, the very tyranny and rage of his.
William Shakespeare (1564 - 1616), The Merchant of Venice, Act IV, sc. 1
Patience is sottish, and impatience does become a dog that's mad.
William Shakespeare (1564 - 1616), Antony and Cleopatra, Act IV, sc. 15
Though patience be a tired mare, yet she will plod.
William Shakespeare (1564 - 1616), Henry V, Act II, sc. 1
Upon the heat and flame of thy distemper sprinkle cool patience.
William Shakespeare (1564 - 1616), Hamlet, Act III, sc. 4

Patriotism

Patriotism is the willingness to kill and be killed for trivial reasons.
Bertrand Russell (1872 - 1970)
The contest, for ages, has been to rescue Liberty from the grasp of executive power.
Daniel Webster (1782 - 1852), Speech in the Senate, May 27, 1834
"My country, right or wrong," is a thing that no patriot would think of saying except in a desperate case. It is like saying, "My mother, drunk or sober."
G. K. Chesterton (1874 - 1936)
Liberty also means responsibility. That is why most men dread it.
George Bernard Shaw (1856 - 1950), Maxims for Revolutionists
Patriotism is your conviction that this country is superior to all other countries because you were born in it.
George Bernard Shaw (1856 - 1950)
You'll never have a quiet world till you knock the patriotism out of the human race.

George Bernard Shaw (1856 - 1950), "Misalliance"
Patriotism is often an arbitrary veneration of real estate above principles.
George Jean Nathan (1882 - 1958)
Don't be a fool and die for your country. Let the other sonofabitch die for his.
George S. Patton (1885 - 1945), (attributed)
Whenever you hear a man speak of his love for his country, it is a sign that he expects to be paid for it.
H. L. Mencken (1880 - 1956), A Mencken Chrestomathy
It is not unseemly for a man to die fighting in defense of his country.
Homer (800 BC - 700 BC), The Iliad
The single best augury is to fight for one's country.
Homer (800 BC - 700 BC), The Iliad
We would rather starve than sell our national honor.
Indira Gandhi (1917 - 1984), Remark in election meeting in Nagpur, India 1967
Our obligations to our country never cease but with our lives.
John Adams (1735 - 1826), Letter to Benjamin Rush, 18 April 1808
And so, my fellow americans: ask not what your country can do for you - ask what you can do for your country. My fellow citizens of the world: ask not what America will do for you, but what together we can do for the freedom of man.
John F. Kennedy (1917 - 1963), Inaugural address, January 20, 1961
Let every nation know, whether it wishes us well or ill, that we shall pay any price, bear any burden, meet any hardship, support any friend, oppose any foe to assure the survival and the success of liberty.
John F. Kennedy (1917 - 1963), Inaugural address, January 20, 1961
How beautiful is death, when earn'd by virtue!
Who would not be that youth? What pity is it
That we can die but once to serve our country!
Joseph Addison (1672 - 1719), "Cato", Act 4, Scene 4, 1713
You're not to be so blind with patriotism that you can't face reality. Wrong is wrong, no matter who does it or says it.
Malcolm X (1925 - 1965)
I only regret that I have but one life to lose for my country.
Nathan Hale (1755 - 1776), last words, 22 September 1776 (attributed)
When a whole nation is roaring Patriotism at the top of its voice, I am fain to explore the cleanness of its hands and purity of its heart.
Ralph Waldo Emerson (1803 - 1882), Journals, 1824
True patriotism sometimes requires of men to act exactly contrary, at one period, to that which it does at another, and the motive which impels themfhe desire to do rightis precisely the same.
Robert E. Lee (1807 - 1870), Letter to General P. G. T. Beauregard, October 3, 1865
Patriotism is the last refuge of a scoundrel.
Samuel Johnson (1709 - 1784), quoted in Boswell's Life of Johnson
When I am abroad, I always make it a rule never to criticize or attack the government of my own country. I make up for lost time when I come home.
Sir Winston Churchill (1874 - 1965)
I would rather be exposed to the inconveniencies attending too much liberty than those attending too small a degree of it.
Thomas Jefferson (1743 - 1826), Letter to Archibald Stuart, December 23, 1791
It behoves every man who values liberty of conscience for himself, to resist invasions of it in the case of others; or their case may, by change of circumstances, become his own.
Thomas Jefferson (1743 - 1826), Letters to Benjamin Rush, April 21, 1803
The flag is the embodiment, not of sentiment, but of history.
Woodrow Wilson (1856 - 1924)
The history of liberty is the history of resistance. The history of liberty is a history of the limitation of governmental power, not the increase of it.
Woodrow Wilson (1856 - 1924), Address to the New York Press Club, September 9, 1912

Peace

We shall find peace. We shall hear the angels, we shall see the sky sparkling with diamonds.
Anton Chekhov (1860 - 1904), 1897
We make war that we may live in peace.
Aristotle (384 BC - 322 BC), Nichomachean Ethics
For peace is not mere absence of war, but is a virtue that springs from the force of character.
Baruch Spinoza (1632 - 1677), Tractatus Politicus
Peace is not an absence of war, it is a virtue, a state of mind, a disposition for benevolence, confidence, justice.
Baruch Spinoza (1632 - 1677)
At present the peace of the world has been preserved, not by statesmen, but by capitalists.
Benjamin Disraeli (1804 - 1881), Letter to Mrs. Sarah Brydges Willyams, October 17, 1863
Peace has never come from dropping bombs. Real peace comes from enlightenment and educating people to behave more in a divine manner.
Carlos Santana, Associated Press interview, September 1, 2004
The name of peace is sweet, and the thing itself is beneficial, but there is a great difference between peace and servitude. Peace is freedom in tranquillity, servitude is the worst of all evils, to be resisted not only by war, but even by death.
Cicero (106 BC - 43 BC)
I like to believe that people in the long run are going to do more to promote peace than our governments. Indeed, I think that people want peace so much that one of these days governments had better get out of the way and let them have it.
Dwight D. Eisenhower (1890 - 1969)
Yes, God and the politicians willing, the United States can declare peace upon the world, and win it.
Ely Culbertson, Must We Fight Russia, chapter 5, 1946

Let him who desires peace prepare for war.
Flavius Vegetius Renatus (~ 375 AD), De Rei Militari
If man does find the solution for world peace it will be the most revolutionary reversal of his record we have ever known.
George C. Marshall (1880 - 1959)
To be prepared for war is one of the most effectual means of preserving peace.
George Washington (1732 - 1799)
Has not peace honours and glories of her own unattended by the dangers of war?
Hermocrates of Syracuse
Peace is not a relationship of nations. It is a condition of mind brought about by a serenity of soul. Peace is not merely the absence of war. It is also a state of mind. Lasting peace can come only to peaceful people.
Jawaharlal Nehru (1889 - 1964)
The only alternative to coexistence is codestruction.
Jawaharlal Nehru (1889 - 1964)
Peace can be a cover whereby evil men can perpetrate diabolical wrongs.
John Foster Dulles
You can't separate peace from freedom because no one can be at peace unless he has his freedom.
Malcolm X (1925 - 1965), Malcolm X Speaks, 1965
If you want to make peace, you don't talk to your friends. You talk to your enemies.
Moshe Dayan (1915 - 1981)
If you want peace, stop fighting. If you want peace of mind, stop fighting with your thoughts.
Peter McWilliams, Life 101, 1991
Every day we do things, we are things that have to do with peace. If we are aware of our life..., our way of looking at things, we will know how to make peace right in the moment, we are alive.
Thich Nhat Hanh
First keep the peace within yourself, then you can also bring peace to others.
Thomas a Kempis (1380 - 1471), 1420
Peace with all nations, and the right which that gives us with respect to all nations, are our object.
Thomas Jefferson (1743 - 1826), Letter to Mr. Dumas, March 24, 1793
That peace, safety, and concord may be the portion of our native land, and be long enjoyed by our fellow-citizens, is the most ardent wish of my heart, and if I can be instrumental in procuring or preserving them, I shall think I have not lived in vain.
Thomas Jefferson (1743 - 1826), letter to Benjamin Waring and others, March 23, 1801
One cannot find peace in work or in pleasure, in the world or in a convent, but only in one's soul.
W. Somerset Maugham (1874 - 1965), The Painted Veil, 1925
Tao. Some of us look for the Way in opium and some in God, some of us in whiskey and some in love. It is all the same Way and it leads nowhither.
W. Somerset Maugham (1874 - 1965), The Painted Veil, 1925
Peace is an unstable equilibrium, which can be preserved only by acknowledged supremacy or equal power.
Will Durant and Arial Durant, The Lessons of History, Chapter 11, 1968
The peace of heaven is theirs that lift their swords, in such a just and charitable war.
William Shakespeare (1564 - 1616)
Only a peace between equals can last. Only a peace the very principle of which is equality and a common participation in a common benefit.
Woodrow Wilson (1856 - 1924), Address to the United States Senate, January 22, 1917

Perfection

I never expect to see a perfect work from imperfect man.
Alexander Hamilton (1755 - 1804), The Federalist
The thing that is really hard, and really amazing, is giving up on being perfect and beginning the work of becoming yourself.
Anna Quindlen (1953 -)
Perfection is achieved, not when there is nothing more to add, but when there is nothing left to take away.
Antoine de Saint-Exupery (1900 - 1944)
Perfection is a road, not a destination. Every time I live, I get an education.
Burk Hudson
Aim for success, not perfection. Never give up your right to be wrong, because then you will lose the ability to learn new things and move forward with your life.
Dr. David M. Burns
Assert your right to make a few mistakes. If people can't accept your imperfections, that's their fault.
Dr. David M. Burns
Remember that fear always lurks behind perfectionism. Confronting your fears and allowing yourself the right to be human can, paradoxically, make you a far happier and more productive person.
Dr. David M. Burns
Artists who seek perfection in everything are those who cannot attain it in anything.
Eugene Delacroix (1798 - 1863)
I do think imperfection's underrated.
Helena Bonham Carter
No one can be perfectly free till all are free; no one can be perfectly moral till all are moral; no one can be perfectly happy till all are happy.
Herbert Spencer (1820 - 1903), Social Statics, part 4, chapter 30 1851
Perfectionism is simply putting a limit on your future. When you have an idea of perfect in your mind, you open the door to constantly comparing what you have now with what you want. That type of self criticism is significantly deterring.
John Eliot, Ph.D., Reverse Psychology for Success

The idea of perfect closes your mind to new standards. When you drive hard toward one ideal, you miss opportunities and paths, not to mention hurting your confidence. Believe in your potential and then go out and explore it; don't limit it.
John Eliot, Ph.D., Reverse Psychology for Success
I don't confuse greatness with perfection. To be great anyhow is...the higher achievement.
Lois McMaster Bujold, "Mirror Dance", 1994
I am careful not to confuse excellence with perfection. Excellence, I can reach for; perfection is God's business.
Michael J. Fox (1961 -), quoted by Lorne A. Adrain in 'The Most Important Thing I Know'
[M]aybe the most any of us can expect of ourselves isn't perfection but progress.
Michelle Burford, O Magazine, 2003
To demand perfection is a sure way to be disappointed in everybody, for you will be bound to think ill of others.
Monica Fairview, Darcy Cousins, 2010
In the eyes of those lovers of perfection, a work is never finished—a word that for them has no sense—but abandoned; and this abandonment, whether to the flames or to the public (and which is the result of weariness or an obligation to deliver) is a kind of an accident to them, like the breaking off of a reflection, which fatigue, irritation, or something similar has made worthless.
Paul Valery (1871 - 1945)
Have patience with all things, but chiefly have patience with yourself. Do not lose courage in considering your own imperfections but instantly set about remedying them - every day begin the task anew.
Saint Francis de Sales (1567 - 1622)
Have no fear of perfection - you'll never reach it.
Salvador Dali (1904 - 1989)
Try as hard as we may for perfection, the net result of our labors is an amazing variety of imperfectness. We are surprised at our own versatility in being able to fail in so many different ways.
Samuel McChord Crothers
If you'd like to be good at something, the first thing to out the window is the notion of perfection.
Scott Berkun, Confessions of a Public Speaker, 2009
You have to let people see what you wrote. It will never be perfect, but perfect is overrated. Perfect is boring.
Tina Fey, Bossypants, 2011
We are all imperfect. We cannot expect perfect government.
William Howard Taft, Address, Washington, D.C., May 8, 1909

Perseverance

By perseverance the snail reached the ark.
Charles Haddon Spurgeon (1834 - 1892)
I think a hero is an ordinary individual who finds strength to persevere and endure in spite of overwhelming obstacles.
Christopher Reeve
The difference between perseverance and obstinacy is that one comes from a strong will; and the other from a strong won't.
Henry Ward Beecher (1813 - 1887), Seven Lectures to a Young Man, 1844
You have to keep plugging away. We are all growing. There is no shortcut. You have to put time into it to build an audience
John Gruber, How to Blog for Money by Learning from Comics, SXSW 2006
Courage and perseverance have a magical talisman, before which difficulties disappear and obstacles vanish into air.
John Quincy Adams (1767 - 1848)
If you wish success in life, make perseverance your bosom friend, experience your wise counselor, caution your elder brother and hope your guardian genius.
Joseph Addison (1672 - 1719)
Victory belongs to the most persevering.
Napoleon Bonaparte (1769 - 1821)
Perseverance is more prevailing than violence; and many things which cannot be overcome when they are together, yield themselves up when taken little by little.
Plutarch (46 AD - 120 AD), Lives
Few things are impossible to diligence and skill. Great works are performed not by strength, but perseverance.
Samuel Johnson (1709 - 1784)

Persistence

Energy and persistence conquer all things.
Benjamin Franklin (1706 - 1790)
Nothing in the world can take the place of Persistence. Talent will not; nothing is more common than unsuccessful men with talent. Genius will not; unrewarded genius is almost a proverb. Education will not; the world is full of educated derelicts. Persistence and determination alone are omnipotent. The slogan 'Press On' has solved and always will solve the problems of the human race.
Calvin Coolidge (1872 - 1933)
You must keep sending work out; you must never let a manuscript do nothing but eat its head off in a drawer. You send that work out again and again, while you're working on another one. If you have talent, you will receive some measure of success - but only if you persist.
Isaac Asimov (1920 - 1992)
That which we persist in doing becomes easier, not that the task itself has become easier, but that our ability to perform it has improved.
Ralph Waldo Emerson (1803 - 1882)
We are made to persist. That's how we find out who we are.
Tobias Wolff, 'In Pharaoh's Army'

Pets

If a dog jumps in your lap, it is because he is fond of you; but if a cat does the same thing, it is because your lap is warmer.
Alfred North Whitehead (1861 - 1947)
We call them dumb animals, and so they are, for they cannot tell us how they feel, but they do not suffer less because they have no words.
Anna Sewell (1820 - 1878), Black Beauty, 1877
I loathe people who keep dogs. They are cowards who haven't got the guts to bite people themselves.
August Strindberg (1849 - 1912), A Madman's Diary, 1895
Yesterday I was a dog. Today I'm a dog. Tomorrow I'll probably still be a dog. Sigh! There's so little hope for advancement.
Charles M. Schulz (1922 - 2000), (Snoopy)
It's funny how dogs and cats know the inside of folks better than other folks do, isn't it?
Eleanor H. Porter (1868 - 1920), Pollyanna, 1912
If you are a dog and your owner suggests that you wear a sweater, suggest that he wear a tail.
Fran Lebowitz (1950 -)
No animal should ever jump up on the dining-room furniture unless absolutely certain that he can hold his own in the conversation.
Fran Lebowitz (1950 -)
Animals are such agreeable friends - they ask no questions, they pass no criticisms.
George Eliot (1819 - 1880), 'Mr. Gilfil's Love Story,' Scenes of Clerical Life, 1857
Cats regard people as warmblooded furniture.
Jacquelyn Mitchard, The Deep End of the Ocean
Cats are smarter than dogs. You can't get eight cats to pull a sled through snow.
Jeff Valdez
Old age means realizing you will never own all the dogs you wanted to.
Joe Gores
My dog is worried about the economy because Alpo is up to 99 cents a can. That's almost $7.00 in dog money.
Joe Weinstein
If you pick up a starving dog and make him prosperous, he will not bite you. This is the principal difference between a dog and a man.
Mark Twain (1835 - 1910)
We are alone, absolutely alone on this chance planet: and, amid all the forms of life that surround us, not one, excepting the dog, has made an alliance with us.
Maurice Maeterlinck (1862 - 1949)
A door is what a dog is perpetually on the wrong side of.
Ogden Nash (1902 - 1971)
On the Internet, nobody knows you're a dog.
Peter Steiner, cartoon in The New Yorker, July 5, 1993
I wonder if other dogs think poodles are members of a weird religious cult.
Rita Rudner
A boy can learn a lot from a dog: obedience, loyalty, and the importance of turning around three times before lying down.
Robert Benchley (1889 - 1945)
I like pigs. Dogs look up to us. Cats look down on us. Pigs treat us as equals.
Sir Winston Churchill (1874 - 1965)
Did you ever walk into a room and forget why you walked in? I think that's how dogs spend their lives.
Sue Murphy
Cats are intended to teach us that not everything in nature has a function.
Unknown

Philosophy

I think we ought always to entertain our opinions with some measure of doubt. I shouldn't wish people dogmatically to believe any philosophy, not even mine.
Bertrand Russell (1872 - 1970)
The point of philosophy is to start with something so simple as not to seem worth stating, and to end with something so paradoxical that no one will believe it.
Bertrand Russell (1872 - 1970), The Philosophy of Logical Atomism
This is patently absurd; but whoever wishes to become a philosopher must learn not to be frightened by absurdities.
Bertrand Russell (1872 - 1970)
There's a difference between a philosophy and a bumper sticker.
Charles M. Schulz (1922 - 2000)
There is nothing so absurd but some philosopher has said it.
Cicero (106 BC - 43 BC), De Divinatione
Who you are isn't tied solely to what you say, even though it may feel that way to you now.
Diane Ackerman, One Hundred Names for Love: A Stroke, A Marriage, and the Language of Healing, 2011
I went off to college planning to major in math or philosophy— of course, both those ideas are really the same idea.
Frank Wilczek (1951 -)
Philosophy consists very largely of one philosopher arguing that all others are jackasses. He usually proves it, and I should add that he also usually proves that he is one himself.
H. L. Mencken (1880 - 1956)
Philosophy is a battle against the bewitchment of our intelligence by means of language.
Ludwig Wittgenstein (1889 - 1951)
One cannot conceive anything so strange and so implausible that it has not already been said by one philosopher or another.

Rene Descartes (1596 - 1650), 'Le Discours de la Methode,' 1637
Philosophers say a great deal about what is absolutely necessary for science, and it is always, so far as one can see, rather naive, and probably wrong.
Richard Feynman (1918 - 1988)
All philosophies, if you ride them, are nonsense, but some are greater nonsense than others.
Samuel Butler (1835 - 1902)
Leisure is the mother of philosophy.
Thomas Hobbes (1588 - 1679)
True philosophy invents nothing; it merely establishes and describes what is.
Victor Cousin (1792 - 1867)
There is only one thing a philosopher can be relied upon to do, and that is to contradict other philosophers.
William James (1842 - 1910)
There are more things in heaven and earth, Horatio,
Than are dreamt of in your philosophy.
William Shakespeare (1564 - 1616), "Hamlet", Act 1 scene 5

Photography

'To the complaint, 'There are no people in these photographs,' I respond, 'There are always two people: the photographer and the viewer.'
Ansel Adams (1902 - 1984)
I have often thought that if photography were difficult in the true sense of the term – meaning that the creation of a simple photograph would entail as much time and effort as the production of a good watercolor or etching – there would be a vast improvement in total output. The sheer ease with which we can produce a superficial image often leads to creative disaster.
Ansel Adams (1902 - 1984)
A photograph is a secret about a secret. The more it tells you the less you know.
Diane Arbus (1923 - 1971), (1923-1971)
Best wide-angle lens? Two steps backward. Look for the 'ah-ha'.
Ernst Haas, Comment in workshop, 1985
The camera doesn't make a bit of difference. All of them can record what you are seeing. But, you have to SEE.
Ernst Haas, Comment in workshop, 1985
We try to grab pieces of our lives as they speed past us. Photographs freeze those pieces and help us remember how we were. We don't know these lost people but if you look around, you'll find someone just like them.
Gene McSweeney, Grey Water Photography, 06-04-2006
Photographers deal in things which are continually vanishing and when they have vanished there is no contrivance on earth which can make them come back again.
Henri Cartier Bresson
Maybe because it's entirely an artist's eye, patience and skill that makes an image and not his tools.
Ken Rockwell, Your Camera Does Not Matter, 2005
No matter how advanced your camera you still need to be responsible for getting it to the right place at the right time and pointing it in the right direction to get the photo you want.
Ken Rockwell, Your Camera Does Not Matter, 2005
The camera's only job is to get out of the way of making photographs.
Ken Rockwell, Your Camera Does Not Matter, 2005
Your equipment DOES NOT affect the quality of your image. The less time and effort you spend worrying about your equipment the more time and effort you can spend creating great images. The right equipment just makes it easier, faster or more convenient for you to get the results you need.
Ken Rockwell, Your Camera Does Not Matter, 2005
No matter how slow the film, Spirit always stands still long enough for the photographer It has chosen.
Minor White
Photography, fortunately, to me has not only been a profession but also a contact between people - to understand human nature and record, if possible, the best in each individual.
Nickolas Muray
Every portrait that is painted with feeling is a portrait of the artist, not of the sitter.
Oscar Wilde (1854 - 1900)
They used to photograph Shirley Temple through gauze. They should photograph me through linoleum.
Tallulah Bankhead (1903 - 1968)

Physics

All science is either physics or stamp collecting.
Ernest Rutherford (1871 - 1937), in J. B. Birks "Rutherford at Manchester" (1962)
In physics, your solution should convince a reasonable person. In math, you have to convince a person who's trying to make trouble. Ultimately, in physics, you're hoping to convince Nature. And I've found Nature to be pretty reasonable.
Frank Wilczek (1951 -)
For the truth of the conclusions of physical science, observation is the supreme Court of Appeal. It does not follow that every item which we confidently accept as physical knowledge has actually been certified by the Court; our confidence is that it would be certified by the Court if it were submitted. But it does follow that every item of physical knowledge is of a form which might be submitted to the Court. It must be such that we can specify (although it may be impracticable to carry out) an observational procedure which would decide whether it is true or not. Clearly a statement cannot be tested by observation unless it is an assertion about the results of observation. Every item of physical knowledge must therefore be an assertion of what has been or would be the result of carrying out a specified observational procedure.

Sir Arthur Eddington (1882 - 1944), The Philosophy of Physical Science
I ask you to look both ways. For the road to a knowledge of the stars leads through the atom; and important knowledge of the atom has been reached through the stars.
Sir Arthur Eddington (1882 - 1944), Stars and Atoms (1928), Lecture 1
It is impossible to trap modern physics into predicting anything with perfect determinism because it deals with probabilities from the outset.
Sir Arthur Eddington (1882 - 1944), In J. R. Newman (ed.) The World of Mathematics, New York: Simon and Schuster, 1956
Not only is the universe stranger than we imagine, it is stranger than we can imagine.
Sir Arthur Eddington (1882 - 1944)
Something unknown is doing we don't know what.
Sir Arthur Eddington (1882 - 1944), comment on the Uncertainty Principle in quantum physics, 1927
We have found a strange footprint on the shores of the unknown. We have devised profound theories, one after another, to account for its origins. At last, we have succeeded in reconstructing the creature that made the footprint. And lo! It is our own.
Sir Arthur Eddington (1882 - 1944), Space, Time, and Gravitation, 1920

Plagiarism

The secret to creativity is knowing how to hide your sources.
Albert Einstein (1879 - 1955)
Don't worry about people stealing an idea. If it's original, you will have to ram it down their throats.
Howard Aiken (1900 - 1973)
I don't like composers who think. It gets in the way of their plagiarism.
Howard Dietz
About the most originality that any writer can hope to achieve honestly is to steal with good judgment.
Josh Billings (1818 - 1885)
Art is either plagiarism or revolution.
Paul Gauguin (1848 - 1903)

Planning

Bite off more than you can chew, then chew it. Plan more than you can do, then do it.
Anonymous
A goal without a plan is just a wish.
Antoine de Saint-Exupery (1900 - 1944)
Make no little plans; they have no magic to stir men's blood...Make big plans, aim high in hope and work.
Daniel H. Burnham (1846 - 1912)
In preparing for battle I have always found that plans are useless, but planning is indispensable.
Dwight D. Eisenhower (1890 - 1969)
A good plan, violently executed now, is better than a perfect plan next week.
George S. Patton (1885 - 1945)
Zeus does not bring all men's plans to fulfillment.
Homer (800 BC - 700 BC), The Iliad
We must be willing to get rid of the life we've planned, so as to have the life that is waiting for us.
Joseph Campbell (1904 - 1987)
Create a definite plan for carrying out your desire and begin at once, whether you are ready or not, to put this plan into action.
Napoleon Hill
Plans are only good intentions unless they immediately degenerate into hard work.
Peter Drucker (1909 - 2005)
It is a bad plan that admits of no modification.
Publilius Syrus (~ 100 BC), Maxims
Self-control is not a problem in the future. It's only a problem NOW when the chocolates is next to us.
Shlomo Bernartzi, TED Talk: Saving for tomorrow, tomorrow, November 2011
Just because something doesn't do what you planned it to do doesn't mean it's useless.
Thomas A. Edison (1847 - 1931)
When we are planning for posterity, we ought to remember that virtue is not hereditary.
Thomas Paine (1737 - 1809)
He who every morning plans the transaction of the day and follows out that plan, carries a thread that will guide him through the maze of the most busy life. But where no plan is laid, where the disposal of time is surrendered merely to the chance of incidence, chaos will soon reign.
Victor Hugo (1802 - 1885)

Poetry

Most people ignore most poetry
because
most poetry ignores most people.
Adrian Mitchell
It's easier to quote poets than to read them.
Allison Barrows, Preteena, 09-30-06
There exist only three beings worthy of respect: the priest, the soldier, the poet. To know, to kill, to create.
Charles Baudelaire (1821 - 1867), Mon Coeur Mis a Nu, XXII
The freedom of poetic license.
Cicero (106 BC - 43 BC), Pro Publio Sestio
A poem is no place for an idea.
Edgar Watson Howe (1853 - 1937), Country Town Sayings, 1911

My poems are hymns of praise to the glory of life.
Edith Sitwell (1887 - 1964), "Some notes on my poetry" Collected Poems, 1957
Poetry is the deification of reality.
Edith Sitwell (1887 - 1964), Life magazine, 01-04-63
All slang is a metaphor, and all metaphor is poetry.
G. K. Chesterton (1874 - 1936), Defendant (1901)
Poets have been mysteriously silent on the subject of cheese.
G. K. Chesterton (1874 - 1936)
A poet more than thirty years old is simply an overgrown child.
H. L. Mencken (1880 - 1956)
Many brave men lived before Agamemnon; but all are overwhelmed in eternal night, unwept, unknown, because they lack a sacred poet.
Horace (65 BC - 8 BC), Odes
It was the misfortune of poetry to be seldom safely enjoyed by those who enjoyed it completely; and that the strong feelings which alone could estimate it truly were the very feelings which ought to taste it but sparingly.
Jane Austen (1775 - 1817), Persuasion, 1818
The worst tragedy for a poet is to be admired through being misunderstood.
Jean Cocteau (1889 - 1963)
One ought, every day at least, to hear a little song, read a good poem, see a fine picture, and if it were possible, to speak a few reasonable words.
Johann Wolfgang von Goethe (1749 - 1832)
You don't have to suffer to be a poet; adolescence is enough suffering for anyone.
John Ciardi (1916 - 1986)
Poetry should please by a fine excess and not by singularity. It should strike the reader as a wording of his own highest thoughts, and appear almost as a remembrance.
John Keats (1795 - 1821)
Poetry often enters through the window of irrelevance.
M. C. Richards
I was working on the proof of one of my poems all the morning, and took out a comma. In the afternoon I put it back again.
Oscar Wilde (1854 - 1900)
In science one tries to tell people, in such a way as to be understood by everyone, something that no one ever knew before. But in poetry, it's the exact opposite.
Paul Dirac (1902 - 1984)
A poem is never finished, only abandoned.
Paul Valery (1871 - 1945)
Every English poet should master the rules of grammar before he attempts to bend or break them.
Robert Graves (1895 - 1985)
A poet who reads his verse in public may have other nasty habits.
Robert Heinlein (1907 - 1988), Time Enough for Love, 1978
A prose writer gets tired of writing prose, and wants to be a poet. So he begins every line with a capital letter, and keeps on writing prose.
Samuel McChord Crothers
A poet ought not to pick nature's pocket. Let him borrow, and so borrow as to repay by the very act of borrowing. Examine nature accurately, but write from recollection, and trust more to the imagination than the memory.
Samuel Taylor Coleridge (1772 - 1834)
A poet's hope: to be,
like some valley cheese,
local, but prized elsewhere.
W. H. Auden (1907 - 1973), Collected Poems
The poet judges not as a judge judges but as the sun falling around a helpless thing.
Walt Whitman (1819 - 1892)

Politicians

A garden, you know, is a very usual refuge of a disappointed politician. Accordingly, I have purchased a few acres about nine miles from town, have built a house, and am cultivating a garden.
Alexander Hamilton (1755 - 1804), Letter to Charles Cotesworth Pinckney
Under every stone lurks a politician.
Aristophanes (450 BC - 388 BC), Thesmophoriazusae, 410 B.C.
You have all the characteristics of a popular politician: a horrible voice, bad breeding, and a vulgar manner.
Aristophanes (450 BC - 388 BC), Knights, 424 B.C.
Now I know what a statesman is; he's a dead politician. We need more statesmen.
Bob Edwards
I have come to the conclusion that politics are too serious a matter to be left to the politicians.
Charles De Gaulle (1890 - 1970)
Since a politician never believes what he says, he is quite surprised to be taken at his word.
Charles De Gaulle (1890 - 1970)
Government is too big and too important to be left to the politicians.
Chester Bowles (1901 - 1986)
Anyone who is capable of getting themselves made President should on no account be allowed to do the job.
Douglas Adams (1952 - 2001), The Hitchhiker's Guide to the Galaxy
Get all the fools on your side and you can be elected to anything.
Frank Dane
Ninety percent of the politicians give the other ten percent a bad reputation.
Henry Kissinger (1923 -)
If I wanted to go crazy I would do it in Washington because it would not be noticed.
Irwin S. Cobb
If God had wanted us to vote, he would have given us candidates.

Jay Leno (1950 -)
Mothers may still want their sons to grow up to be President, but according to a famous Gallup poll of some years ago, some 73 percent do not want them to become politicians in the process.
John F. Kennedy (1917 - 1963), Profiles in Courage, 1956
The reason there are so few female politicians is that it is too much trouble to put makeup on two faces.
Maureen Murphy
Politicians are the same all over. They promise to build a bridge even where there is no river.
Nikita Khrushchev (1894 - 1971)
I once said cynically of a politician, 'He'll doublecross that bridge when he comes to it.'
Oscar Levant (1906 - 1972)
He that would govern others, first should be the master of himself.
Philip Massinger, The Bondman, 1624
The two parties which divide the state, the party of Conservatism and that of Innovation, are very old, and have disputed the possession of the world ever since it was made.
Ralph Waldo Emerson (1803 - 1882), The Conservative, Boston, Massachusetts, December 9, 1841
He has been called a mediocre man; but this is unwarranted flattery. He was a politician of monumental littleness.
Richard M. Nixon (1913 - 1994), Writing of John Tyler, Thomas Hart Benton, chapter 11, 1897
There is no such thing as a nonpolitical speech by a politician.
Richard M. Nixon (1913 - 1994), Address to Radio-Television Executives Society, New York City, September 14, 1955
An honest politician is one who, when he is bought, will stay bought.
Simon Cameron (1799 - 1889)
You've got to vote for someone. It's a shame, but it's got to be done.
Whoopi Goldberg
That's the trouble with a politician's life-somebody is always interrupting it with an election.
Will Rogers (1879 - 1935)

Politics

It is the duty of every citizen according to his best capacities to give validity to his convictions in political affairs.
Albert Einstein (1879 - 1955), 'Treasury for the Free World,' 1946
There is hardly a political question in the United States which doesn't sooner or later turn into a judicial one.
Alexis De Tocqueville (1805 - 1859), Democracy in America, 1835
Crime does not pay ... as well as politics.
Alfred E. Newman
Politics, n. Strife of interests masquerading as a contest of principles.
Ambrose Bierce (1842 - 1914), The Devil's Dictionary
Man is by nature a political animal.
Aristotle (384 BC - 322 BC), Politics
Before we get too depressed about the state of our politics, let's remember our history. The great debates of the past, all stirred great passions. They all made somebody angry, and at least once led to a terrible war. What is amazing, is that despite all the conflict, our experiment in democracy has worked better than any form of government on earth.
Barack Obama (1961 -), University of Michigan Commencement, 2010
If we choose only to expose ourselves to opinions and viewpoints that are in line to our own, we become more polarized, more set in our own ways. It will only reinforce and deepen the political divides in our country. But if we choose to actively seek out information that challenges our assumptions and beliefs, perhaps we can begin to understand where the people who disagree with us are coming from.
Barack Obama (1961 -), University of Michigan Commencement, 2010
Politics has never been for the thin-skinned or the faint of heart, and if you enter the arena , you should expect to get roughed up. Moreover, Democracy in a nation of more than 300 million people is inherently difficult.
Barack Obama (1961 -), University of Michigan Commencement, 2010
I have come to the conclusion that politics are too serious a matter to be left to the politicians.
Charles De Gaulle (1890 - 1970)
Politics is made up largely of irrelevancies.
Dalton Camp
Politics ought to be the part-time profession of every citizen who would protect the rights and privileges of free people and who would preserve what is good and fruitful in our national heritage.
Dwight D. Eisenhower (1890 - 1969), Address recorded for the Republican Lincoln Day dinners, January 28, 1964
Politics is the art of looking for trouble, finding it whether it exists or not, diagnosing it incorrectly, and applying the wrong remedy.
Ernest Benn
Being in politics is like being a football coach. You have to be smart enough to understand the game, and dumb enough to think it's important.
Eugene McCarthy (1916 - 2005)
When the political columnists say 'Every thinking man' they mean themselves, and when candidates appeal to 'Every intelligent voter' they mean everybody who is going to vote for them.
Franklin P. Adams (1881 - 1960), Nods and Becks (1944)
The whole aim of practical politics is to keep the populace alarmed (and hence clamorous to be led to safety) by menacing it with an endless series of hobgoblins, all of them imaginary.

H. L. Mencken (1880 - 1956), Women As Outlaws
Practical politics consists in ignoring facts.
Henry Adams (1838 - 1918), The Education of Henry Adams, 1906
The problem with political jokes is they get elected.
Henry Cate VII
Most people assume the fights are going to be the left versus the right, but it always is
the reasonable versus the jerks.
Jimmy Wales, Keynote Speech, SXSW 2006
The United States Congress, like a lot of rich people, lives in two houses.
John Green, Vlogbrothers, Why Does Congress Suck?, 01-01-13
Nothing is so admirable in politics as a short memory.
John Kenneth Galbraith (1908 - 2006)
Politics is not the art of the possible. It consists in choosing between the disastrous and
the unpalatable.
John Kenneth Galbraith (1908 - 2006)
The word 'politics' is derived from the word 'poly', meaning 'many', and the word
'ticks', meaning 'blood sucking parasites'.
Larry Hardiman
Politics is the skilled use of blunt objects.
Lester B. Pearson (1897 - 1972)
If one morning I walked on top of the water across the Potomac River, the headline
that afternoon would read "President Can't Swim".
Lyndon B. Johnson (1908 - 1973)
Politics is war without bloodshed while war is politics with bloodshed.
Mao Tse-Tung (1893 - 1976)
Politics has less to do with where you live than where your heart is.
Margaret Cho, weblog, 01-18-04
Nothing can so alienate a voter from the political system as backing a winning
candidate.
Mark B. Cohen
Politics is the art of the possible.
Otto Von Bismarck (1815 - 1898), remark, Aug. 11, 1867
Politics is the art of preventing people from taking part in affairs which properly
concern them.
Paul Valery (1871 - 1945), Tel Quel 2 (1943)
In politics you must always keep running with the pack. The moment that you falter
and they sense that you are injured, the rest will turn on you like wolves.
R. A. Butler (1902 - 1982)
Politics is largely a matter of heart.
R. A. Butler (1902 - 1982)
The whole art of politics consists in directing rationally the irrationalities of men.
Reinhold Niebuhr (1892 - 1971)
Politics is perhaps the only profession for which no preparation is thought necessary.
Robert Louis Stevenson (1850 - 1894)
Politics is not a bad profession. If you succeed there are many rewards, if you disgrace
yourself you can always write a book.
Ronald Reagan (1911 - 2004)
Politics is supposed to be the second oldest profession. I have come to realize that it
bears a very close resemblance to the first.
Ronald Reagan (1911 - 2004)
The most practical kind of politics is the politics of decency.
Theodore Roosevelt (1858 - 1919), Remarks to Harvard and Yale undergraduates invited to
Sagamore Hill, Oyster Bay, Long Island, June 1901
Politics is applesauce.
Will Rogers (1879 - 1935)
The more you read and observe about this Politics thing, you got to admit that each
party is worse than the other. The one that's out always looks the best.
Will Rogers (1879 - 1935), Illiterate Digest (1924), "Breaking into the Writing Game"

Possessions

Most things worth having require some sacrifice, usually more than you expect.
Albert Ellis, Michael Abrams, Lidia Dengelegi, The Art & Science of Rational Eating, 1992
We too often let the material things serve as indicators that we're doing well, even
though something inside us tells us that were not doing our best. That we are
avoiding that which is hard, but also necessary. That we are shrinking from rather
than vising to the challenges of the age.
Barack Obama (1961 -), Arizona State Commencement Speech, 2009
The wise man carries his possessions within him.
Bias
I love stuff as much as the next guy, but I've come to understand that, regardless of
the cost of acquiring it, the price of having it is freedom.
Colleen Wainwright, Communicatrix, 06-23-09
Possession is eleven points in the law.
Colley Cibber (1671 - 1757), Woman's Wit, Act 1
I take care of my things. After all, those of us as has few things to begin with must
take care, lest we have fewer.
Erica Eisdorfer, The Wet Nurse's Tale, 2009
Before we set our hearts too much upon anything, let us examine how happy those
are who already possess it.
Francois de La Rochefoucauld (1613 - 1680)
Every increased possession loads us with new weariness.
John Ruskin (1819 - 1900)
To have little is to possess.
To have plenty is to be perplexed.
Lao-tzu (604 BC - 531 BC), The Way of Lao-tzu
Desire makes everything blossom; possession makes everything wither and fade.
Marcel Proust (1871 - 1922), Les Plaisirs et les Jours (1896)

An object in possession seldom retains the same charm that it had in pursuit.
Pliny the Younger (62 AD - 114 AD), Letters
I have everything, yet have nothing; and although I possess nothing, still of nothing
am I in want.
Terence (185 BC - 159 BC), Eunuchus
It is through creating, not possessing, that life is revealed.
Vida D. Scudder

Poverty

Poverty is the schoolmaster of character.
Antiphanes
Poverty is the parent of revolution and crime.
Aristotle (384 BC - 322 BC)
Where justice is denied, where poverty is enforced, where ignorance prevails, and
where any one class is made to feel that society is in an organized conspiracy to
oppress, rob, and degrade them, neither persons nor property will be safe.
Frederick Douglass (1817 - 1895), Speech, April 1886
You are going to let the fear of poverty govern your life and your reward will be that
you will eat, but you will not live.
George Bernard Shaw (1856 - 1950)
It is not the rich man you should properly call happy, but him who knows how to use
with wisdom the blessings of the gods, to endure hard poverty, and who fears
dishonor worse than death, and is not afraid to die for cherished friends or
fatherland.
Horace (65 BC - 8 BC), Odes
Climbing out of poverty by your own efforts that is something on which to pride
yourself, but poverty itself is romanticized only by fools.
J. K. Rowling, Harvard Commencement Address, 2008
It is not an ennobling experience. Poverty entails fear and stress and sometimes
depression. It means a thousand petty humiliations and hardships.
J. K. Rowling, Harvard Commencement Address, 2008
Anyone who had ever struggled with poverty knows how extremely expensive it is to
be poor.
James Baldwin (1924 - 1987), Fifth Avenue Uptown: A Letter from
It is not easy for men to rise whose qualities are thwarted by poverty.
Juvenal (55 AD - 127 AD), Satires
It is pretty hard to tell what does bring happiness; poverty and wealth have both
failed.
Kin Hubbard (1868 - 1930)
That is one consolation when you are poor—there are so many more things you can
imagine about.
L. M. Montgomery (1874 - 1942), Anne of Green Gables, 1908
Wealth is the parent of luxury and indolence, and poverty of meanness and
viciousness, and both of discontent.
Plato (427 BC - 347 BC), The Republic
To be poor and dependent is very nearly an impossibility.
William Cobbett (1763 - 1835), Advice to Young Men, 1829

Power

Far better to think historically, to remember the lessons of the past. Thus, far better to
conceive of power as consisting in part of the knowledge of when not to use all the
power you have. Far better to be one who knows that if you reserve the power not to
use all your power, you will lead others far more successfully and well.
A. Bartlett Giamatti (1938 - 1989), President of Yale University
Nearly all men can stand adversity, but if you want to test a man's character, give him
power.
Abraham Lincoln (1809 - 1865)
You see what power is - holding someone else's fear in your hand and showing it to
them!
Amy Tan (1952 -)
The sole advantage of power is that you can do more good.
Baltasar Gracian, The Art of Worldly Wisdom, 1647
To know the pains of power, we must go to those who have it; to know its pleasures,
we must go to those who are seeking it.
Charles Caleb Colton (1780 - 1832), Lacon, 1825
It is said that power corrupts, but actually it's more true that power attracts the
corruptible. The sane are usually attracted by other things than power.
David Brin (1950 -)
Let not thy will roar, when thy power can but whisper.
Dr. Thomas Fuller (1654 - 1734), Gnomologia, 1732
Ultimately, the only power to which man should aspire is that which he exercises over
himself.
Elie Wiesel (1928 -)
It is when power is wedded to chronic fear that it becomes formidable.
Eric Hoffer (1902 - 1983), The Passionate State of Mind, 1954
There are similarities between absolute power and absolute faith: a demand for
absolute obedience, a readiness to attempt the impossible, a bias for simple
solutionsto cut the knot rather than unravel it, the viewing of compromise as
surrender. Both absolute power and absolute faith are instruments of
dehumanization. Hence, absolute faith corrupts as absolutely as absolute power.
Eric Hoffer (1902 - 1983), The New York Times Magazine, April 25, 1971
If absolute power corrupts absolutely, does absolute powerlessness make you pure?
Harry Shearer
The great secret of power is never to will to do more than you can accomplish.
Henrik Ibsen (1828 - 1906)

Be fit for more than the thing you are now doing. Let everyone know that you have a reserve in yourself; that you have more power than you are now using. If you are not too large for the place you occupy, you are too small for it.
James A. Garfield (1831 - 1881)
The essence of government is power; and power, lodged as it must be in human hands, will ever be liable to abuse.
James Madison (1751 - 1836), Speech in the Virginia constitutional convention, Richmond, Virginia, December 2, 1829
The essence of Government is power; and power, lodged as it must be in human hands, will ever be liable to abuse.
James Madison (1751 - 1836), Speech in the Virginia constitutional convention, Richmond, Virginia, December 2, 1829
We all have the power to choose how we are going to handle every situation we are faced with throughout our lives. We are in control of the decision we make whether it's about work, relationships, parenting, or our health.
Jennifer Hudson, I Got This: How I Changed My Ways and Lost What Weighed Me Down, 2012
Power corrupts. Absolute power is kind of neat.
John Lehman (1942 -), Secretary of the Navy, 1981-1987
One person with a belief is equal to a force of 99 who have only interests.
John Stuart Mill (1806 - 1873)
The secret of all power is - save your force. If you want high pressure you must choke off waste.
Joseph Farrell
The one thing a creator can bring to the table when everybody else has all the money and power is centeredness and the ability to walk away. Never sit at a table you can't walk away from.
Joss Whedon, Entertainment Weekly, 08-30-13
If power was an illusion, wasn't weakness necessarily one also?
Lois McMaster Bujold, A Civil Campaign, 1999
Power tends to corrupt, and absolute power corrupts absolutely.
Lord Acton, Letter to Bishop Mandell Creighton, 1887
The highest proof of virtue is to possess boundless power without abusing it.
Lord Macaulay, review of Lucy Aikin, 'Life and Writings of Addison,' 1943
Power never takes a back step - only in the face of more power.
Malcolm X (1925 - 1965), Malcolm X Speaks, 1965
The problem of power is how to achieve its responsible use rather than its irresponsible and indulgent use - of how to get men of power to live for the public rather than off the public.
Robert F. Kennedy (1925 - 1968), 'I Remember, I Believe,' The Pursuit of Justice, 1964
Most powerful is he who has himself in his own power.
Seneca (5 BC - 65 AD)
Knowledge is power.
Sir Francis Bacon (1561 - 1626), Religious Meditations, Of Heresies, 1597
We thought, because we had power, we had wisdom.
Stephen Vincent Benet (1898 - 1943), Litany for Dictatorships, 1935
We have, I fear, confused power with greatness.
Stewart L. Udall (1920 -), commencement address, Dartmouth College, June 13, 1965
An honest man can feel no pleasure in the exercise of power over his fellow citizens.
Thomas Jefferson (1743 - 1826), letter to John Melish, January 13, 1813
The love of liberty is the love of others; the love of power is the love of ourselves.
William Hazlitt (1778 - 1830)
Power consists in one's capacity to link his will with the purpose of others, to lead by reason and a gift of cooperation.
Woodrow Wilson (1856 - 1924), letter to Mary A. Hulbert, September 21, 1913

Praise

Be thou the first true merit to befriend, his praise is lost who stays till all commend.
Alexander Pope (1688 - 1744)
There are two modes of establishing our reputation: to be praised by honest men, and to be abused by rogues. It is best, however, to secure the former, because it will invariably be accompanied by the latter.
Charles Caleb Colton (1780 - 1832)
Such praise coming from so degraded a source, was degrading to me, its recipient.
Cicero (106 BC - 43 BC)
He who praises you for what you lack wishes to take from you what you have.
Don Juan Manuel (1282 - 1349)
It is a sign of a creeping inner death when we no longer can praise the living.
Eric Hoffer (1902 - 1983)
The meanest, most contemptible kind of praise is that which first speaks well of a man, and then qualifies it with a "but".
Henry Ward Beecher (1813 - 1887)
Praise the young and they will flourish.
Irish Proverb
The praise that comes from love does not make us vain, but more humble.
James M. Barrie (1860 - 1937)
You do ill if you praise, but worse if you censure, what you do not understand.
Leonardo da Vinci (1452 - 1519)
We are always more anxious to be distinguished for a talent which we do not possess, than to be praised for the fifteen which we do possess.
Mark Twain (1835 - 1910), Mark Twain's Autobiography
Don't discuss yourself, for you are bound to lose; if you belittle yourself, you are believed; if you praise yourself, you are disbelieved.
Michel de Montaigne (1533 - 1592)
Praise, like gold and diamonds, owes its value only to its scarcity.
Samuel Johnson (1709 - 1784)
Be not too hasty either with praise or blame; speak always as though you were giving evidence before the judgement-seat of the Gods.

Seneca (5 BC - 65 AD)
You can tell the character of every man when you see how he receives praise.
Seneca (5 BC - 65 AD), Epistles
Praise from the common people is generally false, and rather follows the vain than the virtuous.
Sir Francis Bacon (1561 - 1626)
Real joy comes not from ease or riches or from the praise of men, but from doing something worthwhile.
Sir Wilfred Grenfell (1865 - 1940)
If a man is proud of his wealth, he should not be praised until it is known how he employs it.
Socrates (469 BC - 399 BC)
Think not those faithful who praise all thy words and actions; but those who kindly reprove thy faults.
Socrates (469 BC - 399 BC)
Their silence is sufficient praise.
Terence (185 BC - 159 BC)
I do not confer praise or blame: I accept. I am the measure of all things. I am the centre of the world.
W. Somerset Maugham (1874 - 1965), 'Of Human Bondage', 1915
People ask for criticism, but they only want praise.
W. Somerset Maugham (1874 - 1965), "Of Human Bondage", 1915
I pay no attention whatever to anybody's praise or blame. I simply follow my own feelings.
Wolfgang Amadeus Mozart (1756 - 1791)

Prayer

You must pray that the way be long, full of adventures and experiences.
Constantine Peter Cavafy
Pray as if everything depended upon God and work as if everything depended upon man.
Francis Cardinal Spellman (1889 - 1967)
One single grateful thought raised to heaven is the most perfect prayer.
G. E. Lessing (1729 - 1781)
You can pray for someone even if you don't think God exists.
Gordon Atkinson, RealLivePreacher.com Weblog, July 7, 2003
Prayer indeed is good, but while calling on the gods a man should himself lend a hand.
Hippocrates (460 BC - 377 BC), Regimen
The time to pray is not when we are in a tight spot but just as soon as we get out of it.
Josh Billings (1818 - 1885)
You should pray for a sound mind in a sound body.
Juvenal (55 AD - 127 AD), Satires
If the only prayer you ever say in your whole life is "thank you," that would suffice.
Meister Eckhart
When the gods wish to punish us, they answer our prayers.
Oscar Wilde (1854 - 1900), An Ideal husband, 1893
Do not pray for easy lives. Pray to be stronger men. Do not pray for tasks equal to your powers. Pray for powers equal to your tasks. Then the doing of your work shall be no miracle, but you shall be the miracle.
Phillips Brooks (1835 - 1893)
There are more tears shed over answered prayers than over unanswered prayers.
Saint Theresa of Jesus
I have never made but one prayer to God, a very short one: 'O Lord, make my enemies ridiculous.' And God granted it.
Voltaire (1694 - 1778)

Prejudice

Common sense is the collection of prejudices acquired by age eighteen.
Albert Einstein (1879 - 1955), (attributed)
The greatest friend of Truth is time, her greatest enemy is Prejudice, and her constant companion Humility.
Charles Caleb Colton (1780 - 1832)
Everyone is a prisoner of his own experiences. No one can eliminate prejudices - just recognize them.
Edward R. Murrow (1908 - 1965), television broadcast, December 31, 1955
Opinions founded on prejudice are always sustained with the greatest of violence.
Francis Jeffrey (1773 - 1850)
If we were to wake up some morning and find that everyone was the same race, creed and color, we would find some other cause for prejudice by noon.
George Aiken
Criticism is prejudice made plausible.
H. L. Mencken (1880 - 1956)
It is never too late to give up our prejudices.
Henry David Thoreau (1817 - 1862), 'Economy,' Walden, 1854
When the judgement's weak,
The prejudice is strong.
Kane O'Hara
Education is a method whereby one acquires a higher grade of prejudices.
Laurence J. Peter (1919 - 1988)
Nobody outside of a baby carriage or a judge's chamber believes in an unprejudiced point of view.
Lillian Hellman (1905 - 1984)
There are, in every age, new errors to be rectified and new prejudices to be opposed.
Samuel Johnson (1709 - 1784)

Never try to reason the prejudice out of a man. It was not reasoned into him, and cannot be reasoned out.
Sydney Smith (1771 - 1845)
When faced with sexism or ageism or lookism or even really aggressive Buddhism, ask yourself the following question:"Is this person in between me and what do I want to do?" If the answer is no, ignore it and move on. Your energy is better used doing your work and outpacing people that way. Then, when you're in charge, don't hire the people who were jerky to you.
Tina Fey, Bossypants, 2011
Prejudice is opinion without judgement.
Voltaire (1694 - 1778)
I am free of all prejudice. I hate everyone equally.
W. C. Fields (1880 - 1946)
Without the aid of prejudice and custom I should not be able to find my way across the room.
William Hazlitt (1778 - 1830)
A great many people think they are thinking when they are really rearranging their prejudices.
William James (1842 - 1910)

Pride

To know a man, observe how he wins his object, rather than how he loses it; for when we fail our pride supports us; when we succeed, it betrays us.
Charles Caleb Colton (1780 - 1832)
Pride sullies the noblest character.
Claudianus
When dealing with people, let us remember we are not dealing with creatures of logic. We are dealing with creatures of emotion, creatures bustling with prejudices and motivated by pride and vanity.
Dale Carnegie
The pride of youth is in strength and beauty, the pride of old age is in discretion.
Democritus (460 BC - 370 BC)
Be modest! It is the kind of pride least likely to offend.
Jules Renard (1864 - 1910)
Generosity is giving more than you can, and pride is taking less than you need.
Kahlil Gibran (1883 - 1931)
To find yourself jilted is a blow to your pride. Do your best to forget it and if you don't succeed, at least pretend to.
Moliere (1622 - 1673)
Pride is a powerful narcotic, but it doesn't do much for the auto-immune system.
Stuart Stevens, Northern Exposure, Brains, Know-How, and Native Intelligence, 1990
The charity that hastens to proclaim its good deeds, ceases to be charity, and is only pride and ostentation.
William Hutton

Progress

The path to our destination is not always a straight one. We go down the wrong road, we get lost, we turn back. Maybe it doesn't matter which road we embark on. Maybe what matters is that we embark.
Barbara Hall, Northern Exposure, Rosebud, 1993
The chief obstacle to the progress of the human race is the human race.
Don Marquis (1878 - 1937)
The reasonable man adapts himself to the world; the unreasonable one persists in trying to adapt the world to himself. Therefore all progress depends on the unreasonable man.
George Bernard Shaw (1856 - 1950), Man and Superman (1903) "Maxims for Revolutionists"
The reasonable man adapts himself to the world; the unreasonable one persists in trying to adapt the world to himself. Therefore, all progress depends on the unreasonable man.
George Bernard Shaw (1856 - 1950)
What we call 'Progress' is the exchange of one nuisance for another nuisance.
Havelock Ellis (1859 - 1939)
The advancement of the arts from year to year taxes our credulity, and seems to presage the arrival of that period when human improvement must end.
Henry L. Ellsworth, U.S. commissioner of patents, Annual Report, 1843
Progress might have been all right once, but it has gone on too long.
Ogden Nash (1902 - 1971)
I was to learn later that in life that we tend to meet any new situation by reorganizing; and what a wonderful method it can be for creating the illusion of progress while producing confusion, inefficiency, and demoralization.
Petronius Arbiter
Never discourage anyone...who continually makes progress, no matter how slow.
Plato (427 BC - 347 BC)
Usually, terrible things that are done with the excuse that progress requires them are not really progress at all, but just terrible things.
Russell Baker (1925 -)
All progress is based upon a universal innate desire on the part of every organism to live beyond its income.
Samuel Butler (1835 - 1902), Notebooks, 1912
Every day you may make progress. Every step may be fruitful. Yet there will stretch out before you an ever-lengthening, ever-ascending, ever-improving path. You know you will never get to the end of the journey. But this, so far from discouraging, only adds to the joy and glory of the climb.
Sir Winston Churchill (1874 - 1965)

Progress is the product of human agency. Things get better because we make them better. Things go wrong when we get too comfortable, when we fail to take risks or seize opportunities.
Susan Rice, Stanford University Commencement, 2010

Promises

No wonder Americans hate politics when, year in and year out, they hear politicians make promises that won't come true because they don't even mean them - campaign fantasies that win elections but don't get nations moving again.
Bill Clinton (1946 -), Detroit Economic Club, August 21, 1992
Hypocrisy can afford to be magnificent in its promises; for never intending to go beyond promises; it costs nothing.
Edmund Burke (1729 - 1797)
Promises that you make to yourself are often like the Japanese plum tree - they bear no fruit.
Francis Marion (1732 - 1795)
One must have a good memory to be able to keep the promises one makes.
Friedrich Nietzsche (1844 - 1900)
He that promises most will perform least.
Gaelic Proverb
He who promises more than he is able to perform, is false to himself; and he who does not perform what he has promised, is a traitor to his friend.
George Shelley
When life seems chaotic, you don't need people giving you easy answers or cheap promises. There might not be any answers to your problems. What you need is a safe place where you can bounce with people who have taken some bad hops of their own.
Gordon Atkinson, RealLivePreacher.com Weblog, August 12, 2003
Sometimes people don't understand the promises they're making when they make them. Right, of course. But you keep the promise anyway. That's what love is. Love is keeping the promise anyway.
John Green, The Fault in Our Stars, 2012
You can make those promises with just as much passion the second time around. Such is the regenerative power of the human heart.
Marion Wink, O Magazine, 2003
The woods are lovely, dark, and deep,
But I have promises to keep,
And miles to go before I sleep,
And miles to go before I sleep.
Robert Frost (1874 - 1963), Stopping by Woods on a Snowy Evening
Magnificent promises are always to be suspected.
Theodore Parker (1810 - 1860)

Proverbs

If you refuse to be made straight when you are green, you will not be made straight when you are dry.
African Proverb
When you have given nothing, ask for nothing.
Albanian Proverb
Good habits result from resisting temptation.
Ancient Proverb
Dwell not upon thy weariness, thy strength shall be according to the measure of thy desire.
Arab Proverb
Examine what is said, not him who speaks.
Arab Proverb
Make your bargain before beginning to plow.
Arab Proverb
Don't make use of another's mouth unless it has been lent to you.
Belgian Proverb
Seize opportunity by the beard, for it is bald behind.
Bulgarian Proverb
Be not afraid of growing slowly, be afraid only of standing still.
Chinese Proverb
Do not employ handsome servants.
Chinese Proverb
Do not remove a fly from your friend's forehead with a hatchet.
Chinese Proverb
Give a man a fish and you feed him for a day. Teach a man to fish and you feed him for a lifetime.
Chinese Proverb
He who asks is a fool for five minutes, but he who does not ask remains a fool forever.
Chinese Proverb
If you bow at all, bow low.
Chinese Proverb
Keep your broken arm inside your sleeve.
Chinese Proverb
Raise your sail one foot and you get ten feet of wind.
Chinese Proverb
The gem cannot be polished without friction, nor man perfected without trials.
Chinese Proverb
The palest ink is better than the best memory.
Chinese Proverb
To know the road ahead, ask those coming back.
Chinese Proverb
When you drink the water, remember the spring.

Chinese Proverb
When you have only two pennies left in the world, buy a loaf of bread with one, and a lily with the other.
Chinese Proverb
Do not protect yourself by a fence, but rather by your friends.
Czech Proverb
The big thieves hang the little ones.
Czech Proverb
When you go to buy, use your eyes, not your ears.
Czech Proverb
Ask advice only of your equals.
Danish Proverb
He who would leap high must take a long run.
Danish Proverb
A handful of patience is worth more than a bushel of brains.
Dutch Proverb
A full cup must be carried steadily.
English Proverb
Don't fall before you're pushed.
English Proverb
Use soft words and hard arguments.
English Proverb
Write down the advice of him who loves you, though you like it not at present.
English Proverb
Wait until it is night before saying that it has been a fine day.
French Proverb
A country can be judged by the quality of its proverbs.
German Proverb
Charity sees the need not the cause.
German Proverb
Never give advice unless asked.
German Proverb
Who begins too much accomplishes little.
German Proverb
First secure an independent income, then practice virtue.
Greek Proverb
Call on God, but row away from the rocks.
Indian Proverb
Keep five yards from a carriage, ten yards from a horse, and a hundred yards from an elephant; but the distance one should keep from a wicked man cannot be measured.
Indian Proverb
Praise youth and it will prosper.
Irish Proverb
You've got to do your own growing, no matter how tall your grandfather was.
Irish Proverb
If you scatter thorns, don't go barefoot.
Italian Proverb
It is not enough to aim; you must hit.
Italian Proverb
The best armor is to keep out of range.
Italian Proverb
Don't stay long when the husband is not at home.
Japanese Proverb
Fall seven times, stand up eight.
Japanese Proverb
If you believe everything you read, better not read.
Japanese Proverb
Never rely on the glory of the morning nor the smiles of your mother-in-law.
Japanese Proverb
One kind word can warm three winter months.
Japanese proverb
The reverse side also has a reverse side.
Japanese Proverb
When the character of a man is not clear to you, look at his friends.
Japanese Proverb
Ask about your neighbors, then buy the house.
Jewish Proverb
Don't be sweet, lest you be eaten up; don't be bitter, lest you be spewed out.
Jewish Proverb
Don't live in a town where there are no doctors.
Jewish Proverb
Don't look for more honor than your learning merits.
Jewish Proverb
He that can't endure the bad, will not live to see the good.
Jewish Proverb
If God lived on earth, people would break his windows.
Jewish Proverb
Make sure to be in with your equals if you're going to fall out with your superiors.
Jewish Proverb
Rejoice not at thine enemy's fall - but don't rush to pick him up either.
Jewish Proverb
What you don't see with your eyes, don't invent with your mouth.
Jewish Proverb
Worries go down better with soup than without.
Jewish Proverb
Do not throw the arrow which will return against you.

Kurdish Proverb
If the wind will not serve, take to the oars.
Latin Proverb
It is the part of a good shepherd to shear his flock, not to skin it.
Latin Proverb
Never give a child a sword.
Latin Proverb
A smiling face is half the meal.
Latvian Proverb
Don't think there are no crocodiles because the water is calm.
Malayan Proverb
Trumpet in a herd of elephants; crow in the company of cocks; bleat in a flock of goats.
Malayan Proverb
Never criticize a man until you've walked a mile in his moccasins.
Native American Proverb
Hold a true friend with both hands.
Nigerian Proverb
If you wish your merit to be known, acknowledge that of other people.
Oriental Proverb
Use your enemy's hand to catch a snake.
Persian Proverb
Go often to the house of thy friend; for weeds soon choke up the unused path.
Scandinavian Proverb
Better be ill spoken of by one before all than by all before one.
Scottish Proverb
What may be done at any time will be done at no time.
Scottish Proverb
Speak the truth, but leave immediately after.
Slovenian Proverb
Drink nothing without seeing it; sign nothing without reading it.
Spanish Proverb
If you want to be respected, you must respect yourself.
Spanish Proverb
Never advise anyone to go to war or to marry.
Spanish Proverb
Take hold lightly; let go lightly. This is one of the great secrets of felicity in love.
Spanish Proverb
Whoever gossips to you will gossip about you.
Spanish Proverb
Don't let your sorrow come higher than your knees.
Swedish Proverb
Don't throw away the old bucket until you know whether the new one holds water.
Swedish Proverb
Buy on the rumor; sell on the news.
Wall Street Proverb
Be honorable yourself if you wish to associate with honorable people.
Welsh Proverb
Complain to one who can help you.
Yugoslav Proverb
If you wish to know what a man is, place him in authority.
Yugoslav Proverb

Questioning

The important thing is not to stop questioning. Curiosity has its own reason for existing. One cannot help but be in awe when he contemplates the mysteries of eternity, of life, of the marvelous structure of reality. It is enough if one tries merely to comprehend a little of this mystery every day. Never lose a holy curiosity.
Albert Einstein (1879 - 1955)
You can question somebody's views and their judgment without questioning their motives or patriotism.
Barack Obama (1961 -), University of Michigan Commencement, 2010
In all affairs it's a healthy thing now and then to hang a question mark on the things you have long taken for granted.
Bertrand Russell (1872 - 1970)
Look at all the sentences which seem true and question them.
David Reisman
A thinker sees his own actions as experiments and questions–as attempts to find out something. Success and failure are for him answers above all.
Friedrich Nietzsche (1844 - 1900), The Gay Science, section 41
One's first step in wisdom is to question everything - and one's last is to come to terms with everything.
Georg Christoph Lichtenberg (1742 - 1799)
A young man is embarrassed to question an older one.
Homer (800 BC - 700 BC), The Odyssey
It is better to know some of the questions than all of the answers.
James Thurber (1894 - 1961)
If you ask too many questions, you will find no answers, only more questions.
Monica Fairview, Darcy Cousins, 2010
Ask questions from your heart and you will be answered from the heart.
Omaha Proverb
There are two sides to every question.
Protagoras (485 BC - 421 BC), from Diogenes Laertius, Lives of Eminent Philosophers
It is not every question that deserves an answer.
Publilius Syrus (˜ 100 BC), Maxims
A wise man's question contains half the answer.
Solomon Ibn Gabirol

The most erroneous stories are those we think we know best - and therefore never scrutinize or question.
Stephen Jay Gould (1941 - 2002)
So many men so many questions.
(Quot Homines Tot Sententiae)
Terence (185 BC - 159 BC)
The outcome of any serious research can only be to make two questions grow where only one grew before.
Thorstein Veblen (1857 - 1929)
Judge of a man by his questions rather than by his answers.
Voltaire (1694 - 1778)

Quotations

Everything of importance has been said before by somebody who did not discover it.
Alfred North Whitehead (1861 - 1947)
I have suffered a great deal from writers who have quoted this or that sentence of mine either out of its context or in juxtaposition to some incongruous matter which quite distorted my meaning , or destroyed it altogether.
Alfred North Whitehead (1861 - 1947)
The point of quotations is that one can use another's words to be insulting.
Amanda Cross (1926 -)
Quotation, n: The act of repeating erroneously the words of another.
Ambrose Bierce (1842 - 1914), The Devil's Dictionary
One must be a wise reader to quote wisely and well.
Amos Bronson Alcott (1799 - 1888)
When a thing has been said and well, have no scruple. Take it and copy it.
Anatole France (1844 - 1924)
Be careful – with quotations, you can damn anything.
Andre Malraux (1901 - 1976)
Write a wise saying and your name will live forever.
Anonymous
It is unbecoming for young men to utter maxims.
Aristotle (384 BC - 322 BC)
The wisdom of the wise, and the experience of ages, may be preserved by quotation.
Benjamin Disraeli (1804 - 1881)
A quotation in a speech, article or book is like a rifle in the hands of an infantryman. It speaks with authority.
Brendan Francis
To be amused by what you read–that is the great spring of happy quotations.
C. E. Montague, "A Writer's Notes on His Trade"
I never have found the perfect quote. At best I have been able to find a string of quotations which merely circle the ineffable idea I seek to express.
Caldwell O'Keefe
I improve on misquotation.
Cary Grant (1904 - 1986)
The American people would not want to know of any misquotes that Dan Quayle may or may not make.
Dan Quayle (1947 -)
People will accept your ideas much more readily if you tell them Benjamin Franklin said it first.
David H. Comins
What's the use of a good quotation if you can't change it?
Doctor Who
A facility for quotation covers the absence of original thought.
Dorothy L. Sayers (1893 - 1957), Lord Peter Wimsey in "Gaudy Night"
I might repeat to myself slowly and soothingly, a list of quotations beautiful from minds profound - if I can remember any of the damn things.
Dorothy Parker (1893 - 1967)
Some for renown, on scraps of learning dote,
And think they grow immortal as they quote.
Edward Young (1683 - 1765), Love of Fame (satire I, l. 89)
An epigram often flashes light into regions where reason shines but dimly.
Edwin P. Whipple
If you have any doubts that we live in a society controlled by men, try reading down the index of contributors to a volume of quotations, looking for women's names.
Elaine Gill
I often quote myself. It adds spice to my conversation.
George Bernard Shaw (1856 - 1950)
After all, all he did was string together a lot of old, well-known quotations.
H. L. Mencken (1880 - 1956), on Shakespeare
Misquotation is, in fact, the pride and privilege of the learned. A widely- read man never quotes accurately, for the rather obvious reason that he has read too widely.
Hesketh Pearson, Common Misquotations (1934), Introduction
Misquotations are the only quotations that are never misquoted.
Hesketh Pearson
Life itself is a quotation.
Jorge Luis Borges (1899 - 1986)
A fine quotation is a diamond on the finger of a man of wit, and a pebble in the hand of a fool.
Joseph Roux
What a good thing Adam had. When he said a good thing he knew nobody had said it before.
Mark Twain (1835 - 1910), Notebooks (1935)
I love quotations because it is a joy to find thoughts one might have, beautifully expressed with much authority by someone recognized wiser than oneself.
Marlene Dietrich (1901 - 1992)
A thought is often original, though you have uttered it a hundred times.

Oliver Wendell Holmes (1809 - 1894), The Autocrat of the Breakfast-Table, 1858
Now we sit through Shakespeare in order to recognize the quotations.
Orson Welles (1915 - 1985)
Most people are other people. Their thoughts are someone else's opinions, their lives a mimicry, their passions a quotation.
Oscar Wilde (1854 - 1900), De Profundis, 1905
Have you ever observed that we pay much more attention to a wise passage when it is quoted than when we read it in the original author?
Philip G. Hamerton, "The Intellectual Life"
There is not less wit nor less invention in applying rightly a thought one finds in a book, than in being the first author of that thought.
Pierre Bayle (1647 - 1706), Dictionairre Historique et Critique
Immortality. I notice that as soon as writers broach this question they begin to quote. I hate quotation. Tell me what you know.
Ralph Waldo Emerson (1803 - 1882), Journal (May 1849)
Next to the originator of a good sentence is the first quoter of it.
Ralph Waldo Emerson (1803 - 1882), Letters and Social Aims (Quotation and Originality)
The surest way to make a monkey of a man is to quote him.
Robert Benchley (1889 - 1945)
A quotation, like a pun, should come unsought, and then be welcomed only for some propriety of felicity justifying the intrusion.
Robert Chapman
A book of quotations . . . can never be complete.
Robert M. Hamilton
He wrapped himself in quotations- as a beggar would enfold himself in the purple of Emperors.
Rudyard Kipling (1865 - 1936)
Classical quotation is the parole of literary men all over the world.
Samuel Johnson (1709 - 1784), as quoted in Boswell's Life of Johnson (May 8th, 1781)
Every quotation contributes something to the stability or enlargement of the language.
Samuel Johnson (1709 - 1784)
What is an epigram? A dwarfish whole, its body brevity, and wit its soul.
Samuel Taylor Coleridge (1772 - 1834)
I shall never be ashamed of citing a bad author if the line is good.
Seneca (5 BC - 65 AD)
Famous remarks are very seldom quoted correctly.
Simeon Strunsky (1879 - 1948), No Mean City (1944)
I am reminded of the professor who, in his declining hours, was asked by his devoted pupils for his final counsel. He replied, 'Verify your quotations.'
Sir Winston Churchill (1874 - 1965), quoted in Rudolf Flesch, ed., "The New Book of Unusual Quotations" (NY: Harper & Row, 1966), p. 311
It is a good thing for an uneducated man to read books of quotations. Bartlett's Familiar Quotations is an admirable work, and I studied it intently. The quotations when engraved upon the memory give you good thoughts. They also make you anxious to read the authors and look for more.
Sir Winston Churchill (1874 - 1965), Roving Commission: My Early Life, 1930, Chapter 9
A short saying oft contains much wisdom.
Sophocles (496 BC - 406 BC)
It is better to be quotable than to be honest.
Tom Stoppard (1937 -)
A witty saying proves nothing.
Voltaire (1694 - 1778)
She had a pretty gift for quotation, which is a serviceable substitute for wit.
W. Somerset Maugham (1874 - 1965)
The wisdom of the wise and the experience of the ages is preserved into perpetuity by a nation's proverbs, fables, folk sayings and quotations.
William Feather (1908 - 1976)
I didn't really say everything I said.
Yogi Berra (1925 -)

Reality

Reality is merely an illusion, albeit a very persistent one.
Albert Einstein (1879 - 1955), (attributed)
Everything is a dangerous drug except reality, which is unendurable.
Cyril Connolly (1903 - 1974), "The Unquiet Grave", 1945
You bluffed me! I don't like it when people bluff me. It makes me question my perception of reality.
Diane Frolov and Andrew Schneider, Northern Exposure, Cicely, 1992
Set up as an ideal the facing of reality as honestly and as cheerfully as possible.
Dr. Karl Menninger (1893 - 1990)
Joel: That's the movies, Ed. Try reality.
Ed: No thanks.
Ellen Herman, Northern Exposure, Only You, 1991
I believe in looking reality straight in the eye and denying it.
Garrison Keillor (1942 -)
The real distinction is between those who adapt their purposes to reality and those who seek to mold reality in the light of their purposes.
Henry Kissinger (1923 -)
Realism...has no more to do with reality than anything else.
Hob Broun
Reality is nothing but a collective hunch.
Jane Wagner, Lily Tomlin in "The Search for Signs of Intelligent Life in the Universe"
Reality is the leading cause of stress amongst those in touch with it.
Jane Wagner, (and Lily Tomlin)
Important days don't look like anything special when they start. Invariably, the sun rises and people wake up. Coffee is swilled and eggs are swallowed. Everybody goes

about the business of acting like their lives matter and then, no matter how important the events of the day end up being, the sun invariably sets. The sun rose before the soldiers stormed Omaha Beach on D-Day, and the sun set after Archduke Franz Ferdinand was killed. Sunrises and sunsets are real jerks about putting things in perspective.
Josh Lieb, I am a Genius of Unspeakable Evil and I Want to be Your Class President, 2009
Imagination is the one weapon in the war against reality.
Jules de Gaultier
Reality is a crutch for people who can't cope with drugs.
Lily Tomlin (1939 -)
Reality is something you rise above.
Liza Minnelli (1946 -)
I've wrestled with reality for 35 years, Doctor, and I'm happy to state I finally won out over it.
Mary Chase (1887 - 1973), Jimmy Stewart in "Harvey", 1950
Everything you can imagine is real.
Pablo Picasso (1881 - 1973)
Reality is that which, when you stop believing in it, doesn't go away.
Philip K. Dick (1928 - 1982), "How to Build a Universe That Doesn't Fall Apart Two Days Later", 1978
Humankind cannot stand very much reality.
T. S. Eliot (1888 - 1965)

Reason

A man always has two reasons for what he does–a good one and the real one.
J. Pierpont Morgan
Reason has always existed, but not always in a reasonable form.
Karl Marx (1818 - 1883)
Do not banish reason for inequality; but let your reason serve to make the truth appear where it seems hid, and hide the false seems true.
William Shakespeare (1564 - 1616), Measure for Measure, Act V, sc. 1
Every why hath a wherefore.
William Shakespeare (1564 - 1616), The Comedy of Errors, Act II, sc. 2
His reasons are as two grains of wheat his in two bushels of chaff: you shall seek all day ere you find them, and when you have them, they are not worth the search.
William Shakespeare (1564 - 1616), The Merchant of Venice, Act I, sc. 1
Many that are not mad have, sure, more lack of reason.
William Shakespeare (1564 - 1616), Measure for Measure, Act V, sc. 1
Strong reasons make strong actions.
William Shakespeare (1564 - 1616), King John, Act III, sc. 4
Sure, he that made us with such large discourse, looking before and after, gave us not that capability and god-like reason to fust in us unus'd.
William Shakespeare (1564 - 1616), Hamlet, Act IV, sc. 4

Relaxation

Man is so made that he can only find relaxation from one kind of labor by taking up another.
Anatole France (1844 - 1924), The Crime of Sylvestre Bonnard
To be able to fill leisure intelligently is the last product of civilization, and at present very few people have reached this level.
Bertrand Russell (1872 - 1970), Conquest of Happiness (1930) ch. 14
This art of resting the mind and the power of dismissing from it all care and worry is probably one of the secrets of energy in our great men.
Captain J. A. Hadfield
Acquire inner peace and a multitude will find their salvation near you.
Catherine de Hueck Doherty
Nothing is permanent in this wicked world - not even our troubles.
Charlie Chaplin (1889 - 1977)
Sometimes the cure for restlessness is rest.
Colleen Wainwright, Communicatrix, 08-06-08
Put duties aside at least an hour before bed and perform soothing, quiet activities that will help you relax.
Dianne Hales
No matter how much pressure you feel at work, if you could find ways to relax for at least five minutes every hour, you'd be more productive.
Dr. Joyce Brothers (1928 -)
There is no need to go to India or anywhere else to find peace. You will find that deep place of silence right in your room, your garden or even your bathtub.
Elisabeth Kubler-Ross
We have to fight them daily, like fleas, those many small worries about the morrow, for they sap our energies.
Etty Hillesum, O Magazine, October 2002
Light be the earth upon you, lightly rest.
Euripides (484 BC - 406 BC), Alcestis, 438 B.C.
When we are unable to find tranquility within ourselves, it is useless to seek it elsewhere.
Francois de La Rochefoucauld (1613 - 1680)
During [these] periods of relaxation after concentrated intellectual activity, the intuitive mind seems to take over and can produce the sudden clarifying insights which give so much joy and delight.
Fritjof Capra, physicist
What's the use of worrying? It never was worthwhile.
George Asaf
He enjoys true leisure who has time to improve his soul's estate.
Henry David Thoreau (1817 - 1862), Journal, February 11, 1840

If a man insisted always on being serious, and never allowed himself a bit of fun and relaxation, he would go mad or become unstable without knowing it.
Herodotus (484 BC - 430 BC), The Histories of Herodotus
We spend most of our time and energy in a kind of horizontal thinking. We move along the surface of things [but] there are times when we stop. We sit still. We lose ourselves in a pile of leaves or its memory. We listen and breezes from a whole other world begin to whisper.
James Carroll
To sit in the shade on a fine day, and look upon verdure is the most perfect refreshment.
Jane Austen (1775 - 1817)
Never lose sight of this important truth, that no one can be truly great until he has gained a knowledge of himself, a knowledge which can only be acquired by occasional retirement.
Johann Georg von Zimmermann
I take it that what all men are really after is some form or perhaps only some formula of peace.
Joseph Conrad (1857 - 1924)
If you can attain repose and calm, believe that you have seized happiness.
Julie-Jeanne-Eleonore de Lespinasse, O Magazine, October 2002
Besides the noble art of getting things done, there is a nobler art of leaving things undone. The wisdom of life consists in the elimination of nonessentials.
Lin Yutang
Stress is an ignorant state. It believes that everything is an emergency. Nothing is that important.
Natalie Goldberg
Before you agree to do anything that might add even the smallest amount of stress to your life, ask yourself: What is my truest intention? Give yourself time to let a yes resound within you. When it's right, I guarantee that your entire body will feel it.
Oprah Winfrey (1954 -)
Take rest; a field that has rested gives a bountiful crop.
Ovid (43 BC - 17 AD)
Learning to ignore things is one of the great paths to inner peace.
Robert J. Sawyer (1960 -), "Calculating God", 2000
Working in the garden...gives me a profound feeling of inner peace.
Ruth Stout
Sometimes I sits and thinks, and sometimes I just sits.
Satchel Paige (1906 - 1982)
The time to relax is when you don't have time for it.
Sydney J. Harris

Religion

When I do good, I feel good; when I do bad, I feel bad, and that is my religion.
Abraham Lincoln (1809 - 1865), (attributed)
My religion consists of a humble admiration of the illimitable superior spirit who reveals himself in the slight details we are able to perceive with our frail and feeble mind.
Albert Einstein (1879 - 1955)
Science without religion is lame, religion without science is blind.
Albert Einstein (1879 - 1955), "Science, Philosophy and Religion: a Symposium", 1941
I won't take my religion from any man who never works except with his mouth.
Carl Sandburg (1878 - 1967)
I am determined that my children shall be brought up in their father's religion, if they can find out what it is.
Charles Lamb (1775 - 1834)
It is a fine thing to establish one's own religion in one's heart, not to be dependent on tradition and second-hand ideals. Life will seem to you, later, not a lesser, but a greater thing.
D. H. Lawrence (1885 - 1930)
Rational arguments don't usually work on religious people. Otherwise, there wouldn't be religious people.
Doris Egan, House M.D., The Right Stuff, 2007
Clergymen have much the same in their breeches as other men.
Elizabeth Aston, The Second Mrs. Darcy, 2007
The opposite of the religious fanatic is not the fanatical atheist but the gentle cynic who cares not whether there is a god or not.
Eric Hoffer (1902 - 1983)
Everyone ought to worship God according to his own inclinations, and not to be constrained by force.
Flavius Josephus (37 AD - 100 AD), Life
The secret of a good sermon is to have a good beginning and a good ending, then having the two as close together as possible.
George Burns (1896 - 1996)
For centuries, theologians have been explaining the unknowable in terms of the-not-worth-knowing.
H. L. Mencken (1880 - 1956)
I've often thought the Bible should have a disclaimer in the front saying this is fiction.
Ian McKellen, Interview on the Today Show, May 2006
A myth is a religion in which no one any longer believes.
James Feibleman
Everybody likes to go their own way–to choose their own time and manner of devotion.
Jane Austen (1775 - 1817), Mansfield Park
It will, I believe, be everywhere found, that as the clergy are, or are not what they ought to be, so are the rest of the nation.
Jane Austen (1775 - 1817), Mansfield Park

The home of a clergyman is constantly judged by its parishioners. If it is too large and richly decorated, it is the subject of jealousy. If it is too small and humble, it is the subject of scorn. If it is too clean and orderly, it is considered a museum where charity is untouched and kept in a box. If it is slovenly, it is the subject of disgust.
Laura Moncur (1969 -), The Secret Heart of Charlotte Lucas, 2014
Such evil deeds could religion prompt.
Lucretius (96 BC - 55 BC), De Rerum Natura
I would no more quarrel with a man because of his religion than I would because of his art.
Mary Baker Eddy, "Harvest," 1906
The true meaning of religion is thus not simply morality, but morality touched by emotion.
Matthew Arnold (1822 - 1888), 'Literature and Dogma,' preface to 1883 edition, last words
Those who seek consolation in existing churches often pay for their peace of mind with a tacit agreement to ignore a great deal of what is known about the way the world works.
Mihaly Csikszentmihalyi, Flow: The Psychology of Optimal Experience, 1990
The true mystery of the world is the visible, not the invisible.
Oscar Wilde (1854 - 1900)
Never confuse the faith with the supposedly faithful.
Randy K. Milholland, Something Positive Comic, 10-19-06
The only time anyone's admitted they were a Christian before was when they were busy telling me why they're better than me.
Randy K. Milholland, Something Positive Comic, 10-19-06
The more I study religions the more I am convinced that man never worshipped anything but himself.
Sir Richard Francis Burton (1821 - 1890)
To believe in God or in a guiding force because someone tells you to is the height of stupidity. We are given senses to receive our information within. With our own eyes we see, and with our own skin we feel. With our intelligence, it is intended that we understand. But each person must puzzle it out for himself or herself.
Sophy Burnham
Whatever God's dream about man may be, it seems certain it cannot come true unless man cooperates.
Stella Terrill Mann
With or without religion, you would have good people doing good things and evil people doing evil things. But for good people to do evil things, that takes religion.
Steven Weinberg (1933 -), quoted in The New York Times, April 20, 1999
Say nothing of my religion. It is known to God and myself alone. Its evidence before the world is to be sought in my life: if it has been honest and dutiful to society the religion which has regulated it cannot be a bad one.
Thomas Jefferson (1743 - 1826)
A cult is a religion with no political power.
Tom Wolfe (1931 -)
Angels dancing on the head of a pin dissolve into nothingness at the bedside of a dying child.
Waiter Rant, Waiter Rant weblog, 06-21-05
My mom grew up in Spanish Harlem and the Bronx and gave me an invaluable piece of advice for dealing with people in New York - if someone's bugging you just act crazy. I've modified her approach somewhat. Public displays of religiosity work just as well as feigning psychosis.
Waiter Rant, Waiter Rant, 01-14-10
Religions are born and may die, but superstition in immortal.
Will and Ariel Durant, the Age of reason Begins, 1950, The Age of Reason Begins, 1950

Reputation

There are two modes of establishing our reputation: to be praised by honest men, and to be abused by rogues. It is best, however, to secure the former, because it will invariably be accompanied by the latter.
Charles Caleb Colton (1780 - 1832)
You can't build a reputation on what you are going to do.
Henry Ford (1863 - 1947)
Propriety was a rigid master, but one that must be obeyed if one wanted to keep a sterling reputation.
Lawana Blackwell, The Courtship of the Vicar's Daughter, 1998
A good name, like good will, is got by many actions and lost by one.
Lord Jeffery
Until you've lost your reputation, you never realize what a burden it was.
Margaret Mitchell (1900 - 1949)
One can survive everything, nowadays, except death, and live down everything except a good reputation.
Oscar Wilde (1854 - 1900)
A good reputation is more valuable than money.
Publilius Syrus (~100 BC), Maxims
If I've learned one thing in the 14 years I've been a full-time cartoonist, it's that you can not let anyone else define your professionalism. It has to be a personal ethos to which you adhere despite third party influence or acceptance. The old measuring sticks for professionalism are going away and now more than ever it's time for independent creatives to set the bar. Set it high.
Scott R. Kurtz, PvPonline, 11-28-2011
Regard your good name as the richest jewel you can possibly be possessed of - for credit is like fire; when once you have kindled it you may easily preserve it, but if you once extinguish it, you will find it an arduous task to rekindle it again. The way to gain a good reputation is to endeavor to be what you desire to appear.
Socrates (469 BC - 399 BC)
Good name in man and woman, dear my lord,
Is the immediate jewel of their souls:

Who steals my purse steals trash; 'tis something, nothing;
'Twas mine, 'tis his, and has been slave to thousands;
But he that filches from me my good name
Robs me of that which not enriches him
And makes me poor indeed.
William Shakespeare (1564 - 1616), Othello, Act III, sc. 3
Good name in man and woman, dear my lord,
Is the immediate jewel of their souls:
Who steals my purse steals trash; 'tis something, nothing;
'Twas mine, 'tis his, and has been slave to thousands;
But he that filches from me my good name
Robs me of that which not enriches him
And makes me poor indeed.
William Shakespeare (1564 - 1616), "Othello", Act 3 scene 3
Oh, I have lost my reputation! I have lost the immortal part of myself, and what remains is bestial.
William Shakespeare (1564 - 1616), Othello, Act II, sc. 3
Reputation is an idle and most false imposition; oft got without merit, and lost without deserving.
William Shakespeare (1564 - 1616), Othello, Act II, sc. 3
The purest treasure mortal times afford is spotless reputation; that away, men are but gilded loam or painted clay.
William Shakespeare (1564 - 1616), Richard II, Act I, sc. I

Respect

He removes the greatest ornament of friendship, who takes away from it respect.
Cicero (106 BC - 43 BC)
Respect yourself and others will respect you.
Confucius (551 BC - 479 BC)
The more things a man is ashamed of, the more respectable he is.
George Bernard Shaw (1856 - 1950), "Man and Superman" (1903), act I
Respect a man, he will do the more.
James Howell
Civilization is a method of living, an attitude of equal respect for all men.
Jane Addams (1860 - 1935), Speech, Honolulu (1933)
Loving yourself means caring enough to make the hard decisions in your life.
Jennifer Hudson, I Got This: How I Changed My Ways and Lost What Weighed Me Down, 2012
Self-respect is the cornerstone of all virtue.
John Herschel (1792 - 1871)
Some people have so much respect for their superiors they have none left for themselves.
Peter McArthur
If you want to be respected, you must respect yourself.
Spanish Proverb
The way to procure insults is to submit to them: a man meets with no more respect than he exacts.
William Hazlitt (1778 - 1830)
That you may retain your self-respect, it is better to displease the people by doing what you know is right, than to temporarily please them by doing what you know is wrong.
William J. H. Boetcker

Responsibility

You cannot escape the responsibility of tomorrow by evading it today.
Abraham Lincoln (1809 - 1865)
To give up the task of reforming society is to give up one's responsibility as a free man.
Alan Paton (1903 - 1988)
One can pass on responsibility, but not the discretion that goes with it.
Benvenuto Cellini (1500 - 1571)
I think of a hero as someone who understands the degree of responsibility that comes with his freedom.
Bob Dylan (1941 -)
The perfect bureaucrat everywhere is the man who manages to make no decisions and escape all responsibility.
Brooks Atkinson (1894 - 1984), Once Around the Sun, 1951
There is a mysterious cycle in human events. To some generations much is given. Of other generations much is expected. This generation of Americans has a rendezvous with destiny.
Franklin D. Roosevelt (1882 - 1945)
Action springs not from thought, but from a readiness for responsibility.
G. M. Trevelyan (1876 - 1962)
Liberty means responsibility. That is why most men dread it.
George Bernard Shaw (1856 - 1950), Man and Superman (1903) "Maxims for Revolutionists"
If you don't accept responsibility for your own actions, then you are forever chained to a position of defense.
Holly Lisle, Fire In The Mist, 1992
So many new ideas are at first strange and horrible, though ultimately valuable that a very heavy responsibility rests upon those who would prevent their dissemination.
J. B. S. Haldane (1892 - 1964)
There is an expiry date on blaming your parents for steering you in the wrong direction. The moment you are old enough to take the wheel, the responsibility lies with you.
J. K. Rowling, Harvard Commencement Address, 2008
In every child who is born under no matter what circumstances and of no matter what parents, the potentiality of the human race is born again, and in him, too, once more,

and each of us, our terrific responsibility toward human life: toward the utmost idea of goodness, of the horror of terrorism, and of God.
James Agee (1909 - 1955), Let Us Now Praise Famous Men
Character - the willingness to accept responsibility for one's own life - is the source from which self respect springs.
Joan Didion (1934 -), "Slouching Towards Bethlehem"
I believe that every right implies a responsibility; every opportunity, an obligation; every possession, a duty.
John D. Rockefeller (1839 - 1937), Personal credo
Taking responsibility gives us power and control, because when we recognize the relationship between our choices and their consequences, then the next time we don't like a consequence we can make a different choice.
Julie A., M.A. Ross and Judy Corcoran, Joint Custody with a Jerk: Raising a Child with an Uncooperative Ex, 2011
The more freedom we enjoy, the greater the responsibility we bear, toward others as well as ourselves.
Oscar Arias Sanchez (1941 -)
We are at the very beginning of time for the human race. It is not unreasonable that we grapple with problems. But there are tens of thousands of years in the future. Our responsibility is to do what we can, learn what we can, improve the solutions, and pass them on.
Richard Feynman (1918 - 1988)
The price of greatness is responsibility.
Sir Winston Churchill (1874 - 1965)

Revenge

I tasted too what was called the sweet of revenge - but it was transient, it expired even with the object, that provoked it.
Ann Radcliffe (1764 - 1823), The Mysteries of Udolpho, 1764
There is no revenge so complete as forgiveness.
Josh Billings (1818 - 1885)
An eye for an eye makes the whole world blind.
Mahatma Gandhi (1869 - 1948), (attributed)
If an injury has to be done to a man it should be so severe that his vengeance need not be feared.
Niccolo Machiavelli (1469 - 1527)
Life being what it is, one dreams of revenge.
Paul Gauguin (1848 - 1903)
Nothing inspires forgiveness quite like revenge.
Scott Adams (1957 -)
In taking revenge, a man is but even with his enemy; but in passing it over, he is superior.
Sir Francis Bacon (1561 - 1626)
Revenge is a kind of wild justice, which the more man's nature runs to the more ought law to weed it out.
Sir Francis Bacon (1561 - 1626)
Live well. It is the greatest revenge.
The Talmud

Revolution

The first duty of a revolutionary is to get away with it.
Abbie Hoffman (1936 - 1989)
Poverty is the parent of revolution and crime.
Aristotle (384 BC - 322 BC)
Revolution is not a onetime event.
Audre Lorde
The most radical revolutionary will become a conservative the day after the revolution.
Hannah Arendt (1906 - 1975)
Those who make peaceful revolution impossible will make violent revolution inevitable.
John F. Kennedy (1917 - 1963), In a speech at the White House, 1962
The most important scientific revolutions all include, as their only common feature, the dethronement of human arrogance from one pedestal after another of previous convictions about our centrality in the cosmos.
Stephen Jay Gould (1941 - 2002)

Risk

And the day came when the risk to remain tight in a bud was more painful than the risk it took to blossom.
Anais Nin (1903 - 1977)
I guess what I'm trying to say is, I don't think you can measure life in terms of years. I think longevity doesn't necessarily have anything to do with happiness. I mean happiness comes from facing challenges and going out on a limb and taking risks. If you're not willing to take a risk for something you really care about, you might as well be dead.
Diane Frolov and Andrew Schneider, Northern Exposure, Northern Lights, 1993
Life is a risk.
Diane Von Furstenberg
If you don't risk anything you risk even more.
Erica Jong
Take calculated risks. That is quite different from being rash.
George S. Patton (1885 - 1945)
First weigh the considerations, then take the risks.
Helmuth von Moltke (1800 - 1891)
Great deeds are usually wrought at great risks.

Herodotus (484 BC - 430 BC), The Histories of Herodotus
The policy of being too cautious is the greatest risk of all.
Jawaharlal Nehru (1889 - 1964)
What you risk reveals what you value.
Jeanette Winterson
Be wary of the man who urges an action in which he himself incurs no risk.
Joaquin Setanti
There are risks and costs to a program of action. But they are far less than the long-range risks and costs of comfortable inaction.
John F. Kennedy (1917 - 1963)
If you're never scared or embarrassed or hurt, it means you never take any chances.
Julia Sorel
Risk! Risk anything! Care no more for the opinions of others, for those voices. Do the hardest thing on earth for you. Act for yourself. Face the truth.
Katherine Mansfield (1888 - 1923)
I don't think about risks much. I just do what I want to do. If you gotta go, you gotta go.
Lillian Carter
In order for people to be happy, sometimes they have to take risks. It's true these risks can put them in danger of being hurt.
Meg Cabot, The Boy Next Door, 2002
It seems to me that people have vast potential. Most people can do extraordinary things if they have the confidence or take the risks. Yet most people don't. They sit in front of the telly and treat life as if it goes on forever.
Philip Adams
To win without risk is to triumph without glory.
Pierre Corneille (1606 - 1684), 'The Cid,' 1636
The universe will reward you for taking risks on its behalf.
Shakti Gawain
Our lives improve only when we take chances - and the first and most difficult risk we can take is to be honest with ourselves.
Walter Anderson

Rules

We started off trying to set up a small anarchist community, but people wouldn't obey the rules.
Alan Bennett, Getting On (1972)
It's not enough to create magic. You have to create a price for magic, too. You have to create rules.
Eric A. Burns, Gossamer Commons, 06-15-05
The golden rule is that there are no golden rules.
George Bernard Shaw (1856 - 1950), Man and Superman (1903) "Maxims for Revolutionists"
One of the best rules in conversation is, never to say a thing which any of the company can reasonably wish had been left unsaid.
Jonathan Swift (1667 - 1745)
It is much easier to break the rules when one s surrounded by strangers. One does not know any of them, so one cannot really care for their opinion.
Monica Fairview, Darcy Cousins, 2010
Play by the rules, but be ferocious.
Phil Knight, founder of Nike
Rules are just helpful guidelines for stupid people who can't make up their own minds.
Seth Hoffman, House M.D., 2010
Here's to the crazy ones, the misfits, the rebels, the troublemakers, the round pegs in the square holes... the ones who see things differently – they're not fond of rules... You can quote them, disagree with them, glorify or vilify them, but the only thing you can't do is ignore them because they change things... they push the human race forward, and while some may see them as the crazy ones, we see genius, because the ones who are crazy enough to think that they can change the world, are the ones who do.
Steve Jobs (1955 - 2011)
Hell, there are no rules here– we're trying to accomplish something.
Thomas A. Edison (1847 - 1931)
There are three rules for writing the novel. Unfortunately, no one knows what they are.
W. Somerset Maugham (1874 - 1965)

Sanity

In a mad world only the mad are sane.
Akira Kurosawa (1910 - 1998)
Insanity: doing the same thing over and over again and expecting different results.
Albert Einstein (1879 - 1955), (attributed)
The difference between insanity and genius is success.
Bruce Feirstein, Tomorrow Never Dies
The knowing, I told myself, is only a vapor of the mind, and yet it can wreck havok with one's sanity.
Diane Ackerman, One Hundred Names for Love: A Stroke, A Marriage, and the Language of Healing, 2011
Sometimes the mind, for reasons we don't necessarily understand, just decides to go to the store for a quart of milk.
Diane Frolov and Andrew Schneider, Northern Exposure, Three Doctors, 1993
Insanity in individuals is something rare - but in groups, parties, nations and epochs, it is the rule.
Friedrich Nietzsche (1844 - 1900)
There is always some madness in love. But there is also always some reason in madness.

Friedrich Nietzsche (1844 - 1900), "On Reading and Writing"
Correct me if I'm wrong, but hasn't the fine line between sanity and madness gotten finer?
George Price
Ordinarily he was insane, but he had lucid moments when he was merely stupid.
Heinrich Heine (1797 - 1856)
Truly great madness cannot be achieved without significant intelligence.
Henrik Tikkanen
When dealing with the insane, the best method is to pretend to be sane.
Hermann Hesse (1877 - 1962)
I hate to advocate drugs, alcohol, violence, or insanity to anyone, but they've always worked for me.
Hunter S. Thompson (1939 - 2005)
Part of being sane, is being a little bit crazy.
Janet Long
Sanity calms, but madness is more interesting.
John Russell
I think that maybe in every company today there is always at least one person who is going crazy slowly.
Joseph Heller (1923 - 1999)
A neurosis is a secret that you don't know you are keeping.
Kenneth Tynan
It is no measure of health to be well adjusted to a profoundly sick society.
Krishnamurti
I don't really trust a sane person.
Lyle Alzado (1949 - 1992)
There's a fine line between genius and insanity. I have erased this line.
Oscar Levant (1906 - 1972)
The statistics on sanity are that one out of every four Americans is suffering from some form of mental illness. Think of your three best friends. If they're okay, then it's you.
Rita Mae Brown
You're only given a little spark of madness. You mustn't lose it.
Robin Williams (1951 -)
There is only one difference between a madman and me. I am not mad.
Salvador Dali (1904 - 1989)
There is no great genius without some touch of madness.
Seneca (5 BC - 65 AD), Epistles
Joel: Ed, are you hallucinating?
Ed: Oh, yeah, but not right now.
Sy Rosen and Christian Williams, Northern Exposure, On Your Own, 1992
Howard Hughes was able to afford the luxury of madness, like a man who not only thinks he is Napoleon but hires an army to prove it.
Ted Morgan
Dreaming permits each and every one of us to be quietly and safely insane every night of our lives.
William Dement, in Newsweek, 1959
Canst thou not minister to a mind diseased,
Pluck from the memory a rooted sorrow...
And with some sweet oblivious antidote
Cleanse the stuff'd bosom of that perilous stuff
Which weighs upon the heart?
William Shakespeare (1564 - 1616), Macbeth, Act V, sc. 3
Fetter strong madness in a silken thread.
William Shakespeare (1564 - 1616), Much Ado About Nothing, Act V, sc. 1
Her madness hath the oddest frame of sense, such a dependency of thing on thing, as e'er I heard in madness.
William Shakespeare (1564 - 1616), Measure for Measure, Act V, sc. 1
How comes it, that thou art then estranged from thyself?
William Shakespeare (1564 - 1616), The Comedy of Errors, Act II, sc. 2
Madness in great ones must not unwatch'd go.
William Shakespeare (1564 - 1616), Hamlet, Act III, sc. 1
Matter and impertinency mix'd! Reason in madness!
William Shakespeare (1564 - 1616), King Lear, Act IV, sc. 6
Oh, that way madness lies; let me shun that.
William Shakespeare (1564 - 1616), "King Lear", Act 3 scene 4
That way madness lies.
William Shakespeare (1564 - 1616), King Lear, Act III, sc. 4
Though this be madness, yet there is method in 't.
William Shakespeare (1564 - 1616), "Hamlet", Act 2 scene 2
We are not ourselves when nature, being oppress'd, commands the mind to suffer with the body.
William Shakespeare (1564 - 1616), King Lear, Act II, sc. 4
Were such things here as we do speak about? Or have we eaten on the insane root that takes the reason prisoner?
William Shakespeare (1564 - 1616), King Lear, Act III, sc. 4
Why, this is very midsummer madness.
William Shakespeare (1564 - 1616), Twelfth Night, Act III, sc. 4

Science

Science can only ascertain what is, but not what should be, and outside of its domain value judgements of all kinds remain necessary.
Albert Einstein (1879 - 1955), Out of My Later Years, 1936
Science without religion is lame, religion without science is blind.
Albert Einstein (1879 - 1955), "Science, Philosophy and Religion: a Symposium", 1941

When a distinguished but elderly scientist states that something is possible, he is almost certainly right. When he states that something is impossible, he is very probably wrong.
Arthur C. Clarke (1917 -), Clarke's first law
Science has proof without any certainty. Creationists have certainty without any proof.
Ashley Montague
Science may set limits to knowledge, but should not set limits to imagination.
Bertrand Russell (1872 - 1970)
I maintain there is much more wonder in science than in pseudoscience. And in addition, to whatever measure this term has any meaning, science has the additional virtue, and it is not an inconsiderable one, of being true.
Carl Sagan (1934 - 1996)
All science is either physics or stamp collecting.
Ernest Rutherford (1871 - 1937), in J. B. Birks "Rutherford at Manchester" (1962)
Science is nothing but developed perception, interpreted intent, common sense rounded out and minutely articulated.
George Santayana (1863 - 1952)
Nothing shocks me. I'm a scientist.
Harrison Ford (1942 -), as Indiana Jones
Science is facts; just as houses are made of stones, so is science made of facts; but a pile of stones is not a house and a collection of facts is not necessarily science.
Henri Poincare (1854 - 1912)
There are in fact two things, science and opinion; the former begets knowledge, the latter ignorance.
Hippocrates (460 BC - 377 BC), Law
Science is organized knowledge. Wisdom is organized life.
Immanuel Kant (1724 - 1804)
The most exciting phrase to hear in science, the one that heralds new discoveries, is not 'Eureka!' (I found it!) but 'That's funny ...'
Isaac Asimov (1920 - 1992)
Perfect as the wing of a bird may be, it will never enable the bird to fly if unsupported by the air. Facts are the air of science. Without them a man of science can never rise.
Ivan Pavlov (1849 - 1936)
That is the essence of science: ask an impertinent question, and you are on your way to the pertinent answer.
Jacob Bronowski, The Ascent of Man, 1973
It is a good morning exercise for a research scientist to discard a pet hypothesis every day before breakfast. It keeps him young.
Konrad Lorenz (1903 - 1989)
The cloning of humans is on most of the lists of things to worry about from Science, along with behaviour control, genetic engineering, transplanted heads, computer poetry and the unrestrained growth of plastic flowers.
Lewis Thomas (1913 - 1993)
There are no such things as applied sciences, only applications of science.
Louis Pasteur (1822 - 1895)
As an adolescent I aspired to lasting fame, I craved factual certainty, and I thirsted for a meaningful vision of human life - so I became a scientist. This is like becoming an archbishop so you can meet girls.
M. Cartmill
I am among those who think that science has great beauty. A scientist in his laboratory is not only a technician: he is also a child placed before natural phenomena which impress him like a fairy tale.
Marie Curie (1867 - 1934)
We must not forget that when radium was discovered no one knew that it would prove useful in hospitals. The work was one of pure science. And this is a proof that scientific work must not be considered from the point of view of the direct usefulness of it. It must be done for itself, for the beauty of science, and then there is always the chance that a scientific discovery may become like the radium a benefit for humanity.
Marie Curie (1867 - 1934), Lecture at Vassar College, May 14, 1921
There is something fascinating about science. One gets such wholesale returns of conjecture out of such a trifling investment of fact.
Mark Twain (1835 - 1910)
Our scientific power has outrun our spiritual power. We have guided missiles and misguided men.
Martin Luther King Jr. (1929 - 1968), Strength to Love, 1963
A new scientific truth does not triumph by convincing its opponents and making them see the light, but rather because its opponents eventually die, and a new generation grows up that is familiar with it.
Max Planck, Scientific Autobiography and Other Papers, 1950
As soon as questions of will or decision or reason or choice of action arise, human science is at a loss.
Noam Chomsky (1928 -), in a television interview
In science one tries to tell people, in such a way as to be understood by everyone, something that no one ever knew before. But in poetry, it's the exact opposite.
Paul Dirac (1902 - 1984)
I believe that a scientist looking at nonscientific problems is just as dumb as the next guy.
Richard Feynman (1918 - 1988)
Philosophers say a great deal about what is absolutely necessary for science, and it is always, so far as one can see, rather naive, and probably wrong.
Richard Feynman (1918 - 1988)
Science is one thing, wisdom is another. Science is an edged tool, with which men play like children, and cut their own fingers.
Sir Arthur Eddington (1882 - 1944), Attributed in Robert L. Weber "More Random Walks in Science", 1982
In science the credit goes to the man who convinces the world, not the man to whom the idea first occurs.

Sir Francis Darwin (1848 - 1925), Eugenics Review, April 1914
The important thing in science is not so much to obtain new facts as to discover new ways of thinking about them.
Sir William Bragg (1862 - 1942)
In science, 'fact' can only mean 'confirmed to such a degree that it would be perverse to withhold provisional assent.' I suppose that apples might start to rise tomorrow, but the possibility does not merit equal time in physics classrooms.
Stephen Jay Gould (1941 - 2002)
The most important scientific revolutions all include, as their only common feature, the dethronement of human arrogance from one pedestal after another of previous convictions about our centrality in the cosmos.
Stephen Jay Gould (1941 - 2002)
The effort to understand the universe is one of the very few things that lifts human life a little above the level of farce, and gives it some of the grace of tragedy.
Steven Weinberg (1933 -)
Science is nothing but trained and organized common sense, differing from the latter only as a veteran may differ from a raw recruit: and its methods differ from those of common sense only as far as the guardsman's cut and thrust differ from the manner in which a savage wields his club.
Thomas H. Huxley (1825 - 1895)
The great tragedy of Science - the slaying of a beautiful hypothesis by an ugly fact.
Thomas H. Huxley (1825 - 1895)
If scientific reasoning were limited to the logical processes of arithmetic, we should not get very far in our understanding of the physical world. One might as well attempt to grasp the game of poker entirely by the use of the mathematics of probability.
Vannevar Bush (1890 - 1974)
Every science begins as philosophy and ends as art.
Will Durant (1885 - 1981), The Story of Philosophy, 1926

Secrets

To him that you tell your secret you resign your liberty.
Anonymous, Proverb
Three may keep a secret, if two of them are dead.
Benjamin Franklin (1706 - 1790)
No one gossips about other people's secret virtues.
Bertrand Russell (1872 - 1970)
The best way to divulge a secret is to tell someone not to say anything about it.
Charles Fleischer, TED Talk: All things are Moleeds, February 2005
All secrets are deep. All secrets become dark. That's in the nature of secrets.
Cory Doctorow, Someone Comes To Town, Someone Leaves Town, 2005
If you have to keep something secret it's because you shouldn't be doing it in the first place!
David Nicholls, One Day, 2010
Look in the mirror. The face that pins you with its double gaze reveals a chastening secret.
Diane Ackerman
The first rule of life is to reveal nothing, to be exceptionally cautious in what you say, in whatever company you may find yourself. If you have a secret, you have only to whisper it to your dearest friend with the strictest injunction that it will go no further, and within half a day the story is all over town, and when you do make what would seem to be a perfectly sensible remark, you will find it reported in the most grotesque form, thus incurring no end of criticism to rebound upon you.
Elizabeth Aston, The Darcy Connection, 2008
Trade your secrets and become who you are.
Frank Warren, PostSecret, 09-06-08
There are no secrets better kept than the secrets that everybody guesses.
George Bernard Shaw (1856 - 1950), "Mrs. Warren's Profession" (1893), act III
If you reveal your secrets to the wind you should not blame the wind for revealing them to the trees.
Kahlil Gibran (1883 - 1931)
A neurosis is a secret that you don't know you are keeping.
Kenneth Tynan
The face is the mirror of the mind, and eyes without speaking confess the secrets of the heart.
Saint Jerome (374 AD - 419 AD)
Secret thoughts and open countenance will go safely over the whole world.
Scipione Alberti

Security

The superior man, when resting in safety, does not forget that danger may come. When in a state of security he does not forget the possibility of ruin. When all is orderly, he does not forget that disorder may come. Thus his person is not endangered, and his States and all their clans are preserved.
Confucius (551 BC - 479 BC)
Better be despised for too anxious apprehensions, than ruined by too confident security.
Edmund Burke (1729 - 1797)
There is no security on this earth, there is only opportunity.
General Douglas MacArthur (1880 - 1964)
There is no security on this earth; there is only opportunity.
General Douglas MacArthur (1880 - 1964)
Life is either a daring adventure or nothing. Security does not exist in nature, nor do the children of men as a whole experience it. Avoiding danger is no safer in the long run than exposure.
Helen Keller (1880 - 1968)

Security is mostly a superstition. It does not exist in nature.... Life is either a daring adventure or nothing.
Helen Keller (1880 - 1968), The Open Door (1957)
Too many people are thinking of security instead of opportunity. They seem more afraid of life than death.
James F. Byrnes (1879 - 1972)
The most certain test by which we judge whether a country is really free is the amount of security enjoyed by minorities.
Lord Acton
Security is a kind of death.
Tennessee Williams (1911 - 1983)
No one can build his security upon the nobleness of another person.
Willa Cather (1873 - 1947)

Self-esteem

The reward for doing right is mostly an internal phenomenon: self-respect, dignity, integrity, and self- esteem.
Dr. Laura Schlessinger
So much is a man worth as he esteems himself.
Francois Rabelais (1494 - 1553), 1532
I think high self-esteem is overrated. A little low self-esteem is actually quite good...Maybe you're not the best, so you should work a little harder.
Jay Leno (1950 -), O Magazine, February 2003
A man cannot be comfortable without his own approval.
Mark Twain (1835 - 1910)
Self-esteem is the reputation we acquire with ourselves.
Nathaniel Branden
If you must love your neighbor as yourself, it is at least as fair to love yourself as your neighbor.
Sebastien-Roch Nicolas

Selfishness

To be stupid, selfish, and have good health are three requirements for happiness, though if stupidity is lacking, all is lost.
Gustave Flaubert (1821 - 1880)
Manifest plainness,
Embrace simplicity,
Reduce selfishness,
Have few desires.
Lao-tzu (604 BC - 531 BC), The Way of Lao-tzu
Forgiveness is almost a selfish act because of its immense benefits to the one who forgives.
Lawana Blackwell, The Dowry of Miss Lydia Clark, 1999
Selfishness is not living as one wishes to live, it is asking others to live as one wishes to live.
Oscar Wilde (1854 - 1900)
Glory built on selfish principles is shame and guilt.
William Cowper (1731 - 1800)

Service

Be alert to give service. What counts a great deal in life is what we do for others.
Anonymous
Great services are not canceled by one act or by one single error.
Benjamin Disraeli (1804 - 1881)
While you are not able to serve men, how can you serve spirits [of the dead]?...While you do not know life, how can you know about death?
Confucius (551 BC - 479 BC), The Confucian Analects
Sow good services; sweet remembrances will grow them.
Madame de Stael (1766 - 1817)
I've come to believe that each of us has a personal calling that's as unique as a fingerprint - and that the best way to succeed is to discover what you love and then find a way to offer it to others in the form of service, working hard, and also allowing the energy of the universe to lead you.
Oprah Winfrey (1954 -), O Magazine, September 2002
Be silent as to services you have rendered, but speak of favours you have received.
Seneca (5 BC - 65 AD)

Sex

It is with our passions, as it is with fire and water, they are good servants but bad masters.
Aesop (620 BC - 560 BC)
Confidence is the sexiest thing a woman can have. It's much sexier than any body part.
Aimee Mullins, Oprah Magazine, May 2004
The happiness of a man in this life does not consist in the absence but in the mastery of his passions.
Alfred Lord Tennyson (1809 - 1892)
Any piece of clothing can be sexy with a quietly passionate woman inside it.
Anonymous, O Magazine, The Shy Girl's Guide to Sex, February 2003
Instead of fulfilling the promise of infinite orgasmic bliss, sex in the America of the feminine mystique is becoming a strangely joyless national compulsion, if not a contemptuous mockery.
Betty Friedan (1921 - 2006)
Women need a reason to have sex. Men just need a place.
Billy Crystal (1947 -)

Mortal lovers must not try to remain at the first step; for lasting passion is the dream of a harlot and from it we wake in despair.
C. S. Lewis (1898 - 1963), 'The Pilgrim's Regress'
It's just human. We all have the jungle inside of us. We all have wants and needs and desires, strange as they may seem. If you stop to think about it, we're all pretty creative, cooking up all these fantasies. it's like a kind of poetry.
Diane Frolov and Andrew Schneider, Northern Exposure, Mister Sandman, 1994
I'm too shy to express my sexual needs except over the phone to people I don't know.
Garry Shandling (1949 -)
I can remember when the air was clean and sex was dirty.
George Burns (1896 - 1996)
Sexually,we are all competing for the same seat on the bus and the thing that holds it together is the tightly held conceit that we are all sexual gods. How can I believe in my own uniqueness when there's a cat out there exactly the same as me?
Jeff Melvoin, Northern Exposure, Altered Egos, 1993
A man can sleep around, no questions asked, but if a woman makes nineteen or twenty mistakes she's a tramp.
Joan Rivers (1935 -)
In English, we don't have a word for people who aren't virgins. What the non-virgin lexical gap really made me think was that our obsession with sexual purity is such that once you are no longer this THING, you are indescribable.
John Green, Vlogbrothers, Dumping My 15-Year-Old Girlfriend, 09-24-13
Sexuality is important, but it's certainly not the most interesting or important thing happening to you right now. We live in a world that tells us that there are only two important things. One is the acquisition of goods and the other is either the acquisition or avoidance of sex, but it turns out that the question of who's a virgin and who's a virgout is not the most interesting question.
John Green, Vlogbrothers, Dumping My 15-Year-Old Girlfriend, 09-24-13
In America sex is an obsession, in other parts of the world it is a fact.
Marlene Dietrich (1901 - 1992)
Does it really matter what these affectionate people do– so long as they don't do it in the streets and frighten the horses!
Mrs. Patrick Campbell
One thing I've learned in all these years is not to make love when you really don't feel it; there's probably nothing worse you can do to yourself than that.
Norman Mailer (1923 - 2007)
Life is a sexually transmitted disease.
R. D. Laing
Desperate is not a sexual preference.
Randy K. Milholland, Something Postive, 01-08-09
I know love and lust don't always keep the same company.
Stephenie Meyer, Twilight, 2005
But seduction isn't making someone do what they don't want to do. Seduction is enticing someone into doing what they secretly want to do already.
Waiter Rant, Waiter Rant weblog, 11-29-05
I know nothing about sex because I was always married.
Zsa Zsa Gabor (1919 -)
Silence is a text easy to misread.
A. A. Attanasio, 'The Eagle and the Sword'
'Tis better to be silent and be thought a fool, than to speak and remove all doubt.
Abraham Lincoln (1809 - 1865), (attributed)
Better to remain silent and be thought a fool than to speak out and remove all doubt.
Abraham Lincoln (1809 - 1865)
He who does not know how to be silent will not know how to speak.
Ausonius
The eternal silence of these infinite spaces fills me with dread.
Blaise Pascal (1623 - 1662)
Oppression can only survive through silence.
Carmen de Monteflores
I think the first virtue is to restrain the tongue; he approaches nearest to gods who knows how to be silent, even though he is in the right.
Cato the Elder (234 BC - 149 BC)
Silence is more musical than any song.
Christina Rossetti (1830 - 1894)
A fair request should be followed by the deed in silence.
Dante Alighieri (1265 - 1321), The Divine Comedy
My personal hobbies are reading, listening to music, and silence.
Edith Sitwell (1887 - 1964)
Learn to get in touch with the silence within yourself and know that everything in this life has a purpose.
Elisabeth Kubler-Ross
There is no need to go to India or anywhere else to find peace. You will find that deep place of silence right in your room, your garden or even your bathtub.
Elisabeth Kubler-Ross
Silence is the most perfect expression of scorn.
George Bernard Shaw (1856 - 1950), Back to Methuselah (1921) pt. 5
With silence favor me.
(Favete Linguis)
Horace (65 BC - 8 BC)
A good word is an easy obligation; but not to speak ill, requires only our silence, which costs nothing.
John Tillotson (1630 - 1694)
Silence is one of the hardest arguments to refute.
Josh Billings (1818 - 1885)
I don't want to talk as much. It's nicer to think dear, pretty thoughts and keep them in one's heart, like treasures. I don't like to have them laughed at or wondered over.
L. M. Montgomery (1874 - 1942), Anne of Green Gables, 1908

The most profound statements are often said in silence.
Lynn Johnston (1947 -), For Better or For Worse, 01-15-04
In the attitude of silence the soul finds the path in a clearer light, and what is elusive and deceptive resolves itself into crystal clearness. Our life is a long and arduous quest after Truth.
Mahatma Gandhi (1869 - 1948)
Well-timed silence hath more eloquence than speech.
Martin Farquhar Tupper
In the end, we will remember not the words of our enemies, but the silence of our friends.
Martin Luther King Jr. (1929 - 1968)
Our lives begin to end the day we become silent about things that matter.
Martin Luther King Jr. (1929 - 1968)
In silence man can most readily preserve his integrity.
Meister Eckhart
Silence is golden when you can't think of a good answer.
Muhammad Ali (1942 -), "More Than a Hero"
Not merely an absence of noise, Real Silence begins when a reasonable being withdraws from the noise in order to find peace and order in his inner sanctuary.
Peter Minard
I have often regretted my speech, never my silence.
Publilius Syrus (~ 100 BC), Maxims
It is better to be silent, or to say things of more value than silence. Sooner throw a pearl at hazard than an idle or useless word; and do not say a little in many words, but a great deal in a few.
Pythagoras (582 BC - 507 BC)
The cruelest lies are often told in silence.
Robert Louis Stevenson (1850 - 1894)
Nothing is so good for an ignorant man as silence; and if he was sensible of this he would not be ignorant.
Saadi (1184 - 1291)
Silence propagates itself, and the longer talk has been suspended, the more difficult it is to find anything to say.
Samuel Johnson (1709 - 1784)
It is a great thing to know the season for speech and the season for silence.
Seneca (5 BC - 65 AD)
Silence is the virtue of fools.
Sir Francis Bacon (1561 - 1626)
There are grammatical errors even in his silence.
Stanislaw J. Lec (1909 - 1966), "Unkempt Thoughts"
Words are a heavy thing...they weigh you down. If birds talked, they couldn't fly.
Sy Rosen and Christian Williams, Northern Exposure, On Your Own, 1992
He had occasional flashes of silence, that made his conversation perfectly delightful.
Sydney Smith (1771 - 1845), referring to Macaulay
Their silence is sufficient praise.
Terence (185 BC - 159 BC)
Under all speech that is good for anything there lies a silence that is better. Silence is deep as eternity; speech is as shallow as time.
Thomas Carlyle (1795 - 1881), Essay on Sir Walter Scott, 1881
Under all speech that is good for anything there lies a silence that is better. Silence is deep as Eternity; speech is shallow as Time.
Thomas Carlyle (1795 - 1881)
A man's silence is wonderful to listen to.
Thomas Hardy
Of those who say nothing, few are silent.
Thomas Neill
Silence is one of the great arts of conversation, as allowed by Cicero himself, who says, 'there is not only an art, but an eloquence in it.' A well bred woman may easily and effectually promote the most useful and elegant conversation without speaking a word. The modes of speech are scarcely more variable than the modes of silence.
Tom Blair
There is a wide difference between speaking to deceive, and being silent to be impenetrable.
Voltaire (1694 - 1778)
True silence is the rest of the mind; it is to the spirit what sleep is to the body, nourishment and refreshment.
William Penn (1644 - 1718)
Silence is the perfectest herald of joy: I were but little happy, if I could say how much.
William Shakespeare (1564 - 1616), "Much Ado about Nothing", Act 2 scene 1
The rest is silence.
William Shakespeare (1564 - 1616), "Hamlet", Act 5 scene 2

Simplicity

Everything should be made as simple as possible, but not one bit simpler.
Albert Einstein (1879 - 1955), (attributed)
Seek simplicity, and distrust it.
Alfred North Whitehead (1861 - 1947)
It is simplicity that makes the uneducated more effective than the educated when addressing popular audiences.
Aristotle (384 BC - 322 BC), Rhetoric
Go confidently in the direction of your dreams! Live the life you've imagined. As you simplify your life, the laws of the universe will be simpler.
Henry David Thoreau (1817 - 1862)
Simplicity is the peak of civilization.
Jessie Sampter
Nothing is as simple as we hope it will be.
Jim Horning

Manifest plainness,
Embrace simplicity,
Reduce selfishness,
Have few desires.
Lao-tzu (604 BC - 531 BC), The Way of Lao-tzu
I adore simple pleasures. They are the last refuge of the complex.
Oscar Wilde (1854 - 1900), The Picture of Dorian Gray, 1891

Sincerely

It is dangerous to be sincere unless you are also stupid.
George Bernard Shaw (1856 - 1950), Man and Superman (1903) "Maxims for Revolutionists"
The secret of success is sincerity. Once you can fake that you've got it made.
Jean Giraudoux (1882 - 1944)
Judge thyself with the judgment of sincerity, and thou will judge others with the judgment of charity.
John Mitchell Mason
I am not sincere, even when I say I am not.
Jules Renard (1864 - 1910)
Sincerity is the way of Heaven.
Mencius (371 BC - 289 BC), Works
A little sincerity is a dangerous thing, and a great deal of it is absolutely fatal.
Oscar Wilde (1854 - 1900), The Critic as Artist, part 2, 1891

Sleep

Laugh and the world laughs with you, snore and you sleep alone.
Anthony Burgess (1917 - 1993)
It is better to sleep on things beforehand than lie awake about them afterward.
Baltasar Gracian
Early to bed and early to rise makes a man healthy, wealthy, and wise.
Benjamin Franklin (1706 - 1790)
If you can't sleep, then get up and do something instead of lying there and worrying. It's the worry that gets you, not the loss of sleep.
Dale Carnegie
Life is something that happens when you can't get to sleep.
Fran Lebowitz (1950 -)
There is a time for many words, and there is also a time for sleep.
Homer (800 BC - 700 BC), The Odyssey
To achieve the impossible dream, try going to sleep.
Joan Klempner
People who say they sleep like a baby usually don't have one.
Leo J. Burke
Not being able to sleep is terrible. You have the misery of having partied all night... without the satisfaction.
Lynn Johnston (1947 -), For Better or For Worse, 07-22-06
I have never taken any exercise except sleeping and resting.
Mark Twain (1835 - 1910)
Oh sleep! It is a gentle thing,
Beloved from pole to pole.
Samuel Taylor Coleridge (1772 - 1834)
When I woke up this morning my girlfriend asked me, 'Did you sleep good?' I said 'No, I made a few mistakes.'
Steven Wright (1955 -)
I guess staying up late is good preparation for sweet dreams.
Takayuki Ikkaku, Arisa Hosaka and Toshihiro Kawabata, Animal Crossing: Wild World, 2005
[Sleep is] the golden chain that ties health and our bodies together.
Thomas Dekker (1572 - 1632)
Death's brother, Sleep.
Virgil (70 BC - 19 BC), Aeneid
A great perturbation in nature, to receive at once the benefit of sleep and do the effects of watching!
William Shakespeare (1564 - 1616), Macbeth, Act V, sc. 1
Care keeps his watch in every old man's eye,
And where care lodges, sleep will never lie;
But where unbruised youth with unstuff'd brain
Doth couch his limbs, there golden sleep doth reign.
William Shakespeare (1564 - 1616), Romeo and Juliet, Act II, sc. 3
He that sleeps feels not the tooth-ache.
William Shakespeare (1564 - 1616), Cymbeline, Act V, sc. 4
Methought I heard a voice cry, "Sleep no more! Macbeth does murder sleep!"- the innocent sleep.
William Shakespeare (1564 - 1616), Macbeth, Act II, sc. 2
O sleep, O gentle sleep, nature's soft nurse, how have I frighted thee, that thou no more wilt weigh my eyelids down, and steep my senses in forgetfulness.
William Shakespeare (1564 - 1616), Henry IV, Part II, Act III, sc. 1
O sleep, thou ape of death, lie dull upon her and be her sense but as a monument, thus in a chapel lying.
William Shakespeare (1564 - 1616), Cymbeline, Act II, sc. 2
Shake off this downy sleep, death's counterfeit, and look on death itself.
William Shakespeare (1564 - 1616), Macbeth, Act II, sc. 3
Sleep that knits up the ravell'd sleave of care, the death of each day's life, sore labour's bath, balm of hurt minds, great nature's second course, chief nourisher in life's feast.
William Shakespeare (1564 - 1616), Macbeth, Act II, sc. 2
Sleep, that sometimes shuts up sorrow's eye, steal me awhile from mine own company.
William Shakespeare (1564 - 1616), A Midsummer Night's Dream, Act III, sc. 2

Snow

A lot of people like snow. I find it to be an unnecessary freezing of water.
Carl Reiner
In the bleak midwinter Frosty wind made moan, Earth stood hard as iron, Water like a stone; Snow had fallen, snow on snow, Snow on snow, In the bleak midwinter, Long ago.
Christina Rossetti (1830 - 1894), A Christmas Carol
The aging process has you firmly in its grasp if you never get the urge to throw a snowball.
Doug Larson
Whose woods these are I think I know. His house is in the village though; He will not see me stopping here To watch his woods fill up with snow.
Robert Frost (1874 - 1963), Stopping by Woods on a Snowy Evening

Society

To give up the task of reforming society is to give up one's responsibility as a free man.
Alan Paton (1903 - 1988)
He who is unable to live in society, or who has no need because he is sufficient for himself, must be either a beast or a god.
Aristotle (384 BC - 322 BC), Politics
Society, my dear, is like salt water, good to swim in but hard to swallow.
Arthur Stringer, "The Silver Poppy"
A society of sheep must in time beget a government of wolves.
Bertrand de Jouvenal
We live in a society exquisitely dependent on science and technology, in which hardly anyone knows anything about science and technology.
Carl Sagan (1934 - 1996)
A nation is a society united by a delusion about its ancestry and by common hatred of its neighbors.
Dean William R. Inge
The nature of society is largely determined by the direction in which talent and ambition flow-by the tilt of the social landscape.
Eric Hoffer (1902 - 1983), The Temper of Our Time, 1967
Be very circumspect in the choice of thy company. In the society of thine equals thou shalt enjoy more pleasure; in the society of thy superiors thou shalt find more profit. To be the best in the company is the way to grow worse.
Francis Quarles (1592 - 1644)
What can you say about a society that says that God is dead and Elvis is alive?
Irv Kupcinet
But society has now fairly got the better of individuality; and the danger which threatens human nature is not the excess, but the deficiency, of personal impulses and preferences.
John Stuart Mill (1806 - 1873), On Liberty,chapter 3, 1859
Everyone who receives the protection of society owes a return for the benefit.
John Stuart Mill (1806 - 1873), On Liberty
It is no measure of health to be well adjusted to a profoundly sick society.
Krishnamurti
The needs of society determine its ethics.
Maya Angelou (1928 -)
Do not speak ill of society, Algie. Only people who can't get in do that.
Oscar Wilde (1854 - 1900), The Importance of Being Earnest
I'm against a homogenized society, because I want the cream to rise.
Robert Frost (1874 - 1963)
There is no nonsense so gross that society will not, at some time, make a doctrine of it and defend it with every weapon of communal stupidity.
Robertson Davies
Man seeketh in society comfort, use and protection.
Sir Francis Bacon (1561 - 1626), The Advancement of Learning, 1605
We must beware of trying to build a society in which nobody counts for anything except a politician or an official, a society where enterprise gains no reward and thrift no privileges.
Sir Winston Churchill (1874 - 1965), Radio broadcast, London, March 21, 1943

Speech

Let thy speech be short, comprehending much in a few words.
Aprocrypha
Bore: one who has the power of speech but not the capacity for conversation.
Benjamin Disraeli (1804 - 1881)
Free speech carries with it some freedom to listen.
Bob Marley (1945 - 1981)
Thought is the fountain of speech.
Chrysippus (280 BC - 207 BC)
Great wisdom is generous; petty wisdom is contentious. Great speech is impassioned, small speech cantankerous.
Chuang-tzu (369 BC - 286 BC), On Leveling All Things
The superior man is modest in his speech, but exceeds in his actions.
Confucius (551 BC - 479 BC), The Confucian Analects
All speech is vain and empty unless it be accompanied by action.
Demosthenes (384 BC - 322 BC)
Today's public figures can no longer write their own speeches or books, and there is some evidence that they can't read them either.
Gore Vidal (1925 -)
What this country needs is more free speech worth listening to.
Hansell B. Duckett

Readiness of speech is often inability to hold the tongue.
Jean Baptiste Rousseau
The First Amendment is often inconvenient. But that is besides the point.
Inconvenience does not absolve the government of its obligation to tolerate speech.
Justice Anthony Kennedy (1936 -)
Speak when you are angry–and you will make the best speech you'll ever regret.
Laurence J. Peter (1919 - 1988)
It usually takes more than three weeks to prepare a good impromptu speech.
Mark Twain (1835 - 1910)
Well-timed silence hath more eloquence than speech.
Martin Fraquhar Tupper
Be a craftsman in speech that thou mayest be strong, for the strength of one is the
tongue, and speech is mightier than all fighting.
Maxims of Ptahhotep, 3400 B.C.
Do not fight verbosity with words: speech is given to all, intelligence to few.
Moralia
Tears at times have all the weight of speech.
Ovid (43 BC - 17 AD)
I have often regretted my speech, never my silence.
Publilius Syrus (~ 100 BC), Maxims
Speech is a mirror of the soul: as a man speaks, so is he.
Publilius Syrus (~ 100 BC), Maxims
In anger we should refrain both from speech and action.
Pythagoras (582 BC - 507 BC)
Much talking is the cause of danger. Silence is the means of avoiding misfortune. The
talkative parrot is shut up in a cage. Other birds, without speech, fly freely about.
Saskya Pandita
It is a great thing to know the season for speech and the season for silence.
Seneca (5 BC - 65 AD)
Speech is the mirror of the mind.
(Imago Animi Sermo Est)
Seneca (5 BC - 65 AD)
Where the speech is corrupted, the mind is also.
Seneca (5 BC - 65 AD)
Discretion in speech is more than eloquence.
Sir Francis Bacon (1561 - 1626)
Look wise, say nothing, and grunt. Speech was given to conceal thought.
Sir William Osler (1849 - 1919)
Where there is a great deal of free speech there is always a certain amount of foolish
speech.
Sir Winston Churchill (1874 - 1965)
Much speech is one thing, well-timed speech is another.
Sophocles (496 BC - 406 BC)
Speech is human, silence is divine, yet also brutish and dead: therefore we must learn
both arts.
Thomas Carlyle (1795 - 1881)
In a free state there should be freedom of speech and thought.
Tiberius (42 BC - 37 AD)
If nobody spoke unless he had something to say, the human race would very soon
lose the use of speech.
W. Somerset Maugham (1874 - 1965), The Painted Veil, 1925
The habit of common and continuous speech is a symptom of mental deficiency.
Walter Bagehot (1826 - 1877)
Speak properly, and in as few words as you can, but always plainly; for the end of
speech is not ostentation, but to be understood.
William Penn (1644 - 1718)
Be check'd for silence, but never tax'd for speech.
William Shakespeare (1564 - 1616), All's Well that Ends Well, Act I, sc. 1
Be it art or hap, he hath spoken true.
William Shakespeare (1564 - 1616), Antony and Cleopatra, Act II, sc. 3
Brevity is the soul of wit.
William Shakespeare (1564 - 1616), Hamlet, Act II, sc. 2
How absolute the knave is! we must speak by the card, or equivocation will undo us.
William Shakespeare (1564 - 1616), Hamlet, Act V, sc. 1
I do know of these that... only are reputed wise for saying nothing.
William Shakespeare (1564 - 1616), The Merchant of Venice, Act I, sc. 1
I do not speak to thee in drink but in tears, not in pleasure but in passion, not in
words only, but in woes also.
William Shakespeare (1564 - 1616), Henry IV, Part I, Act II, sc. 4
Ill deeds are doubled with an evil word.
William Shakespeare (1564 - 1616), The Comedy of Errors, Act III, sc. 2
Men of few words are the best men.
William Shakespeare (1564 - 1616), Henry V, Act III, sc. 2
Talkers are no good doers; be assur'd we come to use our hands and not our tongues.
William Shakespeare (1564 - 1616), Richard III, Act I, sc. 3
Things are often spoke and seldom meant.
William Shakespeare (1564 - 1616), Henry VI, Part II, Act III, sc. 1
Though thou speak'st truth, methink thou speak'st not well.
William Shakespeare (1564 - 1616), Coriolanus, Act I, sc. 6
Weighest thy words before thou givest them breath.
William Shakespeare (1564 - 1616), Othello, Act III, sc. 3
I have often regretted my speech, never my silence.
Xenocrates (396 BC - 314 BC)

Sports

Sport is imposing order on what was chaos.
Anthony Starr

Some people think football is a matter of life and death. I don't like that attitude. I
can assure them it is much more serious than that.
Bill Shankly, In Sunday Times (UK) Oct. 4 1981
Anybody who watches three games of football in a row should be declared brain
dead.
Erma Bombeck (1927 - 1996)
Football is a mistake. It combines the two worst elements of American life. Violence
and committee meetings.
George F. Will (1941 -)
Sports serve society by providing vivid examples of excellence.
George F. Will (1941 -)
For when the One Great Scorer comes
To write against your name,
He marks-not that you won or lost-
But how you played the game.
Grantland Rice, "Alumunus Football," Only the Brave and Other Poems, p. 144 (1941)
Sports do not build character. They reveal it.
Heywood Broun (1888 - 1939)
Nobody in the game of football should be called a genius. A genius is somebody like
Norman Einstein.
Joe Theismann, Former quarterback
I started thinking about little kids putting a cylindrical peg through a circular hole,
and how they do it over and over again for months when they figure it out, and how
basketball was basically just a slightly more aerobic version of that same exercise.
John Green, The Fault in Our Stars, 2012
It's not so important who starts the game but who finishes it.
John Wooden (1910 -)
If it weren't for baseball, many kids wouldn't know what a millionaire looked like.
Phyllis Diller
For people to judge a man's worth and his very manhood according to the way he
feels about sport, and not to recognize it for the piddly, inconsequential goings on
that it really is...
Robin Green and Mitchell Burgess, Northern Exposure, Birds of a Feather, 1993
I went to a fight the other night, and a hockey game broke out.
Rodney Dangerfield (1921 - 2004)
Not every age is fit for childish sports.
Titus Maccius Plautus (254 BC - 184 BC)
A good hockey player plays where the puck is. A great hockey player plays where the
puck is going to be.
Wayne Gretzky (1961 -)
If all the year were playing holidays; To sport would be as tedious as to work.
William Shakespeare (1564 - 1616), 'The First Part of King Henry the IV'
Desire is the most important factor in the success of any athlete.
Willie Shoemaker
Baseball is 90% mental, the other half is physical.
Yogi Berra (1925 -)

Spring

If we had no winter, the spring would not be so pleasant: if we did not sometimes
taste of adversity, prosperity would not be so welcome.
Anne Bradstreet (1612 - 1672), 'Meditations Divine and Moral,' 1655
[Spring is] when life's alive in everything.
Christina Rossetti (1830 - 1894)
If there comes a little thaw,
Still the air is chill and raw,
Here and there a patch of snow,
Dirtier than the ground below,
Dribbles down a marshy flood;
Ankle-deep you stick in mud In the meadows while you sing,
"This is Spring."
Christopher Pearce Cranch, A Spring Growl
Well, spring sprang. We've had our state of grace and our little gift of sanctioned
madness, courtesy of Mother Nature. Thanks, Gaia. Much obliged. I guess it's time to
get back to that daily routine of living we like to call normal.
David Assael, Northern Exposure, Spring Break, 1991
Listen, can you hear it? Spring's sweet cantata. The strains of grass pushing through
the snow. The song of buds swelling on the vine. The tender timpani of a baby robin's
heart. Spring.
Diane Frolov and Andrew Schneider, Northern Exposure, Wake Up Call, 1992
Spring is when you feel like whistling even with a shoe full of slush.
Doug Larson
A little Madness in the Spring Is wholesome even for the King.
Emily Dickinson (1830 - 1886), No. 1333
To be interested in the changing seasons is a happier state of mind than to be
hopelessly in love with spring.
George Santayana (1863 - 1952)
[Spring is] a true reconstructionist.
Henry Timrod
If winter comes, can spring be far behind?
Percy Bysshe Shelley (1792 - 1822)
An optimist is the human personification of spring.
Susan J. Bissonette
Winter is on my head, but eternal spring is in my heart.
Victor Hugo (1802 - 1885)
In the spring time, the only pretty ring time, when birds do sing... sweet lovers love
the spring.
William Shakespeare (1564 - 1616), As You Like It, Act V, sc. 3

O, how this spring of love resembleth
The uncertain glory of an April day!
William Shakespeare (1564 - 1616), "The Two Gentlemen of Verona", Act 1 scene 3

Statistics

There are three kinds of lies: lies, damned lies, and statistics.
Benjamin Disraeli (1804 - 1881)
USA Today has come out with a new survey - apparently, three out of every four people make up 75% of the population.
David Letterman (1947 -)
Statistician: A man who believes figures don't lie, but admits that under analysis some of them won't stand up either.
Evan Esar (1899 - 1995), Esar's Comic Dictionary
Statistics: The only science that enables different experts using the same figures to draw different conclusions.
Evan Esar (1899 - 1995), Esar's Comic Dictionary
Smoking is one of the leading causes of statistics.
Fletcher Knebel
I could prove God statistically.
George Gallup (1901 - 1984)
A single death is a tragedy; a million deaths is a statistic.
Joseph Stalin (1879 - 1953)

Stress

Small minds are much distressed by little things. Great minds see them all but are not upset by them.
Francois de La Rochefoucauld (1613 - 1680)
If you ask what is the single most important key to longevity, I would have to say it is avoiding worry, stress and tension. And if you didn't ask me, I'd still have to say it.
George Burns (1896 - 1996)
I deal with stress in two ways because there are two kinds of stress. There's stress that you can take care of and there's stress that you can't. The first one, I take care of it as fast as possible, because putting it off always makes it worse. Things that I can't fix? I think about the fact that I can't fix them. I think about why I can't fix them and I come to terms with the fact that this is a problem that I'm not going to overcome and that the world is not a wish granting factory.
Hank Green, Vlogbrothers, Raw Onion, Twerking, and Speech Jam, 08-30-13
Reality is the leading cause of stress amongst those in touch with it.
Jane Wagner, (and Lily Tomlin)
If you are distressed by anything external, the pain is not due to the thing itself, but to your estimate of it; and this you have the power to revoke at any moment.
Marcus Aurelius Antoninus (121 AD - 180 AD)
It is how people respond to stress that determines whether they will profit from misfortune or be miserable.
Mihaly Csikszentmihalyi, Flow: The Psychology of Optimal Experience, 1990
Stress is an ignorant state. It believes that everything is an emergency. Nothing is that important.
Natalie Goldberg
Before you agree to do anything that might add even the smallest amount of stress to your life, ask yourself: What is my truest intention? Give yourself time to let a yes resound within you. When it's right, I guarantee that your entire body will feel it.
Oprah Winfrey (1954 -)
Throw out an alarming alarm clock. If the ring is loud and strident, you're waking up to instant stress. You shouldn't be bullied out of bed, just reminded that it's time to start your day.
Sharon Gold
If you had to define stress, it would not be far off if you said it was the process of living. The process of living is the process of having stress imposed on you and reacting to it.
Stanley J. Sarnoff, Man Under Stress, 1963
Exercise relieves stress. Nothing relieves exercise.
Takayuki Ikkaku, Arisa Hosaka and Toshihiro Kawabata, Animal Crossing: Wild World, 2005

Stupidity

Only two things are infinite, the universe and human stupidity, and I'm not sure about the former.
Albert Einstein (1879 - 1955)
Genius may have its limitations, but stupidity is not thus handicapped.
Elbert Hubbard (1856 - 1915)
Talk sense to a fool and he calls you foolish.
Euripides (484 BC - 406 BC), The Bacchae, circa 407 B.C.
Get all the fools on your side and you can be elected to anything.
Frank Dane
Against stupidity the gods themselves contend in vain.
Friedrich von Schiller (1759 - 1805)
It is dangerous to be sincere unless you are also stupid.
George Bernard Shaw (1856 - 1950), Man and Superman (1903) "Maxims for Revolutionists"
To be stupid, selfish, and have good health are three requirements for happiness, though if stupidity is lacking, all is lost.
Gustave Flaubert (1821 - 1880)
The two most common elements in the universe are Hydrogen and stupidity.
Harlan Ellison (1934 -)
Ordinarily he was insane, but he had lucid moments when he was merely stupid.
Heinrich Heine (1797 - 1856)
There are more fools in the world than there are people.
Heinrich Heine (1797 - 1856)

There is nothing worse than aggressive stupidity.
Johann Wolfgang von Goethe (1749 - 1832)
Insanity is just what we call stupidity when it doesn't make sense.
Josh Lieb, I am a Genius of Unspeakable Evil and I Want to be Your Class President, 2009
Nothing in all the world is more dangerous than sincere ignorance and conscientious stupidity.
Martin Luther King Jr. (1929 - 1968), Strength to Love, 1963
If there are no stupid questions, then what kind of questions do stupid people ask? Do they get smart just in time to ask questions?
Scott Adams (1957 -)
Strange as it seems, no amount of learning can cure stupidity, and higher education positively fortifies it.
Stephen Vizinczey, An Innocent Millionaire
Artificial Intelligence is no match for natural stupidity.
Unknown
Everyone is entitled to be stupid, but some abuse the privilege.
Unknown
Fools rush in where fools have been before.
Unknown
Never attribute to malice what can be adequately explained by stupidity.
Unknown, Hanlon's Razor
To succeed in the world it is not enough to be stupid, you must also be well-mannered.
Voltaire (1694 - 1778)
Lord, what fools these mortals be!
William Shakespeare (1564 - 1616), "A Midsummer Night's Dream", Act 3 scene 2

Success

Always bear in mind that your own resolution to succeed is more important than any one thing.
Abraham Lincoln (1809 - 1865)
If A is success in life, then A equals x plus y plus z. Work is x; y is play; and z is keeping your mouth shut.
Albert Einstein (1879 - 1955), Observer, Jan. 15, 1950
Try not to become a man of success but rather to become a man of value.
Albert Einstein (1879 - 1955)
A great secret of success is to go through life as a man who never gets used up.
Albert Schweitzer (1875 - 1965)
A discovery is said to be an accident meeting a prepared mind.
Albert Szent-Gyorgyi (1893 - 1986)
Stop seeing the obstacles you face as reasons why you can't do something. See them as a reason why you can. And celebrate your accomplishments on a daily basis.
Ali Vincent, Believe It, Be It: How Being the Biggest Loser Won Me Back My Life, 2009
To think about your life is to create it. You have to take ownership of where you are right now and know where you want to go before you can get there. Keep collecting evidence for your success. You can believe it, and you can be it.
Ali Vincent, Believe It, Be It: How Being the Biggest Loser Won Me Back My Life, 2009
To follow, without halt, one aim: There's the secret of success.
Anna Pavlova (1885 - 1931)
If your success is not on your own terms, if it looks good to the world but does not feel good in your heart, it is not success at all.
Anna Quindlen (1953 -)
Success is the necessary misfortune of life, but it is only to the very unfortunate that it comes early.
Anthony Trollope (1815 - 1882), Orley Farm, chapter 49, 1950
It is possible to fail in many ways...while to succeed is possible only in one way.
Aristotle (384 BC - 322 BC), Nichomachean Ethics
Of course there is no formula for success except perhaps an unconditional acceptance of life and what it brings.
Arthur Rubinstein (1886 - 1982)
Find somebody to be successful for. Raise their hopes. Think of their needs.
Barack Obama (1961 -), Arizona State Commencement Speech, 2009
I've come to embrace the notion that I haven't done enough in my life. I've come to confirm that one's title, even a title like president of the United States, says very little about how well one's life has been led. No matter how much you've done or how successful you've been, there's always more to do, always more to learn, and always more to achieve.
Barack Obama (1961 -), Arizona State Commencement Speech, 2009
That's what building a body of work is all about. It's about the daily labor, the many individual acts, the choices large and small that add up over time, over a lifetime to a lasting legacy. It's about not being satisfied with the latest achievement, the latest gold star, because the one thing I know about a body of work is that it's never finished. It's cumulative. It deepens and expands with each day you give your best. You may have setbacks and you may have failures, but you're not done. You haven't even started.
Barack Obama (1961 -), Arizona State Commencement Speech, 2009
The leaders we revere and the businesses that last are generally not the result of a narrow pursuit of popularity or personal advancement, but of devotion to some bigger purpose. That's the hallmark of real success. The other trapping of success might be the by product of this larger mission, but it can't be the central thing.
Barack Obama (1961 -), Arizona State Commencement Speech, 2009
Why be a man when you can be a success?
Bertolt Brecht (1898 - 1956)
I don't know the key to success, but the key to failure is trying to please everybody.
Bill Cosby (1937 -)
What's money? A man is a success if he gets up in the morning and goes to bed at night and in between does what he wants to do.
Bob Dylan (1941 -)

The person who makes a success of living is the one who see his goal steadily and aims for it unswervingly. That is dedication.
Cecil B. DeMille (1881 - 1959)
Nothing succeeds like the appearance of success.
Christopher Lasch
There is only one success - to be able to spend your life in your own way.
Christopher Morley (1890 - 1957)
There is only one success... to be able to spend your life in your own way, and not to give others absurd maddening claims upon it.
Christopher Morley (1890 - 1957), Where the Blue Begins,1922
The man of virtue makes the difficulty to be overcome his first business, and success only a subsequent consideration.
Confucius (551 BC - 479 BC), The Confucian Analects
Real success is finding your lifework in the work that you love.
David McCullough (1933 -)
Envy was just the tax you paid on success.
David Nicholls, One Day, 2010
Success in business requires training and discipline and hard work. But if you're not frightened by these things, the opportunities are just as great today as they ever were.
David Rockefeller (1915 -)
Aim for success, not perfection. Never give up your right to be wrong, because then you will lose the ability to learn new things and move forward with your life.
Dr. David M. Burns
We succeed only as we identify in life, or in war, or in anything else, a single overriding objective, and make all other considerations bend to that one objective.
Dwight D. Eisenhower (1890 - 1969), speech, April 2, 1957
When I was younger I thought success was something different. I thought, " When I grow up, I want to be famous. I want to be a star. I want to be in movies. When I grow up I want to see the world, drive nice cars. I want to have groupies." But my idea of success is different today. For me, the most important thing in your life is to live your life with integrity and not to give into peer pressure, to try to be something that you're not. To live your life as an honest and compassionate person. To contribute in some way.
Ellen DeGeneres, Tulane Commencement Speech, 2009
Success is counted sweetest by those who ne'er succeed.
Emily Dickinson (1830 - 1886)
Success is really about being ready for the good opportunities that come before you. It's not to have a detailed plan of everything that you're going to do. You can't plan innovation or inspiration, but you can be ready for it, and when you see it, you can jump on it.
Eric Schmidt, University of Pennsylvania Commencement Address, 2009
Now I understand what exhaustion is. It's not just a code word for heroin addiction. People don't teach you how to handle the workload that comes from a little bit of success, and it's something I'd never had to handle, because I'd been rejected for so long.
Felicia Day, The Washington Post, 04-03-12
Success didn't spoil me, I've always been insufferable.
Fran Lebowitz (1950 -)
Nothing changes your opinion of a friend so surely as success - yours or his.
Franklin P. Jones, Saturday Evening Post, November 29, 1953
I owe my success to having listened respectfully to the very best advice, and then going away and doing the exact opposite.
G. K. Chesterton (1874 - 1936)
Nothing fails like success.
Gerald Nachman
To freely bloom - that is my definition of success.
Gerry Spence, How to Argue and Win Every Time
My mother drew a distinction between achievement and success. She said that 'achievement is the knowledge that you have studied and worked hard and done the best that is in you. Success is being praised by others, and that's nice, too, but not as important or satisfying. Always aim for achievement and forget about success.'
Helen Hayes (1900 - 1993)
Men are born to succeed, not fail.
Henry David Thoreau (1817 - 1862)
Success usually comes to those who are too busy to be looking for it.
Henry David Thoreau (1817 - 1862)
Each success only buys an admission ticket to a more difficult problem.
Henry Kissinger (1923 -), Wilson Library Bulletin, March 1979
I can't give you a sure-fire formula for success, but I can give you a formula for failure: try to please everybody all the time.
Herbert Bayard Swope (1882 - 1958)
The toughest thing about success is that you've got to keep on being a success. Talent is only a starting point in this business. You've got to keep on working that talent. Someday I'll reach for it and it won't be there.
Irving Berlin (1888 - 1989), 1958
The secret of success is sincerity. Once you can fake that you've got it made.
Jean Giraudoux (1882 - 1944)
If you can break down those walls you've spent so many years building to protect yourself, you can achieve anything.
Jennifer Hudson, I Got This: How I Changed My Ways and Lost What Weighed Me Down, 2012
If you're... asking yourself why I have this success and you don't, don't be angry with me—stop and ask yourself what your issues are that are holding you back.
Jennifer Hudson, I Got This: How I Changed My Ways and Lost What Weighed Me Down, 2012
We can't let our insecurities own or destroy us. We have to face them head-on. That was part of the challenge that motivated me to take this journey. I wanted to see what I could do and, more important, I wanted to understand everything that was holding me back.
Jennifer Hudson, I Got This: How I Changed My Ways and Lost What Weighed Me Down, 2012
The secret to success in life is known only to those who have not succeeded.
John Churton Collins
What is the point of being alive if you don't at least try to do something remarkable?
John Green, An Abundance of Katherines, 2008
If you wish success in life, make perseverance your bosom friend, experience your wise counselor, caution your elder brother and hope your guardian genius.
Joseph Addison (1672 - 1719)
Having been here before and lost, to be here and win, I've got to tell you, winning is really a lot better than losing. Really a lot better.
Kate Winslet, Oscar Acceptance Speech, 02-22-09
There's no secret about success. Did you ever know a successful man who didn't tell you about it?
Kin Hubbard (1868 - 1930)
A successful individual typically sets his next goal somewhat but not too much above his last achievement. In this way he steadily raises his level of aspiration.
Kurt Lewin (1890 - 1947)
We pay a price for everything we get or take in this world; and although ambitions are well worth having, they are not to be cheaply won, but exact their dues of work and self-denial, anxiety and discouragement.
L. M. Montgomery (1874 - 1942), Anne of Green Gables, 1908
Sometimes in life you don't always feel like a winner, but that doesn't mean you're not a winner.
Lady Gaga (1986 -), Ellen Degeneres Show, 09-08-09
You're probably on the right track if you feel like a sidewalk worm during a rainstorm.
Larry Page, University of Michigan Commencement Address, 2009
All you need in this life is ignorance and confidence; then success is sure.
Mark Twain (1835 - 1910), Letter to Mrs Foote, Dec. 2, 1887
People fail forward to success.
Mary Kay Ash
If you have been touched by the success fairy, people think you know why. People think success breeds enlightenment and you are duty-bound to spread around like manure. Fertilize those young minds!
Meryl Streep (1949 -), Barnard Commencement Speech, 2010
My success has depended wholly on putting things over on people, so I'm not sure that I'm that great a role model. I am, however, an expert on pretending to be an expert on pretending to be an expert.
Meryl Streep (1949 -), Barnard Commencement Speech, 2010
You don't have to be famous. You just have to make your mother and father proud of you.
Meryl Streep (1949 -), Barnard Commencement Speech, 2010
Whenever I hear, 'It can't be done,' I know I'm close to success.
Michael Flatley, (Lord of the Dance) quoted by Eric Celeste
I learned early that sometimes you have to dig through garbage to get anywhere.
Michael Hainey, After Visiting Friends: A Son's Story, 2013
You always pass failure on the way to success.
Mickey Rooney (1920 -)
Success isn't permanent, and failure isn't fatal.
Mike Ditka (1939 -)
Formulate and stamp indelibly on your mind a mental picture of yourself as succeeding. Hold this picture tenaciously. Never permit it to fade. Your mind will seek to develop the picture...Do not build up obstacles in your imagination.
Norman Vincent Peale (1898 - 1993)
Forget about the fast lane. If you really want to fly, harness your power to your passion. Honor your calling. Everybody has one. Trust your heart, and success will come to you.
Oprah Winfrey (1954 -), Stanford Commencement Adress, 2008
How do I define success? Let me tell you, money's pretty nice. But having a lot of money does not automatically make you a successful person. What you want is money and meaning. You want your work to be meaningful, because meaning is what brings the real richness to your life.
Oprah Winfrey (1954 -), Stanford Commencement Adress, 2008
Get on stage. A lot. Try stuff. Make your best stab and keep stabbing. If it's there in your heart, it will eventually find its way out. Or you will give up and have a prudent, contented life doing something else.
Raymond Joseph Teller, Fury Letter written to Brian Brushwood, 10-18-93
I really feel as if the things we create together are not things we devised, but things we discovered, as if, in some sense, they were always there in us, waiting to be revealed, like the figure of Mercury waiting in a rough lump of marble.
Raymond Joseph Teller, Fury Letter written to Brian Brushwood, 10-18-93
We always felt as if every show was the most important thing in the world, but knew if we bombed, we'd live.
Raymond Joseph Teller, Fury Letter written to Brian Brushwood, 10-18-93
We made a solemn vow not to take any job outside of show business. We borrowed money from parents and friends, rather than take that lethal job waiting tables. This forced us to take any job offered to us. Anything. We once did a show in the middle of the Benjamin Franklin Parkway in Philadelphia as part of a fashion show on a hot July night while all around our stage, a race-riot was fully underway. That's how serious we were about our vow.
Raymond Joseph Teller, Fury Letter written to Brian Brushwood, 10-18-93
Success is not the result of spontaneous combustion. You must set yourself on fire.
Reggie Leach
A minute's success pays the failure of years.
Robert Browning (1812 - 1889)

Success is the ability to go from one failure to another with no loss of enthusiasm.
Sir Winston Churchill (1874 - 1965)
Many of life's failures are people who did not realize how close they were to success when they gave up.
Thomas A. Edison (1847 - 1931)
Underpromise; overdeliver.
Tom Peters, in The Chicago Tribune
I don't know what the future of my career holds, but I know that whatever is over the horizon, the road I've traveled to get here is like those Interstates in Texas: everything can look the same, and it can feel like you're not going anywhere, until you suddenly get where you're going and realize that you've been traveling for a long time.
Wil Wheaton, WIL WHEATON dot NET, 12-16-2013
If you enjoyed making a thing, and you're proud of the thing you made, that's enough. Not everyone is going to like it, and that's okay.
Wil Wheaton, WIL WHATON dot NET, 12-07-13
Sometimes, a person who likes your work and a person who don't will show up within milliseconds of each other to let you know how they feel. One does not need to cancel out the other, positively or negatively; if you're proud of the work, and you enjoyed the work, that is what's important.
Wil Wheaton, WIL WHATON dot NET, 12-07-13
I know of only one bird - the parrot - that talks; and it can't fly very high.
Wilbur Wright (1867 - 1912), declining to make a speech in 1908
Eighty percent of success is showing up.
Woody Allen (1935 -)

Suffering
To perceive is to suffer.
Aristotle (384 BC - 322 BC)
But penance need not be paid in suffering...It can be paid in forward motion. Correcting the mistake is a positive move, a nurturing move.
Barbara Hall, A Summons to New Orleans, 2000
In the part of this universe that we know there is great injustice, and often the good suffer, and often the wicked prosper, and one hardly knows which of those is the more annoying.
Bertrand Russell (1872 - 1970)
Never to suffer would never to have been blessed.
Edgar Allan Poe (1809 - 1849)
I felt despair. Though it seems to me now there's two kinds of it: the sort that causes a person to surrender and then the sort I had which made me take risks and make plans.
Erica Eisdorfer, The Wet Nurse's Tale, 2009
I have found that it don't really matter if you're brought up fine or rough, but that it helps to have someone to spill your sorrows to.
Erica Eisdorfer, The Wet Nurse's Tale, 2009
But a somewhat more liberal and sympathetic examination of mankind will convince us that the cross is even older than the gibbet, that voluntary suffering was before and independent of compulsory; and in short that in most important matters a man has always been free to ruin himself if he chose.
G. K. Chesterton (1874 - 1936), What's Wrong With the World; p. 118
Although the world is full of suffering, it is full also of the overcoming of it.
Helen Keller (1880 - 1968)
Character cannot be developed in ease and quiet. Only through experience of trial and suffering can the soul be strengthened, ambition inspired, and success achieved.
Helen Keller (1880 - 1968)
You desire to know the art of living, my friend? It is contained in one phrase: make use of suffering.
Henri-Frédéric Amiel
So long as little children are allowed to suffer, there is no true love in this world.
Isodore Duncan
One does not love a place the less for having suffered in it, unless it has been all suffering, nothing but suffering.
Jane Austen (1775 - 1817), Persuasion, 1818
Man has to suffer. When he has no real afflictions, he invents some.
Jose Marti
A misery is not to be measured from the nature of the evil, but from the temper of the sufferer.
Joseph Addison (1672 - 1719)
I have not yet met with a sorrow that could not be borne, nor with one who's passing did not leave me stronger.
Kathryn L. Nelson, Pemberley Manor, 2006
Whenever evil befalls us, we ought to ask ourselves, after the first suffering, how we can turn it into good. So shall we take occasion, from one bitter root, to raise perhaps many flowers.
Leigh Hunt (1784 - 1859)
I cannot believe that the inscrutable universe turns on an axis of suffering; surely the strange beauty of the world must somewhere rest on pure joy!
Louise Bogan
Crying is the refuge of plain women, but the ruin of pretty ones.
Oscar Wilde (1854 - 1900), Lady Windemere's Fan
People have a hard time letting go of their suffering. Out of a fear of the unknown, they prefer suffering that is familiar.
Thich Nhat Hanh
The truth that many people never understand, until it is too late, is that the more you try to avoid suffering the more you suffer because smaller and more insignificant things begin to torture you in proportion to your fear of being hurt.
Thomas Merton (1915 - 1968)

The sufferings that fate inflicts on us should be borne with patience, what enemies inflict with manly courage.
Thucydides (471 BC - 400 BC)
Pain is inevitable; suffering is optional.
Unknown
If suffer we must, let's suffer on the heights.
Victor Hugo (1802 - 1885), 'Les Malheureux'

Summer
In the depth of winter, I finally learned that within me there lay an invincible summer.
Albert Camus (1913 - 1960)
One swallow does not make a summer.
Aristotle (384 BC - 322 BC), Nichomachean Ethics
There shall be eternal summer in the grateful heart.
Celia Thaxter
Summer afternoon - Summer afternoon... the two most beautiful words in the English language.
Henry James (1843 - 1916)
Summer afternoon-summer afternoon; to me those have always been the two mostTeautiful words in the English language.
Henry James (1843 - 1916)
The tendinous part of the mind, so to speak, is more developed in winter; the fleshy, in summer. I should say winter had given the bone and sinew to literature, summer the tissues and the blood.
John Burroughs (1837 - 1921), The Snow-Walkers
What a beautiful, sunny morning. It makes you happy to be alive, doesn't it? We can't let the sun outshine us! We have to beam, too!
Takayuki Ikkaku, Arisa Hosaka and Toshihiro Kawabata, Animal Crossing: Wild World, 2005
The summer night is like a perfection of thought.
Wallace Stevens (1879 - 1955)
In summer, the song sings itself.
William Carlos Williams (1883 - 1963)
Shall I compare thee to a summer's day?
Thou art more lovely and more temperate:
Rough winds do shake the darling buds of May,
And summer's lease hath all too short a date.
William Shakespeare (1564 - 1616), Sonnet XVIII

Superstition
Faith must have adequate evidence, else it is mere superstition.
Alexander Hodge
I have only one superstition. I touch all the bases when I hit a home run.
Babe Ruth (1895 - 1948)
Fear is the main source of superstition, and one of the main sources of cruelty. To conquer fear is the beginning of wisdom.
Bertrand Russell (1872 - 1970), Unpopular Essays (1950), "Outline of Intellectual Rubbish"
We do not destroy religion by destroying superstition.
Cicero (106 BC - 43 BC)
A superstition is a premature explanation that overstays its time.
George Iles
Security is mostly a superstition. It does not exist in nature.... Life is either a daring adventure or nothing.
Helen Keller (1880 - 1968), The Open Door (1957)
Count Hermann Keyserling once said truly that the greatest American superstition was belief in facts.
John Gunther (1901 - 1970)

Talent
Great ability develops and reveals itself increasingly with every new assignment.
Baltasar Gracian
Put yourself on view. This brings your talents to light.
Baltasar Gracian
Hide not your talents, they for use were made. What's a sun-dial in the shade?
Benjamin Franklin (1706 - 1790)
If you have a talent, use it in every which way possible. Don't hoard it. Don't dole it out like a miser. Spend it lavishly like a millionaire intent on going broke.
Brendan Francis
Natural ability without education has more often attained to glory and virtue than education without natural ability.
Cicero (106 BC - 43 BC)
Everyone has talent. What is rare is the courage to follow the talent to the dark place where it leads.
Erica Jong
Work while you have the light. You are responsible for the talent that has been entrusted to you.
Henri-Frédéric Amiel
Use what talents you possess: the woods would be very silent if no birds sang there except those that sang best.
Henry Van Dyke
Appearance can always be changed, but the talent stays the same.
Jennifer Hudson, I Got This: How I Changed My Ways and Lost What Weighed Me Down, 2012
My focus has always been on talent over looks. This theme of people putting an emphasis on looks first has been a constant reminder throughout my life that most people don't see things in the same way that I do.
Jennifer Hudson, I Got This: How I Changed My Ways and Lost What Weighed Me Down, 2012

The talent should speak for itself.
Jennifer Hudson, I Got This: How I Changed My Ways and Lost What Weighed Me Down, 2012
We believe that if men have the talent to invent need machines that put men out of work, they have the talent to put those men back to work.
John F. Kennedy (1917 - 1963)
It doesn't pay to be good at something unless you are the absolute best at it.
Josh Lieb, I am a Genius of Unspeakable Evil and I Want to be Your Class President, 2009
We are always more anxious to be distinguished for a talent which we do not possess, than to be praised for the fifteen which we do possess.
Mark Twain (1835 - 1910), Mark Twain's Autobiography
You have to have confidence in your ability, and then be tough enough to follow through.
Rosalynn Carter (1927 -)
Toil to make yourself remarkable by some talent or other.
Seneca (5 BC - 65 AD)
Mediocrity knows nothing higher than itself, but talent instantly recognizes genius.
Sir Arthur Conan Doyle (1859 - 1930), (Sherlock Holmes) Valley of Fear, 1915
Getting ahead in a difficult profession requires avid faith in yourself. That is why some people with mediocre talent, but with great inner drive, go much further than people with vastly superior talent.
Sophia Loren (1934 -)
Whatever you are by nature, keep to it; never desert your line of talent. Be what nature intended you for and you will succeed.
Sydney Smith (1771 - 1845)

Taxes

The hardest thing in the world to understand is the income tax.
Albert Einstein (1879 - 1955), (attributed)
The best way to teach your kids about taxes is by eating 30% of their ice cream.
Bill Murray (1950 -)
He who builds a better mousetrap these days runs into material shortages, patent-infringement suits, work stoppages, collusive bidding, discount discrimination–and taxes."
H. E. Martz
Unquestionably, there is progress. The average American now pays out twice as much in taxes as he formerly got in wages.
H. L. Mencken (1880 - 1956)
Income tax returns are the most imaginative fiction being written today.
Herman Wouk (1915 -)
The avoidance of taxes is the only intellectual pursuit that carries any reward.
John Maynard Keynes (1883 - 1946)
When there is an income tax, the just man will pay more and the unjust less on the same amount of income.
Plato (427 BC - 347 BC), The Republic
The income tax has made more liars out of the American people than golf has.
Will Rogers (1879 - 1935), Illiterate Digest (1924), "Helping the Girls with their Income Taxes"

Teaching

I never teach my pupils. I only attempt to provide the conditions in which they can learn.
Albert Einstein (1879 - 1955)
Experience teaches only the teachable.
Aldous Huxley (1894 - 1963)
The true teacher defends his pupils against his own personal influence.
Amos Bronson Alcott (1799 - 1888)
The whole art of teaching is only the art of awakening the natural curiosity of young minds for the purpose of satisfying it afterwards.
Anatole France (1844 - 1924), The Crime of Sylvestre Bonnard
Passive acceptance of the teacher's wisdom is easy to most boys and girls. It involves no effort of independent thought, and seems rational because the teacher knows more than his pupils; it is moreover the way to win the favour of the teacher unless he is a very exceptional man. Yet the habit of passive acceptance is a disastrous one in later life. It causes man to seek and to accept a leader, and to accept as a leader whoever is established in that position.
Bertrand Russell (1872 - 1970)
Teachers open the door. You enter by yourself.
Chinese Proverb
Good teaching is one-fourth preparation and three-fourths theater.
Gail Godwin
He who can, does. He who cannot, teaches.
George Bernard Shaw (1856 - 1950), Man and Superman (1903) "Maxims for Revolutionists"
Teaching is not a lost art, but regard for teaching is a lost tradition.
Jacques Barzun
If you would thoroughly know anything, teach it to others.
Tryon Edwards (1809 - 1894)
For every person who wants to teach there are approximately thirty people who don't want to learn–much.
W. C. Sellar and R. J. Yeatman, And Now All This (1932) introduction

Technology

For a list of all the ways technology has failed to improve the quality of life, please press three.
Alice Kahn
Any sufficiently advanced technology is indistinguishable from magic.
Arthur C. Clarke (1917 -), "Profiles of The Future", 1961 (Clarke's third law)

During my eighty-seven years I have witnessed a whole succession of technological revolutions. But none of them have done away with the need for character in the individual or the ability to think.
Bernard M. Baruch (1870 - 1965)
This is why I loved technology: if you used it right, it could give you power and privacy.
Cory Doctorow, Little Brother, 2008
We make our gadgets our own by the way that we use them, with or without the permission of the manufacturer.
Laura Moncur (1969 -), The Gadgets Page, 07-09-09
Technology is a way of organizing the universe so that man doesn't have to experience it.
Max Frisch
If there is technological advance without social advance, there is, almost automatically, an increase in human misery.
Michael Harrington, The Other America, 1962
Technology is dominated by two types of people: those who understand what they do not manage, and those who manage what they do not understand.
Putt's Law
Humanity is acquiring all the right technology for all the wrong reasons.
R. Buckminster Fuller (1895 - 1983)
For a successful technology, reality must take precedence over public relations, for Nature cannot be fooled.
Richard Feynman (1918 - 1988)
There is an evil tendency underlying all our technology - the tendency to do what is reasonable even when it isn't any good.
Robert Pirsig, Zen and the Art of Motorcycle Maintenance

Television

Television is more interesting than people. If it were not, we would have people standing in the corners of our rooms.
Alan Corenk
Seeing a murder on television... can help work off one's antagonisms. And if you haven't any antagonisms, the commercials will give you some.
Alfred Hitchcock (1899 - 1980)
Television has done much for psychiatry by spreading information about it, as well as contributing to the need for it.
Alfred Hitchcock (1899 - 1980)
Television has proved that people will look at anything rather than each other.
Ann Landers (1918 - 2002)
Television is the first truly democratic culture - the first culture available to everybody and entirely governed by what the people want. The most terrifying thing is what people do want.
Clive Barnes
The one function TV news performs very well is that when there is no news we give it to you with the same emphasis as if there were.
David Brinkley (1920 - 2003)
Television enables you to be entertained in your home by people you wouldn't have in your home.
David Frost
[The television is] an invention that permits you to be entertained in your living room by people you wouldn't have in your home.
David Frost
MTV is the lava lamp of the 1980's.
Doug Ferrari
I can think of nothing more boring for the American people than to have to sit in their living rooms for a whole half hour looking at my face on their television screens.
Dwight D. Eisenhower (1890 - 1969)
Dealing with network executives is like being nibbled to death by ducks.
Eric Sevareid
TV is chewing gum for the eyes.
Frank Lloyd Wright (1869 - 1959)
Imitation is the sincerest form of television.
Fred Allen (1894 - 1956)
Television is a new medium. It's called a medium because nothing is well-done.
Fred Allen (1894 - 1956), on the radio program The Big Show, Dec. 17, 1950
[Television] the triumph of machine over people.
Fred Allen (1894 - 1956)
The great thing about television is that if something important happens anywhere in the world, day or night, you can always change the channel.
From "Taxi"
Don't you wish there was a knob on the TV to turn up the intelligence? There's one marked 'Brightness,' but it doesn't work.
Gallagher
I find television very educating. Every time somebody turns on the set, I go into the other room and read a book.
Groucho Marx (1890 - 1977)
Television news is like a lightning flash. It makes a loud noise, lights up everything around it, leaves everything else in darkness and then is suddenly gone.
Hodding Carter
In general, watching children's television is a dark and surreal descent into madness where the characters on the screen talk directly to you.
John Green, Vlogbrothers, A Surreal Descent into Madness: Reviewing Childrens TV, 04-10-12
If it weren't for Philo T. Farnsworth, inventor of television, we'd still be eating frozen radio dinners.
Johnny Carson (1925 - 2005)

One of the few good things about modern times: If you die horribly on television, you will not have died in vain. You will have entertained us.
Kurt Vonnegut (1922 - 2007), "Cold Turkey", In These Times, May 10, 2004
Thanks to TV and for the convenience of TV, you can only be one of two kinds of human beings, either a liberal or a conservative.
Kurt Vonnegut (1922 - 2007), "Cold Turkey", In These Times, May 10, 2004
If there's anything unsettling to the stomach, it's watching actors on television talk about their personal lives.
Marlon Brando (1924 - 2004)
Imagine what it would be like if TV actually were good. It would be the end of everything we know.
Marvin Minsky
Television is for appearing on - not for looking at.
Noel Coward (1899 - 1973)
My father hated radio and could not wait for television to be invented so he could hate that too.
Peter De Vries
All television is children's television.
Richard P. Adler
It is difficult to produce a television documentary that is both incisive and probing when every twelve minutes one is interrupted by twelve dancing rabbits singing about toilet paper.
Rod Serling (1924 - 1975)
Television has raised writing to a new low.
Samuel Goldwyn (1882 - 1974)
I think that parents only get so offended by television because they rely on it as a babysitter and the sole educator of their kids.
Trey Parker and Matt Stone, South Park, Death, 1997
You know, I think that if parents would spend less time worrying about what their kids watch on TV and more time worrying about what's going on in their kids' lives, this world would be a much better place.
Trey Parker and Matt Stone, South Park, Death, 1997
The human race is faced with a cruel choice: work or daytime television.
Unknown
We are drawn to our television sets each April the way we are drawn to the scene of an accident.
Vincent Canby, on the Academy Awards

Temptation

Good habits result from resisting temptation.
Ancient Proverb
Blessed is the man that endureth temptation: for when he is tried, he shall receive the crown of life.
Bible, New Testament, James, Chapter 1, Verse 12
I never resist temptation because I have found that things that are bad for me do not tempt me.
George Bernard Shaw (1856 - 1950), The Apple Cart (1930)
There is not any memory with less satisfaction than the memory of some temptation we resisted.
James Branch Cabell (1879 - 1958)
Those who flee temptation generally leave a forwarding address.
Lane Olinghouse
I generally avoid temptation unless I can't resist it.
Mae West (1892 - 1980)
There are several good protections against temptations, but the surest is cowardice.
Mark Twain (1835 - 1910), Following the Equator (1897)
I can resist anything but temptation.
Oscar Wilde (1854 - 1900), Lady Windermere's Fan, 1892, Act I
The only way to get rid of a temptation is to yield to it. Resist it, and your soul grows sick with longing for the things it has forbidden to itself.
Oscar Wilde (1854 - 1900), The Picture of Dorian Gray, 1891
Why comes temptation, but for man to meet and master and crouch beneath his foot, and so be pedestaled in triumph?
Robert Browning (1812 - 1889)
Most people would like to be delivered from temptation but would like it to keep in touch.
Robert Orben
The last temptation is the greatest treason: to do the right deed for the wrong reason.
T. S. Eliot (1888 - 1965)
Temptation rarely comes in working hours. It is in their leisure time that men are made or marred.
W. N. Taylor
Often the best way to overcome desire is to satisfy it.
W. Somerset Maugham (1874 - 1965), The Razor's Edge, 1943
It is good to be without vices, but it is not good to be without temptations.
Walter Bagehot (1826 - 1877), "Biographical Studies", 1863

The future

The best way to predict the future is to invent it.
Alan Kay
I never think of the future - it comes soon enough.
Albert Einstein (1879 - 1955)
The future belongs to those who can rise above the confines of the earth.
Alfred North Whitehead (1861 - 1947), From the viewbook of Embry-Riddle Aeronautical University
Change is the process by which the future invades our lives.
Alvin Toffler
In the future everyone will be famous for fifteen minutes.
Andy Warhol (1928 - 1987)
The upper classes are... a nation's past; the middle class is its future.
Ayn Rand (1905 - 1982)
All human situations have their inconveniences. We feel those of the present but neither see nor feel those of the future; and hence we often make troublesome changes without amendment, and frequently for the worse.
Benjamin Franklin (1706 - 1790)
The future is something which everyone reaches at the rate of sixty minutes an hour, whatever he does, whoever he is.
C. S. Lewis (1898 - 1963)
You can't base your life on the past or the present. You have to tell me about your future.
Chuck Palahniuk (1962 -), Invisible Monsters, 1999
Study the past if you would define the future.
Confucius (551 BC - 479 BC)
The time is now, the place is here. Stay in the present. You can do nothing to change the past, and the future will never come exactly as you plan or hope for.
Dan Millman
The future will be better tomorrow.
Dan Quayle (1947 -)
The future is much like the present, only longer.
Dan Quisenberry
The future is no place to place your better days.
Dave Matthews, "Cry Freedom"
The thing to remember is that the future comes one day at a time.
Dean Acheson, Communication Bulletin for Managers & Supervisors, June 2004
A preoccupation with the future not only prevents us from seeing the present as it is but often prompts us to rearrange the past.
Eric Hoffer (1902 - 1983), The Passionate State of Mind, 1954
The function of science fiction is not always to predict the future but sometimes to prevent it.
Frank Herbert (1920 - 1986)
I look to the future because that's where I'm going to spend the rest of my life.
George Burns (1896 - 1996)
There's no present. There's only the immediate future and the recent past.
George Carlin (1937 - 2008)
Because we don't think about future generations, they will never forget us.
Henrik Tikkanen
Not much longer shall we have time for reading lessons of the past. An inexorable present calls us to the defense of a great future.
Henry Luce
The future is uncertain... but this uncertainty is at the very heart of human creativity.
Ilya Prigogine (1917 -)
The consequences of our actions are so complicated, so diverse, that predicting the future is a very difficult business indeed.
J. K. Rowling, Harry Potter and the Prisoner of Azkaban
Children have neither past nor future; they enjoy the present.
Jean de la Bruyere (1645 - 1696)
The future is an opaque mirror. Anyone who tries to look into it sees nothing but the dim outlines of an old and worried face.
Jim Bishop, New York Journal-American, March 14, 1959
We have come too far, we have sacrificed too much, to disdain the future now.
John F. Kennedy (1917 - 1963)
...myopia. He was nearsighted. The future lay before him, inevitable but invisible.
John Green, An Abundance of Katherines, 2008
The future, according to some scientists, will be exactly like the past, only far more expensive.
John Sladek
A man that don't believe in destiny don't need to know what his destiny is.
Laura Moncur (1969 -), Merriton: Twelve Hours from San Francisco, 08-20-08
The future belongs to those who prepare for it today.
Malcolm X (1925 - 1965)
Never let the future disturb you. You will meet it, if you have to, with the same weapons of reason which today arm you against the present.
Marcus Aurelius
When you relinquish the desire to control your future, you can have more happiness.
Nicole Kidman, in The Scotsman
Prediction is very difficult, especially about the future.
Niels Bohr (1885 - 1962)
The trouble with our times is that the future is not what it used to be.
Paul Valery (1871 - 1945)
Long-range planning does not deal with future decisions, but with the future of present decisions.
Peter Drucker (1909 - 2005)
The Past is to be respected and acknowledged, but not to be worshiped. It is our future in which we will find our greatness.
Pierre Trudeau (1919 - 2000)
I have seen the future and it doesn't work.
Robert Fulford
What happens when the future has come and gone?
Robert Half
The world is full of people whose notion of a satisfactory future is, in fact, a return to the idealised past.
Robertson Davies, "A Voice from the Attic", 1960

Time is just something that we assign. You know, past, present, it's just all arbitrary. Most Native Americans, they don't think of time as linear; in time, out of time, I never have enough time, circular time, the Stevens wheel. All moments are happening all the time.
Robin Green and Mitchell Burgess, Northern Exposure, Hello, I Love You, 1994
If you're afraid of the future, then get out of the way, stand aside. The people of this country are ready to move again.
Ronald Reagan (1911 - 2004)
Enjoy present pleasures in such a way as not to injure future ones.
Seneca (5 BC - 65 AD)
If we open a quarrel between the past and the present, we shall find that we have lost the future.
Sir Winston Churchill (1874 - 1965)
The empires of the future are the empires of the mind.
Sir Winston Churchill (1874 - 1965), Speech at Harvard University, September 6, 1943
The past is certain, the future obscure.
Thales (635 BC - 543 BC)
I like the dreams of the future better than the history of the past.
Thomas Jefferson (1743 - 1826)
Life wouldn't be worth living if I worried over the future as well as the present.
W. Somerset Maugham (1874 - 1965), 'Of Human Bondage', 1915
The future is here. It's just not widely distributed yet.
William Gibson (1948 -)
The future ain't what it used to be.
Yogi Berra (1925 -)

The past
This only is denied to God: the power to undo the past.
Agathon (448 BC - 400 BC), from Aristotle, Nicomachean Ethics
Those who cannot remember the past are condemned to repeat it.
George Santayana (1863 - 1952), The Life of Reason, Volume 1, 1905
Look not mournfully into the past. It comes not back again. Wisely improve the present. It is thine. Go forth to meet the shadowy future, without fear.
Henry Wadsworth Longfellow (1807 - 1882)
I tend to live in the past because most of my life is there.
Herb Caen
The farther behind I leave the past, the closer I am to forging my own character.
Isabelle Eberhardt
Ruminating about the past is like trying to drive backward to undo a car accident.
Julie A., M.A. Ross and Judy Corcoran, Joint Custody with a Jerk: Raising a Child with an Uncooperative Ex, 2011
When you get angry at your ex, only about 10 percent of your anger can be attributed to the current situation. The other 90 percent comes from your past experiences with your ex, as well as those with your parents, caregivers, and other significant people in your past. The current situation has simply triggered your past anger and allowed it to resurface. It's been said that if you're hysterical, the cause is probably historical.
Julie A., M.A. Ross and Judy Corcoran, Joint Custody with a Jerk: Raising a Child with an Uncooperative Ex, 2011
We can draw lessons from the past, but we cannot live in it.
Lyndon B. Johnson (1908 - 1973), December 13, 1963
Time is just something that we assign. You know, past, present, it's just all arbitrary. Most Native Americans, they don't think of time as linear; in time, out of time, I never have enough time, circular time, the Stevens wheel. All moments are happening all the time.
Robin Green and Mitchell Burgess, Northern Exposure, Hello, I Love You, 1994
Live neither in the past nor in the future, but let each day's work absorb your entire energies, and satisfy your widest ambition.
Sir William Osler (1849 - 1919), to his students
I don't think of the past. The only thing that matters is the everlasting present.
W. Somerset Maugham (1874 - 1965), The Moon and Sixpence
Events in the past may be roughly divided into those which probably never happened and those which do not matter.
William Ralph Inge (1860 - 1954)

The world
The world is round; it has no point.
Adrienne E. Gusoff
I think the world is run by 'C' students.
Al McGuire
The most incomprehensible thing about the world is that it is at all comprehensible.
Albert Einstein (1879 - 1955)
In the fight between you and the world, back the world.
Frank Zappa (1940 - 1993)
The world's as ugly as sin, and almost as delightful
Frederick Locker-Lampson
The world is a tragedy to those who feel, but a comedy to those who think.
Horace Walpole (1717 - 1797)
All the world's a cage.
Jeanne Phillips
Don't go around saying the world owes you a living. The world owes you nothing. It was here first.
Mark Twain (1835 - 1910)
All the world's a stage and most of us are desperately unrehearsed.
Sean O'Casey (1880 - 1964)

Thoughts
All great deeds and all great thoughts have a ridiculous beginning.
Albert Camus (1913 - 1960), The Myth of Sisyphus
No man deserves punishment for his thoughts.
Anonymous
When I only begin to read, I forget I'm on this world. It lifts me on wings with high thoughts.
Anzia Yezierska
High thoughts must have high language.
Aristophanes (450 BC - 388 BC), Frogs, 405 B.C.
Nurture your mind with great thoughts; to believe in the heroic makes heroes.
Benjamin Disraeli (1804 - 1881)
Only he is free who cultivates his own thoughts, and strives without fear to do justice to them.
Berthold Auerbach (1812 - 1882)
The highest possible stage in moral culture is when we recognize that we ought to control our thoughts.
Charles Darwin (1809 - 1882)
Neither can embellishments of language be found without arrangement and expression of thoughts, nor can thoughts be made to shine without the light of language.
Cicero (106 BC - 43 BC)
Our thoughts are free.
Cicero (106 BC - 43 BC)
Don't think you are going to conceal thoughts by concealing evidence that they ever existed.
Dwight D. Eisenhower (1890 - 1969), speech at Dartmouth College, June 14, 1953
In this world second thoughts, it seems, are best.
Euripides (484 BC - 406 BC), Hippolytus, 428 B.C.
It is not a bad idea to get in the habit of writing down one's thoughts. It saves one having to bother anyone else with them.
Isabel Colegate
You are today where your thoughts have brought you; you will be tomorrow where your thoughts take you.
James Lane Allen
All truly wise thoughts have been thoughts already thousands of times; but to make them truly ours, we must think them over again honestly, till they take root in our personal experience.
Johann Wolfgang von Goethe (1749 - 1832)
If any man wish to write in a clear style, let him be first clear in his thoughts; and if any would write in a noble style, let him first possess a noble soul.
Johann Wolfgang von Goethe (1749 - 1832)
I have always thought the actions of men the best interpreters of their thoughts.
John Locke (1632 - 1704)
The happiness of your life depends upon the quality of your thoughts, therefore guard accordingly; and take care that you entertain no notions unsuitable to virtue, and reasonable nature.
Marcus Aurelius Antoninus (121 AD - 180 AD)
The universe is change; our life is what our thoughts make it.
Marcus Aurelius Antoninus (121 AD - 180 AD), Meditations
When I am attacked by gloomy thoughts, nothing helps me so much as running to my books. They quickly absorb me and banish the clouds from my mind.
Michel de Montaigne (1533 - 1592)
Change your thoughts and you change your world.
Norman Vincent Peale (1898 - 1993)
A man is infinitely more complicated than his thoughts.
Paul Valery (1871 - 1945)
If you want peace, stop fighting. If you want peace of mind, stop fighting with your thoughts.
Peter McWilliams, Life 101, 1991
Thoughts give birth to a creative force that is neither elemental nor sidereal. Thoughts create a new heaven, a new firmament, a new source of energy, from which new arts flow. When a man undertakes to create something, he establishes a new heaven, as it were, and from it the work that he desires to create flows into him. For such is the immensity of man that he is greater than heaven and earth.
Philipus Aureolus Paracelsus (1493 - 1541)
In every work of genius we recognize our own rejected thoughts; they come back to us with a certain alienated majesty.
Ralph Waldo Emerson (1803 - 1882), "Self Reliance"
In every work of genius we see our own rejected thoughts.
Ralph Waldo Emerson (1803 - 1882), Self Reliance
Except our own thoughts, there is nothing absolutely in our power.
Rene Descartes (1596 - 1650)
They are never alone that are accompanied with noble thoughts.
Sir Philip Sidney (1554 - 1586)
Thoughts, like fleas, jump from man to man, but they don't bite everybody.
Stanislaw J. Lec (1909 - 1966)
Watch your thoughts, they become words.
Watch your words, they become actions.
Watch your actions, they become habits.
Watch your habits, they become your character.
Watch your character, it becomes your destiny.
Unknown
There are some that only employ words for the purpose of disguising their thoughts.
Voltaire (1694 - 1778), Dialogue, XIV, "Le Chapon et la Poularde" (1766)
My thoughts are my company; I can bring them together, select them, detain them, dismiss them.

Walter Landor (1775 - 1864)
A thought which, quarter'd, hath but one part wisdom and ever three parts coward.
William Shakespeare (1564 - 1616), Hamlet, Act IV, sc. 4
But thought's the slave of life, and life time's fool.
William Shakespeare (1564 - 1616), Henry IV, Part I, Act V, sc. 4
Call home thy ancient thoughts from banishment.
William Shakespeare (1564 - 1616), The Taming of the Shrew, Induction, sc. 2
Make not your thoughts your prisons.
William Shakespeare (1564 - 1616), Antony and Cleopatra, Act V, sc. 2
My thoughts are whirled like a potter's wheel.
William Shakespeare (1564 - 1616), Henry VI, Part I, Act I, sc. 5
My words fly up, my thoughts remain below.
Words without thoughts never to heaven go.
William Shakespeare (1564 - 1616)
My words fly up, my thoughts remain below:
Words without thoughts never to heaven go.
William Shakespeare (1564 - 1616), "Hamlet", Act 3 scene 3
There is nothing good or bad, but thinking makes it so.
William Shakespeare (1564 - 1616), Hamlet, Act II, sc. 2
Thoughts are but dreams till their effects be tried.
William Shakespeare (1564 - 1616), The Rape of Lucrece

Time

The dogmas of the quiet past, are inadequate to the stormy present. The occasion is piled high with difficulty, and we must rise with the occasion. As our case is new, so we must think anew and act anew. We must disenthrall ourselves, and then we shall save our country.
Abraham Lincoln (1809 - 1865), Annual message to Congress, December 1, 1862
All that really belongs to us is time; even he who has nothing else has that.
Baltasar Gracian
An unhurried sense of time is in itself a form of wealth.
Bonnie Friedman, in New York Times
Time is the coin of your life. It is the only coin you have, and only you can determine how it will be spent. Be careful lest you let other people spend it for you.
Carl Sandburg (1878 - 1967)
Calendars are for careful people, not passionate ones.
Chuck Sigars, The World According to Chuck weblog, September 8, 2003
Time is an illusion. Lunchtime doubly so.
Douglas Adams (1952 - 2001)
Time is a cruel thief to rob us of our former selves. We lose as much to life as we do to death.
Elizabeth Forsythe Hailey, 'A Woman of Independent Means'
All my possessions for a moment of time.
Elizabeth I (1533 - 1603)
The trouble with being punctual is that nobody's there to appreciate it.
Franklin P. Jones
When people go through something rough in life, they say, "I'm taking it one day at a time." Yes, so is everybody. Because that's how time works.
Hannibal Buress
Oh! Do not attack me with your watch. A watch is always too fast or too slow. I cannot be dictated to by a watch.
Jane Austen (1775 - 1817), Mansfield Park
If time flies when you're having fun, it hits the afterburners when you don't think you're having enough.
Jef Mallett, Frazz, 08-01-05
Nothing is as far away as one minute ago.
Jim Bishop
The great French Marshall Lyautey once asked his gardener to plant a tree. The gardener objected that the tree was slow growing and would not reach maturity for 100 years. The Marshall replied, 'In that case, there is no time to lose; plant it this afternoon!'
John F. Kennedy (1917 - 1963)
We must use time as a tool, not as a crutch.
John F. Kennedy (1917 - 1963)
It seemed like forever ago, like we'd had this brief but still infinite forever. Some infinities are bigger than other infinities.
John Green, The Fault in Our Stars, 2012
Time is at once the most valuable and the most perishable of all our possessions.
John Randolph (1773 - 1833)
Our duty is to preserve what the past has had to say for itself, and to say for ourselves what shall be true for the future.
John Ruskin (1819 - 1900)
There is never enough time, unless you're serving it.
Malcolm Forbes (1919 - 1990)
If we take care of the moments, the years will take care of themselves.
Maria Edgeworth, O Magazine, April 2004
Time cools, time clarifies; no mood can be maintained quite unaltered through the course of hours.
Mark Twain (1835 - 1910)
Regret for wasted time is more wasted time.
Mason Cooley, O Magazine, April 2004
Time does not change us. It just unfolds us.
Max Frisch
What very mysterious things days were. Sometimes they fly by, and other times they seem to last forever, yet they are all exactly twenty-four hours. There's quite a lot we don't know about them.
Melanie Benjamin, Alice I Have Been, 2010

So little time and so little to do.
Oscar Levant (1906 - 1972)
A single day is enough to make us a little larger.
Paul Klee (1879 - 1940)
The whole life of man is but a point of time; let us enjoy it.
Plutarch (46 AD - 120 AD)
These times of ours are series and full of calamity, but all times are essentially alike. As soon as there is life there is danger.
Ralph Waldo Emerson (1803 - 1882), Public and Private Education, November 27, 1864
This time, like all times, is a very good one, if we but know what to do with it.
Ralph Waldo Emerson (1803 - 1882)
This time, like all times, is a very good one, if we but know what to do with it.
Ralph Waldo Emerson (1803 - 1882), The American Scholar, August 31, 1837
Doing a thing well is often a waste of time.
Robert Byrne
Time is just something that we assign. You know, past, present, it's just all arbitrary. Most Native Americans, they don't think of time as linear; in time, out of time, I never have enough time, circular time, the Stevens wheel. All moments are happening all the time.
Robin Green and Mitchell Burgess, Northern Exposure, Hello, I Love You, 1994
Nothing is a waste of time if you use the experience wisely.
Rodin (1840 - 1917)
What may be done at any time will be done at no time.
Scottish Proverb
People find life entirely too time-consuming.
Stanislaw J. Lec (1909 - 1966), "Unkempt Thoughts"
I was thinking about how disjointedly time seemed to flow, passing in a blur at times, with single images standing out more clearly than others. And then, at other times, every second was significant, etched in my mind.
Stephenie Meyer, Twilight, 2005
Time present and time past are both perhaps present in time future and time future contained in time past. If all time is eternally present all time is unredeemable.
Swatch, Always Now, 1997
Time is the most valuable thing a man can spend.
Theophrastus (372 BC - 287 BC), from Diogenes Laertius, Lives of Eminent Philosophers
I don't think of the past. The only thing that matters is the everlasting present.
W. Somerset Maugham (1874 - 1965), The Moon and Sixpence
Half our life is spent trying to find something to do with the time we have rushed through life trying to save.
Will Rogers (1879 - 1935), New York Times, Apr. 29, 1930
I wasted time and now doth time waste me.
William Shakespeare (1564 - 1616), Richard II, Act V, sc. 5
Like as the waves make towards the pebbled shore,
So do our minutes hasten to their end.
William Shakespeare (1564 - 1616), Sonnet LX
Nothing 'gainst Times scythe can make defence.
William Shakespeare (1564 - 1616), Sonnet XII
Pleasure and action make the hours seem short.
William Shakespeare (1564 - 1616), Othello, Act II, sc. 3
Ruin has taught me to ruminate,
That Time will come and take my love away.
This thought is as a death, which cannot choose
But weep to have that which it fears to lose.
William Shakespeare (1564 - 1616), Sonnet LXIV
Short time seems long in sorrow's sharp sustaining.
William Shakespeare (1564 - 1616), The Rape of Lucrece
The extreme parts of time extremely forms all causes to the purpose of his speed.
William Shakespeare (1564 - 1616), Love's Labour's Lost, Act V, sc. 2
The time is out of joint : O cursed spite, that ever I was born to set it right!
William Shakespeare (1564 - 1616), Hamlet, Act I, sc. 5
The whirligig of time brings in his revenges.
William Shakespeare (1564 - 1616), Twelfth Night, Act V, sc. 1
Time hath, my lord, a wallet at his back
Wherein he puts alms for oblivion,
A great-sized monster of ingratitudes:
Those scraps are good deeds past, which are devour'd
As fast as they are made, forgot as soon as done.
William Shakespeare (1564 - 1616), Troilus and Cressida, Act III, sc. 3
Time is like a fashionable host
That slightly shakes his parting guest by the hand,
And with his arm outstretch'd, as he would fly,
Grasps in the comer.
William Shakespeare (1564 - 1616), Troilus and Cressida, Act III, sc. 3
Time's glory is to calm contending kings, To unmask falsehood and bring truth to light, To stamp the seal of time in aged things, To wake the morn of sentinel the night, To wrong the wronger till he render right, To ruinate proud buildings with thy hour And smear with dust their glittering golden towers.
William Shakespeare (1564 - 1616), The Rape of Lucrece
Time's the king of men; he's both their parent, and he is their grave, and gives them what he will, not what they crave.
William Shakespeare (1564 - 1616), Pericles, Act II, sc. 3

Tolerance

Laws alone can not secure freedom of expression; in order that every man present his views without penalty there must be spirit of tolerance in the entire population.
Albert Einstein (1879 - 1955)

In the modern world, self-control buys a good life indeed. Having self-control to spare is rare enough nowadays that the marketplace lavishes huge rewards on society's scary new self-control elite, those lords of discipline who not only withstood all that boring stuff in graduate school, but keep themselves thin by carefully regulating what they eat after flogging themselves off to the gym at the crack of dawn. It's as if they got the news ahead of the rest of us-no doubt by waking up earlier-that self-control may well be the most important trait of the twenty-first century.
Daniel Akst, We Have Met the Enemy: Self-Control in an Age of Excess, 2011
Be entirely tolerant or not at all; follow the good path or the evil one. To stand at the crossroads requires more strength than you possess.
Heinrich Heine (1797 - 1856)
The highest result of education is tolerance.
Helen Keller (1880 - 1968), 'Optimism,' 1903
To say the least, a town life makes one more tolerant and liberal in one's judgement of others.
Henry Wadsworth Longfellow (1807 - 1882), Hyperion, 1839
I have learnt silence from the talkative, toleration from the intolerant, and kindness from the unkind; yet strange, I am ungrateful to these teachers.
Kahlil Gibran (1883 - 1931)
The test of courage comes when we are in the minority. The test of tolerance comes when we are in the majority.
Ralph W. Sockman
Once lead this people into war and they will forget there ever was such a thing as tolerance.
Woodrow Wilson (1856 - 1924), in John Dos Passos, "Mr Wilson's War"

Tradition

Traditions are group efforts to keep the unexpected from happening.
Barbara Tober
Traditions are the guideposts driven deep in our subconscious minds. The most powerful ones are those we can't even describe, aren't even aware of.
Ellen Goodman (1941 -)
Tradition means giving votes to the most obscure of all classes, our ancestors. It is the democracy of the dead. Tradition refuses to submit to the small and arrogant oligarchy of those who merely happen to be walking about.
G. K. Chesterton (1874 - 1936), Orthodoxy
Tradition is what you resort to when you don't have the time or the money to do it right.
Kurt Herbert Alder
Traditionalists are pessimists about the future and optimists about the past.
Lewis Mumford (1895 - 1990)
A love for tradition has never weakened a nation, indeed it has strengthened nations in their hour of peril.
Sir Winston Churchill (1874 - 1965)
A love of tradition has never weakened a nation, indeed it has strengthened nations in their hour of peril; but the new view must come, the world must roll forward.
Sir Winston Churchill (1874 - 1965), speech in the House of Commons, November 29, 1944
Tradition is a guide and not a jailer.
W. Somerset Maugham (1874 - 1965)
Men can know more than their ancestors did if they start with a knowledge of what their ancestors had already learned....That is why a society can be progressive only if it conserves its traditions.
Walter Lippmann (1889 - 1974)

Travel

He who would travel happily must travel light.
Antoine de Saint-Exupery (1900 - 1944)
Thanks to the Interstate Highway System, it is now possible to travel from coast to coast without seeing anything.
Charles Kuralt
When you travel, remember that a foreign country is not designed to make you comfortable. It is designed to make its own people comfortable.
Clifton Fadiman (1904 - 1999)
The true traveler is he who goes on foot, and even then, he sits down a lot of the time.
Colette (1873 - 1954), Paris From My Window, 1944
A man travels the world over in search of what he needs and returns home to find it.
George Moore
Before he sets out, the traveler must possess fixed interests and facilities to be served by travel.
George Santayana (1863 - 1952)
The saying "Getting there is half the fun" became obsolete with the advent of commercial airlines.
Henry J. Tillman
There's something wonderful about entertaining people on vacation. Everyone is there to have a good time.
Jennifer Hudson, I Got This: How I Changed My Ways and Lost What Weighed Me Down, 2012
There is not a person in the world who is given the advantage of travel who does not return changed.
Laura Moncur (1969 -), The Secret Heart of Charlotte Lucas, 2014
Travel is fatal to prejudice, bigotry, and narrow-mindedness, and many of our people need it sorely on these accounts. Broad, wholesome, charitable views of men and things cannot be acquired by vegetating in one little corner of the earth all one's lifetime.
Mark Twain (1835 - 1910), The Innocents Abroad
Certainly, travel is more than the seeing of sights; it is a change that goes on, deep and permanent, in the ideas of living.

Miriam Beard
Travel is only glamorous in retrospect.
Paul Theroux (1941 -), in The Washington Post
Everywhere I go I find a poet has been there before me.
Sigmund Freud (1856 - 1939)
Travel only with thy equals or thy betters; if there are none, travel alone.
The Dhammapada
No one travelling on a business trip would be missed if he failed to arrive.
Thorstein Veblen (1857 - 1929)

Trees

Suburbia is where the developer bulldozes out the trees, then names the streets after them.
Bill Vaughan
He plants trees to benefit another generation.
Caecilius Statius (220 BC - 168 BC), Synephebi
Train up a fig tree in the way it should go, and when you are old sit under the shade of it.
Charles Dickens (1812 - 1870)
Trees like to have kids climb on them, but trees are much bigger than we are, and much more forgiving.
Diane Frolov and Andrew Schneider, Northern Exposure, Old Tree, 1993
I speak for the trees, for the trees have no tongues.
Dr. Seuss (1904 - 1991), The Lorax
He that plants trees loves others beside himself.
Dr. Thomas Fuller (1654 - 1734), Gnomologia, 1732
The wrongs done to trees, wrongs of every sort, are done in the darkness of ignorance and unbelief, for when the light comes, the heart of the people is always right.
John Muir (1838 - 1914), My First Summer in the Sierra, 1911
I think that I shall never see
A poem lovely as a tree.
Joyce Kilmer (1886 - 1918), "Trees" (poem), 1914
The trees that are slow to grow bear the best fruit.
Moliere (1622 - 1673)
I think that I shall never see
a billboard lovely as a tree.
Perhaps, unless the billboards fall,
I'll never see a tree at all.
Ogden Nash (1902 - 1971)
There's nothing that keeps its youth,
So far as I know, but a tree and truth.
Oliver Wendell Holmes (1809 - 1894), The Deacon's Masterpiece, 1858
Trees, though they are cut and lopped, grow up again quickly, but if men are destroyed, it is not easy to get them again.
Pericles (490 BC - 429 BC), from Plutarch, Lives
Do not cut down the tree that gives you shade.
Persian Proverb
You should go to a pear tree for pears, not to an elm.
Publilius Syrus (~100 BC), Maxims
You will find something more in woods than in books. Trees and stones will teach you that which you can never learn from masters.
Saint Bernard (1090 - 1153), Epistle
He that climbs the tall tree has won right to the fruit.
Sir Walter Scott (1771 - 1832)
I like trees because they seem more resigned to the way they have to live than other things do.
Willa Cather (1873 - 1947), O Pioneers! (1913)
And this our life, exempt from public haunt,
Finds tongues in trees, books in running brooks,
Sermons in stones, and good in everything.
William Shakespeare (1564 - 1616), As You Like It, Act II, Scene i, Lines 15-17
As the poet said, 'Only God can make a tree' – probably because it's so hard to figure out how to get the bark on.
Woody Allen (1935 -)

Trust

For somehow this is tyranny's disease, to trust no friends.
Aeschylus (525 BC - 456 BC), Prometheus Bound
I never trust people's assertions, I always judge of them by their actions.
Ann Radcliffe (1764 - 1823), The Mysteries of Udolpho, 1764
A human being is only interesting if he's in contact with himself. I learned you have to trust yourself, be what you are, and do what you ought to do the way you should do it. You have got to discover you, what you do, and trust it.
Barbra Streisand (1942 -)
You have got to discover you, what you do, and trust it.
Barbra Streisand (1942 -)
A man who doesn't trust himself can never truly trust anyone else.
Cardinal de Retz, Memoires
Do not trust all men, but trust men of worth; the former course is silly, the latter a mark of prudence.
Democritus (460 BC - 370 BC)
Anyone who goes through life trusting people without making sure they are worthy of trust is a fool. Yet there are people who may be trusted, men as well as women. There are are as many difference in their natures as there are flowers in these meadows.
Elizabeth Aston, The Exploits & Adventures of Miss Alethea Darcy, 2005
In a networked world, trust is the most important currency.

Eric Schmidt, University of Pennsylvania Commencement Address, 2009
You may be deceived if you trust too much, but you will live in torment if you do not trust enough.
Frank Crane
The people I distrust most are those who want to improve our lives but have only one course of action.
Frank Herbert (1920 - 1986)
When you really trust someone, you have to be okay with not understanding some things.
Gordon Atkinson, Real Live Preacher weblog, 07-08-04
It is impossible to go through life without trust: That is to be imprisoned in the worst cell of all, oneself.
Graham Greene, The Ministry of Fear
For it is mutual trust, even more than mutual interest that holds human associations together. Our friends seldom profit us but they make us feel safe... Marriage is a scheme to accomplish exactly that same end.
H. L. Mencken (1880 - 1956)
The chief lesson I have learned in a long life is that the only way to make a man trustworthy is to trust him; and the surest way to make him untrustworthy is to distrust him and show your distrust.
Henry L. Stimson (1867 - 1950)
The only way to make a man trustworthy is to trust him.
Henry Stimson (1867 - 1950)
Never trust anything that can think for itself if you can't see where it keeps its brain.
J. K. Rowling, Harry Potter and The Chamber of Secrets, 1999
A person who trusts no one can't be trusted.
Jerome Blattner
Mistrust the man who finds everything good, the man who finds everything evil and still more the man who is indifferent to everything.
Johann K. Lavater
As soon as you trust yourself, you will know how to live.
Johann Wolfgang von Goethe (1749 - 1832), Faust
But the life that no longer trust another human being and no longer forms ties to the political community is not a human life any longer.
Martha Nussbaum, O Magazine, November 2003
Trust men and they will be true to you; treat them greatly, and they will show themselves great.
Ralph Waldo Emerson (1803 - 1882), Essays, First Series: Prudence, 1841
There are people I know who won't hurt me. I call them corpses.
Randy K. Milholland, Something Positive Comic, 12-06-05
It is better to suffer wrong than to do it, and happier to be sometimes cheated than not to trust.
Samuel Johnson (1709 - 1784)
When I'm trusting and being myself... everything in my life reflects this by falling into place easily, often miraculously.
Shakti Gawain
If we are bound to forgive an enemy, we are not bound to trust him.
Thomas Fuller (1608 - 1661)
Trust thyself only, and another shall not betray thee.
Thomas Fuller (1608 - 1661)
Trust one who has gone through it.
Virgil (70 BC - 19 BC), The Aeneid

Truth

Truth is generally the best vindication against slander.
Abraham Lincoln (1809 - 1865), letter to Secretary of War Edwin Stanton, July 18, 1864
There are few nudities so objectionable as the naked truth.
Agnes Repplier (1855 - 1950)
Believe those who are seeking the truth. Doubt those who find it.
Andre Gide (1869 - 1951)
All truth passes through three stages. First, it is ridiculed. Second, it is violently opposed. Third, it is accepted as being self-evident.
Arthur Schopenhauer (1788 - 1860)
Ye shall know the truth, and the truth shall make you free.
Bible, John 8:32
Chase after truth like hell and you'll free yourself, even though you never touch its coat-tails.
Clarence Darrow (1857 - 1938)
It's a basic truth of the human condition that everybody lies. The only variable is about what. The weird thing about telling someone they're dying is it tends to focus their priorities. You find out what matters to them. What they're willing to die for. What they're willing to lie for.
David Shore, House M.D., Three Stories, 2004
The public will believe anything, so long as it is not founded on truth.
Edith Sitwell (1887 - 1964)
Truth is the only safe ground to stand on.
Elizabeth Cady Stanton (1815 - 1902)
The truth is more important than the facts.
Frank Lloyd Wright (1869 - 1959)
All truths are easy to understand once they are discovered; the point is to discover them.
Galileo Galilei (1564 - 1642)
I have been truthful all along the way. The truth is more interesting, and if you tell the truth you never have to cover your tracks.
Gordon Atkinson, RealLivePreacher.com Weblog, January 04, 2004
The truth that makes men free is for the most part the truth which men prefer not to hear.

Herbert Agar
As scarce as truth is, the supply has always been in excess of the demand.
Josh Billings (1818 - 1885), 'Afturisms from Josh Billings: His Sayings,' 1865
Say not, 'I have found the truth,' but rather, 'I have found a truth.'
Kahlil Gibran (1883 - 1931)
Do not run from the truth. There be nought so hard to live with as a lie.
Kathryn L. Nelson, Pemberley Manor, 2006
A lie told often enough becomes the truth.
Lenin (1870 - 1924)
A lie can travel halfway around the world while the truth is putting on its shoes.
Mark Twain (1835 - 1910), (attributed)
Fiction is obliged to stick to possibilities. Truth isn't.
Mark Twain (1835 - 1910)
The history of our race, and each individual's experience, are sown thick with evidence that a truth is not hard to kill and that a lie told well is immortal.
Mark Twain (1835 - 1910), Advice to Youth
Truth is more of a stranger than fiction.
Mark Twain (1835 - 1910)
Truth sits upon the lips of dying men.
Matthew Arnold (1822 - 1888), 'Sohrab and Rustum,' 1853
The opposite of a correct statement is a false statement. But the opposite of a profound truth may well be another profound truth.
Niels Bohr (1885 - 1962)
The truth is rarely pure and never simple.
Oscar Wilde (1854 - 1900), The Importance of Being Earnest, 1895, Act I
Truth persuades by teaching, but does not teach by persuading.
Quintus Septimius Tertullianus (160 AD - 230 AD), Adversus Valentinianos
Truth is beautiful, without doubt; but so are lies.
Ralph Waldo Emerson (1803 - 1882)
I guess sometimes you have to lie to find the truth.
Scott Westerfeld, Extras, 2007
Turns out if you never lie, there's always someone mad at you.
Scott Westerfeld, Extras, 2007
How often have I said to you that when you have eliminated the impossible, whatever remains, however improbable, must be the truth?
Sir Arthur Conan Doyle (1859 - 1930), (Sherlock Holmes) The Sign of Four, 1890
Men occasionally stumble over the truth, but most of them pick themselves up and hurry off as if nothing ever happened.
Sir Winston Churchill (1874 - 1965)
This does not make the authors of those narratives liars; it makes them servants of fallible human memory and perception.
Tom Bissell, Truth in Oxiana, 2004
The truth is always a compound of two half-truths, and you never reach it, because there is always something more to say.
Tom Stoppard (1937 -)
If you do not tell the truth about yourself you cannot tell it about other people.
Virginia Woolf (1882 - 1941)
Love truth, and pardon error.
Voltaire (1694 - 1778)
The fact that a great many people believe something is no guarantee of its truth.
W. Somerset Maugham (1874 - 1965), The Razor's Edge, 1943
Against my soul's pure truth why labour you to make it wander in an unknown field?
William Shakespeare (1564 - 1616), The Comedy of Errors, Act III, sc. 2
But 'tis strange and oftentimes, to win us to our harm, the instruments of darkness tell us truths, win us with honest trifles, to betray's in deepest consequence.
William Shakespeare (1564 - 1616), Macbeth, Act I, sc. 3
But wonder on, till truth makes all things plain.
William Shakespeare (1564 - 1616), A Midsummer Night's Dream, Act V, sc. 1
They breathe truth that breathe their words in pain.
William Shakespeare (1564 - 1616), Richard II, Act II, sc. 1
Truth is truth
To the end of reckoning.
William Shakespeare (1564 - 1616), "Measure for Measure", Act 5 scene 1
Truth is truth to the end of reckoning.
William Shakespeare (1564 - 1616), Measure for Measure, Act V, sc. 5
Truth will come to light ... at the length, the truth will out.
William Shakespeare (1564 - 1616), The Merchant of Venice, Act II, sc. 2
While you live tell truth and shame the devil.
William Shakespeare (1564 - 1616), Henry IV, Part I, Act III, 1

Uncertainty

Not to be absolutely certain is, I think, one of the essential things in rationality.
Bertrand Russell (1872 - 1970), "Am I An Atheist Or An Agnostic?", 1947
When one admits that nothing is certain one must, I think, also admit that some things are much more nearly certain than others.
Bertrand Russell (1872 - 1970), "Am I An Atheist Or An Agnostic?", 1947
No man can ever be secure until he has been forsaken by Fortune.
Boethius, 522, The Happiness Hypothesis: Finding Modern Truth in Ancient Wisdom, 2005
I believe that uncertainty is really my spirit's way of whispering, "I'm in flux. I can't decide for you. Something is off-balance here."
Oprah Winfrey (1954 -), O Magazine, June 2003
In these matters the only certainty is that nothing is certain.
Pliny the Elder (23 AD - 79 AD)
The only thing that makes life possible is permanent, intolerable uncertainty; not knowing what comes next.
Ursula K. LeGuin
Doubt is not a pleasant condition, but certainty is absurd.

Voltaire (1694 - 1778)

Understanding

Some people will never learn anything because they understand everything too soon.
Alexander Pope (1688 - 1744)
Grown-ups never understand anything for themselves, and it is tiresome for children to be always and forever explaining things to them.
Antoine de Saint-Exupery (1900 - 1944), "The Little Prince", 1943
Language is the source of misunderstandings.
Antoine de Saint-Exupery (1900 - 1944)
Do not weep; do not wax indignant. Understand.
Baruch Spinoza (1632 - 1677)
A stupid man's report of what a clever man says can never be accurate, because he unconsciously translates what he hears into something he can understand.
Bertrand Russell (1872 - 1970)
Everything that irritates us about others can lead us to a better understanding of ourselves.
Carl Jung (1875 - 1961)
It is by universal misunderstanding that all agree. For if, by ill luck, people understood each other, they would never agree.
Charles Baudelaire (1821 - 1867)
The world only goes round by misunderstanding.
Charles Baudelaire (1821 - 1867)
I hear and I forget. I see and I remember. I do and I understand.
Confucius (551 BC - 479 BC)
The people may be made to follow a path of action, but they may not be made to understand it.
Confucius (551 BC - 479 BC), The Confucian Analects
That is what learning is. You suddenly understand something you've understood all your life, but in a new way.
Doris Lessing
The beginning of knowledge is the discovery of something we do not understand.
Frank Herbert (1920 - 1986)
All truths are easy to understand once they are discovered; the point is to discover them.
Galileo Galilei (1564 - 1642)
Before you contradict an old man, my fair friend, you should endeavor to understand him.
George Santayana (1863 - 1952)
When you really trust someone, you have to be okay with not understanding some things.
Gordon Atkinson, Real Live Preacher weblog, 07-08-04
Furious activity is no substitute for understanding.
H. H. Williams
Much learning does not teach understanding.
Heraclitus (540 BC - 480 BC), On the Universe
A man thinks that by mouthing hard words he understands hard things.
Herman Melville (1819 - 1891)
One half of the world cannot understand the pleasures of the other.
Jane Austen (1775 - 1817), Emma
Only if we understand can we care. Only if we care will we help. Only if we help shall they be saved.
Jane Goodall (1934 -)
In mathematics you don't understand things. You just get used to them.
Johann von Neumann (1903 - 1957)
You can see into the future if you have a basic understanding of how people are likely to act.
John Green, An Abundance of Katherines, 2008
It is well to give when asked but it is better to give unasked, through understanding.
Kahlil Gibran (1883 - 1931), 'On Giving,' The Prophet, 1923
You do ill if you praise, but worse if you censure, what you do not understand.
Leonardo da Vinci (1452 - 1519)
Nothing in life is to be feared, it is only to be understood. Now is the time to understand more, so that we may fear less.
Marie Curie (1867 - 1934)
You don't understand anything until you learn it more than one way.
Marvin Minsky
It is not necessary to understand things in order to argue about them.
Pierre Beaumarchais (1732 - 1799)
I can't understand it. I can't even understand the people who can understand it.
Queen Juliana (1909 - 2004), of the Netherlands
It is difficult to get a man to understand something when his job depends on not understanding it.
Upton Sinclair (1878 - 1968)

Values

Happiness is that state of consciousness which proceeds from the achievement of one's values.
Ayn Rand (1905 - 1982)
Pride is the recognition of the fact that you are your own highest value and, like all of man's values, it has to be earned.
Ayn Rand (1905 - 1982), Atlas Shrugged
Education without values, as useful as it is, seems rather to make man a more clever devil.
C. S. Lewis (1898 - 1963)

People everywhere have the same needs and values. They need a place to live and a job. Beyond that, they may need to sell stuff or get a mate.
Craig Newmark (1952 -), Keynote Speech, SXSW 2006
A people that values its privileges above its principles soon loses both.
Dwight D. Eisenhower (1890 - 1969), Inaugural Address, January 20, 1953
It is not our affluence, or our plumbing, or our clogged freeways that grip the imagination of others. Rather, it is the values upon which our system is built. These values imply our adherence not only to liberty and individual freedom, but also to international peace, law and order, and constructive social purpose. When we depart from these value, we do so at our peril.
J. William Fulbright (1905 -), Remarks in the Senate, June 29, 1961
Lasting change is a series of compromises. And compromise is all right, as long your values don't change.
Jane Goodall (1934 -)
Our American values are not luxuries but necessities, not the salt in our bread, but the bread itself. Our common vision of a free and just society is our greatest source of cohesion at home and strength abroad, greater than the bounty of our material blessings.
Jimmy Carter (1924 -)
We live in a time of transition, an uneasy era which is likely to endure for the rest of this century. During the period we may be tempted to abandon some of the time-honored principles and commitments which have been proven during the difficult times of past generations. We must never yield to this temptation. Our American values are not luxuries, but necessities - not the salt in our bread, but the bread itself.
Jimmy Carter (1924 -), in his farewell address
Nearly all legislation involves a weighing of public needs as against private desires; and likewise a weighing of relative social values.
Louis D. Brandeis (1856 - 1941)
If we keep treating our most important values as meaningless relics, that's exactly what they'll become.
Michael Josephson
The secret of a good life is to have the right loyalties and hold them in the right scale of values.
Norman Thomas (1884 - 1968)
The secret of a good life is to have the right loyalties and to hold them in the right scale of values.
Norman Thomas (1884 - 1968)
He who undervalues himself is justly undervalued by others.
William Hazlitt (1778 - 1830)

Vices

It has been my experience that folks who have no vices have very few virtues.
Abraham Lincoln (1809 - 1865)
Search others for their virtues, thyself for thy vices.
Benjamin Franklin (1706 - 1790)
It is a great thing to know our vices.
Cicero (106 BC - 43 BC)
The problem with people who have no vices is that generally you can be pretty sure they're going to have some pretty annoying virtues.
Elizabeth Taylor (1932 -)
Hate no one; hate their vices, not themselves.
J. G. C. Brainard
The greatest minds are capable of the greatest vices as well as of the greatest virtues.
Rene Descartes (1596 - 1650), 'Le Discours de la Methode,' 1637
Nothing is as certain as that the vices of leisure are gotten rid of by being busy.
Seneca (5 BC - 65 AD), Moral Letters to Lucilius, 64 A.D.
He has all the virtues I dislike and none of the vices I admire.
Sir Winston Churchill (1874 - 1965)
Here's a rule I recommend: Never practice two vices at once.
Tallulah Bankhead (1903 - 1968)
It is good to be without vices, but it is not good to be without temptations.
Walter Bagehot (1826 - 1877), "Biographical Studies", 1863
The better part of valour is discretion.
William Shakespeare (1564 - 1616), Henry IV, Part I, Act V, 4
The gods are just, and of our pleasant vices
Make instruments to plague us.
William Shakespeare (1564 - 1616), "King Lear", Act 5 scene 3

Victory

Force is all-conquering, but its victories are short-lived.
Abraham Lincoln (1809 - 1865)
A mind troubled by doubt cannot focus on the course to victory.
Arthur Golden, Memoirs of a Geisha
We improve ourselves by victories over ourself. There must be contests, and you must win.
Edward Gibbon (1737 - 1794)
Be ashamed to die until you have won some victory for humanity.
Horace Mann (1796 - 1859), address at Antioch College, 1859
One of the greatest victories you can gain over someone is to beat him at politeness.
Josh Billings (1818 - 1885)
Exile, for no other motive than ease, would be the last defeat, with no seed of future victory in it.
Lois McMaster Bujold, "Shards of Honor", 1986
There are always survivors at a massacre. Among the victors, if nowhere else.
Lois McMaster Bujold, Ethan of Athos, 1986
Victory attained by violence is tantamount to a defeat, for it is momentary.

Mahatma Gandhi (1869 - 1948), 'Satyagraha Leaflet No. 13,' May 3, 1919
The moment of victory is much too short to live for that and nothing else.
Martina Navratilova (1956 -)
Victory belongs to the most persevering.
Napoleon Bonaparte (1769 - 1821)
Those who know how to win are much more numerous than those who know how to make proper use of their victories.
Polybius (205 BC - 118 BC), History
Another such victory over the Romans, and we are undone.
Pyrrhus (319 BC - 272 BC), from Plutarch, Lives
Be careful that victories do not carry the seed of future defeats.
Ralph W. Sockman
The best victory is when the opponent surrenders of its own accord before there are any actual hostilities...It is best to win without fighting.
Sun-tzu (~ 400 BC), The Art of War, Planning a Siege
Victorious warriors win first and then go to war, while defeated warriors go to war first and then seek to win.
Sun-tzu (~ 400 BC), The Art of War, Strategic Assessments
Far better it is to dare mighty things, to win glorious triumphs even though checkered by failure, than to rank with those poor spirits who neither enjoy nor suffer much because they live in the gray twilight that knows neither victory nor defeat.
Theodore Roosevelt (1858 - 1919)

Violence

Opinions founded on prejudice are always sustained with the greatest of violence.
Francis Jeffrey (1773 - 1850)
Violence is the last refuge of the incompetent.
Isaac Asimov (1920 - 1992), Salvor Hardin in "Foundation"
The only thing that's been a worse flop than the organization of non-violence has been the organization of violence.
Joan Baez (1941 -)
Those who make peaceful revolution impossible will make violent revolution inevitable.
John F. Kennedy (1917 - 1963), In a speech at the White House, 1962
It is better to be violent, if there is violence in our hearts, than to put on the cloak of nonviolence to cover impotence.
Mahatma Gandhi (1869 - 1948)
Victory attained by violence is tantamount to a defeat, for it is momentary.
Mahatma Gandhi (1869 - 1948), 'Satyagraha Leaflet No. 13,' May 3, 1919
There are more pleasant things to do than beat up people.
Muhammad Ali (1942 -)
Perseverance is more prevailing than violence; and many things which cannot be overcome when they are together, yield themselves up when taken little by little.
Plutarch (46 AD - 120 AD), Lives
The right things to do are those that keep our violence in abeyance; the wrong things are those that bring it to the fore.
Robert J. Sawyer (1960 -), "Calculating God", 2000
It is by no means self-evident that human beings are most real when most violently excited; violent physical passions do not in themselves differentiate men from each other, but rather tend to reduce them to the same state.
Thomas Elliot

War

Nations have recently been led to borrow billions for war; no nation has ever borrowed largely for education. Probably, no nation is rich enough to pay for both war and civilization. We must make our choice; we cannot have both.
Abraham Flexner (1866 - 1959), Universities, part 3, 1930
One is left with the horrible feeling now that war settles nothing; that to win a war is as disastrous as to lose one.
Agatha Christie (1890 - 1976), Autobiography (1977)
I know not with what weapons World War III will be fought, but World War IV will be fought with sticks and stones.
Albert Einstein (1879 - 1955)
You cannot simultaneously prevent and prepare for war.
Albert Einstein (1879 - 1955), (attributed)
War is not nice.
Barbara Bush (1925 -)
Sometime they'll give a war and nobody will come.
Carl Sandburg (1878 - 1967), The People, Yes (1936)
People in general are scared to death of the war and all the exhibition have been a failure, because the rich - don't want to buy anything.
Frida Kahlo (1907 - 1954), Letter to Nickolas Muray, 02-27-1939
The quickest way of ending a war is to lose it.
George Orwell (1903 - 1950), Polemic, May 1946, "Second Thoughts on James Burnham"
War is a series of catastrophes that results in a victory.
Georges Clemenceau (1841 - 1929)
War is much too serious a matter to be entrusted to the military.
Georges Clemenceau (1841 - 1929)
In peace, children inter their parents; war violates the order of nature and causes parents to inter their children.
Herodotus (484 BC - 430 BC), The Histories of Herodotus
The outcome of the war is in our hands; the outcome of words is in the council.
Homer (800 BC - 700 BC), The Iliad
You can no more win a war than you can win an earthquake.
Jeannette Rankin (1880 - 1973)

War may sometimes be a necessary evil. But no matter how necessary, it is always an evil, never a good. We will not learn how to live together in peace by killing each other's children.
Jimmy Carter (1924 -)
War is an ugly thing, but not the ugliest of things. The decayed and degraded state of moral and patriotic feeling which thinks that nothing is worth war is much worse. The person who has nothing for which he is willing to fight, nothing which is more important than his own personal safety, is a miserable creature and has no chance of being free unless made and kept so by the exertions of better men than himself.
John Stuart Mill (1806 - 1873)
Neither enemy faces, nor the mothers that love them, come to mind when one is thinking of nothing but endeavouring to survive. Philosophising about war is useless under fire.
Linda Berdoll, Mr. Darcy Takes A Wife, 2004
War is not its own end, except in some catastrophic slide into absolute damnation. It's peace that's wanted. Some better peace than the one you started with.
Lois McMaster Bujold, "The Vor Game", 1990
What difference does it make to the dead, the orphans and the homeless, whether the mad destruction is wrought under the name of totalitarianism or the holy name of liberty or democracy?
Mahatma Gandhi (1869 - 1948), "Non-Violence in Peace and War"
Politics is war without bloodshed while war is politics with bloodshed.
Mao Tse-Tung (1893 - 1976)
I think the mark of a great ruler, is not his ability to make war but to achieve peace.
Monica Fairview, Darcy Cousins, 2010
The way to win an atomic war is to make certain it never starts.
Omar Bradley (1893 - 1981), Speech to Boston Chamber of Commerce, 1948
Either war is obsolete or men are.
R. Buckminster Fuller (1895 - 1983), New Yorker, Jan. 8, 1966
It is well that war is so terrible - otherwise we would grow too fond of it.
Robert E. Lee (1807 - 1870), Statement at the Battle of Fredericksburg (13th December 1862)
Never, never, never believe any war will be smooth and easy, or that anyone who embarks on the strange voyage can measure the tides and hurricanes he will encounter. The statesman who yields to war fever must realize that once the signal is given, he is no longer the master of policy but the slave of unforeseeable and uncontrollable events.
Sir Winston Churchill (1874 - 1965)
One day President Roosevelt told me that he was asking publicly for suggestions about what the war should be called. I said at once 'The Unnecessary War'.
Sir Winston Churchill (1874 - 1965), Second World War (1948)
The only winner in the War of 1812 was Tchaikovsky.
Solomon Short
Wars are, of course, as a rule to be avoided; but they are far better than certain kinds of peace.
Theodore Roosevelt (1858 - 1919), Thomas Hart Benton, Chapter 12, 1897
War is a cowardly escape from the problems of peace.
Thomas Mann (1875 - 1955)
The art of war is simple enough. Find out where your enemy is. Get at him as soon as you can. Strike him as hard as you can, and keep moving on.
Ulysses S. Grant (1822 - 1885)
Wars teach us not to love our enemies, but to hate our allies.
W. L. George
The idea of all-out nuclear war is unsettling.
Walter Goodman
Take the diplomacy out of war and the thing would fall flat in a week.
Will Rogers (1879 - 1935)
You can't say that civilization don't advance, however, for in every war they kill you in a new way.
Will Rogers (1879 - 1935), New York Times, Dec. 23, 1929

Violence

Early to bed and early to rise makes a man healthy, wealthy, and wise.
Benjamin Franklin (1706 - 1790)
If you would be wealthy, think of saving as well as getting.
Benjamin Franklin (1706 - 1790)
An unhurried sense of time is in itself a form of wealth.
Bonnie Friedman, in New York Times
Prefer loss to the wealth of dishonest gain; the former vexes you for a time; the latter will bring you lasting remorse.
Chilo
Maybe it would be better to acknowledge, like the Greeks, that a lot of behavior we call addiction is really a love of pleasure that carries the force of habit. We become addicted mostly because of the central issue in all self-control problems, which is the disproportionate value we place on short-term rewards.
Daniel Akst, We Have Met the Enemy: Self-Control in an Age of Excess, 2011
Anyone may have diamonds: an heirloom is an ornament of quite a different kind.
Elizabeth Aston, Mr. Darcy's Daughters, 2003
It is pretty hard to tell what does bring happiness; poverty and wealth have both failed.
Kin Hubbard (1868 - 1930)
Though I am grateful for the blessings of wealth, it hasn't changed who I am. My feet are still on the ground. I'm just wearing better shoes.
Oprah Winfrey (1954 -), O Magazine
Wealth is the parent of luxury and indolence, and poverty of meanness and viciousness, and both of discontent.
Plato (427 BC - 347 BC), The Republic

Nothing is more admirable than the fortitude with which millionaires tolerate the disadvantages of their wealth.
Rex Stout (1886 - 1975)
It is the sign of a weak mind to be unable to bear wealth.
Seneca (5 BC - 65 AD)
Wealth is the slave of a wise man. The master of a fool.
Seneca (5 BC - 65 AD)
Be charitable before wealth makes thee covetous.
Sir Thomas Browne (1605 - 1682)
Wisdom outweighs any wealth.
Sophocles (496 BC - 406 BC), Antigone

Weather

When all is said and done, the weather and love are the two elements about which one can never be sure.
Alice Hoffman, 'Here on Earth'
Barometer, n.: An ingenious instrument which indicates what kind of weather we are having.
Ambrose Bierce (1842 - 1914), The Devil's Dictionary
Time for the weather report. It's cold out folks. Bonecrushing cold. The kind of cold which will wrench the spirit out of a young man, or forge it into steel.
Diane Frolov and Andrew Schneider, Northern Exposure, Lost and Found, 1992
Weather forecast for tonight: dark. Continued dark overnight, with widely scattered light by morning.
George Carlin (1937 - 2008)
Isn't it interesting that the same people who laugh at science fiction listen to weather forecasts and economists?
Kelvin Throop III
Don't knock the weather. If it didn't change once in a while, nine out of ten people couldn't start a conversation.
Kin Hubbard (1868 - 1930)
No matter how rich you become, how famous or powerful, when you die the size of your funeral will still pretty much depend on the weather.
Michael Pritchard
Money is the opposite of the weather. Nobody talks about it, but everybody does something about it.
Rebecca Johnson, in 'Vogue'

Winter

In the depth of winter, I finally learned that within me there lay an invincible summer.
Albert Camus (1913 - 1960)
If we had no winter, the spring would not be so pleasant: if we did not sometimes taste of adversity, prosperity would not be so welcome.
Anne Bradstreet (1612 - 1672), 'Meditations Divine and Moral,' 1655
Perhaps I am a bear, or some hibernating animal underneath, for the instinct to be half asleep all winter is so strong in me.
Anne Morrow Lindbergh
Every winter, When the great sun has turned his face away, The earth goes down into a vale of grief, And fasts, and weeps, and shrouds herself in sables, Leaving her wedding-garlands to decay– Then leaps in spring to his returning kisses.
Charles Kingsley (1819 - 1875), Saint's Tragedy (act III, sc. 1)
In the bleak midwinter Frosty wind made moan, Earth stood hard as iron, Water like a stone; Snow had fallen, snow on snow, Snow on snow, In the bleak midwinter, Long ago.
Christina Rossetti (1830 - 1894), A Christmas Carol
There's a certain Slant of light, Winter Afternoons– That oppresses, like the Heft Of Cathedral Tunes–
Emily Dickinson (1830 - 1886), No. 258
Every mile is two in winter.
George Herbert (1593 - 1633), Jacula Prudentum
One kind word can warm three winter months.
Japanese proverb
The tendinous part of the mind, so to speak, is more developed in winter; the fleshy, in summer. I should say winter had given the bone and sinew to literature, summer the tissues and the blood.
John Burroughs (1837 - 1921), The Snow-Walkers
When you live in Texas, every single time you see snow it's magical.
Pamela Ribon, Why Girls Are Weird, 2003
When there's snow on the ground, I like to pretend I'm walking on clouds.
Takayuki Ikkaku, Arisa Hosaka and Toshihiro Kawabata, Animal Crossing: Wild World, 2005
Winter is on my head, but eternal spring is in my heart.
Victor Hugo (1802 - 1885)
Winter lies too long in country towns; hangs on until it is stale and shabby, old and sullen.
Willa Cather (1873 - 1947), My Antonia
And for the season it was winter, and they that know the winters of that country know them to be sharp and violent, and subject to cruel and fierce storms.
William Bradford (1590 - 1657), Of Plymouth Plantation
O Winter! ruler of the inverted year, . . . I crown thee king of intimate delights, Fireside enjoyments, home-born happiness, And all the comforts that the lowly roof Of undisturb'd Retirement, and the hours Of long uninterrupted evening, know.
William Cowper (1731 - 1800), Task (bk. IV, l. 120)
Blow, blow, thou winter wind
Thou art not so unkind,
As man's ingratitude.

William Shakespeare (1564 - 1616)
Now is the winter of our discontent
Made glorious summer by this son of York,
And all the clouds that loured upon our house
In the deep bosom of the ocean buried.
William Shakespeare (1564 - 1616), Richard III, Act I, sc. I
Under the greenwood tree who loves to lie with me ... Here shall he see no enemy but winter and rough weather.
William Shakespeare (1564 - 1616), As You Like It, Act II, sc. 5
Winter, which, being full of care, makes summer's welcome thrice more wish'd, more rare.
William Shakespeare (1564 - 1616), Sonnet LVI

Wisdom

Wisdom doesn't automatically come with old age. Nothing does - except wrinkles. It's true, some wines improve with age. But only if the grapes were good in the first place.
Abigail Van Buren (1918 -), 1978
The whole problem with the world is that fools and fanatics are always so certain of themselves, but wiser people so full of doubts.
Bertrand Russell (1872 - 1970)
Wisdom is what's left after we've run out of personal opinions.
Cullen Hightower
Society cannot exist unless a controlling power upon will and appetite be placed somewhere, and the less of it there is within, the more there must be without.
Edmund Burke (1729 - 1797), We Have Met the Enemy: Self-Control in an Age of Excess, 2011
As one grows older, one becomes wiser and more foolish.
Francois de La Rochefoucauld (1613 - 1680), Reflexions ou Sentences et Maximes Morales 1655
One's first step in wisdom is to question everything - and one's last is to come to terms with everything.
Georg Christoph Lichtenberg (1742 - 1799)
The wisest mind has something yet to learn.
George Santayana (1863 - 1952)
The older I grow the more I distrust the familiar doctrine that age brings wisdom.
H. L. Mencken (1880 - 1956)
Force without wisdom falls of its own weight.
Horace (65 BC - 8 BC), Odes
Science is organized knowledge. Wisdom is organized life.
Immanuel Kant (1724 - 1804)
Men are wise in proportion, not to their experience, but to their capacity for experience.
James Boswell (1740 - 1795), Life of Samuel Johnson, 1791
Pain makes man think. Thought makes man wise. Wisdom makes life endurable.
John Patrick, The Teahouse of the August moon, Act I, scene I, 1957
That which seems the height of absurdity in one generation often becomes the height of wisdom in the next.
John Stuart Mill (1806 - 1873)
It is unwise to be too sure of one's own wisdom. It is healthy to be reminded that the strongest might weaken and the wisest might err.
Mahatma Gandhi (1869 - 1948)
We don't receive wisdom; we must discover it for ourselves after a journey that no one can take for us or spare us.
Marcel Proust (1871 - 1922)
To acquire knowledge, one must study; but to acquire wisdom, one must observe.
Marilyn vos Savant
It is not white hair that engenders wisdom.
Menander (342 BC - 292 BC), Unidentified fragment
Inner wisdom is more important than wealth. The more you spend it, the more you gain.
Oprah Winfrey (1954 -), Stanford Commencement Adress, 2008
Those who wish to appear wise among fools, among the wise seem foolish.
Quintilian, De Institutione Oratoria
Like an ability or a muscle, hearing your inner wisdom is strengthened by doing it.
Robbie Gass
Ask counsel of both times-of the ancient time what is best, and of the latter time what is fittest.
Sir Francis Bacon (1561 - 1626), Of Great Place, 1625
Wisdom outweighs any wealth.
Sophocles (496 BC - 406 BC), Antigone
No man is wise enough by himself.
Titus Maccius Plautus (254 BC - 184 BC), Miles Gloriosus
Not by age but by capacity is wisdom acquired.
Titus Maccius Plautus (254 BC - 184 BC), Trinummus
A wise man can see more from the bottom of a well than a fool can from a mountain top .
Unknown
Wisdom is not finally tested in the schools, Wisdom cannot be pass'd from one having it to another not having it, Wisdom is of the soul, is not susceptible of proof, is its own proof.
Walt Whitman (1819 - 1892)
Good people are good because they've come to wisdom through failure.
William Saroyan (1908 - 1981)
The fool doth think he is wise, but the wise man knows himself to be a fool.
William Shakespeare (1564 - 1616), "As You Like It", Act 5 scene 1

Wishes

We would often be sorry if our wishes were gratified.

Aesop (620 BC - 560 BC), The Old Man and Death
Dreams are wishes your heart makes.
American Proverb
Nothing is easier than self-deceit. For what each man wishes, that he also believes to be true.
Demosthenes (384 BC - 322 BC), Third Olynthiac
The easiest thing of all is to deceive one's self; for what a man wishes he generally believes to be true.
Demosthenes (384 BC - 322 BC)
Great minds have purposes, others have wishes.
Washington Irving (1783 - 1859)
If wishes would prevail with me, my purpose should not fail with me.
William Shakespeare (1564 - 1616), Henry V, Act III, sc. 2
Thy wish was father... to that thought.
William Shakespeare (1564 - 1616), Henry IV, Part II, Act IV, 5
Where nothing wants that want itself doth seek.
William Shakespeare (1564 - 1616), Love's Labour's Lost, Act IV, sc. 3
Wishers were ever fools.
William Shakespeare (1564 - 1616), Antony and Cleopatra, Act IV, sc. 15

Work

There has never been but one question in all civilization-how to keep a few men from saying to many men: You work and earn bread and we will eat it.
Abraham Lincoln (1809 - 1865)
A man can only do what he can do. But if he does that each day he can sleep at night and do it again the next day.
Albert Schweitzer (1875 - 1965)
Man is so made that he can only find relaxation from one kind of labor by taking up another.
Anatole France (1844 - 1924), The Crime of Sylvestre Bonnard
All paid jobs absorb and degrade the mind.
Aristotle (384 BC - 322 BC)
Pleasure in the job puts perfection in the work.
Aristotle (384 BC - 322 BC)
You can't rest on your laurels. Your own body of work is yet to come.
Barack Obama (1961 -), Arizona State Commencement Speech, 2009
One of the symptoms of an approaching nervous breakdown is the belief that one's work is terribly important.
Bertrand Russell (1872 - 1970), Conquest of Happiness (1930) ch. 5
It has been my experience that one cannot, in any shape or form, depend on human relations for lasting reward. It is only work that truly satisfies.
Bette Davis (1908 - 1989), The Lonely Life, 1962
You do your best work if you do a job that makes you happy.
Bob Ross (1942 - 1995), Best of Joy of Painting, Winter Elegance
We have too many people who live without working, and we have altogether too many people who work without living.
Charles Reynolds Brown
At least one study of blocked writers has found that they were more productive and more creative when they were essentially forced to write instead of scribbling only when the mood struck them.
Daniel Akst, We Have Met the Enemy: Self-Control in an Age of Excess, 2011
Real success is finding your lifework in the work that you love.
David McCullough (1933 -)
Doing what you love means dealing with things you don't.
David Shore, House M.D., Last Temptation, 2011
Working from home meant we could vary snack and coffee breaks, change our desks or view, goof off, drink on the job, even spend the day in pajamas, and often meet to gossip or share ideas. On the other hand, we bossed ourselves around, set impossible goals, and demanded longer hours than office jobs usually entail. It was the ultimate "flextime," in that it depended on how flexible we felt each day, given deadlines, distractions, and workaholic crescendos.
Diane Ackerman, One Hundred Names for Love: A Stroke, A Marriage, and the Language of Healing, 2011
When a man tells you that he got rich through hard work, ask him: 'Whose?'
Don Marquis (1878 - 1937)
A human being must have occupation if he or she is not to become a nuisance to the world.
Dorothy L. Sayers (1893 - 1957)
Hard work never killed anybody, but why take a chance?
Edgar Bergen (1903 - 1978), (Charlie McCarthy)
Folks who never do more than their paid for, never get paid for any more than they do.
Elbert Hubbard (1856 - 1915)
Get happiness out of your work or you may never know what happiness is.
Elbert Hubbard (1856 - 1915)
Measure not the work until the day's out and the labor done.
Elizabeth Barrett Browning (1806 - 1861)
Our great weariness comes from work not done.
Eric Hoffer (1902 - 1983), The New York Times Magazine, April 25, 1971
A professional is one who does his best work when he feels the least like working.
Frank Lloyd Wright (1869 - 1959)
Getting fired is nature's way to telling you that you had the wrong job in the first place.
Hal Lancaster, in The Wall Street Journal
One kernel is felt in a hogshead; one drop of water helps to swell the ocean; a spark of fire helps to give light to the world. None are too small, too feeble, too poor to be of service. Think of this and act.

Hannah More
I long to accomplish a great and noble task, but it is my chief duty to accomplish humble tasks as though they were great and noble. The world is moved along, not only by the mighty shoves of its heroes, but also by the aggregate of the tiny pushes of each honest worker.
Helen Keller (1880 - 1968)
Derive happiness in oneself from a good day's work, from illuminating the fog that surrounds us.
Henri Matisse (1869 - 1954)
Work while you have the light. You are responsible for the talent that has been entrusted to you.
Henri-Frédéric Amiel
Do not hire a man who does your work for money, but him who does it for love of it.
Henry David Thoreau (1817 - 1862)
When your work speaks for itself, don't interrupt.
Henry J. Kaiser (1882 - 1967)
Life grants nothing to us mortals without hard work.
Horace (65 BC - 8 BC), Satires
People forget how fast you did a job - but they remember how well you did it.
Howard Newton
Nothing is really work unless you would rather be doing something else.
James M. Barrie (1860 - 1937)
By the work one knows the workmen.
Jean De La Fontaine (1621 - 1695)
Your whole life people tell you to do what you love. But if you gotta do something else to pay the bills, you don't automatically have to be miserable.
Jeph Jacques, Questionable Content, Give It Your All, 06-22-12
...in order that a man may be happy, it is necessary that he should not only be capable of his work, but a good judge of his work.
John Ruskin (1819 - 1900)
In order that people may be happy in their work, these three things are needed: They must be fit for it. They must not do too much of it. And they must have a sense of success in it.
John Ruskin (1819 - 1900), Pre-Raphaelitism, 1850
Never continue in a job you don't enjoy. If you're happy in what you're doing, you'll like yourself, you'll have inner peace. And if you have that, along with physical health, you will have had more success than you could possibly have imagined.
Johnny Carson (1925 - 2005)
Genius begins great works; labor alone finishes them.
Joseph Joubert
I'm well aware when they fired the starting gun I was halfway down the track, but I still ran as fast as I could for 25 years.
Joss Whedon, Entertainment Weekly, 08-30-13
Always work hard on something uncomfortably exciting.
Larry Page, University of Michigan Commencement Address, 2009
Iron rusts from disuse; stagnant water loses its purity and in cold weather becomes frozen; even so does inaction sap the vigor of the mind.
Leonardo da Vinci (1452 - 1519), The Notebooks
You have to surrender to the fact that you are of too many in a highly competitive field where it is difficult to stand out. Over time, through your work, you will demonstrate who you are and what you bring to the field. Just stay with it and keep working.
Lisa Kudrow, Vasser Commencement Address, 2010
My work is a game, a very serious game.
M. C. Escher (1898 - 1972)
The sweat of hard work is not to be displayed. It is much more graceful to appear favored by the gods.
Maxine Hong Kingston, The Woman Warrior, 1976
It does not seem to be true that work necessarily needs to be unpleasant. It may always have to be hard, or at least harder than doing nothing at all. But there is ample evidence that work can be enjoyable, and that indeed, it is often the most enjoyable part of life.
Mihaly Csikszentmihalyi, Flow: The Psychology of Optimal Experience, 1990
People who work sitting down get paid more than people who work standing up.
Ogden Nash (1902 - 1971)
When you choose the paradigm of service, it turns everything you do from a job into a gift.
Oprah Winfrey (1954 -), Stanford Commencement Adress, 2008
When you're doing the work you're meant to do, it feels right and every day is a bonus, regardless of what you're getting paid.
Oprah Winfrey (1954 -), Stanford Commencement Adress, 2008
Plans are only good intentions unless they immediately degenerate into hard work.
Peter Drucker (1909 - 2005)
You don't become great by trying to be great. You become great by wanting to do something, and then doing it so hard that you become great in the process.
Randall Munroe, xkcd, Marie Curie, 2011
The more I want to get something done, the less I call it work.
Richard Bach
Anyone can do any amount of work provided it isn't the work he is supposed to be doing at the moment.
Robert Benchley (1889 - 1945)
Anyone who works is a fool. I don't work - I merely inflict myself upon the public.
Robert Morley
Hard work spotlights the character of people: some turn up their sleeves, some turn up their noses, and some don't turn up at all.
Sam Ewing
It's not the hours you put in your work that counts, it's the work you put in the hours.

Sam Ewing
Live neither in the past nor in the future, but let each day's work absorb your entire energies, and satisfy your widest ambition.
Sir William Osler (1849 - 1919), to his students
You've got to find what you love and that is as true for work as it is for lovers. Your work is going to fill a large part of your life and the only way to be truly satisfied is to do what you believe is great work. And the only way to do great work is to love what what you do. If you haven't found it yet, keep looking and don't settle. As with all matters of the heart, you'll know when you've found it.
Steve Jobs (1955 - 2011), Stanford Commencement Adress, 2005
Everybody loves some fun, back-breaking manual labor!
Takayuki Ikkaku, Arisa Hosaka and Toshihiro Kawabata, Animal Crossing: Wild World, 2005
Far and away the best prize that life offers is the chance to work hard at work worth doing.
Theodore Roosevelt (1858 - 1919), Speech in New York, September 7, 1903
Genius is one per cent inspiration, ninety-nine per cent perspiration.
Thomas A. Edison (1847 - 1931), Harper's Monthly, 1932
Genius is one percent inspiration, ninety-nine percent perspiration.
Thomas A. Edison (1847 - 1931), Harper's Monthly, 1932
Blessed is he who has found his work; let him ask no other blessedness.
Thomas Carlyle (1795 - 1881), Past and Present, 1843
I'm a great believer in luck, and I find the harder I work the more I have of it.
Thomas Jefferson (1743 - 1826), (attributed)
In most cases being a good boss means hiring talented people and then getting out of their way. In other cases, to get the best work out of people you may have to pretend you are not their boss and let them treat someone else like the boss, and then that whispers to you behind a fake wall and you tell them what to tell the first person. Contrary to what I believed as a little girl, being the boss almost never involves marching around, waving your arms, and chanting, " I am the boss! I am the boss!"
Tina Fey, Bossypants, 2011
Whoever does not love his work cannot hope that it will please others.
Unknown
Work saves us from three great evils: boredom, vice and need.
Voltaire (1694 - 1778), Candide, 1759
A man ought to work. That's what he's here for. That's how he contributes to the welfare of the community.
W. Somerset Maugham (1874 - 1965), The Razor's Edge, 1943
I like manual labor. Whenever I've got waterlogged with study, I've taken a spell of it and found it spiritually invigorating.
W. Somerset Maugham (1874 - 1965), The Razor's Edge, 1943
The secret of greatness is simple: do better work than any other man in your field - and keep on doing it.
Wilfred A. Peterson
Whenever it is in any way possible, every boy and girl should choose as his life work some occupation which he should like to do anyhow, even if he did not need the money.
William Lyon Phelps

Worries

Do not anticipate trouble, or worry about what may never happen. Keep in the sunlight.
Benjamin Franklin (1706 - 1790)
That's the secret to life... replace one worry with another....
Charles M. Schulz (1922 - 2000), Charlie Brown
What worries you masters you.
Haddon W. Robinson
Worries go down better with soup than without.
Jewish Proverb
Worrying helps you some—it seems as if you were doing something when you're worrying.
L. M. Montgomery (1874 - 1942), Anne of Green Gables, 1908
Worry a little bit every day and in a lifetime you will lose a couple of years. If something is wrong, fix it if you can. But train yourself not to worry. Worry never fixes anything.
Mary Hemingway
It is generally true that, the more preparations one has for an event, the more inconveniently fast the event will occur.
Monica Fairview, Darcy Cousins, 2010
If you can solve your problem, then what is the need of worrying? If you cannot solve it, then what is the use of worrying?
Shantideva
We have been taught to believe that negative equals realistic and positive equals unrealistic.
Susan Jeffers

Writing

I've always believed in writing without a collaborator, because where two people are writing the same book, each believes he gets all the worries and only half the royalties.
Agatha Christie (1890 - 1976)
I always wrote with the idea that what I put out there is going to stay there. Once I publish something, it has been published. I've never deleted more than one or two posts from my site. I don't think that there are takebacks. I don't feel right about it.
Alison Headley, Digital Preservation and Blogs, SXSW 2006
If the weak hand, that has recorded this tale, has, by its scenes, beguiled the mourner of one hour of sorrow, or, by its moral, taught him to sustain it - the effort, however humble, has not been vain, nor is the writer unrewarded.
Ann Radcliffe (1764 - 1823), The Mysteries of Udolpho, 1764
The best way to become acquainted with a subject is to write a book about it.
Benjamin Disraeli (1804 - 1881)
Not every story has explosions and car chases. That's why they have nudity and espionage.
Bill Barnes and Gene Ambaum, Unshelved, 09-14-08
I have made this [letter] longer, because I have not had the time to make it shorter.
Blaise Pascal (1623 - 1662), "Lettres provinciales", letter 16, 1657
All of us learn to write in the second grade. Most of us go on to greater things.
Bobby Knight (1940 -)
Don't use words too big for the subject. Don't say 'infinitely' when you mean 'very'; otherwise you'll have no word left when you want to talk about something really infinite.
C. S. Lewis (1898 - 1963)
Even in literature and art, no man who bothers about originality will ever be original: whereas if you simply try to tell the truth (without caring twopence how often it has been told before) you will, nine times out of ten, become original without ever having noticed it.
C. S. Lewis (1898 - 1963)
Words, once they are printed, have a life of their own.
Carol Burnett (1936 -)
Many books require no thought from those who read them, and for a very simple reason; they made no such demand upon those who wrote them.
Charles Caleb Colton (1780 - 1832), Lacon, 1820
An author is a fool who, not content with boring those he lives with, insists on boring future generations.
Charles de Montesquieu (1689 - 1755)
This is pretty much what journals are all about, at least to me. I knew as I wrote them that even though they provided an excellent place for brain (and heart, and psyche) dump, they were mainly a map of me.
Colleen Wainwright, communicatrix, 03-23-2006
Better to write for yourself and have no public, than to write for the public and have no self.
Cyril Connolly (1903 - 1974)
Writers should be read, but neither seen nor heard.
Daphne du Maurier (1907 - 1989)
Maybe that's just what happens; you start out wanting to change the world through language, and end up thinking it's enough to tell a few jokes.
David Nicholls, One Day, 2010
She was discovering once again that reading and writing were not the same-you couldn't just soak it up then squeeze it out again.
David Nicholls, One Day, 2010
Sometimes, when it's going badly, she wonders if what she believes to be a love of the written word is really just a fetish for stationary. The true writer, the born writer, will scribble words on scraps of litter, the back of a bus ticket, on the wall of a cell.
David Nicholls, One Day, 2010
Writing gives you the illusion of control, and then you realize it's just an illusion, that people are going to bring their own stuff into it.
David Sedaris, interview in Louisville Courier-Journal, June 5, 2005
A classic is classic not because it conforms to certain structural rules, or fits certain definitions (of which its author had quite probably never heard). It is classic because of a certain eternal and irrepressible freshness.
Edith Wharton (1862 - 1937)
Beneath the rule of men entirely great,
The pen is mightier than the sword.
Edward Bulwer-Lytton (1803 - 1873), Richelieu
Unprovided with original learning, unformed in the habits of thinking, unskilled in the arts of composition, I resolved to write a book.
Edward Gibbon (1737 - 1794)
The skill of writing is to create a context in which other people can think.
Edwin Schlossberg
If writers stopped writing about what happened to them, then there would be a lot of empty pages.
Elaine Liner, We Got Naked, Now What, SXSW 2006
Please write again soon. Though my own life is filled with activity, letters encourage momentary escape into others lives and I come back to my own with greater contentment.
Elizabeth Forsythe Hailey, 'A Woman of Independent Means'
It's not enough to create magic. You have to create a price for magic, too. You have to create rules.
Eric A. Burns, Gossamer Commons, 06-15-05
You ask me why I do not write something....I think one's feelings waste themselves in words, they ought all to be distilled into actions and into actions which bring results.
Florence Nightingale (1820 - 1910), in Cecil Woodham-Smith, Florence Nightingale, 1951
Your life story would not make a good book. Don't even try.
Fran Lebowitz (1950 -)
After being Turned Down by numerous Publishers, he had decided to write for Posterity.
George Ade (1866 - 1944), "Fables in Slang", 1899
The man who writes about himself and his own time is the only man who writes about all people and all time.
George Bernard Shaw (1856 - 1950)
This is the sixth book I've written, which isn't bad for a guy who's only read two.
George Burns (1896 - 1996)

A scrupulous writer, in every sentence that he writes, will ask himself at least four questions, thus: 1. What am I trying to say? 2. What words will express it? 3. What image or idiom will make it clearer? 4. Is this image fresh enough to have an effect?
George Orwell (1903 - 1950), "Politics and the English Language", 1946
In certain kinds of writing, particularly in art criticism and literary criticism, it is normal to come across long passages which are almost completely lacking in meaning.
George Orwell (1903 - 1950), "Politics and the English Language", 1946
Good writing takes more than just time; it wants your best moments and the best of you.
Gordon Atkinson, RealLivePreacher.com weblog, 10-09-04
I think people want their illusions and writers are mostly illusion. When you read their words, you read a flattened, incomplete version of the writer.
Gordon Atkinson, RealLivePreacher.com Weblog, January 05, 2004
I write because I'm afraid to say some things out loud.
Gordon Atkinson, Real Live Preacher weblog, 03-13-05
If you want to write you must have faith in yourself. Faith enough to believe that if a thing is true about you, it is likely true about many people. And if you can have faith in your integrity and your motives, then you can write about yourself without fear.
Gordon Atkinson, Real Live Preacher weblog, 07-25-06
See things as they are and write about them. Don't waste your creative energy trying to make things up. Even if you are writing fiction, write the things you see and know.
Gordon Atkinson, Real Live Preacher weblog, 07-25-06
This is the challenge of writing. You have to be very emotionally engaged in what you're doing, or it comes out flat. You can't fake your way through this.
Gordon Atkinson, RealLivePreacher.com Weblog, January 29, 2004
No passion in the world is equal to the passion to alter someone else's draft.
H. G. Wells (1866 - 1946)
Keep writing. Keep doing it and doing it. Even in the moments when it's so hurtful to think about writing.
Heather Armstrong, Keynote Speech, SXSW 2006
How vain it is to sit down to write when you have not stood up to live.
Henry David Thoreau (1817 - 1862)
Be generous, be delicate, and always pursue the prize.
Henry James (1843 - 1916), from his essay about the rules of writing
I am a galley slave to pen and ink.
Honore de Balzac (1799 - 1850)
The cure for writer's cramp is writer's block.
Inigo DeLeon
You must keep sending work out; you must never let a manuscript do nothing but eat its head off in a drawer. You send that work out again and again, while you're working on another one. If you have talent, you will receive some measure of success - but only if you persist.
Isaac Asimov (1920 - 1992)
It is not a bad idea to get in the habit of writing down one's thoughts. It saves one having to bother anyone else with them.
Isabel Colegate
Writing well means never having to say, 'I guess you had to be there.'
Jef Mallett, Frazz, 07-29-07
The first step in blogging is not writing them but reading them.
Jeff Jarvis, BuzzMachine, 07-10-2006
Write something to suit yourself and many people will like it; write something to suit everybody and scarcely anyone will care for it.
Jesse Stuart
I write entirely to find out what I'm thinking, what I'm looking at, what I see and what it means. What I want and what I fear.
Joan Didion (1934 -)
If any man wish to write in a clear style, let him be first clear in his thoughts; and if any would write in a noble style, let him first possess a noble soul.
Johann Wolfgang von Goethe (1749 - 1832)
The tendinous part of the mind, so to speak, is more developed in winter; the fleshy, in summer. I should say winter had given the bone and sinew to literature, summer the tissues and the blood.
John Burroughs (1837 - 1921), The Snow-Walkers
Stories don't just make us matter to each other—maybe they're also the only way to the infinite mattering he'd been after for so long.
John Green, An Abundance of Katherines, 2008
There is this unwritten contract between author and reader and I think not ending your book kind of violates that contract.
John Green, The Fault in Our Stars, 2012
You have a choice in this world, I believe, about how to tell sad stories.
John Green, The Fault in Our Stars, 2012
The way you define yourself as a writer is that you write every time you have a free minute. If you didn't behave that way you would never do anything.
John Irving (1942 -)
You can't think yourself out of a writing block, you have to write yourself out of a thinking block.
John Rogers, Kung Fu Monkey, 06-25-11
Say all you have to say in the fewest possible words, or your reader will be sure to skip them; and in the plainest possible words or he will certainly misunderstand them.
John Ruskin (1819 - 1900)
About the most originality that any writer can hope to achieve honestly is to steal with good judgment.
Josh Billings (1818 - 1885)
I go to movies expecting to have a whole experience. If I want a movie that doesn't end, I'll go to a French movie. A movie has to be complete within itself; it can't just build off the first one or play variations.

Joss Whedon, Entertainment Weekly, 08-30-13
I'm the least confident person in so many ways. But I believed that if somebody gave me the chance to tell a story, I would tell a story [well enough] that the person who gave me the chance would get their money back.
Joss Whedon, Entertainment Weekly, 08-30-13
If I wrote what I really think, I would be so sad all the time. We create to fill a gap - not just to avoid the idea of dying, it's to fill some particular gap in ourselves.
Joss Whedon, Entertainment Weekly, 08-30-13
It's very important that we start creating new content again. We can only build on nostalgia so much before we have nothing left to build on.
Joss Whedon, Entertainment Weekly, 08-30-13
You go to movies to see people you love suffer - that's why you go to the movies. You don't go to see a movie about a guy who already knows he has a wonderful life.
Joss Whedon, Entertainment Weekly, 08-30-13
No letter from a lover is ever more welcome, brings more joy, than a publisher's expression of interest does to a new author!
Judith Brocklehurst, Darcy And Anne
Literature is an occupation in which you have to keep proving your talent to people who have none.
Jules Renard (1864 - 1910)
Writing is the only profession where no one considers you ridiculous if you earn no money.
Jules Renard (1864 - 1910)
A writer is a writer not because she writes well and easily, because she has amazing talent, because everything she does is golden. In my view, a writer is a writer because even when there is no hope, even when nothing you do shows any sign of promise, you keep writing anyway.
Junot Diaz, O Magazine, November 2009
Thus, in a real sense, I am constantly writing autobiography, but I have to turn it into fiction in order to give it credibility.
Katherine Paterson, The Spying Heart, 1989
Reading stories is bad enough but writing them is worse.
L. M. Montgomery (1874 - 1942), Anne of Green Gables, 1908
The only reason for being a professional writer is that you can't help it.
Leo Rosten (1908 -)
Inspiration is wonderful when it happens, but the writer must develop an approach for the rest of the time... The wait is simply too long.
Leonard Bernstein (1918 - 1990)
Learn as much by writing as by reading.
Lord Acton
I take the view, and always have, that if you cannot say what you are going to say in twenty minutes you ought to go away and write a book about it.
Lord Brabazon (1884 - 1964)
First you're an unknown, then you write one book and you move up to obscurity.
Martin Myers
When you write things down, they sometimes take you places you hadn't planned.
Melanie Benjamin, Alice I Have Been, 2010
There's always something to write about. If there's not then you need to live life more aggressively.
Min Kim, Better Blogging Brainstorming, SXSW 2006
I was working on the proof of one of my poems all the morning, and took out a comma. In the afternoon I put it back again.
Oscar Wilde (1854 - 1900)
I love being a writer. What I can't stand is the paperwork.
Peter De Vries
In comparing various authors with one another, I have discovered that some of the gravest and latest writers have transcribed, word for word, from former works, without making acknowledgment.
Pliny the Elder (23 AD - 79 AD), Natural History
There is nothing to write about, you say. Well then, write and let me know just this - that there is nothing to write about; or tell me in the good old style if you are well. That's right. I am quite well.
Pliny the Younger (62 AD - 114 AD), Letters
Typos are very important to all written form. It gives the reader something to look for so they aren't distracted by the total lack of content in your writing.
Randy K. Milholland, Something Positive Comic, 07-03-05
I have never thought of writing as hard work, but I have worked hard to find a voice.
Randy Pausch, Carnegie Mellon Commencement Speech, 2008
The most difficult part of writing a book is not devising a plot which will captivate the reader. It's not developing characters the reader will have strong feelings for or against. It is not finding a setting which will take the reader to a place he or she has never been. It is not the research, whether in fiction or non-fiction. The most difficult task facing a writer is to find the voice in which to tell the story.
Randy Pausch, Carnegie Mellon Commencement Speech, 2008
You have to know how to accept rejection and reject acceptance.
Ray Bradbury (1920 -), advice to writers
At least half the mystery novels published violate the law that the solution, once revealed, must seem to be inevitable.
Raymond Chandler (1888 - 1959)
The key to non-anxious sermon-writing is that it's not about me. It's about the congregation. I honor the fact that the listeners bring more to the sermon than I do. I remind myself of the hundreds of times someone says, 'I loved how you said...' and then tell me things that they heard that were nowhere in my text and that I never said. But they heard what they needed to hear.
Reverend Sean Parker Dennison, Ministrare, 04-07-2006

Detail makes the difference between boring and terrific writing. It's the difference between a pencil sketch and a lush oil painting. As a writer, words are your paint. Use all the colors.
Rhys Alexander, Writing Gooder, 12-09-05
A good many young writers make the mistake of enclosing a stamped, self-addressed envelope, big enough for the manuscript to come back in. This is too much of a temptation to the editor.
Ring Lardner (1885 - 1933), "How to Write Short Stories"
It took me fifteen years to discover that I had no talent for writing, but I couldn't give it up because by that time I was too famous.
Robert Benchley (1889 - 1945)
Writing is not necessarily something to be ashamed of, but do it in private and wash your hands afterwards.
Robert Heinlein (1907 - 1988)
Politics is not a bad profession. If you succeed there are many rewards, if you disgrace yourself you can always write a book.
Ronald Reagan (1911 - 2004)
Every journalist has a novel in him, which is an excellent place for it.
Russel Lynes
The only thing I was fit for was to be a writer, and this notion rested solely on my suspicion that I would never be fit for real work, and that writing didn't require any.
Russell Baker (1925 -)
I don't think anyone should write their autobiography until after they're dead.
Samuel Goldwyn (1882 - 1974)
Read over your compositions, and wherever you meet with a passage which you think is particularly fine, strike it out.
Samuel Johnson (1709 - 1784), from Boswell's Life of Johnson
Your manuscript is both good and original, but the part that is good is not original and the part that is original is not good.
Samuel Johnson (1709 - 1784), (attributed)
A poet ought not to pick nature's pocket. Let him borrow, and so borrow as to repay by the very act of borrowing. Examine nature accurately, but write from recollection, and trust more to the imagination than the memory.
Samuel Taylor Coleridge (1772 - 1834)
There are a lot of people who can't write and maybe shouldn't write.
Sarah Hepola, How To Add Video To Your Blog, SXSW 2006
Even writers need relief from words.
Sarah Vowell, O Magazine, March 2009
There is only one way to defeat the enemy, and that is to write as well as one can. The best argument is an undeniably good book.
Saul Bellow (1915 - 2005)
Reading maketh a full man, conference a ready man, and writing an exact man.
Sir Francis Bacon (1561 - 1626)
The reserve of modern assertions is sometimes pushed to extremes, in which the fear of being contradicted leads the writer to strip himself of almost all sense and meaning.
Sir Winston Churchill (1874 - 1965)
I'm all in favor of keeping dangerous weapons out of the hands of fools. Let's start with typewriters.
Solomon Short
Advice to writers: Sometimes you just have to stop writing. Even before you begin.
Stanislaw J. Lec (1909 - 1966), "Unkempt Thoughts"
I never feel that I have comprehended an emotion, or fully lived even the smallest events, until I have reflected upon it in my journal; my pen is my truest confidant, holding in check the passions and disappointments that I dare not share even with my beloved.
Stephanie Barron, Jane and the Unpleasantness at Scargrave Manor, 1996
Any word you have to hunt for in a thesaurus is the wrong word. There are no exceptions to this rule.
Stephen King (1947 -), "Everything You Need to Know About Writing Successfully - in Ten Minutes", 1988
If you don't have the time to read, you don't have the time or the tools to write.
Stephen King (1947 -), On Writing, p. 147
You can approach the act of writing with nervousness, excitement, hopefulness, or even despairâ€”the sense that you can never completely put on the page whatâ€™s in your mind and heart. You can come to the act with your fists clenched and your eyes narrowed, ready to kick ass and take down names. You can come to it because you want a girl to marry you or because you want to change the world. Come to it any way but lightly. Let me say it again: you must not come lightly to the blank page.
Stephen King (1947 -), On Writing: A Memoir of the Craft, 2000
You must not come lightly to the blank page.
Stephen King (1947 -), On Writing: A Memoir of the Craft, 2000
Some editors are failed writers, but so are most writers.
T. S. Eliot (1888 - 1965)
All a good letter has to do is make you feel special.
Takayuki Ikkaku, Arisa Hosaka and Toshihiro Kawabata, Animal Crossing: Wild World, 2005
It's not about the writing. It's about the feelings behind the words.
Takayuki Ikkaku, Arisa Hosaka and Toshihiro Kawabata, Animal Crossing: Wild World, 2005
Why do writers write? Because it isn't there.
Thomas Berger
A writer is a person for whom writing is more difficult than it is for other people.
Thomas Mann (1875 - 1955)
A great writer reveals the truth even when he or she does not wish to.
Tom Bissell, Truth in Oxiana, 2004
I believe more in the scissors than I do in the pencil.
Truman Capote (1924 - 1984)

If a writer wrote merely for his time, I would have to break my pen and throw it away.
Victor Hugo (1802 - 1885)
An author spends months writing a book, and maybe puts his heart's blood into it, and then it lies about unread till the reader has nothing else in the world to do.
W. Somerset Maugham (1874 - 1965), The Razor's Edge, 1943
People do tell a writer things that they don't tell others. I don't know why, unless it is that having read one or two of his books they feel on peculiarly intimate terms with him; or it may be that they dramatize themselves and, seeing themselves as it were as characters in a novel, are ready to be as open with him as they imagine the characters of his invention are.
W. Somerset Maugham (1874 - 1965), The Razor's Edge, 1943
There are three rules for writing the novel. Unfortunately, no one knows what they are.
W. Somerset Maugham (1874 - 1965)
We do not write because we want to; we write because we have to.
W. Somerset Maugham (1874 - 1965)
The reason why so few good books are written is that so few people who can write know anything.
Walter Bagehot (1826 - 1877)
Journalism is just a gun. It's only got one bullet in it, but if you aim right, that's all you need. Aim it right and you can blow a kneecap off the world.
Warren Ellis, Transmetropolitan: Back On The Street
Vigorous writing is concise.
William Strunk Jr., "The Elements of Style", 1919

Youth

The deepest definition of youth is life as yet untouched by tragedy.
Alfred North Whitehead (1861 - 1947)
The secret of eternal youth is arrested development.
Alice Roosevelt Longworth (1884 - 1980)
The young know how truly difficult and dreadful youth can be. Their youth is wasted on everyone else, that's the horror. The young have no authority, no respect.
Anne Rice (1941 -), "Tale of the Body Thief"
Young people are in a condition like permanent intoxication, because youth is sweet and they are growing.
Aristotle (384 BC - 322 BC), 'Nicomachean Ethics'
Never suffer youth to be an excuse for inadequacy, nor age and fame to be an excuse for indolence.
Benjamin Haydon
Youth is something very new: twenty years ago no one mentioned it.
Coco Chanel (1883 - 1971)
You can only be young once. But you can always be immature.
Dave Barry (1947 -)
The foundation of every state is the education of its youth.
Diogenes Laertius
What a mistake to suppose that the passions are strongest in youth! The passions are not stronger, but the control over them is weaker! They are more easily excited, they are more violent and apparent; but they have less energy, less durability, less intense and concentrated power than in the maturer life.
Edward Bulwer-Lytton (1803 - 1873)
Yes is how you get your first job, and your next job, and your spouse, and even your kids. Even it it's a bit edgy, a bit out of your comfort zone, saying yes means that you will do something new, meet someone new and make a difference.
Eric Schmidt
What is youth except a man or a woman before it is ready or fit to be seen?
Evelyn Waugh (1903 - 1966)
We cannot always build the future for our youth, but we can build our youth for the future.
Franklin D. Roosevelt (1882 - 1945)
The surest way to corrupt a youth is to instruct him to hold in higher esteem those who think alike than those who think differently.
Friedrich Nietzsche (1844 - 1900), The Dawn, Sec. 297
Keep true to the dreams of thy youth.
Friedrich von Schiller (1759 - 1805)
Youth is a wonderful thing. What a crime to waste it on children.
George Bernard Shaw (1856 - 1950)
Youth, which is forgiven everything, forgives itself nothing: age, which forgives itself everything, is forgiven nothing.
George Bernard Shaw (1856 - 1950), Man and Superman (1903) "Maxims for Revolutionists"
If youth only knew: if age only could.
Henri Estienne (1470 - 1520)
Youth would be an ideal state if it came a little later in life.
Herbert Henry Asquith (1852 - 1928)
Praise youth and it will prosper.
Irish Proverb
Age is foolish and forgetful when it underestimates youth.
J. K. Rowling, Harry Potter and the Half-Blood Prince, 2005
Youth cannot know how age thinks and feels. But old men are guilty if they forget what it was to be young.
J. K. Rowling, Harry Potter and the Order of the Phoenix, 2003
I'm youth, I'm joy, I'm a little bird that has broken out of the egg.
James M. Barrie (1860 - 1937)
No wise man ever wished to be younger.
Jonathan Swift (1667 - 1745)
Youth isn't always all it's touted to be.
Lawana Blackwell, The Dowry of Miss Lydia Clark, 1999

Don't laugh at a youth for his affectations; he is only trying on one face after another to find his own.
Logan Pearsall Smith (1865 - 1946)
In youth we learn; in age we understand.
Marie Ebner von Eschenbach
There's nothing that keeps its youth,
So far as I know, but a tree and truth.
Oliver Wendell Holmes (1809 - 1894), The Deacon's Masterpiece, 1858
I am not young enough to know everything.
Oscar Wilde (1854 - 1900)
To get back my youth I would do anything in the world, except take exercise, get up early, or be respectable.
Oscar Wilde (1854 - 1900), The Picture of Dorian Gray, 1891
Boyhood, like measles, is one of those complaints which a man should catch young and have done with, for when it comes in middle life it is apt to be serious.
P. G. Wodehouse (1881 - 1975), Uneasy Money
In case you're worried about what's going to become of the younger generation, it's going to grow up and start worrying about the younger generation.
Roger Allen
Nothing can be so amusingly arrogant as a young man who has just discovered an old idea and thinks it is his own.
Sidney J. Harris
There's something amazing about the passion of youth and its power to sustain. If there's a more powerful energy source, I don't know about it.
Takayuki Ikkaku, Arisa Hosaka and Toshihiro Kawabata, Animal Crossing: Wild World, 2005
We are none of us infallible—not even the youngest of us.
W. H. Thompson
It is an illusion that youth is happy, an illusion of those who have lost it; but the young know they are wretched for they are full of the truthless ideal which have been instilled into them, and each time they come in contact with the real, they are bruised and wounded.
W. Somerset Maugham (1874 - 1965), 'Of Human Bondage', 1915
The dead might as well try to speak to the living as the old to the young.
Willa Cather (1873 - 1947)
We have some salt of our youth in us.
William Shakespeare (1564 - 1616), "The Merry Wives of Windsor", Act 2 scene 3